The Cross
in
The New Testament

The Cross
in
The New Testament

by

Leon Morris

William B. Eerdmans Publishing Company
Grand Rapids, Michigan

Library of Congress catalog card number, 64-22026

ISBN 0-8028-3199-0

Printed in the United States of America

Reprinted, March 1980

Preface

This is principally a book about the cross, since in the New Testament salvation centres on the cross. The Christian salvation was won by Christ's atoning work. Books on the atonement are legion, but it has been some time since anyone in the evangelical tradition attempted to survey the general teaching of the New Testament on the subject. In view of the way theological knowledge advances, it is well that from time to time someone should seek to evaluate the total witness of the scripture to this key doctrine. The atonement is the crucial doctrine of the faith.[1] Unless we are right here it matters little, or so it seems to me, what we are like elsewhere.[2]

That does not mean that a carefully articulated doctrine of the atonement is a necessity before a man can be called a Christian.

---

[1] Cf. Dyson Hague, 'The Atonement is Christianity in epitome. It is the heart of Christianity as a system; it is the distinguishing mark of the Christian religion. For Christianity is more than a revelation; it is more than an ethic. Christianity is uniquely a religion of redemption' (*The Fundamentals,* xi, Chicago, n. d., p. 23).

[2] E. Brunner can say, 'He who understands the Cross aright . . . understands the Bible, he understands Jesus Christ.' He then quotes Luther, 'Therefore this text — "He bore our sins" — must be understood particularly thoroughly, as the foundation upon which stands the whole of the New Testament or the Gospel, as that which alone distinguishes us and our religion from all other religions' (*The Mediator,* London, 1946, pp. 435f.).

5

But it does mean that, whether we can put it into words or not, our relationship to Christ and therefore to God depends on the way we view the cross.   If we feel that Christ has really put our sins out of the way, effectively and finally, our view of the faith will be very different from what would be the case if we felt that He had simply given us an example, or had won a spectacular victory which has little regard for the rights of the case.   Our view of the atonement and our view of God are inextricably interwoven.

In my discussion of the contribution of the Gospels to our understanding of this subject I have assumed the authenticity of many sayings. I have of set purpose eschewed the discussion of such questions as 'How far are the Gospels reliable witnesses to what Jesus thought about His death?'   In adopting this course I am impressed with the position so well expressed by R. H. Fuller, who asks, 'Can we say with certainty that they represent the teaching of Jesus himself?' and who answers, 'This is a question which in the nature of the case it is not possible to answer conclusively, for in a very real sense it is not possible to get back behind the apostolic witness'.[3] I know that some very eminent scholars have made the attempt, but, with all respect, I am not convinced by the results. Unless the Gospels are substantially reliable we cannot know what Jesus thought and said and did.   If it be accepted that the Evangelists give us an adequate picture of Jesus, what I have said will cause no trouble.   If it be held that every saying must be authenticated, then the work would have to be extended very greatly.   Most (including myself) will feel that it is already too long.   I can only ask such a critic to take this book as pointing to what the early church taught about the cross.   The teaching is there, by whomever it was originated.[4]

This book then is to be taken as a survey of what the New Testament has to say about the atonement. It is my conviction that there is a substantial unity in New Testament thought on this topic, as well as considerable variety, and I have tried to do justice to both. It is also my conviction that there is a much more solid weight of scriptural teaching behind the view that Christ was in some sense our Substitute than most modern scholars will allow.   I have tried

[3] *The Mission and Achievement of Jesus*, London, 1954, p. 59.

[4] Cf. H. Conzelmann's explanation of his procedure: 'This study of St. Luke's theology is, by its approach to the problems, for the most part not dependent on any particular literary theories about St. Luke's Gospel and the Acts of the Apostles, for it is concerned with the whole of Luke's writings as they stand. If these form a self-contained scheme, then for our purpose literary critical analysis is only of secondary importance . . . . our aim is to elucidate Luke's work in its present form, not to enquire into possible sources or into the historical facts which provide the material' (*The Theology of St. Luke,* London, 1960, p. 9).

to bring some of this out, as well as to indicate that this idea is necessary as well as scriptural.

This book arose out of the John A. McElwain Lectures which I delivered at Gordon Divinity School, Beverly Farms, Massachusetts, in March, 1960. I had been thinking on the subject for some years, and this Lectureship gave me the opportunity of setting my thoughts in order. Since then I have worked steadily at the manuscript and have added many notes. I would like to express my sincere thanks to the Dean and Faculty of the Gordon Divinity School, both for the honor they paid me in extending the invitation to deliver the lectures, and also for their hospitality and their many kindnesses while I was at the school. I benefited greatly from the discussions I had with them.

Normally quotations are made from the Revised Version, though occasionally I have made my own translation without comment.

—LEON MORRIS

Contents

Abbreviations

AG   *A Greek-English Lexicon of the New Testament and other Early Christian Literature* by W. F. Arndt and F. W. Gingrich (Cambridge, 1957).

ANT   *The Atonement in New Testament Teaching* by Vincent Taylor (London, 1946).

AS   *A Manual Greek Lexicon of the New Testament* by G. Abbott-Smith (Edinburgh, 1954).

AV   English Authorized Version (King James).

BDS   *The Bible Doctrine of Salvation* by C. Ryder Smith (London, 1946).

BS   *Bible Studies* by A. Deissmann (Edinburgh, 1901).

CC   *The Cruciality of the Cross* by P. T. Forsyth (London, 1948).

CDDR   *Church Dogmatics,* vol. iv, *The Doctrine of Reconciliation,* Part I, by Karl Barth, translated by G. W. Bromiley (Edinburgh, 1956).

CDR   *The Christian Doctrine of Reconciliation* by James Denney (London, 1918).

DC   *The Death of Christ* by James Denney (London, 1903).

11

ERE   *Encyclopaedia of Religion and Ethics,* edited by J. Hastings.

ET   *The Expository Times.*

GT   *A Greek-English Lexicon of the New Testament,* being Grimm's Wilke's *Clavis Novi Testamenti,* translated, revised, and enlarged by J. H. Thayer (Edinburgh, 1888).

HDCG   *Hastings Dictionary of Christ and the Gospels.*

HDAC   *Hastings Dictionary of the Apostolic Church.*

IB   *The Interpreter's Bible.*

ICC   *The International Critical Commentary.*

IFG   *The Interpretation of the Fourth Gospel* by C. H. Dodd (Cambridge, 1953).

JBL   *The Journal of Biblical Literature.*

JG   *The Justification of God* by P. T. Forsyth (London, 1916).

JS   *Jesus and His Sacrifice* by Vincent Taylor (London, 1939).

JTS   *The Journal of Theological Studies.*

LAE   *Light from the Ancient East* by A. Deissmann (London, 1927).

LS   *A Greek-English Lexicon,* compiled by H. G. Liddell and R. Scott; new edition revised by H. S. Jones and R. McKenzie (Oxford, 1940).

LXX   Septuagint Version.

MM   *The Vocabulary of the Greek Testament* by J. H. Moulton and G. Milligan (London, 1914-29).

MNTC   *The Moffatt New Testament Commentary.*

NEB   *The New English Bible.*

NTS   *New Testament Studies*

NICNT   *The New International Commentary on the New Testament.*

PP   *Positive Preaching and the Modern Mind* by P. T. Forsyth (London, 1909).

RSV   American Revised Standard Version, 1946.

RV   English Revised Version, 1881.

SE   *Studia Evangelica,* edited by K. Aland *et al.* (Berlin, 1959).

SJT   *The Scottish Journal of Theology.*

ST   *Studies in Theology* by James Denney (New York, 1895).

TWBB   *A Theological Word Book of the Bible,* edited by A. Richardson (London, 1950).

TWNT   *Theologisches Wörterbuch zum neuen Testament,* edited by G. Kittel and G. Friedrich (Stuttgart, 1928—).

WOC   *The Work of Christ* by P. T. Forsyth (London, 1948).

WThJ   *The Westminster Theological Journal.*

CHAPTER ONE

The Cross in Matthew and Mark

'The Gospel of the Son of God Crucified' is the title of an article
in which John A. Allan seeks to make clear the main thrust of St.
Mark's Gospel.[1] Thereby he brings out the very important truth
that, although there is very little specific teaching on the atonement
in this Gospel (as, for that matter, in many other parts of the New
Testament), this means no more than that it lacks a formal statement of the way in which atonement is effected. The fact of the
atonement underlies the whole. It is not too much to say that the
Gospels are books about the atonement.[2] Their authors select their

---

[1] *Interpretation*, ix, pp. 131-43.

[2] This is sometimes overlooked. It is curious to notice, for example, that
A. M. Hunter in his very fine little book, *Introducing New Testament Theology*
(London, 1957), has no chapter on the cross or the atonement, though
he has one on the resurrection. Perhaps even more illuminating is E. Basil
Redlich's Introduction to his *St. Mark's Gospel: A Modern Commentary*
(London, 1948). He begins by saying, 'The main purpose of this volume
is to emphasize the crucial importance of the opening verse of *St. Mark's*

incidents and choose the words in which they describe them specifically to bring out the great saving act of God in Christ.   The Gospels
are not biographies.   It has become almost a commonplace in recent
writing that they are documents written with a theological purpose.
That theological purpose is to convey to men the good news of
what God has done for their salvation,[3] and for the evangelists
the cross is in the centre of that good news.   It is not all of what
God has done, and thus the cross is not the sole topic.   But it is the
most important thing, and the evangelists emphasize it accordingly.
They have thought long and deeply[4] on the significance of the person
and work of Jesus, and the Gospels express something of this significance.   The Gospels are not objective histories.   They are not works
of literary art, examples of *belles lettres*.   They are in fact — Gospels.
It does not need much more than a cursory examination to make
plain that they are written round the cross.[5]   Everything before leads
up to this climax.   From about one-sixth to one-third of the whole
space is devoted to the events associated with the Passion.   These
are the events of absorbing interest, the events on account of which
the whole was set down.[6]

Gospel, "the beginning of the gospel of Jesus Christ, the Son of God"'.   Then
he goes on to summarize 'the good news', but his summary has not one word
about the cross.   His choice of adjective ('the crucial importance') completely
gives his case away.
   [3] C. H. Dodd thinks of 'Gospel' as 'a virtual equivalent for *kerygma.*'   He
proceeds, 'Mark therefore conceived himself as writing a form of *kerygma,*
and that his Gospel is in fact a rendering of the apostolic Preaching will
become clear from an analysis of the book itself' (*The Apostolic Preaching
and its Developments,* London, 1944, p. 47).   O. Piper is somewhat critical
of this thesis, asking, 'how are we to explain the fact that none of the evangelists gave a total presentation of the material available?' (JBL, lxxviii,
p. 121).   But this does not dispose of Dodd's main point that Mark is primarily interested in the *kerygma.*   Moreover Piper insists that Matthew was
written 'to proclaim a saving truth,' and sees this in the expression βίβλος
γενέσεως (Mt. 1:1) equally with ἀρχὴ τοῦ εὐαγγελίου (Mk. 1:1) (*op. cit.,*
p. 122).
   [4] 'A full heart does not necessarily mean an empty mind.   The first
disciples would never have begun to preach at all unless they had believed
that their experience was of universal significance' (G. B. Caird, *The Apostolic
Age,* London, 1955, p. 38).
   [5] 'The crucified Messiah, as the fulfilment of God's promise to His people,
is also the chief theme of St. Mark's gospel' (R. H. Lightfoot, *The Gospel
Message of St. Mark,* Oxford, 1950, p. 31).
   [6] Cf. D. E. H. Nineham, 'St. Mark's Gospel, as I sometimes say to my
students, is rather like a tadpole — a large head with a comparatively short
tail.   The head of the Gospel is what theologians call the Passion Narrative — the account of the last few days in Jerusalem when Jesus suffered
and died.   Here is the heart of the Gospel, its centre of gravity . . . not only
has Mark given to the passion the position of pre-eminence and climax in the
Gospel — he has so selected and arranged the rest of his material that, for all

If then we are interested in what the Gospel writers have to say
about the atonement, we must give attention to a great part of their
writings. We must examine a good deal more than those sayings
which refer to the cross in so many words. Other passages, even
whole themes, may well have a bearing on the whole. To receive
the total impression we must study not the central part of the canvas
alone, but also those subsidiary motifs which direct us toward the
centre. They are not inserted aimlessly.

It is usual for the first three Gospels to be considered together.
They give us recognizably the same picture of Jesus and of His work.
But for our purpose there is much to be said for treating the third
Gospel separately. Luke has his own way of bringing out the meaning of the atonement, and it is not quite the same way as that
adopted by Matthew and Mark. Despite some differences, these two
do tackle the problem in essentially the same manner. We shall
therefore consider Matthew and Mark together, and postpone Luke
to another chapter.

SALVATION IS ALL OF GOD

Mark expressly tells us what he is about in his opening words, 'The
beginning of the gospel of Jesus Christ'. A few verses later he
comes back to this same concept of 'gospel' when he speaks of
Jesus as 'preaching the gospel of God' (Mk. 1:14), and calling on
men to 'believe in the gospel' (Mk. 1:15). This word 'gospel' is
not self-explanatory. Etymologically it means 'good news'. In
the classics it was used for the reward given to the messenger who
brought good news,[7] and sometimes, too, for the good news itself.
But to the uninstructed an expression like 'God's good news' or
'Christ's good news' would not mean much. Why should God be
receiving or sending good news? What could such good news conceivably be? Who was Christ? How did He come to be involved
in this thing? Questions would multiply. In a Christian context,

---

its importance, it is seen to be subordinate to what happened in Jerusalem.
If you read the earlier part of the Gospel attentively, you will see that
practically everything in it is in some way introductory to the passion
of Jesus; the aim throughout is quite single-minded — to help the reader
to see Jesus on the Cross' (*Theology*, lx, p. 269). Cf. M. Kähler's description
of the Gospels as 'Passion narratives with extended introduction' (cited by
G. Bornkamm, *Jesus of Nazareth*, London, 1960, p. 17).

[7] GT gives as the first meaning of εὐαγγέλιον 'a reward for good tidings',
and illustrates with τὰ διδασκάλια, the fees given the διδάσκαλος. Similarly
LS, *'reward of good tidings*, given to the messenger', and proceeds to notice
that in Attic the word is always plural. The term is examined by G. Milligan,
St. Paul's Epistles to the Thessalonians, London, 1908, pp. 141-44. See also
G. Friedrich, TWNT, ii, pp. 705-735.

however, the answers would not be hard to find. There 'the' good news could mean nothing else than the good news of what God has done in Christ to bring men salvation. 'God's good news' (or 'the gospel of God', as our translation runs) means that it takes its origin in God. 'Christ's good news' ('the gospel of Jesus Christ') signifies that it is mediated through Christ, and that His action is central to the content of the good news.

When Mark, then, tells us that he is writing about 'the good news', he is laying it down uncompromisingly right at the very beginning that his central topic is the salvation wrought by Christ. He is not writing a history. He is not stringing together an edifying collection of stories or sayings.[8] He is telling men the good news of God's action in dealing with their sin. On his own showing, that, and nothing else, is what he is about.

Matthew begins in a somewhat different fashion, but in his own way he makes essentially the same opening point. He begins with a genealogy. To modern men this is nothing more than a dry-as-dust list, and they do not read it. But to Matthew it is important. At the very threshold of his narrative he wants it to be clear that Jesus is of the line of Abraham, God's chosen man, and of the royal house of David, through whom the Messiah would come. The links are preserved (though Matthew does not choose to put them all down). This is the One whom God has planned to send from centuries back. And He has been pleased to send Him to bring salvation, for immediately Matthew comes to his narrative proper; he tells the birth story and stresses that the Child that would be sent to Mary should be called Jesus, 'for it is he that shall save his people from their sins' (Mt. 1:21).[9] He proceeds to cite the prophecy of a virgin bearing a son, 'And they shall call his name Immanuel; which is, being interpreted, God with us' (Mt. 1:23). The salvation of which he writes is of divine origin. In Jesus, God was coming to men — a truth which is behind the story of the Wise Men which Matthew tells next. For Matthew, as for Mark, it is important to show at the very beginning what he is about. He is writing a book which shows that salvation comes from what God does, and not from any human effort whatever.

The thought is continued throughout both Gospels and is developed in various ways. The word 'gospel' recurs. Jesus preached 'the gospel of the kingdom' (Mt. 4:23; 9:35), and said it would be preached throughout the world (Mt. 24:14; 26:13; Mk. 13:10;

---

8 A string of sayings in the manner of the so-called 'Gospel of Thomas' is not a Gospel in the New Testament sense of the word. It belongs to a different literary genre altogether.

9 'Jesus' is, of course, the English equivalent of the Greek 'Ιησοῦς, which corresponds to the Hebrew yehoshua' (the form yeshua' also occurs), meaning 'The Lord saves'.

14:9). He called on men to make sacrifices 'for my sake and the gospel's' (Mk. 8:35; 10:29). All this means that God's kingdom is bound up with the good news and this good news accordingly is neither temporary nor unimportant. It is God's final word to man. It must be proclaimed throughout the length and breadth of this world.

Or consider the demand Jesus made for conversion, and the implications of this demand. Matthew quotes our Lord as saying, 'Except ye turn (AV, "be converted"), and become as little children, ye shall in no wise enter into the kingdom of heaven' (Mt. 18:3). Both evangelists speak of the necessity of conversion as they recount the parable of the Sower (Mt. 13:15; Mk. 4:12). While it is true that conversion involves a human activity it is also true that in the New Testament it always points to that other truth that salvation comes from God.[10] Men are not saved because they turn over a new leaf. Conversion is not a meritorious action which ought to be suitably rewarded. Conversion, as the New Testament understands it, means a wholehearted turning away from sin. It means a ceasing to rely on one's own strong right arm. It means a coming to rely entirely on the mercy of God. Apart from that mercy conversion would be aimless, futile, meaningless. Conversion roots salvation squarely in the action of God, and it takes its meaning from the action of God.[11]

The same thing must, of course, be said about repentance. This is demanded from the beginning (Mk. 1:4, 15), and its absence is reprobated in the strongest terms (Mt. 11:20ff.). But unless repentance is linked with a forgiving act of God it effects nothing, and can effect nothing. Nowhere do the Gospels countenance any such view as that repentance *in itself* is meritorious. But the repentant cast themselves on the forgiving love of God, and it is this which is significant.

The divine initiative is implied once more in the parable of the Labourers in the Vineyard (Mt. 20:1-16). This story is not without its difficulties, most of which stem from our conviction that justice is not being done. Deep down we feel that those who complained that they had borne 'the burden of the day and the scorching heat' (v. 12) and therefore should be treated differently from the men who worked for no more than one hour, really have legitimate cause for

---

[10] In an article entitled 'Conversion' (SJT, iii, pp. 352-62) Stephen C. Neill says, 'Christian life, in whatever form, is always response to the gracious activity of God in Christ. The initiative always rests with God, who approaches man as Redeemer, and not with the individual, whatever his seeking and striving after God' (*op. cit.*, p. 357).

[11] Cf. Julius Schniewind, 'This then is conversion: to accept the death-sentence and the acquittal of God' (SJT, v, p. 276).

complaint. They are not being treated on a basis of equity. They are not receiving common justice.

But that is Jesus' whole point. God does not treat men on the basis of a cold, even-handed justice. If He did, we should all be in difficulty.[12] But we are not treated strictly according to our deserts. We are treated on the basis of God's grace. The parable underlines the truth that God's way is the way of grace. God's way cannot be reduced to some variant of the human way, a way of estimation of merit.[13] In this same spirit Matthew records for us the wonderful invitation of Jesus, 'Come unto me, all ye that labour and are heavy laden, and I will give you rest. Take my yoke upon you, and learn of me; for I am meek and lowly in heart: and ye shall find rest unto your souls' (Mt. 11:28f.). Those worn by hard labour and bowed under the burdens of life are in no position to effect their own salvation. They are helpless in the face of ultimate issues. But they find rest for their souls by coming to Christ and by relying on Him. The saying springs from the assurance that He is well able to meet their need, and that He will meet it.[14] And it is in connection with salvation that we need the words, 'with God all things are possible' (Mt. 19:26; Mk. 10:27). None are beyond His power. This does not mean that salvation comes easily. Matthew sombrely records the words of the mockers, 'He saved

12 Cf. Shakespeare, 'Use every man after his desert, and who should 'scape whipping?' (*Hamlet*, II, 2, 561).

13 A. H. McNeile in his commentary on this passage adds a Rabbinic parable from Jer. *Berak.* 2:5c, 'Like a king who had hired many labourers, one of whom so distinguished himself by industry and skill that the king took him by the hand and walked up and down with him. In the evening the labourers came, and the skilful one among them, to receive their pay. The king gave them all the same pay. Wherefore those who had worked the whole day murmured, and spake: We have worked the whole day, and this man only two hours, and yet he also has received his whole pay. The king answered: This man hath wrought more in two hours than you in the whole day.' (The same parable is found also in *Ecc. Rab.* V. 11. 5 and *Song of Songs Rab.* VI. 2. 6.) It is clear that the story made a great appeal to the Rabbis, and equally clear that they put their emphasis on merit. Indeed, the Rabbinic parable strikingly illustrates the way the mind of the natural man instinctively turns to the way of merit. Our Lord's parable is directed specifically against this tendency. T. W. Manson reminds us that it would have been possible to pay all the workers exactly what they had earned. 'There is such a thing as the twelfth part of a denar. It was called a *pondion*. But there is no such thing as a twelfth part of the love of God' (*The Sayings of Jesus*, London, 1949, p. 220).

14 T. W. Manson points out that any language resembling these words in Judaism represents an encouragement to study the Law. 'It thus appears that Jesus claims to do for men what the Law claimed to do; but in a different way' (*op. cit.*, p. 186). The radical novelty of this and the magnitude and nature of the claim should not be overlooked.

others; himself he cannot save' (Mt. 27:42). We cannot doubt that he saw in these words truth as well as mockery.[15] Salvation is at cost. But the big point is that the cost has been met. The price has been paid. Salvation is a reality. It is a reality because God can and does bring it about.

References to the 'elect' (Mt. 24:22, 24, 31; Mk. 13:20, 22, etc.), or to being 'chosen' (Mt. 22:14) also point to God's saving act. Men do not 'elect' or 'choose' themselves.[16] There is in the essential meaning of the words the thought of the divine initiative. Unless God chooses to intervene and make some men His own, none will ever be saved. There is a tendency in some recent writing to minimize the significance of election. It is not surprising that, in a man-centred age, some writers put their emphasis on what men may be expected to do. The term may be retained, but its meaning tortured out of all recognition. It must be insisted upon that the Gospels speak of an election in which God, not man, is sovereign.

There is an air of finality about the gospel. God's action in saving men is not a temporary device, as though He chose this way for the men of Christ's day, and another for other men. The gospel must be proclaimed among all the nations (Mk. 13:10; 14:9[17]; cf. Mt. 28:19f.). God is in it. It is His final answer to the ever-present problem of man's sin. It is as relevant to us as to the men of the first century. We cannot look for a modification one of these days of the basic word of the gospel, that therein salvation is procured by God Himself.

Before we look more closely at this salvation, let us notice two things by way of introduction, the first that sin is a serious matter

[15] 'He was held, not by the nails, but by His will to save them' (A. Plummer, *An Exegetical Commentary on the Gospel according to S. Matthew,* London, 1910, p. 397).

[16] H. H. Rowley reminds us that the doctrine of election 'would seem to be fundamental to the thought of the Bible in both Old and New Testaments' (*The Biblical Doctrine of Election,* London, 1952, p. 15). Of church members in the New Testament he says, 'They were not men and women who chose to be Christians, or who of their own initiative decided to attach themselves to the Church, but men and women on whom the constraint of God had been laid, who were chosen in Christ and redeemed by Him, and who in individual loyalty had responded to that grace and pledged themselves without reserve to the obedience of their Lord' (*op. cit.,* p. 170).

[17] G. D. Kilpatrick, in a study entitled 'The Gentile Mission in Mark and Mark 13:9-11' (*Studies in the Gospels,* ed. D. E. Nineham, Oxford, 1955, pp. 145-158), argues that these passages contain no necessary thought of preaching *to* the Gentiles; the passages may mean a preaching to Jews scattered among the nations (as we see in Acts). But he agrees that there are 'significant elements in the Gospel for the breakdown of particularism' (*op. cit.,* p. 157), i.e., he agrees that Mark sees the gospel as applying to all men.

involving dire consequences, the second that suffering is not wholly evil, but may be the pathway to good. Both these ideas are strange to this generation, so we must give good heed to what the evangelists say.

SIN MERITS PUNISHMENT

Matthew and Mark set their 'good news' against a sombre background. Jesus does not save men from some imaginary danger, but from very real peril. The Gospel writers bring this out by insisting that sin is a serious business, serious in itself and serious in its consequences. Men may not be deeply concerned about it, but God is. We may see a very good illustration of this in the preaching of John the Baptist. Basically John spoke of the coming of the Messiah, of Him in whom the purposes of God were to be worked out. Matthew and Mark saw in the coming and the work of this Messiah the outworking of God's love and of His willingness to save. But the former records that John said plainly that His 'fan is in his hand, and he will thoroughly cleanse his threshing-floor; and he will gather his wheat into the garner, but the chaff he will burn up with unquenchable fire' (Mt. 3:12). The baptism 'with fire' may well be a baptism of judgment[18] as opposed to baptism 'with the Holy Ghost', which points rather to the mercies of God.[19] The religious activities of the day are inadequate. The Pharisees and Sadducees are addressed as 'Ye offspring of vipers', and are warned of 'the wrath to come' (Mt. 3:7). They are told that descent from Abraham will be of no avail, for the axe 'is . . . laid unto the root of the trees' (Mt. 3:9f.). The narrative is heavy with impending judgment.

Mark does not use the same language, but his picture of John leaves us with essentially the same impression. Mark sees him as calling on men to get ready because the Lord is coming (Mk. 1:3), as preaching 'the baptism of repentance unto remission of sins' (v. 4), as having men confess (v. 5), as proclaiming that the Coming One was so mighty that he, John, was not worthy to stoop down and unloose His sandal straps (v. 7). Early in both these Gospels

---

[18] W. H. Brownlee cites from the Qumran scrolls a vivid passage on the eschatological river of fire and comments, 'The finding of this passage in an ancient Jewish document of Palestine makes it seem quite reasonable to suppose that the baptism of fire of which John spoke may have been in the torrents of hell so vividly described here' (*The Scrolls and the New Testament*, ed. K. Stendahl, London, 1958, p. 42. Cf. also H. J. Flowers, ET, lxiv, p. 156; E. Schweizer, ET, lxv, p. 29; L. W. Barnard, JTS, n. s., viii, p. 107).

[19] It points also to the truth we saw in our last section, that salvation comes from God. 'It implies, as indeed the whole Bible does, that men cannot save themselves, but that they need something that comes from God' (C. Ryder Smith, BDS, p. 131).

the thought is made quite plain that God will have no truck with sin.[20] Sin can bring nothing but punishment from Him.

This stern note continues. It is seen in the recognition that the ministry of Jesus is 'to them which sat in the region and shadow of death' (Mt. 4:16). The objects of His mission are men in mortal peril. It is seen in Christ's unfailing demand for repentance (Mt. 9:13; Mk. 1:15; 2:17, etc.), which implies that men will find nothing but condemnation if they continue in their sins. Sometimes this thought becomes explicit, as when Jesus proclaims His 'Woes' to the cities in which He has worked, not so much because of the terrible nature of their sins (though this, of course, is implied) as 'because they repented not' (Mt. 11:20). Repentance is the first note struck alike in the preaching of John, of Jesus Himself, and of the disciples (Mt. 3:1f.; 4:17; Mk. 6:12).

We might profitably consider the implications of this. If men are to undergo a wholehearted repentance, that means a complete end to sin. The message of Jesus will not countenance evil in any shape or form. This differentiates Christianity from all religions of law. In a religion of law, such as Judaism, all that is necessary is that a man should acquire a balance of good deeds over bad.[21] He must, so to speak, keep his account in credit. As long as he does this a few small sins are neither here nor there. It is worth noticing in passing that this probably explains much of modern man's indifference to sin. He does not understand that Christianity is a religion of grace, a religion of redemption. He has reduced it to a religion of law. He thinks of it as 'living a good life', and he hopes by his good life to attain heaven. He knows that he is not perfect, but he is not troubled by the fact. He knows of no such outstanding evil as would wipe out his credit balance (as he sees it) of good deeds.

But Jesus did not call on men to lead a 'good' life in this sense.

---

[20] Cf. Floyd V. Filson, 'There was something fundamentally true and thoroughly wholesome in such an uncompromising assertion of the righteousness of God. No man or age that takes sin lightly can live worthily.' He goes on to point out that 'The Gospel of grace is protected from moral laxity or indifference . . . only when the world is known to be subject to God's rule and judgment' (*One Lord One Faith*, Philadelphia, 1943, pp. 109f.).

[21] J. Klausner claims this as a mark of the superiority of Judaism to Christianity, affirming again and again that the Christian ethic is an ideal, whereas that of Judaism can be attained. 'Judaism also knows the ideal of love for the enemy . . . but Judaism never emphasized it to such a degree that it ultimately became too high an ideal for ordinary mankind, and even too high for the man of more than average moral calibre' (*Jesus of Nazareth*, London, 1928, pp. 392f.); 'Judaism will never allow itself to reach even in theory the ethical extremeness characteristic of Christianity; this extremeness has no place in the world of reality' (*From Jesus to Paul*, London, 1946, p. 609).

He did not point them to a law and ask them to keep it more often than not. He never suggested by word or deed that man's whole duty is to perform a certain quota of good deeds. He demanded perfection (Mt. 5:48). And if men came short of perfection in even the slightest degree, He demanded repentance. Which means that He demanded repentance of every man. Men must make a complete break with every evil thing. So long as they have evil about them they cannot enter God's heaven or be numbered among God's people here on earth. Sin is a serious business indeed.

Or consider the implications of the righteousness that Jesus demanded. He said that the way to life is through a 'narrow gate' and along a 'straitened way' (Mt. 7:14). Men will not find themselves safe if they simply drift along through life. A study of the Sermon on the Mount is a disturbing exercise. There are some passages in it which are very comforting, but the total impact of the Sermon is devastating. It demands from men a standard of righteousness which none of us attains.[22] The lustful look breaks the command on adultery. The angry word breaks that on murder. Then the positive righteousness that Jesus demands is frightening. Men are to go the second mile (Mt. 5:41). They are to love their enemies (Mt. 5:44). Their duty is summed up shortly by saying that they are to be perfect, perfect as God is perfect (Mt. 5:48). This standard is so high that no one, of course, attains it. Jesus accepts universal sinfulness as something that can be taken for granted. Speaking about men's good deeds He says, 'If ye then, being evil, know how to give good gifts unto your children . . .' (Mt. 7:11). Notice how quietly 'being evil' is slipped in. It is basic. It does not need to be argued. It can be assumed. But if Jesus is sure that men are naturally sinful He is not complacent about the consequences. There is such a thing as 'the judgment' (Mt. 5:21, 22; 7:1ff.). There is such a thing as 'the hell of fire' (Mt. 5:22). 'Every tree that bringeth not forth good fruit is hewn down,' He says, 'and cast into the fire' (Mt. 7:19).

The Sermon teaches many things. Two of them are important for our present purpose. The one is that the standard God requires is so high that men do not, in fact, attain it. The other is that this failure is serious, for it brings the punishment of God down upon them.

Nor should we overlook the fact that some of the parables which expressly teach us about mercy and the like are intelligible only

---

[22] 'From time to time one hears people declare that they "like" the Sermon on the Mount. It is in fact the most terrible indictment of human nature in all literature . . . . Who is sufficient for these merciless moral demands? . . . If that is the ideal, God have mercy on us all, sinners' (A. M. Hunter, *The Unity of the New Testament*, London, 1944, pp. 84f.).

against a background of judgment. Thus the parable of the Unmerciful Servant (Mt. 18:23-35) primarily inculcates the necessity for men to practise forgiveness. Yet it concludes on the note of punishment.[23] The servant who had no mercy is delivered to the 'tormentors'. Lest we should feel that this is no more than a detail necessary to the coherence of the story but irrelevant to the spiritual interpretation, there is a little addition. The disciples are warned that the heavenly Father will do likewise to them if they sin in the same fashion. The parable of the Wicked Husbandmen (Mt. 21:33-45; Mk. 12:1-12) also concludes on the note of judgment. There is forbearance in the story. When He might well have inflicted punishment, the Lord of the vineyard sent His Son. But when even this tender divine gesture is misunderstood, considered as the basis of a scheme for personal profit, and made the springboard for a further outbreak of evil, when the Son is rejected and slain, then there is nothing left but judgment. 'He will miserably destroy those miserable men'.[24] In the end judgment is inevitable.

Blasphemy against the Holy Spirit is so serious that it never has forgiveness (Mt. 12:32; Mk. 3:28f.). This sin is not explained in detail, but it is clear enough that men may resist and oppose the divine leading and that this rebellion is serious.[25] Both our evangelists record Jesus' words with reference to the sin of Judas, 'good were it for that man if he had not been born' (Mt. 26:24; Mk. 14:21). Of another sinner Jesus said that it would be better for him to have a millstone hanged about his neck and be cast into the sea than to have committed his sin (Mt. 18:6). Similarly the loss of a foot or an eye is to be preferred to hell fire (Mt. 5:29f.; Mk. 9:43ff.). The longer ending to Mark was probably not penned by the original writer, but it faithfully reflects his thought when it says, 'he that dis-

---

23 Cf. E. Fuchs, SE, p. 493.

24 C. Ryder Smith makes a similar point when dealing with the Old Testament doctrine of the wrath of God: 'An attempt has been made to show that Jesus himself did not accept this doctrine, on the ground that (except in Luke xxi. 23) He uses neither of the Greek *words* translated "wrath" or "anger", but this is to be a slave of the letter. Without the *concept,* some Parables — such as those of the Wheat and Tares, or of the Man who Built on Sand, or of the Sheep and Goats — mean nothing. Without it, much of the apocalyptic teaching of Jesus would hardly make sense. Without it, such phrases as "eternal fire", "the outer darkness", "Gehenna", and "where their worm dieth not and the fire is not quenched" would not only be symbolic, but symbolic of nothing. Without it Jesus' use of the word "perish" would lose its meaning' (BDS, p. 127).

25 Cf. Alan Richardson, 'to reject the inbreaking Aeon (the Kingdom of God) and to dismiss the signs of its arrival — such as the exorcisms which demonstrate the overthrow of Satan's counter-kingdom — as the work of Beelzebub, is to reject the salvation which God is bringing and is in fact to be guilty of unforgivable sin against the New Age' (*An Introduction to the Theology of the New Testament,* London, 1958, p. 108).

believeth shall be condemned' (Mk. 16:16). This points to final
judgment, and the thought occurs elsewhere. The parable of the
Tares carries an explanation from which we find that in the last day
the angels will gather all evildoers 'and shall cast them into the
furnace of fire' (Mt. 13:42). So also with the parable of the Net
(Mt. 13:47f.). There are references to 'the outer darkness' (Mt.
8:12; 22:13; 25:30), to the fact that many are called but few
chosen (Mt. 22:14), to 'weeping and gnashing of teeth' (Mt. 8:12;
22:13; 24:51; 25:30). We read of hell repeatedly (Mt. 5:22, 29,
30; 10:28; 18:9; 23:15, 33; Mk. 9:43, 45, 47). Eternal issues
hang on the final judgment where men will be dealt with on the
basis of their deeds (Mt. 16:27; 25:31-46[26]). To deny Christ on
this earth means finally to be denied before the Father (Mt. 10:33;
Mk. 8:38). Nor may men hope to hide their deeds in that day.
Everything will be made known (Mt. 10:26; Mk. 4:22), even 'every
idle word that men shall speak' (Mt. 12:36). Plainly these evangelists regard the final results of sin with horror. They faithfully record all sorts of sayings which make this plain. And they
think of an eventual crisis which means the end of man's opportunity
to put things right, as we see from statements like these from the
parables: 'the door was shut' (Mt. 25:10); 'straightway he putteth
forth the sickle' (Mk. 4:29). There is an air of utter finality about
such words.

An important feature of this part of the evangelists' message is
their frequent warning of the peril in which the nation, the people of
God, and more especially its religious leaders, stood. Jesus sent
His disciples to 'the lost sheep of the house of Israel' (Mt. 10:6).
The lost state of these lost sheep is brought out in several ways.
Isaiah 6:10 is quoted with respect to them, 'this people's heart is
waxed gross . . .' (Mt. 13:15). They are characterized as 'An evil
and adulterous generation' (Mt. 12:39). They are told that in the
day of judgment it will be better for cities like Tyre, Sidon, and
Sodom, than for those in which Christ has done His mighty works
(Mt. 11:20-24). Jesus warned against the teaching of the scribes and
Pharisees and Sadducees (Mt. 16:6ff.; Mk. 7:6ff.; 8:15ff.). He told
the chief priests and elders that the publicans and harlots would
enter the kingdom before they would (Mt. 21:31). He reserved His
most spectacular denunciations for religious men, saying repeatedly,
'Woe unto you, scribes and Pharisees, hypocrites' (Mt. 23, *passim;*
cf. Mk. 12:38ff.). The parable of the Wicked Husbandmen, to

---

[26] Theo Preiss sees in this passage what he calls 'the element of juridical
substitution' (*Life in Christ*, London, 1954, p. 46). He sees this concept as
important for an understanding of the atonement, for a little later he speaks
of Christ as freely identifying Himself 'with each of the wretched ones by
an act of substitution' (*op. cit.,* p. 53).

which we have already referred, is spoken against the religious leaders (Mt. 21:33-45; Mk. 12:1-12), and the incident of the barren fig tree appears to be an acted parable directed against the same group (Mt. 21:18f.; Mk. 11:13f., 20f.). There is menace behind Jesus' words, 'Every plant which my heavenly Father planted not, shall be rooted up' (Mt. 15:13), spoken as they were in a context of Pharisaic opposition. Jesus sees 'the sons of the kingdom . . . cast forth into the outer darkness: there shall be the weeping and gnashing of teeth' (Mt. 8:12).

From all this it is abundantly clear that in these two Gospels sin is uniformly thought of as a very horrible thing. It is horrible in itself and it is horrible in its consequences.

A BENEDICTION ON SUFFERING

Now let us take notice of the way these writers view suffering. Their view is not the same as ours. We take it for granted that suffering is an evil. We go to great lengths to avoid it, both for others and for ourselves. It is not, and I imagine never can be, attractive. Yet the Gospels do not regard it as an unmitigated evil. An evil it is, but suffering may also be the path to blessing as when Jesus said, 'Blessed are ye when men shall reproach you, and persecute you, and say all manner of evil against you falsely, for my sake. Rejoice, and be exceeding glad' (Mt. 5:11f.). So much depends on the attitude of the sufferer. It is possible to complain and to rebel and to hit out wildly, thus increasing the amount of suffering and evil. But it is also possible to accept suffering, and in the acceptance to turn it into good and the means of good.[27] Suffering may be meaningful, and when it is accepted as such it is fruitful for good.[28] It is in any case an inevitable part of life, especially for believers. Christians must accept the fact that 'tribulation

---

[27] Leonard Hodgson points out that when a man has been sinned against he may react vindictively, thus increasing the sum of evil in the world. Or he may absorb in himself consequences of the sin of the other, forgiving the injury. In this case 'he will have taken the pain which is the child of sin and made it the parent not of further evil, but of good; he will have taken the pain which is the product of sin and treated it as raw material for increasing the world's output of goodness' (*The Doctrine of the Atonement,* London, 1951, p. 62).

[28] H. N. Wieman distinguishes between pain, which is meaningless or nearly so, and suffering, which 'always adds some meaning, since it is essentially the meaning and not the present event alone that is the suffering' (*The Source of Human Good,* Chicago, 1946, p. 96). And he reminds us that 'suffering, even more than happiness, leads to that kind of communication whereby creativity increases the good of life . . . . If great art teaches us anything about the nature of man and the good of life, it tells us that suffering is intrinsic and essential to the increase of qualitative meaning' (*op. cit.,* pp. 96f.).

or persecution' will arise 'because of the word' (Mk. 4:17). Christians will be delivered up to councils and beaten in synagogues (Mk. 13:9). Christians will be 'hated of all men for my name's sake' (Mk. 13:13). This is a condition of Christian service, and is not subject to modification. This is the kind of life to which Christ calls His people. Notice that nothing is said in these Gospels by way of rebellion against all this. Suffering is not treated as something to be shunned. Nor is it regarded as a hindrance to Christian service. It is part of the Christian's lot. He must simply get used to it. He must bear in mind the cost of discipleship. Jesus reminded one would-be follower that He Himself had less 'security' than the foxes or the birds, and to another who wanted to stay at home until he had buried his father, He said, 'leave the dead to bury their own dead' (Mt. 8:19-22). More than once He called on those who would follow Him to take up their cross or to lose their life for His sake (Mt. 10:38; 16:24; Mk. 8:34). He told the rich young ruler to sell all that he had (Mt. 19:21; Mk. 10:21). An element of renunciation is integral to Christian service. It is not a cruel accident to be endured with as good a grace as possible. It is of the very essence of discipleship.

The truth is that, for the Christian, suffering has been trans-formed by the fact that his Master came to suffer. Both our Gospels have a good deal to say about the sufferings of Christ, and these sufferings have saving power. These sufferings cannot be regarded as no more than the outcome of the machinations of wicked men. They are that. But they are also, and more importantly, the means whereby God brings blessing to mankind. The pathway to salva-tion lies through sufferings, the sufferings of the Son of God Himself. By these sufferings Christ has consecrated suffering for His followers. It is not palatable, but the truth is that suffering is the pathway to blessing both for the sufferer himself and for others.

We even have an indication that in some sense the disciple may share the Master's sufferings. Jesus asked the sons of Zebedee, 'Are ye able to drink the cup that I drink? or to be baptized with the baptism that I am baptized with?' and He went on to assure them that 'The cup that I drink ye shall drink; and with the baptism that I am baptized withal shall ye be baptized' (Mk. 10:38f.). This may also be behind the appeal to the three close intimates to watch with the Lord in Gethsemane (Mt. 26:38). Jesus surely did not want them to act as sentinels to guard against a surprise attack. He wanted them to share with Him as He prayed through His hour of agony. We are dealing with a mystery here and we must not be dogmatic. It is in any case impossible to hold that any sufferings of the disciples are to be thought of as atoning. But if we must not exaggerate the significance of the words, we must not minimize it either. Jesus is holding out to His followers the prospect of sharing to some degree in His sufferings.

THE WILL OF THE FATHER

Sometimes in the history of theology the atonement has been described in such a way as almost to imply that Jesus was saving men from the Father. The Father is depicted as a stern Judge, as One who insists that men should keep His laws and pay the due penalty for any and every transgression. He is willing to forgive, but only on condition that His darling laws be honoured, only when all His demands are met up to the hilt. Into this picture comes Jesus, the loving Son. By His atoning death He fully satisfies the demands of the Father, and turns away His wrath. This can only be dismissed as a caricature. This is not the picture that is found in Scripture. There the atonement is not described as something wrung by desperate means from the Father. It is something that is wrought expressly because of Him. The atonement proceeds from His loving heart. It is *His* way of saving men.

We shall see this brought out throughout the New Testament. In our two Gospels it is implied, for example, in passages which speak of the passion as fulfilling prophecy (e.g., Mt. 26:24, 54, 56; Mk. 14:21,[29] 27, 49). If what is happening is fulfilment of prophecy, then clearly the events are simply following the course that God has laid down. His will is being done. Vincent Taylor brings this out by drawing attention to the prophecy 'I will smite the shepherd' cited from Zechariah 13:7 in Mark 14:27. Jesus' 'suffering and death are not merely events compassed by men, but rather the fulfilment of a purpose deep in the counsels of God.'[29a] The God who inspired the prophecies is bringing to pass their fulfilment. What is taking place, then, is not in defiance of His will, but on account of His will.

The same implication must be drawn from these passages which say that the Son of man *must* (Gk. δεῖ) suffer (Mt. 16:21; Mk. 8:31). There is a compelling divine necessity about this 'must'. It is not simply advisable. It is not merely expedient. It is not the best way under the circumstances. The expression shows that there is no other possibility. The hand of God is in it, and this rules all else out. Even where the word 'must' does not occur statements about the inevitability of the cross can scarcely be understood otherwise (see Mt. 17:22f.; 20:18f.; Mk. 9:31; 10:33f.). As early

---

[29] The words 'woe unto that man . . .' bring home Judas' responsibility. Yet in the same action we may see the working out of the divine purpose. God overrules evil to bring to pass His will. In our preoccupation with the evil we should not be blind to the deeper issue.

[29a] JS, p. 147.

as his third chapter Mark records a discussion among the Pharisees and the Herodians as to how they could 'destroy' Jesus (Mk. 3:6). From the earliest days the shadow of the cross lay over the Christ.

Perhaps clearest of all is the prayer of our Lord in the Garden. The cross loomed very large. He experienced to the full the natural human shrinking from the horror that lay ahead. His prayer came from the agony of His soul,[30] yet with complete submission to the Father's will: 'not what I will, but what thou wilt' (Mk. 14:36); 'thy will be done' (Mt. 26:42). It is impossible to understand this other than as signifying that the ordeal that lay ahead was the will of the heavenly Father for the Son. The death that Jesus would die is a death in which the fatherly purpose of God would be done. It was not a process whereby an unwilling pardon was wrung from Him.

From all this it is abundantly clear that both Matthew and Mark understand the atonement as something that proceeds ultimately from the Father. They do not obtrude the thought, but throughout their Gospels there is the consistent idea that God wrought out His will in what Christ underwent for men. In the work of salvation the Father and the Son were completely at one.

DEATH AND THE MISSION OF CHRIST

It is this thought of the purpose of God which leads on to the idea that the death of Jesus represents an integral part of His mission. More, it is the very heart and core of His mission. He came to die.[31]

Some today understand the Gospels as though the death of Jesus was a tragedy. They picture Him as a prophet[32] setting out with

---

[30] Lesslie Newbigin contrasts the ease of creation with the cost of redemption: 'the Son of God, the Word of God made flesh, kneels in the garden of Gethsemane. He wrestles in prayer. His sweat falls like great drops of blood. He cries out in an agony: "Not my will, but thine be done". That is what it costs God to deal with man's sin. To create the heavens and the earth costs Him no labour, no anguish; to take away the sin of the world costs Him His own life-blood' (Sin and Salvation, London, 1946, p. 32).

[31] 'What the Gospels tell us is that Jesus saw His death not as a glorious after-thought which would move men's hearts by its splendour of self-sacrifice but as the very soul of His vocation — the thing God sent Him into the world to do' (A. M. Hunter, The Work and Words of Jesus, London, 1956, p. 92).

[32] Paul E. Davies in an article, 'Did Jesus Die as a Martyr-Prophet?', in Biblical Research, ii, pp. 19-30, argues that there was a firm tradition that a prophet would suffer. He quotes F. W. Young, 'In a sense prophetic death as well as prophetic life was typed'; 'It was commonly known that if a prophet followed the pattern of the venerated prophets of old, then he

high hopes that by His teaching and His living He would bring His nation to see that He was the One appointed by God to bring in the Kingdom. As the crowds thronged around Him it seemed that He was well on the way to effecting this aim. But then events took a sinister turn. People, especially the vested interests in politics and religion, turned against Him. He came to be regarded as dangerous. His enemies conspired against Him. He was betrayed by one who should have obeyed. He was handed over by His own nation. He was slain as the result of a sordid combination of treachery, cowardice, and cynical political expediency. The story is a miserable one, with its one redeeming feature the bearing of the Martyr who endured so much without complaint. It is all inexpressibly sad.

But that is not the way it appeared to Matthew and Mark. There are some elements of truth even in this reconstruction, but the main thrust is quite at variance with what the Gospels actually say. Matthew pictures Jesus as facing the possibility of worldly success right at the beginning of His ministry, and as rejecting it. He thought of turning stones into bread, of working spectacular but empty miracles, of establishing a magnificent world-wide kingdom. And He dismissed all three as nothing more than the temptation of the devil (Mt. 4:1-11). The sayings about putting a patch of un-dressed cloth on an old garment, and about pouring new wine into old wineskins (Mt. 9:16f.; Mk. 2:21f.) both emphasize that Jesus did not come merely to patch up an old system. Rather He came to do something radically new. Specifically the evangelists do not see the death of Jesus as an unmitigated tragedy. It is a tragedy in some senses. It is a tragedy that Judas should betray his Lord. It is a tragedy that the chief priests should conspire against Him to whom their Scriptures pointed. It is a tragedy that Pilate should let him-self be brow-beaten into acquiescence in a deed that he knew to be wrong. Nothing can alter the fact that these things *are* tragic. Nor that the tragedy is the supremely significant thing for Judas, and for the chief priests, and for Pilate (little though the last-mentioned two suspected it). But the tragedy is not the really significant thing about Calvary. For Matthew and Mark there is a much deeper truth than that. Jesus came to die. That was His mission. That was the purpose of His coming.

This is sometimes brought out by the recording of sayings of the type, 'the Son of man must suffer' (Mk. 8:31). The important

---

inevitably was faced with martyrdom' (*ibid.*, p. 26). Thus the acceptance of the role of the prophet pointed inexorably to the cross (Davies agrees that this recognition does not rule out the possibility that Jesus also under-stood His death as a ransom or a sacrifice; others do not go so far).

thing here is the linking of the expression 'the Son of man'[33] with suffering. 'The Son of man' is a curious expression, and it is just as unusual in Greek as it is in English. It is a slavishly literal translation of an Aramaic expression, and the scholars are not at all agreed as to its exact significance. Some things, however, are clear. One of them is that it is Jesus' own name for Himself. The expression is used by Him more than eighty times, and nobody else refers to Him in this way with the solitary exception of Stephen (Acts 7:56). It is found in all the strata discerned by modern critics in the four Gospels. There cannot be the slightest doubt that this is the way Jesus delighted to refer to Himself, nor that it is peculiarly His own. Other people do not use the expression. That is to say, it was not a widely used title, known and accepted by all. It was not an accepted designation of the Messiah. Jesus could use it without people thereby thinking that He was claiming to be the political Messiah of popular expectation. Clearly it expressed His own sense of mission, of vocation.[34] He had come to fulfil all that 'the Son of man' implies. What 'the Son of man' was to do, Jesus was to do.[35]

If we seek to find out what this involves we naturally turn to the Old Testament. There the expression is found in some Psalms (as Ps. 8:4), and in the book of Ezekiel, as synonym for 'man'. Usually in these places the thought is of man in his weakness, his creatureliness (though this is combined with a certain glory, and a sense of mission). It is not impossible that Jesus should have used the expression on occasion to denote that He was meek and lowly. But He certainly did not do this always or habitually.[36] In Mark 14:62 He says, 'ye shall see the Son of man sitting at the right hand of power, and coming with the clouds of heaven.' This awakens memories rather of Daniel 7:13f., 'behold, there came with the clouds of heaven one like unto a son of man, and he came even to the ancient of days, and they brought him near before him. And

[33] There is a very useful summary of recent writing on 'the Son of man' by A. J. B. Higgins in *New Testament Essays, Studies in Memory of Thomas Walter Manson*, ed. A. J. B. Higgins, Manchester, 1959, pp. 119-35. See also S. Mowinckel, *He that Cometh*, Oxford, 1956, pp. 346-450.

[34] E. Schweizer sees the term as gathering together a number of Jewish ideas, as well as being of central importance to Jesus (JBL, lxxix, p. 122).

[35] See further Leon Morris, *The Lord from Heaven*, London and Grand Rapids, 1958, pp. 26-29.

[36] E. Stauffer notes the view of some that the expression signifies 'the complete unpretentiousness of the historical Jesus who was, and wanted to be, no more than a man among men.' He proceeds, 'But the contribution of the history of religions has taught us better than that. "Son of Man" is just about the most pretentious piece of self-description that any man in the ancient East could possibly have used!' (*New Testament Theology*, London, 1955, p. 108).

there was given him dominion, and glory, and a kingdom, that all
the peoples, nations, and languages should serve him: his dominion
is an everlasting dominion, which shall not pass away, and his kingdom that which shall not be destroyed'. Most scholars today see
in this glorious figure the origin of our Lord's idea. Here the
Son of man is a being of heavenly origin, one who will bring in
God's kingdom (Jesus' favourite topic of teaching was 'the kingdom of God'), a kingdom that will never pass away.

To associate suffering with this glorious being is to set forth a
striking paradox.[37]   In Daniel and in non-canonical Jewish literature
the Son of man is a figure of majesty and splendour. He is accorded universal honour and acclaim.[38] Jesus knew Himself to
fulfil this aspect of the Son of man's work, as His eschatological
references abundantly illustrate. But He also knew that the path
to glory for the Son of man was by way of the cross. If He saw
Himself as the Son of man He saw Himself no less clearly as the
Suffering Servant of Isaiah 53. He does not quote from this
chapter very often, but allusions are often to be detected.[39]   For
example, in Mark 10:45 we have the word 'minister' (which
means 'serve'), the phrase 'for many' ('many' occurs four times in
the Servant poem[40]), and the substitutionary giving of life (which
is the theme of Isaiah 53). Few students of the Gospels doubt that
Jesus saw Isaiah fulfilled in the manner and purpose of His death.[41]

[37] Some have argued that others than Jesus made this equation. H. H.
Rowley's careful examination, however, indicates that this is not the case
(*The Servant of the Lord*, London, 1952, p. 13, n. 5, pp. 74ff.). See also
H. Wheeler Robinson, *Redemption and Revelation*, London, 1943, p. 199;
S. Mowinckel, *op. cit.*, pp. 327 and n., 328f., 410, 448f.; H. J. Schoeps,
Paul, London, 1961, p. 140; M. Black, SJT, vi, p. 11, etc.

[38] C. F. D. Moule thinks the term points to 'vindication after defeat. But
it means more than being vindicated: it means vindicating; for on any showing the term is to this extent a collective one that the person of Jesus is
representative, inclusive, incorporative; and therefore if his course is vindicated,
then with it he becomes the Vindex of the body of people whom he represents
and sums up' (*Studiorum Novi Testamenti Societas, Bulletin III*, Oxford,
1952, p. 46).

[39] For a list of passages which contain such allusions see W. Zimmerli and
J. Jeremias, *The Servant of God*, London, 1957, pp. 98f.   Matthew specifically
quotes Servant passages and applies them to Jesus (Mt. 8:17; 12:18-21).   C. J.
Cadoux lists the passages which convince him that Jesus applied the Servant
passages to Himself (*The Historic Mission of Jesus*, London, 1941, pp. 37f.).

[40] Of this expression in Is. 53 S. Mowinckel says, ' "The many" (not "many";
the article is omitted in poetical style) is the community as contrasted with
the single individual, and so = "all" ' (*op. cit.*, p. 202, n. 1).

[41] Morna Hooker is an exception.   She argues that Jesus did not think of
Himself as the Servant, nor did the early church as a whole, the identification
being first clearly made in 1 Peter (*Jesus and the Servant*, London, 1959; for
the last point see p. 127).   She agrees that 'Christian experience . . . has
shown the rightness of the Church's interpretation' (*op. cit.*, p. 163), and

Now the combination of these two ideas is important. If Jesus was to suffer, and if at the same time Jesus was the Son of man and suffered as the Son of man, then suffering was of the very essence of His mission.[42] 'The Son of man' was, so to speak, His official title. It was the way He described Himself in the light of His mission. He came to be the glorious Son of man. But these passages show that He would reach His true glory precisely by suffering. And nothing illuminates the nature and the meaning of His suffering like the great Servant passage in Isaiah 53. This embodies a distinctive view of suffering.[43] He did not only suffer: He suffered vicariously, substitutionarily.[44] He bore the penalty for the sins of others.[45] S. H. Hooke sums up the work of the Servant in Isaiah 53 in this way:

> First of all we have the emphasis laid on the divine initiative, an initiative of which the Servant is fully conscious, "Jahveh called me from the womb, from the bowels of my mother he made mention of my name", words which recall Jeremiah's similar expression of

---

thus leaves herself open to Vincent Taylor's penetrating question, 'In interpreting the Servant concept was the Church more discerning than Jesus?' (ET, lxx, p. 301). For references to scholars on both sides see E. Schweizer, *Lordship and Discipleship*, London, 1960, p. 49n.

[42] Cf. C. R. North, 'The essential likeness between the Servant and Jesus lies in this: that whereas prophets like Jeremiah suffered in the course of, or as a result of, their witness, for both the Servant and Jesus suffering is the means whereby they fulfil their mission and bring it to a triumphant conclusion' (*The Suffering Servant in Deutero-Isaiah*, Oxford, 1948, p. 208).

[43] E. J. Young points this out: 'The righteous Servant suffering for the sins of those who are unrighteous . . . involves the truth that salvation from the guilt of sin is by grace and not by man. It is a conception which is to be found only in the Bible. In the religions of antiquity, and, for that matter, in those of the modern world, it does not appear' (WThJ, xiii, p. 32).

[44] T. H. Hughes thinks that Jesus 'interpreted the vocation and task of the Messiah in the light of vicarious sacrifice and death of the Servant. The Servant vicariously bears the sufferings caused by his people's sin, and gives himself to death as a substitute for others. In this way a vicarious and substitutionary element enters into the very fibre of Christ's self consciousness' (*The Atonement*, London, 1949, p. 167). Cf. also H. C. Thomson, 'The Servant is made an *'asham* for the guilty people; he is the substitute who gives his life and so preserves theirs, and by his sacrifice their guilt is expiated' (*Transactions of the Glasgow University Oriental Society*, xiv, p. 26). J. Morgenstern thinks the Servant's mission was 'to offer himself as the substitute-sacrifice, the sin-offering, i.e., then as the scapegoat, for the redemption of errant mankind' (*Vetus Testamentum*, xi, p. 410).

[45] J. S. Whale emphasizes the penal aspect of the sufferings described in Isa. 53: 'the song makes twelve distinct and explicit statements that the servant suffers the *penalty* of other men's sins: not only vicarious suffering but penal substitution is the plain meaning of its fourth, fifth and sixth verses. These may not be precise statements of Western forensic ideas, but they are clearly concerned with penalty, inflicted through various forms of punishment which the Servant endured on other men's behalf and in their stead, because the Lord so ordained' (*Victor and Victim*, Cambridge, 1960, pp. 69f.).

his sense of the divine mission. Secondly, by this experience of
the divine choice he is marked out as Jahveh's agent and representative, his function is to carry out the will of Jahveh. Thirdly,
he is seen as voluntarily offering himself, "Truly he gave himself
as a guilt offering." Fourthly, he carries the experience of Ezekiel,
the bearing of Israel's sins, to the ultimate limit of death and
descent into the underworld. Fifthly, we have the declaration put
into the mouth of those for whom this divine activity of substitution has been wrought, "The chastisement leading to our welfare
was upon him, and by means of his stripes there is healing for us."
Finally, whether in figure or reality, the poet prophet sees in
resurrection and return to light Jahveh's acceptance of the Servant's
substitutionary work and the pledge of his success.[46]

Small wonder that from New Testament times on Christians have
found in the Servant a satisfying conception for the setting forth
of the meaning of Christ's death. This idea that Christ suffered in
the stead of sinners is, for those who follow Him, the deepest truth
about Him as it is about suffering.[47]

This is brought out also in other ways. There is an early passage
in which He deals with the question of fasting (Mt. 9:15; Mk. 2:19f.).
He explains that His disciples cannot fast while He is with them.
'But the days will come, when the bridegroom shall be taken away
from them, and then will they fast in that day.' There cannot be
the slightest doubt but that 'taken away' refers to Jesus' death by
violence (the bridegroom is not 'taken away' at a wedding: this
is an alien element and not part of the figure). The linking of this
violence with the messianic title 'the Bridegroom' indicates that the
death is part of Jesus' messianic calling. He does not see it as
something alien to His mission.[48]

So with the question, 'how is it written of the Son of man, that
he should suffer many things and be set at nought?' (Mk. 9:12)
asked by Jesus as He descended with the disciples from the mount
of transfiguration (Matthew has the saying in the form of a statement, 'Even so shall the Son of man also suffer of them,' Mt. 17:12).
The disciples have just said, 'The scribes say that Elijah must first
come.' That is to say, Jesus' words are set in a messianic context.
The coming of Elijah was associated firmly in Jewish expectation
with the coming of the Messiah. It is clear that both Jesus and

[46] *Vetus Testamentum*, ii, pp. 15f.
[47] J. Jeremias thinks that the absence of references to the Servant in
sayings peculiar to Matthew and Luke shows that this was Jesus' teaching
to His disciples and not His public preaching (Zimmerli and Jeremias,
op. cit., p. 104).
[48] A. M. Hunter makes the point that this saying shows that from very
early days Jesus faced death as that to which He was called (*op. cit.*, pp. 93f.).

the disciples are thinking in terms of messiahship. And His thoughts go to suffering.[49]

We should also bear in mind Jesus' reaction to the request of the sons of Zebedee for the supreme places. He asked whether they could drink the cup that He would drink, and be baptized with the baptism with which He would be baptized (Mt. 20:22; Mk. 10:38). These words clearly point to the death of Christ, but they equally clearly point to the fulfilment of the high calling wherewith He was called. He is not speaking of something extraneous, but of that towards which He had set His face. We might here consider also Jesus' response to the anointing at Bethany. When the woman poured the unguent over His head and became the target of criticism, Jesus defended her. Among other things, He said, 'she hath anointed my body aforehand for the burying' (Mk. 14:8; cf. Mt. 26:12). Now anointing was a common custom at feasts and the like. The normal associations aroused by the term would have been those of joy and festivity. Jesus' words show that He was very much occupied with the thought of His death. It was at the centre of His thinking.[50] The saying also shows that Jesus was anticipating that His death would be that of a criminal. Only so would it be expected that there would be no anointing.[51]

Mark has a wonderful word picture of the scene as Jesus went up to Jerusalem. 'And they were in the way, going up to Jerusalem; and Jesus was going before them: and they were amazed; and they that followed were afraid' (Mk. 10:32). What a subject for an artist! The amazement, the fear indicate that something in the bearing of Jesus intimidated them[52] as He strode purposefully

[49] See Vincent Taylor's discussion of this passage, JS, pp. 91-7. He examines and refutes objections to the authenticity of the saying, and concludes: 'The saying is of the greatest importance. It confirms the view that Jesus believed He must suffer as the Son of Man, and that He had taught this truth to His disciples. . . . the saying shows that Jesus thought of His Messianic suffering in relation to the coming of the Kingdom. He had faced the problem created by the expectation of the return of Elijah before the Parousia, and had solved it by identifying Elijah with John; but He had also faced a problem not contemplated in the thought of the time — the necessity of the suffering of the Son of Man before the perfecting of the Rule of God. This problem He had solved in the certainty of His own suffering and rejection.'

[50] 'Only a dominating interest can account for this reference' (Vincent Taylor, JS, p. 11).

[51] So Zimmerli and Jeremias, op. cit., pp. 99, 103.

[52] C. H. Turner arbitrarily changes the text to read 'he was amazed', and proceeds, 'or rather, since "amazed" in our modern English use of the word is quite inadequate to represent the Greek, "he was overcome with consternation." A stronger compound of the same verb is used of the Agony in Gethsemane (14:33): it is a foretaste of that moment' (A New Commentary on Holy Scripture, ed. C. Gore, H. L. Goudge, A. Guillaume, London and New York, 1928, in loc.; see also Turner's The Study of the New Testament, Oxford, 1926,

at the head of the little band of His followers as He went up to Jerusalem — to die. Here there is no thought that Jesus regarded His passion as something negative, some calamity imposed from without, something to be endured with what fortitude He could muster, the initiative being in the hands of His enemies. On the contrary, it is in the passion that He is active, positive, supremely the Master of the situation. There as nowhere else He accomplishes His mission.

The triumphal entry to Jerusalem is to be considered here. Matthew and Mark use it to introduce the events of the last week of Jesus' life, those leading up to the cross. They do not picture Jesus as deceived for one moment by the enthusiasm of the crowds. He recognized it for what it was, the shallow enthusiasm of people who understood neither His mission nor His message. But the triumphal entry has its place all the same. It represents the making of a formal, public, open, almost official claim to being the King prophesied in Zechariah 9.[53] The royalty of Jesus was not the royalty dreamed of and looked for by the excited multitude. It was a royalty that was leading to a cross, a royalty that would be revealed, for those who had eyes to see, in the cross. But the important point is that it *was* royalty. Matthew and Mark see Jesus as indeed fulfilling the prophecy. Though He was on the way to die, He was a King. The two are one, for He came to establish the kingdom through His death. The same thing shines through the entire passion narrative. Consider Jesus as He stands before the High Priest. With the certainty that His condemnation to death by crucifixion lay in the immediate future, Jesus could answer the question of Caiaphas, 'Art thou the Christ, the Son of the Blessed?' in the words, 'I am: and ye shall see the Son of man sitting at the right hand of power, and coming with the clouds of heaven' (Mk. 14:61f.; cf. Mt. 26:63f.). The certainty of the cross meant no diminution of the glory. With the cross in immediate prospect, Jesus makes His most explicit claims to heavenly royalty.

All along He had, of course, made much of the idea of God's

---

p. 62). This seems to me to be a complete misunderstanding of the situation, as well as being a high-handed treatment of the text.

[53] 'Jesus entered Jerusalem for the last time in a manner which showed that He was none other than the Messiah, the Son of David, who was coming to Sion to claim the city as His own' (R. V. G. Tasker, *Tyndale Commentary on the Gospel According to St. Matthew,* London, 1961, p. 197). Tasker has a section in which he develops the theme that this Gospel is the 'Royal' Gospel (*op. cit.,* pp. 17-26). *Inter alia* he says, 'it is obviously very relevant to describe the Gospel of Matthew as "the apologetic", "the liturgical" and "the ecclesiastical" Gospel. But if we are looking for a single epithet to describe its dominant characteristic perhaps the best available for our purpose is the word "royal"; for, as McNeile well says (p. xvii), "the special impression which Matthew embodies is that of royalty" ' (*op. cit.,* p. 19).

Kingdom. Though He uses the term Kingdom 'of God' or 'of heaven'[54] that is not to be interpreted as though He had nothing to do with it. As He began His ministry Jesus could call on men to repent 'for the kingdom of heaven is at hand' (Mt. 4:17; similarly Mk. 1:15).[55] John the Baptist, whom Matthew sees as pointing forward to the coming of Jesus, used a similar expression (Mt. 3:2), and Jesus told the disciples to make this the burden of their preaching (Mt. 10:7). All this indicates that the Kingdom and the mission of Jesus were connected in the closest fashion. In some sense the mission inaugurates the Kingdom. This, too, is the implication of the expression 'the gospel of the kingdom' (Mt. 4:23; 9:35; 24: 14; 'the word of the kingdom', Mt. 13:19, means much the same). The good news that Jesus brought centered in the Kingdom.

It is emphasized in much recent writing that the basic meaning of the word for 'Kingdom', alike in Greek, Aramaic, and Hebrew, is 'reign', rather than 'realm'. It is a dynamic, not a static concept. The Kingdom of God, then, is God's rule in action. But various hindrances disqualify men from entering the Kingdom (Mt. 5:20; 7:21; 18:3; 19:23ff.; Mk. 10:23ff.). The very fact that the evangelists mention these things shows that they hold it to be desirable that men should enter. Matthew preserves a command to seek the Kingdom first of all (Mt. 6:33), and his words about the 'scribe who hath been made a disciple to the kingdom of heaven' that he 'bringeth forth out of his treasure things new and old' (Mt. 13:52) show that it is an enriching experience. He can use the expression 'the sons of the kingdom' to denote those in right relationship to God (Mt. 13:38), though this use is not invariable (Mt. 8:12). Mark sees the Kingdom as supremely desirable, so that it is well gained even if a man has to lose an eye to do it (Mk. 9:47). This last passage shows that entering the Kingdom and entering into life mean much the same, for the two expressions are used in parallel

---

[54] G. E. Ladd points out that there is no real difference of meaning between the two expressions, and that Jesus' use is a new one. 'The "kingdom of heaven" does not appear anywhere in Jewish-Greek writings before it is found in Matthew's Gospel. However, the equivalent phrase is found in the talmudic literature quite frequently: *malkuth shamayim*. This literature cannot be taken as antecedent to the time of our Lord's ministry even though some old traditions may be preserved in it. It does reflect the fact that during the succeeding centuries, the phrase became deeply imbedded in Jewish idiom. The phrase, the kingdom of God, occurs infrequently in the Jewish literature known to antedate the New Testament. The concept of the kingdom constantly recurs, but the idiom itself rarely is found' (*Crucial Questions about the Kingdom of God*, Grand Rapids, 1954, pp. 121f.).

[55] That the verb ἐγγίζω in such passages means 'has come' is contended by W. R. Hutton (ET, lxiv, pp. 89ff.; see also M. A. Simpson, ET, lxiv, p. 188). This would signify that the Kingdom had already come in the person of Jesus. It is difficult to square this, however, with John the Baptist's use of the same expression (Mt. 3:2).

(Mk. 9:43, 45, 47). Both our evangelists indicate that a childlike attitude is the right one for those who would enter the Kingdom (Mt. 19:14; Mk. 10:14f.).

The Kingdom is in some sense future, for the Lord's Prayer includes a petition for its coming (Mt. 6:10), and Jesus looks forward to a time when some will sit down in it (Mt. 8:11). All is not straightforward about the Kingdom, for there are mysteries concerning it which are not made known to all, though they are made known to Jesus' disciples (Mt. 13:11; Mk. 4:11). Matthew has a good deal to say about the Kingdom in a series of parables in chapter 13, and elsewhere (see 19:23ff.; 20:1ff.; 22:2ff.; 25:1ff.). These emphasize the worth of the Kingdom, its connection with Jesus, and the importance of entering it by a right attitude toward Him.[56] The important point for our present study is the connection with Jesus. If there is a Kingdom of God, and if Jesus is linked in the closest fashion with this Kingdom, and with God as His Father, then He shares in the royalty. He holds the highest place.

And it is no coincidence that Mark records the words of the centurion as he saw Jesus die, 'Truly this man was the Son of God' (Mk. 15:39). The cross does not contradict the divine Sonship. The cross is not some major obstacle to be reconciled with difficulty with the divine Sonship. The cross reveals the divine Sonship.

THE DEATH OF THE INNOCENT

The cross means suffering, and, indeed, the Gospel writers ascribe central importance to the sufferings of Christ. But they are writing about sufferings which were significant. They were for the salvation of Christ's people. Thus the evangelists make it clear that His death was not in any sense due to personal demerit. His death was for our sins, not for His, for He had none. They picture Him as innocent of any crime or sin, as the spotless One. This point is important, for unless He were without sin Jesus could not have been the Saviour of sinful man. He would Himself have needed to be saved. So our evangelists show us One who is qualified to be our Saviour. This is implicit in the whole manner of the life they describe. They do not say in so many words that Jesus was sinless

---

56 Cf. J. Jeremias, 'In attempting to recover the original significance of the parables, one thing above all becomes evident: it is that all the parables of Jesus compel his hearers to come to a decision about his person and mission. For they are all full of "the secret of the Kingdom of God" (Mk. iv, 11), that is to say, the recognition of "an eschatology that is in process of realization". The hour of fulfilment is come, that is the urgent note that sounds through them all' (*The Parables of Jesus,* London, 1954, p. 159). C. H. Dodd also stresses the demand for decision implied in the parables (*The Parables of the Kingdom,* London, 1938, pp. 197f.)

(though the temptation narratives may well be held to imply this). They simply show Him going about doing good.[57]

But particularly in the passion narrative they draw attention to the absence of any crime that could be brought against Jesus. Judas declares that he has sinned in betraying 'innocent blood' (Mt. 27:4). Pilate inquires, 'Why, what evil hath he done?' (Mt. 27:23; Mk. 15:14). This man knew that the chief priests had delivered Jesus up, not on account of any sins He might have committed, but 'for envy' (Mt. 27:18). Matthew also records Pilate's attempt to deny responsibility for the crucifixion by taking water and washing his hands before the crowd with the words, 'I am innocent of the blood of this righteous man' (Mt. 27:24). It is possible also that Mark's repeated references to Jesus as 'King of the Jews' in connection with the crucifixion are meant to teach the same thing (Mk. 15:2, 9, 12, 18, 26, 32). Jesus was crucified as a criminal. He was actually a King. Could His innocence be more emphatically asserted?[58]

CHRIST AND SINNERS

But if Christ is depicted as personally innocent, He is also shown to us as One who was closely linked with sinful men. He was the Friend of sinners. This means more than that He mingled with sinners from time to time. Occasions when He did just this are reported (e.g., Mt. 9:10ff.; Mk. 2:15ff.), and His choice of Matthew the publican among His apostles is significant (Mt. 9:9; Mk. 2:14). Table fellowship with such people may well, as J. Jeremias thinks, imply an offer of salvation.[59] At the very least it indicates an attitude foreign

---

[57] I have drawn out the evidence for this point a little more fully in *The Lord from Heaven,* London and Grand Rapids, 1958, pp. 21-24.

[58] Yet it is to be borne in mind that Mark records no declaration of Jesus' innocence on the part of Pilate. Nor does he mention any attempt by Jesus to clear Himself before the governor. As Mark sees it, there is an air of inevitability about the proceedings. Jesus must suffer. Cf. T. H. Robinson, 'In a very real sense Jesus threw His life away. Though the final stroke of violence which deprived Him of life came from the hands of others, yet it was His own act, calculated and determined, which armed those hands with their destructive power. It is in full accord with the whole of this scene that He is represented elsewhere as saying of His life "No man taketh it from me, but I lay it down of myself"' (*St. Mark's Life of Jesus,* London, 1941, p. 125).

[59] 'Orientals, to whom symbolic actions mean more than to us, immediately understood that the admission of the outcasts to table fellowship with Jesus meant an offer of salvation to the guilty sinners, and the assurance of forgiveness. Hence the passionate objections of the Pharisees . . . who assumed that the pious could have table fellowship only with the righteous. In this way they revealed an understanding of our Lord's intention to accord to sinners worth before God, and they objected to the placing of the sinners on the same level as the righteous' (*The Eucharistic Words of Jesus,* Oxford, 1955, p. 136).

to the usual religious views of the day. At best Judaism thought of God as exercising His love and His mercy to those who repent. Jesus sought out sinners. It had been obvious to thinking men that contemporary Israel was far from being the people of God in any meaningful sense. But the usual remedies were withdrawal. The Qumran sect did this literally, withdrawing into the wilderness. The Pharisees did it in a different fashion, living among the people but separating themselves in thought. They despised others and thought of themselves as standing especially close to God. Such groups regarded 'sinners' as hopeless. Jesus' attitude is in sharp contrast. For Him sinners are not to be rejected out of hand. They are to be sought out and ministered to. It is impossible to see in His warmth toward them anything less than an indication that they might enter into the salvation He came to bring. It is significant that His whole ministry was concerned with sinners, not with righteous men (Mt. 9:12f.; Mk. 2:17).

For our present purpose, however, even more important than this is the fact that Jesus accepted treatment as a sinner. Of set purpose He included Himself in the number of the sinners. Take, for example, the perplexing fact of His seeking baptism at the hands of John. John's baptism was a 'baptism of repentance' (Mk. 1:4). Now we have already noticed that our evangelists firmly repudiate any thought of sin in Jesus. Therefore a baptism connected with repentance could have no relevance to Jesus Himself. The sinless Son of God could have no need of such a rite. It is impossible to understand this baptism other than along the lines that thereby Jesus took up a position among sinners. His baptism allied Him firmly with sinners. It put Him where sinners stand. It numbered Him among sinful men.[60]

But there is probably more to the baptism than this. There is general agreement among modern students of the Gospel that Jesus saw His vocation in terms, partly at least, of the Suffering Servant of Isaiah 53.[61] There is also agreement that the baptism represents the beginning of His work, the time of dedication, the time of hearing the divine voice.[62] This being so, it is not

---

[60] Cf. James Denney, 'It would not have been astonishing if Jesus had come from Galilee to baptize along with John, if He had taken His stand by John's side confronting the people; the astonishing thing is that being what He was He came to be baptized, and took His stand side by side with the people. He identified Himself with them. . . . It is as though He had looked on them under the oppression of their sin, and said: On Me let all that burden, all that responsibility descend' (DC, p. 20).

[61] See above, pp. 31ff.

[62] The divine voice (Mt. 3:17; Mk. 1:11) commends Jesus in words which remind us of the commendation of the Servant in Is. 42:1. But the words are even closer to those used of Isaac in Gen. 22:2, so that the thought of the passage may be that Jesus is fulfilling all that is implied in the offering of

surprising that many recent students have come to the conclusion
that the baptism sees Jesus not only taking His place with sinners,
but doing this in the role of the Servant who would bring them salvation. Thus O. Cullmann can say,

> At the moment of his Baptism he receives the commission to under-
> take the rôle of the suffering Servant of God, who takes on him-
> self the sins of his people. Other Jews come to Jordan to be
> baptised by John for their *own* sins. Jesus, on the contrary, at the
> very moment when he is baptised like other people hears a voice
> which fundamentally declares: *Thou* art baptised not for *thine own*
> sins but for those of the whole people. For thou art he of whom
> Isaiah prophesied, that he must suffer representatively for the sins
> of the people. This means that Jesus is baptised in view of his
> death, which effects forgiveness of sins for all men. For this
> reason Jesus must unite himself in solidarity with his whole people,
> and go down himself to Jordan, that "all righteousness might be
> fulfilled."[63]

If we can say all this we can say more. The acceptance of the
role of the Suffering Servant means an acceptance of death. This
is implied also in the fact that Jesus numbered Himself not merely
with sinners, but with sinners standing under judgment. What
gave urgency to John's preaching was precisely the certainty of
judgment, the recognition of the ill desert of sin. Moreover, the
symbolism of the baptism he practised points in the same direction.
Putting all this together we reach the conclusion, with J. A. T.
Robinson, that 'Jesus' acceptance of baptism at the hands of John
is therefore the beginning of that baptism of vicarious suffering which
could only be completed in the Cross'.[64]

Now let us notice a saying recorded only in the first Gospel.
When Jesus came to John for baptism, that stern man of the deserts
tried to prevent Him from submitting to the ordinance. Jesus replied, 'Suffer it now: for thus it becometh us to fulfil all righteousness'
(Mt. 3:15). This saying has always perplexed Christians, and its
meaning is far from obvious. Some see in it a way of referring to the
truths we have already examined, the taking of a place with sinners,

---

Isaac. The Rabbis appear to have taught that Isaac willingly offered himself for sacrifice, and, indeed, that the willingness was the reason for a
special efficacy attaching to this. See G. Vermes, *Scripture and Tradition in
Judaism*, Leiden, 1961, pp. 193-227; J. Klausner, *From Jesus to Paul*, London,
1946, p. 265, n. 1.

[63] *Baptism in the New Testament*, London, 1950, p. 18. See also *The
Christology of the New Testament*, London, 1959, pp. 66ff.; W. F. Flemington,
The New Testament Doctrine of Baptism, London, 1948, p. 27; G. W. H.
Lampe, SJT, v, pp. 167f.

[64] SJT, vi, p. 261. See also J. Warns, *Baptism*, London, 1957, pp. 20, 21.

and the like.[65] But 'fulfil all righteousness' seems to imply something more. A. E. Garvie long ago suggested that the right way to understand this expression is in the light of Isaiah 53.[66] We have already seen other indications that this chapter must be in mind in interpreting the incident, and it seems logical accordingly that this very unusual expression be interpreted in the same way. Garvie points out that the righteousness that Jesus in point of fact set Himself to fulfil throughout His ministry is not explicable in terms of the righteousness of the Pharisees (an observance of rites and precepts), nor of that of John (repentance). It is much more likely that the righteousness He has in mind is that of Isaiah 53:11. Garvie says,

> The righteous Servant shall justify many because He shall bear their iniquities. It is in His vicarious consciousness and the sacrifice which this would ultimately involve that Jesus fulfilled all righteousness. There is a higher righteousness than being justified by one's own works, a higher even than depending on God's forgiveness; and that belongs to Him who undertakes by His own loving sacrifice for sinners to secure God's forgiveness on their behalf.[67]

In other words, at this moment Jesus set Himself to fulfil that righteousness that meant justifying sinful men. Understood in this way, the baptism of our Lord, taken in conjunction with the interpretative comment that Matthew records, is seen to be a most significant prelude to the ministry. It indicates the pattern that was to be followed, a pattern that began with our Lord's numbering Himself with sinners, and ended with His obtaining eternal justification for them on the cross.[68]

The Transfiguration (Mt. 17:1-8; Mk. 9:2-8) is usually understood as a revelation of the glory of Jesus, that and nothing more.

---

[65] E.g., C. Ryder Smith, BDS, p. 149; F. D. Coggan, ET, lx, p. 258. D. R. Griffiths, however, prefers to take the term in an ethical sense, ET, lxii, pp. 155-57.

[66] So, more recently, C. E. B. Cranfield, 'The righteousness that Jesus was determined to fulfil to the uttermost was the role of the Suffering Servant of the Lord' (SJT, viii, p. 54).

[67] The Expositor, VI, 5 (1902), p. 375.

[68] Cf. G. W. H. Lampe, 'It may not be too much to claim that this saying shows that Jesus is regarded by St. Matthew as interpreting His Sonship and Messianic anointing in such a way as to identify Himself with the righteous Remnant of Israel and, as its representative, to unite Himself with those who are undergoing John's baptism in order that they may be constituted a renewed community of the "saints". Perhaps we may go even further and see a deeper meaning in the words of Jesus; the Servant who is to suffer vicariously and "bear the sin of many" will procure a general justification, or declaration of righteousness, for His people' (The Seal of the Spirit, London, 1951, pp. 37f.).

Moses and Elijah appear in this understanding of it all as the representatives of the Law and the Prophets. This may well be so. But it should not be overlooked, as C. Ryder Smith reminds us, that both these were men who agonized over the sins of their people, men who, while not personally sharing in the people's sin, yet felt themselves very much one with the people.[69] The words that came from heaven in this mountain are practically identical with those spoken at the baptism when Jesus made Himself one with sinners, and they may well be meant to commend essentially the same attitude. And we should not forget that, as the little band went down the mountainside, their talk was of the death of the Lord and of the resurrection of the Lord and of the place of John the Baptist in this sequence of events.

In the crucifixion narrative the same truth is brought out. The evangelists tell us that Jesus was crucified between two thieves. This no doubt was due to the malice of His enemies, but the fact that the evangelists choose to record it indicates that they saw a deeper significance in it than that. The position in the centre makes it impossible to overlook the fact that He is right among sinful men. In His death He is not apart from sinful men. He is executed as sinful men are executed. Through all His ministry He had sought out sinful men. At the climax of it all He is clearly one with them.[70]

SEPARATION FROM THE FATHER

'Nobody lays such emphasis on the fact that His followers "all forsook him and fled", on the Lord's utter dereliction in the hour of death, so that even the two thieves crucified with Him retire into the background of the narrative. The despairing cry of Psalm 22

---

[69] 'With both there had been an agony of years . . . . The chief element in the imperfect salvation that they wrought was the fact that they so loved their people that they "must" identify themselves with them, yet must all the time refuse to sin with them. This means that in their degree they shared both in Jehovah's love for Israel and in His abhorrence of their sins, and that the two passions tore them in two. This is the very tension of salvation. When our Lord was about to "set his face to go to Jerusalem", it helped Him to think of those who had won a smaller yet similar battle' (BDS, p. 154).

[70] Heinrich Vogel sees in this the heart of the gospel and the rationale of substitution. If someone were to be executed in place of a criminal, he says, 'you will see there is a lie involved; fundamentally it is unreal and ineffective; for no one can remove the actual guilt from the condemned man . . . . it is not within the power or the will of man.' He proceeds, 'God can do it, simply because he is omnipotent, so that with him the impossible is possible. God is willing to do it; for in his mercy he became one of us, in Christ. Christ alone really stands in our place. He lives our life, stamped with the curse of death; he dies our death; he, the only innocent one, became guilty in our stead; he became the accursed one under God's Wrath. Everything you read about him in the Gospel you must accept through this fact: for us, in our place' (*The Iron Ration of a Christian,* London, 1941, p. 140).

underlines the dereliction even more clearly. On the cross the Christ is utterly alone.'[71] In these words J. V. Langmead Casserley brings out the stress Mark places on the forsakenness of Jesus in the hour of His death. And this brings us to one of the most difficult problems in biblical interpretation, namely the meaning we are to assign to the cry of dereliction, 'My God, my God, why hast thou forsaken me?' (Mt. 27:46; Mk. 15:34).

Some find the plain sense of the words so frankly incredible that some other meaning must be found. They think it quite impossible for the Son ever to have been forsaken of the Father. The words then are taken to refer to a feeling of desolation and deep depression which came over Jesus' soul at this difficult time. The words of T. R. Glover are often cited with approval, 'I have sometimes thought there never was an utterance that reveals more amazingly the distance between feeling and fact.'[72] This type of explanation seems to me basically unsatisfactory. It will account for our own feelings of desolation. We often think in our self-pity (and self-importance) that God has forsaken us, only to return in our better moments to the realization that He never does leave His erring children. So we come to understand that our moments of spiritual weakness do not give us the measure of the divine presence.

But it is impossible to ascribe to Jesus our weakness. In point of fact this very saying shows that His faith was strong. He still addresses God as 'my' God. We must not impute to Him the spiritual blindness that is part and parcel of ourselves. He could not be mistaken in a matter of this kind. If He said that God had forsaken Him, then the hitherto unbroken communion between the Father and the Son must have been clouded over. We must not water down an unpalatable saying. Vincent Taylor examines the passage and says (in my judgment, rightly), 'it appears to be an inescapable inference that Jesus so closely identified Himself with sinners, and experienced the horror of sin to such a degree, that for a time the closeness of His communion with the Father was broken, so that His face was obscured'.[73] But then he adds, 'and He seemed to be forsaken by Him.' Why 'seemed'? Jesus said He

---

[71] J. V. Langmead Casserley, *Christian Community*, London, 1960, p. 14. See also L. W. Grensted, 'It is as perfect man that He has assured communion with the Father, unbroken save for that terrible moment of darkness upon the Cross, when, that He might be wholly one with man even in man's sin, He knew the full horror of the loneliness which man has made for himself' (*The Person of Christ*, London, 1933, p. 239).

[72] *The Jesus of History*, London, 1917, p. 192. Halford E. Luccock takes some of the sting out of the words by citing as a position which has won much agreement, 'we have here "not an expression of the feeling of dereliction" or abandonment by God, but rather of loneliness and perplexity over the betrayal, the desertion, and the Cross' (IB on Mk. 15:34).

[73] JS, p. 162.

was forsaken.[74] Can we really believe that a modern student of
the Gospels knows more of the realities of such a situation than did
Jesus Himself?[75] In saying this I am not unmindful of the very real
difficulty of the saying. The words raise difficult problems not only
with regard to the atonement but also concerning our Lord's Person,
and the doctrine of the Trinity. I find this 'an hard saying.' Frankly,
from some points of view, I would find the situation much more
tolerable if these words did not stand in the record.[76] But they are
there, and I see no merit in attempting to empty them of their force.

Other scholars remind us that the words are the opening words
of Psalm 22. M. Dibelius, for example, points this out, and goes on
to say that this is 'a Psalm which opened up to Christians the true
understanding of the Passion in a quite essential way . . . . A Bible
word on the lips of a dying man means a religious reverence for the
Bible, and, in any case, union with God.'[77] Dibelius is developing
the point that the events of the Passion were offensive,[78] and that
the Christians gave them meaning by thinking of them as the will
of God and finding Old Testament passages where they were foretold. I do not think that this is the right way of understanding the
situation, but even if we were to grant that Dibelius' reconstruction
is sound, the question would immediately arise, Why are *these* words
chosen? Look at them. They express neither 'religious reverence

[74] E. Stauffer contrasts the psalmist of Qumran: 'In the Qumran psalms
the "teacher of righteousness" confesses again and again: "Thou hast not
forsaken me, *lo asabthani.*" ' He proceeds to point out the significance of
this, 'no expositor may blunt the edge of this word. It is a *skandalon* — a
"stumbling block". No Qumran heretic was ever so god-forsaken and solitary
as the crucified heretic on Golgotha' (*Jesus and His Story,* London, 1960, pp.
114, 115).

[75] R. W. Dale takes up a more satisfactory position. 'I shrink from saying
that even in my calmest and brightest hours I have a knowledge of God
and the ways of God which is truer than Christ had, even in His agony. I
dare not stand before His cross and tell Him that even for a moment He
imagines something concerning God which is not a fact and cannot be a
fact' (*The Atonement,* London, 1902, p. xli).

[76] There is, of course, that other point of view so well stated by Canon
Peter Green, 'nothing could make up for the loss of these precious words
from the Bible' (*Studies in the Cross,* London, 1917, p. 81). He points out
that the worst part of the punishment of sin is the cutting off of the sinner
from God, and he asks, 'suppose He had paid all the rest of the price of
sin, the suffering, the submission and breaking of pride, and the hatred of sin,
and left this unpaid, would it not have been as if He had paid the farthings,
pence, and shillings of some vast debt but left the pounds for us to pay?'
(*op. cit.,* p. 101). The cry of dereliction shows that the price of sin has been
paid in full.

[77] *From Tradition to Gospel,* London, 1934, pp. 193f.

[78] 'What happened in Jerusalem at that time must have been so offensive
and ignominious that a record of these things could only seem a document of
shame and disgrace' (*op. cit.,* p. 184).

for the Bible' nor 'union with God.' As plainly as words can they
express the very opposite of union.

Another way of trying to ease the difficulty is to point out that,
while this Psalm begins with the troubles of the Psalmist it proceeds
to an expression of trust, 'I will declare thy name unto my
brethren . . . He hath not despised nor abhorred the affliction of
the afflicted; neither hath he hid his face from him; but when
he cried unto him, he heard' (vv. 22-24). The suggestion now is
that Jesus in His hour of need consoled Himself by reciting this
Psalm. The evangelists have recorded no more than the opening
verse. But we should understand the later expressions of trust to
be included. Against this interpretation H. Maynard Smith force-
fully objects, 'the awful cry which startled the onlookers cannot
be reconciled with a devotional exercise.'[79] The evangelists do not
give the impression that they are recording a pious meditation.
There is also the point that, if this is what Matthew and Mark mean,
it is pertinent to ask, Why do they not say so? It would not have
taken them many words to explain that Jesus was reciting a whole
Psalm.[80] If brevity was of the essence of the matter, they might
have cited a verse which gives plainer expression to the thought of
trust. They could hardly have chosen a worse one if that was in
their mind. We should not forget that these are the only words from
the cross recorded by the first two evangelists. They must have
selected them for a purpose. As they stand the words can scarcely
be taken as anything other than a declaration that in the manner
of His death Jesus was cut off from the Father.[81] And our
evangelists graphically express the same thought when they tell us
that there was darkness over all the land as Jesus died. An event
so terrible must be shrouded in gloom (Mt. 27:45; Mk. 15:33).

A position with the definite ring of the modern world is that of
E. Basil Redlich, who explains it all on psychological principles.

---

[79] *Atonement,* London, 1925, p. 155.

[80] It is not certain that Jesus was quoting the Psalm at all. William Blight
points to the habit, common among those who are steeped in Scripture, of
expressing their feelings in Bible language: 'when on the Cross He felt
acutely His isolation from God and man. "Cursed is every one that hangeth
on a cross" was a statement with which He had long been familiar. He felt
alone, deserted: and He said so: in Scriptural words. But He was not
quoting at all' (ET, lxviii, p. 285).

[81] Cf. John Marsh, 'in our view the desolation expressed in this cry was
one which faced Jesus because He was dying *as a man.* To have died our
physical death and not tasted its spiritual awfulness in the final separation
from God that spiritual death means, would have been to have missed the
characteristic "sting" of death for man. It would have been to cease to be man
at this point of man's death.' He quotes 2 Cor. 5:21, and proceeds, 'Though
sinless, he died the sinner's death and tasted the bitterness of its desolation'
(*The Fulness of Time,* London, 1952, p. 100, n. 1).

The explanation of the cry is given by modern psychology, where it is known that a pure-minded woman, for example, who in conscious life has repressed evil thoughts into the subconscious often gives utterance to those very thoughts when she is in a state of semi-consciousness. Then those thoughts which she has refused to harbour well out from the unconscious and could easily mislead the hearers as to her true character. Jesus in the Garden of Gethsemane was sore troubled with thoughts of God's love, fought them down, and emerged victorious from the mental conflict. And now on the Cross the thoughts He had repressed in the Garden find their way out when He is semi-conscious.[82]

This position is objectionable for several reasons. In the first place it means in plain language that Jesus did not know what He was talking about; He was completely in error. In the second, what took place in the Garden was not repression. There Jesus did not simply put away unwelcome possibilities. He faced reality squarely and won through to a victory.[83] In the third, Jesus was not semi-conscious as He uttered the words. Redlich himself has said on the previous page that the loud cry with which Jesus died 'indicated that Jesus was in full possession of His faculties at death.' Redlich's psychological theory is completely untenable.

The cry of dereliction must be considered in conjunction with the agony in Gethsemane. There, as Jesus prayed, His soul was in veritable torment. 'He . . . began to be greatly amazed, and sore troubled' (Mk. 14:33).[84] This is very forceful language. Of the word translated 'sore troubled', J. B. Lightfoot says it 'describes the confused, restless, half-distracted state, which is produced by physical derangement, or by mental distress, as grief, shame, disappointment',[85] and H. B. Swete refers to it as conveying 'the distress which follows a great shock.'[86] The language is vivid, almost shocking. Clearly

---

[82] Op. cit., p. 177.

[83] Cf. the definition of repression given in a standard work, 'But there is another type of unconscious fact — one which has proved distasteful to the ego and has been disowned by it. The forgetting of such facts occurs in an automatic way, and this process is known as repression' (Sir David Henderson, R. D. Gillespie, and Ivor R. C. Batchelor, A Text-Book of Psychiatry, London, 1956, p. 138). This is not a description of what happened in Gethsemane. David Cox quotes from a law report to show how repression works, ' "Even politicians", he said, "sometimes said or did something which they afterwards wished they had not done. All that he, counsel, suggested against the plaintiff was that his mind had worked in the following way: It was a silly thing to do; I wish I had never done it: I could not have been such a fool; of course, I did not do it. . . . And finally the plaintiff had come into the witness box fully persuaded that he had not agreed to go" ' (Jung and St. Paul, London, 1959, p. 134). It is impossible to understand the cry of dereliction along such lines.

[84] Moffatt translates, 'he began to feel appalled and agitated'.

[85] Commentary on Phil. 2:26.

[86] Commentary on Mk. 14:33.

the evangelists were describing no ordinary perturbation. Jesus was in agony as He faced death. Why? Death is never a pleasant prospect, but many have faced it calmly. Significantly, many of Jesus' own followers have faced their death without a qualm, some even with exultation.[87] Jesus was no coward, as many incidents in His life amply testify. It is impossible to hold that He was afraid of leaving this life. It was not death as such that He feared. It was the particular death that He was to die,[88] that death which is 'the wages of sin' as Paul puts it (Rom. 6:23), the death in which He was at one with sinners, sharing their lot, bearing their sins, dying their death. There is a kind of anticipation of this also in Jesus' horror at being 'betrayed into the hands of *sinners*' (Mt. 26:45; Mk. 14:41), and at being arrested by men who came against Him 'as against a robber' (Mt. 26:55; Mk. 14:48).[89] Nor should we overlook His reference to drinking the 'cup' (Mt. 20:22f.; 26:39; Mk. 10:38f.; 14:36). This is usually taken as no more than a metaphor for suffering, but C. E. B. Cranfield has pointed out that 'in the O. T. the metaphorical use of "cup" refers predominantly to God's punishment of human sin'. He concludes that 'His cup is the cup of God's wrath against sin. We must connect Mk 14.36 with the Cry of Dereliction on the Cross, which marks the veritable descent into hell of the sinless Son of God — His descent into the hell of utter separation from the Father — and with 2 Co. 5.21 or Ga. 3.13.'[90]

The cry of dereliction must not be watered down.[91] It is a

---

[87] 'The absence of all fear, in fact, is one of the notes of the early Church'; 'For weeks before the fatal issue, we find the martyrs living in a state of ecstasy' (H. B. Workman, *Persecution in the Early Church*, London, 1923, pp. 305, 321). D. W. Riddle's curious book, *The Martyrs*, Chicago, 1931, regards the martyrdoms as purely sociological phenomena, and the deeds of the martyrs as 'the results of attitudes socially produced' (*op. cit.*, p. vii). The author never asks whether what the martyrs (or the church) said had any truth in it. But he amply documents the martyrs' readiness for, even eagerness for, death.

[88] 'It was not with such feelings that the martyrs faced death, and the only tenable explanation of the words is one which recognizes that it was the prospect of death *as Jesus interpreted it* which tortured His soul in this hour' (JS, p. 149; Taylor's italics).

[89] J. Jeremias sees something of this also in Jesus' vow of abstinence (Mt. 26:29; Mk. 14:15). By this 'Jesus may have intended to make clear to His disciples that His decision to open the way for the kingdom of God by His vicarious suffering was irrevocable. . . . Beneath His resolution there is already something of the dreadful tension of the struggle at Gethsemane, and of the depth of His dereliction on the Cross' (*The Eucharistic Words of Jesus*, Oxford, 1955, p. 171).

[90] ET, lix, p. 138. Cranfield thinks that the term is used of the disciples only in a weakened sense.

[91] In his commentary on Mark, C. E. B. Cranfield rejects 'softening explanations' and goes on: 'The burden of the world's sin, his complete self-

shocking statement, and we must beware of trying to render it innocuous.[92] The death that Jesus died was full of horror, and no understanding of the atonement can be satisfactory which does not reckon with that. It is the terrible nature of the death that He died that is significant, and not merely the fact that He did die. M. Goguel reminds us that

> it is not without significance that the earliest account of the Passion has not attempted (as it would have been easy to do) to emphasize the physical torture which Jesus endured, while it has retained so accurate and precise a recollection of his spiritual agony; for the sense of being abandoned by God must have caused unfathomable pain to him whose whole life had been supported by the experience of the presence of God.[93]

That this presence was withdrawn is the measure of the horror of Jesus' death. This shows us, as nothing else does, the cost of atonement. Centuries earlier the prophet Habbakuk had prayed, 'Thou that art of purer eyes than to behold evil, and that canst not look on perverseness' (Hb. 1:13). It is here, it seems to me, that we must seek our explanation of the saying. So terrible is it to bear the sin of the world that it led to this awful separation. Sin separates from God (Is. 59:2), and so it would seem does sin-bearing.[94] J. K. S. Reid says forthrightly, 'Christ as reprobate bears damnation on His shoulders to defend and shelter those who

---

identification with sinners, involved not merely a felt, but a real, abandonment by his Father' (*in loc.*).

[92] J. P. Hickinbotham reminds us that 'A cry so liable to misunderstanding would probably not be recorded at all, certainly would not be recorded in splendid isolation, unless it were charged with theological meaning. . . . We cannot doubt that St. Mark intends us to understand that the Three Hours of Darkness symbolize a real darkness in the soul of Jesus: a real consequence of being forsaken by God which finds its expression in the Cry of Dereliction. It is this spiritual desolation which makes plain the significance of His Death' (*The Churchman,* lviii, p. 56). He later says, 'the desolation Christ suffered *was our penalty transferred to Him*' (*op. cit.,* p. 57; Hickinbotham's italics; his article is written to show that the theory underlying St. Mark's Gospel 'is such as can only be rightly described in terms of penal substitution', *op. cit.,* p. 52).

[93] *The Life of Jesus,* London, 1958, p. 541. He has earlier noted the remarkable brevity of the description of the crucifixion, 'a word or two, and that is all' (*op. cit.,* p. 534), and he proceeds to show how remarkable this is by detailing with the aid of a long quotation from Albert Réville the horrors of this mode of execution.

[94] 'It would seem then that atonement could not be complete, the experience would be unfulfilled, unless He had also been where sin is "when it is finished" — the death of the soul. This is hell — separation from God — and many have felt with Calvin that these words from the Cross are the best commentary on the profession of the Creed: "He descended into hell"' (D. H. C. Reid, ET, lxviii, p. 262).

are in Him from it, however merited.'[95] While perhaps not every-one would choose exactly this way of expressing it, something like this does seem to be demanded by the scriptural language.

This, of course, must be held in such a way as not to obscure that other truth that the unity of the Trinity is unbroken and unbreakable.[96] No one wants to speak of a rupture within the depths of the divine Being. But the incarnation means something. It means among other things that it became possible for Christ to die. And if it became possible for Him to die it became possible for Him to die the most bitter of deaths, the death of God-forsakenness. There is paradox here, and both sides of the paradox are important. One side emphasizes the truth that Jesus Christ, perfect man, has drunk to the very dregs the cup of our sins. He has endured their consequences to the uttermost extent. So fully did He make Himself one with sinful man that He entered into the God-forsakenness that is the lot of sinners. He died their death. The other side of the paradox we might put in Temple's words: 'No further entry of the Supreme God into the tangle and bewilderment of finitude can be conceived. All that we can suffer of physical or mental anguish is within the divine experience; He has known it all Himself. He does not leave this world to suffer while He remains at ease apart; all the suffering of the world is His.'[97] Because it is a paradox it is not surprising that many have surrendered one side or the other. The history of the doctrine of the atonement is plentifully be-sprinkled with examples of those who have taken the easy way by opting for the one view and jettisoning the other. But the Gospel writers express their paradox and we neglect either side to our loss.

REMISSION OF SINS

After all this, it is not surprising to find that these writers have a deep interest in the forgiveness of sins. As early as Mark 1:4 we read that John preached his baptism of repentance 'unto remission of sins.' The interest in forgiveness shown thus early is seen

---

[95] SJT, i, p. 181. Interestingly, J. H. Newman also saw in this cry 'the agony of hell itself' (cited in W. J. Sparrow Simpson, *The Redeemer*, London, 1937, p. 110).

[96] Cf. C. E. B. Cranfield, 'It is, of course, theologically important to main-tain the paradox that, while this God-forsakenness was utterly real, the unity of the Blessed Trinity was even then unbroken' (on Mk. 15:34).

[97] *Christus Veritas*, London, 1949, p. 270. Cf. also R. W. Dale, 'The mysterious unity of the Father and the Son rendered it possible for God at once to endure and to inflict penal suffering, and to do both under conditions which constitute the infliction and the endurance the grandest moment in the moral history of God' (*The Atonement*, London, 1902, p. 393). While he is not speaking primarily of this passage his words apply to it.

throughout both Gospels. An interesting early example comes from the story of the paralyzed man brought to Jesus by his four friends. When they let him down through the roof in front of the Master He said to him, 'Son, thy sins are forgiven' (Mk. 2:5; so also Mt. 9:2).[98] This is so strange to modern ideas that it is worth closer consideration. We today are very much concerned with the problem of suffering. We build and equip large and expensive hospitals. We regard it as almost axiomatic that sickness should be attended to. We would regard with the gravest suspicion any clergyman who insisted upon talking about a sick man's sins before allowing the medical man to do something about his paralysis. We would not discount the spiritual, but we would insist on keeping it in its 'proper' place. Jesus insisted on that, too, but His understanding of the 'proper' place was not ours. He first neglected the paralysis and concentrated on that which was of prime importance. He dealt with the sin. Only then did He turn His attention to the man's bodily ailment.[99] For twentieth-century men there is food for thought here.

Forgiveness is not something to be taken for granted. It does not come about automatically. Indeed, both Matthew and Mark record some words of Christ about a sin which cannot be forgiven (Mt. 12:31f.; Mk. 3:28ff.). The explanation given to the parable of the Sower reveals that the use of the parabolic method is connected with the fact that some will not be forgiven (Mk. 4:12; Matthew has 'lest haply they should . . . turn again, and I should heal them,' Mt. 13:15, which amounts to the same thing). Both evangelists stress the importance of men's exercising forgiveness of their fellow-men, and connect this with the Father's forgiveness of them (Mt. 6:14f.; 18:21-35; Mk. 11:25).[100] The insistent demand for repentance which we noted earlier has its relevance here. Repentance and remission complement one another. Neither can be well understood apart from the other. A reference to the one implies the other.

Matthew records an important saying concerning the attitude to

---

[98] A. Cole is of the opinion that the sick man 'was not so much conscious of his physical need as of his spiritual burden' (*Tyndale Commentary, in loc.*).

[99] Cf. Karl Heim, 'The forgiveness of guilt is the decisive victory on which everything depends. The overcoming of the power of disease is merely secondary evidence that that victory has been won' (*Jesus the World's Perfecter*, Edinburgh, 1959, p. 31).

[100] 'Here there is no idea of a bargain. The pardon which is received does not pay for the pardon given; it is due to a sense of guilt, which is necessary in order that the pardon offered by God can be grasped and appropriated by man' (Maurice Goguel, *op. cit.*, p. 579).

be adopted when one of the brethren sins against another: 'And if thy brother sin against thee, go, shew him his fault between thee and him alone: if he hear thee, thou hast gained thy brother' (Mt. 18:15). Jesus does not simply say that the offended brother is to be ready to forgive when the sinner is penitent. He himself must take the initiative. He is to seek the sinner out, and try to effect a reconciliation. While this is not explicitly posited of God, it is impossible to think that Jesus asked men to do more than God Himself does. Moreover, the divine seeking out of sinners is evident in every line of this Gospel, recording the ministry of Jesus in the way it does. The saying points us to the source of the initiative in forgiveness.

The death of Christ is explicitly linked with forgiveness in these two Gospels only in Matthew 26:28, 'this is my blood of the covenant, which is shed for many unto remission of sins'. Since the words about remission are absent from the corresponding passage in Mark, and since Matthew gives the impression that at this point in his narrative he is basically dependent on Mark, most modern scholars doubt whether they can be thought of as authentic. The point is interesting, but since most also agree that they are a faithful representation of our Lord's thought, with Matthew doing no more than drawing out the implications of Mark,[101] it hardly seems necessary to discuss it. The 'blood of the covenant' must be interpreted in the light of the new covenant of Jeremiah 31:31ff., probably with a side glance at certain Isaianic passages which likewise refer to a covenant.[102] Whether the word 'new' be accepted as the true reading in either account or not (some manuscripts have it and some do not in both Gospels), a covenant which is being initiated in blood so many hundred years after the other cannot be any other than a 'new' covenant. And Jeremiah gives as a feature of the new covenant that he foresaw, 'I will forgive their iniquity, and their sin will I remember no more.' To say then that Jesus is shedding His blood to inaugurate such a covenant is to

[101] E.g., Vincent Taylor, *Forgiveness and Reconciliation*, London, 1946, p. 12.

[102] Alan Richardson links the saying with the Jeremiah passage, and also with Isa. 42:6 ('I . . . will . . . give thee for a covenant of the people, for a light of the Gentiles'), and 49:8 ('in a day of salvation have I helped thee: and I will preserve thee, and give thee for a covenant of the people'). 'It is clear that, if our Lord understood his own mission in terms of the prophecy of Isaiah, as the evidence undoubtedly shows that he did, he would inevitably think of his death as necessary, as expiatory, and as establishing a new covenant between God and a new people, which would include the "enlightened" Gentiles' (*op. cit.*, p. 231). See also M. Black, ET, lvii, pp. 277f.; R. N. Flew, *Jesus and His Church*, London, 1938, p. 104; R. H. Fuller, *The Mission and Achievement of Jesus*, London, 1954, pp. 74f.

say that He is shedding[103] His blood that men's sins might be forgiven. It is to ascribe atoning value to His death.[104]

A RANSOM FOR MANY

There is one passage in these Gospels wherein Jesus described His death as a ransom. 'The Son of man came not to be ministered unto, but to minister, and to give his life a ransom for many' (Mt. 20:28; Mk. 10:45). The saying arises from the incident in which the sons of Zebedee seek the chief places in the coming kingdom. Jesus counters by asking whether they can drink the cup that He drinks, and be baptized with the baptism with which He will be baptized. They assure Him that they can. He tells them that they will indeed drink such a cup and receive such a baptism, but that the places they seek will be given to them for whom they have been prepared.

This incident provokes the ten to indignation, and Jesus proceeds to give them a lesson on the essential nature of Christian service. 'Whosoever would become great among you, shall be your minister (or "servant"; Gk. διάκονος).' The Christian is not to seek greatness as the world seeks greatness. For him is rather the lowly way, the way of making himself a servant to his fellows. 'Whosoever would be first among you, shall be servant (or "slave"; Gk. δοῦλος) of all.' Paradoxically the foremost Christian is the one who is slave of all the others! Then Jesus explains how this comes to be. If His own mission is to serve, then how much more that of His followers. He proceeds to show the extent of His own service by referring to the giving of His life as a ransom. This is the supreme example of service.

In the ancient world the 'ransom' was the price paid for release.

---

[103] E. D. Burton points out that ἐκχυννόμενον, 'poured out' or 'shed' in Mk. 14:24 is used in the Septuagint not of the killing of a sacrificial victim, but '(a) of the shedding of blood in murder (Gen. 9:6) and (b) of the pouring out of the blood of the sacrifice at the base of the altar'. He sees the most probable understanding of it as combining 'a reference to the burnt-offering and peace-offering, by which the covenant between God and Israel was ratified, with a reference to the sin-offering' (op. cit., pp. 121f.). I am not persuaded that all this detail can be derived from the expression, but at least it does point us to the truth that Jesus fulfilled all that the sacrificial system implied with respect to covenant sacrifice.

[104] J. Jeremias examines the words τὸ ἐκχυννόμενον ὑπὲρ πολλῶν and concludes that the meaning is 'which is going to be shed for the whole world' (op. cit., p. 151). He later says, 'The often repeated assertion that it is unthinkable that Jesus should have ascribed atoning power to His death, and that such statements belong much rather to the dogmatizing of the Primitive Church or of the Apostle Paul, will astonish anyone who knows the Palestinian sources . . . . The sources compel the conclusion that it is unthinkable for Jesus not to have thought about the atoning effect of His death' (op. cit., p. 152).

It applied widely to the release of prisoners of war or of slaves. The Old Testament adds another use. In certain circumstances a man under sentence of death might be released on payment of ransom (Ex. 21:30). Apart from metaphorical passages, these three groupings give us the uniform usage in antiquity. There is always a plight into which a man has fallen, be it captivity or slavery or condemnation. There is always the payment of the price which effects release, and it is this price that is called the 'ransom'.[105]

Each of the above situations has point in the Christian scheme. Like the prisoner of war, man is in the power of the enemy. Christ has paid the ransom, freeing him and bringing him back where he belongs. The sinner is a slave. He is in bondage to his sins. Christ has paid the price, His life, which brings release to the sinner. As a result he is a free man. The sinner is under sentence of death on account of his sin. His life is forfeit. But 'the forfeited lives of many are liberated by the surrender of Christ's life.'[106]

Some deny the authenticity of the ransom saying. The fullest case against it still seems to be that of Hastings Rashdall, but as I have discussed this elsewhere it may suffice to refer to that discussion.[107] Vincent Taylor has a careful examination of the saying, and concerning certain objections he says, 'the idea that no act of requital is due to a Holy God, or is needed by men, is a modern notion which it would be a libel to attribute to the ancient world; and to say that Jesus cannot have spoken of His death in this way is to modernize His figure and His thought. Jesus is a stranger to the thought-world of the twentieth century.'[108] We must always be on our guard against accepting only those New Testament ideas which are congenial to us. Those who see no significance in the mention of 'ransom', but generalize the saying into no more than an advocacy of the duty of service to others should heed the warning of W. F. Howard, that 'modern exposition is rather in danger of reducing the logion to a pious platitude.'[109]

Along with many others,[110] Howard sees in this verse a reference

---

[105] See further the discussion in my *The Apostolic Preaching of the Cross*, London and Grand Rapids, 1955, Ch. I.

[106] James Denney, DC, p. 45.

[107] *Op. cit.*, pp. 26-35.

[108] JS, p. 105. He also has a judicious note on the passage in his commentary on *The Gospel According to St. Mark* (London, 1952), where he cites opinions *pro* and *con,* and concludes, 'The strength of the argument is on the affirmative side.' He says further, 'It is wise never to forget that λύτρον is used metaphorically, but it is equally wise to remember that a metaphor is used to convey an arresting thought' (*op. cit.*, p. 446).

[109] ET, 1, p. 107.

[110] E.g., Alan Richardson, who says dogmatically, 'In Mark 10. 45 he is alluding to Isa. 53. 10f.' (*op. cit.*, p. 220). R. Mackintosh thinks that 'this crucial saying may include an echo of Isa. liii. 12 — the great Sufferer "bare

to Isaiah 53. He points out that the choice of words is very significant. 'The Son of man' is important, for, in the words of Rudolph Otto, Jesus 'knew Himself to be the one who had to suffer, not as an ordinary, chance, private individual, nor as a mere martyr, but as the Son of Man.' 'Came' is surely not used here in a light, casual way, but in the deeper sense of 'a mission to be fulfilled'. 'Serve'[111] in this context 'compels us to recognize that a life-time of service is to find its climax in suffering and death for the sake of "many".' And the word 'ransom' with its cognates, he reminds us, 'is used nearly one hundred and forty times in the LXX, generally with the thought of the payment of compensation, or of deliverance from prison, or the offering of a substitute.'[112]

He might have added that the preposition $\dot{\alpha}\nu\tau\acute{\iota}$, 'for', is the preposition of substitution. Of itself it does not prove that the atonement is substitutionary, but it lends its measure of support to the other indications that this is in mind.[113] Indeed, the whole saying is substitutionary, for it tells us that in His death Jesus paid the price that sets men free. He took our place. He gave His life that our lives be no longer forfeit.[114] C. K. Barrett is more than doubtful whether it is right to see Isaiah 53 as the background of the saying, but he clearly recognizes that the language

---

the sins of *many*" — but it throws us back upon the teaching of Ps. xlix in regard to "ransom" from death' (*Historic Theories of Atonement,* London, 1920, p. 49).

111 P. H. Boulton in an article entitled 'Διακονέω and its Cognates in the Four Gospels' (SE, pp. 415-22), complains that insufficient attention is given to the verb. His examination leads him to say, 'In the crucial saying of Mark 10, 45, διακονέω (with its cognate διάκονος) is understood as expressing the complete fulfilment of a complete sacrifice — the giving of one's life. . . . "Here", as Beyer remarks, "διακονεῖν attains its ultimate theological profundity" ' (*op. cit.,* p. 421).

112 *Op. cit.,* p. 109. R. H. Fuller sees the expression δοῦναι τὴν ψυχὴν αὐτοῦ λύτρον as pointing to Is. 53:10, *'im tāsîm 'asham naphshô.* He proceeds, 'λύτρον is a perfectly adequate rendering of *'āshām*, the meaning of which in this passage is given by Brown, Driver and Briggs s.v. as: "the Messianic servant offers himself as an *'āshām in compensation for the sins of the people, interposing for them as their substitute" ' (op. cit.,* p. 57).

113 'It would be rash to find here a doctrine of the Atonement; yet the preposition used (ἀντί, "instead of") clearly implies substitution, as the echoes of Isa. liii imply representative and redemptive suffering' (A. M. Hunter, *op. cit.,* p. 98).

114 'Addressed by Jewish lips to Jewish ears the words would not be startling or obscure. Jesus was going deliberately to death, knowing that since His own Person was unique, in that He was the Son of the Father, and destined to be revealed as the Son of Man, His surrendered life would be an equivalent for many lives' (A. H. McNeile, on Mt. 20:28).

points us to substitution.[115] It speaks of Christ as suffering in our stead[116] that He might bring us deliverance, deliverance from the consequences of our sins, and deliverance also from our sins themselves.

VICTORY OVER EVIL

A feature of the Synoptic Gospels which is not particularly congenial to modern men, but which has attracted a good deal of attention in recent theological writing, is the continuing conflict with demons.[117] We do not see how demons could take possession of a man, and therefore we conclude that it is impossible. We notice that some of the features of demon possession are not unlike those of illness, often of mental illness, and we assert accordingly that demon possession is no more than that. We feel that what we would with greater exactness describe as sickness the Gospel writers more picturesquely call demon possession.[118]

But the Gospel writers in fact make a distinction between the effects of demon possession and the effects of illness. The fact that we cannot see on what basis they distinguished between the two should not blind us to the truth that they do make the

[115] See his article, 'The Background of Mark 10:45' in *New Testament Essays, Studies in Memory of Thomas Walter Manson*, ed. A. J. B. Higgins, Manchester, 1959. *Inter alia* he says, 'In λύτρον the idea of equivalence is central'; 'This sense of equivalence, or substitution, is proper to λύτρον' (*op. cit.*, p. 6). So also Julius Schniewind, 'Jesus Himself gives His own life as substitute for our lost life' (*op. cit.*, p. 272).

[116] Cf. J. Burnier, 'From what will He liberate them? According to the Gospel of St. Mark it can only be that He will rescue them from their alienation from God, from the sin which subjugates and enslaves them. He will effect this liberation by undergoing in their stead the death which was meant for them, death in stark loneliness and abandonment by God' (*Vocabulary of the Bible*, ed. J. J. von Allmen, London, 1958, p. 350).

[117] Cf. the suggestive title of an article by J. S. Stewart when he deals with the demonic, 'On a Neglected Emphasis in New Testament Theology' (SJT, iv, pp. 292-301). He says, *inter alia*, 'Christ's coming to earth, says Dibelius, was an advance into enemy occupied territory (*ein Vordringen ins feindliche Lager*). It was only by meeting these forces on their own ground, only, that is, by getting into history where they were entrenched, that He could break their power' (*op. cit.*, p. 297). Ragnar Leivestad has shown that the ideas of conflict and victory are to be discerned throughout the New Testament (*Christ the Conqueror*, London, 1954). C. T. Chapman is another to stress the importance of the conflict with evil, in his *The Conflict of the Kingdoms*, London, 1951.

[118] Marguerite Crookes argues for the reality of possession in some cases: 'The rejection of the New Testament accounts of devil-possession is based on an entirely inadequate knowledge of this difficult and complex subject.' She quotes from L. Bendit, 'In our opinion dangerous psychic entities do exist in their own right,' and Osterreich, 'it is impossible to avoid the impression that we are dealing with a tradition which is veracious' (ET, lxiii, pp. 233f.).

distinction (e.g., Mt. 4:23f.; 8:16; 10:8; Mk. 6:13). Moreover, we should not imagine that the Bible is full of cases of demon possession. It is not. It does not seem to occur in the Old Testament at all (though 1 Sa. 16:14ff.; 1 Ki. 22:22ff. are similar), while in the New Testament the phenomenon is referred to only twice outside the Gospels. 'Demon-possession is a phenomenon which occurred almost exclusively, but then to be sure on an amazing scale, during Jesus' appearance on earth and to a lesser extent during the activity of the apostles.'[119]   The conclusion is inescapable that the Gospel writers see this as part of the war between Jesus and the hosts of evil. Jesus was assaulted by the devil at the threshold of His ministry. And from then on, the battle was joined. One theme of the Gospels is this battle, and Jesus is victorious.[120]

As early as Mark 1:21-27 we read of a conflict between Jesus and an unclean spirit. The spirit cried out saying, 'What have we to do with thee, thou Jesus of Nazareth? art thou come to destroy us?' The second question is significant. There did not have to be any formal declaration of war. The unclean spirit recognized Jesus as 'the Holy One of God' and automatically ranked himself in opposition.[121] Throughout the Gospels the same thing is repeated. Whenever Jesus came into contact with demons there was opposition, and He cast them out (Mt. 9:33; 12:22; 17:18; Mk. 1:34, 39; 3:14f.; 5:2ff.; 9:25f.). He set Himself the task of binding 'the strong man' (Mt. 12:29; Mk. 3:27). The parable of the Tares depicts Jesus as in conflict with Satan (Mt. 13:24ff.; cf. 'the sons of the evil one', v. 38).

In His conflict with the demons Jesus did not behave like a typical exorcist. Such a man would have techniques, spells, incantations, and the like.[122]   The Gospel writers do not picture

[119] N. Geldenhuys, *Commentary on the Gospel of Luke,* London, 1952, p. 174. Cf. E. Langton, *Essentials of Demonology,* London, 1949.

[120] Cf. A. M. Hunter, 'Only if we see the Galilean Ministry thus, do we see it aright; and the emergent picture of the Chief Figure in the campaign, so far from being that of a high-souled teacher patiently indoctrinating the multitudes with truths of timeless wisdom, is rather that of the strong Son of God, armed with his Father's power, spear-heading the attack against the devil and all his works, and calling men to decide on whose side of the battle they will be' (*Introducing New Testament Theology,* London, 1957, p. 18).

[121] A. D. Galloway sees in the treatment of the subject in Mark 'convincing evidence that Mark saw the overcoming of the demonic forces as the central activity of the ministry of Jesus. This impression is confirmed by the fact that from a merely quantitative point of view, the main bulk of the Gospel of Mark is devoted to accounts of healing of the sick and the casting out of demons' (*The Cosmic Christ,* London, 1951, p. 38).

[122] For example, Josephus recounts an exorcism performed by a certain Eleazar in the presence of Vespasian, 'and this was the manner of the cure:

Jesus as just another of this type. 'What is this?' men said when He cast out a devil in the synagogue at Capernaum, 'a new teaching! with authority he commandeth even the unclean spirits, and they obey him' (Mk. 1:27). There is indeed a conflict with the demons, but our Gospel writers do not think of Jesus as in a position anything like that of the magicians. He stood in a place all His own. He was uniquely the object of Satanic opposition. He was unique in the methods He used to defeat it. And He was unique in the completeness of His victory.

Sometimes the disciples are associated with Him in this conflict (Mt. 10:1, 8; Mk. 3:15; 6:7), though our information is not sufficient to determine their part in it with any exactness. The petition in the Lord's Prayer, 'deliver us from the evil one' (Mt. 6:13), probably refers to this conflict.[123] On one occasion 'they cast out many devils' (Mk. 6:13). However, face to face with the unclean spirit and the epileptic boy, they were powerless (Mk. 9:18). Why they should be able to cast out devils on some occasions and not on others we do not know. What we do know is that the followers of Jesus were caught up in the Master's struggle against evil. Sometimes even those outside Jesus' immediate circle cast out devils in the Master's name (Mk. 9:38).

The note of triumph is sounded in places other than the struggle with the demons.[124] Thus, at the end of the parable of the Labourers in the Vineyard, Jesus recalled the Scripture, 'The stone which the builders rejected, the same was made the head of the corner: this was from the Lord, and it is marvellous in our eyes' (Mt. 21:42; Mk. 12:10f.). He is thinking of the cross. He will be rejected, and that by His own nation. But that is not the

---

he put to the nose of the possessed man a ring which had under its seal one of the roots prescribed by Solomon, and then, as the man smelled it, drew out the demon through his nostrils, and, when the man at once fell down, adjured the demon never to come back into him, speaking Solomon's name and reciting the incantations which he had composed. Then, wishing to convince the bystanders and prove to them that he had this power, Eleazar placed a cup or footbasin full of water a little way off and commanded the demon, as it went out of the man, to overturn it and make known to the spectators that he had left the man' (Ant. VIII. ii. 5; Loeb translation).

[123] The Greek, ἀπὸ τοῦ πονηροῦ, could, of course, be understood as AV, 'from evil', but most recent discussions agree that a personal reference is more likely. Cf. T. W. Manson, 'The petition asks not for deliverance from distress or suffering, but for deliverance from the arch-enemy of God and men' (op. cit., p. 170).

[124] Some understand the story of the Magi (Mt. 2) in this way, seeing it as the triumph of Christ over the magicians. For an exposition of this point of view see W. K. Lowther Clarke, 'The Rout of the Magi', Theology, xxvii, pp. 72-80.

end of the story. It is little more than the beginning. In the
end there will be triumph.

The Last Supper is the occasion for another indication of the
Lord's victory. To the words about the cup's being His 'blood of
the covenant' Jesus adds, 'I will no more drink of the fruit of
the vine, until that day when I drink it new in the kingdom of God'
(Mk. 14:25; cf. Mt. 26:29).[125]   In the very moment when He
spoke of the significance of His death, Jesus could look right through
that death to the final triumphant establishment of God's kingdom. It
is not too much to see in this the assurance of His triumph through
His death.

The conflict leads inexorably to the cross. But our evangelists
do not see that as defeat. They record the confession of the
centurion as he watched Jesus die, 'Truly this man was the Son of
God' (Mk. 15:39; so also Mt. 27:54). Dibelius notes the significance of this:

> It is not the word or the virtue of a man which is operative, but
> the saving power of Christ's death as a whole. Thus the record
> of this conversion is not an edifying legend with which the death
> of Jesus was adorned, but the last proof of the supernatural sending
> of Jesus to earth, and thus a "sign". The first Gentile was con-
> verted and in his word the Gentiles give their answer to the death
> of Jesus.[126]

The rending of the temple veil (Mt. 27:51; Mk. 15:38), the earthquake[127] and the raising of the saints (Mt. 27:51f.) are further
indications of the same thing.[128]   The evangelists are speaking of

[125] On the authenticity of the Last Supper and specifically of this saying
John Knox says, 'not only may it be said that all of this is credible, but one
may also ask whether subsequent events would be understandable at all if
all of this, or something like it, did not occur' (*The Death of Christ*, London,
1959, p. 122).

[126] *Op. cit.*, p. 195.

[127] Abraham Kuyper sees in the earthquake a reference to the oneness of
Christ's body of flesh with nature, 'If now this flesh is related to all of
nature, how could it be otherwise than that also *in nature* the dying of the
Savior must have its afterthrill' (*His Decease at Jerusalem*, Grand Rapids,
1928, p. 293). More specifically, he relates it to the curse pronounced on
nature as the result of the fall (cf. Rom. 8:19ff.), 'How then could you say,
that a nature, which with the advent of sin dons the garment of mourning, and
still groaning ever waits for the revelation of glory which is to come, should
not have quaked, when the great suit also regarding *her* future was decided,
and the Mediator, who was also her Creator, died away in the death on the
cross' (*op. cit.*, p. 295).

[128] Cf. C. K. Barrett, 'Whatever connotation these occurrences may have
in detail, the general impression which they convey, and were no doubt intended to convey, is of a unique event in this world, which nevertheless
belongs as much to the other, spiritual, world as to this; in fact, of a cosmologi-
cal act (a defeat of Satan) whose decisive actor was yet visible in the

a decisive happening. They describe not defeat but victory.

And when the Gospels come to the cross they do not stop there. They go on to a resounding climax in the story of the resurrection. There we see Christ triumphant over every force of evil, yea over death itself. The repeated forecasts of the resurrection (Mt. 16:21; 17:22f.; Mk. 8:31; 9:31; 10:34) make this all the more impressive. Jesus knew that He would die. But He was in perfect command of the situation. He knew that the death He was dying was the worst that the forces of evil could do to Him, and He knew that He would rise triumphant. He said that He would rise, and He made His words good. The last picture that the Gospels give us of Jesus is that of the Mighty Conqueror.[129] Matthew tells us that He commissioned His followers to preach the gospel and to make disciples, adding, 'lo, I am with you alway, even unto the end of the world' (Mt. 28:20; cf. Mk. 16:15ff.). His triumph does not cease. It continues in the mission of His followers. The eschatological discourse in Mark 13 envisages struggle and difficulty for Christian men until the end of time. But the dominant thought is not difficulty. It is the final triumph of Christ.

FAITH

How are men to have their share in the triumph won by Christ? The New Testament gives but one answer to this question. They are to believe. This is plainer in some places than in others, but it is taught everywhere. In the first two Gospels, as elsewhere, there is no alternative to faith.

We are familar with the expression which recurs in the Gospels, 'thy faith had made thee whole (lit. "saved thee")' (Mk. 5:34; 10:52, etc.). Some think that this means no more than faith in Jesus as the great Healer. Jesus was able to perform miracles, but He could do this only in response to faith, and therefore He looked for men to have faith in His wonder-working powers. This does not square with the Gospel picture. The evangelists make it clear, for example, that, while faith was commonly antecedent to the miracles, it was not absolutely necessary. Sometimes Jesus wrought miracles quite apart from men's faith (e.g., the lame man of John 5). Even at Nazareth, where His mighty works were somewhat inhibited through unbelief, 'he laid his hands upon a few sick

---

world of space and time' (*The Holy Spirit and the Gospel Tradition*, London, 1947, p. 67).

[129] John Knox stresses the point that this is one of the two great New Testament concepts of the meaning of Christ's death (*op. cit.*, pp. 146ff.; the other is the offering of an atonement for sin).

folk, and healed them' (Mk. 6:5). Jesus did not seek to astonish men, but to save them. Hence the call for faith.

Faith must be taken to mean a genuine trust[130] in Jesus Himself, or in the Father (to really trust the One is to trust the Other also). Let us consider the implications of the incident of the epileptic boy, encountered immediately after the Transfiguration (Mk. 9:14ff.). When the man came to Jesus saying that the disciples could not cure the boy, Jesus said, 'O faithless (Matthew adds "and perverse") generation, how long shall I be with you?' The father went on to say to Jesus, 'If thou canst do anything, have compassion on us, and help us.' Jesus replied, 'If thou canst! All things are possible to him that believeth.' The father's reply shows genuine spiritual insight: 'I believe; help thou mine unbelief.' Jesus cast out the demon, and subsequently was asked by the disciples why they could not cast it out. 'Because of your little faith,' answered the Lord, 'for verily I say unto you, If ye have faith as a grain of mustard seed, ye shall say unto this mountain, Remove hence to yonder place; and it shall remove; and nothing shall be impossible unto you' (Mt. 17:20). Faith is demanded right through this incident. The need for healing is in mind throughout, so that there is no question but that faith in Jesus as Healer is in mind. But it is impossible to hold that Jesus' deep emotion is aroused only because He is concerned to work a miracle. He is concerned with a whole attitude of life of which the attitude toward the miracle is but one symptom. He looks for men to trust Him wholly, and, trusting Him, to trust God. 'All things are possible to him that believeth' is a striking statement, and takes us beyond the immediate incident. So does the reference to moving mountains, a figure which occurs elsewhere, significantly after the injunction, 'Have faith in God' (Mk. 11:22;[131] cf. Mt. 21:21). Men must trust God.

We may see a little more of the significance of this by referring to a passage wherein belief is connected with John the Baptist. 'John came unto you in the way of righteousness, and ye believed him not: but the publicans and the harlots believed him: and ye, when ye saw it, did not even repent yourselves afterward,

[130] 'It is important to realise that "faith" in the Synoptic Gospels is not — as some have mistakenly imagined — a mere confidence that Jesus can perform the particular miracle in question, not "faith" merely in the sense in which it is used in modern faith-healing, but faith in the characteristic New Testament sense' (C. E. B. Cranfield, SJT, iii, p. 65).

[131] On this passage B. Harvie Branscomb comments, 'The observation of the withering of the fig tree is used by the evangelist as an occasion for presenting several sayings on the power of faith. It appears that he has such sayings available in some numbers, and presents some of them whenever his text especially suggests it' (in loc.). If this observation is sound it will indicate that faith was a frequent subject in Jesus' teaching.

that ye might believe him' (Mt. 21:32). Here belief is spoken of and praised, while unbelief is blamed. But it is accepting John's words as true and acting on this acceptance that is meant, nothing more than that. When Jesus said to Peter, 'O thou of little faith' (Mt. 14:31), and to all the disciples, 'O ye of little faith' (Mt. 16:8), or 'have ye not yet faith' (Mk. 4:40), when He spoke of the men of His day as a 'faithless (and perverse) generation' (Mt. 17:17; Mk. 9:19), faith means more than mere credence. Jesus looked for more in their attitude toward Him than in that toward John the Baptist. He looked for trust. In this spirit He commended the faith of the centurion (Mt. 8:10), that of the woman with the hemorrhage (Mt. 9:22; Mk. 5:34), that of blind Bartimaeus (Mt. 9:29; Mk. 10:52), and that of the Syrophoenician woman (Mt. 15:28; Mark has 'For this saying go thy way,' Mk. 7:29, but the implication is the same). This demand was there from the first as Mark makes clear with his account of Jesus' first preaching, 'repent ye, and believe in the gospel' (Mk. 1:15). And saving faith is plainly required in the longer ending of Mark's Gospel, where we read, 'he that believeth and is baptized shall be saved' (Mk. 16:16). This plainly inculcates the necessity for trust in Jesus. It looks for the faith that relies on Him alone. This is implied also in such an earlier passage as Mark 10:14f., 'of such (children) is the kingdom of God'. The characteristic of childhood is a trust that has no reservations. When a child trusts, he trusts with all his heart. That is the attitude that Christ seeks in His followers.

One aspect of the narrative of the Last Supper falls to be considered here. When Jesus invited His followers to share the bread, saying to them, 'This is my body,' and to partake of the wine, with the words, 'This is my blood,' He was referring to His death for them, but He was doing more. He was inviting them to appropriate that death, to take it so to speak into their very being, to make it their own. His sacrifice is not something to be viewed from afar. It is something that His children are to make their very own. And they do so by faith.

It cannot be said that in these two Gospels faith is spoken of as fully or in quite the same way as it is in, for example, the Pauline Epistles. But the same basic attitude is there. The call of the disciples to leave everything and follow Jesus requires an attitude which we may recognize also in the Pauline expression, 'that life which I now live in the flesh I live in faith, the faith which is in the Son of God' (Gal. 2:20). The terminology is different. The underlying experience is much the same.

From all this it is apparent that these two evangelists have a very far-reaching understanding of the atonement, even though they do not choose to expound it in set terms. But they see salvation as something which God and none less effects. They think of sin as universal and serious, so that the judgment of God may be expected to rest upon all sinners. But they think that suffering may affect this situation, and specifically the suffering of Christ. His sufferings, in conformity with their great thought of the priority of the divine, they see as proceeding from the will of the Father. It is the God who has been worshipped from of old, the God who spoke through the prophets, who has sent His Son to suffer and so to effect salvation. This is His mission, the reason for His being sent to earth. Himself personally innocent, He became one with sinners in the utmost consequence of their sin, namely in being forsaken of the Father. So He wrought out remission of sins, He effected a ransom for the many. So He won the victory. And throughout these Gospels there is the appeal for faith, the call to men to cast in their lot with Christ, and be numbered among His people.

No one would maintain that this is the full New Testament teaching on the atonement. There is much more that remains to be contributed to our understanding of this central doctrine. But it is important to be clear that these writers do have a very great deal to say on the subject. It is simply untrue to affirm that they are not concerned with the significance of the cross. Even this brief survey is sufficient to indicate that the contrary is the case. They see it as God's great act, and they see it as efficacious for men's salvation. By way of interpretation they have some important insights, the thought of ransom, of the place of dereliction, of victory, of remission of sins. They are giving expression in their own way to that great central saving truth that we shall meet throughout the New Testament.

CHAPTER TWO

The Cross in the Lukan Writings

I. THE GOSPEL

Luke begins his two-volume work with a stress on its factualness. He claims to have accurate information, and to be setting it down so that others may know the truth. Many writers today are insisting that Luke was theologically-minded. They say that he has made no attempt to give us a merely factual historical account.[1] He has written out of his own spiritual experience to convey to others who might be interested the certainty concerning the things in which they have been instructed. This is certainly so.[2] It is

---

[1] 'He writes as one for whom Christ alone makes history intelligible' (A. R. C. Leaney, *A Commentary on the Gospel according to St. Luke*, London, 1958, p. 9).

[2] N. B. Stonehouse concludes his survey of this Gospel by remarking, 'That living, abiding, dynamic faith of Luke gives perspective to his entire undertaking in proclaiming Jesus as the One "that died, yea rather was raised from the dead" (cf. Rom. viii. 34)' (*The Witness of Luke to Christ,*

clear to the sympathetic reader of his writings that there is theology in Luke, just as there is in John, or, for that matter, in Matthew and Mark. The methods, the thought processes, the language, the approach may be different, but the underlying intentions are much the same.

But though all this be accepted, we should not overlook the force of Luke's preface. He tells us that he is not engaging merely in edifying discourse. He is not setting out to compose a pious work of fiction, nor even to take the Christian tradition and modify it with a didactic purpose. He may be selecting his facts to bring out the truths he wishes to present, but he insists that it is with facts that he is concerned.[3] He claims that he has 'traced the course of all things accurately[4] from the first', and that he has received his information from them 'which from the beginning were eye-witnesses and ministers[5] of the word' (Lk. 1:2f.). This claim should be taken all the more seriously in view of the extent to which modern research has confirmed the accuracy of much that Luke wrote.[6] In an earlier day many scholars regarded Luke as a very second-rate historian. It is difficult to take up this position now.

London and Grand Rapids, 1951, p. 151). So also N. Geldenhuys, *Commentary on the Gospel of Luke,* London, 1952, pp. 42, 43; W. Manson, *The Gospel of Luke,* London, 1937, p. xii.

[3] 'Luke did not believe that religious devotion flourished in the absence of earnest meditation upon historical truth' (N. B. Stonehouse, *op. cit.,* p. 177).

[4] On this word J. Baker says: 'There is no mistaking the force of ἀκριβῶς here — "accurately, exactly." Here we see a man giving a guarantee of his integrity at the bar of truth. However strong the faith he holds, Luke is determined that his account of the life of his Lord shall be as unbiassed as he can make it, depending for its effect upon the power of the truth, and its appeal to man's reason. And he does this, we believe, with the awareness of a critical, logical mind' (ET, lxviii, p. 123).

[5] Cf. A. M. Ramsey, 'This twofold description of them is a clue to the character of the traditions, and to the motive in preserving them. "Eye-witnesses": there is the concern for historic facts. "Servants of the Word": the historic facts are important because God speaks through them a message about salvation' (SE, p. 35).

[6] A. Ehrhardt finds it 'almost incomprehensible how lightly theologians have dismissed the thesis of Eduard Meyer, who maintained that St. Luke figures as the one great historian who joins the last of the genuinely Greek historians, Polybius, to the first great Christian historian, perhaps the greatest of all, Eusebius of Caesarea.' He proceeds to remind us that 'The man who proposed this view was after all the last European scholar who possessed the learning to write an Ancient History of his own' (*Studia Theologica,* xii, p. 45). See also Sir William Ramsay, *The Bearing of Recent Discovery on the Trustworthiness of the New Testament,* London, 1920, pp. 80, 81, 222, 294; C. S. C. Williams, *A Commentary on the Acts of the Apostles,* London, 1957, pp. 30f.; E. M. Blaiklock, *The Acts of the Apostles,* London, 1959, p. 16; F. F. Bruce, *Are the New Testament Documents Reliable?,* London, 1946, p. 90.

All this has its relevance to his teaching on the atonement as to all else. He is not recording a beautiful myth which will enable us to see something of what in his view God expects of us. He is recording what God actually did in Christ for the salvation of mankind. As we approach his work we must be clear on what he is setting out to do. His preface gives the guiding rules. This applies, of course, to both volumes, that which we call his Gospel, and that which we call the Acts of the Apostles. For the remainder of this chapter we shall concentrate our attention on the Gospel.

THE CHANGED SET OF THE LIFE

First, let us notice that Luke, like Matthew and Mark, stresses the seriousness of sin. But he has his own way of doing it. Especially does he draw attention to the radical reformation that must be brought about if men are to be saved. Basic to what he writes is the conviction that men are on the wrong track altogether. They do not even approve (let alone follow) the right things, but 'that which is exalted among men is an abomination in the sight of God' (Lk. 16:15). And as for their achievement, at best they are 'unprofitable servants' (Lk. 17:10). Under these circumstances if men are to be saved at all it is not a matter of tidying up a little, correcting a few errors here, getting rid of some bad habits there, and the like. The evil is deep-rooted. The whole set of the life must be altered. The remedy must be drastic.

Quite early Luke tells us that it was to be the work of John the Baptist to 'turn the hearts of the fathers to the children' (Lk. 1:17). The 'fathers' are the great forbears of the race, Abraham, Isaac, and the rest. 'The hearts of the fathers' were against the children. That is to say, 'the hearts of the fathers' could not but condemn children whose ways were so far removed from the right paths that were dear to the fathers. The children must be radically renewed. They must learn to walk in right paths. Then the hearts of the fathers will react differently. Their hearts will be 'turned' towards the children.[7] A similar activity is envisaged by the further statement that John was 'to make ready for the Lord a people prepared for him' (Lk. 1:17). This clearly indicates that, as they are, the people are in no fit state to confront their God. They are not 'ready.' They are not 'prepared.' This

---

[7]Cf. Godet, 'Abraham and Jacob, in the place of their rest, had blushed at the sight of their guilty descendants, and turned away their faces from them; but now they would turn again towards them with satisfaction in consequence of the change produced by the ministry of John' (in loc.). He proceeds to cite Jn. 8:56, 'Abraham rejoiced to see my day, and he saw it, and was glad.'

must be altered. John's mission was to initiate a reversal of the whole state of affairs that he encountered.

This reversal of human values is further brought out in the *Magnificat*:

> He hath shewed strength with his arm;
> He hath scattered the proud in the imagination of their heart.
> He hath put down princes from their thrones,
> And hath exalted them of low degree.
> The hungry he hath filled with good things;
> And the rich he hath sent empty away (Lk. 1:51ff.).

In these democratic days we take it as axiomatic that one man is as good as another. But we should not read this attitude back to the first century. The men of Mary's day regarded the rich and those in high places with feelings akin to awe and reverence. Such exalted beings must be accorded due deference. They must be looked up to. The poor must keep their proper station. But Mary's song shows no such deference and respect. Human standards do not apply. Mary is singing about the salvation that God will bring. Before men can be saved, human standards must be turned on their heads.[8] It will never do to think that salvation can come by merely following human ideas to their logical conclusion.

Luke brings this out in his report of Jesus' Sermon on the Plain. There we read of blessings pronounced on the poor, the hungry, those that weep, those that are reproached. In the same vein He speaks woe[9] to the rich, to the full, to those that laugh, and to them that are well spoken of (Lk. 6:20-26).[10] Such words are often neglected today, or perhaps treated as material for crusades for social reform. Neither course fits Luke's intention. These words are too revolutionary to fit into a tidy acceptance of the *status quo*. They will not allow us to acquiesce in things as they are. They jolt and disturb us. Nor are they much easier if we try to interpret them in terms merely of social uplift. This whole Gospel makes it abundantly clear that Jesus was not interested simply in the correction of social abuses. He was deeply concerned to bring in the Kingdom of God. He wanted men to have 'the true riches' and these he explicitly contrasts with 'the unrighteous mammon' which men value so highly (Lk. 16:11). Disturbing sayings like those we have cited hammer home the truth that in God's Kingdom man's judgments and man's methods

---

[8] 'There is loveliness in the *Magnificat* but in that loveliness there is dynamite. Christianity begets a revolution in each man, and a revolution in the world' (William Barclay, *The Gospel of Luke,* Edinburgh, 1961, p. 10).

[9] 'The word is not so much a curse as an expression of pity, "Alas for"' (H. K. Luce, *in loc.*).

[10] Notice that while Matthew has a larger number of Beatitudes than has Luke, the Woes are peculiar to the Third Gospel.

and man's whole outlook have no place. They simply do not apply. God rudely shatters and disrupts man's accepted order. His Kingdom is incompatible with the situation that man has brought about. And as Jesus has come to bring in the Kingdom that situation must go.

Like the other Synoptists[11] Luke dwells on the necessity for repentance. He records the Baptist's clarion call (Lk. 3:3f.). He tells us that Jesus came to call sinners to repentance (Lk. 5:32). He says that men are evil (Lk. 11:13). At best they are no more than 'unprofitable servants' (Lk. 17:10). No man at all is good (Lk. 18:19). Thus men must repent (Lk. 13:3, 5). There is no other way. The universality of sin and the harmfulness of sin taken together mean that repentance is not to be escaped. Again we have a reversal of the situation that men have created for themselves. And this reversal must be thoroughgoing, for true repentance is more than merely a form of words. If it is genuine, repentance is an attitude of the whole man. It reaches out into all of life. Luke shows what it means when he is dealing with the preaching of John the Baptist. Like Matthew, he records John's demands for 'fruits worthy of repentance' (Lk. 3:8). But he goes beyond Matthew. He alone records John's detailed advice to the people in general that they share things like clothing and food, to the publicans that they exact no more than their just dues, and to the soldiers that they refrain from violence, from extortion by false accusation and from discontent with their pay (Lk. 3:10ff.). Men are responsible beings. God expects them to take their responsibility seriously[12] and to turn from every evil thing. Luke sees the importance of this and he will not let us miss the demands made on men by repentance. He spells them out in full. In the same vein he tells us that Jesus demanded that the forgiven practise the virtue of forgiveness (Lk. 11:4; 17:3f.). There must be changed lives.

Luke often sounds the note of urgency. Indeed, his note of urgency is practically all-pervasive. 'Let your loins be girded about,' said Jesus, 'and your lamps burning; and be ye yourselves like unto men looking for their lord' (Lk. 12:35f.). The axe is laid at the root of the trees (Lk. 3:9), a grim reminder of the

---

[11] Perhaps it ought to be made clear that by treating the Third Gospel separately from the first two I do not mean that everything that Luke says is distinctive other than when the contrary is specifically mentioned. Luke makes use of some of the material we have already considered in chapter I; Mark, and especially Matthew, use some of that in this chapter. In both I am concerned rather with the general picture than with exact delineation of what is peculiar and what is common.

[12] Karl Barth sees this passage as showing that 'the baptism of John is therefore the sign of penitent expectation of the Judge and His *dies irae*' (CDDR, p. 218).

imminence of judgment. As does Matthew, Luke records the Baptist's words about Jesus' fan being in His hand. Judgment is approaching. This is seen also in the words of the Lord, 'Judge not, and ye shall not be judged: and condemn not, and ye shall not be condemned: release, and ye shall be released: give, and it shall be given you; good measure, pressed down, shaken together, running over, shall they give into your bosom. For with what measure ye mete it shall be measured to you again' (Lk. 6:37f.). All men's deeds stand under the judgment of God. The natural optimism of man leads him to believe, or at any rate to hope, that somehow only that which is favourable will come out at the last. But Luke records the words, 'nothing is hid, that shall not be made manifest; nor anything secret, that shall not be known and come to light' (Lk. 8:17; cf. also 12:2). God's is a searching judgment. In it nothing can be hid. Again, contact with the Son of man is universally thought to be the source of blessing, but Luke reminds us of other possibilities. The man who is ashamed of the Son of man and of His teaching now will find himself in a serious situation when the Son returns with His angels. Then the Son of man will be ashamed of *him* (Lk. 9:26). From another angle, men who carry on the momentum of evil inherited from the past will be held responsible for all that evil with which they associate themselves. The men of Jesus' generation will be called on to account for the blood of all the prophets (Lk. 11:49-51). So serious is this that Jesus repeats the solemn saying, 'yea, I say unto you, it shall be required of this generation'. This makes the charge personal and brings it home. The note of personal challenge is sounded in the 'which of you . . . ?' so characteristic of the introduction to parables and parabolic sayings in this Gospel, and which appears to be unparalleled.[13]

There are no half measures. The alternatives are to save life or to kill (Lk. 6:9). Men may not be neutral. They cannot take refuge in some half-way house where they refrain from active opposition to Jesus and all He stands for, but refrain also from the discomfort of casting in their lot with Him. The man who is not with Christ is against Him (Lk. 11:23).[14] Luke is painting a picture

[13] It is found in 11:5, 11; 12:25; 14:5, 28; 15:4, 8; 17:7 (also three times in Matthew). Cf. G. Bornkamm, 'Many of the metaphors and parables of Jesus begin, therefore, with the disturbing question, a question which grips one right away, without any preliminaries: "Which of you . . .?" — a form of parable for which, remarkably enough, there is not a single parallel in rabbinic lore. It is always a question aimed straight at the hearer himself . . . . the hearer is gripped just where he really is' (*Jesus of Nazareth,* London, 1960, p. 70).

[14] This is not contradicted by that other saying, 'he that is not against you is for you' (Lk. ix. 50). This tells us that a man who does not voice all our shibboleths is not on that account to be esteemed as an enemy. Our verse emphasizes that if a man tries to step out of the conflict he is in effect

of the divine Lord come to earth to establish the Kingdom of God. When men come to see what is being claimed and done they cannot be neutral. If their lips profess neutrality their lives proclaim their real decision.[15]

Again and again Jesus cuts across the accepted ideas of the day. He agrees that almsgiving is praiseworthy, but says, 'give for alms those things which are within' (Lk. 11:41). What is usually thought of as acceptable is not sufficient for His exacting standards. He tells men that they will be 'sons of the Most High' if they love their enemies (Lk. 6:35). Against man's natural tendency to assert himself and to take the highest place to which his merits entitle him (and a higher one if he can) Jesus tells His followers to take the lower place (Lk. 14:7-11). He warns them that they must not exercise lordship in the manner of the Gentiles (Lk. 22:24-27). And Jesus Himself set the example. When His foes came to arrest Him, and one of His followers struck the servant of the high priest, the Master, so Luke alone tells us, touched the man's ear and healed him (Lk. 22:51; Luke also tells us that it was the man's right ear). Another detail peculiar to Luke's Gospel is Jesus' prayer for those who crucified Him, 'Father, forgive them; for they know not what they do' (Lk. 23:34).[16] This word of the dying Saviour is not out of line with Luke's interests. He has a great deal to say about forgiveness throughout his Gospel. In addition to this prayer, he records the prayer that Christ taught His followers to

---

allowing evil to triumph. He is in fact against Christ. In this sense there is no such thing as neutrality. A man must be positively for Christ else he is in effect in the opposite camp. Cf. Lagrange, 'In these absolute propositions all depends on the way in which one begins. Neutrality is not contemplated. If then someone is not for me, it is the case that he is against me. But if someone is not against me, it is the case that he is for me. The ancients, more accustomed to logic, recognized that the two propositions, contradictory as they appear, both together shew that one must decide for or against Jesus' (cited by H. K. Luce, in loc.).

[15] Cf. W. Manson, 'there is no middle course between evil and good, darkness and light, Satan and God' (on Lk. 11:23).

[16] Cf. J. Jeremias, 'for late Judaism the expiatory vow of the criminal is a formal part of the execution ("May my death expiate all my sins"), which Jesus reverses, but so as to transfer the expiatory virtue of his death to his tormentors' (The Servant of God, London, 1957, p. 102). Cf. also Is. 53:12. The authenticity of the saying is disputed. It is omitted by a strong group of manuscripts including א⁣ᶜ B D* W θ syrˢⁱⁿ, but attested by א* A Dᶜ f1 f13 Mcion Ir Or etc. B. H. Streeter accepts the saying, reasoning that it would appear to a second-century copyist that the Jews ought not to have been forgiven. There would thus be a strong tendency to omit the words (The Four Gospels, London, 1930, pp. 138f.). This position is accepted by very many, and it does not seem to be adequately countered by affirming that no copyist would purposely omit such words.

pray, wherein they seek forgiveness (Lk. 11:4);[17] he tells us of occasions when men were forgiven (Lk. 5:20, 24; 7:47f.), he includes the charge that 'repentance and remission of sins' should be preached throughout the world (Lk. 24:47), and he looks through to the last day and speaks of what will and what will not be forgiven then (Lk. 12:10). Now if men need forgiveness, then clearly their own way is not good enough. And the place Luke gives forgiveness shows the importance he attaches to it. It all fits in with his demand for radical renewal.

Some of this is not peculiar to Luke, though a good deal is. But whether he is using his own material or that which is found in the other Synoptists, he impresses his own stamp on the whole. He incorporates the old, and he brings in the new. The result is a strong emphasis on the truth that the way of the natural man is not the way of salvation. However men are to be saved, it will not be by their own effort. There must be a radical transformation of all that man stands for. The divine way is not the human way, not even the human way dusted up a little.

SIN AND JUDGMENT

Luke tells us that Jesus made use of contemporary happenings to hammer home the ill desert of sin. Some Galileans had been killed by Pilate in a particularly horrible way; their blood was mixed with that of their sacrifices. In Siloam a tower collapsed, killing eighteen men in its fall. Jesus told His hearers that those who died in ways such as these were not ·singled out by God on account of their extreme sinfulness. But He did say that judgment was a reality. He warned His hearers that unless they repented they would perish (Lk. 13:1-5).

Luke follows this piece of teaching with the parable of the Barren Fig Tree. This tells of an owner who speaks of cutting the useless tree down. It produces nothing, and it occupies ground that could be made to produce. The vinedresser is reluctant to comply. He secures a postponement of the sentence, promising to take appropriate steps to bring the tree into production. The parable stresses the divine reluctance to punish sinners.[18] God delays punishment while every resource of mercy and grace is exhausted. But in the end, if the fig tree, in spite of everything, remains barren, then there can await it no other fate than destruction. There is a limit to the postponement of God's judgments. The moral for sinners is plain. T. W. Manson ends his comment on this story with 'if it is

---

[17] He also emphasizes the duty of the forgiven to forgive (Lk. 17:3f.).

[18] A small point in the wording of Luke's narrative emphasizes the vinedresser's unwillingness to take action. If all fails he does not say, 'I will cut it down', but 'thou shalt cut it down'.

madness to fly in the face of His justice, it is desperate wickedness to flout His mercy'.[19] And that desperate wickedness will not go forever unnoticed and unrequited.

Other parables have the same underlying implication. Luke recounts for us the story of the Rich Man and Lazarus (Lk. 16:19-31). While the thrust of the parable concerns the use that men make of their lives, yet the story is incomprehensible other than against a background of judgment. A serious fate for the finally impenitent is presupposed. Unless there is such a dread reality, then neither the rich man nor his brothers are in any danger. They may as well continue with their godless living. Another aspect of our responsibility is brought out in the parable of the Pounds (Lk. 19:12-27). It is not a matter of indifference how we live out our lives. When God gives men good gifts then those gifts must be used. And the unpalatable truth is that punishment awaits those who do not use them.[20] The whole picture of the studious application of God's good gifts in the midst of difficult circumstances is peculiarly applicable to the world of our own day.

The parable of the Wicked Husbandmen (Lk. 20:9-18) hammers home the truth that evil-doers cannot look for immunity. This story finishes with the wicked men being destroyed, and Jesus immediately comments that the Stone will break to pieces all who fall on it and grind to dust those on whom it falls. The parable of the Rich Fool (Lk. 12:16-21) is a warning to have regard to true values, particularly in the light of Jesus' mission. Men's actions have eternal significance, and it is a thousand pities when they hold so fast to things temporal that they finally lose the things eternal. The parable of the Unjust Steward (Lk. 16:1-13) is notoriously difficult. But at least it is plain that we face a reckoning with Almighty God, and this parable urges us with a powerful voice that we face it realistically.[21] For the steward the gaining of a little money was

---

[19] *The Sayings of Jesus,* London, 1949, p. 275.

[20] Some maintain that the words about the slaying of the enemies in verse 27 formed no part of the original parable. Whatever be the truth of this, Luke has recorded them. If we are trying to understand his thought we cannot overlook the fact that he concludes this parable with words of fearful judgment. T. W. Manson has a comment on the slaying of the enemies: 'We may be horrified by the fierceness of the conclusion; but beneath the grim imagery is an equally grim fact, the fact that the coming of Jesus to the world puts every man to the test, compels every man to a decision. And that decision is no light matter. It is a matter of life and death' (*op. cit.,* p. 317).

[21] 'Our Lord is urging us to face these facts, and to be more frank than we are wont to be in admitting to ourselves the strangely uncertain nature of our hold on this present life . . . . These days we pride ourselves on our frankness in matters which to previous generations were taboo, especially in matters of sex; nevertheless we are not nearly so frank as our fathers were

useless. It would be taken from him to pay his defalcations. He needed friends — urgently. And he acted with decision and energy to get them.[22]

There is a good deal in Luke about the eternal consequences of men's actions. He tells us of Jesus' prophecy that Capernaum will be 'brought down unto Hades' (Lk. 10:15).[23] He records the Master's exhortation: 'Fear him, which after he hath killed hath power to cast into hell; yea, I say unto you, Fear him' (Lk. 12:5). God is to be feared, but not because it is in His power to terminate a man's life here on earth. He is to be feared because life on this earth is not the whole story. There is a hell into which men may be cast, and this gives an awful solemnity to the whole business of living. Those who deny Jesus on earth will be 'denied in the presence of the angels of God' (Lk. 12:9). Blasphemy against the Holy Spirit will never be forgiven (Lk. 12:10). Throughout His ministry Jesus had nothing but unsparing condemnation for those who made a religious profession and failed to back it up with lives given over to the service of God and man. For those who 'devour widows' houses', He said, there will be 'greater condemnation' (Lk. 20:47). And He spoke solemnly of the coming of the 'days of vengeance', the addition, 'that all things which are written may be fulfilled' (Lk. 21:22), indicating that this is rooted squarely in the will of God.

---

in facing up realistically to the transitory nature of this present world' (Ronald S. Wallace, *Many Things in Parables,* London, 1955, p. 74).

[22] J. Duncan M. Derrett argues convincingly that the parable is to be explained in the light of Jewish law and custom (NTS, vii, pp. 198-219). The steward had been using loopholes in the law to obtain usury. Faced with dismissal, he cancelled the usurious contracts and issued others in their place. This gained him friends and at the same time was in accordance with the moral law. The steward would be presumed to have acted in accordance with his master's wishes unless his action was repudiated. Theoretically the master could disown the steward's action, but practically he could not. 'That the steward's prudence was beneficial to the steward was evident; that it redounded to his master's reputation with the public was obvious. An ungracious repudiation was out of the question' (*op. cit.,* p. 217). Derrett sees the meaning of the words, 'his lord commended the unrighteous steward because he had done wisely' (Lk. 16:8) as, 'He did not merely praise the steward, he adopted the latter's acts' (*op. cit.,* p. 216). Derrett agrees with those who see the point of the parable in the steward's prompt action while he still had authority, ' "right action while there is time" is a great part of the lesson which it seeks to impart' (*op. cit.,* p. 216, n. 6).

[23] Cf. Geldenhuys, 'For the people of Capernaum, too, who had had abundant opportunity (Matt. iv. 18-22, ix. 1; John ii. 12) of seeing and accepting the kingly dominion of God in Jesus, an inexorable execution of judgment is awaiting. In the Roman-Jewish war this prophecy was partially fulfilled. But the final fulfilment waits until the last judgment' (*in loc.*).

Jesus does not, in this Gospel, enunciate the truth made so much of by John, that judgment is something which takes place here and now. But Luke does make it clear that the coming of Jesus forces men to a decision which takes place here and now and which has lasting consequences. 'I came to cast fire upon the earth' (Lk. 12:49) may point us to the fire of division.[24] If it be held, with a number of commentators, that the 'fire' is holiness, faith, judgment, the spiritual power exercised by the Lord,[25] or something similar, in any case it is plain that the fire bodes no good for sinners. They are being warned. They should make use of their opportunity while they have it. And shortly Jesus goes on to say unambiguously, 'Think ye that I am come to give peace in the earth? I tell you, Nay; but rather division: for there shall be from henceforth five in one house divided, three against two, and two against three. They shall be divided, father against son, and son against father; mother against daughter, and daughter against her mother; mother in law against her daughter in law, and daughter in law against her mother in law' (Lk. 12:51-53). There is an ineluctable element of decision involved in His whole mission. His coming divides men.[26] And the implication is that those who reject Him will eventually rue their decision. For Jerusalem the day of reckoning is near 'because thou knewest not the time of thy visitation' (Lk. 19:44). It is a solemn matter to be visited by the Christ. His offer of salvation is to be taken seriously. A day will come when many 'shall seek to enter in, and shall not be able' (Lk. 13:24). Clearly Luke wants us to see that important issues are posed. There is a judgment hanging over all men. Jesus presents them with the possibility of escape. Let them not neglect their day of opportunity.

'GOD MY SAVIOUR'

But if Luke is insistent that the judgment of God is a stern reality, he is also clear that God has provided the way whereby men may be saved. Again and again he brings out the point that God is the Author of a salvation that is available for all men. Salvation is his

---

[24] See H. K. Luce, *in loc.*, A. Plummer, *in loc.*

[25] Geldenhuys maintains that it is 'not merely the symbol of holiness (Plummer), or of faith (Zahn), or of dissension (Creed), or of judgment (Klostermann), but more generally of the spiritual power exercised by the Lord through His Word and Spirit on the strength of His completed work of redemption — to the undoing of those who reject Him and to the refining of those who believe in Him' (*in loc.*). The last words show that this commentator also recognizes the divisive effect of the 'fire' in question.

[26] 'Judgment is inherent in the response made to Jesus . . . . The cross is crucial to the problem of judgment for it separates the enemies of Jesus from the believers' (E. C. Colwell and E. L. Titus, *The Gospel of the Spirit*, New York, 1953, p. 171; they are speaking with special reference to the Fourth Gospel).

great theme from beginning to end, from the infancy narratives (Lk. 1:47) right through to Paul's preaching in Rome (Acts 28:28). And everywhere he ascribes it to God.

He begins his Gospel by telling his readers that he is writing about the things which have been 'fulfilled' (πεπληροφορημένων). This word is somewhat unexpected. Some have taken it to mean 'surely believed' and others 'completed'. But it is likely, as Geldenhuys suggests, that it 'points to the fact that in Jesus the divine promises of the Old Dispensation have been fulfilled and that a new era has been inaugurated. The fullness of the saving purpose of God has been revealed and the glad tidings must be proclaimed.'[27] Luke is pointing to the fulfilment of the purpose of God.

A feature of the early chapters of this Gospel is the series of beautiful hymns that Luke records. While they are not professedly songs about salvation, there is much about salvation in them. Indeed, it could be said that basically they all deal in one way or another with that salvation. Mary begins her song, for example, by praising God whom she describes as 'God my Saviour' (Lk. 1:47), and she goes on to sing of the way in which God's mercy is being worked out. The Song of Zacharias, which might be expected to be primarily a song of gladness over the birth of the aged priest's little son, begins with, 'Blessed be the Lord, the God of Israel; for he hath visited and wrought redemption for his people, and hath raised up a horn of salvation for us in the house of his servant David' (Lk. 1:68f.). The burden of his song is not his own overflowing happiness, not even the work that the infant before him would accomplish, but the great salvation that God is working out for His people. When eventually Zacharias comes to speak of his own little son he sings of him in relation to the God-given salvation. The Babe's task will be 'to give knowledge of salvation unto his people in the remission of their sins, because of the tender mercy of our God, whereby the dayspring from on high shall visit us'. The song of the angels has to do with the good tidings of the birth of 'a Saviour, which is Christ the Lord' (Lk. 2:11). Simeon can declare his readiness to depart when he has looked upon the Christ child, 'For mine eyes have seen thy salvation' (Lk. 2:30). He also reveals something of the cost of it all by his words to Mary, 'Yea and a sword shall pierce through thine own soul' (Lk. 2:35).

The songs, then, stress what God is doing for men's salvation. They speak of a peace which comes from God, a peace with a divine reference, and not simply a peace between man and man (Lk. 1:79; 2:14).[28] They sing of His mercy (Lk. 1:50, 54, 72, 78).

[27] In loc.

[28] In this verse RV, 'peace among men in whom he is well pleased', is to be preferred to AV, 'on earth peace, good will toward men'. The latter may

They stress that the promise made to Abraham is now receiving its fulfilment (Lk. 1:55, 72f.). God's gracious purpose, declared as long ago as the days of the great patriarch and father of the people, was now coming to its climax.

Other expressions indicate that the salvation was promised from of old. The redemption of which Zacharias sings (Lk. 1:68) has been looked for (and longed for) by pious people for long enough (Lk. 2:38; cf. also 21:28; 24:21). 'The consolation of Israel' (Lk. 2:25) points us to very much the same thing, as does 'thy salvation, which thou hast prepared before the face of all peoples' (Lk. 2:30f.). There is no thought that he was consciously looking for it, but the same salvation is surely that which Zacchaeus found, when Jesus said to him, 'Today is salvation come to this house' (Lk. 19:9). All these passages refer in one way or another to a salvation that was looked for from God. He had planned it. In His own way and time He would bring it to pass. And Luke is telling us that in Jesus He has brought it to pass.

The same essential idea underlies the references to fulfilled prophecy.[29] This may be what is meant when Luke speaks in his opening sentence of 'those matters which have been fulfilled among us' (Lk. 1:1).[30] Or he may have in mind the inner logic of those events which found fulfilment in Christ's work. Either way, he is thinking of a divine plan as unfolding in Jesus' ministry. Luke, with an eye to Gentile readers, does not appeal to the Old Testament as often as does Matthew, but the appeal is there nevertheless. Zacharias saw the coming of salvation 'As he spake by the mouth of his holy prophets' (Lk. 1:70). Luke points out that Scripture

---

be (and often is) understood of a general benovolence towards one's fellow-men. Luke is not speaking about this, nor is he saying that the birth of the Babe means peace to everyone, including those who, entrenched within their sinfulness, exude a genial good-fellowship to all. He is saying that the coming of Christ means peace to those on whom God sets His good pleasure, i.e., to the elect, those who are saved. NEB renders, 'on earth his peace for men on whom his favour rests.'

[29] That the fulfilment of prophecy was a major interest of Luke's is convincingly demonstrated by P. Schubert in his article in *Neutestamentliche Studien für Rudolf Bultmann*, Berlin, 1957, pp. 165-186. He goes so far as to say 'this proof-from-prophecy theology is Luke's central theological idea throughout the two-volume work' (*op. cit.*, p. 176; Schubert includes prophecies uttered by Jesus and others, as Gabriel, Elizabeth, etc., as well as the prophets of the Old Testament. Thus he can say, 'It is apparent that for Luke Jesus' own predictions of his suffering, death and resurrection, continuing, confirming and elaborating Scriptural prophecies, are regarded as the decisive proof that Jesus is the Christ, and that God has raised him from the dead', *op. cit.*, p. 174).

[30] $\pi\lambda\eta\rho o\phi o\rho\acute{\epsilon}\omega$ need not necessarily mean more than 'complete' but it is difficult to think that Luke has chosen so sonorous a word to convey a minimal meaning.

was fulfilled when Jesus went to Nazareth (Lk. 4:16, 21). He records our Lord's statements that in His passion 'all the things that
are written' must be fulfilled (Lk. 18:31; 21:22). Specifically
Luke sees fulfilment of prophecy in the fact that 'he was reckoned
with transgressors' (Lk. 22:37). This reference to Christ's death
is sharpened if the concluding words of the verse be rendered 'Yes,
for My course is run',[31] a very possible translation. In his concluding chapter Luke has many references to the fulfilments of
prophecy in the passion (Lk. 24:25, 27, 44, 45, 46).[32] Evidently
when the passion had been accomplished the believers speedily
began to search the Scriptures for enlightenment as to the significance
of what had happened.

We should draw a similar conclusion from Jesus' predictions of
His passion.[33] Like the other Synoptists, Luke thinks of this as
following immediately on Peter's confession of faith at Caesarea
Philippi. But he ties in the passion more closely. Immediately after
Peter had said that Jesus is 'The Christ of God' Luke tells us that
Jesus 'charged them, and commanded them to tell this to no man;
saying, The Son of man must suffer. . .' (Lk. 9:20ff.). The word
'saying' links the prediction of the passion which follows very closely
with what precedes. The one arises from the other. It is a small
touch, but it helps us to see the way Luke's mind was running. We
have similar Lukan touches in the transfiguration narrative a little
later in the same chapter. This story is introduced (as the parallels
in Matthew and Mark are not) by a statement that it took place
'about eight days after these sayings' (Lk. 9:28). This links it among
other things to the prediction of the passion which was one of the
'sayings'.[34] Again Luke tells us, as the others do not, that the subject of the conversation between Jesus and the heavenly visitants was
'his decease which he was about to accomplish at Jerusalem' (Lk.

---

[31] So Luce, in loc., Cf. Rieu's translation, 'Indeed for me the course is
run'. The Greek is καὶ γὰρ τὸ περὶ ἐμοῦ τέλος ἔχει.

[32] 'It was to the Cross that all the scriptures looked forward. The Cross
was not forced on God; it was not an emergency measure when all else
had failed and when the scheme of things had gone wrong. It was part of
the plan of God, for the Cross is the one place on earth, where in a moment
of time, we see the eternal love of God' (W. Barclay, op. cit., p. 312).

[33] Cf. W. Barclay, 'if we place any reliance on the story of the Gospels,
there never was a time in his earthly life when Jesus was not aware that
at the end of the road there stood the Cross. We can trace this consciousness
of Jesus backwards through the story' (Crucified and Crowned, London, 1961,
p. 91).

[34] Cf. P. Schubert, 'the transfiguration scene is not so much linked to
Peter's confession (as is the case in Mark and Matthew); rather it is more
specifically and very deftly linked to the prediction of the passion, death and
resurrection (vs. 22) and to the attending sayings about the nature of true
discipleship (vss. 23-27)' (op. cit., p. 181).

9:31). On the surface of it the transfiguration is an episode connected rather with glory and majesty than with death, but Luke's
predominant interests show out.[35] Such touches help reveal to us
Luke's deep interest in the passion and all that concerns it. In
particular, it helps us to see it as he did, as something that was in the
plan of God long before it became evident to men on the stage of
history. This is probably also behind Luke's statement that 'when
the days were well-nigh come that he should be received up, he
stedfastly set his face to go to Jerusalem' (Lk. 9:51). The passion
did not take Jesus unawares. He went up as God determined. He
went up stedfastly, purposefully. He went up to fulfil that for
which He had come.[36]

The divine initiative is brought out with freshness and power
in a trilogy of parables peculiar to this Gospel. In chapter 15 the
evangelist recounts the stories of the Lost Sheep, the Lost Coin, and
the Lost Son. Together they give an unforgettable picture of the
infinite divine mercy by which alone men are saved. The first two
of them also have the thought of the divine initiative (which is not
far from the third also: clearly the father was on the watch for his
son, and when he saw him, he ran to him, and from that point
directed all that happened). This is tremendously important and
a radical novelty. Judaism has the thought of search after a lost coin,
but the seeker is man, not God, and what he finds is 'the words of

---

[35] H. Conzelmann goes so far as to say, 'The purpose behind the heavenly
manifestation is the announcement of the Passion, and by this means the proof
is given that the Passion is something decreed by God' (*The Theology of St.
Luke*, London, 1960, p. 57).

[36] Sometimes rather strange conclusions are drawn from Luke's handling
of his material, as in J. M. Creed's frequently quoted dictum, 'There is indeed no *theologia crucis* beyond the affirmation that the Christ must suffer,
since so the prophetic scriptures had foretold' (*The Gospel according to St.
Luke*, London, 1950, p. lxxii). Creed does not face the fact that there is
other evidence than the fulfilment of prophecy, he assumes that the longer
text in the narrative of the institution of the Lord's Supper is not authentic
(to get rid of the words referring to the cup as the new covenant in Christ's
blood), and he does not follow out the implications of the fact he admits,
that Luke did regard Christ's death as fulfilling prophecy. It seems to me
somewhat cavalier to admit that Luke saw Christ's death as fulfilling prophecies
God had inspired and to refuse to regard this as significant. C. K. Barrett
regards Creed's statement as 'not the whole truth, but it is not lightly to be
set aside' (*Luke the Historian in Recent Study*, London, 1961, p. 23). But
elsewhere he can make such statements as '. . . [Luke's two-volume work] sets
forth Jesus Christ, crucified and risen, as the one means of salvation';
'It is the theme of his work that the outcome of the life and death of Jesus
was a community which expanded from Jerusalem to fill the world' (*op. cit.*,
pp. 67, 74). The fact is that Luke has his own way of making his point. But
it is seriously to misunderstand him to say that he under-valued the place and
significance of the cross.

the Torah'.[37] There is no thought that God in His eagerness to bring men salvation actually goes out after men to seek them and bring them in as in the parable of the Lost Sheep. We are so familiar with this story that it is easy for us to miss the revolutionary note it introduced into men's understanding of the nature of God. Up till then, the best thought of Judaism was eloquent of God's readiness to respond to the penitent, forgiving him his sins and restoring him to place. But the first move had to come from the sinner. Until he showed penitence nothing could happen. The parable of the Lost Sheep put the initiative with God. C. G. Montefiore brings this out. 'The virtues of repentance are gloriously praised in the Rabbinical literature,' he says, 'but this direct search for, and appeal to, the sinner, are new and moving notes of high import and significance. The good shepherd who searches for the lost sheep, and reclaims it and rejoices over it, is a new figure . . . .'[38] That God should stoop to seek out sinful men and bring them back to Himself is a profoundly moving idea. We cannot dispense with the thought of the divine initiative.

The story of the Prodigal Son has a place all its own in Christian affections. It speaks to the depths of man's soul. And it emphasizes that there is nothing, nothing at all, in man to justify his salvation. That depends on the sheer mercy of God. Apart from His forgiving grace there could be salvation for no one. But He loves mankind, and out of His love flows the readiness to receive sinners of which this parable speaks so eloquently. As Helmut Thielicke puts it, 'The fact that the lost son was taken back again is not attributable to his greater maturity, but solely to the miracle of God's love. Here a man has no claim whatsoever upon God. Here a man can only be surprised and seized by God'.[39] This is an integral part of the gospel message. Until we learn that there is nothing at all in man to merit salvation, we cannot begin to com-

---

[37] 'If a man loses a *sela‘* or an *obol* in his house, he lights lamp after lamp, wick after wick, till he finds it. Now does it not stand to reason: if for these things which are only ephemeral and of this world a man will light so many lamps and lights till he finds where they are hidden, for the words of the Torah which are the life both of this world and of the next world, ought you not to search as for hidden treasures?' (*Cant.* R. I. 1. 9; Soncino translation).

[38] *The Synoptic Gospels,* ii, London, 1927, p. 520. He also says, 'This we may regard as a new, original, and historic feature in his teaching. And it is just here that opposition comes in and begins. To call sinners to repentance, to denounce vice generally, is one thing. To have intercourse with sinners and seek their conversion by seeming to countenance them and by comforting them — that is quite another thing' (*op. cit.,* i, p. cxviii). Cf. G. S. Duncan, *Jesus, Son of Man,* London, 1947, p. 162.

[39] *The Waiting Father,* New York, 1959, p. 27.

prehend the meaning of salvation by God's grace.[40]   A. Nygren has
an interesting discussion of Jülicher's interpretation of this parable
wherein the latter suggests that 'that is how it really happens in
life' and draws the conclusion, 'Therefore, God cannot deal otherwise with the sinner; He must receive him and give him His forgiveness'.[41]   Nygren points out that such an understanding can be
confronted with another story wherein the Father refused to receive
the son until he had produced some honest work, and the son
presently returned to thank the father 'for the unyielding severity
that had led to his recovery, unlike the foolish softness and weak
indulgence of some other fathers'.[42]   It cannot be denied that it
sometimes happens like this in real life, but we do not reason that
therefore God acts so.   Thus Nygren makes his point that we cannot
reason from men to God in this way.   In Jülicher's method 'God's
love is measured by human standards; God is made in the image of
man.   But the Parable of the Prodigal Son takes the opposite course.
God's attitude is the primary thing, and the father in the Parable is
made in the image of God.'[43]

Sometimes exegetes have pointed out that this parable speaks of
no atoning work, and have hastened to draw the conclusion[44]
that all that is necessary for forgiveness is repentance and confession.
This overlooks several things.   The argument proves too much, for
if there is no atonement there is also no Christ in the parable.   Nor
does the Father go out to seek the son (he awaits his return before
running to meet him).   Nor is there any reference to a repugnance
to sin on the part of the Father.   Nor do we find any mention of
subsequent amendment of life on the part of the prodigal.   In short,
the parable demonstrably says nothing about a number of things
universally held to be important in the Christian scheme of things.
This parable, like all the parables, is there to teach us one lesson.
It emphasizes God's readiness to forgive, but on any showing it
does not tell us everything.[45]   We must consider it in the light of

[40] Lesslie Newbigin comments on this parable, 'You cannot be both a coolie
and a son.   You cannot both earn God's favour as a right, like a workman
earning his wages, and also enjoy His love like a son in his father's home.
If you want to have a righteousness of your own, the righteousness which
comes by law, then you are certainly shut out of the righteousness of God, that
which is by grace' (Sin and Salvation, London, 1956, p. 107).

[41] Agape and Eros, London, 1953, p. 82.

[42] Op. cit., p. 84.

[43] Op. cit., p. 86.

[44] E.g., A. Sabatier, The Doctrine of the Atonement, London, 1904, p. 36;
Hastings Rashdall, The Idea of Atonement in Christian Theology, London,
1919, p. 26.

[45] A. J. Tait remarks, 'The plain fact is that the parable of the Prodigal
Son provides the most moving picture of the welcoming and forgiving love
of God, but has nothing whatever to contribute about His redeeming love.

all that the Gospels have to tell us. It is to be understood in relation to the rest of Jesus' teaching, and not in isolation from it.
We must not overlook the force of the fact that it is Jesus who tells
us this story, and that He elsewhere makes it clear that the cross
is integral to the way of salvation.[46]

From another angle the parable of the Pharisee and the Publican
stresses the impossibility of the human element counting for anything in the process of salvation. The Pharisee is pictured as an
outwardly religious man who could rejoice in his 'godly' standing.
He congratulated the Deity on the excellence of His servant. He
preened himself in the holy place. By contrast the publican would
not even raise his eyes toward heaven. In a gesture of deep contri-
tion he smote himself on the breast as he exclaimed, 'God, be pro-
pitiated[47] to me a sinner' (Lk. 18:13, mg.). 'This man,' said Jesus,
'went down to his house justified'. We misinterpret this parable if
we say to ourselves, 'Poor, deluded Pharisee. How little he knew of
what he really had accomplished!' Now it is true that the Pharisee
did not grasp the basic realities of the situation. But the trouble is
not that he exaggerated what he had done. Go through the parable
again and you will see that every word that he said about himself
was true. Like it or not, he simply was not as other men. He
might be a keen man of business but he was not extortionate. 'Unjust'? The typical Pharisee was the soul of fairness. 'Adulterers'?
His moral life was above reproach. 'Or even as this publican'? No
one in his wildest moments would have dreamed of lumping them
together. 'I fast twice in the week'. He did, too, and that is no
small self-discipline.[48] 'I give tithes of all that I get.' He *was*
systematic in his giving to God. You see his words are no exaggeration. They describe the situation as it was. The trouble with the
Pharisee was not that he was not as far along the road as he thought

---

That did not enter into its purpose.' Acutely he adds, 'Hence the argument
(i.e. the argument that the parable shows that no atoning work of Christ
is necessary) would be as inimical to the position of Abelard as to that of
St. Anselm' (*The Atonement in History and Life*, ed. L. W. Grensted, London,
1936, p. 124).

[46] Cf. W. Manson, 'the measure of the gospel is constituted not by any one
parable or word but by the sum-total of the aspects under which Jesus is
revealed, and if these elsewhere include the sense of a redeeming or expiatory purpose to be effected by the sufferings and death of the Messiah, the
parable of the Lost Son, perfect illustration as it is of the joy of God over
a sinner's repentance, is not to be pressed to the exclusion of that conception'
(*in loc.*).

[47] The Greek is ἱλάσθητι. The significance of this choice of expression
should not be overlooked in assessing the teaching of this Gospel on the
atonement.

[48] It was also a work of supererogation. The only fast in the Law was
that on the day of Atonement.

he was. The trouble was that he was on the wrong road altogether.[49] It did not matter how far he went along that road. He would never reach his destination that way. Whereas the publican cast himself on the mercy of God,[50] the Pharisee relied on his own merit.

Systematically the Pharisees made the same mistake. They are castigated because they 'rejected for themselves the counsel of God' (Lk. 7:30). By reason of their special position they might have been expected to have grasped the important truths concerning salvation. But they rejected them and went on in their own self-opinionated way. God's people, God's real children, are everywhere in contrast. The 'elect' rely on God to avenge them (Lk. 18:7), and this is but a symptom of their habitual attitude. Basically they are those that rely on God. Everywhere Luke has the thought that men may rely on God, indeed that they must rely on Him. They can never be saved in their own strength.

This last point comes out in many ways. It is behind the parable of the Friend at Midnight, and that of the Unjust Judge.[51] In each case the central figure is one who is conscious of his need, and of the fact that that need can be met by one person alone. The importunity of which these parables speak is meaningless apart from this. The relevance of the point to salvation is plain.

John the Baptist pointed out that men may not trust in their earthly position. Descent from Abraham in a merely outward sense is vain (Lk. 3:8). The Jews were proud of their lineage. Proud, too, of their whole system with its emphasis on salvation through upright living. They put tremendous stress on keeping the Law,

---

[49] Cf. Rudolf Bultmann, 'The Pharisee was not condemned because he spoke falsely in what he said; but the fact that he compared himself with others, that he desired to exhibit his virtue before God, showed that he did not rightly understand what God's grace meant. For God's grace can be known only when a man realizes his utter helplessness, and perceives nothing more in himself to which he can appeal' (*Jesus and the Word*, London, 1935, pp. 200f.).

[50] T. W. Manson emphasizes this point. 'It is a great mistake to regard the publican as a decent sort of fellow, who knew his own limitations and did not pretend to be better than he was. It is one of the marks of our time that the Pharisee and the publican have changed places; and it is the modern equivalent of the publican who may be heard thanking God that he is not like those canting humbugs, hypocrites, and killjoys, whose chief offence is that they take their religion seriously. This publican was a rotter; and he knew it. He asked for God's mercy because mercy was the only thing he dared ask for' (*op. cit.*, p. 312).

[51] Cf. Theo Preiss, 'Is it not significant that exegesis still fails to recognize that the parable of the Wicked Judge (Luke 18:1-8), just as much as its twin sister concerning the Pharisee and the tax-gatherer, treats of justification, but of its objective aspect, of the great clash between God and his elect on the one hand and Satan and his partisans on the other?' (*Life in Christ*, London, 1954, p. 14).

i. e., on man's service of God. Jesus did not come to preach merely a revised version of Judaism. His message was so radically new that it could never be accommodated within such a system. He pointed out that men do not tear a piece of cloth from a new garment to patch up an old one. Such a piece of housekeeping means spoiling the new from which the patch is taken without making good the deficiencies of the old. The new patch does not match, and in any case when it shrinks it pulls the old garment and sets up strains which result in a worse tear. New wine does not go into old wineskins. If it does there is loss both ways. The old skins are burst, and the new wine is lost (Luke 5:36ff.). Reliance on God — on God alone — for salvation is not a truth which can be grafted on to a religion which stresses the necessity for a man to earn his salvation by his own meritorious works. The two are incompatible. Systematically Jesus castigated men for relying on the merely outward. The formalism of the scribes and Pharisees came in for strong condemnation (Lk. 11:39-52). So He said that those who claimed to have eaten and drunk in His presence and to have had Him teach in their streets, would be disowned at the end (Lk. 13:25-30). The parable of the Excuses (Lk. 14:15-24) exposes the hollowness of the religion of the day from another angle. It is clear enough that Luke is trying to present us with something radically new. And it is equally clear that the radical element is the disowning of the characteristic Jewish approach and the replacing it with a complete reliance upon God, upon God alone, for salvation.[52]

In common with the other Synoptics, Luke has a good deal to say about the Kingdom of God. He speaks of it as 'good tidings' (Lk. 8:1).[53] He tells us that it is to be the burden of the message of Jesus' followers (Lk. 9:2, 6). In the person and the ministry of Jesus the Kingdom has come near to men (Lk. 10:9, 11). Men are urged to pray for the Kingdom's coming (Lk. 11:2), to seek the Kingdom rather than the things of the material life (Lk. 12:31). They need not fear lest they seek it in vain, 'for it is your Father's

[52] Cf. Ronald S. Wallace, 'The Pharisee thought of the Kingdom of God as something that had to be prepared, and prepared for. He thought of it as something that required the efforts of good men like himself to complete. The Kingdom of God would come when all religious men like himself kept the law of God perfectly, but God must wait until then.' Jesus, by contrast, 'did not speak of our building up the Kingdom, but only of our receiving it and entering it. That is all a man can do. The final consummation of all things in this world, and the manifestation of the Kingdom in all its glory, await only God's word, God's decision, not our efforts' (op. cit., pp. 66f.).

[53] Cf. L. S. Thornton, 'the kingdom of God as embodied in the words and life of Christ was a manifestation of the redeeming activity of God. . . . The synoptic gospels make it clear that Christ had a mission to forgive sins and that He gave His life a ransom for sinners . . .' (The Incarnate Lord, London, 1928, p. 171).

good pleasure to give you the kingdom' (Lk. 12:32; notice that it is not something that men bring about, but rather something that they receive as a gift from God). The Kingdom is not something that men will see coming. It is 'among' or perhaps 'within' men (Lk. 17:21).[54] There are parables which liken the Kingdom to a mustard seed growing into a large plant, or to leaven working silently (Lk. 13:19, 21). Those who are in the Kingdom may be likened to little children (Lk. 18:16). He that does not receive the Kingdom (again the thought is of the gift of God) as a little child will certainly not enter into it (Lk. 18:17). The Kingdom is never thought of as brought in as a result of human endeavour. In modern times some have had the thought that Christian people should labour together to bring in the Kingdom. This is a lofty ideal, and not to be disparaged. But it is not the idea we see in the Gospels. There the Kingdom is connected with the mission of Jesus. Though Luke does not explicitly link the two, he leaves us with no doubt but that the Kingdom is to be brought in by the death of the Lord.[55] Only through this death could men be in that right relationship to God which the concept of the Kingdom represents.[56]

THE FATHER'S BUSINESS

Along with the idea that salvation comes from God alone, we should take the other idea that Jesus was ceaselessly occupied with the work of God. When Mary gently rebuked her Son for remaining behind in the temple instead of going back to Nazareth in the cavalcade of returning pilgrims, the child Jesus answered, 'How is it that ye

[54] For a discussion of the point, see the note by J. M. Creed, *in loc.* Most commentators agree that 'among' is the more probable rendering, for Jesus is not talking about a Kingdom that consists of an inner state of soul, but rather a Kingdom intimately bound up with His person and work. See further C. H. Roberts, *Harvard Theological Review,* xli, pp. 1ff.; W. G. Kümmel, *Promise and Fulfilment,* London, 1957, pp. 33-35.

[55] Cf. Hugh Martin, 'To understand Jesus, the Kingdom must never be separated from the Cross. The Messiah — impossible thought as it was to the Jews — had to die' (*Luke's Portrait of Jesus,* London, 1949, p. 45). Cf. also N. B. Stonehouse, 'The primary feature of the gospel, without which the other (i.e. the social implications of the kingdom) is meaningless, concerns the tidings of the crucified and risen Saviour in whose name repentance and remission of sins were to be proclaimed (cf. Lk. xxiv. 46, 47). The realization of the kingdom was therefore inconceivable without the accomplishment of the Messiah's task, and the fulfilment of the messianic mission gave assurance of the coming of the kingdom' (*op. cit.,* pp. 164f.).

[56] Cf. G. Dalman, 'When He, who was appointed to be the Head of the Kingdom (sovereignty) of God among men, died, in order that they might take part in God's "covenant" by which this Kingdom could be fully established, it is clear that men could not enter this Kingdom unless they recognized that it was their sin that caused His Death, and thereby admit that the righteousness of God has to be satisfied' (*Jesus-Jeshua,* London, 1929, p. 176).

sought me? wist ye not that I must be about my Father's business?'
(Lk. 2:49, mg.). The note struck thus early is carried on throughout the Gospel. Jesus told the devil that 'Man shall not live by
bread alone' (Lk. 4:4), and whether the words 'but by every word
of God' be added or not,[57] they must be understood. Jesus is affirming His entire dedication to the will of God. Bread and all it stands
for cannot be allowed to interfere with the necessity for doing that
will. Similarly He rejected the temptations to establish an earthly
kingdom (Lk. 4:5ff.), and to be a spectacular miracle-worker (Lk.
4:9ff.).[58] These things did not harmonize with the Father's will.
And anything out of keeping with that will can have no place
in the task to which He is setting His hand.

Luke has many references to the things which Jesus *must* do.
It is never said in so many words whence this necessity arises, but
no one is left in any real doubt but that this is the divine will. If
God has determined that a thing be done, then it remains only
for Jesus to fulfil it. In this strain, He must preach the Kingdom
to certain cities (Lk. 4:43). He must suffer.[59] Sometimes in this
connection Luke records sayings found in other Gospels (Lk. 9:
22), sometimes he speaks in a way the others do not (Lk. 17:
25;[60] 24:7, 26, [61] 44). He tells us that Jesus goes as it has been

[57] They are read by ADΘ fam 1, fam 13, etc., but are omitted by אBW.
In view of their occurrence in Dt. 8:3, it would be natural for scribes to
insert the words here if they found them lacking in MSS they were copying.
Consequently, the omission by three such important MSS is usually held
to be significant.

[58] A. Ritschl acutely remarks, 'no man of moral worth will find a temptation
in a situation in which he from the outset recognizes Satan.' He goes on,
'Those experiences of Christ must therefore be understood to mean that the
impulses which became temptations to Him, because they at first appeared
legitimate, were in due time condemned by Him because their satisfaction
would entangle Him in the kingdom of evil' (*Justification and Reconciliation,*
Edinburgh, 1902, p. 573).

[59] Conzelmann sees Luke's use of δεῖ as especially significant in the way
he brings out the necessity for the passion (*op. cit.,* p. 153; the whole of the
section headed 'God's Plan,' pp. 151-4, is important).

[60] Vincent Taylor draws attention to the importance of this saying,
pointing out that it is largely ignored by the commentaries, which take the
line that it is probably an interpolation. Taylor thinks it likely that in its
present context it is an interpolation, but this does not dispose of the
problem of the origin of the words. He finds good reason for tracing the
saying to Luke's special source. This is important. Unlike other sayings of
similar import, this does not go back to Mark. Independently of that
evangelist, Luke had good reason for thinking of the passion as inevitable
(JS, pp. 172-5). Goguel argues for the saying's authenticity, saying that it
'cannot have been invented by tradition' (*The Life of Jesus,* London, 1958,
p. 390).

[61] 'Behoved' in this verse renders the Greek ἔδει. Where we have the
present of this verb instead of the past it is translated 'must'. The term is a
strong one.

determined (Lk. 22:22). Clearly Luke wants us to think of Jesus as One who saw it as part of His vocation that He should suffer. That was the will of God for Him. Suffering was not merely a crass accident, but it was integral to the conception of Messiahship as He saw it. Maurice Goguel has said that Jesus 'did not think that (God's purpose) would be realized in spite of his failure and in spite of his rejection, but by his sufferings and by his rejection. . . . Jesus did not believe that he was the Messiah *although* he had to suffer; he believed that he was the Messiah *because* he had to suffer. This is the great paradox, the great originality of his Gospel.'[62]

Jesus' foreknowledge of His betrayal fits into this pattern (Lk. 22:22). We should notice that this evangelist has some expressions of his own with regard to the passion. He tells us that Jesus spoke of it as 'a baptism to be baptized with' adding 'how am I straitened till it be accomplished' (Lk. 12:50).[63] Elsewhere we may read of the passion as a 'baptism', but the words about being 'straitened' (which we do not find elsewhere) give a sense of urgency to the situation. Again, Luke speaks of Jesus as being 'perfected' on the third day (Lk. 13:32). The verb shows us Jesus' ministry coming to its appointed culmination.[64] The Pharisees have been warning Jesus that Herod 'would fain kill' Him. His reply shows that He knows He will die. But it also reveals the calm confidence that this will take place as and when the Father determines. God and not Herod has the decision in this matter. With a sense of irony justified by the long history of the city He adds, 'it cannot be that a prophet perish out of Jerusalem' (Lk. 13:33).[65] Throughout this discussion the death of Jesus is continuously in mind,

---

[62] *Op. cit.*, p. 392. Goguel is not speaking specifically of the Lukan picture but his words are relevant to the Third Gospel.

[63] 'These words indicate that Jesus' death is not just an epilogue, but an integrating essential part of his work' (O. Cullmann, *The Christology of the New Testament*, London, 1959, p. 62).

[64] C. P. M. Jones sees many 'points of contact between Hebrews and the Lukan writings. So, of this verb, he says, 'τελειοῦμαι is best taken in the sense common in Hebrews, of the attainment of heavenly perfection through suffering and death' (*Studies in the Gospels*, ed. D. E. Nineham, Oxford, 1955, p. 128).

[65] Cf. W. Barclay, 'It is life's bitterest tragedy to give one's heart to someone only to have it broken. That is what happened to Jesus in Jerusalem; and still He comes to men, and still men reject Him. But the fact remains that to reject the love of God is in the end to be in peril of the wrath of God' (*The Gospel of Luke*, Edinburgh, 1961, p. 192). On the reference to the holy city, R. H. Fuller says, 'It may be that the meaning behind this insistence that he must perish at Jerusalem is that Jerusalem is the place of revelation, the centre from which the redemptive activity of God is to go forth to the world, and that therefore the death of Jesus is to be the culmination of the sacred history of God's dealings with his people' (*The Mission and Achievement of Jesus*, London, 1954, p. 64).

and throughout the discussion the will of the heavenly Father is thought of as being done by Jesus. The life of Jesus was one long doing of the Father's will, and He was still about the Father's business in the act and the manner of His death. In harmony with this, Luke tells us that it was when 'the days were well-nigh come that he should be received up' that Jesus 'stedfastly set his face to go to Jerusalem' (Lk. 9:51). 'Received up', as Creed notes, 'perhaps connotes the various stages by which Jesus passed from an earthly to a heavenly existence . . . rather than the single incident of the Ascension into heaven.'[66] The expression indicates that the events surrounding the passion and culminating in the ascension were determined,[67] and that Jesus' stedfastness in going to Jerusalem represented a courageous acceptance of it all. Nor should we overlook the fact that Luke (and Luke alone) tells us that Jesus died with the words upon His lips, 'Father, into thy hands I commend my spirit' (Lk. 23:46). This does not give us justification for slurring over the cry of dereliction in Matthew and Mark. But Luke makes his own contribution to our understanding of the way Jesus died. At the very last He was at one with the Father.[68]

THE DIGNITY OF THE SAVIOUR

We can gain some idea of the importance and of the significance of a piece of work from the kind of person who accomplishes it. So in the Gospels the person and the work of Jesus interpenetrate.[69] The one can scarcely be understood apart from the other. Thus it is not without its significance for our inquiry that Luke has a good deal to say about the nature of Jesus.

Very early in his Gospel he records that the angel messenger sent to Mary spoke of the child that was to be born as 'the Son of God' (Lk. 1:35). Sometimes the expression 'son of God' means no more than that a man is in right relation to God, and perhaps also that he is serving God faithfully (as when Solomon is spoken of in this way, 1 Ch. 22:10, or when believers have this title, 1 Jn. 3:1f.). But

[66] In loc. The word ἀνάλημψις is usually held to mean 'ascension', but AG cite evidence that it can also mean 'death'.

[67] Introducing the section Lk. 9:51-19:28, W. Manson comments, 'The evangelist, by commencing the section with the words, "As the time for his assumption was now due" (cf. ix. 31), places all its contents under the solemn shadow of the Cross' (in loc.).

[68] Cf. McLeod Campbell's well-known saying that Christ offered 'a perfect Amen in humanity to the judgment of God on the sin of man' (The Nature of the Atonement, Cambridge, 1856, p. 134).

[69] 'The right approach to the Christology of the New Testament is through its soteriology . . . . There is in the New Testament no speculative Christology divorced from the Gospel of the Saviour and of the salvation He brings' (J. K. Mozley, in Mysterium Christi, ed. G. K. A. Bell and A. Deissmann, London, 1930, p. 171).

it can mean more. And in this context there cannot be the slightest doubt that it does mean more. The angel is explaining to Mary the way in which the child is to be born. There will be the intervention of no male whatever. Instead 'The Holy Ghost shall come upon thee, and the power of the Most High shall overshadow thee'. It is because of this that the Child is to be called holy, and 'the Son of God'.[70] The context demands that the expression be given as full a content as it will take. Luke never loses sight of this high dignity of the Saviour.

So he records Elizabeth's words to Mary, 'blessed is the fruit of thy womb' (Lk. 1:42), and he tells us that she greeted Mary as the mother of 'my Lord' (Lk. 1:43). Even though the Child was as yet unborn, Luke records those sayings that will impress on us the high dignity that was to be His.

Or again, he pictures for us a Jesus who impressed men as deity impresses them. Take, for example, the effect of the miracles. These might conceivably have been displays of mighty power, but Luke does not leave us with this impression. When John the Baptist sent messengers to Jesus with a question about His mission, the miracles are cited as evidence that He is the One long awaited, the Messiah (Lk. 7:20f.). Fear came on men who saw the miracles as they realized that God had visited His people (Lk. 7:16). Those who saw them were 'astonished at the majesty of God' (Lk. 9:43). Before the miracles men glorified God (Lk. 17:15-18).

From a somewhat different point of view, we see the same thing in the effect on Peter of the miraculous draught of fishes. He and his companions, professional fishermen though they were, had been able to catch nothing at the time that they recognized as the best for this work. Then at Jesus' instigation, they let down their nets at a time that they held to be not so advantageous, and they caught a vast multitude of fish. Peter recognized the hand of God. The recognition brought no immediate sense of joy or exultation, but the surprising ejaculation, 'Depart from me; for I am a sinful man, O Lord' (Lk. 5:8). Peter reacted as in the presence of the very holiness of God. His joy in the catch was swamped by the realization that he was a sinner.[71]

[70] W. Manson comments, 'It is obvious that in this context "Son of God" is to be explained no longer in a purely spiritual but in a physical or hyperphysical sense. Jesus is *Son of God* because a new constitutive principle, the creative energy of God enters into and determines his nature before he is born' (*in loc.*).

[71] 'This miracle has brought home to him a new sense, both of his own sinfulness and of Christ's holiness' (A. Plummer, *in loc.*). Plummer notices that Peter had seen other miracles, but points out that 'this was a miracle in Peter's own craft, and therefore was likely to make a special impression on him.'

At the end of the story of the healing of the Gadarene demoniac there is a little touch which we might well consider here. Jesus told the man to go home and tell the people what God had done for him. So he went and told them what Jesus had done for him (Lk. 8:39). What Jesus did and what God did are the same.

Luke records Jesus as exercising the divine prerogative of forgiving sins and the amazement of men when they heard Him doing this (Lk. 7:49). He tells us that the events of the ministry of Jesus are such that 'many prophets and kings' had wanted to see them, but had not had the privileged position of the men of Jesus' day (Lk. 10:24). Like the other Synoptists he tells the story of the triumphal entry in a way which shows that Jesus was a King, the King foretold by the prophet Zechariah. The men who shouted acclamation may not have known exactly what it was that they were doing; indeed, they certainly did not. But there is no doubt in Luke's account of the story. He is writing about a King.[72] It is not without significance that the cry of the multitude (Lk. 19:38) is recorded in words which remind us of the song of the angels (Lk. 2:14).[73] Luke now and then looks beyond this life to the time when the Son of man will confess men or not confess them before the angels (Lk. 12:8). Or he can think of Him as coming in glory with the angels (Lk. 9:26). He will sit 'at the right hand of the power of God' (Lk. 22:69). Revealing, too, are the words he records of those who walked to Emmaus. They did not appreciate either the fact or the significance of the resurrection. They thought of their Lord as yet dead. But they could say that He was 'mighty

[72] A. R. C. Leaney puts a good deal of emphasis on Luke's view of Jesus as King: 'his central theme is the kingship of Jesus, which appears to be his own contribution'; 'his theme was the reign of Christ, how it is established, how it must be maintained . . . he introduces the Kingdom of God as the object of the Lord's work in Marcan contexts not containing it (e.g. Mark i. 38 and Luke iv. 43; Mark vi. 7 and Luke ix. 2), he makes explicit the content of the *euangelion* as the kingdom (viii. 1; xvi. 16; Acts viii. 12), he narrates the birth of one who is to inherit the throne of David, he deliberately allows Jesus to enter Jerusalem as a king (xix. 38), and represents him as bequeathing a kingdom to the Apostles on the eve of his death (xxii. 18)' (*op. cit.*, pp. 32, 34).

[73] 'Glory in the highest' occurs in both, as does a reference to 'peace'. Cf. G. W. H. Lampe, 'the song of the angels at the announcement of the birth of the Messianic king is echoed by the crowds who greet Jesus, according to St. Luke, as the king who comes in the name of the Lord. His kingship, proclaimed at his birth, is realized through the suffering and death which await him in the stronghold of his enemies' (*op. cit.*, p. 183). Karl Barth sees significance in the Lukan addition of ἐν οὐρανῷ εἰρήνη καὶ δόξα ἐν ὑψίστοις to the ὡσαννά ἐν ὑψίστοις of Matthew and Mark in the disciples' song of praise on the entry into Jerusalem, thus giving to the event a clear significance for God Himself. Preceding everything that the event can mean for men, there is obviously something prior and higher at which we have to rejoice' (CDDR, p. 212).

in deed and word before God and all the people' (Lk. 24:19).
Though they might not rise to an understanding of all that Jesus was,
they could not but see this.

Luke, then, thought of no mean Saviour. For Him, Jesus plainly
occupied the highest place of all. And, as we cannot well separate
the person from the work, this helps us to see something of the
stupendous nature of the salvation that Luke is writing about. If
it required for its due accomplishment such a One as this, then it was
indeed a work of tremendous significance. It was a divinely wrought
salvation.

JESUS AND SINNERS

But though Luke speaks of such a wonderfully exalted Person, he
does not speak of One who was aloof. A striking feature of Luke's
portrait of Jesus is the way he brings out our Lord's close contact
with sinful men. This was in strong contrast with the usual attitude
of the religious leaders of the day. They held themselves scrupulously
(and contemptuously) aloof from 'the people of the land'.[74] This
expression was used in a derogatory sense of the great mass of common people who made no attempt to conform to Pharisaic tradition.[75]
This did not necessarily denote that they were irreligious (though
the term did include the irreligious). 'The tradition of the elders'
by this time amounted to a voluminous code of regulations. Intended originally to help men keep the divine law, it grew and
grew until it became a vexatious mass of petty, complicated, and
time-absorbing rules. The sheer bulk of the tradition made it difficult even to know what ought to be done, and the character of the
ritual requirements which were demanded meant that observance was
quite out of the question for ordinary men who had to earn their living. Labouring men simply did not have the time for all these things.
Given the best will in the world, they could hardly have kept up
with them. But they did not have the best will in the world. The

[74] Danby defines the term as 'The name given to those Jews who were
ignorant of the Law and who failed to observe the rules of cleanness and
uncleanness and were not scrupulous in setting apart Tithes from the
produce (namely, Heave-offering, First Tithe, Second Tithe, and Poor-man's
Tithe)' (The Mishnah, Oxford, 1933, p. 793).
[75] There is a very valuable note on this subject by George F. Moore in
The Beginnings of Christianity, i, London, 1920, pp. 439-445. He points out
that the educated 'looked down on the masses not only as unlearned but as
ill-bred, rude, and dirty' (op. cit., p. 439). He cites a Baraitha which shows
the way they were regarded: 'Six things are laid down by the rabbis about the
am ha-ares: Entrust no testimony to him, take no testimony from him, trust
him with no secret, do not appoint him guardian of an orphan, do not make
him the custodian of charitable funds, do not accompany him on a journey;
many add, do not inform him if you have found something belonging to him'
(op. cit., p. 443).

evidence, as far as we have it, is that they turned away from all this.[76] And as they rejected the tradition, the Pharisees rejected them.[77] The reaction on both sides is quite understandable. But it meant that ordinary men ceased to be religious in the best sense of the term.

The revolutionary thing in the practice of Jesus was His readiness to identify Himself with ordinary men. He did not take up a position anything like that of the general run of religious leaders.[78] He did not blame or despise men for failing to keep the traditions. He did not regard Himself as too holy to come into contact with them. He did not thank God that He was not like other men. Instead He sought them out. He talked with them. He dined with them. He made Himself one with them.

Right from the beginning this attitude is apparent. We have discussed the baptism of Jesus in connection with the witness of Matthew and Mark.[79] Luke also records this incident. He did not think of Jesus as needing for Himself that baptism which he describes as one 'of repentance unto remission of sins' (Lk. 3:3), for he regards Jesus as without fault (Lk. 23:4, etc.). It is possible that the Greek rendered 'when all the people were baptized' (Lk. 3:21) gives us the clue. It seems to indicate that Jesus was a little apart from the others while yet sharing the rite that they underwent.[80] In other words He was not a sinner, not one of them. But He made Himself one with them. He shared their lot.[81]

Luke records a number of occasions when Jesus had close contact with sinners. He speaks of the time in Levi's house when 'there was a great multitude of publicans and of others that were

---

[76] See G. H. C. MacGregor and A. C. Purdy, *Jew and Greek: Tutors Unto Christ*, London, 1937, pp. 125f.

[77] The great Hillel could say, 'No ignorant man (*Am-ha-Areç*) is religious' (*Ab.* ii. 5; cited in MacGregor and Purdy, *op. cit.*, p. 127).

[78] 'There can be no common ground between a religion which sees the sinner as a man to be avoided at all costs and a religion which sees the sinner as a man to be sought out at all costs, between a religion which sees the sinner as a man to be saved and a religion which sees the sinner as a man to be destroyed' (W. Barclay, *The Mind of Jesus*, London, 1960, p. 166).

[79] See above, pp. 39ff.

[80] Plummer renders ἐν τῷ βαπτισθῆναι ἄπαντα τὸν λαόν '*After* all the people had been baptized', and rejects '*while* they were being baptized'. He points out that the latter would require ἐν τῷ with the present infinitive. He thinks that 'Possibly Jesus waited until He could be alone with John' (*in loc.*).

[81] Barclay comments on the baptism in this Gospel, 'in His baptism Jesus realized, first, that He was the Messiah, God's Anointed King; and, second, that that involved not power and glory, but suffering and a Cross. The Cross did not come on Jesus unawares; from the first moment of realization He saw that Cross ahead. The baptism shows us Jesus asking for God's approval and receiving the destiny of the Cross' (*The Gospel of Luke*, Edinburgh, 1961, p. 33).

sitting at meat with them' (Lk. 5:29). This provoked the Pharisees and their scribes to ask, 'Why do ye eat and drink with the publicans and sinners?' They would never have done such a thing.[82] Jesus' reply makes it clear that His business is with sinners. He came not 'to call the righteous but sinners to repentance.'[83]

But Jesus did not confine His meals to such homes. Luke tells us of an occasion when He dined with Simon the Pharisee (Lk. 7: 36ff.). At this dinner a woman, described as 'a sinner', came behind Him as He reclined, and proceeded to wash His feet with her tears, wipe them with the hair of her head, kiss them, and anoint them with a precious unguent. Simon was most critical of this, and more particularly of the fact that Jesus did nothing to discourage the woman. But Jesus rebuked the Pharisee and encouraged the woman, saying to her, 'Thy sins are forgiven'. In other words, when the division became clear, Jesus took His stand with her that was called sinful, not with him who was esteemed righteous.

Here we might notice also Jesus' contact with Zacchaeus. By their collaboration with the conquering Romans, the tax-collectors put themselves out of court with all patriotic souls, and this included the religious parties. Religion and politics were practically inseparable in that day. Certainly a man who was engaged on the sort of work that occupied Zacchaeus would have been completely unacceptable to the Pharisees and their ilk. But Jesus not only spoke kindly to him, but invited Himself to Zacchaeus' home for a meal. That this was not popular is shown by the reaction of the crowd. They all complained, 'He is gone in to lodge with a man that is a sinner' (Lk. 19:7).[84]

The effect of all this must have been tremendous. Ordinary people had never experienced anything like it in a religious leader. Small wonder that 'all the publicans and sinners were drawing near unto him' (Lk. 15:1). They did not draw near to Pharisees or scribes or Sadducees. Spontaneously, naturally, they drew near to Jesus. And Luke records all this as though it were significant. Not only was it a fact, but it was a fact which expressed something of what Jesus came to do. He made Himself one with sinners because

[82] The Talmud explicitly provides that there be no table fellowship with the people of the land. Cf. also Mekilta Ex. 18. 1, 'the sages said: Let a man never associate with a wicked person, not even for the purpose of bringing him near to the Torah' (ed. J. Z. Lauterbach, Philadelphia, ii, 1933, p. 166).

[83] Cf. W. Manson, 'Over against the Pharisaic idea of salvation by segregation he sets up the new principle of salvation by association' (in loc.).

[84] M. J. Lagrange (in loc.) thinks Luke's use of πᾶς here is significant. It is not the Pharisees but the crowd who murmur. He proceeds, 'they took exception to the fact that instead of staying with a person of godliness and learning, Jesus asks hospitality of a sinner'. On verse 10 he comments, 'It is the putting into practice of the parables of ch. 15'.

His mission concerned sinners, because He came to do for them that which was vitally necessary, but which they could not do for themselves.

Like the other Synoptists, Luke records the agony in Gethsemane. In our earlier discussion of this incident we saw that the agony is meaningful only on the understanding that in the death that He died Jesus would be identified with sinners. Luke contributes to the picture with the detail that as He prayed, 'his sweat became as it were great drops of blood falling down upon the ground' (Lk. 22: 44). This detail is the more impressive when we recall that the night was so cold that those in the high priest's courtyard lit a fire to warm themselves (Mk. 14:54; Lk. 22:55). He also tells us that an angel came to strengthen Him. Though his narrative is rather abbreviated (he does not mention the threefold coming to the disciples with the Lord's command that they should watch and pray), yet he brings out more fully than the others the depths of the Saviour's agony.

It is in connection with this incident that we should perhaps consider the earlier sayings, 'I came to cast fire upon the earth; and what will I, if it is already kindled? But I have a baptism to be baptized with; and how am I straitened till it be accomplished!' (Lk. 12:49f.). The 'fire' of the first part of the saying we have discussed above.[85] Whatever its precise meaning, the saying as a whole is to be understood in the light of the passion, as the concluding words plainly show.[86] Jesus is speaking of His death,[87] and He is not speaking calmly. 'In His full humanity the horror of what is in front of Him presses heavily on His soul.'[88] The saying gives expression to some of the shrinking which marks out the death set before Jesus as no ordinary death. It was possessed of terrors of its own. Vincent Taylor points out that the verb rendered 'straitened' ($\sigma\upsilon\nu\acute{\epsilon}\chi o\mu\alpha\iota$) 'suggests the idea of a constraining impulse which brooks no delay and can tolerate no obstacle, but there is about the word in this saying an atmosphere of distress which is well expressed by Moffatt's translation: "I have a baptism to undergo. How I am distressed till it is all over!" In this respect the saying anticipates the experiences of Gethsemane.'[89]

[85] See p. 73.

[86] B. S. Easton renders, 'I must pass through dark waters; how great is my trouble until this is accomplished' (What Jesus Thought, New York, 1938, p. 57).

[87] Cf. R. H. Fuller, commenting on this passage, 'the death of Jesus as a baptism is a category running through the whole New Testament, and we may say with a tolerable degree of certainty that it has its origins in the teaching of our Lord himself' (op. cit., p. 61).

[88] H. K. Luce, in loc. Luce also speaks of 'The weariness and sadness of these two verses' and points out that Jesus 'longs for the coming of the Kingdom, but knows that it can only come through His own death'.

[89] JS, p. 167.

Luke is not depicting for us a death to be taken calmly, but one full of indescribable horror.

Like Matthew and Mark, Luke tells us that Jesus was crucified with two thieves, 'one on the right hand and the other on the left' (Lk. 23:33). As He died, Christ was in the very midst of sinners. His position symbolically set forth the significance of His death.[90] Lest we should miss the significance of this, he includes in his narrative of the Last Supper a note which sees in the death of the Lord the fulfilment of the prophecy of Isaiah, 'And he was reckoned with transgressors' (Lk. 22:37; cf. Is. 53:12).[91] This note is set in a context in which Jesus recalls the early days when he had sent the disciples out 'without purse, and wallet, and shoes', and contrasts them with the present 'he that hath a purse, let him take it, and likewise a wallet: and he that hath none, let him sell his cloke, and buy a sword'. Of this verse T. W. Manson says,

> The grim irony of v. 36 is the utterance of a broken heart . . . . Now nobody will give them a crust or a copper, and he who kills them will think he does God a service. The "friend of publicans and sinners" will be "reckoned with transgressors," and His life will end in defeat and ignominy. Jesus Himself has already accepted this necessity and found its meaning in the prophecies concerning the Servant of Jehovah . . . . The disciples cannot see this . . . . They and He are at cross purposes; and Jesus breaks off the conversation. He must die alone.[92]

CONSISTENT OPPOSITION

As Jesus moves towards this death, the pattern Luke weaves is one of continuing opposition. We might understand this, in part at least, as akin to the pattern we have seen in Matthew and Mark, with the forces of the demons locked in battle with the forces of God.

---

[90] Cf. Karl Barth, 'He is with us *as we are*, yes, He is Himself what we are. He has assumed our nature; He has made our sin His own, and He has made our death His . . . . He took upon Himself our fate, our godlessness, yea, the torture of our hell. Our deepest misery is His misery also. Yes, exactly in the depths of our misery He intercedes for us, and substitutes Himself for us, warding off the wages justly due us and suffering and making restitution what we could not suffer and where we could not make restitution' (*God in Action*, Edinburgh, 1936, pp. 16f.).

[91] W. Manson introduces his comment on Lk. 23:32-38 by saying: 'Luke relates the final tragedy with sustained reserve. The circumstances on which he dwells, the crucifixion along with Jesus of the two criminals, the prayer of Jesus for his executioners, "Father, forgive them, they do not know what they are doing," the drawing of lots for Christ's garments, the cruel sport of the soldiers, the mockery of the inscription placed on the cross, all these in the dying hour of the Son of man remind us that he was "numbered with the transgressors" and "bore the sins of many" ' (*in loc.*).

[92] *The Sayings of Jesus*, London, 1949, p. 341.

Or we might think of it as Jesus moving towards a death that is inevitable in the nature of things, inevitable, that is to say, because of what He was and because of what His enemies were and because of the relentless hostility that always exists between good and evil. What is clear enough is that Luke thinks of an opposition that begins early and is unrelenting. Thus when Jesus went back to Nazareth after His first brief spell of public ministry Luke recounts an attempt to kill Him (Lk. 4:28-30). That the attempt was abortive should not disguise from us the implied rejection of all that Jesus stood for.

It was not long before Jesus was prophesying that 'the bridegroom shall be taken away from them' (Lk. 5:35), which must be understood with respect to His death. After the healing of the man with the withered hand the enemies of Jesus discussed what they could do against Him (Lk. 6:11). Significantly, Luke ends his list of the Twelve with 'Judas Iscariot, which was the traitor' (Lk. 6:16). For the present stage of his narrative there is no necessity to insert this detail. But it belongs in the overall pattern. When Jesus is called 'a gluttonous man, and a winebibber, a friend of publicans and sinners!' (Lk. 7:34) there is the continuing note of hostility. There is no threat of violence here, but there is a rejection of all that Jesus stood for. This is so also in the scene pictured in Luke 11:53 where the scribes and Pharisees heckle Jesus, hoping to trap Him into a damaging statement.

In keeping with this, there is the detail in the transfiguration story which tells us that the topic of Moses and Elijah was 'his decease[93] which he was about to accomplish at Jerusalem' (Lk. 9:31; as we noted earlier this point is peculiar to Luke). Again, Jesus prophesied that He would be delivered up into the hands of men (Lk. 9:44). There is also a wonderful sentence in which Luke informs us that 'when the days were well-nigh come that he should be received up, he stedfastly set his face to go to Jerusalem' (Lk. 9:51). The inevitability of Jesus' death shines through all such sayings. The enemies of Jesus were so constant and so bitter that His death was certain. But there is also the thought that the purpose of God was being worked out. He is not defeated by the wickedness of evil men.

Sometimes there is the added thought that the followers of Jesus enter into all this, and that they are to accept suffering as a necessary part of their vocation. The beatitudes in Luke 6 ascribe blessedness to those who hunger, those who weep, those who are hated, and those whose name is cast out (vv. 21f.). The disciples are called

---

[93] Many recent writers interpret this saying in terms of the Exodus, e.g. J. Mánek, *Novum Testamentum*, ii, pp. 8-23; A. Cole, *Tyndale Commentary on Mark 9:4*; A. G. Hebert, *When Israel Came Out of Egypt*, London, 1961, p. 112. The starting point, of course, is the use of the term ἔξοδος.

upon to bless those who curse them; they are to pray for those who treat them badly; they are to turn the other cheek (Lk. 6:28f.). Clearly the followers of Jesus are not expected to react as do the men of this world to suffering and ill-treatment. Their Master accepted suffering. They must accept it, too.

THE TRIUMPH OF THE CHRIST

The constant opposition that Jesus encounters is viewed at times as a struggle between Jesus and all the denizens of hell. Just as in the other Synoptists, there are stories of exorcism (Lk. 4:33-37, 41; 6:18; 8:2, 27-39; 13:11-16). Let us take one example of such, and see how the whole ministry of Jesus stands out when it is regarded against this background. In chapter 11 Luke describes the casting out of a devil (v. 14). This led some of Jesus' enemies to ascribe His power to Beelzebub, the chief of the devils. Jesus replied by showing that a divided house or kingdom is powerless. In any case His opponents' sons practiced exorcism. If His enemies were correct in their reasoning, then it followed that they had the emissaries of the evil one in their very households. Their contention proved too much. Then Jesus pointed out the consequences of recognizing the divine origin of His exorcisms. 'But if I by the finger of God cast out devils, then is the kingdom of God come upon you' (v. 20). If it is the power of God that is seen in the expulsion of the demons, then nothing less than the Kingdom has descended upon them, and that a Kingdom come with power. Jesus went on to tell the little parable of the strong man armed whose goods are in peace, and of the stronger than he who defeats and spoils him. In this vivid way He described the conflict in which He was engaged. From there He went on to the impossibility of neutrality. Men must be on the side of God or that of Satan.[94] Ultimately there is no other. And the section concludes with the little story of the unclean spirit who goes out of a man, and subsequently returns with seven other spirits more wicked than himself, thus making the last state of the man worse than the first. This describes not a victory over the unclean spirit, but a temporary lull in the conflict. Satan for a time leaves the man alone, giving him respite to conduct a little moral reformation. But a little moral reformation is not Jesus' aim. This is not the activity in which He is engaged. In such a case the basic situation is unchanged.

---

[94] The importance of personal commitment should not be overlooked. Cf. Trevor Ling, who asks with respect to Christ's triumph over the demons, 'But what does this mean so far as the individual is concerned? How am I implicated in Christ's conquest of the demonic forces, if at all? Or am I merely a delighted spectator? The manner in which the Christus Victor theme is sometimes preached suggests the latter' (Theology, lvi, p. 329).

The man still belongs to Satan.[95] Rather Jesus' theme is the forcible expulsion of Satan by One who is stronger than he. Throughout this entire section the theme is the conflict with Satan, and this is not one isolated incident. There is a continuing warfare, a battle which does not cease.[96] The coming of the Kingdom has precipitated a struggle. Satan and all his cohorts are ranged in opposition to Christ. They are locked in mortal combat, but it is a combat in which Christ is triumphant.

The disciples are called into this struggle. They cannot stand aside when their Master is engaged in such a conflict. So He gives them power over demons (Lk. 9:1; 10:19f.). The seventy return from their mission and are greeted with the words, 'I beheld Satan fallen as lightning from heaven' (Lk. 10:18). There is no mention of Satan in the story of the mission. The disciples are charged to do such things as proclaim peace, heal the sick and announce judgment. But in this activity, whether they know it or not, they are engaged in the struggle against the evil one. Consequently, their successful discharge of the task represents a hard blow struck against Satan. This seems to me to be the most likely interpretation of the

[95] The unclean spirit, after going out of the man, can still speak of him as 'my house' (v. 24). However it may seem to the man, the evil spirit is clear that the fundamental situation is unchanged. He can take possession whenever he wishes.

[96] I cannot follow H. Conzelmann in his contention that in this Gospel Satan plays no part between the temptation and the passion. He says, 'The Temptation is finished decisively ($\pi\acute{a}\nu\tau a$), and the devil departs. A question of principle is involved here, for it means that where Jesus is from now on, there Satan is no more' (op. cit., p. 28); 'Satan does not enter as a factor in the saving events. In fact the only part he plays is the negative one of being excluded from the period of Jesus' ministry. Between the "Temptation" and the Passion he is absent' (op. cit., p. 156; see also p. 188). He dismisses the passage I have just discussed in a sentence, 'passages such as Luke xi, 17-23 do not mean that there is a constant conflict with Satan during Jesus' ministry; they have a symbolic meaning and are meant primarily to be a comfort to the Church of Luke's time' (op. cit., p. 188, n. 4). All this appears to me to be pure assertion. No reason is cited for the view. And it ignores a number of facts. Thus in the passage under discussion Jesus defends Himself against the accusation of casting out devils by Beelzebub by asking, 'if Satan also is divided against himself, how shall his kingdom stand?' (Lk. 11:18), which at the least indicates Satanic activity. So does the following reference to 'the strong man' (v. 21). So does Jesus' reference to 'Satan fallen as lightning from heaven' in connection with the mission of the seventy (Lk. 10:18). So does the description of a woman whom Jesus healed in a synagogue as 'a daughter of Abraham, whom Satan had bound' (Lk. 13:16). So does the reference to the devil in the parable of the Sower (Lk. 8:12). So does the conflict with demons and unclean spirits which Luke attests so faithfully, for even Conzelmann admits that there is a clear connection between Satan and the evil spirits in this Gospel (op. cit., p. 157). Cf. also the statement of K. Heim cited on p. 97, n. 98.

passage,[97] though it is possible also to understand it as meaning that Satan had, prior to the mission of the disciples, been thrown down, and that this was the reason for their success. Either way the unspectacular activities of the little band are meaningful in the overall struggle of Christ against Satan. That Satan is mindful of the position and activities of believers is seen also in the explanation given to the parable of the Sower. Satan takes the good word out of men's hearts lest they believe and be saved (Lk. 8:12). He is totally opposed to men's best interests.

It is possible that some, at any rate, of Jesus' attitude to the Sabbath is explicable in terms of this conflict. Luke tells us of a woman possessed by 'a spirit of infirmity' (Lk. 13:10-17), and says that Jesus described her as 'a daughter of Abraham, whom Satan had bound, lo, these eighteen years'. Confronted with a work of the evil one, Jesus must take action, sabbath or no sabbath. The Jews persistently censured Jesus for His attitude to the sabbath, but they did not understand the situation. He was engaged in an unrelenting struggle with the very prince of hell. As Satan works seven days a week, so must those who seek to thwart his purpose.

Especially are Satan's activities seen in the events associated with the passion. He 'entered into Judas' (Lk. 22:3). When Jesus was arrested He could say, 'this is your hour, and the power of darkness' (Lk. 22:53). These words might be understood as, 'This is your hour, and yet it is the power of darkness', in which case it would point up the contrast between the joyous triumph of those who had arrested the Lord and the realities of the situation. More likely the words are to be understood of Satan. Moffatt translates, 'This is your hour, and the dark Power has its way.' This is the supreme moment in the struggle against the evil one.[98]

---

[97] 'Fallen' is aorist, πεσόντα. C. A. Webster has a note on this passage in which he claims this aorist as constative, citing J. H. Moulton and A. T. Robertson in support. The former speaks of 'the original timeless character' of the aorist participle, and says of our passage, ' "I watched him fall" will be the meaning, the Aorist being constative: πίπτοντα "falling" (cf. Vulg. cadentem) would have been much weaker, suggesting the possibility of recovery' (ET, lvii, p. 53).

[98] Karl Heim reviews a number of sayings culminating in this one and proceeds, 'The mortal suffering which He faces is therefore not vocational suffering caused by human misunderstanding and resistance. Neither is it a struggle between ideas, e.g. between a national-political and a purely religious concept of the Messiah. On the contrary, according to Jesus' own assertion it is the final battle, terrible and decisive, of the war that fills the whole of His life, against the satanic power that wants to dethrone God . . . . the thought of an anti-godly power against which this war is waged cannot be eliminated from the mind of Jesus as an unimportant concept to be attributed to popular ideas of His time. On the contrary: this is the fundamental conviction that makes His whole life-work from the beginning to the

But this is not the end. Jesus rose triumphant on the third day. Luke is not in the resurrection narrative using material derived from the other evangelists nor, apparently, their sources. He records events like the walk to Emmaus which the others do not, and he describes the whole resurrection event in his own way. If the resurrection of which he speaks is certainly the same resurrection as that described elsewhere, the song of resurrection triumph is Luke's own composition.

Luke does not think of the resurrection as coming completely out of the clear blue sky. He records prophecies that the Lord would rise (Lk. 9:22; 11:29f.; 18:33). Indeed, before the Saviour was ever born Luke has the angel saying to Mary concerning Him, 'the Lord God shall give unto him the throne of his father David: and he shall reign over the house of Jacob for ever; and of his kingdom there shall be no end' (Lk. 1:32f.). If this cannot be adduced as showing the expectation of a resurrection it does show that the note of triumph was there from the very beginning. And we see it again during Jesus' ministry in the defeats of death when Jairus' daughter was brought back to life (Lk. 8:41-56), and again when Jesus raised the son of the widow of Nain (Lk. 7:11-15). Jesus' words of reassurance to Peter at the Last Supper also fall to be considered here. They arise out of the Lord's realization that Peter was the object of Satan's attack at this critical moment. 'Simon, Simon,' says Jesus solemnly, 'behold, Satan asked to have you, that he might sift you as wheat' (Lk. 22:31). It is impossible to interpret these words other than as a reference to the dark hours when the disciples would all forsake their Lord and flee,[99] and when Peter himself would three times deny that he even knew Him. In full knowledge of all this, Jesus assures Peter of His prayers for him, and He says, 'do thou, when once thou hast turned again, stablish thy brethren' (Lk. 22:32). Even in that hour Jesus looked for the survival of His little band and for Peter's continuing ministry. Later, at the tomb, the angel reminded the women that Jesus had looked for triumph indeed, but for nothing other than the triumph that comes out of crucifixion with all that that means, and then resurrection (Lk. 24:6f.).

An interesting group of passages extends the ultimate triumph to the followers of Jesus. They will have a share in resurrection itself (Lk. 20:35, 37). Associated with this is the heavenly reward of those who follow Christ, that reward which is 'great in heaven' (Lk. 6:23). So important is this whole idea that it is no gain if a

---

terrible end into a fierce war with an invisible enemy' (*Jesus the Lord*, Edinburgh and London, 1959, pp. 90f.).

[99] 'You' is plural, ὑμᾶς, and refers to others than Peter. But the pronoun is singular when He says, 'I made supplication for thee (περὶ σοῦ)'.

man could acquire the whole world and in the process lose his soul (Lk. 9:25). Nor is it any better to substitute achievements of a spiritual character here on earth for material prosperity. It is better to have one's name written in heaven than to have a spectacular power over evil spirits (Lk. 10:20). John the Baptist was a very great man. Indeed, Jesus said that he was the greatest of men. Yet he that is 'but little' in God's kingdom is greater than he (Lk. 7:28).[100] There is a general reference to being recompensed 'in the resurrection of the just' (Lk. 14:14), and another which assures those who forsake comforts for Jesus' sake in this life that they will receive 'manifold more in this time, and in the world to come eternal life' (Lk. 18:30). There is also the specific assurance given by Jesus to the dying thief as they hung on their crosses, that he would be with Him in Paradise (Lk. 23:43).

Nor does the story end even there. Luke looks beyond the resurrection to the eschatological messianic banquet. He tells us that at the Last Supper Jesus said, 'With desire I have desired to eat this passover with you before I suffer: for I say unto you, I will not eat it, until it be fulfilled in the kingdom of God' (Lk. 22:15f.). Luke proceeds, 'And he received a cup, and when he had given thanks, he said, Take this, and divide it among yourselves: for I say unto you, I will not drink from henceforth of the fruit of the vine, until the kingdom of God shall come.' These verses have been much discussed in connection with the difficult questions of whether the Last Supper was a passover meal or not, and of just how Luke understands the Holy Communion to have been instituted. But neither of these is our immediate concern. It is enough for us to notice that thoughts of the passover were certainly in Jesus' mind as He thought of His death. As of old the shedding of the blood of the passover victim brought deliverance to the people of God, so would it be now. All that the passover prefigured and symbolized, Jesus perfectly fulfilled.

But more is implied. Jesus looks past His suffering and past His resurrection and ascension to the culmination of all things in the Kingdom of God, a culmination that His sufferings would in due course bring about. The death is clearly in mind. 'I will not drink from henceforth of the fruit of the vine' is a word of farewell. Jesus is speaking of His death. What follows cannot be separated from that. But the death is not the end. It is the beginning. And what follows is rooted in the death. His sufferings will bring about all that is involved in the fulfilment of the Kingdom of God. Vincent

---

[100] This saying has implications beyond the immediate question of John the Baptist. W. Manson says that it 'presupposes on Jesus' part not merely the highest estimate of John . . . but a consciousness of the *finality* of his own mission to Israel' (*in loc.*).

Taylor sees the importance of this saying in 'the close association it establishes between the Supper, the approaching death, and the consummation of the Kingdom in the thought of Jesus . . . . What Lk. xxii. 17f. does permit us to say is that the connexion is intimate and that, in the expression of fellowship, death is faced with unconquered hope and certainty.'[101]

There is a similar ring of certainty in Jesus' promise of 'a kingdom' to His followers. He said further that they would eat and drink at His table in His kingdom and 'sit on thrones judging the twelve tribes of Israel' (Lk. 22:29f.). Jesus is facing death. He has just been speaking about it. He has inaugurated the solemn sacrament in which believers will remember His death. But with quiet assurance He speaks now of His own dominion and of the authority He will bestow on His own in due course.[102]   Death is not defeat.

Thus right through this Gospel we hear the note of victory. There is a never-ceasing strife against evil, but there is never any suggestion that the issue is in doubt. Evil will be defeated resoundingly, and the means of that defeat is, paradoxically, the death of the Lord. For this leads on to the mighty resurrection. There cannot be the slightest doubt but that it was important to Luke that his Master was triumphant. There are other aspects of the atonement, but the aspect of victory is real and it is important.

ENTERING LIFE

It remains to ask how the benefits of Christ's death become available to His people. How do men enter into life? When the question was put to Jesus, 'Master, what shall I do to inherit eternal life?' (Lk. 10:25) He directed the attention of His questioner to the Law.[103]   He did the same when the rich young ruler put a similar

---

101 JS, pp. 185f.

102 'That such convictions should be expressed in such an hour is inexplicable unless He believes that His suffering and death manifest His lordship and in some way are necessary to the consummation of the Divine Rule' (Vincent Taylor, JS, p. 190).

103 E. S. G. Wickham sees this incident as pointing us to justification. He begins a study of Lk. 10:29 with: 'The doctrine of justification by faith does not come alive easily as presented in the abstract by its chief exponent St Paul. Can it be approached, imaginatively and man to man rather than theologically, by dwelling on the one incident in the Gospel story in which we read of a lawyer in the presence of Jesus "desiring to justify himself"?'   He ends his discussion with an emphasis on faith, 'faith which because it is a response to divine initiative in and through Christ is the acceptance of a divine gift — faith which is not so much man's acceptance of Christ as his acceptance of Christ's prior acceptance of himself' (Theology, lx, pp. 417f.). That such a discussion is possible shows that Jesus certainly is doing something more than recommend a barren adherence to the doctrine of salvation by human merit.

question to Him (Lk. 18:18ff.). But before we jump to the conclusion that He thought of salvation as coming to men as a result of
faithful Law-keeping we must notice His explicit statement, 'none
is good, save one, even God' (Lk. 18:19). If this is the case no
man can merit his salvation by works of law. The parable of the
Good Samaritan should not be understood as teaching salvation by
deeds of compassion. The parable is not an answer to the question
'What must I do to be saved?', but to quite another, 'And who is
my neighbour?'[104] Its application to the mode of salvation is
better understood when it is applied to what Jesus has done on men's
behalf.[105] Jesus' words about Law, then, are not to be taken as out-
lining the way in which men in point of fact are saved. Rather they
draw attention to the importance of living wholeheartedly for God.
Of Mary of Bethany He said, 'but one thing is needful: for Mary
hath chosen the good part, which shall not be taken away from her'
(Lk. 10:42; Moffatt renders, 'she is not to be dragged away from
it').[106] Such words indicate that discipleship is no easy affair. It
involves serious choice, and wholehearted, concentrated service.

Jesus made it clear that division is an inevitable result of His
message (Lk. 12:51-53). When a man enters into life a barrier
is raised between him and those who refuse the life-giving message.
Indeed, before Jesus was more than a tiny Babe, old Simeon had
said, 'Behold, this child is set for the falling and rising up of many
in Israel; and for a sign which is spoken against' (Lk. 2:34). This
thought is also behind the warning that no man can serve two masters
(Lk. 16:13), and it is not out of mind in the saying, 'If any man
cometh unto me, and hateth not his own father, and mother, and wife,
and children, and brethren, and sisters, yea, and his own life also,
he cannot be my disciple' (Lk. 14:26). It is hardly necessary to
point out that literal hatred of one's closest kin is not being incul-
cated. But Jesus is calling for a loyalty and a love beside which
all earthly loyalties pale into insignificance, and all earthly loves
look like hatred. Small wonder that He urged people to count the

[104] Plummer makes this point, and objects to the thought that the parable
teaches salvation by works of benevolence (in loc.).

[105] For this point of view see R. S. Wallace, op. cit., p. 109; H. Thielicke,
op. cit., p. 168.

[106] 'The contrast is between Martha, immersed in the business of her little
corner of the workaday world, and Mary, who is of the kind that leave all to
follow Christ. It could be urged, and Martha makes the point, that in leaving
all Mary has mostly left her duties in the house. A similar criticism could,
however, have been made by Peter's wife or the father of James and John;
and it can be said that the progress of the Gospel in the world would not have
been what it was if there had not been those who heard a call that
cancelled all other obligations' (T. W. Manson, op. cit., pp. 264f.). It is
this last point which is so significant.

cost (Lk. 14:28-33).[107]   Such an adventure is not to be undertaken lightly.

None of this means salvation by human merit. Nothing in this Gospel suggests that one way of merit is being exchanged for another. The whole of the preceding part of this chapter has shown that Luke puts the divine action of God in Christ at the root of salvation. But this does not mean that all men are saved. It opens the door. But if men are to enter it is necessary that they should receive this salvation. This means that their attitude must be that of wholehearted submission to God, which is what the passages we are now noticing indicate. Luke sometimes points to this in terms of faith. He tells us that Jesus praised the faith of the centurion (Lk. 7:9).[108] He speaks of saving faith in those who came to be healed (Lk. 8:48; 17:19; 18:42). But he tells us also that on the occasion of the stilling of the storm Jesus inquired of the disciples, 'Where is your faith?' (Lk. 8:25). This is not so much the miracle-seeking faith as that which reposes on a person and that Person the Lord Himself. The disciples had learned something of the lesson when they prayed, 'Lord, increase our faith' (Lk. 17:5). And to the woman whose sins He had just forgiven Jesus said, 'Thy faith hath saved thee' (Lk. 7:50).[109] By contrast there is castigation for faithlessness (Lk. 9:41). It is fairly clear then that Jesus in this Gospel is seen as demanding from men an attitude, an attitude of trust, an attitude of wholehearted trust. We see it in the invitation, 'If any man would come after me, let him deny himself, and take up his cross daily, and follow me' (Lk. 9:23; cf. 14:27). The Saviour took up His cross. If a man would be saved he must look to the Saviour and follow Him.

Salvation then comes from faith, from that faith that leads to a wholehearted following of Christ. It is not some great complicated system like that of the Pharisees. On the contrary, anyone can understand it. It is very simple.

But it is not easy.

[107] Cf. Helmut Thielicke, 'Can we really imagine that he died on his cross . . . for the flimflam of respectable Christianity? He wants to bring us on to the straight road to the Father in order that we may get back to his heart. In no case does he want people who do nothing but run around in circles, people who want the Father but won't let go of the devil and therefore get nowhere' (op. cit., p. 151).

[108] Of this man William Barclay says, 'He came with that perfect confidence which looks up and says, "Lord, I know you can do this." If we only had a faith like that for us too the miracle would happen and life would become new' (op. cit., p. 84).

[109] 'Jesus does not say "thy love hath saved thee", but "thy faith" — not because "faith" is a merit, but because it is her faith that appropriates the forgiveness which grace has bestowed' (Geldenhuys, in loc.). W. Manson speaks of her love as 'the proof of her forgiveness, not its ground' (in loc.).

A UNIVERSAL SALVATION

> All four Evangelists tell us that the good tidings are sent to "all
> the nations" . . . . But no one teaches this so fully and persistently
> as S. Luke. He gives us, not so much the Messiah of the O.T.,
> as the Saviour of all mankind and the Satisfier of all human needs.
> Again and again he shows us that forgiveness and salvation are
> offered to all, and offered freely, independently of privileges of
> birth or legal observances.[110]

This special interest in the universal application of the gospel
comes out quite early, as when he records the words of Simeon
with reference to the Christ-child, that He would be 'a light for
revelation to the Gentiles' (Lk. 2:32), though he does not overlook
God's ancient people, for he adds immediately, 'the glory of thy
people Israel'. If God sends His Son, then it is fairly obvious that
His mission concerns all mankind. But Luke does not leave us to
guess. He tells us of this 'revelation to the Gentiles'. As does
Matthew, he records the prophecy from Isaiah 40, but he continues
to a point after that at which Matthew stops so that he can include
the words, 'all flesh shall see the salvation of God' (Lk. 3:6). He
records the words of Jesus with respect to the Gentile centurion, 'I
have not found so great faith, no, not in Israel' (Lk. 7:9), and in another connection those other words, 'And they shall come from the
east and west, and from the north and south, and shall sit down in the
kingdom of God' (Lk. 13:29).

So again it is Luke who points out the significance of the stories
of Naaman and of the widow of Sarepta (Lk. 4:26f.). There were
many possible objects of the divine bounty within Israel in the days
of these two. But in each case God chose to work out His purpose
outside the borders of His chosen people. Similar to this is Luke's
interest in the Samaritans. He mentions the gentle response of Jesus
to the hostile Samaritan villagers (Lk. 9:51-6), and he recounts the
parable of the Good Samaritan (Lk. 10:30-37) and the story of
the ten lepers with its singling out of the Samaritan for commendation (Lk. 17:11-19).

Luke does not emphasize it beyond what is seemly,[111] but the place

---

110 A. Plummer, op. cit., p. xlii.

111 Indeed N. Q. King can speak of Luke's 'positive Jewishness' and maintain that it is 'only after the Resurrection that there is an unequivocal reference to the gentile mission which advances beyond the Old Testament
teaching' (SE, pp. 203, 204). I am not fully persuaded that he has made
out his case for the complete absence of emphasis on the Gentiles before the
resurrection, and in any case he seems to recognize something more when he
begins his final summing up with, 'Clearly St. Luke was universalistic in his
outlook in that he envisaged the gospel's being carried to non-Jews . . . . He
indicates that the preaching to the gentiles is to come after the Jews have
done their worst to the Messiah and he has triumphed in the power of God'

of the Gentiles clearly meant much to him. It is significant that
when he gives our Lord's genealogy he traces the line back not
to Abraham, as does Matthew the Jew, but to 'Adam, the son of God'
(Lk. 3:38).[112]   And in the great eschatological discourse he speaks
of Jerusalem as being 'trodden down of the Gentiles, until the times
of the Gentiles be fulfilled' (Lk. 21:24).   Salvation is, of course,
not in mind here, but the reference shows us something of Luke's
interest.   At the very end of his Gospel he tells us that Christ commanded His followers that 'repentance and remission of sins should
be preached in his name unto all the nations' (Lk. 24:47).

His universalism comes out also in his frequent references to people
who would usually be ignored by the religious men of the day.   Thus
it is in the Third Gospel above all others that we read of the women
who are associated in one way or another with the Lord: the Virgin,
Elizabeth, Anna, the widow of Nain, the sinner in the house of
Simon the Pharisee, Joanna the wife of Chuza, Susanna, the woman
with an issue, Mary Magdalene, Martha and her sister Mary, the
widow casting her two mites into the temple treasury, the 'daughters
of Jerusalem' and the women at the tomb.   Clearly this aspect of
Jesus' ministry made a deep appeal to Luke.[113]   His wide interests
come out also in his references to the disreputable of various kinds.
He begins with those who came to John (Lk. 3:12f.), and goes on
to those who find a welcome with Jesus (Lk. 5:27-32; 7:37ff.; 15:1f.,
11ff.; 18:9-14; 19:2-10; 23:39-43).   He does not forget the respectable, for he notices how Jesus sought them out, too, though he has
no such response to record as in the case of the outcasts (Lk. 7:36ff.;
11:37; 14:1ff.).   He has similarly a deep interest in the poor
(Lk. 1:52f.; 2:7ff., 24; 4:18; 6:20f.; 7:22; 14:13, 21; 16:20), and
a rather less interest in the rich (Lk. 19:2ff.; 23:50ff.).

From all this it is plain that Luke sees the gospel message as something relevant to the needs of all men.   He is writing of no petty
thing, done in a corner and of no especial significance.   He is
writing of a gospel world-wide in its grasp and scope.   He is writing

---

(*ibid.*, pp. 204f.).   It is certainly the case that Luke does not envisage the
preaching to the Gentiles as taking place before the resurrection.   The point
on which I am concerned to insist is that he did see the Gentiles as having
their place in the salvation God wrought out in Christ.

[112] Cf. Bishop Cassian, Luke 'was a universalist.   Salvation in Christ
belongs to all.   But the universalism of Luke is different from that of
Matthew.   St. Matthew has his feet in the Old Testament.   His gospel is a
revelation of the promised Messianic Kingdom in the Church under the law
of love.   This message is historical in its origin and in its essence.   Luke is
not rooted in history.   His universalistic conception of salvation is the
universalism of the loving mercy of God in Christ' (SE, p. 141).

[113] The Rabbis assigned women a very low place.   To this day the
orthodox Jew thanks God that He did not make him a woman.

of God's remedy for the sinful condition of all mankind. He is writing of a gospel that must be taken to the very ends of the earth.[114]

From all this it appears that Luke has essentially the same view of the atonement as have Matthew and Mark, though he has his own way of putting things and his own emphases. More than does either of the other two, he stresses the factualness of his narrative. It is important that it be understood that these things *happened*. Luke is not dealing in myths and fables, but in events, those events in which it pleased God to effect man's salvation. In this Luke sees God as overthrowing human values and as doing what pleased Himself. He puts some emphasis on the fact that God's ways are not our ways, a point which it is important to keep in mind, for in some theories of the atonement confidently advanced in modern times there is more than the suspicion that it is our ways rather than God's which receive attention. It is the unreflecting pride of modern man that his way of understanding things must needs be the right way. Luke would not agree. He sees God as acting according to the norms of His own holy nature, and man has no reason for thinking that God's norms are his. As soon as we drag it out into the open, we see that the contrary is certain to be the case. Since we are not divine, we will not think as God thinks. This is all so very obvious that it would be hardly worth stating were it not that in practice it is so often ignored. This particular Lukan emphasis ought to keep us humble.

Sometimes a good deal of emphasis is placed on Luke's omissions. Thus he has no equivalent of the ransom saying of Mark 10:45, nor of Matthew's connection of Jesus' covenant blood with remission of sins (Mt. 26:28). He does not connect forgiveness with Jesus' death. H. Conzelmann goes so far as to say that in Luke there is no 'direct soteriological significance drawn from Jesus' suffering or death. There is no suggestion of a connection with the forgiveness of sins.'[115] But this leaves us with a wrong impression. Though Luke does not

---

[114] Some maintain that the reference to 'seventy' in Luke points to the mission to the Gentiles because seventy was held to be the number of the nations (e.g., H. Burton, *The Gospel according to St. Luke,* London, 1890, p. 5). But the textual variant 'seventy-two' may be right and point to Israel (T. W. Manson, *op. cit.,* p. 257), or 'seventy' may indicate the elders of Israel (Ex. 24:1; Nu. 11:16). No weight can be placed on the passage.

Another possibility is that the parable of the Pounds is meant as a condemnation of exclusivism. Thus A. M. Hunter sees typified in 'the barren rascal' who kept his pound hidden in a napkin 'the pious Pharisee who hoarded the light God gave him (the Law) and kept for himself what was meant for mankind. Such a policy of selfish exclusivism yields God no interest on his capital; it is tantamount to defrauding him and must incur his judgment' (*op. cit.,* p. 81).

[115] *Op. cit.,* p. 201. A similar position is taken up by H. J. Cadbury, *The Making of Luke-Acts,* London, 1958, pp. 280f.

speak of these matters as specifically as do his fellow evangelists yet it must be recognized that he puts a great deal of emphasis on the passion, introducing it into contexts where the others do not (e.g., the transfiguration), that he consistently pictures it as taking place in accordance with God's will and plan, that he thinks of Jesus as the Saviour, that he pictures Him as making Himself one with sinful men, that he shows us Jesus as viewing His death with something like horror. In the light of all this it is very difficult indeed to deny that Luke sees soteriological significance in Christ's death. And if he does not see soteriological significance, the question arises, What significance does he see? That he sees some significance is manifest, for he devotes so much space to it. And if he does not expressly speak of the death as soteriological, it is also true that he does not express-ly describe it in any other way.[116] He does not refer to it as the death of a martyr, for example. We are left to draw our conclusions from the kind of thing I have just noted. And at the very least such state-ments are more consonant with an atoning death than with any other kind of death. There is no essential difference here between Luke on the one hand and Matthew and Mark on the other.

Like the first and second evangelists, the third sees sin as a serious business, since the judgment of God is against all those who commit sin. Like them he sees salvation as consequent on God's action, and he delights to dwell on this in song and story. He stresses that Jesus was about the Father's business, which roots salva-tion in the will of God. He thinks of Jesus as divine in the fullest sense, which does the same. He sees Jesus' method as one in which He makes Himself one with sinners, identifying Himself with them. The Lord faces strong and consistent opposition, and that from sources both human and demonic, but Luke sees Him as winning through to glorious triumph. So He makes available to all men a wonderful salvation. Luke likes to notice the universality of its scope, for this is the salvation of God's people everywhere, not simply among the Jews. And Luke looks for men to make the appropriate response to the offer of salvation. It is not something that comes to men automatically. There is a division, a sifting. Men must decide for Christ. Men must take Him as their Leader. Men must believe with all their heart.

---

[116] C. K. Barrett thinks Luke's references to the cross suggest 'a temporary reverse, not unforeseen, and speedily retrieved' (op. cit., p. 60). But this is surely an estimate never derived from Luke. It ignores Luke's emphasis on the cross, and his references to the working out of the divine plan. Barrett himself can refer to 'Luke's representation of the divine plan of redemptive history' (op. cit., p. 66), and this is a reality.

CHAPTER THREE

The Cross in the Lukan Writings

II. THE ACTS

Luke carries on the story he began in the Gospel by narrating in Acts the experiences of the early church. We are used to thinking of Luke's Gospel and Acts as two separate works. But they are really one book in two volumes. The preface at the beginning of the Gospel is the preface to Acts as well as to the Gospel.[1] It is still

---

[1] The importance of this is brought out by H. J. Cadbury, 'Luke i. 1-4 therefore is not merely of indirect value to the student of Acts as an introduction to another work written by the same author and addressed to the same patron. It is the real preface to Acts as well as to the Gospel, written by the author when he contemplated not merely one but both volumes . . . . It is as necessary to apply the phraseology of the preface to Acts as to the Gospel; and to recognize that references to previous writers, to "eye-witnesses and ministers of the word," to the author's own intimate knowledge of the subjects treated, are equally applicable to both books' (*The Beginnings of Christianity,* ii, London, 1922, p. 492).

the same story.   As R. R. Williams puts it, 'Luke is telling the story of a mighty event, and this event has two stages, both of which are supernatural.   The Gospel tells how God "visited and redeemed his people" by sending His Son, Jesus Christ.   The Acts tells how this event became "a light to lighten the Gentiles" through the witness of the Spirit-filled Church.'[2]   So Luke tells how Jesus commanded His followers to wait in Jerusalem for the promised gift, how the Holy Spirit of God came down at Pentecost to galvanize the little group of believers into vigorous life, and how the first preachers went about their task of proclaiming the gospel.   We read of high adventure, of experiences grave and gay, of men who were persecuted for being Christians and of one who fell asleep during a sermon, of conversions, of men who halted between two opinions, and of men who turned away.   We learn of some who gave themselves wholeheartedly to the proclamation of the message, and of some who threw their energies into opposing it.   And through all this there runs the same purpose as we saw in the Gospel.   Luke is not simply a historian narrating history, though there is history here. He is first and foremost a believer.   He is writing about how God worked in the early church to accomplish His purpose.[3]

For all his profound theological interest, Luke does not give us a carefully thought-out system of theology, more particularly with respect to the atonement.   But just as the death of Christ underlay everything in the Gospel, so does it underlie everything in Acts. Nothing here makes sense apart from the cross whereon men's salvation was accomplished.   Luke pictures faithfully for us the comparatively simple, more or less unreflecting theology of the first days of the Christian Church.   He shows us men caught up in the first fine flush of a new enthusiasm.   The wonder of the resurrection gripped their minds and their imaginations.[4]   The new-found power of the indwelling Spirit of God transformed their innermost being.   They lived out the power of the gospel.   They preached to others with directness and certainty and won them for Christ.   The exploration of the great depths in the message was not their immediate concern.

---

[2] *The Acts of the Apostles,* London, 1953, p. 26.

[3] Cf. M. Dibelius, 'it was the Acts of the Apostles which first tried to form from traditional material the continuous account of an actual period in history. Many details, however, especially the speeches, will make it clear to the reader that this is not the ultimate object of the book, which aims also to preach and to show what the Christian belief is and what effects it has' (*Studies in the Acts of the Apostles,* London, 1956, p. 102).

[4] Cf. Erich Sauer, faith 'was only re-established by the bodily resurrection of the Lord and His subsequent appearances as the Risen One . . . . Without the bodily resurrection no thinking man would ever have believed upon the Crucified One; for His end would have contradicted His own prior announcements of His resurrection and triumph' (*The Triumph of the Crucified,* London, 1951, p. 41).

They were practical evangelists and pastors. Later would come theologians like Paul and John and the writer of the Epistle to the Hebrews. These profound and restless minds would probe into the message and bring to light its implications. But for the present, Luke pictures the preachers as practical men, concentrating on the task in hand. They told men what God had done and they called men to respond in repentance and faith. They ransacked their vocabulary to find some way of conveying to their hearers a little of the immense significance they found in Jesus Christ and in the work that He had done for men. So, as we follow Luke through his narrative, we shall not expect to find a consistently thought-out system. The thought will not be slipshod, but it will not be worked into a system. We shall see men acting under the conviction that the salvation that is being proclaimed is adequate for all the needs of men. And we shall find it proclaimed in terms which are meaningful for those who want to understand the first appeal of the message.[5] We shall see much that was said in the Gospel restated in this second volume. But we shall also see that additional points of importance are brought out.

THE SERIOUSNESS OF SIN

As in the former volume, the seriousness of sin is everywhere assumed. Luke does not regard sin as a minor misunderstanding which will speedily or easily be put right. He stresses that it has important implications. In particular, he makes three points.

(1) A Demand for Repentance and Conversion

Sin must be utterly forsaken. There can be no trifling with it. As early as the very first sermon that Luke records, that of Peter on the day of Pentecost immediately after the gift of the Spirit, we read of a strong appeal for men to forsake sin. 'Repent ye, and be baptized every one of you', said Peter.[6] 'Save yourselves from this crooked generation' (Acts 2:38, 40). 'Repent ye therefore, and turn again,' he said at the Gate Beautiful after the lame man had been healed, 'that your sins may be blotted out, that so there may come seasons of refreshing from the presence of the Lord' (Acts 3:19). These 'seasons' could not be expected without a wholehearted repentance. Luke does not think of this as a requirement that may

---

[5] C. F. Evans sums up much when he speaks of 'The basic pattern of the resurrection and exaltation of the crucified Jesus, through whom repentance and remission of sins is preached' (JTS, n. s., vii, pp. 38f.). A great deal of Acts is intelligible when regarded as the proclamation of this message.

[6] 'It must be underscored that Peter's basic and primary demand is for *repentance*' (N. B. Stonehouse, *Paul before the Areopagus*, Grand Rapids, 1957, p. 84).

be waived now and then. He reports Paul's message to the Athenians, that God 'commandeth men that they should all everywhere repent' (Acts 17:30). This command is urgent. It brooks no delay. God has in past days overlooked 'the times of ignorance', but the situation is changed with the coming of the Gospel. Repentance may no longer be deferred (*ibid.*). This is the same note of urgency that was struck in the Gospel. Luke is explicit that repentance is a universal as well as an immediate requirement, for in addition to the passage we have just noted he tells us that Paul reminded the elders of the Ephesian church that when he was among them he had testified 'both to Jews and to Greeks repentance toward God, and faith toward our Lord Jesus Christ' (Acts 20:21).[7] With this should be taken his statement before Agrippa that he had 'declared both to them of Damascus first, and at Jerusalem, and throughout all the country of Judaea, and also to the Gentiles, that they should repent and turn to God, doing works worthy of repentance' (Acts 26:20). Two things are noteworthy about this. The one is that the enumeration of the various people to whom Paul had preached in this way shows that it was Paul's habitual message. The other is that the repentance he sought was not one merely in name or in words, but one that was expressed in deeds.[8] Men must produce 'works worthy of repentance'. We are reminded of the way Luke reports John the Baptist's demand for just such works.

This teaching on repentance is complemented by a similar insistence on conversion. Peter, in one breath, urged both on the men of Jerusalem. 'Repent ye therefore, and turn again' (Acts 3:19). Barnabas and Paul told the crowds at Lystra who wanted to make gods out of them that their message was 'that ye should turn from these vain things unto the living God' (Acts 14:15). Luke tells us that the same apostles described their work as 'declaring the conversion of the Gentiles' (Acts 15:3; cf. also 15:19; 26:20). This is all of a piece with the teaching in his Gospel that the whole set of a man's life must be changed. Conversion is a turning, a turning away from the old with its emphasis on the here and now and on the things which profit the individual, however widely 'profit' be

---

[7] Note that repentance and faith are linked. Cf. E. L. Kendall, 'Repentance, as it is set forth in the New Testament, involves more than turning away from sin. It involves the active acceptance of faith implied in the Lord's command "Repent ye and believe the Gospel", without which positive direction of intention there is always the danger that the power of the devil to do harm may be renewed with sevenfold intensity' (*A Living Sacrifice*, London, 1960, p. 137).

[8] Cf. B. Gärtner, 'Μετανοεῖν always implies a radical conversion, which involves condemnation of what is being discarded, and a total adoption of something new' (*The Areopagus Speech and Natural Revelation*, Uppsala, 1955, p. 237).

interpreted. It is a turning to things eternal, to the service of that God who made all men to be His own. It means that the life ceases to be self-centred and becomes God-centred.

Luke brings this out also with an interesting name for Christianity, namely, 'the Way' (Acts 9:2; 19:9, 23; 22:4; 24:14, 22). If Christianity is 'the Way' then it is not concerned with isolated incidents. It is not concerned with certain compartments of life. It is concerned with the whole of life.[9] It is 'the' way of living. The same expression may well point us to another truth. It is the way to God and it may be understood accordingly as the way of God, i.e., 'the way of the Lord' spoken of in the prophets. Christians were preparing the way for His coming.[10]

Vincent Taylor has brought out a very important point in connection with the passages calling for repentance and the like. He points out that they follow on passages dealing with the sufferings of Christ. 'It is not because of some prophetic word which Jesus has spoken that men are to repent, but because of what He is and does.'[11] Being such a One as He is, the Suffering Servant of prophecy, and having done what He did, suffered on the cross for men's forgiveness, exhortations to repentance and conversion are natural enough. But they would have no basis were there no connection between the sufferings and the sins. Since Jesus' death deals with men's sins, makes atonement for them, provides the way of forgiveness, in the light of the narration of that death men may be called upon to make a response which concerns their sins. As Christ has died for them, they must die to them. Lampe points out that 'although repentance had been proclaimed by Jesus during his ministry, it is far more strongly emphasized after Pentecost in the missionary

---

[9] Cf. AG, the term is used 'of the whole way of life fr. a moral and relig. viewpoint, *the Way, teaching* in the most comprehensive sense' (*sub ὁδός*). Some hold that the title was given to the Christians by the Jews because of their peculiar practices. If this is the case, the Christians speedily adopted the term as their own, as Luke's use shows.

[10] S. Vernon McCasland in án article called 'the Way' (JBL, lxxvii, pp. 222-230) examines the expression in the light of the use of the term in the Dead Sea Scrolls. He maintains that IQS 9. 16-21 shows that it refers to 'the way of the Lord' (Is. 40:3), a passage cited in each of the four Gospels. He says, 'We conclude therefore that the Way (ἡ ὁδός, הדרך) as a designation of Christianity was derived from Isa 40. 3 and that it is an abbreviated form of "the way of the Lord"; that the idiom הדרך was used in a similar sense by Qumran as a designation of its life; that Christians probably derived the idiom ultimately from Qumran; and that the agent of the transmission was John the Baptist' (*op. cit.*, p. 230). The important point is the first. The 'Way' for the early Christians was 'the way of the Lord'. They must live acceptably to Him.

[11] ANT, p. 19. He also says, 'the exhortations . . . imply a close connexion between the suffering and service of Jesus and the facts of human sin' (*loc. cit.*).

preaching of the apostles'.[12] Forgiveness depended upon Christ's atoning work, and thus it is after the death and resurrection that it receives its fullest proclamation.

The novelty of all this must be stressed. In the New Testament period there were gods many and lords many, but repentance and conversion were not common demands. It is impossible to envisage a demand for the forsaking of sin in faiths where the very deities were of dubious morality. Even a slight acquaintance with the myths of Greece and Rome is enough to make us see the impossibility of the adherents of the classical gods taking moral demands seriously.[13] But the God of the New Testament has no truck with any unclean thing. He is a high and holy God. He has no trace of impurity in Himself, and He demands that His worshippers turn from all evil. The Gentiles to whom the gospel was preached would find this a strange demand. The Christian attitude was distinctive. And Luke leaves us in no doubt as to what it was.

(2) The Punishment of Sinners

Sometimes Luke draws attention to the seriousness of sin by recording the punishment that actually fell upon certain sinners. These stories present a difficulty to our age, because we prefer to dwell on the tenderness and love of God.[14] But Luke records them in the sure conviction that sin is an evil thing deserving (and sometimes getting) severe punishment. The deaths of Ananias and Sapphira (Acts 5:1-11) are instructive in this connection. There are mysteries in the story, but it is clear enough that the deaths of these two sinners made a profound impression on the infant Church. This was a punishment not of the heathen but of believers. They had no special immunity. All sin, wherever found, is a horrible thing. Its punishment, whether in the here and now or in the hereafter, is certain and severe. All sin among the brethren was not punished as obviously or immediately as this, but the lesson was striking. It is not surprising that Luke concludes the incident by saying, 'great fear came upon the whole church, and upon all that heard these things.'[15]

---

[12] *Studies in the Gospels,* ed. D. E. Nineham, Oxford, 1955, p. 186. He says, 'In this, as in so many other departments of St. Luke's teaching, the fact is strongly emphasized that the coming of the Spirit and the gifts which result therefrom and which are aspects of the Kingdom of God waited upon the death and exaltation of Christ' (*op. cit.,* pp. 186f.).

[13] W. K. C. Guthrie cites Teiresias, 'Dionysius compels no woman to be chaste' (*The Greeks and their Gods,* Boston, 1956, p. 149).

[14] P. T. Forsyth speaks scathingly of those who think of 'the God of the children', and hold that 'The Saviour must wear soft raiment' (JG, pp. 30f.).

[15] William Telfer uses the imagery of a people at war to characterize the attitude of the early church to sin, 'And it is the sense of war to the death that provides the atmosphere in which we can rightly view the horrific picture

Another outstanding example is that of the sorcerer Elymas. When the proconsul Sergius Paulus was being drawn to the gospel message, Elymas resisted the divine work and tried to turn him aside from the faith. This led Paul to say to him, 'O full of all guile and all villainy, thou son of the devil, thou enemy of all righteousness, wilt thou not cease to pervert the right ways of the Lord? And now, behold, the hand of the Lord is upon thee, and thou shalt be blind, not seeing the sun for a season.' As a result of this 'there fell on him a mist and a darkness' (Acts 13:10f.). Again, it cannot be said that all who opposed the preaching of the gospel received this punishment or anything like it, but Luke's recording of the incident shows that he recognized the serious nature of the offence. More, he saw that sin *deserves* punishment.[16] Along the same lines he records the danger that Simon Magus found himself in as a result of his rash attempt to buy the ability to confer the Holy Spirit (Acts 8:20ff.). Simon Magus is a sinner. It follows with remorseless logic that he is in danger. In Paul's first recorded sermon there occurs a passage in which the preacher reminds his hearers of the perils in which sinners find themselves. 'Beware therefore, lest that come upon you, which is spoken in the prophets; Behold, ye despisers, and wonder and perish . . .' (Acts 13:40f.). This roots it deep in the counsels of God. The prophet in days of old had spoken of punishment. Now the despisers bring it upon themselves.[17] It was no sudden or new-fangled thing. It was God's settled purpose. The death of Judas is probably recorded as a concrete illustration of the working out of the same principle. Luke does not explicitly say that this took place as the result of a divine judgment on Judas. But he hardly needs to. The revolting detail he describes is sufficient. It is plain enough that sin leads only to disaster. That is Luke's point.[18]

---

of the deceit and death of Ananias and Sapphira' (*The Forgiveness of Sins*, London, 1959, p. 21).

[16] See further pp. 385ff. below.

[17] 'Great as was the disaster that overtook those who ignored the warnings of the prophets, an even greater disaster will fall upon those who refuse the gospel' (F. F. Bruce, NICNT, *in loc.*).

[18] Lesslie Newbigin has an apt comment. He points to the extraordinary variety represented in those who destroyed Jesus, 'religious Pharisees and worldly Sadducees, Herodians and Romans, the governor at one end of the scale and the rabble in the street at the other . . . . The practically unanimous judgment of mankind was that he should be crucified. There was no room for Jesus and his claims if human life was to go on. Mankind had seen its maker face to face and with swift and murderous determination had destroyed him.' Newbigin adds, 'In that terrible nadir of man's history, there was one silent comment, the suicide of Judas. How shall man live if he is indeed his maker's murderer?' (*A Faith for this One World?* London, 1961, p. 70).

(3) The Last Judgment

The third way in which Luke stresses the serious character of sin is to speak of the judgment of God at the end of the world. Sin did bring about the death of the Lord and is thus a proper basis of a call to repentance. It is an evil which is sometimes punished with exemplary severity. These things are true, but they do not exhaust the consequences of sin. Luke also sees sin as having effects which last through time and will still be in force when men finally stand before God. Sin has lasting significance. A man will find his sins rising up against him at the last great day. And on that last great day he will be confronted by his Judge, not in the person of some hitherto unknown deity emerging from a remote obscurity, but with the Lord Jesus Christ Himself. He it is who is 'ordained of God to be the Judge of quick and dead' (Acts 10:42). God 'hath appointed a day, in the which he will judge the world in righteousness by the man whom he hath ordained' (Acts 17:31). There is an implication underlying this that ought not to be missed. If Jesus came to earth and lived and died precisely to save men from their sins He cannot be expected to regard it as unimportant when a man treats sin lightly and spurns the dearly bought salvation. This is rebellion against the divine.[19] The very identity of the Judge adds seriousness to the whole idea of the judgment. For believers, it is true, there is comfort in the thought that their Judge is the One who has already done so much for them. How can they fear facing Him? But there is nothing but terror in the prospect for those who reject His love. And this is no minor matter, the concern of an insignificant few. All are included within its scope. It is 'the world' that will be judged. Paul could proclaim this truth before the highest in the land. He stood before Felix and 'reasoned of righteousness, and temperance, and the judgement to come' (Acts 24:25). None may escape.

From all this it is clear that Luke still has his burning sense of the danger in which sinful men stand. The expression of the thought is rather different in the Acts from what we saw in the Gospel, but the basic thought is essentially the same. Let sinners beware, says Luke. Sin will not forever go unpunished.

THE ACCOUNTABILITY OF MEN

Luke also brings out the truth that men are accountable. This is really much the same thought as that which occupied us in the last

---

[19] Karl Heim points out that it is this which makes sin so very serious: 'every form of guilt, whatever it may consist of, is never guilt before men or before some reality of this world but a rebellion aimed immediately at God' (*Jesus the World's Perfecter*, Edinburgh and London, 1959, p. 16).

section, but here I have in mind passages in which the writer speaks of specific sins, especially that of crucifying Jesus, as being blameworthy. In the first Christian preaching side by side with the insistence that God wrought out His will on Calvary there runs an emphasis on the truth that those who delivered up Jesus to His death were reprehensible. On the one hand, God used the wicked acts of evil men to work out His purpose. God is not mocked. No man can defy His will and prevent Him from bringing it to pass. God will always overrule evil and out of it bring that which is good. But, on the other hand, the acts in question are evil acts. The men who do them are wicked men. They are held accountable before God for the evil that they do. They are not mere tools in the hands of a blind Fate. They are responsible beings. And therefore their evil deeds are to be reprobated in the strongest fashion.

It is a remarkable feature of the first Christian preaching, in view of the danger in which it involved the preachers, that Peter and his companions keep on insisting that the Jewish leaders are to be blamed for their murder of Jesus. Peter told the Jerusalemites in his first sermon that 'him, being delivered up by the determinate counsel and foreknowledge of God, ye by the hand of lawless men did crucify and slay' (Acts 2:23). Here is a clear recognition that what God purposed was done. But there is also the plain accusation that his hearers were responsible for the slaying of the Lord. And Peter not only made the charge so plainly that there could be no mistake. He repeated it. In the same sermon he went on to speak of God's action in making Him 'both Lord and Christ', and he immediately adds, 'this Jesus whom ye crucified' (Acts 2:36). The context did not demand it. He could have made his essential point without this reference. But it was important that the guilt of his hearers be made plain and thus Peter goes out of his way to emphasize it. He begins his next sermon with, 'The God of Abraham, and of Isaac, and of Jacob, the God of our fathers, hath glorified his Servant Jesus; whom ye delivered up, and denied before the face of Pilate, when he had determined to release him' (Acts 3:13). He will not leave the point, for he continues, 'But ye denied the Holy and Righteous One,[20] and asked for a murderer to be granted unto you, and killed the Prince of life . . . .' Nor does he confine this kind of speaking to the mob. They might seek to evade responsibility by reasoning that the directive had come from higher

---

[20] Lev. Gillet examines this term in an article called, 'The Just' (ET, lvi, pp. 277-9). He thinks that between the Testaments 'Jewish thought had more or less associated the notions of Just and Messiah'. But 'Christ is the only true and perfect Righteous, *the* Just One. He is the Jewish *tsadik* in the fullest sense by His mediatory and saving power' (*op. cit.*, p. 279). That is to say, even a term like this, which on the surface is a title of honor, has undertones which link it with salvation, and that by way of mediation.

up. When examined before the highest Jewish authorities, namely, the rulers and the elders, the high priest and his kindred, Peter explained that the miracle of healing of the lame man was done in the name of Jesus Christ 'whom ye crucified' (Acts 4:10). Not surprisingly, the high priest complains a little later that 'ye have filled Jerusalem with your teaching, and intend to bring this man's blood upon us' (Acts 5:28). Without hesitation Peter accepts the charge. He speaks of 'Jesus, whom ye slew, hanging him on a tree' (Acts 5:30). In the house of Cornelius he comes back to the theme (Acts 10:39). It is apparently a consistent strand in Peter's proclamation of the message. The men responsible must be made to see that their deed cannot be overlooked. They are guilty men.

Nor is this confined to Peter. Stephen could upbraid the court that tried him as 'betrayers and murderers' of the Righteous One (Acts 7:52). Paul brings it home to them 'that dwell in Jerusalem, and their rulers' (Acts 13:27f.). This aspect of the first preaching is striking. When the guilt of the men of Jerusalem was stressed in Jerusalem itself, this could not but put the lives of the preachers in jeopardy. It was dangerous talk. Yet they did not keep quiet on the issue. They insisted in season and out of season on the guilt of those responsible.

It is probably well for us to reflect that this has wider implications, especially when we remember that it is a consistent strand of New Testament teaching that Christ died for the sins of all men. We must beware of trying to shift responsibility to others. There is a story of an African chieftain who heard the crucifixion story for the first time. He was deeply moved and irresistibly attracted by the Christ who went so courageously to death for others. But he was stirred also by the cowardice of Jesus' followers. He burst out, 'Ah, if we had been there, I and my men, we would have saved Him!' There is the natural human reaction. We think of ourselves as on the side of Christ. We think of those responsible for putting Him to death as the enemy, as those on the other side. If we had been there, it would have been different.

But we *were* there, you and I, in all that matters. We were not there bodily, but we were there effectively. And we did not rescue Him. Far from it. We crucified Him.[21] When we are dealing with this element of human responsibility, let us never lose sight of the fact that it was our sin that put Him on the tree. The strong words of the early Christian preachers on this matter are not words that should instill into us a comfortable feeling that we at any rate

---

[21] Cf. A. C. Bouquet, 'The diverse motives of the men and women who brought Jesus to the gallows are the common motives of mankind. Indirectly we all find ourselves at some time or other "assistants at the Passion" ' (*Jesus: A New Outline and Estimate*, Cambridge, 1933, p. 198).

are guiltless. We are verily guilty men, and our responsibility is heavy.[22]

> Who was the guilty? Who brought this upon Thee?
> Alas, my treason, Jesu, hath undone thee;
> 'Twas I, Lord Jesu, I it was denied thee:
> I crucified Thee.[23]

SALVATION IS ALL OF GOD

The idea that salvation depends essentially on God, and that man can do no more than call on Him runs through the early chapters of Acts. 'Whosoever shall call on the name of the Lord', said Peter, quoting from the prophet Joel, 'shall be saved' (Acts 2:21). Notice the reference to 'the name' of the Lord. Such references abound. It was 'the name' that healed the lame man at the Gate Beautiful (Acts 3:16; 4:10). The disciples preached 'the name' or 'in the name' (Acts 8:12; 9:27, 29). By contrast, those who sought to hinder their work forbade them to speak 'in this name' (Acts 4:17f.; 5:28, 40). When the first prohibition was reported among the brethren they 'lifted up their voice to God with one accord' (Acts 4:24), and they included in their prayer a petition 'that signs and wonders may be done through the name of thy holy Servant Jesus' (v. 30). It is a teaching of the prophets that 'through his name every one that believeth on him shall receive remission of sins' (Acts 10:43).

For men of antiquity, of course, the 'name' meant far more than it does with us.[24] In modern times a name is little more than a label, a convenient way of distinguishing one person from another. But the world of the first century did not distinguish very sharply between the name and the person. The name expressed the person.[25] The

[22] D. R. Davies reminds us that such evil deeds as the crucifixion always require the action of 'good' men. The evil, unaided, can never accomplish such things (*The Art of Dodging Repentance,* London, 1952, pp. 34f.). He also says that we of all men can never claim that we are guiltless. He speaks of 'the generation of our blood-soaked, cruelty-ridden world' and proceeds, 'Of all the men who have lived and died since Calvary, we men of today can least pretend to the possession of superior virtue, of a deeper, finer, more responsible morality. The unnumbered millions done to death and the millions condemned to a living death in remote spaces scream denial of any such pretension. No century has more clearly recrucified Christ than the twentieth' (*op. cit.,* p. 41).

[23] Johann Heermann, par. Robert Bridges.

[24] Cf. O. S. Rankin, 'In the thought of the ancient world a name does not merely distinguish a person from other persons, but is closely related to the nature of its bearer. Particularly in the case of such powerful persons as deities, the name is regarded as part of the being of the divinity so named and of his character and powers' (TWBB, p. 157).

[25] Cf. H. Conzelmann, 'We can go so far as to say that to speak of the efficacy of the name is the specifically Lucan way of describing the presence

name summed up the whole man. To 'call upon the name' thus meant a good deal more than simply to utter the sounds which make up the name. It meant to invoke all that the name stands for, to trust the personality expressed in the name. F. F. Bruce comments on Acts 3:16, 'There was no merely magical efficacy in the sounds which Peter pronounced when he commanded the cripple to walk in Jesus' name; the cripple would have known no benefit had he not responded in faith to what Peter said'. It is not the sound that is efficacious. 'But,' Professor Bruce goes on, 'once this response was made, the power of the risen Christ filled his body with health and strength.'[26] Similarly passages which speak of salvation through 'the name' mean nothing other than salvation through the bearer of that name.[27] We might deduce that this means that there is but one source of salvation, but we are not left to conjecture. We are told that it is by the name of Jesus Christ and by that name only that men are saved. 'And in none other is there salvation: for neither is there any other name under heaven, that is given among men, wherein we must be saved' (Acts 4:12).[28] Luke is sure that what God has done in Christ is unique. He is not speaking of one among many ways of salvation. He is speaking of the only way.

When believers were added to the infant church it was the Lord who added them (Acts 2:47). To the casual Jerusalemite it might appear that these people had decided to join the new community.

---

of Christ' (*The Theology of St. Luke,* London, 1960, p. 178). But he goes on to say, 'it is not without meaning to evoke it and to use it as a formula. When this formula is used God acts' (*loc. cit.*). In the light of the incident when the sons of Sceva invoked the name but only to their own harm and discredit (Acts 19:13ff.), this can scarcely stand. The name is never a mere formula. There is no power in it other than in line with the purposes for which Jesus stands.

[26] NICNT, *in loc.* Cf. also R. B. Rackham on Acts 4:10, '*made whole, by the name of Jesus Christ of Nazareth,* i.e. the power contained in the revelation of Jesus of Nazareth as the Messiah'.

[27] C. Biber thinks that in the New Testament the name of Jesus 'indicates the acceptance pure and simple, astonished but confident, persevering and audacious, of the manifestation of God in Jesus Christ . . . . In this name one believes, and that indicates the entrance into the ways of God' (*Vocabulary of the Bible,* ed. J. J. Von Allmen, London, 1958, p. 280).

[28] H. G. G. Herklots connects this with the idea held in antiquity, that 'If the soul were to make its progress to the seventh heaven it must know the right names of the door-keepers at each successive stage; and there were many worried people uncertain whether they could remember the difficult names aright. Some of these were later to welcome with relief the confident assertion that there was no name given under ' :aven by which men must be saved except the one name Jesus Christ' (*A Fresh Approach to the New Testament,* London, 1950, pp. 37f.). This may be a little too confident, but at least it is plain that this clear affirmation of the one name stands in marked contrast to the complexities of paganism.

He would take it as a purely human activity. But that was not the way it seemed to Luke. The divine initiative is important to him. The decisive part in salvation is all God's. So when men are saved, He it is who has added them to the Church. In keeping with this, the gospel is spoken of as 'the gospel of the grace of God' (Acts 20:24). Of itself 'gospel', of course, conveys the thought of 'the good news of what God has done in Christ', and when 'of grace' is added there is a further emphasis on the priority of the divine. The same emphasis is seen when the work of preaching is called 'speaking boldly in the Lord' (Acts 14:3). While it is true that men speak, it is also true that the really important thing is that it is God who enables and directs them. And the thought of God's grace recurs. When men did speak boldly in the Lord He 'bare witness unto the word of his grace, granting signs and wonders to be done by their hands' (Acts 14:3). That is to say, the power of God is active in the gospel. 'The word of his grace' is far-reaching in its effects, and goes beyond the initial work of salvation. When Paul was taking his farewell of the Ephesians, he said, 'And now I commend you to God, and to the word of his grace, which is able to build you up, and to give you the inheritance among all them that are sanctified' (Acts 20:32).[29] God not only begins a work of salvation in men in calling them out of darkness into His most marvellous light, but He also carries on that work of salvation. Day by day the believer is indebted to God for 'the word of his grace'. Sometimes the grace in question is linked with Jesus, as when we read, 'we believe that we shall be saved through the grace of the Lord Jesus' (Acts 15:11). This, of course, does but bring out the implications of the other passages. It links the 'grace' with the saving mission of Jesus Christ, and reminds us of what He did to bring us salvation.

It is this which is in mind, too, when Paul tells the men of Pisidian Antioch that 'Of (David's) seed hath God according to promise brought unto Israel a Saviour, Jesus' (Acts 13:23). The very word 'Saviour' indicates that men do not save themselves. They are saved by Another. This is behind Peter's sermon also when he speaks of 'seasons of refreshing' which he says come 'from the

---

[29] The expression, 'the word of his grace', is found only in the Lukan writings. Moffatt sees in this, together with 'the gospel of the grace of God' (Acts 20:24), Luke's originality in handling the concept of grace. This expression goes beyond anything in the Pauline writings, 'although this would have been an apt formula for him'. The point can scarcely stand in the form given by Moffatt, for in some cases Luke is reporting Pauline speeches. But when full allowance is made for this it remains that Luke does not simply repeat other people's ideas about grace. God's grace means much to him and he makes his distinctive contribution to our understanding of it. Moffatt also feels that these passages 'carry a distinct reference to the Christian mission as including non-Jews', and he notes the significance of Acts 20:21 in this connection (*Grace in the New Testament*, London, 1931, pp. 362f.).

presence of the Lord' (Acts 3:19), or again when he speaks of
God's sending of His Son to bless men. 'Unto you first God, having
raised up his Servant, sent him to bless you, in turning away every one
of you from your iniquities' (Acts 3:26). The expression 'seasons
of refreshing' is not a common one, and is not, for example, an
accepted term for the times of the Messiah, or the like.[30]   But it
clearly points to a blessing that God will give.[31]   The blessing is
further defined in terms of turning men from their iniquities.   This
'turning' obviously is not done by men.   It is done by God in Christ
('his Servant').   Again there is the thought that it is God and
God alone who brings salvation (the expression may also be meant
to evoke memories of the cross).

A revealing expression occurs at the end of the discussion held on
Peter's handling of the Cornelius situation.   When the apostle was
called to account by them 'that were of the circumcision' (Acts 11:
2) he patiently went over the whole incident.   He told of the vision
thrice repeated, of the Spirit's bidding him go with Cornelius'
emissaries, of the falling of the Spirit on the Gentiles.   And his
hearers, when he finished, 'held their peace, and glorified God,
saying, Then to the Gentiles also hath God granted repentance unto
life' (v. 18).   Repentance is not here considered as a purely human
activity.   The Gentiles repented only because God gave them the
gift of repentance.   And just as He granted it to them, so also did
He give this gift to Israel (Acts 5:31).   Repentance is always a
divine gift.   Left to himself, the sinner would prefer to stay in his
sins.   He does not know what the salvation which he is missing is,
and he is not willing to undergo the sharp pain of separation from
his sin.[32]   It takes a miracle in a man's soul for him even to want to

[30] Cf. Lake and Cadbury, 'This phrase does not appear to be used in
Rabbinical or other literature as a synonym for the Messianic period. . . .
The context seems to show that the writer used it as a description of the
coming of the Anointed One from heaven' (in loc.).

[31] Rackham thinks that the word recalls 'the wealthy place' of Ps. 66:12
'into which Israel was brought after passing through fire and water, and
so it takes us back in thought to the Exodus' (in loc.).   Some such thought
may be present, though it should be noted that the word in the Psalm is not
that used here (as Rackham affirms that it is), but a cognate word.   Here we
have ἀνάψυξις, in the Psalm ἀναψυχή.

[32] C. S. Lewis brings out this point by picturing evil as a reptile seated on
the shoulder of a ghostly, unsubstantial figure.   An angel urges the ghost
to allow him to kill the reptile.   Eventually the ghost agrees.   'Next moment
the Ghost gave a scream of agony such as I never heard on Earth.   The
Burning One closed his crimson grip on the reptile: twisted it, while it bit
and writhed, and then flung it, broken backed, on the turf.   "Ow!   That's
done for me," gasped the Ghost, reeling backwards.'   Then Lewis goes on to
describe the Ghost's metamorphosis into a genuinely heavenly being (The
Great Divorce, London, 1945, pp. 92f.).   So he makes his point that a painful
break with evil is the necessary prelude to an entrance into real life.

turn away from evil. And the teaching of the Acts is that God in
Christ does work that miracle. He gives repentance.

We might draw a similar conclusion from the references to the
sacraments. Several times we hear of people being baptized, from
the first preaching on (Acts 2:38, 41; 8:12, 13, 16, 38, etc.),
while the continual observance of the Lord's Supper is implied in
'they continued stedfastly in . . . the breaking of bread' (Acts 2:42).[33]
Now neither of these ordinances makes sense on a view which roots
salvation in man. They both witness to what God has done, and
they both witness to man's dependence on God for His good gift.
Specifically, they point us to Christ's death. 'There is nothing in
Christianity more primitive than the Sacraments, and the Sacraments,
wherever they exist, are witnesses to the connection between the
death of Christ and the forgiveness of sins.'[34] Holy Communion is
obviously meaningless apart from the death of Christ. It is explicitly
a sacrament of the body and blood of Christ, and this means His
death. And, quite apart from Romans 6, the New Testament view
of baptism is always one which connects it with the atoning death
of Christ and with the forgiveness won by Christ.[35] Peter called
on the people after his day of Pentecost sermon in these words,
'Repent ye, and be baptized every one of you in the name of Jesus
Christ unto the remission of your sins' (Acts 2:38). Paul tells
us that Ananias urged him to baptism with the words, 'arise, and be
baptized, and wash away thy sins, calling on his name' (Acts 22:
16). Both sacraments are meaningful only because of the death
of Christ to which they point. Both depend on the gift of God.

All this is the more impressive in that it must be seen against the
Jewish idea of salvation on the basis of works. There was no controversy among the Jews on this point. There might be differences
as to the right way of interpreting the Law, but as to the fact that
men must keep the Law the Jews were unanimous. Right from the
first the Christians probably had to face the question of whether they
took a similar attitude to the Law. Certainly in time (and quite
early) it became an issue, and Luke devotes his fifteenth chapter to
detailing how the controversy was resolved. The case did not go

[33] 'The "breaking of bread" here denotes something more than the ordinary
partaking of food together: the regular observance of the Lord's Supper is no
doubt indicated' (F. F. Bruce, NICNT, *in loc.*).

[34] James Denney, DC, p. 84.

[35] Cf. H. Vogel, 'In so far as it is incorporation into the body of Christ . . .
it is essentially my baptism, the beginning which God makes with me. In a
divine appropriation there takes place to me that which has already taken place
for me. For that reason I am made a partaker of the mystery of substitution,
I am seized and sealed as a man with Jesus Christ, as one who has died and
been raised again with Him' (SJT, vii, p. 45). He also says, 'As a sacrament
instituted by the risen Christ baptism is based upon the substitutionary baptism
in blood in Christ crucified' (*op. cit.,* p. 41).

by default. Responsible Christian leaders met in solemn conclave
and debated whether all converts should be circumcised and taught
to keep the whole law of Moses. Should the Law be held to be
an integral part of the Christian way? The consideration that finally
weighed was that expressed in the concluding words of Peter's speech,
'why tempt ye God, that ye should put a yoke upon the neck of the
disciples, which neither our fathers nor we were able to bear? But
we believe that we shall be saved through the grace of the Lord Jesus,
in like manner as they' (Acts 15:10f.). The most representative
gathering of Christians described in the whole New Testament gave
careful consideration to the matter and came up with the decision that
no practice could be imposed which obscured the fundamental truth
that men do not laboriously earn their salvation.[36] They receive it
as the gift of God. The Council's verdict was an affirmation that
men are saved by grace.[37]

It is clear, then, that just as in his Gospel Luke has his way of
stressing the divine initiative in salvation, so is it in the Acts. It
is not the same way, but it is the same underlying idea. Luke was
quite clear in affirming that God works out men's salvation as He
pleases. And in both his volumes he gives expression to this idea.

THE PURPOSE OF GOD IN THE CROSS

Luke gives expression, too, to his certainty that in the cross God
was working out His purpose of salvation. We have already noticed
that he often speaks of men's accountability in this matter. Here
our concern is with the other side of the picture, with the way in which
the divine is seen to have the priority. The salvation that is all of
God is a salvation wrought out on a cross, by a death which perfectly accorded with God's purpose.

One of the strongest expressions of all occurs in the first address
of all. Then Peter told the men of Jerusalem that Jesus was 'de-

---

[36] Johannes Munck makes an acute observation on the church in Acts: 'it
has been usual to assume that the first disciples in Jerusalem did not differ
from the other Jews, except by their belief that the coming Messiah was identical with the crucified Jesus. It does not seem to have been clearly realized
that that difference was great enough to make the Jerusalem Christians differ
from their fellow-countrymen on all other points too' (*Paul and the Salvation
of Mankind*, London, 1959, p. 214). Their relation to the crucified Lord affected
all their other relationships. If men are saved by what Christ has done for
them, then the very central tenet of Judaism is flatly rejected.

[37] Notice that this distinguishes Christianity not only from Judaism, but
from all other religions. Cf. Emil Brunner, 'all other forms of religion —
not to mention philosophy — deal with the problem of guilt apart from the
intervention of God, and therefore they come to a "cheap" conclusion. In
them man is spared the final humiliation of knowing that the Mediator
must bear the punishment instead of him . . . . He is not stripped absolutely
naked' (*The Mediator*, London, 1946, p. 474).

livered up by the determinate counsel and foreknowledge of God'
(Acts 2:23). This means more than that God knew beforehand
what would happen. He determined beforehand what would happen.
He planned that the Messiah should be given over to death. The
purpose of God was wrought out in that death. No way of viewing
Calvary which regards it primarily as a tragedy, a martyrdom, or
the like, is adequate to these words. They point us to a deeper
truth. God's will was done that day. The prayer meeting in Acts 4
reiterates this truth. All concerned, Herod, Pilate, Gentiles and
Israelites alike, the praying group affirmed, 'were gathered together,
to do whatsoever thy hand and thy counsel foreordained to come to
pass' (Acts 4:27f.). The cross must be seen as the accomplishment
of the divine purpose, however that purpose be understood.

The same thought underlies the many passages which refer to the
cross as the fulfilment of the prophecies of Scripture. 'The scripture
should be fulfilled', said Peter, 'which the Holy Ghost spake before by
the mouth of David concerning Judas, who was guide to them that
took Jesus' (Acts 1:16). Notice that the fulfilment here concerns not
simply the general idea, not even the main event, but the detail of
Judas' part in the betrayal. The whole thing was minutely planned
by God. Peter again sees Christ undergoing those things 'which
God foreshewed by the mouth of all the prophets, that his Christ
should suffer' (Acts 3:18), while Paul could maintain that he said
'nothing but what the prophets and Moses did say should come; how
that the Christ must suffer . . .' (Acts 26:22f.; cf. also 28:23). That
this was the accepted early Christian understanding of the situation is seen in the episode of Philip and the Ethiopian eunuch. Philip
found the man reading from Isaiah 53, 'And Philip opened his mouth,
and beginning from this scripture, preached unto him Jesus' (Acts
8:35). This is completely impromptu. Philip, until he approached
the chariot, had no inkling of what the man was reading. But as
soon as he heard the prophecy, he spoke of Jesus. There cannot
be the slightest doubt but that the early Christians as a whole understood the passage to refer to Jesus and specifically to foretell the
manner and the meaning of the passion. Now if Christ's death was in
fulfilment of prophecies made centuries beforehand, then clearly the
primary thing is the will of Him who caused those prophecies to be
made. The events which culminated in the crucifixion on the hill
called Calvary cannot be said to have taken place by chance.

Sometimes the divine purpose is brought out with the thought of
God's call. The promise is to 'as many as the Lord our God shall
call' (Acts 2:39). Paul is spoken of as a 'chosen vessel' (Acts 9:15),
and as 'appointed' to know God's will (Acts 22:14). Throughout
his ministry the divine purpose is emphasized. At Antioch in Pisidia
'as many as were ordained to eternal life believed' (Acts 13:48).

At Corinth, God encouraged His servant in a time of difficulty with the words, 'I have much people in this city' (Acts 18:10). Paul could assure the Ephesians, 'I shrank not from declaring unto you the whole counsel of God' (Acts 20:27).

At Thessalonica he reasoned from the scriptures, 'opening and alleging, that it behoved the Christ to suffer . . .' (Acts 17:3). This is a strong expression. It indicates that Christ's suffering took place as the result of a compelling divine necessity. The crucifixion was inevitable. There was no way of avoiding it. The human element was not the really significant one.

It is important to be clear on this in view of the suggestion often made that the preaching of the apostles was heavily conditioned by the Jewish rejection of the entire concept of the crucified Messiah. Since this was a critical stumbling block, some way around it had to be found, and the suggestion is that the apostles found their way by pointing to a useful purpose that was accomplished by the cross. Their preaching of the cross on this view was negative, a mere rebuttal of damaging criticisms. They found it useful to be able to cite Scripture speaking of messianic suffering. This had the effect of transforming Christ's sufferings from a grievous handicap into something intellectually respectable, the very expression of the will of God. E. D. Burton, for example, maintains that passages like those we have cited are 'a defense of Jesus against the assumption, natural to a Jewish mind, that death on the cross indicated his rejection by God. As against this interpretation of Jesus' death, the early Christian preachers contended that this death was predetermined by God, that it was a part of the divine plan.'[38] This idea has been widely held in recent times. Many are acutely conscious of the stumbling block a crucified Messiah would have been to the Jews, and therefore to the first Christians, themselves Jews.

There is an element of truth here. The apostles undoubtedly encountered this Jewish objection, and felt the difficulty. Equally undoubtedly they took steps to meet it, including that of pointing to prophecy to show that the divine will was done when Jesus was crucified. But it is impossible to read the Acts and conclude that this particular strand of Christian preaching was entirely, or even primarily, negative, a defence against certain Jewish allegations. We do not know of a time when Christian preachers did not give expression to this thought. It goes back to the very first Christian sermon that is recorded, and therefore back to a time before the objection could be urged (Acts 2:23). And it goes back, as we saw in the earlier chapters, to the teaching of Jesus Himself. It is not put forward from any idea that it was good teaching, or good

[38] *Biblical Idea of Atonement,* Chicago, 1909, p. 150.

strategy, or that it could meet a damaging criticism.[39] It was put forward because it was held to be true. And not only true, but the significant truth about the atonement. It is far too central to be the reaction to sniping from carping critics. In any event, it no doubt proved a useful line to take with the Jews. But there is not one scintilla of evidence that it was evolved to meet the objections of the Jews. From the first the truth of it gripped the minds of the preachers. If the cross is not the working out of the purpose of God, then the whole New Testament teaching on it must be scrapped. It is this truth, that God is in it, that gives the message of the cross its power. This is the vital, positive truth about the atonement. It must on no account be surrendered.[40]

THE GENTILES

A noteworthy feature of Acts is the way in which it shows that the salvation wrought in Christ is for all mankind. This comes out in the opening scene when the Risen Lord tells His followers: 'ye shall be my witnesses both in Jerusalem, and in all Judaea and Samaria, and unto the uttermost part of the earth' (Acts 1:8). The rest of the book may be regarded as the unfolding of the implications of all this.[41] And it should not be overlooked that while the witnessing was being made 'in Jerusalem' there were hints of a wider ministry.

---

[39] John Knox notes that the cross did present a stumbling block, and goes on, 'But however true and pertinent this may be, it is obvious that such considerations are quite inadequate to account for the place of the Cross in the New Testament and in the community life for which it speaks. The death of Christ was, to be sure, a problem for faith (in the more intellectual meaning of that term); but it was also (in another and profounder sense) the very centre of faith. Indeed, it could become so acute a problem for thought only because it was already so crucial a fact within the life of the community' (*The Death of Christ*, London, 1959, p. 132).

[40] Cf. James Denney, the idea, 'that the cross *in itself,* is nothing but a scandal, and that all the New Testament interpretations of it are but ways of getting over the scandal, cannot be too emphatically rejected'. 'A doctrine of the death of Jesus, which was merely the solution of an abstract difficulty — the answer to a conundrum — could never have become what the doctrine of the death of Jesus is in the New Testament — the centre of gravity in the Christian world. It could never have had stored up in it the redeeming virtue of the gospel. It could never have been the hiding-place of God's power, the inspiration of all Christian praise. Whatever the doctrine of Jesus' death may be, it is the feeblest of all misconceptions to trace it to the necessity of saying something about the death which should as far as possible remove the scandal of it' (DC, pp. 78, 79). The New Testament writers did not apologize for the cross. They gloried in it (Gal. 6:14).

[41] J. C. O'Neill thinks of Acts (together with Luke's Gospel) as having been written with a view to the conversion of Gentiles, especially those in Rome. The last words of his book are 'he wrote Luke-Acts to persuade men at the centre of power to abandon their lives to the service of the kingdom of God' (*The Theology of Acts*, London, 1961, p. 177).

Thus in Acts 2:5ff. Luke makes it clear that the Jews who heard the first preaching came 'from every nation under heaven'. Peter's quotation from Joel goes on as far as 'and it shall be, that whosoever shall call on the name of the Lord shall be saved' (Acts 2:21), and he later makes it clear to his hearers that 'the promise' is not only for them and their children, but also 'to all that are afar off, even as many as the Lord our God shall call unto him' (Acts 2:39).

Luke goes on to recount the reception of Samaritans into the church (Acts 8). This was initiated by a persecution set on foot by the Jews (Acts 8:1), a persecution which, incidentally, demonstrated convincingly that Christianity was not identical with or a mere variant of Judaism. But, though he went to Samaria as a result of the persecution, Philip's mission to the Samaritans does not read like a mere reaction to persecution. He enters energetically into the propagation of the gospel among the Samaritans and wins many converts. Luke records approval of this at the highest Christian level. The apostles at Jerusalem sent Peter and John to the city, and these leaders laid hands on the Samaritan believers and prayed for them so that they might receive the Holy Spirit (Acts 8:14ff.).

A big step forward was taken with the baptism of Cornelius and his associates (Acts 10:48). Previously, proselytes had been accepted (Acts 6:5), but Cornelius was a Gentile. The difficulty in the way of receiving such into the church is seen in the fact that it took a divine vision, thrice repeated (Acts 10:9-16), to induce Peter to take the necessary action. But the point is that the action was taken. Gentiles were admitted.[42]

Sometimes the church seems to have been driven into a step that it did not contemplate. Thus the Jerusalem Christians sent Barnabas to Antioch to look into a report that certain men had been preaching to Gentiles (Acts 11:22). But the upshot was that Barnabas led a mission which resulted in the extension of the Christian way among Gentile cities (Acts 13:1ff.). There is no indication that the men of Jerusalem had anticipated anything so startling. But Luke says clearly that this was the leading of the Holy Spirit. It was of God that the gospel was preached among the Gentiles. From this point onwards Acts is taken up with such work, and Luke especially gives himself over to recounting the deeds of Paul, the great apostle of the Gentiles. But it is important to notice that the Gentile mission was not the creation of Paul, though he did so much to

---

[42] Cf. M. Dibelius, 'This, then, is what the reference to the conversion of Cornelius means. It is not a conversion-story of the usual type, nor is it meant to show that Peter is glorified by the consequences of the knowledge which he gained through a vision. It shows the revelation of God's will that the Gentiles should be received into the Church without obligation to the law. This is what the story of Cornelius means, at least for Luke' (op. cit., p. 117).

forward it.[43] Inherent in the very nature of the gospel message, it was sooner or later bound to make itself manifest. The general pattern was preaching among the Jews at first (Acts 13:14ff.; 17:2), but when the Jews rejected the message the preachers went to the Gentiles (Acts 13:46). This procedure was called in question by some (Acts 15:1), but endorsed by the Jerusalem council (Acts 15:13ff.). Indeed the declaration that this was a fulfilment of prophecy (Acts 15:15ff.) is an assertion that it is the divine will.[44]

All this means that the atonement wrought in Christ was world-wide in its scope. If it is the divine answer to the problem of men's sin, then the gospel must be proclaimed to all. This is what Luke speaks of. He writes as he does because of his deep conviction that the atonement is not meant for a small handful of Jews but for men who should be saved throughout the whole world.[45]

THE PLACE OF SUFFERING

The purpose of God for man's salvation was wrought out through suffering. The Acts makes it clear that Christ's sufferings are the pathway to Christian blessings. This does not mean that these sufferings are dwelt upon or magnified in any way. A typical allusion is the first one, which refers to the apostles 'to whom he also shewed himself alive after his passion by many proofs . . .' (Acts 1:3). Here the awful agonies of crucifixion are dealt with in one word. The references to the prophetic predictions of the passion to which we have just been referring are of the same type. So are the passages in which the early preachers referred to them, such as Paul's statement to Agrippa that he used to say 'nothing but what the prophets and Moses did say should come; how that the

[43] Cf. Floyd V. Filson, 'This extension of horizon was essentially achieved, though its recognition and effective defense were still far from complete, before Paul became the outstanding figure of the Gentile mission. The entire development implies that most early Jewish Christians were aware of the gracious and actively redemptive character of God, and grew in their grasp of the breadth of God's quest' (*One Lord — One Faith*, Philadelphia, 1943, pp. 119f.).

[44] Conzelmann sees this in the happenings at Pentecost, 'The connection of the Church with the Old Testament promises implies the universal missionary task. This can be seen in the story of Pentecost, which links the Spirit and the mission with prophecy' (*op. cit.*, p. 213).

[45] B. Gärtner brings this out for the Areopagus address in his chapter entitled 'Universalism and the aspect of the divine plan of salvation' (*op. cit.*, ch. viii). He also gives the fourth of the seven standard topics of preaching he discerns in the speeches in Acts in these terms: 'The apostolic message is also to the Gentiles. We can assume this article to have been part of the regular preaching, since the Diaspora communities all had their proselytes and "God-fearers", by whom the unrestricted universalism of the *Kerygma* must have been joyfully received' (*op. cit.*, p. 31).

Christ must suffer, and how that he first by the resurrection of the dead should proclaim light both to the people and to the Gentiles' (Acts 26:22f.).

There is a noteworthy restraint in all this. Crucifixion was one of the most painful methods of execution invented by man. Those who endured it had to undergo excruciating agonies. But these early Christians say little of all this. They know of it, but they make no attempt to play it up. This is in striking contrast to the exaggerated interest that popular Christian piety, both Catholic and Protestant, has often shown in the physical sufferings of the Saviour. What is more curious than the misunderstandings of popular piety is the way eminent scholars go astray at this point. Thus John Knox, who incidentally takes delight in castigating conservatives for reading meanings into the scripture that are not there, or even for accepting some which are plainly there, shows a strange readiness to read his own ideas back into the early writers in this matter. He says,

> One must take into account also the exigencies of the Christian preaching . . . . The Crucifixion had to be *pictured*. Men must see and feel it, imaginatively entering into the sufferings of Christ and sensing the awful significance of what happened on Calvary. The story of the Passion must be told in such fashion that the stark reality of it be felt . . . .[46]

This is pretty well what naive piety has often thought. An elementary acquaintance with hymnology is sufficient to bring to light many examples, some of which border on the morbid. But it is passing strange to find great scholars putting forth essentially the same misconception. For, if our records are at all reliable, the

---

[46] *Op. cit.*, p. 19. He later returns to the theme, 'the terrible circumstances of the death — the anguish of it, the ignominy, the violence and brutality of the means of it, the awful anomaly that one such as he should be made the victim of such cruelty and malignity — all of this would have had the effect of accentuating the emotional impact of the death and of making even more certain that thenceforth to remember Jesus was to remember first of all his Cross' (*op. cit.*, p. 139). This may be how and why Knox preaches the cross, but it is not derived from the New Testament. There is no tendency there to play on men's heartstrings. M. Dibelius can say of Mark's account, 'If we read, say, the story of the arrest or the trial before Pilate without reading any construction into the text, we shall be astonished at the bareness of the description and the absence of any traits that show the feelings of those who took part and that work upon the feelings of the readers' (*From Tradition to Gospel*, London, 1934, pp. 185f.). Similarly Edgar J. Goodspeed, 'Mark's narrative proceeds with a stern restraint that is positively amazing. It is strangely objective; all the more poignant because no pity, no sympathy find expression in it' (*A Life of Jesus,* New York, 1950, p. 217). And what is true of Mark is true of all the others. The New Testament writers show marked restraint. And it is not true that they found a meaning for Christ's death because they remembered it so poignantly. They remembered it because they found such meaning in it.

early preachers made no attempt at all to dwell on the agonies of Christ. Nowhere in the New Testament are these sufferings highlighted. On the contrary, they are always treated with the greatest reserve. In particular, Luke did not engage in any sentimentality. He knew that Christ's sufferings were important and he said so. But he left it at that. We may legitimately infer that the physical sufferings, great though they undoubtedly were, were not the really significant thing.[47] To dwell unnecessarily on the physical might well have obscured the central truth that 'the suffering of His soul was the soul of His suffering'.

In our study of Luke's Gospel, we noticed that he suggests the idea that suffering is not altogether an unmixed evil. Suffering was the pathway the Christ must tread to bring to the world its greatest good. And in their measure Christians enter into this. Of them, too, it has often proved true that their greatest contribution to the service of God and of their fellows has been along the path of suffering. Luke tells us that the apostles 'departed from the presence of the council, rejoicing that they were counted worthy to suffer dishonour for the Name' (Acts 5:41). They did not endure suffering stoically, putting the best face possible on something that could not be avoided. They departed from their tormentors *rejoicing* that they were given the privilege of suffering. Nor was this something confined to the apostles. Paul and Barnabas warned their converts that 'through many tribulations we must enter into the kingdom of God' (Acts 14:22). Suffering is the common lot of the servants of God, and through it God works out His sovereign will.[48]

This is especially clear in the case of Paul. From the time of his conversion, the way of suffering was marked out for him. God spoke to Ananias about him saying, 'he is a chosen vessel unto me, to bear my name before the Gentiles and kings, and the children of Israel: for I will shew him how many things he must suffer for my name's sake' (Acts 9:15f.). We do not normally think of

[47] W. Eason Robinson's *Emotional Aspects of the Atonement*, London, 1948, is a study of the way the church has tended to dwell on the physical sufferings of Christ through the centuries. He begins by expressing surprise at the absence of 'the element of feeling' from the New Testament accounts of the passion. 'We should all agree that never before or since were writers given such wonderful material as the events which the last days of the Son of Man supplied. Here there was a wealth of opportunity for the introduction of sublime pathos, deep passion, and intense emotional reaction, yet these things are entirely absent' (*op. cit.,* p. 1).

[48] G. W. H. Lampe makes the point that this takes place through the power of the Spirit: 'St. Luke wishes to show how, as the result of the gift of the Spirit, the disciples who once could not understand that the Messiah must die, are now able to enter into his trials and death through the Spirit's power and to reproduce them in their own persons' (*op. cit.,* p. 196).

our Christian vocation in terms like this. We can follow the reference
to bearing God's name before Gentiles and kings and Israelites.
That is the kind of thing that we envisage for God's chosen servants. But suffering? We find these words strange. We do not
like them, and we do not usually take much notice of them. And
yet the fundamental truth is plain. Christ suffered. He said that
anyone who comes after Him must take up a cross. And if that does
not mean suffering it means nothing.

The words about Paul were not empty sound. He professed
himself as ready to be bound and even to die for the sake of Jesus
if need be (Acts 21:13; cf. 20:23). His life bears out this readiness.
Luke records that he was stoned at Lystra and left for dead (Acts
14:19). At Philippi he was beaten with rods, put in the dungeon
and had his feet fastened in the stocks (Acts 16:22ff.). The Jerusalem rabble mobbed him and beat him and tried to kill him (Acts
21:31f.; 22:22; 23:21). Others came to recognize that this kind
of thing was the will of the Lord for him (Acts 21:14).[49] There
is a mystery here. After all these centuries we do not seem to be
much nearer an understanding of why suffering should be necessary
for the follower of Christ. But at least we ought to be clear on the
basis of Scripture that, whether we understand it or not, the
fact is there. God has ordained that the pathway to blessing is
usually through suffering. This has its applicability to the atoning
work of Christ. Since God uses suffering so widely to bring about
His good purposes we need not be quite so astonished that the
way of atonement was a way of suffering.

VICTORY

But suffering is not the last word. Suffering is not the end, but
the means to the end, and that end is victory. Perhaps the dominant
note of the Acts is the note of victory.[50] The first Christians were
men who had passed through the shattering experience of that first
Good Friday when Jesus died. They had set their hopes on Him,
and His death came as a hammer blow. But then there came the

---

[49] Johannes Munck develops the thought that there are many parallels
between the Passion narrative at the climax of the Gospels and Paul's trial
at the climax of Acts (op. cit., pp. 320ff.). This may be part of the way Luke
emphasizes his point that those who follow a suffering Saviour must expect
to be suffering servants.

[50] 'Through death to the heavenly throne. This is the picture of Christ's
work which Luke is most concerned to show us' (G. W. H. Lampe, New Testament Studies, ii, p. 167). Lampe sees the difference between this and 'the
familiar Old Testament pattern of disaster and restoration' in the identification of Jesus with the Servant, and in the fact that 'he suffers and ascends as
the ἀρχηγός of his people. He goes on before as the guarantor of his followers' own entry' (loc. cit.).

totally unexpected resurrection. They took a little time to readjust
themselves to this new fact. At first they found difficulty in believing
it. But once they became sure of it, their whole outlook was transformed. The message of the resurrection runs through the whole
of the early preaching. It clearly gripped the imagination of the
preachers, and they proclaimed it with power and conviction.

As early as the third verse of this book Luke speaks of Jesus as
having 'shewed himself alive after his passion by many proofs'.
Later in the same chapter he tells us that the function of the new
apostle who was to replace Judas was to 'become a witness with us
of his resurrection' (Acts 1:22). Peter made quite a feature of the
resurrection in his first sermon (Acts 2:24-36), and in his second
(Acts 3:15, 26). In his little summary in Acts 4:32ff. Luke
speaks of the apostolic preaching this way: 'And with great power
gave the apostles their witness of the resurrection of the Lord Jesus:
and great grace was upon them all'.

The resurrection is rooted in the same compelling divine necessity
as the death of the Lord. The two are linked in Paul's message at
Thessalonica, where he says that 'it behoved the Christ to suffer,
and to rise again from the dead' (Acts 17:3). In similar strain
is Peter's conviction that 'it was not possible that he should be
holden' of death (Acts 2:24). The impossibility we may perhaps
see explained in the title given to Jesus in Acts 3:15, 'the Prince of
life'.[51] It is unthinkable that One who stands in this relationship
to life should be permanently subjected by death. The title implies
not only that Jesus *did* rise, but also that He *must* rise.

It is this necessity that is behind the prophecies concerning the
resurrection. Peter pointed out to the men of Jerusalem that David
spoke in Psalm 16 of not being left in Hades and not seeing corruption. But David himself did die and was buried, and his tomb
remained. Peter explains the passage thus, 'Being therefore a
prophet, and knowing that God had sworn with an oath to him, that
of the fruit of his loins he would set one upon his throne; he foreseeing this spake of the resurrection of the Christ, that neither was
he left in Hades, nor did his flesh see corruption.' Peter adds, 'This
Jesus did God raise up' (Acts 2:30ff.). Paul has the same argument
in Acts 26:22f., though without specific mention of passages. If a
thing is foretold in Scripture it must come to pass. The fact that we
do not always find it easy to see the resurrection in Old Testament passages should not blind us to the interest of the men of the
New Testament. They knew that the resurrection took place as the

---

[51] Rackham explains this term as 'the victorious Captain who "brought
to nought him that had the power of death" and who "brought life and immortality to light"' (*in loc.*). The term ἀρχηγός combines the thoughts of
priority in time and priority in importance ('pioneer' and 'prince').

result of the outworking of the divine purpose, and they delighted accordingly to see the foreshadowing of this event in the ancient scriptures. It is a measure of their certainty that the hand of God was in it. In this spirit they tell us over and over again that God raised Jesus up (not simply that Jesus arose). See Acts 2:32; 3:15, 26; 4:10; 5:30; 10:40; 13:30, 33, 34, 37; 17:31. The resurrection is the triumph of God.[52]

With this we must take references to the exaltation of Jesus. 'Being therefore by the right hand of God exalted, and having received of the Father the promise of the Holy Ghost, he hath poured forth this, which ye see and hear', said Peter (Acts 2:33). Jesus was not raised to resume the life He had left when He was crucified. He was exalted to highest heaven, and from there was in a position to send gifts to His people. So we read, 'Him did God exalt with his right hand to be a Prince and a Saviour' (Acts 5:31); 'God . . . hath glorified his Servant Jesus' (Acts 3:13); He has made Him 'both Lord and Christ' (Acts 2:36). The exaltation is a very real part of the early Christian message. It represents the truth that after the events associated with the Passion Jesus was an altogether glorious Being. His triumph was complete.

One part of the early proclamation which must have meant much to the first Christians, but which we easily overlook in modern times, is that which stresses victory over the demons. The ancient world was demon-ridden to a degree which we find difficult to comprehend. This is not quite the same point as is made in the Gospels, though, of course, it is akin to it. There our concern was with demon possession, here with the haunting fear of demonic forces. While the extent to which the Bible speaks of men as demon-possessed is sometimes today exaggerated, the extent to which demons haunted life is as often overlooked. Demons lurked everywhere, and men resorted to all kinds of devices in the attempt to escape their baleful influences. Spells and incantations were the common weapons as men fought to keep the demons at bay. But always at the back of men's minds was a lurking fear, for in the last resort demons were stronger and more versatile than any human force. The point of using sorceries and spells was that they were thought to enlist supernatural power. But, at best, this kind of thing afforded only temporary protection. Even when the magic was successful, none could tell when the repulsed demons or their friends might return.

---

[52] Cf. Karl Barth, 'The resurrection is marked off from the death of Jesus Christ as a new and specific act of God by the fact that in it there is pronounced the verdict of God the Father on the obedience of the Son: His gracious and almighty approval of the Son's representing of the human race; His acceptance of His suffering and death as it took place for the race . . .' (CDDR, p. 354).

To such a demon-ridden world the Christians came telling about One who not only 'went about doing good', but also 'healing all that were oppressed of the devil; for God was with him' (Acts 10:38).[53] Men who came to Him need fear demons no more. And He left to His followers an unusual power over demons. They could even expel demons from the demon-possessed. At Philippi Paul, being plagued by a girl possessed in this way, 'turned and said to the spirit, I charge thee in the name of Jesus Christ to come out of her. And it came out that very hour' (Acts 16:18).

There was nothing magical or automatic about this power. The ancient world, as we have noticed, attributed a great value to spells and enchantments. But there everything depended on the correct performance of the ritual and the right enunciation of the words. The mere invocation of a powerful name was thought to be what was required to give the speaker power over all that the name represented.[54] In this spirit certain 'strolling Jews' tried to use the name of Jesus. They had seen Paul use it with singular effect, and Luke describes their attempt to take over what must have seemed to them an extremely potent form of magic.

> But certain also of the strolling Jews, exorcists, took upon them to name over them which had the evil spirits the name of the Lord Jesus, saying, I adjure you by Jesus whom Paul preacheth. And there were seven sons of one Sceva, a Jew, a chief priest, which did this. And the evil spirit answered and said unto them, Jesus I know, and Paul I know; but who are ye? And the man in whom the evil spirit was leaped on them, and mastered both of them, and prevailed against them, so that they fled out of that house naked and wounded (Acts 19:13ff.).

The incident is Luke's way of demonstrating graphically that, while the name of Jesus does indeed give power over every evil thing, the power is not magical. It is not available to those who come in the wrong attitude. Men must believe. And believing means committing themselves to the service of Jesus as Paul did. The power does not come to lovers of the spectacular, or to those who are seeking success for themselves, or to any who are outside Christ. It is the

---

[53] 'It is scarcely possible to over-emphasize the extent to which Jesus appeared to his immediate followers as the great conqueror of the devil and of demons' (Lake and Cadbury, in loc.; Edward Langton has a statement almost word for word with this, *Essentials of Demonology*, London, 1949, p. 182).

[54] Some of the magical papyri that have come down to us contain long strings of what appear to be nonsense syllables conjoined with all sorts of names (see the examples given by A. Deissmann, LAE, pp. 255-63, etc.). The theory lying behind this appears to be that if in such a list the wizard managed to include the name of some spirit then the spirit must do his bidding. To have the name (even though unwittingly) was to have power over all that the name represents.

power of God and it is available only to set forward the purposes
of God.

The triumph may also be seen against the obstacles that the first
Christians encountered so constantly. Throughout the book of
Acts, the preaching of the gospel is attended with difficulties.
Humanly speaking the task must often have appeared quite hopeless. But the difficulties are never the determining factor. The
opposition is never triumphant. God's purposes are worked out, and
the triumph of His workers enshrines a profound truth. We might
perhaps take Paul's ministry as an illustration. Luke pictures him
as opposed on every hand. He was persecuted, stoned, hindered
from preaching, arrested. But despite all this God's purpose went
forward. Indeed, it was through such things that God's purpose was
advanced. Take, for example, Paul's arrest. That looked very
much like a major hindrance to Paul's service of God. But it
did not work out quite that way. It proved to be the means of bringing Paul to Rome to preach the gospel there. The very last words of
Acts are symbolic. There Luke shows us Paul preaching in the
capital of the world, 'none forbidding him' (Acts 28:31).[55]

Sometimes the preachers looked forward to a life beyond this
one, and then they thought of Jesus as the source of their own resurrection. This is implied in the expression 'Prince of Life' (Acts
3:15), which has already occupied us. It comes out also in the
subject of the preaching given in Acts 4:2, where they 'proclaimed
in Jesus the resurrection from the dead.' This note is not struck
very commonly, but it is there. As Christ's resurrection so dominated
their minds, it is not at all surprising that their own resurrection
should claim a measure of attention, too. Nor that it should be
so closely linked with what Christ had done for them.

Thus, in a variety of ways, Luke shows us Jesus triumphant.
Not all the forces of this world or the next could stand against
Him, not kings and princes, not death and hell itself. There
is no despondency about the lowly place of the Christians. There
is no hesitation or uncertainty either. These believers are men
with the deep-seated conviction that their Lord is victorious. They
might be beset by dangers and trials and difficulties innumerable.
But ultimate triumph was sure.

---

[55] R. R. Williams sees Paul as walking in the steps of his Master in all
this. 'It is not, of course, that Paul's escape and arrival at Rome are, in
theological importance, in any way comparable to the Passion and Resurrection
of Christ. It is true, however, that the *pattern* of failure followed by success,
defeat followed by victory, weakness swallowed up in strength is considered by
Luke to lie at the heart of God's dealing with men through the gospel' (*op. cit.*,
p. 32).

THE PLACE OF FAITH

The attitude of trust that we saw demanded in the Gospel continues to be required in Acts. The difference is that the noun 'faith' and the verb 'believe' are used more freely. Faith may still be connected with healing (Acts 3:16), though even here there is the suspicion that more than a belief that Jesus can heal is meant. And certainly this is the case when Stephen is said to be 'a man full of faith and of the Holy Spirit' (Acts 6:5), or when a similar description is given of Barnabas (Acts 11:24). The opening of 'a door of faith unto the Gentiles' (Acts 14:27) points us to saving faith, and this is explicitly connected with the Lord Jesus Christ on a number of occasions (Acts 20:21; 24:24; 26:18). So characteristic of the followers of Jesus is faith that the whole Christian system may be called 'the faith' (Acts 6:7; 13:8; 14:22; 16:5). Along the same lines those who are Christ's are called 'believers' or are said to have 'believed'. Indeed, throughout the book the usual way of saying that someone has become a Christian is simply to say that he has 'believed'.[56] Sometimes the object is added and people are said to have believed 'on the Lord' (or similar expression, Acts 9:42, etc.). But there is really no need. Where faith is so fundamental there is no necessity to specify the Object of faith.[57] There can be no doubt on such a matter.

Perhaps the classic passage in this connection is in the account of the visit of Paul and Silas to Philippi. The Philippian jailor asked the apostles, 'Sirs, what must I do to be saved?' and received the simple answer, 'Believe on the Lord Jesus, and thou shalt be saved' (Acts 16:30f.). No deeds of law are urged, no works of righteousness, no ritual act, no devotional exercise. Important as these are in their own place, they cannot be mentioned in answer to such a question. Faith in the Lord Jesus is the one demand. It is by believing and it is only by believing that men receive the divine provision for their need in Christ.

---

[56] Cf. Karl Barth, 'faith is *the* act of the Christian life to the extent that in all the activity and individual acts of a man it is the most inward and central and decisive act of his heart, the one which — if it takes place — characterises them all as Christian . . .' (CDDR, p. 757).

[57] W. Lillie makes the point that the New Testament emphasis on trust in a Person is a complete reversal of the usual attitude. 'In Greek thought a statement was true, because it was logically based on another true statement, and *pistis* was inferior to reasoned knowledge, because the statements accepted by *pistis* were not so logically deduced. In the Bible, the statements accepted by faith are the statements with the most certain foundation, and so superior to all others; they are based on the faithfulness and truth of God. This is why "believing *in* God" is primary' (SJT, x, p. 144).

BLESSINGS FROM CHRIST

When men believe they are introduced to the sphere in which the blessings of God are made available to His people. One such blessing is forgiveness. This is stressed from the very beginning:[58] 'And Peter said unto them, Repent ye, and be baptized every one of you in the name of Jesus Christ unto the remission of your sins' (Acts 2:38). Or again, 'through his name every one that believeth on him shall receive remission of sins' (Acts 10:43). The idea that forgiveness comes through Christ and what He did for men is found continually.[59] Luke saw the whole mission of Jesus as connected with putting right the situation caused by men's sins. This involves forgiveness from the divine side, and it involves a whole-hearted forsaking of sin from the human side. It is the heart of the purpose of God in Christ. So Peter told his hearers that God raised up 'his Servant' and 'sent him to bless you'. Then he describes this blessing, the whole purpose of God's raising up Jesus and sending Him, as consisting in 'turning away every one of you from your iniquities' (Acts 3:26). This means both that God provided forgiveness in what He did in Christ, and that He intends that those who believe should turn decisively away from their sins. It is true that forgiveness is not explicitly connected with the death of Jesus in this passage, but it is not possible to make sense out of Luke's various statements on the matter apart from such connection.[60]

---

[58] Floyd V. Filson sees this as the experience of the disciples immediately after the crucifixion, 'In spite of their miserable failure they had benefited from the death of Jesus. He had suffered for them. A teaching of forgiveness by his death was near at hand.' He goes on to point out that this yields the idea of substitution: 'The Primitive Church had no single or fully developed line of thought about the suffering of Jesus, but it turned easily to the idea that his death was a vicarious suffering for the spiritual benefit of men. There is an element of substitution in this idea' (*op. cit.*, p. 172).

[59] Christ's saving act is not otiose. There is nothing automatic or mechanical about forgiveness. It is not inevitable. Something has to be done before it is possible. Cf. Henry W. Clark, 'precisely in proportion as we have actual direct personal responsibility for any one's moral and spiritual welfare does it become impossible to cancel a transgressor's account by writing "pardoned" in its margin and then permitting the matter to slide. The relations between members of a family and its head (to take one of the most obvious examples) cannot be so lightly ruled. A father on whom the sense of parental duty lies with adequate weight knows that he dare not, when his child has offended, always or often content himself with saying "I forgive"' (*The Cross and the Eternal Order*, London, 1943, p. 35). There is a real basis for the forgiveness of which Luke writes.

[60] Cf. James Denney, on the necessity for postulating such a connection, 'it is self-evident to any one who believes that there is such a thing as Christianity as a whole, and that it is coherent and consistent with itself, and who reads with a Christian mind. The assumption of such a connection at once articulates all the ideas of the book into a system, and shows it to be

Peace comes by Jesus Christ. The gospel is 'The word which he sent unto the children of Israel, preaching good tidings of peace by Jesus Christ' (Acts 10:36). In the New Testament, peace is to be understood in the sense it bears in the Old Testament, and not in the sense we commonly give the term. Our understanding of peace derives from the Greeks, with whom it was a negative idea. They thought of peace as the absence of war or strife.[61] But for the Hebrews peace was positive. It meant the prosperity of the whole man, more especially his spiritual prosperity.[62] Indeed, without spiritual prosperity there can be no real prosperity of any sort. So the Hebrew looked to be at peace with God, for only then could he expect to flourish in the widest sense. In the New Testament we get the thought that Christ brings man peace. That is to say He ends man's alienation from God. He brings man into the closest and warmest relation of personal fellowship with God.[63] In this new fellowship, man can and does receive the fulness of blessing.[64]

Now and then the good gift of God is thought of as an inheritance. 'I commend you to God,' said Paul to the elders of Ephesus, 'and to the word of his grace, which is able to build you up, and to give you the inheritance among all them that are sanctified' (Acts 20:32). The natural way of obtaining an inheritance is by the death of the testator, so there is probably a reference here to the death of Christ as the means whereby the gift comes. We cannot insist on this last point, for in biblical Greek the word was sometimes used of a possession without strict regard to the way in which it was obtained.[65] But it does remind us that God gives liberally. And in the case of the Christian inheritance there is surely a for-

---

at one with the gospels and epistles; and such an assumption, for that very reason, vindicates itself' (DC, p. 83).

[61] W. Foerster begins the article on εἰρήνη, TWNT, ii, p. 398, by saying, 'It is fundamental for the Greek εἰρήνη - concept, that this word denotes primarily neither a relationship between several people nor an attitude, but a state: *the time of peace, the state of peace,* originally understood only as an interruption of the perpetual state of war.' He proceeds to cite Pseud. - Plat. Def. 413a, εἰρήνη ἡσυχία ἀπ' ἔχθρας πολεμικῆς.

[62] Cf. the detailed note on εἰρήνη, E. de W. Burton, *I.C.C. on Galatians,* Edinburgh, 1921, pp. 424ff.

[63] G. A. F. Knight emphasizes the continuity between the two Testaments in this connection (*Law and Grace,* London, 1962, p. 89).

[64] Foerster sees three possibilities for the meaning of εἰρήνη in the New Testament: 'a. the psychological: peace as a feeling of peace and calm of mind, -b. peace as a state of being reconciled to God, -c. peace as the "existence of salvation" (*Heilsein*) of the whole man, as ultimately an eschatological conception. All three possibilities are realized in the New Testament, but in such a way that the third forms the foundation' (TWNT, ii, p. 410).

[65] See the note in B. F. Westcott, *The Epistle to the Hebrews,* London, 1892, pp. 167-9; so also F. J. A. Hort, *The First Epistle of St. Peter,* London, 1898, p. 35.

ward look to the heavenly reward. There is more in our inheritance than we yet dream of.

Occasionally, too, Luke records that salvation is viewed as justification. Significantly, we find it in the report of Paul's sermon at Pisidian Antioch, where the apostle said, 'by him (i.e. Jesus) every one that believeth is justified from all things, from which ye could not be justified by the law of Moses' (Acts 13:39).[66] This topic will come up for more extended treatment when we come to consider Paul's views. Here we simply notice that justification is basically a legal term and that it means more than pardon. It indicates that the person concerned is treated as innocent, as having been acquitted at the bar of God's justice. Christ's death is the means of conferring on us the status of being righteous in God's sight.

The idea of covenant is central to the Old Testament. The thing that stamped Israel off from every other nation was the fact that she stood in covenant relation to Yahweh. He was her God. She was His people. But the Israelites failed again and again to fulfil their covenant obligations. Over and over the prophets denounced them for the evils they had committed. Evil ways have no place among the people of God. By walking in such ways, the nation forfeited its right to be called God's people, and opened the way for a new covenant, which was foretold by a number of prophets, notably Jeremiah. In Acts we see the idea that the true Israel is the Christian group, not Israel after the flesh. All that the covenant implies is fulfilled in the tiny new community. 'Ye are the sons of the prophets,' said Peter at the Gate Beautiful, 'and of the covenant which God made with your fathers, saying unto Abraham, And in thy seed shall all the families of the earth be blessed' (Acts 3:25).[67] Plainly Peter is seeing the fulfilment of this prophecy in the work of Christ, and equally plainly he is inviting the people to be 'the sons of the prophets' in the fullest sense, by linking themselves with the Church. This thought permeates the speech of Stephen in Acts 7. This speech is not an easy one to interpret. But it is plain enough that the first martyr held firmly that Israel had forfeited her place, and that the Church was now God's people. He sees the Church as the descendant of the Old Testament people of God. And for Stephen, as for all the

---

[66] This does not mean that the law of Moses justified from some things, but Jesus from more. Rather, the meaning is 'forgiveness for everything — which the Law never offered' (Lake and Cadbury, in loc.).

[67] This quotation is from Gn. 22:18, the consummation of the story of Abraham's offering of Isaac. In Rabbinic tradition Isaac was pictured as fully cooperating, and great efficacy was attached to this. On the present passage G. Vermes comments, 'Targumic tradition ascribes this blessing to Isaac's sacrifice, but Peter reinterprets it of Jesus, as Paul does in Galatians iii' (*Scripture and Tradition in Judaism*, Leiden, 1961, p. 221).

others, the cross was the critical point. It marked the place of transition.[68]

The character involved in this separation to be the people of God is not overlooked. At the Council of Jerusalem, Peter spoke of God as putting no difference between Jew and Gentile. Of the latter, as of the former, he could say, 'cleansing their hearts by faith' (Acts 15:9). The atonement should not be thought of as purely negative. It is not confined to such matters as forgiveness, as putting away sin and condemnation. It includes the thought that those for whom atonement is made go on to have purified hearts and clean hands. Their lives are transformed. Something similar is probably implied in the affirmation that Christ 'by the resurrection of the dead should proclaim light both to the people and to the Gentiles' (Acts 26:23). Life now is illuminated by what Christ has done. There is light that was not there before He came.

THE HOLY SPIRIT OF GOD

The activity of the Holy Spirit so pervades Acts that this book has been termed, not unjustly, 'The Acts of the Holy Spirit'. Certainly the work of the Spirit is far more important in it than anything the apostles do. In the first chapter the disciples are pictured as waiting. In the second chapter the Spirit comes. The rest of the book is the story of the Spirit acting through Spirit-filled men engaging in a Spirit-directed and Spirit-dominated ministry.[69] The enthusiasm of the Spirit suffuses everything. There is no section of this entire book which does not tell of the presence and the power of God the Holy Spirit.

Now the Holy Spirit is directly connected with the work that Jesus accomplished. The risen Jesus told His followers to await the gift (Acts 1:4, 8). He spoke of it in terms of being 'baptized with the Holy Ghost' (Acts 1:5), which links it with His whole mission, for John the Baptist had prophesied that He would baptize with the Holy Ghost (Lk. 3:16). Now this had become a reality. Peter explicitly says that it is the exalted Christ who has 'poured forth this, which ye see and hear' (Acts 2:33).[70] The gift is the

---

[68] It is worth noticing, too, that Stephen's calm acceptance of death ('Lord Jesus, receive my spirit', Acts 7:59) marks another gift of God. Not so did others than Christians in general face their death.

[69] 'The "gospel" of the Acts is the gift of the Spirit . . . . The gift of the Spirit, then, makes the Christian' (Rackham, op. cit., p. lxxv).

[70] 'Salvation and the power of the Spirit stand in so close a relation to each other in St. Luke's thought, that the exaltation of Jesus and his reception of the Father's promise (to bestow it in turn upon his followers) must of necessity be the source of the salvation which can thenceforth be preached to the ends of the earth' (G. W. H. Lampe, op. cit., p. 180). Lampe sees in this the essence of Christ's kingship. 'His kingship is equivalent to

culmination of the work of Jesus and follows immediately on the completion of that work.[71]

We should not overlook the fact that the adjective usually linked with 'Spirit' is 'Holy'. He might have been called 'the Spirit of power' or the like. Or, good prophetic precedent might have been followed, and a name selected from Isaiah's list, 'the spirit of wisdom and understanding, the spirit of counsel and might, the spirit of knowledge and of the fear of the Lord' (Is. 11:2). But the *Holy* Spirit puts the emphasis on separation. This is both positive, separation to God, and negative, separation from sin. The Spirit is the very antithesis of all that sin means. And the Spirit-dominated man will likewise take up his stand against sin. The atonement does not stop with forgiveness of past sin. It introduces men to a life of war against present sin. They are 'saints' (Acts 9:13, 32, 41; 26:10). This term, which is to become so prominent in the later parts of the New Testament, signifies the separation to the service of God which is the characteristic of those who believe. Alternatively they can be said to be 'sanctified' (Acts 20:32; 26:18). Nowhere does Acts sit loose to the obligations of discipleship. They are plainly brought out. It is anticipated that in the power of the Holy Spirit those who have come to Christ will live lives of purity in the service of their God.

THE PURCHASE OF GOD

The early preachers were much more taken up with the wonder of what Christ had done for them than with trying to explain how He had done it. But sometimes there is a venture on explanation. For example, we read in Acts 20:28, 'Take heed unto yourselves, and to all the flock, in the which the Holy Ghost hath made you bishops, to feed the church of God, which he purchased with his own blood.' Here the imagery is that of purchase. The Church is bought, as in a commercial transaction, with the blood of Christ. The metaphor of purchase was destined to play a big part in the understanding of the cross for centuries. But Paul's words should not be understood as implying or even countenancing the bizarre interpretations of purchase so common in patristic theology. What

---

his reception from the Father of the promise of the Holy Spirit, and as the result of his exaltation the kingdom which was operative in him on earth through the power of the Spirit becomes effective in the Spirit among his disciples and their converts' (*op. cit.,* p. 183).

[71] C. Ryder Smith says that for the apostles 'the Death, Resurrection, Ascension, and the gift of the Spirit, were an organic whole' (BDS, p. 186). The gift of the Spirit is not to be thought of as unrelated to the saving work of Christ. He is 'the Spirit of Jesus' (Acts 16:7).

he means is that the Church became God's own at great cost. For our salvation Christ shed His blood.

THE SERVANT OF THE LORD

Sometimes the sufferings of Christ are interpreted along the lines of Isaiah 53. Vincent Taylor thinks that this was the case from the first.[72] He examines the speech of Peter in Acts 2 and concludes, 'Already in this discourse it is clear that the dominating conception is that of the Servant, humiliated in death and exalted by God in the fulfilment of his supreme service for men. This claim is valid even though the Servant has not yet been mentioned.'[73] This seems a not unfair statement of the position. Certainly it is not long before the Servant is mentioned explicitly (Acts 3:13, 26; 4:27, 30).[74] It is likely also that the references to Jesus as 'the Righteous One' (Acts 3:14; 7:52; 22:14) point back to Isaiah 53:11, as Jeremias thinks.[75] It is not without its importance that Luke nowhere explains how and why the term 'Servant' began to be applied to Jesus. He could take this as accepted. It was a basic concept,[76]

---

[72] So does Joachim Jeremias. He points out that the application of παῖς to Jesus is confined to Acts 3 and 4 and says it 'belongs to a very ancient stratum of the tradition' (*The Servant of God*, London, 1957, p. 91). He also says, 'it must on balance appear probable that the predication of Jesus as the servant of God is meant from the start to characterize him as the servant of the Lord prophesied in Isa. 42 and 53' (*op. cit.*, p. 86). I find unconvincing the suggestion of J. C. O'Neill, that the term does not represent a Servant Christology and that Luke has confined the use of παῖς to this section of his book because he knew it to be an ancient liturgical form (*op. cit.*, pp. 133ff., especially p. 139). O. Cullmann conjectures that it is from Peter that this understanding of Christ's death found its way into the early church, Peter having derived it from his Lord (*The Christology of the New Testament*, London, 1959, pp. 74f.). If this is so, then the interpretation is very early indeed. Elsewhere Cullmann notes passages in Acts where 'Jesus openly receives the very title *ebed Yahweh*, "Servant of God," in the Greek rendering, *pais tou theou*. In the Septuagint the latter phrase translates the expression which Deutero-Isaiah uses for the Suffering Servant of God who takes upon himself in a substitutionary way the sins of the people' (*Peter, Disciple — Apostle — Martyr*, London, 1953, p. 67).

[73] ANT, p. 18.

[74] K. Lake and H. J. Cadbury reject any reference to Is. 53 (*The Beginnings of Christianity*, London, 1933, iv, p. 47, v, pp. 366ff.). But their reasoning does not commend itself. As W. L. Knox says, their treatment seems 'unduly sceptical and to rest on a failure to recognise the extent to which the prophecy of Isa. liii underlies the N.T. . . . The strand of prophecy could hardly be more freely used in the N.T. than it is, unless the authors are to be expected to reiterate the appeal to the same testimony an indefinite number of times' (*The Acts of the Apostles*, 1948, p. 79, n. 2).

[75] *Op. cit.*, p. 91.

[76] Cf. W. L. Knox, 'The death of Our Lord is regarded by non-Pauline Christianity as a fulfilment of the prophecy of Isaiah liii. This implies that Our Lord is the Righteous Servant of God, whose death is the atonement for

and had evidently been derived from the Master Himself. Thus when Philip talked with the man from Ethiopia, he had no hesitation in claiming the great Servant passage as referring to the Lord. From all this, we may fairly claim that the first Christians thought of the death of Jesus as doing all that the death of the Servant does in Isaiah 53. This means that they thought of His death as substitutionary ('he was wounded for our transgressions, he was bruised for our iniquities . . . . the Lord hath laid on him the iniquity of us all'). He stood in men's place. He bore their sins and they bear them no more.

BEARING THE CURSE

On three occasions Luke refers to the cross as a 'tree' (Acts 5: 30; 10:39; 13:29), and he specifically says that Jesus was 'hanged' on it on the first two of them. 'The cruel tree' has become part of the language of Christian devotion, so we never stop to think that this is an exceedingly curious way to describe crucifixion. A cross is not a tree, and it is not usually called one.[77] But the expression occurs in Deuteronomy 21:22f. of the criminal executed by hanging on a tree and who is said to have been accursed as a result. It is difficult to escape the impression that Luke is alluding to this. If he did not think of Jesus as bearing our curse, I see no reason why he should three times employ a very unusual form of speech which would invite men to think of Jesus as having died accursed. To say that there were other ways of describing the crucifixion is to understate the case. Luke has to go out of his way to describe it in this fashion.[78] It seems impossible to escape

---

the sins of many. . . . This is a point of primary importance. It implies that Christianity had before S. Paul's conversion a doctrine of the atonement, based on a terminology which S. Paul himself did not care to use. To the fact of Our Lord's Resurrection must be added the belief that His death is the atonement for the sins of others' (*St. Paul and the Church of Jerusalem,* Cambridge, 1925, p. 30).

[77] ξύλον properly means 'wood' and it is used of all manner of objects made of wood, as well as of trees. Thus it is used of cudgels (e.g. Mt. 26:47; Lk. 22:52) and of instruments of punishment like stocks (Acts 16:24). It is even used of gallows, but LS cite no example of its use for a cross outside the New Testament.

[78] On this expression G. B. Caird says, 'This is not a description of the Crucifixion which would naturally occur to a bystander. It is a quotation from Deuteronomy xxi. 22f.: "If a man has committed a capital crime and is put to death, and you hang him on a tree, his body shall not remain all night upon the tree, but you shall bury him the same day; for he that is hanged is under God's curse". Surely no Christian preacher would have chosen to describe the death of Jesus in terms which drew attention to the curse of God resting upon the executed criminal, unless he had first faced the scandal of the Cross and had come to believe that Jesus had borne the curse

the conclusion that he does this meaningfully. He knows that Jesus has borne our curse and he chooses this way of making the point.[79]

In Acts, then, Luke repeats most of the teaching of the Gospel on the cross, though sometimes with a different emphasis. He sees the seriousness of sin and stresses it with his reminder of God's judgment, both present and to come. He calls for repentance, but there is an advance on the Gospel in that this demand is linked with the death on the cross. It is because of what Christ did for them that men should repent and believe. Another new note is that of the accountability of men for their evil, more particularly that of crucifying the Christ. As in the Gospel, he makes the point that salvation comes from God, that God worked out His purpose in the cross. This latter point is emphasized with some very forthright statements about predestination. Luke sees suffering as the means of bringing men salvation, first the suffering of Christ, which is atoning suffering, and then the suffering of the servants of Christ, which is not atoning but is the means of bringing the message to others. Luke sees the whole world as coming within the scope of the gospel message, and he records the progressive widening of the circles in which the gospel was preached. Christ's death, though apparent defeat, was really a resounding victory, as the resurrection makes clear. Acts puts a new emphasis on the response expected of men, with its teaching about believing. This is plainly the important thing. When Luke speaks of the salvation wrought by Christ, he thinks of it as bringing forgiveness and peace and an inheritance and justification. It is the realization of the covenant promised from of old, so that believers are the people of God. They live as the people of God, which means that they have a new strength. Few things are more distinctive of Acts than the place it gives to the Holy Spirit. His work is not separate from the work of Christ, but an integral part of it, its necessary climax. Christ died not only that the past might be cancelled, but that the future might be won for God. The Holy Spirit makes all things new. Luke sees Christ as having purchased His people, a note which reminds us of the ransom saying in the first two Gospels. And he thinks of Christ as having fulfilled all that is implied in His calling as the Servant of Isaiah 53. This means that the Christian salvation, as Luke sees it, is something wherein the cross is central. There God effectively dealt with sin and brought men into a new life.

---

on behalf of others' (*The Apostolic Age*, London, 1955, p. 40).

[79] It is an almost peculiarly Lukan point. Ξύλον is used of the cross outside Acts only in Gal. 3:13; I Pet. 2:24.

CHAPTER FOUR

The Cross in the Gospel According to St. John

John clearly was a man of subtle and penetrating mind. He was moreover profoundly spiritual, and he had given a great deal of thought to the significance of Christ. In his Gospel he tells us something of what the Spirit had taught him about Christ and about the ways of God. He does this in his own inimitable way, for he was not one for walking in the accustomed paths or repeating stereotyped formulas. He wrote as he saw, and he saw clearly but deeply. His writings accordingly are a mixture of clarity and profundity. On the one hand, the humblest child of God can read them and understand them.[1] It is no coincidence that Evangelist Billy Graham advises the newly-converted to begin their Bible reading with the Gospel according to St. John. On the other hand,

---

[1] 'The critic may range the gospel with Philo and the Alexandrian philosophers; but, and the question is important, did the poor and the ignorant, when they lay a-dying ever ask their Rabbis to read to them out of the voluminous writings of Philo or of those like him?' (E. C. Hoskyns, *The Fourth Gospel*, London, 1950, p. 20).

these simple words carry such profound meaning that the wisest scholar or the holiest saint will scarcely feel that he has even begun to explore their significance.[2] Accordingly we shall be able to see some of John's thought, but we must expect that the writer has greater depths of meaning than we can plumb.

And if this is so in general, it applies in particular to the matter of man's salvation, for the Gospel is full of it.[3] By this I do not mean that John has as much to say about the specific topic of salvation as other New Testament writers, for he has not. The number of his themes is not large, and the bulk of his specific references to the atonement is not great. He has not the same richness and variety of thought on the subject, for example, as has Paul. There is nothing in John like Romans 3:21ff., where in a few verses Paul draws on justification, redemption, propitiation, the righteousness of God, the blood of Christ, and more, to bring out his meaning. This is not John's way. His themes are fewer, but they run through his Gospel. And all that he writes is written in the light of Christ's work for men. Whenever he speaks of love, it is love illuminated by the cross that he has in mind. Whenever he speaks of life, it is the life that has been won by Christ to which he refers. And so throughout. His themes may not be many, but they are all seen only in the light of the cross. They are accordingly of tremendous importance.[4] They do not keep us on the surface, but take us to the deep things of God and of God's salvation.

[2] 'Someone has described the remarkable character of this Gospel by saying that it is a book in which a child can wade and an elephant can swim' (P. F. Barackman, *Interpretation,* vi, p. 63).

[3] Cf. C. Ryder Smith, 'the whole of the Fourth Gospel is a Book of Salvation' (BDS, p. 241). So also W. F. Lofthouse, 'He does not mention the words reconciliation, atonement. But the thing is everywhere' (*The Father and the Son,* London, 1934, p. 125). Or C. K. Barrett, 'The history he records is the history of God's saving activity, directed to the need of men, and he never thinks of it in other terms' (*The Gospel according to St. John,* London, 1955, p. 66). Or Bishop Cassian, 'the theme of the Passion is put from the very beginning of the Gospel as one of its central themes' (SE, p. 143). Or P. Gardner-Smith, 'In a sense the whole Gospel is a passion narrative' (*Saint John and the Synoptic Gospels,* Cambridge, 1938, p. 42).

[4] Cf. Vincent Taylor, 'The Johannine teaching (*sc.* on the atonement) is of imperishable value to the Church and to the individual believer. It has fewer notes than Pauline teaching, but they have a deep diapason quality with which instinctively many readers of the New Testament find themselves to be in harmony' (ET, lviii, pp. 258f.). So also Theo Preiss, 'In a style of grandiose monotony, [the thought of John] develops a few unchanging themes: Father, Son, love, life and death, light and darkness, truth and falsehood, judgment, witness. Looked at closely, its poverty is extreme, like those melodies of only three or four notes. And yet on this reduced keyboard we hear a music of infinitely varied harmonies, each note evoking so many reverberations that even the most attentive ear cannot capture them all at once' (*Life in Christ,* London, 1954, p. 10).

THE PRESENT JUDGMENT

John has his own way of bringing out the seriousness of sin. At the outset let us notice that he is much more concerned with the problem of sin than is any other of the Gospel writers. It is not without significance that he uses the word 'sin' more often than Matthew and Mark combined.[5] This is sometimes overlooked.[6] The idea is tolerably common that John is primarily concerned to depict the revelation that God made in Christ. His Gospel is seen as preeminently the Gospel of revelation.[7] His concern for sin is minimized. It is surprising how widespread is the idea that, whereas Paul is concerned with salvation from sin, John's interest by contrast is rather the incarnation, the unfolding of the implications of the Word made flesh.[8] This is a false antithesis. We need turn only to Philippians 2:5-11 to discover Paul's deep interest in the incarnation. And while John's interest in the incarnation is plain for all to see, his concern for the problems of salvation is no less real.

To begin with, John makes it quite clear that unless sin is dealt with men will perish eternally. The giving of the only begotten Son preserves believers from this, but the plain implication of John 3:16 is that those who do not believe do not have everlasting life. They 'perish'. The text is usually cited to show God's love and the wonder of the provision He has made for man's salvation in 'Christ, but it should not be overlooked that the love of which it speaks is directed towards saving men from a dire fate, not playacting in a situation where there is no real peril. For John the possibility of perishing is a very real one indeed. And his reference to 'the world' shows that this is no restricted thing. All men stand

---

[5] Matthew uses the noun 7 times and the verb 3 times; for Mark the figures are 6 and 0, and for John, 17 and 3. In the face of this it is curious to read in Lofthouse, 'The references to sin in the Fourth Gospel are both rare and, it would seem, incidental' (*op. cit.,* p. 156). This writer later on says, 'there lay at the heart of His message the thought of men, of the whole world, as alienated from God' (*op. cit.,* p. 164). In this he concedes the essential point, namely that John is deeply concerned with the problem of human sin.

[6] E. F. Scott does this. He says, for example, 'The fact of sin ceases to be the dominant fact in (John's) theology, but here and there he recognises it and makes some partial attempt to connect it with his own doctrine of the work of Christ'; 'the doctrine of sin, in the sense that it meets us elsewhere in the New Testament, is almost wholly absent from the Fourth Gospel'; 'The problem of sin, which was central in the mind of Paul, to John appeared something secondary' (*The Fourth Gospel,* Edinburgh, 1906, pp. 218, 221, 225). All this is simply not in accord with the facts. It ignores John's usage. It may be how Scott interprets the kind of theology we see in the Fourth Gospel, but it is not the position that John himself takes up.

[7] So, for example, G. W. Wade, *New Testament History,* London, 1922, p. 677.

[8] See W. F. Howard, *Christianity according to St. John,* London, 1943, p. 97; E. F. Scott, *op. cit.,* p. 206, etc.

in danger.[9] Another way of expressing the same truth is to speak of the wrath of God. 'He that believeth on the Son hath eternal life; but he that obeyeth not the Son shall not see life, but the wrath of God abideth on him' (Jn. 3:36). The unrepentant sinner excludes himself from life. He shuts himself up to the wrath of God, and the present tense, 'abideth', a tense denoting continuous action, shows that this is no passing phenomenon.[10] It is permanent. In keeping with this the worst of calamities appears to be the horrible, though undefined, fate of dying in sin. 'For except ye believe that I am he,' said Jesus, 'ye shall die in your sins' (Jn. 8:24). There is a similar expression in the Old Testament (e.g. Ezek. 18:14), but neither there nor here is it defined. The horror is all the greater for being nameless. From all this, it is clear that John views sin very seriously. He understands it as having far-reaching consequences. It merits a terrible punishment in the hereafter.

It also has its consequences in the here and now. It was commonly held in the first century that sin brings temporal penalties upon the sinner, and sometimes on those in some way connected with him. This idea is at the back, for example, of the disciples' question, 'Rabbi, who did sin, this man, or his parents, that he should be born blind?' (Jn. 9:2). Jesus' answer shows that both suggestions are faulty. Sin and sin's penalty are not connected in so simple a fashion. There are temporal afflictions that have nothing to do with sin.

Nevertheless this Gospel makes a great deal of the thought that sin's consequences become apparent in the here and now. The present judgment is a spiritual state rather than temporal calamity,[11] but it is very real: 'He that believeth on him is not judged: he that believeth not hath been judged already, because he hath not believed on the name of the only begotten Son of God. And this is the judgment, that the light is come into the world, and men loved the darkness rather than the light' (Jn. 3:18f.). This present

[9] 'If salvation is for the whole world, the whole world must stand in need of it; all men must be regarded as sinful' (G. B. Stevens, *The Theology of the New Testament,* Edinburgh, 1901, p. 192).

[10] Paul Tillich comments on the modern distaste for the whole concept of wrath in God. 'The idea of the Divine wrath has become strange to our time. We have rejected a religion which seemed to make God a furious tyrant, an individual with passions and desires who committed arbitrary acts.' But he goes on, 'This is not what the wrath of God means. It means the inescapable and unavoidable reaction against every distortion of the law of life, and above all against human pride and arrogance' (*The Shaking of the Foundations,* New York, 1948, p. 71). See also K. Barth, *Credo,* London, 1936, p. 46.

[11] And yet it may mean temporal calamity. See W. Robinson, SJT, iv, p. 145; H. Wheeler Robinson, *The Christian Doctrine of Man,* Edinburgh, 1926, pp. 310f.

judgment of the man who rejects the revelation that God has made in His Son does not exclude the thought of a final punishment in the world to come. We have already noticed references to 'perishing', to dying in sin, and to 'the wrath of God' as remaining continually on unbelievers. In similar fashion the judgment passage in John 5:27-29 looks forward to the Son's activity at the last day in connection with the final judgment on evil men. But though judgment is a future reality, it is not *only* a future reality. Final judgment is already in operation. It is true that the impenitent man will one day meet God's judgment. But it is also true that he is 'judged already'! His preference for darkness over light has shut him up to darkness. He cannot have light, and that precisely because he has chosen darkness. His own action means that here and now he is under judgment, none the less real because self-imposed. It should not be overlooked that John's word for 'judgment' is *krisis,* which denotes the process.[12] John is not saying, 'This is the sentence God has passed on sinners', but 'This is the way judgment works', 'This is the process whereby men judge themselves'.[13]

The same truth may be expressed in other ways. Thus the man who persists in sin can be spoken of as a slave (Jn. 8:34).[14] The lot of the slave to sin is far from pleasant, and the slave cannot break free. The imagery stresses the present ill plight of the sinner, a condemnation in the here and now brought about by the fact of his sin. Sin might bring on a man a 'worse thing' than lifelong lameness (Jn. 5:14). This may well refer to a penalty after death, but it is at least possible that it has reference also to a present disaster, just as the lameness to which it is compared is a present disaster. Men divide according to their attitude to Christ. So characteristic is this of Christ's impact on men that He can be said to have come into the world expressly for judgment: 'For judgement came I into this

---

[12] The sentence would be rather κρίμα.

[13] Dorothy Sayers points out that 'There is a difference between saying: "If you hold your finger in the fire you will get burned" and saying, "if you whistle at your work I shall beat you, because the noise gets on my nerves".' She adds, "The God of the Christians is too often looked upon as an old gentleman of irritable nerves who beats people for whistling. This is the result of a confusion between arbitrary "law" and the "laws" which are statements of fact. Breach of the first is "punished" by edict; but breach of the second, by judgment' (*The Mind of the Maker,* London, 1941, p. 9). This is not the whole truth. But it is an important part of the truth.

[14] 'When men sin, they do it gladly with the feeling that they have control over their action; another time they can decide in the opposite way and do what is right. But this consciousness of freedom which accompanies sin is nothing but an illusion. "He who sins, is a slave to sin." It is not mankind which is the master of sin, but it is sin which is the master of mankind. By nature we all stand under this terrible dominion. We live in an occupied country, and even if we imagine that we are free, we are still under an alien power' (A. Nygren, SJT, iv, p. 367).

world, that they which see not may see; and that they which see may become blind' (Jn. 9:39).[15] This does not mean that it was Jesus' purpose to condemn men any more than it is the purpose of the sun that shadows be cast. Yet when the sun shines shadows are inevitable. And when light is come into the world it is equally inevitable that those who prefer darkness are shown up for what they are (Jn. 3:19). Their own attitude excludes any other possibility than their condemnation. Not staying for the sentence of God on judgment day, they hasten to pass sentence on themselves now.

This is profoundly important. While it is true in one sense that God passes sentence of condemnation on sinners (they have broken His laws and they are sentenced accordingly), it is just as true in another sense that men condemn themselves.

> Still, as of old,
> Man by himself is priced.
> For thirty pieces Judas sold
> Himself, not Christ.[16]

Sinners believe that they secure their end by their sin. And, indeed, they do secure their end. Like Judas, they obtain their thirty pieces. But what they do not see, and what John makes us see with painful clarity, is that in their very success lies their condemnation. Precisely that on which they congratulate themselves, the pinnacle of their success, as they see it, is their penalty. Their successful pursuit of darkness means that they shut themselves off forever from the light. The light streams forth from the love so vividly set forth on Calvary. If a man prefers anything whatever to surrendering to such love he has not secured a gain, but utter loss whether he sees it or whether he does not.

> . . . Judas sold
> Himself, not Christ.

THE PRESENT SALVATION

If John thinks of condemnation as present, he is equally sure that salvation is the present possession of the believer. Early in the Gospel, John the Baptist salutes Jesus as 'the Lamb of God, which taketh away the sin of the world' (Jn. 1:29; cf. v. 36). There are difficulties in understanding the expression, 'Lamb of God',[17] but for our present purpose we need note only that the application of this atoning work to the believer is not something that must await a distant judgment day. It is a present reality. 'He that

[15] 'Judgement is the obverse of salvation; it is the form salvation takes for men who will have none of it' (C. K. Barrett, op. cit., p. 68).
[16] C. J. Wright, Jesus the Revelation of God, London, 1950, p. 164.
[17] See below, pp. 174f.

heareth my word, and believeth him that sent me, hath eternal life'
(Jn. 5:24). The present tense, 'hath', is significant. This is not
to deny that John sees a glorious future awaiting the believer in a
life beyond death. But it is to affirm that the believer has present
possession of a life that death cannot destroy. Death is concerned
with the body. Eternal life is nonetheless real and nonetheless permanent because its possessor will one day pass through the gateway we
call death. Again and again John brings out the truth that this life
is a present possession.[18] See John 1:12; 3:16, 36; 6:33, 40, 47, etc.

This salvation is not at men's disposal. It is not given at men's
whims and fancies. It is a divine gift, and John associates each of
the Persons of the Trinity with it. He tells us that before men can
be saved it is necessary that the Spirit convict them (Jn. 16:8f.).
Left to themselves, men do not want to be saved, as every preacher
of the gospel knows. Men do not think of themselves as sinners and
therefore they see no need of a Saviour. It requires a divine work
within them before they can see themselves as they really are before
God. Only as the Spirit of God works within them do they become convicted. 'Convicted' may refer to a change in outlook whereby they realize their sin, or it may mean that the Spirit condemns
them.[19] Either way, it is a divine work. Men simply do not see
themselves as sinners. And the Spirit's work does not cease with
convicting men. John tells us that salvation is a process of rebirth
and that this is brought about by the Spirit. 'Except a man be born
of water and the Spirit, he cannot enter into the kingdom of God'
(Jn. 3:5; cf. v. 8, 'so is every one that is born of the Spirit').
These words, it should be noted, are addressed not to some un-
usually sinful being, but to Nicodemus, a leading Pharisee, and evidently chosen by John as typifying the way of salvation by the keeping of the Law. To this eminent representative of Jewish orthodoxy,
Jesus makes it clear that the way into the Kingdom is not by human
striving. It is by the way of rebirth, rebirth through the activity of
the divine Spirit. A man *must* be reborn if he would see the Kingdom. This process of being born all over again is first brought up
in the Prologue, when it is insisted that the 'children of God' are
those who are born, 'not of blood, nor of the will of the flesh, nor
of the will of man, but of God' (Jn. 1:13). It is in mind again

[18] 'The great change, then, in a man's life does not take place at death, but
at the moment when he submits himself to Christ, the Son of God. By en-
trusting his life to Him, believing in Him, he becomes partaker of eternal life,
and this happens in this earthly existence, under present conditions. It is an
eternal "Now", reaching out into the future' (W. H. Rigg, *The Fourth Gospel
and its Message for To-day*, London, 1952, p. 83).

[19] Cf. R. H. Strachan, 'It is not said that they will feel themselves guilty,
but the Paraclete as judge and strengthener of the persecuted pronounces
them guilty of the charge that *they believe not on me*' (*The Fourth Gospel*,
London, 1955, p. 294).

when the activity of Jesus is spoken of as baptizing with the Holy Ghost (Jn. 1:33). There is emphasis on the necessity of this work of the Spirit within, re-creating men so that they can be said to have been born all over again if they are to be saved.

And if the Spirit must work this work within them, John insists that the Father must in like manner do a work within them. He must draw them if they are to come. 'No man can come to me, except the Father which sent me draw him', said Jesus (Jn. 6:44), and He repeated it with emphasis, 'no man can come unto me, except it be given unto him of the Father' (Jn. 6:65).[20] It is the fallacy of the procrastinator that he can come to Christ whenever he wishes. He thinks he can defer that step until he is good and ready, and that then he can come. He cannot. He can come only when the Father draws him. Perception in spiritual things, and a readiness to take the step of faith are not natural attributes. They come only as God's good gift.

And the other Person of the Trinity is also involved in this process, for Jesus said, 'And I, if I be lifted up from the earth, will draw all men unto myself' (Jn. 12:32). 'Lifting up' in this Gospel always refers to the lifting up on the cross (Jn. 3:14; 8:28; 12:32, 34). Jesus is speaking of His atoning death for sinners. In that death He will draw men to Himself. Again there is the thought that the initiative is with the divine. It is not simply that men decide that they will come to Christ. Something similar is perhaps implied in the words of Jesus to Nathanael, 'Verily, verily, I say unto you (the first occurrence of this emphatic formula), Ye shall see the heaven opened, and the angels of God ascending and descending upon the Son of man' (Jn. 1:51). There are mysteries here, but at the least the saying means that Jesus will be the means of communication between earth and heaven.[21] No one else has ever ascended to heaven (Jn. 3:13). He only, then, is the means of raising men to heaven. Which is another way of saying that salvation depends on

---

[20] This should be noted over against a tendency in some quarters to think that if only Christ be set forth in all His beauty men would naturally flock to Him. Cf. C. J. Barker, 'Even Jesus confessed impotence — No man can come unto me except the Father draw him . . . . This denial of inherent magnetism in Himself is startling on the lips of Christ . . . . There is a strain of pessimism in the Fourth Gospel which needs to be squarely faced. It is the contretemps to the assurance which declares "I, if I be lifted up, will draw all men unto me"' (*Studies in the Fourth Gospel*, ed. F. L. Cross, London, 1957, p. 50). Cf. J. Jocz, *A Theology of Election*, London, 1958, pp. 190ff.

[21] 'The place of the stone in the ancient story is now taken by the flesh and blood of Jesus the Son of man. He is the Door (x. 7, 9), the Way to the heavenly mansions of God (xiv. 1-7), the place where the vision of God is vouchsafed to men (xiv. 8-10). Through Him the will of God is made known . . .' (Hoskyns, *op. cit.*, p. 183).

Him and not on man. This is the thought also when He rejects the possibility of salvation through John the Baptist, whose function was no more than that of bearing witness to the truth (Jn. 5:33). Jesus insists, 'I say these things, that ye may be saved' (Jn. 5:34). Again He says, 'The Son also quickeneth whom he will' (Jn. 5:21). The divine initiative is strongly insisted upon.

Negatively we read, 'ye will not come to me, that ye may have life' (Jn. 5:40). 'Will' here is not the simple future, but the verb θέλω, 'you have set your will against coming to me'. Salvation is so closely connected with Christ, that when a man's will is against coming to Him, then that man is excluded from the possibility of salvation. Throughout this Gospel the priority of the divine is insisted upon. Salvation is simply not a human possibility at all. John's whole Gospel is concerned with the way in which God has brought men life through the sending of His Son (Jn. 20:31).

THE WILL OF GOD

This is expressed also in the contrast of grace with law. 'For the law was given by Moses; grace and truth came by Jesus Christ' (Jn. 1:17). There are moreover the strong statements about grace in the Prologue, 'And the Word became flesh, and dwelt among us (and we beheld his glory, glory as of the only begotten from the Father), full of grace and truth' (Jn. 1:14); 'For of his fulness we all received, and grace for grace' (Jn. 1:16).[22] Though John uses the word grace these four times only in his Gospel, the idea behind it is everywhere, as its mention in the Prologue may be meant to indicate. Now the very idea of grace means the priority of the divine. Grace is one of the great Christian words, and it is pregnant with the thought of the unmerited favour that God extends to men. Unmerited. The very idea of merit excludes that of grace. Wherever, then, we get the thought of grace, we get that of the divine action to bring men salvation quite apart from man's deservings.

When John reminds us that the Law was given by Moses, he is directing attention to the very antithesis of grace. The Jews were very proud of Moses and of their place as the custodians of the Law that he gave. And they interpreted the Law as pointing men to salvation by their own merits.[23] John saw it differently. He did not

---

[22] This 'is another way of saying "By the grace of God I am what I am"' (J. Moffatt, *Grace in the New Testament*, London, 1931, p. 367).

[23] J. O. F. Murray speaks of 'a fundamental distinction between the old dispensation and the new. The pride of the Jew centred in the Law which had been given him on tables of stone through Moses. It gave him an opportunity of acquiring merit by conforming to external regulations. But all its ordinances were only "shadows of the true". With the new order a new relation of free favour with God came flooding in' (*Jesus According to S. John*, London, 1936, pp. 44f.).

deny that the Law given to Moses was of divine origin. His Gospel shows that he was always more than respectful of it. But he saw it as pointing, not to salvation by human merit, but to Christ. He tells us that Philip told Nathanael, 'We have found him, of whom Moses in the law, and the prophets, did write, Jesus of Nazareth' (Jn. 1:45). The whole Old Testament on John's view prepares the way for the coming of Jesus. Those who read it aright will welcome Him, just as did Philip and then his friend, Nathanael. The same truth lies behind our Lord's words in John 5:39. There is doubt whether we should translate 'Ye search the scriptures' or 'Search the scriptures' in the opening part of the verse, but there is no doubt about the conclusion, 'these are they which bear witness of me'. John tells us that his aim in writing the Gospel was 'that ye may believe that Jesus is the Christ' (i.e. the Messiah, Jn. 20:31). Now the Christ is a figure foretold in the Old Testament. The Jews lovingly went through the prophecies that spoke of His coming, and they looked and longed for Him. When John speaks of his aim as showing that Jesus was the Christ, then, he spoke of the way in which he understood the scripture to foretell His coming, and of the fact that he saw that coming as the will of God.

It is in this spirit that he records the turning of the water into wine (Jn. 2). There has been much discussion as to exactly what happened here, and what it is that John is trying to teach us. Though we do not try to go into the matter at all fully, it seems that one thing that John was doing, at any rate, was showing the superiority of Christianity to Judaism.[24] While there is no reason to doubt that John had set himself the task of recording something that had happened (he was not adapting a pagan legend or manufacturing an edifying allegory), yet it is significant that he records that it was water 'set there after the Jews' manner of purifying' (v. 6) that was changed into wine. The water of Judaism, under the influence of Christ, became the wine of Christianity.[25] And it is possible that the cleansing of the temple which John records in the same chapter points us in the same direction. Many commentators agree that this incident reflects a dissatisfaction with the temple system, the heart of Judaism, and a determination to replace it with something better.

In none of this is there a repudiation of the Old Testament or a denial that the Jews were the people of God. But there is the thought that the Old Testament is not God's final word. It is the preparation for a fuller revelation. And the same thing may be said about the

[24] 'The Christ is the dispenser of the life of God, the author and giver of eternal life, which He offers to the world through His death and through the mission of His disciples. This is the fulfilment of Judaism, of which the miracle of Cana is a sign' (Hoskyns, *op. cit.*, pp. 190f.).

[25] 'Jesus, by His coming, turned the imperfection of the law into the perfection of grace' (William Barclay, *The Gospel of John*, i, Edinburgh, 1956, p. 89).

religion of the Old Testament. It was divine in origin, but it looked forward to the coming of the Christ and the new way that He would inaugurate. The purpose of God is foreshadowed in the Old Testament and its religion, but that purpose is realized in Jesus Christ. Therefore, for John, everything must be evaluated in the light of Christ. There we see God's purpose as we see it nowhere else.

Specifically, John sees the will of God to issue in the cross. In the best-known text in the whole of Scripture, we read, 'For God so loved the world, that he gave his only begotten Son, that whosoever believeth on him should not perish, but have eternal life' (Jn. 3:16). Salvation is not something wrung from an unwilling God by the desperate intervention of a compassionate Son who took pity on those subject to His Father's destroying wrath. Salvation proceeds rather from the loving heart of God the Father Himself.[26] It is an expression at once of His love and of His righteousness. This is a precious truth, and it must never be lost sight of.

But it is not always noticed that if the cross is an expression of God's love it is also an expression of His righteousness. If there were nothing but His love to be considered, it would be difficult to see why the cross should be necessary at all (indeed, the logic of the position of some scholars seems to render it unnecessary). The cross is as eloquent of God's concern for moral law as it is of His love.[27]

In line with all this, John makes it clear that Jesus' will was perfectly at one with the will of the Father: 'I do nothing of myself', He said (Jn. 8:28); 'I can of myself do nothing: as I hear, I judge: and my judgment is righteous; because I seek not mine own will, but the will of him that sent me' (Jn. 5:30). We are not to think of Jesus as willing one thing and the Father another, so that in the end He had to bow in submission. The two see things the same way.[28] So close was His unity with the Father that Jesus could

[26] Cf. R. V. G. Tasker, 'He will hang on a cross like a condemned criminal. But His subjection to that particular form of death will not be due to some mischance. He will die in that way, precisely because it is in that way that God has chosen to reveal His love for sinners. He has given His Son to pay the penalty of their sins' (*in loc.*).

[27] Cf. P. T. Forsyth, 'God so loved the world, we read, that He gave His Son as a propitiation to His own holiness. He gave His holy Self in His Son. But God so loved the world, we are now taught, that He was not going to let His holiness interfere with its salvation. He had means to hush that holiness, or salve it, but we should not speak of satisfying it. Satisfaction is obsolete theology. At any rate He took it less seriously than His pity. But surely that is a non-moral creed, one which is but sympathetic, one therefore which must issue in an immoral society, first delightful, then debased. Room must be made for a real judgment . . .' (JG, p. 110).

[28] Cf. C. H. Dodd, on Jn. 5:19-30. 'It seems clear that it is intended to rule out any suspicion that Christ claims to be δεύτερος θεός, or a "second principle" over against the one God . . . . The sole condition on which the Son exercises divine functions is that He acts in complete unity with the Father, a unity

say, 'I and the Father are one' (Jn. 10:30). Anyone who has seen Him has seen the Father (Jn. 14:9). To know Him is to know the Father (Jn. 14:7). Those who have not known the Father have not known Christ (Jn. 16:3). Those who have seen and hated Christ have seen and hated the Father (Jn. 15:24). The works that Jesus did He did not of Himself, but because the Father was within Him (Jn. 5:19). Indeed, the Father could be said to do the works Himself, 'the Father abiding in me doeth his works' (Jn. 14:10).

John could hardly make the point more emphatically. He speaks of a real incarnation, and is at pains to show that Jesus was true man.[29] But it is the incarnation of One who is true God, and John emphasizes the community of will which illustrates this. What the Father willed the Son willed. This means that the salvation that Jesus dies to bring is divinely appointed. It does not rest on any human wisdom or any human contriving, not even that of Jesus considered as a man. It is that to which all the preparation in the ancient scriptures pointed. It is that in which the will of the heavenly Father is perfectly revealed. Those, then, who believe on Jesus Christ, and see in Him the Son of God, have the deep-seated certainty that the way of salvation in which they have been led is the way that God planned from of old whereby men might be saved.

CHRIST'S DELIBERATE CHOICE OF DEATH

In the last section we noticed that part of the will of God which Jesus fulfilled, and a most important part, was the manner of His death for sinners. Here we take up this point once more, for it is a most important point in the Fourth Gospel. John emphasizes in many ways the truth that the death Jesus died was not simply the result of the raging of wicked men, but was the divine plan for men's salvation. This is not a side issue. It is the very heart of the story.

One way John does this is to show that Jesus was sinless. The implication, of course, is that His death could not have been the penalty of personal demerit. John treats this both positively and negatively. Positively he records that Jesus said, 'I do always the things that are pleasing to him' (Jn. 8:29).[30] This is an assertion of a conformity to God's will which is both perfect and constant.

---

which has the form of unqualified obedience to the Father's will. Given such unity, every act which the Son performs is an act of the Father' (IFG, p. 327).

[29] J. E. Davey emphasizes the point, so that the main section of his book brings out Jesus' dependence on the Father (*The Jesus of St. John*, London, 1958).

[30] R. H. Strachan sees in this verse the 'moral supremacy' of Jesus. He prefers this term to 'sinlessness,' which is negative (*op. cit.*, pp. 213f.).

There is a remarkable scene depicted later in the same chapter when
Jesus asked, 'Which of you convicteth me of sin?' (Jn. 8:46). No
one took up the challenge.[31] Familiarity with the passage sometimes
prevents us from seeing that this is a very remarkable challenge indeed. We cannot imagine any other figure in the whole of history
making it. And if the issuing of the challenge is remarkable,
even more so is the failure of even bitter enemies to take it up.
Jesus' words show a perfectly cloudless and serene conscience.[32] The
absence of a reply shows that this corresponds to reality.

The same point comes out in the story of the man born blind. On
that occasion some of the Pharisees said that Jesus was not of God,
but John records the question others of them asked, 'How can a
man that is a sinner do such signs?' (Jn. 9:16). Once again there
is no answer. The fact of the miracles is clear. The absence of
sin is therefore established. There can be little doubt that John
understood this (and means his readers to understand it) in fuller
fashion than the Pharisees who spoke the words. They meant no
more than that Jesus was not conspicuously a sinner if He did
miracles of this kind. John means that Jesus was not a sinner in
any sense. He proceeds to bring the same point out a little later in
the same incident. The man who had been healed was told that the
leaders did not know where Jesus came from in contrast with Moses,
who came from God, as everyone knew. This provoked the retort,
'Why, herein is the marvel, that ye know not whence he is, and yet
he opened mine eyes. We know that God heareth not sinners:
but if any man be a worshipper of God, and do his will, him he
heareth' (Jn. 9:30f.). God certainly heard Jesus on this occasion,
runs the reasoning. Therefore Jesus is not a sinner. The repetition
is impressive. John does not want us to miss the point. Jesus was
the Sinless One. Therefore His death was the death of the Sinless
One. However it be understood, it must be understood this way.
Right to the end John stresses this point. He puts it on record that
three times over Pilate testified that he found no fault whatever
in the Prisoner who stood before him (Jn. 18:38; 19:4, 6). This
emphasis cannot be without point. We may infer, as does Dietrich

---

[31] Cf. J. H. Bernard, 'His hearers did not understand, of course, that Jesus
was literally χωρὶς ἁμαρτίας (Heb. 4:15); but they could prove nothing to the
contrary, and they knew it' (in loc.).

[32] Cf. F. Godet, 'The perfect holiness of Christ is proved in this passage,
not by the silence of the Jews, who might very well have ignored the sins of
their interlocutor, but by the assurance with which Jesus lays this question
before them. Without the immediate consciousness which Christ had of the
perfect purity of His life, and on the supposition that He was only a more
holy man than other men, a moral sense so delicate as that which such a
state would imply, would not have suffered the least stain to pass unnoticed,
either in His life, or in His heart' (in loc.).

Bonhoeffer, that sinlessness is a necessary qualification in One who is to bear the guilt of others.[33]

But despite His sinlessness Jesus knew that He was appointed unto death. When Lazarus was reported as very sick and Jesus proposed going to Bethany, the disciples reminded Him of the danger: 'the Jews were but now seeking to stone thee; and goest thou thither again?' (Jn. 11:8). They had no doubt about what a trip to the neighbourhood of Jesusalem meant for Jesus and those associated with Him at just that time. When they saw that He was determined to make the journey, Thomas urged his fellows not to forsake the Master in the grim words, 'Let us also go, that we may die with him' (Jn. 11:16). To go up, it was clear to all, meant death. And Jesus went up.

Jesus taught the disciples the necessity for His death by talking about the ear of wheat. 'Except a grain of wheat fall into the earth and die, it abideth by itself alone; but if it die, it beareth much fruit' (Jn. 12:24). This means that the indispensable condition of fruitfulness in the case of a grain is that it 'fall into the earth and die'. And the indispensable condition in the case of One who would bear fruit among men is similar. He must die. So Jesus could not pray that the Father would save Him from death. Death was the very purpose of His coming into the world. 'Now is my soul troubled,' He said, 'and what shall I say? Father, save me from this hour. But for this cause came I unto this hour' (Jn. 12:27). There was no avoiding that for which He had come into the world. This same troubling of soul in the prospect of death is found in John 13:21, where Jesus speaks of His betrayal by Judas.[34] This is the Johannine equivalent of the strand of Synoptic teaching in which Jesus shrinks from that death wherein He is identified with sinners. But this is the way whereby Jesus will accomplish His appointed task.[35]

---

[33] He says, 'As one who acts responsibly in the historical existence of men Jesus becomes guilty. It must be emphasized that it is solely His love which makes Him incur guilt. From His selfless love, from His freedom from sin, Jesus enters into the guilt of men and takes this guilt upon Himself. Freedom from sin and the question of guilt are inseparable in Him. It is as the one who is without sin that Jesus takes upon Himself the guilt of His brothers, and it is under the burden of this guilt that He shows Himself to be without sin' (*Ethics*, London, 1955, p. 210). Or again, 'real innocence shows itself precisely in a man's entering into the fellowship of guilt for the sake of other men' (*loc. cit.*).

[34] John says ἐταράχθη τῷ πνεύματι. This is not serenity, but dread. What Jesus faced was no ordinary death, but something full of horror.

[35] Cf. Lord Charnwood, 'He is represented, and beyond all reasonable doubt truly represented, in this passage, with the foreknowledge suddenly made full, of torture and ignominy and death immediately before Him, and with the resolute conviction that somehow this is His success' (*According to Saint John*, London, n. d., p. 107).

The divine necessity for Jesus' death underlies the conversation Jesus had with the governor. Pilate, conscious of his supreme position as holding the power of life and death in his hands, said to his Prisoner, when He did not make answer as Pilate thought He should, 'knowest thou not that I have power to release thee, and have power to crucify thee?' But Jesus replied, 'Thou wouldest have no power against me, except it were given thee from above' (Jn. 19:10f.). But clearly this power was given Pilate 'from above', for he proceeded to sentence Jesus and send Him forth to death. It is impossible to avoid the implication that God's hand is to be discerned in Christ's death.

We should take notice of a remarkable series of passages dealing with Jesus' 'hour' or His 'time'. These begin in the story of the wedding at Cana, when Jesus says to His mother, 'mine hour is not yet come' (Jn. 2:4). They continue in Jesus' words to His brothers, 'My time is not yet come', 'my time is not yet fulfilled' (Jn. 7:6, 8). His enemies could not arrest Him at the feast 'because his hour was not yet come' (Jn. 7:30). Exactly the same reason is given for their not arresting Him 'in the treasury, as he taught in the temple' (Jn. 8:20). But with the cross in immediate prospect, Jesus could say, 'The hour is come', 'for this cause came I unto this hour' (Jn. 12:23, 27; similar expressions recur in Jn. 13:1; 16:32; 17:1). This catena of passages is unobtrusive, but nonetheless convincing for that. From the very beginning, John makes it clear that there was an appointed hour for Jesus. Till that hour came He was perfectly safe. He could not die. He could not even be arrested. He was safe from men. But when His hour was come, nothing could prevent His death. The Gospel moves inevitably, remorselessly, to its predetermined climax.

As in the New Testament writings generally, the death of Christ is seen as a fulfilment of Scripture.[36] John sees even comparatively minor details of the passion as foreshadowed in the prophecies of Scripture. The fact that there was a traitor among the Twelve fulfilled Psalm 41:9. John brings this out by reporting that Jesus excluded Judas from the scope of certain things He was saying about the other apostles with the words, 'I speak not of you all: I know whom I have chosen: but that the scripture may be fulfilled, He that

---

[36] R. H. Strachan cites Burkitt, 'The argument from Prophecy is ultimately an attempt to show that the life and mission of Jesus was no Divine freak or caprice, but a part of a well-ordered whole. To the pious Jew, the utterances of the Prophets had very much the same place in their idea of the world as what we call the laws of Nature have for us: they were things which had been formulated by men, yet they were not constituted by man, but by God.' He adds, 'The Christian Church took over this conception of Prophecy. In the utterances of the prophets they heard the expression of God's eternal will and purpose' (op. cit., p. 260).

eateth my bread lifted up his heel against me' (Jn. 13:18).[37]   Similarly scripture was fulfilled in the soldiers' gambling for Jesus' seamless robe rather than tearing it into pieces (Jn. 19:24), in Jesus' thirst as He hung on the cross (Jn. 19:28), in the failure to break His legs, and in the piercing of His side (Jn. 19:36f.). Particularly important is the fulfilment of Isaiah 53:1, mentioned in John 12:38, for it shows that John, like the Synoptists, understood Christ to be the Suffering Servant.

Sometimes we get the thought that Jesus' own words were fulfilled.[38]   Thus the Jews refused to judge Him according to their own law, as Pilate suggested, and John tells us that this happened 'that the word of Jesus might be fulfilled, which he spake, signifying by what manner of death he should die' (Jn. 18:32).

Both the fulfilment of scripture and the fulfilment of Jesus' own words yield the thought of a death which took place according to the will of God.   John's emphasis on minute details indicates that he thought of God as watching over everything that took place.   Nothing escaped Him, and nothing was too small for Him to be concerned with it.   All must be done, and all was done exactly according to His will.   This was the divinely ordained way whereby men must be saved.

THE SAVIOUR OF THE WORLD

Because it is God who is working out His purpose in the events associated with Calvary, and because there is but one God, the salvation there wrought out is effective for all mankind.   Thus Christ is spoken of not in terms of any restricted group, but of all mankind.   The Samaritan believers refer to Him as 'indeed the Saviour of the world' (Jn. 4:42).   John tells us explicitly that 'God sent not the Son into the world to judge the world; but that the world should be saved through him' (Jn. 3:17).   Christ's 'flesh' is given (undoubtedly a reference to Calvary) 'for the life of the world' (Jn. 6:51).   Universality is implied moreover in the reference to the 'other sheep' which are 'not of this fold', but of whom Christ could say, 'I lay down my life for the sheep' (Jn. 10:15f.).   At the very least this extends the mission of Jesus beyond the Jewish nation, and once started on the Gentiles who is to say where it will

---

[37] 'The quotation would not only strengthen Jesus' own soul, but it would be of apologetic use to the church as showing that even Judas' treachery was not outside the horizon of God's providence' (R. H. Strachan, *op. cit.*, p. 269).

[38] Cf. J. H. Bernard, John 'twice comments on recorded words of Jesus in the same way; that is, he speaks of them as if they were inevitable of fulfilment, like words of Scripture' (*The Gospel according to St. John*, I. C. C., i, New York, 1929, p. clv).

end?[39] John's comment on Caiaphas' unconscious prophecy is revealing, 'he prophesied that Jesus should die for the nation; and not for the nation only, but that he might also gather together into one the children of God that are scattered abroad' (Jn. 11:51f.). John saw potential 'children of God' scattered throughout the world. And the means whereby they would be brought together into their rightful place is the death of the Saviour.[40] Nothing less is implied by Jesus' statement, 'I, if I be lifted up from the earth, will draw all men unto myself' (Jn. 12:32). This is not the propagation of a doctrine of universalism, but it does mean that there are many who are to be drawn to the Christ. We draw a similar conclusion from the reference to giving 'eternal life' to as many as God has given Him in the same breath as the assurance that He has been given 'authority over all flesh' (Jn. 17:2). These words mean that Jesus will give life to men of all nations, and the preceding statement, 'the hour is come', links this with the cross. And this is implied surely in the 'whosoever' of passages like John 3:16, 'whosoever believeth on him should not perish, but have eternal life'. 'Whosoever' is wide enough to include anyone at all, not only the members of one nation.

From all this it is clear enough that John thought of Jesus as the Saviour of all those who are saved. His saving act is God's saving act. John has a wide vision. He sees the whole world as in need of salvation, and as coming within the scope of what was done on Calvary. Christ's work was bigger than Judaism. It occupied a larger canvas than any one nation could supply. It meant hope for all men and all nations.

It meant also that there was no hope for any man outside of Christ.

CHRIST THE SOURCE OF LIFE

One of the great themes of the Fourth Gospel is that of life, divine life, divine life made available for men. And everywhere that life is

[39] 'Here is opened up the vast panorama of the mission to the Gentiles, to which the Evangelist returns at the conclusion of the gospel under the imagery of *fish* and *sheep* and *lambs* (xxi. 1-17 . . .). The mission is the mission of Jesus. They are His sheep, led by Him from wheresoever they may hitherto have been confined . . . . The whole company of the faithful, whatever may have been their original condition, shall form one flock, because all are under the care of one shepherd. There is no other bond of union' (Hoskyns, *op. cit.,* p. 378).

[40] Cf. C. J. Wright, 'the death of Jesus was to be fruitful in a way none of the priests in His day ever dreamed . . . . (Caiaphas') words are pregnant with a meaning which was true, both to the conscious mission of Jesus and to the experience of His disciples. That mission was for the spiritual well-being, not of one nation only, but of all nations. The Cross, which consummated that mission, would be a message to all the scattered families of men; and would gather them "into one" . . . . The unifying power of humanity will be the Cross, and all for which it stands' (*op. cit.,* pp. 263ff.).

associated with Christ.[41]   John knows nothing of any life worthy of the name which is not a life in Christ and with Christ and from Christ.   As early as the fourth verse of the first chapter we read, 'In him was life; and the life was the light of men'.   The theme thus prominently set forth in the Prologue is developed throughout the Gospel.

First let us notice the way this life is persistently associated with Christ and the Father.   Indeed, there is something of a definition of this life in Christ's great high priestly prayer, 'this is life eternal, that they should know thee the only true God, and him whom thou didst send, even Jesus Christ' (Jn. 17:3).[42]   Life is the gift of Christ (Jn. 6:33; 10:28; 17:2).   This is probably the meaning also of the expression in which men are enjoined: 'Work not for the meat which perisheth, but for the meat which abideth unto eternal life, which the Son of man shall give unto you' (Jn. 6:27).   They who 'hear' him, even the dead, will live (Jn. 5:25).   Men get life by coming to Christ (Jn. 6:35) and they do not get life when they will not come to Him (Jn. 5:40).   Seeing Him (Jn. 6:40) and hearing Him (Jn. 5:24) are likewise linked with life.

But that which above all is said to be the cause of life is believing in Christ.   Believing is linked with the seeing and hearing mentioned in the last two passages cited.   God gave His Son so that 'whosoever believeth on him should not perish, but have eternal life' (Jn. 3:16), while in the discourse on the Bread of Life Jesus said simply, 'He that believeth hath eternal life' (Jn. 6:47).   Again, He could assure Martha, 'he that believeth on me, though he die, yet shall he live' (Jn. 11:25; cf. also 3:14f., 36).   John brings this matter of believing into

[41] C. K. Barrett makes essentially this point when he says, 'What John perceived with far greater clarity than any of his predecessors was that Jesus *is* the Gospel, and that the Gospel *is* Jesus.   It was through the life, and especially through the death and resurrection, of Jesus that men had been admitted to the blessings of the messianic kingdom, and the highest blessing of that kingdom was, as Paul had already seen, the life of communion with Christ Himself: "for me, to live is Christ" (Phil. 1:21).   That is, when the Gospel was offered to men it was Christ himself who was offered to them, and received by them' (*op. cit.*, p. 58).

[42] Cf. William Temple, 'We constantly miss the spiritual value of the greatest religious phrases by failing to recall their true meaning.   At one time I was much troubled that the climax of the *Veni Creator* should be

Teach us to know the Father, Son,
And Thee, of Both, to be but One.

It seemed to suggest that the ultimate purpose of the coming of the Holy Spirit was to persuade us of the truth of an orthodox formula.   But that is mere thoughtlessness.   If a man once knows the Spirit within him, the source of all his aspiration after holiness, as indeed the Spirit of Jesus Christ, and if he knows this Spirit of Jesus Christ within himself as none other than the Spirit of the Eternal and Almighty God, what more can he want? *This is the eternal life*' (*op. cit.*, p. 310).

his statement of his purpose in writing his Gospel at all (Jn. 20:31). He wrote in order that men might believe that Jesus is the Christ, and believing have eternal life. It is central to his understanding of things and not on the periphery. Negatively, men will not get life, but will die in their sins if they do not believe (Jn. 8:24).

Other expressions may be used which amount to much the same. For example, Jesus speaks of men eating His flesh and drinking His blood if they are to obtain life (Jn. 6:54), or more simply of eating Him: 'he that eateth me, he also shall live because of me' (Jn. 6:57). So also following Him is to have 'the light of life' (Jn. 8:12). Such passages mean essentially that men must be in right relationship to Christ if they are to be the recipients of the life of which He speaks.[43]   And the right relationship is that of faith. Sometimes this is linked with Christ's 'words'. Thus when many went back and ceased to be Christ's followers and the Lord challenged the little band with, 'Would ye also go away?' Peter's magnificent response was, 'Lord, to whom shall we go? thou hast the words of eternal life' (Jn. 6:67f.). On the surface of it, 'words' is a curious term to use in this connection. But Jesus has just said, 'the words that I have spoken unto you are spirit, and are life' (v. 63), and earlier He said that the dead would hear Him and live (Jn. 5:25). Later He told the Jews, 'If a man keep my word, he shall never see death' (Jn. 8:51f.), and again, that the Father's commandment 'is life eternal' (Jn. 12:50). All this appears to be a way of emphasizing the newness and the complete reliability of the teaching of Jesus about life. He was not merely enunciating what all men took for granted, so His words had to be noted. But those words were entirely reliable, so that heeding them led to eternal life. To believe the words was to trust the speaker. In other words these passages, too, imply the necessity for believing in Christ. There is no other way to life.[44]

Sometimes Jesus uses imagery which brings out the fact and meaning of this life. We have already noticed in another connection His discussion with Nicodemus, the Pharisee leader, on divine rebirth.

---

[43] Cf. G. Smeaton, 'the words, "eating the flesh and drinking the blood" of Christ for life, announce that we do not bring, but receive; that we do not work for life, but enter into a finished work, the already accomplished death of Christ' (*The Doctrine of the Atonement as Taught by Christ Himself*, Grand Rapids, 1953, p. 280).

[44] 'Eternal life is simply *the life*, — the life which is truly such, — life after the divine ideal. It is realized by coming into right relations to God. Entrance into these relations and the maintenance of them may be called by various terms, such as faith, obedience, fellowship, love. They all mean the same thing, or various aspects of the same thing' (G. B. Stevens, *op. cit.*, p. 231).

There we were concerned with the priority of the divine in salvation, here with the similar truth that life comes as Christ's gift. The way into the Kingdom is the way of rebirth, birth from above. And birth means life. Those who have been born into the heavenly family have life that those outside know nothing of. For the first time they know that life that is life indeed. Or again, Jesus may speak of 'living' water. As He spoke to the woman of Samaria He said, 'If thou knewest the gift of God, and who it is that saith to thee, Give me to drink; thou wouldest have asked of him, and he would have given thee living water' (Jn. 4:10). In any one who drinks of it this water will become 'a well of water springing up unto eternal life' (v. 14). The imagery is unusual. 'Living water' among the Jews of the time usually denoted water in motion (for example, in a stream), over against stagnant water (which we see in a pond). Moreover where they employed the symbolism of water, it was generally to point men to the Law.[45] Jesus' statement was quite new. We get a little further light a little later, when, after Jesus refers to 'living water' once more, John adds an explanation: 'this spake he of the Spirit, which they that believed on him were to receive: for the Spirit was not yet given; because Jesus was not yet glorified' (Jn. 7:39). From this we see that the life is the gift of Jesus, and that it is linked with His atoning work. We also see in the imagery of 'springing up' something of the vigor of the new life, and in the assurance that whoever drinks of the living water will never thirst (Jn. 4:14) evidence of its permanently satisfying character.

In a discourse full of rich symbolism Jesus describes Himself as 'the true bread' (Jn. 6:32), 'the bread of life' (vv. 35, 48),[46] 'the bread which cometh down out of heaven' (v. 50), 'the living bread which came down out of heaven' (v. 51). He also repeatedly invites men to partake of this bread (vv. 51, 54, 57). Bread was the staple article of diet in Palestine of that day, and language of this kind points us to Jesus as the continual Sustenance for the souls of those who come to Him. The allegory points to the completely satisfying nature of the life that Christ gives (v. 35), and we are told that the life that is given thereby is a life from which men do not die (v. 50). There are references to the giving of the flesh of Christ which should not be overlooked: 'the bread which I will give is my flesh, for the life of the world' (v. 51). Nor

---

[45] See H. L. Strack and P. Billerbeck, *Kommentar zum Neuen Testament aus Talmud und Midrasch,* ii, München, 1924, pp. 433-6.

[46] 'The words "I am the bread of life" reveal that the Lord Himself is the gift which He brings. The genitive is qualitative, as is shown by the synonym "living bread" . . . but the expression should be understood as including the power to bring life into being; life proceeds from life' (R. H. Lightfoot, *St. John's Gospel,* Oxford, 1957, p. 167).

should that to His flesh and blood in separation (vv. 53 etc.).
There are certain difficulties here and some points will remain uncertain. But what is beyond doubt is that such words point us
to the death of Christ. The life that He would give is purchased at
the cost of His own life.

This point is made elsewhere. Life through death is one of
John's great themes. The discussion on the new birth leads on
into a statement of the atonement, 'as Moses lifted up the serpent
in the wilderness, even so must the Son of man be lifted up: that
whosoever believeth may in him have eternal life' (Jn. 3:14f.).
We have seen that the 'bread of life' discourse carries the thought
of the death of Christ. So does that of the Good Shepherd. Jesus
says that He came 'that they may have life, and may have it
abundantly' and immediately goes on, 'I am the good shepherd:
the good shepherd layeth down his life for the sheep' (Jn. 10:10f.).[47]
The miracle of the raising of Lazarus which sets forth Christ as
the great Giver of life, as One supreme over death, leads in logical
sequence (the chief priests and others 'therefore' gathered together)
to the council at which Caiaphas laid down the necessity that one
man should die for the people (Jn. 11:50). Jesus spoke of the
grain of wheat. Unless it 'fall into the earth and die, it abideth by
itself alone; but if it die, it beareth much fruit' (Jn. 12:24). The
context makes it plain that the primary reference is to His own
death.[48] It is clear that in this Gospel the death of Christ is
closely linked with the gift of life in Christ. Our life is purchased
at the cost of His death.

Let us notice two more points. The first is that the life is linked
with Christ in the most thoroughgoing fashion. Twice He said
that He *is* life. To Martha He said, 'I am the resurrection, and
the life' (Jn. 11:25), and to the disciples in the upper room, 'I am
the way, and the truth, and the life' (Jn. 14:6).[49] He has 'life
in himself' which is the gift of the Father and which is like the

---

[47] Cf. W. Lüthi, 'The servant protects the sheep, but in the end he runs
away because his own life is worth more to him than the animals in his care.
That is his right as a hireling. But the shepherd who owns the sheep does not
run away. He is prepared to protect what belongs to him with his very life'
(*St. John's Gospel,* Edinburgh, 1960, p. 133).

[48] The context also includes a voice from heaven, and H. C. Mabie points
out that on each of the three occasions when the Gospels record a heavenly
voice there is some reference to Christ's death: at the baptism in the river
Jordan it was symbolically enacted, on the mount of transfiguration it was
the theme of the conversation with Moses and Elijah, and here it runs right
through Jesus' discourse (*How Does the Death of Christ Save Us?* London,
1908, pp. 49ff.).

[49] James P. Berkeley points out that in these words Jesus offers Himself, and
that the offer calls for a personal response (*Reading the Gospel of John,*
Philadelphia, 1958, pp. 187f.).

life which the Father has, also 'in himself' (Jn. 5:26).[50] He lives
'because of the Father' (Jn. 6:57). All this stresses the uniqueness
of the life that He gives. No one else is in a position to give life,
for no one else has life in this way. So it is that believers live because He lives (Jn. 14:19). He gives life where He will (Jn. 5:21).

The final point is that the life Christ gives is 'eternal life'. The
adjective is not always supplied, but it is always implied. There
is no difference in this Gospel between 'life' as a gift of Christ
and 'eternal life'. 'Eternal' is the adjective derived from the Greek
word for 'age'. But the age in question is not this present age,
but the age to come, so that the adjective means 'pertaining to the
age to come'. One aspect of this age is that it does not end, and
thus John sometimes refers to men as living for ever (Jn. 6:51,
58), or as never dying (Jn. 8:51f.; 10:28; 11:26). He speaks of
the resurrection of life (Jn. 5:29), and of raising up certain
people at the last day (Jn. 6:39, 40, 44, 54). This aspect of such
life is obviously important to John, but it is equally clear that he
does not think of it as the only thing, or even the most important
thing. When he speaks of life as knowing the Father and the Son
(Jn. 17:3) it is obvious that it is a quality rather than a quantity of
life that is in mind.[51] This is apparent in such a passage as John
15 with its frequent references to 'abiding' in Christ. Though it
is a present possession of the believer (note the tense in such a
passage as Jn. 5:24), the significant thing about eternal life is that
it is the life that is appropriate to the coming age. It is no mere
earthly gift.

THE SAVIOUR LIFTED UP

We have already noticed the unusual expression in John 3:14,
where there is a reference to Christ's being 'lifted up'. We see
it again in John 12:32, 'And I, if I be lifted up from the earth,

[50] Cf. E. C. Colwell and E. L. Titus, 'To understand the nature of eternal
life it is necessary to keep in mind that for the fourth evangelist Jesus is God.
The life which resides in him is essential, elemental life.' They go on to quote
Jn. 1:12f. and say, 'Belief in Jesus makes possible this birth from above, this
change of nature, this sharing in the nature of Christ and God' (*The Gospel
of the Spirit*, New York, 1953, p. 174).

[51] Barclay reminds us that endless life could as easily be hell as heaven.
'The idea behind eternal life is the idea of a certain quality, a certain kind
of life. What kind of life? There is only one person who can properly be
described by this adjective eternal (*aiōnios*) and that one person is God.
Eternal life is the kind of life that God lives; it is God's life. To enter into
eternal life is to enter into possession of that kind of life which is the life
of God. It is to be lifted up above merely human, temporary, passing,
transient things, into that joy and peace which belong only to God' (*op. cit.,*
i, p. 118).

will draw all men unto myself'. The addition of 'from the earth' to the being 'lifted up' indicates plainly that it is not a metaphorical lifting up that is meant, but a physical one. In fact, it is a reference to being lifted up on the cross.[52] To make quite sure that the point is grasped John adds, 'this he said, signifying by what manner of death he should die.' This meaning is clear also in John 8:28, where Jesus says to His enemies, 'When ye have lifted up the Son of man, then shall ye know that I am he, and that I do nothing of myself'. For the only way the enemies of Jesus would lift Him up would be on the cross. They would have no interest in 'exalting' Him. It is true that the addition 'then shall ye know . . .' indicates that the 'lifting up' has a revelatory function. It shows Jesus to be what He really is. But this does not affect the fact that the 'lifting up' means the crucifixion. Until the cross what Jesus was was not fully known. Only in the cross was He truly revealed in His essential character and being.

In modern times men often speak of 'lifting up' Jesus in other senses. The expression is frequently used of Christ-centered preaching, for example. This is a perfectly intelligible and legitimate use of language, but we must beware of reading it back into John's story. There the 'lifting up' applies strictly to the lifting up on the cross.

And yet John was probably not unmindful of the fact that the verb could be used of exaltation in the sense of ascribing to a person an exalted place. Indeed, this double use of the term may explain why John uses it in the way he does.[53] For 'lifting up' is not really a natural or unambiguous way of referring to crucifixion. But it is quite a habit of John's to use words which might be understood in more ways than one. And he thinks of Jesus as exalted, indeed. Though He was so lowly to outward appearance, yet the seal of the Father's approval rested upon Him. This happened at the baptism, when the Spirit descended upon Him as the Father had said (Jn. 1:33). Indeed, it can be said to have happened in all the witness that the Father bore to Him (Jn. 5:37), and of which this Gospel is so full. It happened at the voice from heaven which perplexed

[52] J. C. Ryle says the words mean 'that the death of Christ on the cross would have a drawing effect on all mankind. His death as our Substitute, and the Sacrifice for our sins, would draw multitudes out of every nation to believe on Him and receive Him as their Saviour. By being crucified for us, and not by ascending a temporal throne, He would set up a kingdom in the world, and gather subjects to Himself' (*in loc.*).

[53] Cf. C. K. Barrett, 'In Mark the suffering and glorification are chronologically distinguished; in John one word is used to express both. ὑψοῦν has this double meaning at each place in the gospel in which it is used, and further it is always used of the Son of man' (*op. cit.*, pp. 178f.) 'Jesus was lifted up in execution on the cross and thereby exalted in glory' (*op. cit.*, p. 356).

some people (Jn. 12:28). John is in no doubt that Jesus is a glorious Being. And the crucifixion does not alter this in any way. The crucifixion is no denial of the exaltation of Jesus. In fact, paradoxically, the crucifixion *is* the exaltation. Though to men it might seem the very depth of degradation, yet in His humiliation the Son of God made life available to men. His humiliation was the means to their salvation. The hour of His suffering is thus paradoxically the hour of His greatest glory. The glory may be hidden from the sons of men. But the glory is there nonetheless. In the fullest sense, the exaltation took place when the Son of God died for sinful men. John sees nothing to apologize for in the cross.

Sometimes he sees it in terms of glory. To some it might be so repulsive as to be a stumblingblock, but to him it is glorious as nothing else is glorious.[54] Glory is another of the great themes of the Gospel.[55] As with other dominant motifs, it is introduced in the Prologue where John speaks of seeing Christ's glory, 'glory as of the only begotten from the Father' (Jn. 1:14). This glory is seen in the earthly life of Jesus, as, for example, in the miracle at Cana when He 'manifested his glory' (Jn. 2:11). He did not receive glory from men (Jn. 5:41), but contrasted this with 'the glory that cometh from the only God' (v. 44). Lazarus' sickness was 'for the glory of God, that the Son of God may be glorified thereby' (Jn. 11:4). But preeminently the glory is seen in the cross. With Calvary in immediate prospect Jesus says, 'The hour is come, that the Son of man should be glorified' (Jn. 12:23).[56] The idea that the death of Christ is supremely glory dominates this particular section of the narrative (Jn. 12:16, 28, 41). And likewise, when the traitor went out to do what might well be thought of as his foul business, Jesus could say, 'Now is the Son of man glorified, and God is glorified in him' (Jn. 13:31).[57] For John the thoughts of

---

[54] Cf. William Barclay, 'Jesus came to the Jews with a new view of life. They looked on glory as conquest, the acquisition of power, the right to rule. He looked on glory as a cross. He taught men that only by death comes life; that only by spending life do we retain life; that only by service comes greatness' (*op. cit.,* ii, p. 145). But even this misses the point that the glorious salvation of God is realized through the death of His only Son.

[55] Cf. the two articles by Paula von Mirtow, 'The Glory of Christ in the Fourth Gospel', *Theology,* xlix, pp. 336-40, 359-65.

[56] D. M. Mackinnon sees this as Christ's acceptance of all that was to follow, 'The hour of Jesus in the upper room is presented by John as an hour of glory. . . . if there is anything in my interpretation, it can be seen as the hour of Jesus' absolute self-giving to which the resurrection is the crown. What immediately follows, betrayal, mockery, trial and death, is in the upper room embraced and taken by Christ into the very substance of his being' (*Studies in the Gospels,* ed. D. E. Nineham, Oxford, 1955, p. 204).

[57] 'The "glorifying" of Jesus always means His dying (xiii. 31). It is God Who thus glorifies Him, and in His dying God Himself is glorified. The Cross is the complete manifestation of God's glory, revealing His goodness or

the lifting up of Jesus, of His exaltation, and of His glory are all intertwined. But none of them is explicable except in terms of the cross. There, and there only, is the true glory to be seen.

A CONFLICT WITH EVIL

The imagery of light and darkness is used in the Fourth Gospel to great effect. Once again we go to the Prologue for the enunciation of the thought. There we read that 'the light shineth in the darkness; and the darkness apprehended it not' (Jn. 1:5). There is some dispute as to the exact meaning to be assigned to the Greek word translated 'apprehended',[58] but it seems to me that it ought to be rendered by 'overcame' or the like. John is thinking of light and darkness as locked in bitter conflict. The darkness strives against the light. The darkness tries to extinguish the light. But the darkness is not successful. The light 'shineth' (present tense) in the darkness.[59] Precisely there. The light, which this Gospel shows to be Christ, is victorious against the darkness. There are many places in this Gospel where Christ is linked with light. Preeminently He is 'the light of the world' (Jn. 8:12). All such references, in view of the Prologue, are probably to be taken as referring in part at least to this conflict. Christ is the Light. His mission is to combat darkness. Wherever He encounters it, He dispels it.

Another aspect of the conflict comes before us in the Prologue. There we read that the Word 'came unto his own, and they that were his own received him not' (Jn. 1:11). His very own people would have nothing to do with Him. This conflict, too, runs through the Gospel.[60] As John unfolds his story, he shows us how 'the Jews' are in perpetual opposition to Jesus. They resist

---

love to the utmost . . .' (R. H. Strachan, *op. cit.,* p. 106). Or again, ' "Glory" in this Gospel is God in action through Jesus Christ, bringing the whole "weight" or riches (*kābôd*) of the love of the Father to bear on the world of men' (*loc. cit.*).

[58] The verb is κατέλαβεν. This verb means basically to lay hold on something so that it becomes one's own. It is used in this way of 'obtaining' or 'attaining' the prize (1 Cor. 9:24). From this arise translations like that of RV. But such meanings do not readily fit into this context. John does not usually picture darkness as trying to understand light but as warring with it. Thus the less usual (but attested) meaning 'overcame' seems required.

[59] Cf. B. F. Westcott, 'The relation of darkness to light is one of essential antagonism . . . . The existence of the darkness is affirmed, and at the same time the unbroken energy of the light. But the victory of the light is set forth as the result of a past struggle; and the abrupt alteration of tense brings into prominence the change which has passed over the world' (*in loc.*).

[60] Lord Charnwood sees this as a major interest. John is occupied 'with a double theme, how Jesus Christ was rejected by the mass of those who should have been "His own," and what He imparted to the few who "received Him." The two central acts, as it were, of his drama are respectively concerned in the main with the two sides of this contrast' (*op. cit.,* p. 105).

Him at every turn. They seek to hinder Him in His mission. They try to thwart His purposes. They more than once try to arrest Him. And eventually they bring about His death.

Sometimes this opposition is set before us in strange ways. Thus even when Jesus won a temporary popularity the opposition is still to be seen on a deep level. After the feeding of the multitude on the loaves and the fishes they said, 'This is of a truth the prophet that cometh into the world' (Jn. 6:14). But this does not mean acceptance of Jesus. In the next verse we read of their trying to make a King out of Jesus, but this is not acceptance either. Their idea of a King was a King concerned with food and armies and pomp and splendour. In their apparent acceptance of Jesus, even enthusiasm for Him, there is a deep-seated rejection of all that He really stood for. They were interested not in His purposes but in their own. John shows for us a picture of Jesus ceaselessly at work doing the will of the Father, and as ceaselessly being rejected in this capacity, however He might be sought out for other reasons.

Another aspect of the struggle comes before us in such a passage as John 3:19, 'This is the judgement, that the light is come into the world, and men loved the darkness rather than the light; for their works were evil'. John sees Satan as actively at work among men. Satan continually tempts them to do his wicked will. Some men yield to him so continually that he may be said to be their father (Jn. 8:44). And if in the end men come under condemnation ('judgement'), then it is because they have heeded his blandishments, because in the last resort they preferred the darkness of sin and of Satan to the light of Christ. Moreover, John does not see their decisions as isolated, individual, insignificant happenings. They are stages in the age-old struggle between good and evil. They are episodes in Christ's conflict with the evil one. Men aid the powers of darkness, or they support the cause of Christ.

Especially does John see the conflict raging in connection with the death of Christ on Calvary. With the cross in immediate prospect Jesus can say, 'Now is the judgment of this world: now shall the prince of this world be cast out' (Jn. 12:31). The treachery of Judas is viewed in this light. It was Satan who put the desire into his heart (Jn. 13:2). Satan entered Judas (Jn. 13:27). When Judas went out from the Upper Room, John adds the detail that 'it was night' (Jn. 13:30). It was night round about the men in the Upper Room (though night mitigated by the flickering light of the lamps). It was night over the city of Jerusalem (though night illuminated by the shining of the Paschal full moon). And it was night, unrelieved black night in the heart of Judas Iscariot.[61]

---

[61] Cf. J. S. Billings, 'The dramatic phrase ἦν δὲ νύξ is surely a peep into the black soul of Judas, and an indication that the Evil One needs blackness

John sees the struggle carried on upon the cross. Indeed, there it comes to its climax. With respect to His death Jesus said, 'the prince of the world cometh' (Jn. 14:30). At Calvary the very powers of hell were arrayed against Him. But the victory was not with Satan and darkness and death. The victory was with Christ and light and life.[62] To the world, no doubt, it seemed that Christ was defeated. Nothing seems further from victory than a corpse on a cross. Small wonder that even to the disciples it seemed that evil was triumphant as the prophecy of Jesus was fulfilled that they would be scattered and leave Him alone (Jn. 16:32), and that other that they would weep and lament while the world rejoiced (Jn. 16:20; cf. Jn. 20:11, and the reference to their fear of the Jews in Jn. 20:19). But of that death Jesus had already said, 'the prince of this world hath been judged' (Jn. 16:11). 'Judged' here is used in an Old Testament sense which conveys the thought of victory over an enemy. In the ancient scriptures the basic thought in judgment is that of discrimination followed by decisive action. This will mean vindicating those who are in the right and punishing those who are in the wrong. We see a good example of this latter use in the request of Ahimaaz the son of Zadok that he might bear tidings to David 'how that the Lord hath avenged him (mg. judged him from the hand) of his enemies' (2 Sa. 18:19). To 'judge' a wicked man was to overthrow his purposes, to defeat his cunning plans. It was to vindicate the right. It was in this way that Jesus 'judged' Satan on Calvary. He completely defeated him and overthrew his purposes. That action, which to the outward eye seemed Satan's complete victory, in reality represented his complete overthrow. Whatever else Calvary may mean, in one aspect it is the defeat of all the forces of evil.

---

to carry out his work. In writing it, St. John must have recollected how our Lord had called Himself "the Light of the World"; and he points the contrast' (ET, li, p. 156). Billings thinks of Judas, as this Gospel depicts him, as being the incarnation of the Evil One, but this is going too far.

[62] Karl Heim reminds us of the antinomy, so strongly stressed by Luther, 'God acts in Satan. The devil is God's devil. God has given him his power. . . . And yet we must not detract from the fact that the satanic power is God's mortal enemy, that is to say not merely an intermediate stage on the way to the divine end of the world but the radically evil against which a total war must be waged' (*Jesus the World's Perfecter*, Edinburgh and London, 1959, p. 38). On the cross, as nowhere else, do we see the radical opposition and the supremacy of God. Heim later goes on to suggest that here is where we find the central truth in the atonement: 'the victory over God's mortal enemy must not appear as a mere subsidiary result of the doctrine of reconciliation . . . . On the contrary this ultimate aim of Jesus' struggle must provide the central content for the whole interpretation of the Cross. Everything else that we have to say by way of explanation must be subordinated to this leading aspect' (*op. cit.*, p. 70).

The defeat is brought to its consummation in the resurrection. John brings this note into his Gospel quite early, when he records Jesus' words to the Jews, 'Destroy this temple, and in three days I will raise it up' (Jn. 2:19). John goes on to speak of the way the Jews misunderstood these words, and then he gives the true explanation, 'he spake of the temple of his body' (v. 21). There are difficulties attaching to this prophecy, but what is quite clear is that John understands the words as referring to the resurrection. From the very beginning the issue of the conflict was never in doubt.[63] And as John begins his Gospel by making this point, so he rounds it off with the resurrection narratives. The empty tomb is described with its neatly folded graveclothes, and the effect on the beloved disciple is given: 'he saw, and believed' (Jn. 20:8). The resurrection appearances lead up to Thomas' magnificent cry of faith, 'My Lord and my God' (Jn. 20:28). For John there can be no doubt about the completeness of the victory won.

THE LOVE OF GOD IN CHRIST

That God is love is a precious truth, and one which is accepted throughout Christendom as practically axiomatic today. But the meaning we put into 'love' is not always that of the Bible writers. Modern men often confuse love with sentimentality, and they see love as a general benevolence which is interested in nothing other than happiness. If God is love, they feel, then He must be concerned with our happiness as with nothing else. It follows that we need not take sin very seriously, since to punish men for sin is certainly not to make them happy. Not only the popular notion of hell but every notion of hell is dismissed, since it is so difficult to fit it in with celestial benevolence.

John has a good deal to say about love.[64] It is clearly a most important idea for him. But his ideas on the subject must be understood according to his own expressions and not according to modern thought. And he relates love specifically to the cross. 'God so loved the world, that he gave his only begotten Son, that whosoever believeth on him should not perish, but have eternal life' (Jn. 3:16). 'Greater love hath no man than this, that a man lay down his

---

[63] J. Daniélou reminds us that this is a very different view from the one so popular in contemporary thought that we can expect progress only along the line of evolutionary processes. 'All evolutionary illusions are thus dissipated by one blow. Henceforth, no progress can carry us toward what we already possess in Christ, since in Him the goal beyond progress is already present' (SE, p. 27).

[64] G. B. Stevens quotes a saying of Augustine's concerning John, *Locutus est multa, sed prope omnia de caritate* (*The Christian Doctrine of Salvation,* Edinburgh, 1930, p. 281, n. 1).

life for his friends' (Jn. 15:13). 'Jesus knowing that his hour was come that he should depart out of this world unto the Father, having loved his own which were in the world, he loved them unto the end' (Jn. 13:1). In these three passages there is manifestly the thought that it is the cross which shows us the love. But the cross is not thought of as simply a demonstration of love. It is more than that. It is the means of bringing men life.[65] It saves men.[66] Apart from the cross they would 'perish'. In other words the cross which shows us the love of God is the very thing that shows us also the concern God has for righteousness, and the peril that men are in on account of their sin. Love, as John sees it, is not indiscriminate sentimentality. It has a due regard for moral purposes, and for the moral law that sinners have broken.

It has also a concern for the attitude of the beloved. 'He that hath my commandments, and keepeth them, he it is that loveth me,' said Jesus, 'and he that loveth me shall be loved of my Father, and I will love him . . .' (Jn. 14:21; so also 16:27). He told the disciples that He loved them as the Father loved Him, and urged them to abide in that love of His. How were they to do that? By keeping His commandments (Jn. 15:9f.).[67] This does not mean, of course, that God does not love all those whom He has created. We have already seen that He loves 'the world'. But these passages mean nothing unless they mean that our reaction to that love of God is significant. That unless there is the appropriate reaction we do not come within the shelter of its provision for men. Again there is the thought that God's love is not indifferent to moral considerations. However we understand the divine love we must not regard it as a way of taking sin lightly, as esteeming sin a thing that can simply be ignored.

Love is to be the characteristic thing about Jesus' followers. 'By this shall all men know that ye are my disciples, if ye have love one to another' (Jn. 13:35). This is not a truism; Jesus calls it 'a new commandment' that He lays upon them. Love of the kind that He displays, a love for sinners which at the same time does not condone the sin, but bears it and makes atonement for it, is a new thing in the world. Therefore the commandment that the disciples should love as Christ loved (Jn. 13:34) is radically new. Repeatedly love of the kind that Christ enjoins is linked with keeping His commandments (Jn. 14:15, 21, 23f.; 15:10). There is a

[65] 'The love of God is thrown into the sharpest relief as the initiating and effective cause of life and of forgiveness' (W. F. Howard, op. cit., p. 104).

[66] 'Salvation was conceived by the love of God. The Father planned salvation; the Son executed it; and the Holy Spirit applies it' (E. J. Carnell, 'Love', Baker's Dictionary of Theology, Grand Rapids, 1960, p. 332).

[67] Lofthouse speaks of the 'vital connection between love and obedience, as if the two were but different sides of the same thing' (op. cit., p. 219).

moral energy in love which is of the very essence of love as John understands it.[68]

All this means that when John thinks of the atonement as proceeding from the divine love he does not think of it along the lines of the 'moral' or 'subjective' theories. For him the love of God is seen in saving men from a very real danger. It copes with the situation posed by man's sin in such a way that neither the divine demand for righteousness nor the sinner's best interests are overlooked.

CHRIST OUR SUBSTITUTE

John puts a certain emphasis on the thought that in His death Jesus took the place of sinners. Let us notice, for example, the way he deals with the cynical remark of Caiaphas, 'it is expedient for you that one man should die for the people, and that the whole nation perish not' (Jn. 11:50). These words are spoken by a politician without illusions and without scruples. He urges upon the Sanhedrin the consideration that it is better by far that one man, however innocent, should die than that the whole nation be put in jeopardy. The death of Jesus is the logical conclusion.

But John records the words, not because he wants to show up Caiaphas for the cynical sinner he was, but because he sees in the words a fuller, deeper meaning. Christ did, indeed, die as Caiaphas said He should, and, because He did, the whole nation did not perish. But He died for the nation in a way that Caiaphas could not possibly understand. He died in place of the nation, and, says John, not in place of that nation only, but in that of the whole world. Caiaphas spoke out of a worldly-wise political realism, but John saw in the words an unconscious act of prophecy, a prophecy expressing the truth that Christ died as our Substitute. All men were under condemnation on account of their sin. But Christ took their place, and made a way of escape for them.[69] That John took this very

---

[68] Clayton R. Bowen emphasizes the Johannine stress on love within the brotherhood, and he deplores the lack of passages about love for outsiders ('Love in the Fourth Gospel', *Journal of Religion,* xiii, pp. 39-49). But of the love of which John speaks he says, 'There is, indeed, a truth, a practicality, a value, even a grandeur in this Johannine love within the household of faith' (*op. cit.,* p. 48).

[69] Cf. P. T. Forsyth, 'The consummation of this historic union of grace and judgment was in the death of Christ. And as the grace of God was on Christ, and not only through Christ on us, so also the judgment of God was on Christ and not only through Christ on us. That is the serious solemn point, disputed by many, and to be pressed only with a grave sense that it alone meets the moral demand of holiness and completes it. Christ not only exercises the judgment of God on us; He absorbs it, so that we are judged not only by Him but in Him. And so in Him we are judged unto salvation. "The chastisement of our peace was on Him" ' (PP, p. 314).

seriously is seen by his repetition of the statement, for, when later he wishes to speak of this same Caiaphas, once again he characterizes him with reference to this prophecy. 'Now Caiaphas was he which gave counsel to the Jews, that it was expedient that one man should die for the people' (Jn. 18:14).

The same truth is elsewhere expressed otherwise. For example, Jesus said, 'Greater love hath no man than this, that a man lay down his life for his friends' (Jn. 15:13). The words are capable of wide application. But, when Jesus spoke on the eve of the cruci- fixion of laying down His life for His friends, there can be little doubt but that He meant that He died in order that they might not die. In other words, He took their place. The language is not un- ambiguously substitutionary, but the thought of the passage, I think, is.

In this connection we should notice passages which refer to Christ's death in sacrificial terms. Thus in our Lord's high priestly prayer He said, 'for their sakes I sanctify myself' (Jn. 17:19). Now 'sanctify' is a term common in the sacrificial vocabulary of the day.[70] It means to set apart for sacrifice. When He uses the term, Christ is solemnly setting Himself apart as a sacrifice for men.

The thought that Christ's death was sacrificial is implied also in some words of John the Baptist, 'Behold, the Lamb of God, which taketh away the sin of the world!' (Jn. 1:29). While the precise mean- ing of this expression is in dispute,[71] and while cogent objections may be urged against a facile equation with any one of the sacrificial vic- tims (as the passover), yet some things are clear. John is referring to the death of Jesus[72] and to that death as a means of taking away sin.[73] Most students agree that he is thinking of that death in

---

[70] Cf. C. K. Barrett, 'The language is equally appropriate to the prepara- tion of a priest and the preparation of a sacrifice; it is therefore doubly ap- propriate to Christ' (in loc.). So also J. H. Bernard, 'In His death He was both Priest and Victim' (in loc.).

[71] Many hold the expression to refer to the passover, some think of a reference to Is. 53:7, or to the general idea of the Servant. Others suggest the lamb of the morning and evening burnt offerings, or the gentle lamb of Jer. 11:19, or the lamb Abraham thought of as provided by God (Gen. 22:8), or the triumphant lamb of the apocalypses. There is no shortage of suggestions, and more or less cogent arguments may be brought against them all. It seems likely that the expression is purposely vague, so as not to tie up the reference to one particular sacrifice, but rather to sum up all that is suggested by the various sacrifices.

[72] G. Florovsky, in his article, 'The Lamb of God' (SJT, iv, pp. 13-28), emphasizes this point. 'Salvation is completed on Golgotha, not on Tabor, and the Cross of Jesus was foretold even on Tabor (cf. Luke 9:31). The redeem- ing death is the ultimate purpose of the Incarnation' (op. cit., p. 20).

[73] The verb is αἴρω, the equivalent of the Hebrew נשׂא, on which T. J. Crawford comments, 'as used in this passage it is highly significant, implying that Christ took upon Himself the burden of our sin, and in this way removed

sacrificial terms. For my part, I am convinced that the term is vague of set purpose, so that the allusion is not to be tied down to any one sacrifice, be it passover, or sin offering, or any other.[74] It is a way of bringing before the mind the sacrificial system as a whole. What all the ancient sacrifices dimly foreshadowed, that Christ effectively accomplished.

Now this, to my mind, means substitution. Christ took our place, as the sacrificial victim took the place of the worshipper. I realize that the significance of sacrifice is widely disputed, and that there are some who reject any substitutionary aspect. Here there is no space to go into the matter fully. I can only state dogmatically that in my judgment sacrifice cannot be satisfactorily understood without including an aspect of substitution.[75] And as Christ died as our sacrifice, He died accordingly as our Substitute.

FAITH IN CHRIST

In John, as elsewhere in the New Testament, the saving work of Christ is appropriated by faith. Therefore believing in Christ is a fundamental concept for him, and he has a great deal to say about it. Strangely, this is sometimes overlooked or even denied outright, as when E. F. Scott maintains that John looks for 'the acceptance of a given dogma' rather than 'an inward disposition of trust and

---

it from us' (The Doctrine of Holy Scripture Respecting the Atonement, Edinburgh, 1871, p. 45).

[74] Alan Richardson takes a similar position, 'In the mind of Jews in NT days a multiple image would be found, and it is hardly possible to determine which of its components would be dominant in any particular NT passage in which Jesus is spoken of as a lamb or as the "Lamb of God". In all such cases, where a rich variety of images has contributed to NT usage, it is unwise to ask which of them is in the mind of the writer in any particular passage. They are probably all present, consciously or subconsciously' (An Introduction to the Theology of the New Testament, London, 1958, p. 226).

[75] This point is brought out by K. J. Foreman in his volume on Romans, I, II Corinthians (London, 1962) in the Layman's Bible Commentaries: 'Sacrifice is a complex problem, but it is clear that in the Old Testament the word had many meanings and intentions. The Early Church, following Paul's lead, singled out one of these as basic — namely, substitution. The one who made a sacrifice of a living animal imaginatively identified himself with the sacrifice. The killing of the beast signified the wrath of God; in other words, the repenting man felt he deserved to die — the universe would be better off if his own bad life were destroyed. But God allowed him to make the sacrifice as a substitute for himself. The purpose was not simply to wipe the slate clean, it was to give him a fresh start and restore him to fellowship with God. So Christ above all is the final and all-availing sacrifice which brings sinning man back to God' (op. cit., p. 31).

obedience'.[76]   Nothing could be further from the truth. John continually demands an attitude of love and trust and loyalty. He looks for men to give to Christ their wholehearted allegiance.[77] He speaks of their 'abiding' in Christ as well as of 'believing' in Him. We are not going too far when, with Vincent Taylor, we speak of 'mystical union with Christ'.[78]

Something that has not been satisfactorily explained is that John never uses the noun 'faith', though he uses the verb 'to believe' more than ninety times. Probably we should understand this, at least — that for John faith is something dynamic. It is not passive but active. Moreover, John sees it from various aspects, as we see from the variety of constructions he employs. Sometimes he speaks of 'believing that . . .', i.e. he gives us the content of faith. Or he may speak of believing εἰς, 'believing into', where faith, so to speak, takes a man out of himself and places him in Christ.[79] He may speak of believing Christ, or believing the Father, or of believing into the name of Christ. And so fundamental is faith that sometimes he speaks simply of believing. It would be unwise to place too hard and fast a distinction between these various constructions, but they should be noted, for they show us that for John faith is many-sided.

The passages which speak of 'believing that' are probably those that impress Scott. They should not be overlooked, and they do stress the fact that faith has content. It is not a general credulity. It is not a meaningless trust. John saw believers as men with definite convictions, finally held. Thus Peter could say, 'we have believed and know that thou art the Holy One of God' (Jn. 6:69), and this sets the pattern. John sees faith as connected with the person of Christ and with His relationship to the Father. Men must believe 'that I am he' (Jn. 8:24), that He is 'the Christ, the Son of God, even he that cometh into the world' (Jn. 11:27, so also

---

[76] He says, 'It is evident, however, even to a superficial reader, that the "believing" so constantly insisted on by John is something much narrower and poorer than the Pauline "faith." It implies not so much an inward disposition of trust and obedience, as the acceptance of a given dogma' (*op. cit.*, p. 267).

[77] Cf. B. W. Bacon, 'Neither here, nor in Paul, nor in the Epistle of James, is faith a mere matter of intellectual assent. In all cases its primary element is loyalty — personal adherence' (*The Gospel of the Hellenists*, New York, 1933, p. 342).

[78] 'Faith, in the Johannine sense . . . is mystical union with Christ, fellowship with Him, and, in 1 John, fellowship also with God or with the Father' (ANT, p. 139).

[79] James I. Packer speaks of this construction as 'conveying the thought of a movement of trust going out to, and laying hold of, the object of its confidence' ('Faith', *Baker's Dictionary of Theology*, Grand Rapids, 1960, p. 208).

20:31), that He is in the Father and the Father in Him (Jn. 14:10f.). Several times there are references to believing that Jesus 'came forth' from the Father, or was 'sent' by Him (Jn. 11:42; 16: 27, 30; 17:8, 21). It is important to be clear that faith is not some nebulous credulity, a trust in one knows not what. As John sees it, faith is essentially dependent on God, on the God who sent His Son.[80] Apart from that divine act and all its consequences faith would be meaningless.

But John does not stop there. He speaks repeatedly of believing 'in' or 'on' (εἰς) Christ (Jn. 3:18; 4:39; 7:31, 38f.; 17:20, etc.). This is John's characteristic construction. It is found in all 45 times in the New Testament, 37 of them being in John. As we have noted, the thought is that of the faith that takes one out of one-self, and adheres to the Object. And it is in line with this that John is the writer above all who speaks of 'abiding' in Christ (e.g., Jn. 15:4ff.). As he understands it, faith is a very thorough-going attachment to a person.[81] Believing 'on the name' of Christ (Jn. 1:12; 2:23) means much the same, 'the name' being a designation of the whole person.

Sometimes also John thinks of simple credence, when he speaks of believing Christ or believing the Father (using the dative). There are several references to believing Christ (Jn. 5:46f.; 8:31, etc.). One reference to believing the Father is very forthright: 'He that hear-eth my word', said Jesus, 'and believeth him that sent me, hath eternal life, and cometh not into judgement, but hath passed out of death into life' (Jn. 5:24). This indicates that the most far-reaching con-sequences follow from believing the Father. If we believe Him, if we really believe Him, then we accept the way of salvation He has provided. In other words, to believe, in the sense of credence, if genuine, means to believe in the sense of trust. The two cannot really be separated. Similarly there is little difference between be-lieving on and believing. The man born blind asked who the Son of God was 'that I may believe on him'. When he found out he said, 'Lord, I believe' (Jn. 9:36, 38). In similar fashion John 16:30f. shows that there is no real distinction between 'believing that' and 'believing'. The disciples use the former construction, and Jesus replies with the latter.

Another point that John makes is that faith is not a purely

---

[80] Cf. Packer, 'Throughout the Bible, trust in God is made to rest on belief of what he has revealed concerning his character and purposes. In the NT, where faith is defined as trust in Christ, the acknowledgment of Jesus as the expected Messiah and the incarnate Son of God is regarded as basic to it' (op. cit., p. 209).

[81] Cf. Augustine, 'What then is "to believe on Him"? By believing to love Him, by believing to esteem highly, by believing to go into Him and to be incorporated in His members' (On the Gospel of St. John, Tractate xxix, 6).

human activity. Jesus told certain people, 'ye believe not, because ye are not of my sheep' (Jn. 10:26).[82] John tells us that others 'could not believe', for they were the objects of a certain prophecy (Jn. 12:39). This is all of a piece with his usual emphasis on the priority of the divine. Faith is not an activity generated by some human will to believe. It comes about because God first works in a man.

Finally let us notice that faith is connected with the great saving acts, the death and the resurrection. For the first point we adduce John 3:16, 'God . . . gave his only begotten Son (i.e., on Calvary), that whosoever believeth on him should not perish. . . .' For the second, the disciple whom Jesus loved, when he came into the empty tomb, 'saw, and believed' (Jn. 20:8). Thomas refused at first to believe (Jn. 20:25), was summoned by the risen Lord to 'be not faithless, but believing' (Jn. 20:27), and so entered into faith (Jn. 20:29).

UNITY

John sees the death of Christ as a unifying force. There is much talk of unity today, and John speaks here to our age. But the unity he sees is not a vague one, based on general principles, or a desire for fellowship, or a distaste for schism. It is the unity of those who are saved in Christ.[83] As Jesus spoke of Himself as the Good Shepherd, He said, 'I lay down my life for the sheep. And other sheep I have, which are not of this fold: them also I must bring, and they shall hear my voice; and they shall become one flock, one shepherd' (Jn. 10:15f.). This passion for unity comes out also in our Lord's saying, 'I, if I be lifted up from the earth, will draw all men unto myself' (Jn. 12:32), and in the prayer that His followers be one (Jn. 17:21). John sees this also in Caiaphas' unconscious prophecy, which he explains as that Christ should die not only for Israel, 'but that he might also gather together into one the children of God that are scattered abroad' (Jn. 11:52). The thought is not expressed in the same language as when Paul in

---

[82] 'His disciples, like the sheep of the parable, hear His voice, follow Him, and will never perish, that is, they will survive the final judgement. This ultimate security is not, however, the reward of human achievement: it is the gift of Jesus who knows His faithful disciples and gives them now and at once that life which belongs to the age which is to be, and which, consequently, will enable them to pass unscathed through the final judgment of God' (Hoskyns, *op. cit.*, p. 387).

[83] 'They are one in Jesus Christ as the one who reconciled them by dying and rising again in their stead. As divided men they first meet in his crucified body, in which their old life is put to death and destroyed' (Geoffrey W. Bromiley, 'Unity', *Baker's Dictionary of Theology,* Grand Rapids, 1960, p. 538).

Ephesians 2:13ff. speaks of breaking down the middle wall of partition, but it is essentially the same thought. True unity among men depends on true salvation. When men get right with God, then and only then may we except them to be right with each other.

From all this it is clear that the cross is the mighty climax to which all else leads up. For John, Jesus is the divine Son of God, come to earth expressly in order to bring about man's salvation. In this capacity he depicts Him as perpetually in conflict with all the forces of darkness, and as especially in conflict with them in His death. So much does John stress all this that when the dying Saviour cries, 'It is finished' (Jn. 19:30)[84], John sees no need for further explanation. This is the moment to which the whole Gospel leads with the remorseless logic of a Greek tragedy. But John does not see it as a tragedy. It is no coincidence that it is in the very passion narrative that Jesus is confronted with Pilate, the representative of earthly power and dominion. One by one all the other characters drop out, and John lets us see Christ confronted by the representative of the world's most eminent kingdoms. In this way His own kingship is brought out (Jn. 18:37, 39; 19: 3, 14, 15, 19, 21f.). The repeated references to the King is John's way of hammering this point home. It is an important idea for John. The kingship of Jesus is seen precisely in the cross.[85] As the Fathers liked to think, He reigned from the tree.[86]

---

[84] On this expression A. M. Hunter says, 'In Christ's own picture-phrases this means: "I have drained the cup. I have travelled the road. I have paid the price." Metaphors all of them, no doubt; perhaps only in metaphors could our Lord describe his work ere it was done. But the work was finished, and of the results of that finished work Christians all down the centuries have never doubted' (ET, lxiii, p. 186).

[85] Even such a radical writer as Charles Guignebert sees this in John: 'for the Jesus of John, the Christ, the cross becomes a kingly throne' (*Jesus,* London, 1935, p. 412), though his idea that this involves the elimination of 'every trace of the human element' is not in accord with the facts.

[86] B. F. Westcott says of John's passion narrative, 'It is from the beginning to the end a revelation of majesty. No voice of suffering, no horror of thick darkness, find a place in it' (*The Victory of the Cross,* London, 1889, p. 95); 'the Cross is the symbol of Christ's throne from which He reigns, till the last enemy shall be subdued, with a sovereignty new, and universal, and present, and divine' (*op. cit.,* p. 97).

CHAPTER FIVE

The Cross in the Pauline Epistles

I. THE PLIGHT OF MAN

The sheer bulk of Paul's teaching on the atonement makes it difficult to deal at all adequately with his thought. The apostle was an exceedingly able man, and his whole life had been transformed by his contact with the risen Lord on the Damascus road.[1] That encounter gave him a new orientation.[2] From then on he

[1] A. M. Hunter speaks of 'one fact of palmary importance — his conversion' and goes on, 'Somebody has said Paul's faith bears not so much the grammarian's as the sinner's touch. It is the theology of a converted man, of one who could say, "By the grace of God I am what I am" (1 Cor. 15:10)' (*Interpreting Paul's Gospel*, London, 1960, p. 19). He later says that certain 'convictions, born of his encounter with Christ on the Damascus Road, were to colour deeply his later thinking and theology' (*op. cit.*, p. 20).

[2] Or, as F. C. Grant puts it, 'He had fathomed the dark, unplumbed depths of alienation from God, and he had returned, had been brought back to life again by the gracious act of God in Christ' (*An Introduction to New Testament Thought*, New York, 1950, p. 174).

was Christ's man. Whereas he had been 'a blasphemer, and a persecutor, and injurious' (1 Tim. 1:13), now he became, as he liked to express it, Christ's 'slave' (Rom. 1:1, etc.).

This radical change meant a rethinking of his fundamental theological beliefs. Just how soon he came to perceive the centrality of the cross we do not know. But we do know that when he had reached a settled theological position he saw that he owed everything to Christ not as a teacher, not as an example, not as a revealer of mysteries from God (though He was all these), but as Saviour and Redeemer. Paul knew a power in his life that had not been there before, and he associated this power with the cross.[3] The cross was not merely a miscarriage of justice, not only a martyrdom. It was an act of God. It was *the* act of God. It was absolutely central.[4] All that Paul was, and all that Paul hoped for centred on the action of God in the cross.[5]

Behind all that Paul says about the atonement, then, is this conversion which transformed him. His passionate letters are the outcome of what God had done for him in Christ. They are the expression of the experience of this man of profound intellect, boundless energy, and spiritual depth who had come to see in the cross the centre of all things.

As we consider his thoughts we begin with his understanding of the plight from which Christ rescued men. It was basic to Paul that sinners are in an unenviable position.[6] They face a calamitous eternity. He regards the atonement accordingly as a very real work of rescue. It is not simply the means whereby God conveyed to men the thought of His love, or assured them of His perpetual readiness to forgive the penitent, or gave them the certainty that

---

[3] Paul loves to dwell on the power of God, and to contrast this with mere words, and to link it with the cross. See, for example, 1 Cor. 1:17f. 'For Christ sent me not to baptize, but to preach the gospel: not in wisdom of words, lest the cross of Christ should be made void. For the word of the cross is to them that are perishing foolishness; but unto us which are being saved it is the power of God.' See also Rom. 1:16; 1 Cor. 2:4f.; 4:20; 2 Cor. 13:4; Eph. 3:20; 1 Thes. 1:5, etc.

[4] 'All that is essential in the work of Christ is summed up in his death on the Cross. The Cross is the essence of the wisdom and the power of God, of salvation, of the preaching of the Apostle' (Maurice Goguel, *The Life of Jesus*, London, 1958, p. 110).

[5] 'Paul's whole soul was aflame with the conviction that Jesus, crucified but now exalted to God's right hand, was God's appointed Messiah for the salvation and the judgment not of Israel merely, but of all mankind' (G. S. Duncan, SJT, ii, p. 5).

[6] Cf. T. R. Glover, 'There is, as Wendland says, a unity in Paul's fundamental thoughts, an inner connexion. Before Damascus he hated Jesus; after Damascus he loved him; but, before and after, he knew what sin was — from experience; and he knew, from what it meant to himself, that God could not compromise with it' (*Paul of Tarsus*, London, 1925, p. 75).

everything would come out all right in the end. It was one of Paul's fundamental convictions that, apart from Christ, nothing would come out all right, ever. Man left to himself is doomed. That is why Christ's work on the cross is so very important, and that is why the proclamation of the gospel is so urgent. Christ can deliver men. But men, of their own endeavors, can never break free from various tyrants that hold them in, and confine them to a miserable slavery.

SLAVES TO SIN

No biblical writer makes the point that all men are sinful more emphatically than does Paul. This is the thrust, for example, of the whole opening argument of the most systematic of his writings, the Epistle to the Romans. He is out to show that all alike, Gentile as well as Jew, are sinners. So, after the usual greetings and a brief statement of the essential content of the gospel, he wastes no time in declaring that God's wrath is revealed against all unrighteousness (Rom. 1:18). Then he proceeds to show that all men in point of fact are unrighteous, and so come under this condemnation. He begins with the Gentiles. These are 'without excuse' (Rom. 1:20). 'Without excuse' not because they have broken the Law of the Old Testament, not because they have failed to keep the Ten Commandments, but because 'the invisible things of him since the creation of the world are clearly seen, being perceived through the things that are made' and thus, 'knowing God, they glorified him not as God' (Rom. 1:20f.). In other words they are condemned not for some abstract crime, like failing to keep a holy law of which they had never heard, but for the extremely practical reason that they have sinned against the light they have. We might put Paul's point by saying that no man lives up to the highest and best that he knows. But Paul maintains that he should. God expects him to. And because he does not, he is a sinner in God's eyes, whatever he may be in his own.

Now sin has consequences, and step by step Paul unfolds the terrible story. Remorselessly he brings out the sin and the sins of the Gentiles, together with the inevitable results. He concentrates for the most part on the consequences here and now, but his threefold 'God gave them up' (Rom. 1:24, 26, 28) shows that he is not thinking of automatic sequence so much as the divine sentence.[7] This is a moral universe and God has so made it that

---

[7] Cf. W. P. DuBose, 'it is true that God hardened Pharaoh's heart. Pharaoh's sin was his own, but its hardening effect upon himself was the working of a natural law, which was not his doing but God's. And these natural results of sin in the sinner are judicial; they are God's judgments upon sin, God's punishment for sin' (*The Soteriology of the New Testament*, London, 1910, pp. 48f.).

sin cannot but reap its reward.[8] And at the end of the chapter Paul reminds his readers that it is God's ordinance 'that they which practise such things are worthy of death' (Rom. 1:32).

In the next chapter he turns his attention to the Jews. Jewish readers would have approved all that he had to say about the Gentiles, but would have prided themselves on being different. They were in a special sense God's people. To them God had given the Law. They were not like the Gentiles. They might undergo the fatherly discipline of God, but they were in no serious danger.[9] Paul stresses deeds to them. 'Not the hearers of a law are just before God, but the doers of a law shall be justified' (Rom. 2:13). He does not deny, here or elsewhere, the privileges of the Jew. But he asserts that the Law was given, not so that the Jew could preen himself on his privileged position, but in order to be kept. And the Jew had not kept it. He did the same things as the Gentile (Rom. 2:1, 3). Accordingly Paul can address the Jew in these terms: 'but after thy hardness and impenitent heart treasurest up for thyself wrath in the day of wrath and revelation of the righteous judgement of God' (Rom. 2:5). While the Jews have received the Law, they have not kept it. They, too, are sinners. Therefore they, too, stand under the condemnation of God.

Thus Paul has shown that men on both sides of the great religious division of mankind are sinners. All are 'under sin' (Rom. 3:9). With a long catena of quotations from the Old Testament the apostle hammers home the point that nobody, nobody at all, is righteous (Rom. 3:10-18). Every mouth is stopped (Rom. 3:19). All the world lies under God's judgment (*ibid.*). 'There is no distinction; for all have sinned, and fall short of the glory of God' (Rom. 3:22f.).

Paul's position is made clearer in the massive argument in Romans than in any other passage in his writings. But the essential position is the same everywhere. To him it is fundamental that all men are

---

[8] R. S. Franks reminds us of the seriousness of this. While a man may enter into the experience of forgiveness through the mercy of God, this does not wipe out all the temporal consequences of his sin. 'It is clear that the Divine forgiveness does not remove directly either the physical or the social consequence of our sins. The forgiven man may still have to bear the penalty of his wrong-doing in enfeebled health' (*The Atonement*, London, 1934, p. 159). So also H. Maldwyn Hughes, 'Sin is punished according to the operation of universal laws, which reconciliation does not suspend' (*What is the Atonement?*, London, n.d., p. 19).

[9] This point is well brought out in a passage in Wisdom wherein the temporal afflictions that befall Israel are contrasted with those that fall on the Gentiles: 'While therefore thou dost chasten us, thou scourgest our enemies ten thousand times more, to the intent that we may ponder thy goodness when we judge, and when we are judged may look for mercy. Wherefore also the unrighteous that lived in folly of life thou didst torment through their own abominations . . .' (Wisdom 12:22f.).

sinners, and that this is serious. The gospel is meaningful for Paul because it is seen against this background. Always he thinks of men as sinful. Always he thinks of them as unable to do anything about their sinfulness. Always he thinks of Christ as the only Deliverer.

It cannot be denied that in our modern society Paul's teaching is usually ignored. And the basic reason is probably that modern man does not see himself as Paul sees him, and he does not see God as Paul sees Him. This despite the fact that our modern society provides us with almost a classical illustration of Paul's view of the self-defeating nature of the sinful life. Man rejects God's way and chooses his own pleasures, his own success, only to find that the self-centered life has forfeited all the values it sought to conserve. This is a pleasure-seeking generation, but never before have so many men been jaded, blasé, bored, and unhappy. Men have made success their ideal, and while their material achievements are impressive there is a widespread consciousness of failure at the deepest levels of life. In his fear man pursues security, and no generation has ever felt less secure. Sin carries with it a built-in frustration. But the typical modern man does not think deeply about such matters. He sees himself as on the whole a good fellow, a remarkably decent citizen. There may be a few minor peccadilloes, lapses understandable in the light of the limitations of the human frame, but nothing he thinks of as 'sin'. He is not deeply concerned about sin.[10] Indeed, sin is a word he uses but rarely. He leaves that to parsons and religious cranks. He himself knows of nothing worse than failings, more or less excusable.[11] These he sees as his fate, not his fault.[12] And he does not see God as a moral God, as pure and holy

---

[10] He would agree with Sir Oliver Lodge, 'the higher man of to-day is not worrying about his sins at all, still less about their punishment. His mission, if he is good for anything, is to be up and doing' (*Man and the Universe*, London, 1909, p. 220).

[11] G. O. Griffith brings out the contrast between such views and that of the Apostle: 'But sin, as Paul sees it, is not merely delinquency, or neurosis, or egoism, it is man's self-will *in rebellion against the holy God;* and as such, it constitutes a problem not only on the human side but on the divine side also' (*St. Paul's Gospel to the Romans*, Oxford, 1949, p. 109).

[12] Karl Heim objects very strongly to the whole concept of fate and insists on the reality and seriousness of guilt (*Jesus the World's Perfecter*, Edinburgh and London, 1959, chs. I-III). He approves of Kant's conclusion that guilt 'is due to a simply inexcusable, inexplicable, baseless decision, an "intelligible act" which is prior to any experience and by which the intelligible ego has decided to give priority to the sensual instincts over the commandment of reason. Kant's doctrine of the radically evil is merely a philosophical description of what Jesus calls the satanic' (*op. cit.*, p. 9). He firmly rejects 'the attempt to take away the sting from guilt and to alter it into a tragic fate in which we have got caught on account of our human constitution, our sensuous inclinations or the history of our people' (*op. cit.*, p. 12). There can

and righteous as Paul sees Him. His god is celestial good nature, a benevolent hander-out of prizes for all. And because he has manufactured a complaisant god to replace the God who insists on morality, he dismisses Paul's teaching as hopelessly irrelevant.[13]

There is need for clear thinking here. God is not a being conjured up in the minds of modern men and shaped according to their will. He is the God of the Bible. He is the sovereign God. He is a righteous God and he demands righteousness in His people.[14] Sin against Him is a grim and dreadful affair. We cannot begin to understand the thought of Paul or for that matter of the other biblical writers, until we get this clear.

Not only are men sinners, they can no longer help being sinners. Paul speaks of them as 'slaves' to sin (Rom. 6:17, 20). They are 'sold under sin' (Rom. 7:14), sold as under a cruel slave master, sold into a captivity from which they can never escape. They are brought 'into captivity under the law of sin' (Rom. 7:23). Though in their mind they may seek to serve God and His law, yet 'with the flesh' they serve only 'the law of sin' (Rom. 7:25). How can a man break free from a captivity like this?

Sometimes Paul takes this further. Man's plight is serious not only because of what he *does,* but also because of what he *is,* a sinner by nature as well as by choice.[15] 'In Adam all die', he

---

be no doubt but that in all this he is opposing something very characteristic of the modern world.

[13] We should not overlook the case of such men as C. E. M. Joad, who was so impressed by the fact of evil with all its implications that he came to say 'I am willing, as I once was not, to bank on the religious hypothesis being true' (*God and Evil,* London, 1945, p. 360). He brings this out more fully in *The Recovery of Belief,* London, 1952, in which he says, for example, 'To me, at any rate, the view of evil implied by Marxism, expressed by Shaw and maintained by modern psychotherapy, a view which regards evil as the by-product of circumstances, which circumstances can, therefore, alter and even eliminate, has come to seem intolerably shallow and the contrary view of it as endemic in man, more particularly in its Christian form, the doctrine of original sin, to express a deep and essential insight into human nature' (*op. cit.,* p. 63). But his pilgrimage is distinctly exceptional.

[14] Markus Barth emphasizes the importance of God's kingship in this connection. 'Paul's way of speaking about sin is a decisive and indispensable part of the gospel of God's righteousness. Just as John the Baptist — according to the synoptic Gospels — called everybody to repentance only because he had to announce the coming king, so Paul's chapters, that deal so fiercely with man's unrighteousness, are an evangelistic interpretation of God's kingship over subjects such as we are' (SJT, viii, p. 296).

[15] Cf. G. Aulén, 'the doctrine of original sin is concerned with man as a whole. Sin does not have reference to something external and peripheral in man, nor to something "accidental"; it has its "seat" in his inner being, in the inclination of the will, and applies, therefore, to man as a whole' (*The Faith of the Christian Church,* London, 1954, pp. 272f.).

says succinctly (1 Cor. 15:22), while in Romans 5:12-21 he develops the argument that Adam's sin had calamitous effects on all his posterity. 'By the trespass of the one the many died' (Rom. 5:15); 'through one trespass the judgement came unto all men to condemnation' (Rom. 5:18); 'through the one man's disobedience the many were made (κατεστάθησαν)[16] sinners' (Rom. 5:19); 'sin reigned in death' (Rom. 5:21).

From such passages the idea of original sin is derived. The basic idea in this concept is that the nature that mankind inherits is not the innocent nature of the unfallen Adam, but that stained by sin as the result of the Fall. G. O. Griffith has a very useful illustration of what this means when he says, 'Original sin is sin that is original to man's fallen *nature,* as distinct from sins committed by each individual man's *will.* A tiger cub, before he has fleshed his teeth in his first "kill", is already a beast of prey, for he has inherited a predatory nature.'[17] In the same way man is a sinner because he has inherited a sinful nature. It is no more possible to regard him as anything other than a sinner than it is to regard a tiger cub as anything other than a beast of prey.

We cannot and we do not feel guiltless about this. Karl Heim reminds us that when we hear of calamity overtaking a rival our first reaction is apt to be 'malicious joy'. After this, 'ethical considerations set in, and prohibitions due to education become active. I am ashamed of my mean feeling. I am really sorry for the man and with sincere sympathy inquire from his relations how he is.' Similarly our first feeling at the promotion of another is often envy, and only later do we get round to sincere congratulations. Heim proceeds: 'The question now arises: can we, because there is no question here of any conscious decision of the will, decline all responsibility for these nasty inclinations of malicious joy, envy, hatred and rage? Are we innocent of them?' The answer of course is that we cannot do anything of the sort. Indeed we feel particularly responsible for them: 'it is particularly these entirely instinctive and involuntary inclinations of mean professional, commercial and artistic rivalry, of outright, almost sadistic malicious joy in the misery of someone else, which arise in me during the first unguarded moments, that make me feel even more ashamed than wrong decisions taken

---

[16] Cf. N. P. Williams, 'It is clear that the transgression of Adam is conceived as standing in a *causal* relation to the subsequent death, sin, and condemnation of his descendants — nothing less than this can be meant by the word κατεστάθησαν ("were constituted") in *v.* 19 — though the exact nature of the link between this primal cause and its multitudinous effects is not expressly indicated' (*The Ideas of the Fall and of Original Sin,* London, 1927, p. 131).

[17] *Op. cit.,* p. 181.

after clear deliberation.'[18]   Precisely here I know myself to be evil
at the core. I know myself guilty, and I am ashamed of what I am.
This concept underlies a good deal of what Paul says. Thus in
Romans 7 he thinks of sin as something located within man's very
being. Take, for example, verses 19f., 'For the good which I would
I do not: but the evil which I would not, that I practise. But if
what I would not, that I do, it is no more I that do it, but sin which
dwelleth in me.'[19] A little later he speaks of being brought 'into
captivity under the law of sin which is in my members' (Rom. 7:23).
Elsewhere he tells us that men are 'by nature children of wrath'
(Eph. 2:3), and that children not sanctified by the faith of a parent
are 'unclean' (1 Cor. 7:14).[20] His idea of the 'flesh' as evil, lusting
against the Spirit (Gal. 5:17) and producing the 'works of the
flesh' (Gal. 5:19ff.) points in the same direction.

The idea of original sin has not been popular in modern times,
though quite recently it has been making something of a come-
back (aided, interestingly, by some contributions of the psycholo-
gists).[21] We like to think of ourselves as free and responsible, and

[18] *Jesus the Lord,* Edinburgh and London, 1959, pp. 113f. He further
says, 'I am shocked at the abysmal meanness which reveals itself in these
feelings, and of which I had not thought myself capable. But I cannot accept
the dark instincts to which I am subject indifferently as if they were merely
a fate. I know only too well that they are the impulses of my own heart.
I feel stained by them. I regret them as one regrets a fault' (*op. cit.,* p. 114).

[19] Cf. Lesslie Newbigin, 'Each man in himself is not a unity. His mind
is a republic in which many forces are battling against one another . . . .
Fears, ambitions, envies, hatreds arise in his mind which conflict with one
another and with his own purposes, and threaten to ruin him. Above all,
there is in every man a great division between what he knows he ought to
do, and what he actually does' (*Sin and Salvation,* London, 1956, p. 13).

[20] J. S. Bezzant has an observation on babies in this connection: 'Babies,
so far as we can judge, have no self-consciousness, knowledge or conscious
volition. But when moral consciousness is attained we find already present
a tendency to lawlessness, the source of which is plainly racial rather than
individual or personal . . . . The *condition,* being prior to self-consciousness,
is manifestly inherited, not subsequently acquired; quite independently of any
theological dogma, it has an indisputably adequate psychological basis' (*Theology,* lxii, p. 448).

[21] Cf. J. W. D. Smith's article, 'A Study of Sin and Salvation in terms of
C. G. Jung's Psychology', SJT, iii, pp. 397-408. *Inter alia* he says that man's
life 'had lost its true centre in God and, in consequence, there was conflict
within his own nature and competitive strife in society. This self-centred
fear is transmitted to each new generation through the parents and through
society as a whole. The egocentricity of the parents is visited upon the
children unto the third and fourth generation. It intensifies the bonds of
infantile dependence and the pressure of a tainted social tradition cooperates
with it in the distortion of each new life. Original sin is thus a fact of man's
social inheritance. The child is shaped in iniquity from birth even if it be
not conceived in sin' (*op. cit.,* p. 404). However inadequate this may be as
a summary of biblical teaching, it is not without its interest as showing a

the concept of original sin does not please us accordingly. But we must bear in mind, as John Burnaby reminds us, that 'Neither freedom nor responsibility has lost its meaning; but freedom is exercised in a frame that is given, and responsibility is limited by the limitations upon freedom.'[22]   Whether we like it or not we are subject to limitations not of our choosing, and one of those limitations is that our nature is not neutral, but sinful.[23]   Men have always found the pursuit of virtue strenuous.   It does not come to us naturally to do good, whereas sin is much easier.   We can drift into sin, but we cannot drift into virtue.   It is this which points us to the important truth that sin is part of our nature, and not simply the result of our environment.   Basically we sin because we are the kind of people we are, and not simply because we see others sinning.[24] The idea of original sin must be retained, for it corresponds both to the teaching of St. Paul, and to the facts of life.[25]

This concept also reminds us of the solidarity of the race.   'We are members one of another' (Eph. 4:25).   The community aspect of life cannot be overlooked.   The race is more than a collection of independent atoms.   Now while we owe a good deal to environment it is also true that there is such a thing as national temperament.   And on the wider scale the human race is united at a deep level.   Together we are sharers in sin.[26]   This is all too obvious in our group

---

trend in psychology.   Cf. also David Cox's study, *Jung and St. Paul,* London, 1959.

[22] *Theology,* lxii, p. 14.

[23] In Judaism Paul found the doctrine of the *yetzer ha-ra,* 'the evil inclination' (see C. G. Montefiore and H. Loewe, *A Rabbinic Anthology,* London, 1938, pp. 295-314, for passages setting forth this idea).   Many scholars have felt that this is the background to such passages as Rom. 7 with its struggle between the good and the evil within.   This may well be the case, but it should be noted that Paul does not use this terminology, nor can his ideas on the subject be constrained within the Jewish concept.

[24] N. P. Williams in his classic treatment of the subject lays it down as his fifth major proposition that 'Ever since this first human transgression, our nature has displayed an inherent moral weakness or bias towards sin', and as his seventh, 'This quality of "weakness of will," or defective control of appetites, inheres in the human stock as a hereditary character transmitted from parent to offspring through biological and not merely through what is called social heredity' (*op. cit.,* pp. 456, 460).

[25] Cf. William Hordern, 'the term, despite its misuses, must be retained. It points up the fact that all man's sins stem from his original sin, the sin that is logically first.   Man sins because he is a sinner in the wrong relationship with God; he sins because he has tried to place himself, his concerns, his insights, at the center of his life, where God ought to be.   It is also original in the sense that it describes a situation that we inherit . . . . Sin is something that has somehow got its hold upon the human race as a whole' (*The Case for a New Reformation Theology,* Philadelphia, 1959, p. 130).

[26] Cf. John Burnaby, 'But if sin is resistance to the will of God, it seems impossible to *confine* the field of that resistance to the operation of personal

relationships. On the international level we accept without question standards of conduct that we would never dream of applying in our personal relationships. All our altruism appears to be exhausted at the local level. Groups of men of every kind act unashamedly on the basis of self-interest and the like, and even good men stoutly defend the practice. Clearly something is wrong in the race as a whole.

THE WRATH OF GOD

Not only are men sinners and slaves to sin, but they are in jeopardy as a result. Paul speaks of a dreadful reality which he calls 'the wrath of God', or simply 'the wrath', and which he tells us is visited upon sinners. This idea is not at all congenial to the men of our day, partly at least, as Paul Tillich reminds us,[27] because they have not understood it. Thus there are many who seek to explain it away. Sometimes we are told that 'the wrath' is an impersonal expression, meant to point us to a process of cause and effect,[28] but not to indicate that God is personally active in deeds of wrath.[29] This does

---

freedom. The resistance is present already in the many-threaded web by which the individual is bound up with the society in which he is placed, and ultimately with the species to which he belongs . . . . one can hardly contemplate the apparently incorrigible self-righteousness, the shameless Pharisaism which is exhibited in the *collective* behaviour of every human group — social, political, national, or ecclesiastical — without being compelled to acknowledge that in human nature as we see it there is a hard core which everywhere opposes itself to the Spirit's persuasion' (*op. cit.*, p. 15). Cf. also James Denney, 'the unity or solidarity of the human race in sin is involved in the vital organic connection of all men with each other, and in the disproportion which actually appears, in all men who have come to moral responsibility, between what they are, and what they know they should be' (CDR, p. 201).

[27] Cf. the statement of his cited above, p. 147, n. 10.

[28] Some trace this idea back to the Old Testament, but against this cf. W. Eichrodt, *Theology of the Old Testament*, i, London, 1961, pp. 258-69. *Inter alia* he says that wrath 'signifies, when applied to God, the emphatically personal character of the Deity' (*op. cit.*, p. 258) and he speaks of 'this conception of the divine displeasure as an act of real feeling' (*op. cit.*, p. 265). So also Th. C. Vriezen, 'God's wrath exists because of sin: suffering is the punishment God inflicts because of sin' (*An Outline of Old Testament Theology*, Oxford, 1958, p. 157). He also says, 'According to the prophets the worst of all is that in their wicked self-conceit men say that God cannot be angry (Amos ix. 10; Isa. v. 18ff.; Mic. ii. 7; Zeph. i. 12)' (*op. cit.*, p. 158). E. Jacob notes that wrath is ascribed to Yahweh in the Old Testament more often than to men. He says, 'the Israelite really believed in the wrath of Yahweh and did not project it upon God from the testings and punishments which he himself had passed through' (*Theology of the Old Testament*, London, 1958, p. 114).

[29] Thus C. H. Dodd says that Paul 'constantly uses "wrath" or "the Wrath" in a curiously impersonal way' (*Romans*, MNTC, p. 21); and that he retains

not do justice to Paul's thought. There are no grounds for distinguishing between 'the wrath of God' and 'the wrath' in his writings, or for that matter, anywhere in the New Testament.[30] It is impossible to think that God is anything other than vigorously active in such a process as that described in Romans 2:5ff.,

> but after thy hardness and impenitent heart
> treasurest up for thyself wrath in the day
> of wrath and revelation of the righteous
> judgement of God; who will render to every
> man according to his works . . . unto them that
> are factious, and obey not the truth, but

---

the term, 'the Wrath of God', 'not to describe the attitude of God to man, but to describe an inevitable process of cause and effect in a moral universe' (*op. cit.,* p. 23). Similarly R. P. C. Hanson maintains that 'in all the uses of (*orgē* and *thumos*) wrath is carefully treated as something ordained and controlled by God indeed, but distinct from him' (*God: Creator, Saviour, Spirit,* London, 1960, p. 46). No one has argued this point of view more thoroughly than A. T. Hanson. His book abounds in statements like 'The wrath was not an emotion or attitude of God, it was simply a word for what happened to those who broke God's moral laws. It was in fact the "principle of retribution in a moral universe" ' (*The Wrath of the Lamb,* London, 1957, p. 109). He even manages to see the words 'God gave them up' (Rom. 1:24) as 'evidence not of a personal, but an impersonal reaction' (*op. cit.,* p. 193)! Hanson frequently complains that those who argue in favour of the view that the wrath of God is personal do not face the kind of evidence that he adduces. Yet he himself does not face the strength of the opposing point of view. He does not face the question of the meaning to be attached to an impersonal process of wrath in a genuinely theistic universe. Nor does he seriously grapple with the meaning of the passages which explicitly speak of the wrath 'of God'. Nor does he face passages like 2 Thes. 1:8ff. which do not mention 'wrath' but which do speak of personal divine revulsion to evil in the strongest terms. There are other defects. It is possible that we have the clue to his procedure in his statement: 'If we once allow ourselves to be led into thinking that a reference to the wrath of God in the New Testament means that God is conceived of as angry, we cannot avoid some sort of theory of expiation. We cannot avoid maintaining that in some sense the Son endured the wrath of the Father, we cannot avoid thinking in forensic terms' (*op. cit.,* p. 193). If we are determined to be rid of all ideas of expiation and all forensic terms we will probably be compelled to jettison the idea of a personal wrath. But whether we are justified in doing so on New Testament terms is another matter.

[30] Cf. Alan Richardson, 'In Paul, as in the NT generally, though the expression ἡ ὀργή is used absolutely, it always means "the wrath *of God*" and not a kind of impersonal "inevitable process of cause and effect in a moral universe"; we can rationalize the idea in that way, if we like, but it would be a mistake to suppose that the NT writers did so' (*An Introduction to the Theology of the New Testament,* London, 1958, p. 76). A. M. Hunter notices that Paul 'speaks often of "the Wrath" without naming God' and proceeds to ask, 'Is this because he thinks of it impersonally? Is it not rather because he finds it unnecessary to say whose wrath it is?' (*op. cit.,* p. 79).

obey unrighteousness, shall be wrath and
indignation, tribulation and anguish, upon
every soul of man that worketh evil.

It is difficult to see how words could state more emphatically that
God is personally opposed to evil and to evil men.[31] The words
describe a positive revulsion.[32] Moreover they speak of God's
activity in the day of judgment. That is to say, His personal, vigorous
opposition is not exhausted in His present judgments on our sins.
It continues to the very end of time and beyond.[33]

Paul does not speak of his views on the wrath of God as the
result of his personal evaluation of the situation. He says, 'the
wrath of God is revealed from heaven against all ungodliness and
unrighteousness of men' (Rom. 1:18). This is not a truism. It is
something that is 'revealed'. Some religions, like that of the Greeks
in its more philosophical form, did not think of a divine anger but
regarded the gods as passionless. The Greek philosophers did not
think of a wrath of God.[34] Divine wrath is something that God
has made known, and because He has revealed it, it is sure and
certain. Moreover it is far-reaching, for the words of Romans 1:18

[31] William Temple objects to the view that God hates the sin but loves
the sinner. Sin, he says, 'is not an accretion attached to my real self; it is
myself, as that self now exists . . . . He loves me even while I sin; but it
cannot be said too strongly that there is a wrath of God against me as sinning;
God's Will is set one way and mine is set against it. There is a collision of
wills; and God's Will is not passive in that collision' (Christus Veritas,
London, 1925, p. 258).

[32] Daniel Lamont points out that to overlook this may lead to disastrous
consequences: 'it is partly true that sin brings its own penalty, but it is far
from true that God has nothing to do with it, for this would exclude God
from the operation of the moral law which is His own law. Such a view
is a product of that disastrous modern humanism which has led to the
widespread departure from the living God which we find in the world of
to-day. When God is regarded as having nothing to do with the working
out of the moral law it is an easy transition to the notion that He has
nothing to do with anything that happens on earth' (God the Redeemer,
London, 1944, p. 7).

[33] John Knox notices C. H. Dodd's view that 'the wrath' is to be taken
as impersonal, and proceeds, 'But actually there is no way to eliminate the
evidence that Paul also thought of death as a punishment of sin and of "the
wrath" as the righteous judgment of God upon those who have disobeyed his
will' (The Death of Christ, London, 1959, p. 155).

[34] Cf. E. Bevan, 'Greek philosophy had long ago repudiated emphatically
the conception common to primitive and popular Greek religion and to the
Old Testament. Anger was a weak and discreditable emotion, it taught, in
men, and to attribute such an emotion to a divine being was absurd and
blasphemous. Deity, every novice in Greek philosophy knew as an axiom,
must be apathēs, without disturbing emotions of any kind. The idea of the
Divine anger was not something which penetrated into Christianity from its
pagan environment: it was something which the Church maintained in the
face of adverse pagan criticism' (Symbolism and Belief, London, 1938, p. 210).

apply it to every 'ungodliness and unrighteousness of men'. We saw in the previous section that Paul sees all men as sinners; this means that the wrath of God must be expected to be directed against all men. This is the implication also of other statements. Thus by nature we all are 'children of wrath' (Eph. 2:3). God's wrath comes upon 'the sons of disobedience' (Eph. 5:6; Col. 3:6). This wrath is not exhausted in this life, for Paul can speak of 'the wrath to come' (1 Thes. 1:10). Clearly Paul thought of God as implacably opposed to sin in every shape and form, and as exerting Himself in opposition to it.[35] To gloss over this is to manufacture a god who is not the God of the Bible.[36]

Sometimes the same truth is expressed in other terminology. Thus Paul may speak of men as 'alienated' from God (Eph. 4:18; Col. 1:21), or as 'enemies' of God (Rom. 5:10; Phil. 3:18; Col. 1:21). Such expressions do not mean that there is a slight coolness between God and sinners. They mean that they are in opposite camps. Sinners range themselves against God. They must expect nothing but hostility from the God whose enemies they have become. The language is vigorous. The meaning is not in doubt.

Paul thus makes it clear in many ways that God is in total opposition to every form of evil. He leaves no room for complacency.[37] No one who has grasped the implications of his teaching on wrath and kindred subjects can regard sin with equanimity.[38]

[35] Gustav Wingren insists that the wrath is God's even when the manifestation is human: 'Even though wrath and judgment come upon sinful man in the course of human life, and even though it is in his relations to his fellow men, whether Christians or not, that wrath is most frequently to be seen and his egoism stands self-accused, it is always *God's* wrath. The guilt of sinful man is revealed and judged in these person-to-person relationships, but it is guilt *coram deo* — man's guilt comes between Him and God, and is the guilt of the Last Judgment . . . . God's *opus alienum*, even though it is painfully connected with person-to-person relationships and guilty memories of injuries done or inflicted, is *God's* wrath throughout' (*Creation and Law*, Edinburgh and London, 1961, pp. 55f.).

[36] P. T. Forsyth stresses that to water down Paul's teaching on the wrath of God has serious consequences for our understanding of the character of God. He complains of the attitude that 'empties of meaning the wrath of God' that it 'reduces the holy law of His nature to a bye-law He can suspend, or a habit He can break' (PP, pp. 353f.). Again, he says, 'Any conception of God which exalts His Fatherhood at the cost of His holiness, or to its neglect, unsettles the moral throne of the universe' (*op. cit.*, p. 354).

[37] W. F. Lofthouse points out that 'To be angry simply because I have been injured, to wreak my vengeance like a spoiled child on the person or thing that has thwarted me, — there is no morality in that.' He goes on, 'But anger may be the highest form of altruism. When the mind is irradiated with the flame of anger against tyranny or meanness, high-handed violence or slavish cunning, anger is then simply virtue in operation' (*Ethics and Atonement*, London, 1906, p. 161).

[38] R. Otto sees wrath somewhat differently. To the men of the Old Testament, he says, 'the Wrath of God, so far from being a diminution of

DEATH

'The wages of sin is death,' says Paul starkly (Rom. 6:23). Sin's earnings are grim. Paul does not gloss over the situation.[39] He often links sin with death in close fashion. Thus he can speak of being slaves 'of sin unto death' (Rom. 6:16), i. e., to become slaves of sin leads to death. He brings this out further a little later when he says, 'the end of those things (i. e., the sinful things of which he has just been speaking) is death' (Rom. 6:21). Along the same lines we must understand his statement that 'the sinful passions, which were through the law, wrought in our members to bring forth fruit unto death' (Rom. 7:5), and again, 'sin, that it might be shewn to be sin, by working death to me . . .' (Rom. 7:13). All such passages carry the thought that sin can never be considered an entity in itself. It has results which are inescapable. And among them is death. Sin and death are linked in the closest fashion, and in the relationship of cause and effect. This is not fortuitous. It is 'the ordinance of God' that those who 'practise such things are worthy of death' (Rom. 1:32).[40] Repentance, with all that that implies in the Christian scene, would alter things, but it must be genuine Christian repentance, for 'the sorrow of the world worketh death' (2 Cor. 7:10).

There is a mystery here. Bodies such as ours seem destined to die. It is difficult to conceive of them as lasting indefinitely. Yet we must not overlook the other truth that man instinctively shrinks from death. He cannot regard it as simply another physical fact. It is unnatural, a horror. What Paul is saying is that the thing that makes it unnatural, that gives it its 'sting' is sin (1 Cor. 15:56). Had there been no sin there would doubtless have been a transition

---

His Godhead, appears as a natural expression of it, an element of "holiness" itself, and a quite indispensable one. And in this they are entirely right' (*The Idea of the Holy*, London, 1936, pp. 18f.). He later says, 'naive as it may be, the analogy is most disconcertingly apt and striking; so much so that it will always retain its value, and for us no less than for the men of old be an inevitable way of expressing one element in the religious emotion. It cannot be doubted that, despite the protest of Schleiermacher and Ritschl, Christianity also has something to teach of the "Wrath of God" ' (*op. cit.*, p. 19).

[39] Cf. James Denney, 'This is not mythology, nor pseudo-science; it is the testimony of conscience that all sin, and all who identify themselves with sin, must confront the annihilating judgment of God' (CDR, p. 146).

[40] Cf. Paul Tillich, 'It is not that we are mortal which creates the ultimate fear of death, but rather that we have lost our eternity beyond our natural and inescapable mortality; that we have lost it by sinful separation from the Eternal; and that we are guilty of this separation . . . . We are slaves of fear, not because we have to die, but because we deserve to die!' (*The Shaking of the Foundations*, New York, 1948, p. 171).

from this world to the next, but of another kind than that which we must face.[41]

A slightly different aspect of the subject comes before us in the notable discussion in Romans 5:12-21. There we learn that death entered the world through sin (v. 12), that 'by the trespass of the one many died' (v. 15). Here is the causal relationship we have just been examining. But there is the additional thought that 'death reigned from Adam until Moses' (v. 14), that 'by the trespass of the one, death reigned through the one' (v. 17). Just as Paul thinks of sin as a slave master to whom the sinner is sold, so he personifies death as a monarch, holding sway over the sinner. Both pieces of imagery emphasize the lost condition of the sinner. He is not autonomous. He is under the control of forces initially set in motion by his sin.

We ought not to overlook the expression, 'the law of sin and of death' (Rom. 8:2). While it does not equate the two it reveals them as close allies. And death has other allies. Paul almost gives us a definition of death when he tells us that 'the mind of the flesh is death' (Rom. 8:6). He does not say 'brings death' but 'is death'. Throughout the New Testament the only life that is worth calling life is the life that is lived in close fellowship with God. The sinner, by the very fact of his sin, cuts himself off from that fellowship. He places himself into a condition of death. He is 'dead in trespasses and sins' (Eph. 2:1, 5; Col. 2:13). The body is the means whereby all this is brought about, and thus Paul once speaks of 'the body of this death' (Rom. 7:24).[42] This is not to deny that fundamentally the body is of value. It is 'a temple of the Holy Ghost' (1 Cor. 6:19), and Paul sees it as having such values that he looks for it to be raised at the last day. But he is a very realistic man. And men do sin with their bodies. Therefore he can think of death as specially linked with the body (cf. also the references to the body as 'mortal' [Rom. 6:12; 8:11; 2 Cor. 4:11]).

Sometimes Paul puts the same truth in other terms. Thus he may speak of 'perishing', which is just the same as if he had introduced

---

[41] J. E. L. Oulton suggests that had there been no sin, 'Man might have passed from this world to the next naturally and fearlessly just as we pass from one room to another. There would have been no fear of the loss of personal identity, no fear of a break in continuity, no fear of separation from God and loved ones' (*The Mystery of the Cross*, London, 1957, p. 35). He thinks that the Transfiguration shows 'how Jesus, the Sinless One, might have made the great transition', and goes on to ask, 'who can measure the courage of him who having known the bliss of the Transfiguration faced the anguish of the Cross?' (*op. cit.*, pp. 35, 36).

[42] C. K. Barrett translates, 'this body of death', and comments, ' "The body of this death" is grammatically possible but scarcely makes sense. Paul means the body or human nature which through sin and law has fallen under the dominion of death' (*in loc.*).

the word 'death'. There is not much difference between the passages we have seen which connect sin and death and Romans 2:12, 'as many as have sinned without law shall also perish without law' (cf. also 1 Cor. 1:18; 2 Cor. 2:15; 2 Thes. 2:10). The 'end' of the enemies of Christ's cross is 'perdition' (Phil. 3:18f.). So those who do not obey the gospel 'shall suffer punishment, even eternal destruction from the face of the Lord' (2 Thes. 1:9).

Paul thinks of death, not as something natural and to be accepted, but as something hostile. It is not strong enough to separate us from the love of God (Rom. 8:38f.), but the implication is that it might be expected to do so, or at least to militate in that direction. Right to the end it is hostile. It is 'the last enemy that shall be abolished' (1 Cor. 15:26).[43]

To this it might perhaps be added that the ancient world as a whole viewed death with utter despondency.[44] Everywhere it thought of death as the end of that life which is really life, and as completely powerful. When death comes for a man there is nothing he can do about it. There is universal hopelessness in the face of death. For Christians Christ transformed all this, as we shall see in a later section. Here it is enough to notice that the passages we have cited from Paul are typical of the ancient world apart from Christ. Death is strong. Death is triumphant.[45] And for those of a serious cast of mind the situation was complicated by the fact of sin. The linkage of sin with death could not but fill men with deep horror.

[43] Karl Heim reminds us that men escape their responsibility to other men when they die. 'There is the place where no human claim can follow me any longer. There I am safe from it as in an unassailable fortress.' But with God it is different. 'God is the only One before whom there is no place of escape. I cannot even escape from Him when I die. Even in death I continue to fall into His hands' (*Jesus the World's Perfecter*, Edinburgh, 1959, p. 19).

[44] 'Greek epitaphs are well known to reflect an almost universal pessimism with regard to any life beyond the grave . . . . the only kind of immortality possible is to live on in the memory of posterity' (W. K. C. Guthrie, *The Greeks and their Gods*, Boston, 1956, p. 260).

[45] This has its counterpart in the modern world. Man's fear of death is such that he has outlawed death. He avoids speaking about it. He avoids thinking about it. Concern over it he regards as morbid. Children are shielded from all reference to it. Funerals are conducted in such a way as gloss over the naked reality. And death wreaks a grim vengeance. Never have there been so many cheap books and magazines full of violence and death. Crimes of violence culminating in murder are common. And world wars have exacted a terrible toll of human life. Where men will not face the reality squarely they must expect unfortunate results. Cf. William J. Wolf, 'Modern man banishes death from polite conversation, calling such consideration "morbid," apparently unaware that what is truly "morbid" is just the refusal to face so obvious and inevitable a fact as death' (*No Cross, No Crown*, New York, 1957, p. 29).

THE LAW

Paul uses the term 'law' with a bewildering variety of meaning, as we see from such a passage as Romans 7:22f., 'For I delight in the law of God after the inward man: but I see a different law in my members, warring against the law of my mind, and bringing me into captivity under the law of sin which is in my members.' Clearly 'law' is used here in several different ways, and equally clearly 'law', for Paul, is an exceedingly complex idea.　In this section of our study we are not concerned to trace out the full complexity of the Pauline concept, but rather to concentrate on the way Paul thought of the law of the Old Testament, and more particularly of the law considered as bringing men salvation.

For the Pharisees, as for the Jews in general, the law was the high point of Scripture, the supreme revelation of God.　Man's whole duty was to keep the law.　It is plain that Paul had accepted this idea in his days as a Pharisee.　He tells us that he had been 'as touching the law, a Pharisee . . . as touching the righteousness which is in the law, found blameless' (Phil. 3:5f.).　In time he came to see that this was an exaggerated estimate of his standing with God. Keeping the law could never really constitute a man 'blameless'. But if he came to modify his idea about what the law could achieve he never lost his reverence for the law as divinely given, and as expressing the truth of God.　He tells us that 'the law is holy, and the commandment holy, and righteous, and good' (Rom. 7:12); that 'the law is spiritual' (Rom. 7:14); that it is 'good' (Rom. 7:16; 1 Tim. 1:8); and he vigorously repudiates any suggestion that it is 'against the promises of God' (Gal. 3:21).　From all this it is plain that when he says 'I delight in the law of God after the inward man' (Rom. 7:22) he merely states the fact.　For Paul the God-given law held a place all its own.　It must never be depreciated.[46]

But it must never be exaggerated either.　The trouble was that the Jews thought of the law as the way of salvation.　Keep the commands of God and you will merit eternal bliss, was their idea. But Paul saw that if a man receives circumcision 'he is a debtor to do the whole law' (Gal. 5:3).　And that is just the difficulty.　No man keeps the whole law.　Paul is firmly convinced that every man alive is a sinner.　This means that there is no salvation along these lines.　'By the works of the law shall no flesh be justified' (Rom.

---

[46] There is a sense in which the law remains indispensable to a right approach to God. Cf. Paul Tillich, 'The majesty of God is challenged, when we make Him the loving Father before we have recognized Him as the condemning law' (op. cit., pp. 134f.). Although we do not think of salvation by works of law, the place of law should not be overlooked.

3:20, and so Gal. 2:16; 3:11).[47]   So far from freeing men from sin, the law caused sin to abound (Rom. 5:20).   It brought men into bondage (Gal. 2:4).   The real function of the law in the scheme of salvation is temporary and preparatory.   It was 'added . . . till the seed should come' (Gal. 3:19).   It was 'our tutor to bring us unto Christ, that we might be justified by faith' (Gal. 3:24).   It could show men their sinfulness and thus prepare them for the salvation that Christ alone could give.   Thus rightly understood it could issue in salvation.   But it could never bring salvation of itself.

Indeed, it could be thought of as the very antithesis of the way of salvation.   Paul several times sets the way of law over against the better way which he describes in terms of grace or promise or the like.   Thus he tells us that 'the law is not of faith; but, He that doeth them shall live in them' (Gal. 3:12).   Here he explicitly contrasts the way of faith, which rests on Christ's work for men, and the way of law, which rests on human achievement.[48]   The gift of the Spirit comes by faith not law (Gal. 3:2, 5; cf. 5:18).   'If the inheritance is of the law, it is no more of promise' (Gal. 3:18).   If men are heirs because they are 'of the law' then 'faith is made void, and the promise is made of none effect' (Rom. 4:14).   The law is not the way.   To be justified by law is to fall away from grace (Gal. 5:4).   Paul contrasts the states of being 'under law' and 'under grace' (Rom. 6:14f.; cf. also 11:6).   The law, he reminds us, 'came four hundred and thirty years after' the covenant with Abraham (Gal. 3:17), a covenant which laid down the principle that God deals with men on the basis of trust, of grace.   For believers, 'Christ is the end of the law unto righteousness' (Rom. 10:4).   His death is effective, whereas if men obtained their righteousness by the way of the law, 'then Christ died for nought' (Gal. 2:21).[49]   These

---

[47] In all of these passages νόμος is anarthrous.   That is to say, Paul's words might be understood in the most general way.   Not only is it true that men are not justified by the works of the Jewish law, but they are not justified by 'works of law' of any kind.   But the primary application is to the law of the Old Testament.

[48] Cf. G. S. Duncan, 'Paul does not mean that faith and the scrupulous observance of ordinances are wholly incompatible *in practice* . . . . What Paul does insist on is that faith and the observance of Law are incompatible as grounds of *justification*.   The Law in itself takes no account of the religious attitude of those who are under its authority; it is concerned merely with the question of performance or non-performance' (*in loc.*).

[49] Cf. Martin Luther, 'But we do constantly affirm with Paul (for we will not reject the grace of God) that either Christ died in vain, or else the law justifieth not.   But Christ died not in vain: therefore the law justifieth not.   Christ the Son of God, of his own free grace and mercy hath justified us: therefore the law could not justify us; for if it could, then had Christ done unwisely in that he gave himself for our sins, that we thereby might be justified.   We conclude therefore, that we are justified neither by our

vigorous passages make it abundantly clear that Paul did not see the law as the means whereby men enter into salvation. It had its place, and a large place, but its place is not that.

We have already noticed that he saw the law as showing men their shortcomings. 'Through the law cometh the knowledge of sin' (Rom. 3:20; so also 7:7). The trenchant argument of Romans 2 is that the law serves to condemn men, not to give them grounds for confidence. 'Not the hearers of a law are just before God, but the doers of a law shall be justified' (Rom. 2:13; cf. also 10:5), but his point is that nobody ever does 'do' the law completely. The law shows up men for what they are, sinners. So strongly does Paul hold this that he can even say 'the power of sin is the law' (1 Cor. 15:56). This is because 'sin is not imputed when there is no law' (Rom. 5:13). Thus he gives us the well-known picture of the man who, not knowing the law, is untroubled by sin. 'I was alive apart from the law once'. But the picture is radically altered when the law comes in. 'When the commandment came, sin revived, and I died' (Rom. 7:9). The point is important and he repeats it in a slightly different form: 'the commandment . . . I found to be unto death: for sin, finding occasion, through the commandment beguiled me, and through it slew me' (Rom. 7:10f.). Indeed, apart from the law sin can be called 'dead' (Rom. 7:8). It derives its strength from the law. Paul can even say, 'the law came in beside, that the trespass might abound' (Rom. 5:20). He categorically denies that the law is sin (Rom. 7:7). The law is good. But, man being what he is, sin works through the law, and would be gravely handicapped, even impotent, apart from the law. There is more to it even than this. The law, considered as the Jews considered it, as a way of salvation, could not but be misleading. Men are not saved that way. Those who trust in law-keeping for their salvation are headed for disaster. The law has become an enemy.[50]

Thus just as Paul has seen sin in alliance with wrath and with death, so he sees it as linked with law. Indeed all these are united in hostility to man. We have already seen the link between the law and sin, and the law and death. Paul also tells us that 'the law

---

own works and merits before grace or after, nor by our cross and afflictions, nor yet by the law, but by faith only in Christ' (*A Commentary on St. Paul's Epistle to the Galatians*, London, 1953, p. 183).

[50] Cf. G. Aulén, 'That the Law is counted as a hostile power does not depend only or chiefly on the fact that the Law inexorably condemns sin. The real reason lies deeper. The way of legal righteousness which the Law recommends, or, rather, demands, can never lead to salvation and life. It leads, like the way of human merit, not to God, but away from God, and deeper and deeper into sin . . . . Thus the Law is an enemy, from whose tyranny Christ has come to save us' (*Christus Victor*, London, 1937, p. 84).

worketh wrath' (Rom. 4:15). Man under the law is man in a dreadful predicament, for the upshot is to bring him under a curse, 'for it is written, Cursed is everyone which continueth not in all things that are written in the book of the law, to do them' (Gal. 3:10).

Allied to this is the thought that men are under condemnation. While this basically signifies a legal sentence, it is not usually related in set terms to the law. For example, Paul speaks of believers as not 'condemned with the world' (1 Cor. 11:32), and of the unworthy recipient of the holy communion as one who 'eateth and drinketh judgment unto himself' (1 Cor. 11:29). The references to condemnation coming through the sin of Adam (Rom. 5:16, 18) necessarily exclude the law, for the happening in question took place prior to the giving of the law. We are a little nearer when we read 'he that resisteth the power, withstandeth the ordinance of God: and they that withstand shall receive to themselves judgement' (Rom. 13: 2; for another example of condemnation for a specific offence see Rom. 3:8). The importance of all this is that it extends the scope of condemnation and makes it as applicable to Gentiles as to Jews. Paul puts the principle clearly: 'he that doeth wrong shall receive again for the wrong that he hath done' (Col. 3:25). Whether under the law or not, all men in their natural state stand under condemnation.

THE FLESH

Like 'law', 'flesh' is a term which is used with several varieties of meaning.[51] Basically it refers to the most important constituent of the physical body, as in the expression 'flesh and blood' (1 Cor. 15:50). So it can denote the whole of this earthly life, for Paul contrasts departing this life with abiding 'in the flesh' (Phil. 1:23f.). This can lead to the thought of weakness. Paul speaks of 'the infirmity of your flesh' (Rom. 6:19), and of the law as being 'weak through the flesh' (Rom. 8:3). This last expression is not far from affirming an ethical weakness in men's flesh, and other passages bring this out. It is this aspect of flesh that is our concern. Just as Paul thought of sin, death, wrath, and law as all in one way or another exercising a harmful sway over men, so is it with flesh. We cannot escape the flesh. As long as we live we are circum-

[51] Kenneth Grayston reminds us that 'The wide range of meanings for *sarx* have not been reduced to a uniform terminology' (TWBB, p. 84). This must constantly be borne in mind. There is a sense in which believers are 'in the flesh' (Gal. 2:20) and a sense in which they are not (Rom. 8:9). There is no difficulty in following such statements, but we must be on our guard against assuming a uniform usage of the term 'flesh'. For a study of this term see William Barclay, *Flesh and Spirit*, London, 1962, pp. 18ff.

scribed by it.[52]   And it, too, turns out to be a tyrant, too strong for man to overcome and operating to his detriment.

In one sense there is no escaping the flesh.   Paul can speak of himself with regard to flesh: 'in me, that is, in my flesh' (Rom. 7:18); 'though we walk in the flesh . . .' (2 Cor. 10:3).   But in this latter passage he makes an important distinction, 'though we walk in the flesh, we do not war according to the flesh'.   While we must live out our lives here and now in the flesh we need not live them in accordance with the standards that our lower nature would set.   The flesh has its appetites, and these all too easily become the occasion of sin.   There are references to 'the lusts of the flesh', a particularly instructive one being Ephesians 2:3, 'we also all once lived in the lusts of our flesh, doing the desires of the flesh and of the mind, and were by nature children of wrath, even as the rest'.   To do the lusts of the flesh, then, is the natural thing.   All unregenerate men do this. Paul explains it as 'doing the desires of the flesh and of the mind', i.e., living the self-centred life, whether this is on what men would call a high or a low level.   It matters not whether a man lives in crude and blatant lust, or in a refined intellectuality, if he is basically concerned to carry out his own desires (even though these desires seem to him 'good') he is living 'in the lusts of the flesh'.   It is not easy for us to grasp the truth that, man being what he is, there is an element of sin even in his 'good' works.[53]   But Paul makes it clear that man's 'flesh' is corrupt.   It is in opposition to the things of God, for 'the flesh lusteth against the Spirit, and the Spirit against the flesh; for these are contrary the one to the other' (Gal. 5:17). Paul goes on to give a terrible list of what he calls 'the works of the flesh' (Gal. 5:19ff.).

It is characteristic of the Christian that he does not live on this level.   He has taken up a radically new position with regard to the flesh.   He has 'crucified' it together with its passions and lusts (Gal. 5:24).   He has put off the whole body of flesh (Col. 2:11),[54]

---

[52] Cf. W. J. Phythian-Adams, 'According to St. Paul (Rom. vii), sin is rooted in the "flesh," in the very *being* of man, thwarting the aspirations of his mind and making the whole organism a "body of death" ' (*The Way of At-one-ment*, London, 1944, pp. 34f.).

[53] Cf. Article 13 of the Anglican Thirty-Nine Articles: 'Works done before the grace of Christ, and the Inspiration of his Spirit, are not pleasant to God, forasmuch as they spring not of faith in Jesus Christ . . . . yea rather, for that they are not done as God hath willed and commanded them to be done, we doubt not but they have the nature of sin.'

[54] On the expressions σῶμα τῆς σαρκός in this verse and σῶμα τῆς ἁμαρτίας in Rom. 6:6, Karl Barth says, 'Can we avoid the comparison that it is not by the giving of medicine, or by an operation, but by the killing of the patient that help is brought?   No word of separating him from his sin, or his sin from him.   He stands or falls with it.   If it disappears, he disappears. And that is what happened on Golgotha' (CDDR, p. 296).

which means that he has rejected the whole concept of living according to the dictates of the flesh. He makes no provision to fulfil its lusts (Rom. 13:14). He recognizes that it is worth destroying the flesh if so the spirit be saved (1 Cor. 5:5). He enjoys liberty, but he does not make that an excuse for pandering to the flesh (Gal. 5:13). Rather he walks in the Spirit (or by the Spirit) and does not fulfil the lust of the flesh (Gal. 5:16). This does not mean asceticism. The New Testament everywhere witnesses to the conviction that life in the body is God-given good, and there is no thought of inflicting hardness on the body for hardness' sake. It means rather that when the power of the Holy Spirit of God is operative within a man there is total renewal.[55] That man is no longer 'in the flesh' (Rom. 8:9). He is no longer dominated by his lower nature. He no longer lives to do his own will. In the power of the Spirit of God he lives to do the will of God.

Flesh is associated closely with sin. A man in his mind may serve the law of God, 'but with the flesh the law of sin' (Rom. 7:25). There is a close tie here. So flesh can be called 'sinful flesh' (Rom. 8:3). Those in the flesh are subject to 'sinful passions' which work in their 'members' (Rom. 7:5). Paul can sum all this up by saying, 'in me, that is, in my flesh, dwelleth no good thing' (Rom. 7:18). The flesh, as flesh, leads to sin and not to goodness.[56]

It is really saying the same thing to say that the flesh leads men into opposition to God, for God is opposed to everything that is evil. Paul tells us simply that 'they that are in the flesh cannot please God' (Rom. 8:8). And he means the same thing, essentially, when he says that 'they that are after the flesh do mind the things of the flesh; but they that are after the spirit the things of the spirit' (Rom. 8:5). He does not shrink from speaking of outright hostility, 'The mind of the flesh is enmity against God' (Rom. 8:7). The flesh stands for man in his creatureliness as a rebel against God. It is

---

[55] David Cox points out that 'St. Paul says, "We know not how to pray as we ought", and then goes on to explain that Christian prayer is only adequate because "The Spirit Himself maketh intercession with our spirit".' He goes on, 'In other words, even when a man is justified his high impulses (in this case the impulse to pray) do not lead him aright, and if this is so the high impulses of natural man must be even less trustworthy' (op. cit., p. 157). Cox insists repeatedly that even the good will of the natural man is sinful, and he cites an impressive catena of Christian writers to show that 'the Christian teaching has always been that the good will of natural man cannot be trusted' (op. cit., p. 158).

[56] W. David Stacey sums up Paul's view in this way: 'Though the flesh is not itself evil, sin invades man through it, finding the easiest entry there. Sin may then grow strong in the flesh and cause havoc in every department of life. It may create a lower nature in the flesh to war constantly with the divine inspiration and to bring about a state of tension and self-contradiction' (The Pauline View of Man, London, 1956, p. 162).

man in the totality of his being, but his unregenerate being. And man in the flesh is doomed. 'He that soweth unto his own flesh shall of the flesh reap corruption' (Gal. 6:8). How can he reap anything else? What else ultimately has the flesh to offer? Sombrely Paul holds out to those in the way of the flesh nothing but death. 'When we were in the flesh,' he says, 'the sinful passions, which were through the law, wrought in our members to bring forth fruit unto death' (Rom. 7:5). 'The mind of the flesh is death' (Rom. 8:6). 'If ye live after the flesh, ye must die' (Rom. 8:13). And man un-aided is not able to resist the flesh. The result of the striving of the flesh against the Spirit is that 'ye may not do the things that ye would' (Gal. 5:17).[57] Paul leaves us with a picture of man as helpless in the grip of his own lower nature, a grip which will at the last lead him to disaster. Outside Christ he sees no hope.

THE ELEMENTAL SPIRITS

The men of antiquity in general had no doubts that the universe is peopled with a host of spirits, some good and some evil.[58] The spirits exercised influences beneficial or baleful on the lives of men. Sometimes they were offered worship;[59] this might seem an elementary precaution. Everywhere the tendency was to treat them with respect. Who could tell when some spirit's activity might not impinge on his own affairs?

Paul has no doubt about the reality of this spirit world.[60] He refers to the spirits on occasion, as when he tells the Corinthians that the sacrifices which the heathen offer to idols they actually 'sacrifice to devils' (1 Cor. 10:20). These appear to be beings subordinate to Satan, whom he also mentions (Rom. 16:20; 2 Cor. 11:14; 1 Thes. 2:18, etc.). This same being is probably meant also by 'the prince of the power of the air' (Eph. 2:2).

[57] Exegetes such as H. N. Ridderbos (NICNT, *in loc.*) and J. B. Lightfoot see here the view that even believers do not completely overcome the flesh. M. A. C. Warren, however, thinks that the verse speaks of the way 'the over-mastering power of the Spirit prevents the triumph of the flesh' (*The Gospel of Victory*, London, 1955, p. 99; so also G. S. Duncan and J. Allan). Whichever interpretation we accept, Paul thinks of victory over the flesh as impossible for man. It is actual only in the power of the Spirit.

[58] See, for example, the discussion by Clinton D. Morrison in *The Powers That Be*, London, 1960.

[59] J. MacQuarrie in two articles under the title 'Demonology and the Classic Idea of Atonement' (ET, lxviii, pp. 3-6, 60-63) argues for 'the identification of the demons with the gods of the pagan world' (*op. cit.,* p. 61).

[60] Cf. G. B. Caird, 'the idea of sinister world powers and their subjugation by Christ is built into the very fabric of Paul's thought, and some mention of them is found in every epistle except Philemon' (*Principalities and Powers,* Oxford, 1956, p. viii).

Other passages almost certainly point us to the spirit world. Thus in Galatians 4:3 we read, 'we also, when we were children, were held in bondage under the rudiments (mg. elements) of the world'. Most scholars see in this a reference to the elemental spirits. The word translated 'rudiments' does refer to the elements, and thus may go on to mean the ABC. But it may also denote the spirits who inhabited the elements, and this is likely to be Paul's meaning here. He uses the same word in Colossians 2:8, and many take the same meaning there.[61] There, however, he speaks of 'philosophy and vain deceit' and of 'the tradition of men', and I incline to the view that his emphasis on man makes a meaning like 'rudimentary religions' or the like slightly more probable.[62]

The expression 'principalities and powers' is found a number of times in Paul. Sometimes at any rate it must refer to spirit beings, as when Paul writes, 'our wrestling is not against flesh and blood, but against the principalities, against the powers, against the world-rulers of this darkness, against the spiritual hosts of wickedness in the heavenly places' (Eph. 6:12). Here it is clear that the expression refers to spirits who are hostile to God and to man's best interests, and who must be resisted stoutly. While the expression can on occasion refer to men (Tit. 3:1), it usually seems to refer to spirits. These are included among the forces that cannot separate us from the love of God (Rom. 8:38f.), the implication being that they might be expected to try. They are created beings (Col. 1:16), and Christ is supreme over them (Col. 2:10).

Paul's major interest in the demons is the fact that they have been completely defeated by Christ. But he apparently regards them as unchecked outside Christ. Without Christ, men are subject to all the perils the spirit world could mount. And the spirits are antagonists that no man can tame. The plight of men in bondage to them is indeed a sorry one.[63]

THE JUDGMENT OF GOD

We have noticed that Paul thinks of the opposition of God to evil in terms of wrath. But this does not exhaust his thought. Like many men in antiquity, Paul delights in legal imagery, and he sometimes thinks of God as visiting the sinner with judgment. This was so from

---

[61] E. g., F. F. Bruce, NICNT, in loc.

[62] So also F. C. Synge, in loc.

[63] A. M. Hunter reminds us of the revival of belief in the demonic in recent times. He cites Otto Piper, Paul Tillich and C. S. Lewis as men who accept this and who are 'not lightly to be labelled obscurantists or charged with fundamentalism. It is the cosmic range and the sheer malignity of the evil they have seen in our world which have led them to re-espouse the Pauline view' (op. cit., p. 75).

the very beginning. He can speak of God's action on the occasion of Adam's sin in these terms: 'for the judgment came of one unto condemnation' (Rom. 5:16). God dealt judicially with Adam and his posterity.

Somewhat in the Johannine manner, Paul thinks of judgment as a present reality. This comes out clearly in the latter part of Romans 1. Here Paul is speaking of the consequences of the sins in which the Gentiles indulge, and three times he says that 'God gave them up' to these consequences (Rom. 1:24, 26, 28). The earthly-minded would see in these things nothing more than the natural consequences of the sins in which the Gentiles engaged. To a man like Paul, with his vivid consciousness of the divine government of all the affairs of men, there are no such things as purely 'natural consequences'. Many today find no difficulty in the thought of an impersonal process of cause and effect operating quite apart from God. For Paul this would have been an intolerable thought. For him nothing operates apart from God. If men sin, and evil consequences follow, then that is because God has willed it so.[64] God punishes men by those consequences.

There is a good example of the extremes to which Paul will take this in his Thessalonian correspondence. He refers to certain people who 'received not the love of the truth, that they might be saved' and proceeds, 'God sendeth them a working of error, that they should believe a lie' (2 Thes. 2:10f.). Most men today would be inclined to say that these people turned their backs on the love of the truth, and because they rejected truth they naturally came to believe a lie. But Paul does not hesitate to say that the hand of God is to be seen in this process. God judges them by shutting them up to the delusion they choose in preference to the truth.[65] There are mysteries here, but Paul thinks of the judgments of God as 'unsearchable' (Rom. 11:33). The principle behind all this is 'whatsoever a man soweth, that shall he also reap' (Gal. 6:7). Paul is sure that, while there is no automatic process at work and man is not able to discern the full process by any means, yet the judgments of God are being worked out in men's lives. And God's judgment is a righteous judgment (2 Thes. 1:5).

But he does not think of God's judgment as being exhausted in what takes place here and now. He has a good deal to say about 'the day when God shall judge the secrets of men, according to

---

[64] E. H. Gifford sees a reference to the 'natural consequences' of sin, but adds, 'what the Apostle further teaches us is that this law of our moral nature is a law of the living God, who Himself works in and by it' (*The Epistle of St. Paul to the Romans*, London, 1886, p. 65).

[65] 'Men who reject the Gospel of God are bound to end by accepting evil as truth. Thereby God uses Satan as the means of punishing them' (*Tyndale Commentary, in loc.*).

my gospel, by Jesus Christ' (Rom. 2:16). He ridicules the idea
that some men might escape judgment (Rom. 2:3), and solemnly
reminds his readers that 'each one of us shall give account of himself to God' (Rom. 14:12), 'each shall receive his own reward
according to his own labour' (1 Cor. 3:8; see also 4:5). Out of this
conviction he can tell the Galatians that 'he that troubleth you shall
bear his judgement, whosoever he be' (Gal. 5:10). But men may
have confidence in the prospect of that judgment, for it will not be
an imperfect judgment like the judgments of earth, even at best. It
is 'according to truth' (Rom. 2:2). Those who do the things for
which punishment is meted out 'are worthy of death' (Rom. 1:32).
There will be no 'respect of persons' (Eph. 6:9). Paul can speak
indifferently of all men as standing before the judgment seat of God
(Rom. 14:10f.), or of Christ (2 Cor. 5:10). That does not matter.
What matters is that judgment is certain.[66] And in the light of
it Paul can say, 'Knowing therefore the fear of the Lord . . .'
(2 Cor. 5:11). The fear of the Lord is a very present factor for
Paul, and one to be used in sizing up many situations. It is especially
relevant to the truth that no man shall escape judgment.

OTHER CONSIDERATIONS

The foregoing represent the chief ways Paul saw man as in a difficult position. But they do not exhaust the apostle's thought,
and we will notice in this section of our study one or two other
facets. One which is very relevant to modern man is that Paul
sometimes thinks of man, as indeed of the whole creation, as being
in bondage to futility. 'The creation', he says, 'was subjected to
vanity' (Rom. 8:20), and again 'we know that the whole creation
groaneth and travaileth in pain together until now' (Rom. 8:22).
His thought is that, apart from Christ, there is a meaninglessness in
life, and this meaninglessness runs right through creation. Nor is
it removed by intellectual depth, for Paul has many references to the
emptiness of merely worldly wisdom. This is behind his argument
in 1 Corinthians 1 and 2, a massive argument in which he dismisses
intellectual pretension, no matter how glittering. So he warns the
Colossians against 'philosophy and vain deceit' (Col. 2:8), and
against the man who is 'vainly puffed up by his fleshly mind' (Col.
2:18). He admonishes the Ephesians, 'Let no man deceive you
with empty words' (Eph. 5:6), and reminds them that the Gentiles
walk 'in the vanity of their mind' (Eph. 4:17).[67] He exhorts the

66 Cf. H. L. Goudge, 'How God's judgment will one day be exercised we
do not know; but that it will be exercised, our consciences surely bear
witness. A world in which justice was not at last done would not be
God's world at all' (Sin and Redemption, London, 1919, p. 29).
67 Cf. E. K. Simpson, 'Professing wisdom, ancient culture had branded
itself with the stigma of downright futility. Its fatal hollowness could no

Galatians and the Philippians to avoid 'vainglory' (Gal. 5:26; Phil. 2:3). It is plain from such citations from several epistles that one strand of Paul's teaching may be summed up in his quotation from the Psalms, 'The Lord knoweth the reasonings of the wise, that they are vain' (1 Cor. 3:20; cf. 1 Tim. 6:20; 2 Tim. 2:16).

All this speaks to the generation that has known the 'beatniks,' the 'teddy boys', the 'bodgies', and the 'widgies', and many more. There is a pointlessness about life for most people, an aimlessness, a futility.[68] We may deceive ourselves temporarily by activism or the like, but it is there. Paul felt it, and we feel it, too.

Allied to this is Paul's thought about this 'world'. We have already noticed that he thinks little of this world's wisdom. He says bluntly that 'the wisdom of this world is foolishness with God' (1 Cor. 3:19), and with a rhetorical flourish he asks, 'hath not God made foolish the wisdom of the world?' (1 Cor. 1:20). His main point here is that the world in its wisdom cannot know God (1 Cor. 1:21). Sometimes he thinks of the sheer ignorance of this world's wise men, as when they crucified the Lord, a thing they would never have done had they realized that He was 'the Lord of glory' (1 Cor. 2:8). Sometimes it is the transitoriness of this world (1 Cor. 7:31). Sometimes it is its powerlessness to produce anything other than death (2 Cor. 7:10). Ultimately it can receive nothing other than condemnation (1 Cor. 11:32).

The world may arouse in men such a love that they forsake their duty (2 Tim. 4:10). Accordingly it is not surprising that we sometimes find the world thought of as 'this present evil world' (Gal. 1:4). Or it may be associated with evil powers, as in our conflict with 'the world-rulers of this darkness' (Eph. 6:12), or when we read that 'the god of this world hath blinded the minds of the unbelieving' (2 Cor. 4:4; cf. also Gal. 4:3). Whether Colossians 2:8 be understood of the elemental spirits of the world or not, its mention of 'world' puts it in opposition to the things of God.

---

longer be hid. Its sapient insipidities of diet supplied nothing to sate the gnawing hunger of the human heart' (NICNT, *in loc.*).

[68] Cf. Lewis Mumford, 'The period through which we are living presents itself as one of unmitigated confusion and disintegration: a period of paralyzing economic depressions, of unrestrained butcheries and enslavements, and of world-ravaging wars: a period whose evil fulfillments have betrayed all its beneficent promises. But behind all these phenomena of physical destruction we can detect an earlier and perhaps more fundamental series of changes: a loss of communion between classes and peoples, a breakdown in stable behaviour, a loss of form and purpose in many of the arts, with a growing emphasis on the accidental and the trivial: in short, the earliest form of this crisis was an internal "schism of the soul," as Toynbee calls it, and a break-up of the over-all pattern of meaning' (*The Condition of Man*, London, 1944, p. 14).

Now and then Paul can speak of such things as 'the bondage of corruption' (Rom. 8:21; cf. I Cor. 6:12; 15:42). Or he can talk about 'affliction' which he finds so much a part of this life (2 Cor. 2:4; 4:17; 6:4; 8:2, etc.).

It is very clear that he thinks of life in this world as necessarily involving subjection to the futilities of existence, and of what passes with this world for wisdom. Inherent in the very nature of life in this world is subjection of this kind. Man left to himself is bound up to it. He cannot break away.

Paul's teaching on the atonement must be understood against this background. Modern men often have a rather shallow view of life, and are not one whit disturbed.[69] They do not see themselves as being in any really great danger, and therefore they see no need of salvation. Of what need is salvation to the safe? But Paul's analysis of the situation in which man, modern man as well as ancient man, finds himself is much more profound. He takes with seriousness life as he finds it, and he sees that man's existence is limited by various of the influences we have been considering in this chapter. But not only do these things constitute limitations. They constitute also a threat. As long as life is like this, man is in grave and imminent danger. Paul thought of Christ as one who can and does deliver His people. But we cannot understand the deliverance unless we first see what His people are delivered from.

[69] A. M. Hunter cites Niebuhr as speaking of men who 'put their trust in a God without wrath who brings men without sin into a kingdom without judgment through the ministrations of a Christ without a Cross' (*op. cit.*, p. 73).

CHAPTER SIX

The Cross in the Pauline Epistles

II. THE SALVATION OF GOD

The preceding chapter has made it plain that Paul takes a very serious view of man's plight. Sin he sees as pregnant with dire consequences, and it is allied to wrath, death, and other forces hostile to man. He has no illusions about human goodness nor about what lies in store for sinners. It is impossible to exaggerate the dangers in which man stands, as Paul sees the situation.

But his writings are not a series of gloomy meditations on horrors present and to come. Paul is no pessimist. If he faces sin and sin's consequences realistically, he looks equally realistically at God's remedy for sin. His writings are a veritable torrent of enthusiasm as he struggles with the inadequacy of mere words to convey the mighty deliverance that meant so much to him. God has wrought salvation for men, a salvation adequate to deal with every aspect of man's need. So Paul sets forth for all to read the wonder of what God has done, the manifold variety of the salvation that God has

wrought, and the consequences for man both now and in the hereafter. And the cross is right at the centre. It was on the cross that
the divine salvation was wrought out. It is there that Paul sees
God's will to save men as he sees it nowhere else. And if his
thought on the atonement is complex, the complexity is the natural
result of what we have seen in the preceding chapter. Man's plight
is far from simple. He is involved in a veritable maze of horrors.
So the cross, which deals with that plight in the most thoroughgoing
fashion, while from one point of view delightfully simple ('the Son
of God . . . loved me, and gave himself up for me', Gal. 2:20),
is complicated with all the complexity that the situation demanded.

THE FULFILMENT OF SCRIPTURE

We begin with Paul's way of finding his teachings in Holy Writ.
He was not conscious of being an innovator. He was simply drawing men's attention to what God had revealed and done. He thought
of God as active in the atoning work of Christ, and if God was
active then God's purpose was being wrought out. Now God had
revealed His purposes for men in the pages of the Scripture, so
nothing could be more natural for Paul than to find the work of
Christ and the way of salvation generally foreshadowed in his Bible.
Over and over again he points to the Old Testament to show how the
saving events of Christ's life and death were there set forth.

Thus he begins the Epistle to the Romans by informing his
readers that he had been 'separated unto the gospel of God, which
he promised afore by his prophets in the holy scriptures' (Rom.
1:1f.).[1] He does not waste a moment before making it plain to
these believers in the great city he had never seen that the message
he set forth was one grounded in the Bible. The gospel he proclaimed was no personal invention, but that 'promised afore by
his prophets'. We have already seen that Paul gave a very large place
in his scheme of things to the sin that had marred men's lives. But
that is nothing to be surprised at, for 'the scripture hath shut up all
things under sin' (Gal. 3:22). Once his eyes were open to the
realities of the situation, he saw that the Bible pointed forward
to it. He saw the great central acts of the passion as foretold in the
same holy writings. 'Christ died for our sins according to the

---

[1] F. J. Leenhardt comments, 'In speaking of the gospel of God, Paul
already connects the proclamation of Jesus Christ with the plan of God
which the prophets first disclosed. There is only one God, who speaks
differently according to the diversity of times and seasons: but His message is eternally the same, for He is true; and He ever pursues the same work,
for He is faithful. His veracity and His fidelity culminate in Jesus the
Christ . . . . The end illuminates the meaning of the process which led up
to it. Thus Holy Scripture in its totality arranges itself into a meaningful
pattern' (*in loc.*).

scriptures', he tells the Corinthians, as a truth of supreme importance (1 Cor. 15:3).[2] So also the resurrection was foretold: 'he hath been raised on the third day according to the scriptures' (1 Cor. 15:4).

It is not only the significant events and details of the passion that Paul sees as foretold in the Scripture, but also the broad general plan of salvation. Thus he can say, 'the scripture, foreseeing that God would justify the Gentiles by faith, preached the gospel beforehand unto Abraham, saying, In thee shall all the nations be blessed' (Gal. 3:8). Justification by faith is by common consent one of Paul's very central topics. It is fundamental to his understanding of salvation. And here the Scripture foresees it, and preaches the gospel that involved it, to Abraham. That this is no casual expression is indicated by the fact that his extended treatment of Abraham in Romans 4 proceeds on basically the same assumption. God has always worked on this principle and Abraham is the classical example. Rightly understood, the scripture gives the clue to the interpretation of the great events associated with Christ. Along the same lines we notice that Paul was always calling on men to believe; and faith, too, he saw as a truth of scripture, 'For the scripture saith, Whosoever believeth on him shall not be put to shame' (Rom. 10:11). Small wonder that he should write to Timothy, 'from a babe thou hast known the sacred writings which are able to make thee wise unto salvation' (2 Tim. 3:15).

It may be that we should take another point of importance from Paul's references to the blessing promised to the Gentiles through Abraham's seed (Gal. 3:8, 13f.). Rabbinic exegesis made much of Isaac's willingness to.be sacrificed and of the consequent superlative worth of his offering. The Rabbis attached all manner of blessings to this sacrifice. If, as may well be the case, Paul has this Rabbinic interpretation of Scripture in mind, then he is saying that the realization of all of Israel's hope of redemption, foreshadowed from of old, lies in the perfect sacrifice of Jesus.[3] It is possible that a reference to the

---

[2] The expression ἐν πρώτοις, rendered 'first of all' probably does not mean that this was the first thing Paul said to the Corinthians. It signifies rather that this was 'first in importance'.

[3] G. Vermes argues strongly that Paul's view of Christ's saving work is based on the Jewish idea of the binding of Isaac (*Scripture and Tradition in Judaism*, Leiden, 1961, pp. 219f.). So also H. J. Schoeps, *Paul*, London, 1961, p. 141. I. Speyart van Woerden, in an article entitled, "The Iconography of the Sacrifice of Abraham" (*Vigiliae Christianae*, xv, pp. 214-255), suggests that the frequency with which this scene is depicted by ecclesiastics implies that they attached great importance to it. On the other hand, C. K. Barrett thinks that Paul made no serious use of the conception (*A Commentary on the Epistle to the Romans*, London, 1957, p. 99). If Paul did have it in mind as much as the former writers maintain, one wonders why he was not a little more explicit.

binding of Isaac is often to be discerned, for the Rabbis connected it with the suffering servant passages, with the Passover, and with the blowing of the trumpet at the New Year celebrations.

Paul is an inveterate quoter of Scripture. For him the Bible was verily the word of God, and its authority was unquestioned. He looked to it for guidance on the deep matters of life, and specifically on the way men must be saved. When he gave out his teaching he was not conscious of introducing anything totally new. He realized that there was novelty, even radical novelty, but not the kind of novelty that sweeps away everything that precedes it. There is a newness in his message, but it is firmly rooted in the old. The gospel is that to which the Old Testament pointed throughout, and what is new is the fulfilment, not the principle. The gospel he saw as no afterthought, but God's eternal plan to bring about man's salvation. God had always intended to save men by the way of the cross. Therefore Paul sees this way foreshadowed, indeed, foretold with minute accuracy in the Bible. The fulfilment of scripture was the guarantee that this is truly the purpose of God that is being done.

PREDESTINATION

A strand of Pauline teaching which is uncongenial to modern man is that wherein he speaks of election, predestination, and the like. In this democratic age we like to think that we cast our own vote to determine our final destination, be it heaven or hell. We do not care to delegate this to another, not even to God. And it scarcely occurs to us to inquire whether the matter is in our hands at all. Nor do we like the element of unfairness we think we detect in the doctrine. We do not consider it 'just' that God alone should choose His elect. So we roundly deny it. But Paul is untroubled by our modern fastidiousness. He takes it as axiomatic that the almighty God[4] does what He pleases, in the matter of salvation as in all else. He rejoices in the thought that it is God, none less, who has chosen him, Paul, for salvation and for service.[5] He sees in this

---

[4] Cf. Gwilym O. Griffith, 'when Paul says "God" he means God; not a seedling Divinity in process of germination, or a gradually evolving Being in quest of "experience," but God, than whom Paul can think of nothing higher, and great beyond all his conceiving . . . . Paul will ascribe to Him all foreknowledge. An unprescient God, says Augustine, deeply learned in Paul, were no God at all . . . . So Paul will ascribe to Him predestinative purpose. Divine foreknowledge is servant to Divine Holiness and Grace. Every attribute of God is active. Whom He did foreknow them He also did predestinate' (*St. Paul's Life of Christ*, London, 1925, pp. 204f.).

[5] Cf. the statement in Article 17 of the Anglican Thirty-Nine Articles, 'the godly consideration of Predestination, and our Election in Christ, is full of sweet, pleasant, and unspeakable comfort to godly persons . . . .'

the grounds for an optimism that could not exist were men to be the masters of their own fate.[6]

Let us first notice that Paul speaks often of the will of God as being done. He sees this, for example, in his own apostolate as he repeatedly assures us (1 Cor. 1:1; Eph. 1:1; Col. 1:1). He sees it notably in the death of the Lord, 'who gave himself for our sins . . . according to the will of our God and Father' (Gal. 1:4). In the opening section of Ephesians there is a very noteworthy discussion of predestination in which there are repeated references to the will of God as being done. Paul goes as far as to speak of 'the purpose of him who worketh all things after the counsel of his will' (Eph. 1:11). Later he refers to 'the eternal purpose which he purposed in Christ Jesus our Lord' (Eph. 3:11), where he clearly has in mind the death of Christ for our salvation. So also we read that 'Christ Jesus came into the world to save sinners' (1 Tim. 1:15). Much more could be cited. It is not germane to our purpose to go through the complex argument of such a passage as Romans 9-11, but we should not overlook the fact that through it all Paul stresses that the will of God is done.[7] This is one of the apostle's leading ideas. God works out His purposes. He does His will, whatever men may think about it. And the purpose of God culminates in the cross.

Sometimes Paul uses a very expressive term to describe the whole message of salvation, when he calls it a 'mystery'. The Greek term *mysterion* does not denote the mysterious in our sense of the term, i. e., some problem which it is very difficult for men to work out. The *mysterion* is something which men could not work out at all. It points to something quite beyond men's capacity for solving. But there is the added thought that God has now been pleased to reveal it.[8] Paul can use the term of such things as 'the mystery of lawlessness' (2 Thes. 2:7), but his special use of the term is for 'the mystery of the gospel' (Eph. 6:19). Who could have guessed that for man's salvation God Himself would become incarnate and die a felon's death? Such a truth is the reverse of what human wisdom might devise. It cannot be deduced by the intellect. It is made known by revelation, or it is not known at all. Paul's task

---

[6] Cf. A. Barr, SJT, iii, pp. 68-77.

[7] Cf. E. F. Scott, 'We are not to read the chapters as if they had reference only to the controversy of Jew and Gentile which agitated the church in Paul's day and is now a thing of the past. In the light of one specific instance we are meant to perceive how the divine purpose fulfils itself in the whole life of the world' (*Paul's Epistle to the Romans,* London, 1947, p. 56).

[8] The New Testament 'uses it to mean the secret thoughts, plans, and dispensations of God which are hidden fr. the human reason, as well as fr. all other comprehension below the divine level, and hence must be revealed to those for whom they are intended' (AG *sub voc.*).

is 'to make all men see what is the dispensation of the mystery which from all ages hath been hid in God' (Eph. 3:9), to which statement he adds the rider that the purpose of this is that 'unto the principalities and the powers in the heavenly places might be made known through the church the manifold wisdom of God, according to the eternal purpose which he purposed in Christ Jesus our Lord' (Eph. 3:10f.). That is to say, when the gospel is proclaimed in power and men are brought into salvation, then God's wise dealings are made plain and open for all to see. There is wisdom in the mystery of the gospel, though it is not a wisdom devised by man. It is the thought of the divine wisdom in the mystery that is before Paul also in 1 Corinthians 2:7, where he adds the thought that it is 'the wisdom that hath been hidden, which God foreordained before the worlds unto our glory'. So also it was 'kept in silence through times eternal, but now is manifested' (Rom. 16:25f.). This is the thought also when Paul speaks of the mystery as made known to himself 'by revelation', but that it 'in other generations was not made known unto the sons of men, as it hath now been revealed unto his holy apostles and prophets in the Spirit' (Eph. 3: 3, 5; cf. also 1:9). In this passage the thought that the gospel is for the Gentiles as well as the Jews is prominent, and it is found also in a notable statement in Colossians where Paul speaks of the mystery as 'hid from all ages and generations: but now hath it been manifested to his saints'. Then he goes on to speak of 'the riches of the glory of this mystery among the Gentiles, which is Christ in you, the hope of glory' (Col. 1:26f.). Throughout all these passages there run several key thoughts: (1) God works out His purpose in the gospel. (2) It was an eternal purpose, purposed before the ages began. (3) It is hid from men, and nobody can know it except by way of revelation. (4) But Paul's big point is that now it has been made known. God has revealed it. The way of the cross is made plain and open, at least to the saints of God. And therein God brings salvation to Gentile as to Jew.

Often Paul speaks of men as being predestined to salvation. The purpose of God, he says, is 'according to election . . . not of works' (Rom. 9:11),[9] and a good deal of his writings are given over to drawing out the meaning of this. The saved can be spoken of simply as 'the election' (Rom. 11:5, 7, 28; cf. also 1 Thes. 1:4). When he is combating the pretensions of the Corinthians, Paul emphasizes the truth that election does not take place on the

---

[9] Johannes Munck, dealing with the argument of Rom. 9-11 says, 'in Paul's view God by his free grace took Israel into his care, afterwards making the disobedient nation hard-hearted, and again taking it into his care before the end of the world. That line of thought presupposes a plan of salvation, a living God who acts in human history . . .' (*Paul and the Salvation of Mankind*, London, 1959, p. 48).

basis of human excellence. If all believers were men of super-lative excellence then it might be held that God chose out those best qualified in the world. But God chose not the great of this world but 'the foolish things of the world . . . the weak things of the world . . . the base things of the world, and the things that are despised . . . yea and the things that are not' (1 Cor. 1:27f.). The reason for His choice remains with God. Believers are those who have been 'fore-ordained . . . unto adoption as sons through Jesus Christ', who have been 'foreordained according to the purpose of him who worketh all things after the counsel of his will' (Eph. 1:5, 11). God 'chose us in him before the foundation of the world' (Eph. 1:4), He 'chose you from the beginning unto salvation' (2 Thes. 2:13). Eternal life is something which 'God, who cannot lie, promised before times eternal' (Tit. 1:2). Many times Paul refers to the promises of God as being fulfilled in believers (e. g., 2 Cor. 1:20; 7:1). He refers to the faithfulness of God (1 Thes. 5:24; 2 Thes. 3:3). In the end men are saved, not because of any merit or deed or attitude of their own but because God chooses to save them.[10] In the last resort we can only say, 'The Lord knoweth them that are his' (2 Tim. 2:19).

Since this doctrine is so often rejected, misunderstood and opposed it may be as well to add one or two points. One is that election is an act of divine love. Paul can write to the Thessalonians, 'know-ing, brethren beloved of God, your election' (1 Thes. 1:4). The popular caricature of predestination sees it as a process wherein God sentences some men to damnation before they are born, with-out ever giving them a chance. This is not the teaching of the Bible. There election is a means of saving men, not of sentencing them. It proceeds from God's love and His deep concern for men. The connection of predestination with love should never be over-looked.[11]

The second thing is that the thought of predestination is some-thing that gives assurance. If we were dependent on our own effort for salvation we would never know whether we had done enough. If we were saved by Christ, but were dependent on retaining our hold on Him we could never be sure that we would not weaken. But Paul can say, 'whom he foreknew, he also foreordained to be

---

[10] Cf. Karl Heim, 'Certainly every conversion to Christ takes place by means of a conscious decision of the will which is made as the result of the message of a living witness. But everyone who does reach an inward change will discover afterwards that he made no decision of his own but that a decision was made concerning him from all eternity, that is to say in a supra-temporal fashion. His surrender to Christ depends on a supra-temporal calling which became an act on the temporal level and has its effect on the ethical level in the form of a surrender of our will' (*Jesus the World's Perfecter*, Edinburgh and London, 1959, p. 230).

[11] See further pp. 237f. below.

conformed to the image of his Son . . . and whom he foreordained, them he also called: and whom he called, them he also justified: and whom he justified, them he also glorified' (Rom. 8:29f.). The sequence goes on with splendid inevitability to glorification. Those who have been predestined will not fall by the way. 'God never goes back upon his . . . call' (Rom. 11:29, Moffatt). It should not be overlooked that we tend to regard predestination as a part of a philosophical theory. For us it is the answer to the question, 'Are all things determined or not?' For Paul it is the answer to quite another question, 'How much of our salvation is due to God?' It is part of man's make-up that he likes to think that he earns his salvation. When he sees that the cross rules out the way of human merit and that he is saved by grace, by God's free gift, he tries to salvage something from the wreck. He thinks that at any rate he deserves some credit. He made the right decision. He decided to be a Christian. He chose God. The doctrine of predestination takes this last prop from under him. He could not decide this, left to himself. The reason he is a believer is not that he chose God but that God chose him. Predestination is the assurance that *all* of our salvation, from the very beginning to the end, is of God. We ought never to think of it other than in relation to salvation. That is where Paul sets it. It assures me that my salvation is no improvised affair, brought into being by a more or less fortuitous decision of my own. I am saved because none less than God willed it and pre-destined me before all the ages. Nothing at all can give the believer assurance like this great truth.

And thirdly predestination is related to ethical ends. Paul can exhort the Colossians, 'Put on therefore, as God's elect, holy and beloved, a heart of compassion . . .' (Col. 3:12). Precisely because they are elect they are to produce qualities of character. If a man says, 'I am predestined to salvation, therefore it does not matter what kind of life I live' he shows that he does not understand the biblical doctrine of predestination. Predestination does not encourage ethical sloth. Believers are not spiritually lazy. Believers are 'created in Christ Jesus for good works, which God afore prepared that we should walk in them' (Eph. 2:10). The good life of the people of God and their election are not two separate subjects. Election is for the purpose of doing the good works that God has prepared for His people to do.[12]

---

[12] H. H. Rowley emphasizes that 'Election is for service . . . it is never primarily for the privilege but for the service that the elect are chosen' (*The Biblical Doctrine of Election,* London, 1952, p. 45). He says, 'The Biblical doctrine of election is therefore penetrated through and through with warning. To be the elect of God is not to be His pampered favourite. It is to be challenged to a loyalty and a service and a sacrifice

So Paul continually stresses the divine initiative. It is God who 'saved us, and called us' (2 Tim. 1:9). 'By grace have ye been saved through faith; and that not of yourselves: it is the gift of God' (Eph. 2:8). He has freely given us grace 'in the Beloved' (Eph. 1:6). Indeed, Paul's whole stress on grace should be very much borne in mind in this connection.[13] Grace and predestination are not two disparate things, but two different ways of looking at the same divine action. Along the same lines Paul speaks of there being but one foundation, and of Christ as having laid it (1 Cor. 3:11). He tells us that it is God 'which worketh in you' (Phil. 2: 13). Much more could be quoted. It is plain that Paul thought of God as working out His will in the whole process of salvation, from its beginning before eternity in His own secret counsel to its culmination in eternity in the bliss of heaven. He was not taken by surprise by men's sin. In Christ He carried out His predetermined plan to overcome it.[14] And He brought His elect to salvation.

THE DEATH OF CHRIST

For Paul the death of Christ is the great fact on which salvation for all believers depends. For him it is absolutely central. He is always speaking about it, and he ransacks his vocabulary to bring out something of the richness of its meaning. So much of what he says has passed into the common stock of Christian knowledge that it is difficult to estimate at all fully our debt to him. It comes as

---

that knows no limits, and to feel the constraint of the Divine love to such a degree that no response can seem adequate and no service worthy' (*op. cit.,* p. 168).

[13] J. K. S. Reid argues strongly that the place of Christ in predestination should not be minimized (SJT, i, pp. 5-19, 166-183). He stresses that Christ is the Chosen, for which he cites Mt. 17:5, and that believers are chosen in Christ before the foundation of the world, Eph. 1:4 (*op. cit.,* pp. 179f.). He says, 'Predestination is *sola gratia.* It is the eternal determination of God's will towards men, in total disregard of any considerations but those of grace . . . . Predestination is simply grace traced, if we may so put it, to its earliest source, and found to be already deposited safely within an eternal decision' (*op. cit.,* pp. 174f.).

[14] D. E. H. Whiteley says that 'much of the offence of the doctrine (i. e., predestination) is due to the fact that we understand it in a mechanistic fashion as a system of depersonalized mechanical necessities . . . . Unfortunately, theologians have strained out the personal element' (SE, p. 105). It is right to insist that predestination deals with persons, not things, and that in the Bible it is far from being a mechanical process. Yet we must not take this so far that we empty the doctrine of meaning. As Whiteley goes on, 'Yet we cannot evade the question "Is God's purpose for the world to be achieved or is it not?" And if we are Christians we are bound to say that God's purpose will be achieved, that God is powerful over all, παντοκράτωρ' (*loc. cit.*).

something of a surprise, for example, to find that, apart from the crucifixion narrative and one verse in Hebrews, Paul is the only New Testament writer to speak about 'the cross'. We find it difficult to talk for long about Jesus without mentioning 'the cross', and this is the measure of the way Paul has influenced all subsequent Christian vocabulary. We would imagine that there are many New Testament references to the death of Christ. But, outside of Paul, there are not. That is to say, there are not many which use the noun 'death' (references to 'the blood' of Christ, which mean much the same thing, are more frequent). Paul has a good deal to say about 'the death of his Son' (Rom. 5:10), but this is not a common New Testament form of expression. And it is not only a question of terminology. There are great ideas in connection with Christ's work for men which are found only or mainly in the apostle's writings. Thus it is to Paul that we owe great concepts like justification,[15] imputation, reconciliation, adoption, the state of being 'in Christ', and a good deal more. Even the bare recital of a list like this is enough to indicate something of the richness of Paul's thought about the cross, and of the very great debt that we owe him.

Repeatedly Paul says that Christ died for sin and that he died for men. For the first point let us notice that He was 'delivered up for our trespasses' (Rom. 4:25), that He 'died for our sins' (1 Cor. 15:3), that He 'gave himself for our sins' (Gal. 1:4), that 'the death that he died, he died unto sin once for all' (Rom. 6:10, mg.), that God sent Him 'in the likeness of sinful flesh[16] and as an offering for sin' (Rom. 8:4). For the second point, 'Christ died for the ungodly' (Rom. 5:6), or for 'sinners' (Rom. 5:8). He 'died for all' (2 Cor. 5:14). He 'died for us' (1 Thes. 5:10). It is clear that both thoughts mean a good deal for Paul, and that they are connected, as when he speaks of Christ's death for 'sinners'. It is probable that he gives us the connection as he sees it when he tells us that 'the wages of sin is death' (Rom. 6:23). He repeatedly links death with sin in a causal fashion (Rom. 5:12ff.; 1 Cor. 15:21). This is not a simple thought because physical death and a state of

---

[15] Justification is mentioned once in the Gospels (in the sense of acceptance before God), namely when Jesus said that the publican 'went down to his house justified' (Lk. 18:14), twice in Acts (in a speech of Paul, Acts 13:39), and three times in James in what is evidently an echo of the controversy aroused by Paul's teaching (Jas. 2:21, 24, 25). While the terminology is not absolutely confined to Paul it is plain that the basic idea was developed by him and by no one else in the New Testament.

[16] On this expression G. Smeaton says, 'His human nature never existed apart from personal union to the Son of God, nor apart from sin-bearing; and hence He appeared in the likeness of the flesh of sin, not by a mere arbitrary assimilation to us men, but because He bore in His own body the weight of imputed sin' (*The Apostles' Doctrine of the Atonement*, Grand Rapids, 1957, p. 173).

soul seem both to be involved. It is impossible to understand either Romans 5 or 1 Corinthians 15 without the thought of physical death. But it is impossible to think of physical death as exhausting the thought of either passage. Death is both mortality, a liability to physical death, and also separation from God, an alienation from that life which alone is worth calling life ('the mind of the flesh is death' whereas 'the mind of the spirit is life', Rom. 8:6).

This close connection between sin and death for Paul demanded that Christ's saving act should deal with death. As James Denney puts it, 'It was sin which made death, and not something else, necessary as a demonstration of God's love and Christ's. Why was this so? The answer of the apostle is that it was so because sin had involved *us* in death, and there was no possibility of Christ's dealing with sin effectually except by taking *our* responsibility in it on himself — that is, except by dying for it.'[17] In dying then Christ died that death which is the wages of sin. His death is effective to deal with the consequences of our sin. We had involved ourselves in death. Christ took over our involvement and freed us from it.

Paul can sum up his message by saying 'we preach Christ crucified' (1 Cor. 1:23). When he came to Corinth he had reached a determination not only not to preach, but also 'not to know anything among you, save Jesus Christ and him crucified' (1 Cor. 2:2). Likewise among the Galatians 'Jesus Christ was openly set forth (or "placarded") crucified' (Gal. 3:1). Each of these passages shows that the crucified Christ was primary in Paul's preaching. In each case 'crucified' is the perfect participle, which means that Paul preached not only that Christ was once crucified (which would be the aorist), but that He continues in His character as the crucified One. The crucifixion is a fact of permanent significance and not simply a historical curiosity.[18] It is this firm conviction of the permanent efficacy of the crucifixion that leads Paul to say that he will glory only in the cross (Gal. 6:14).

Sometimes he prefers to speak of 'the blood' of Christ, as when he tells us that God set Him forth 'to be a propitiation, through faith, by his blood' (Rom. 3:25), or when he refers to 'being now justified by his blood' (Rom. 5:9). It is 'through his blood' that we have redemption (Eph. 1:7). Yet another of Paul's great concepts, reconciliation, is related to 'the blood', for it was the Father's

---

[17] DC, p. 126.

[18] On this participle in 1 Cor. 1:23, R. St. J. Parry says, 'The perf. part. marks at once the fact and the triumph over the fact, its inclusion in the renewed and larger life of the risen Lord: so Gal. iii. 1; the aorist is used where the bare fact and its circumstances are referred to . . . but here the thought is of the abiding significance of the fact under the conditions of the ascended Life. Neither Person nor fact is merely of the past: they are both of the eternal present' (*in loc.*).

good pleasure 'through him to reconcile all things unto himself, having made peace through the blood of his cross' (Col. 1:20; cf. Eph. 2:13). He speaks of the use of the chalice in the holy communion as 'a communion of (or "participation in", as mg.) the blood of Christ' (1 Cor. 10:16), and he reports the words of Christ at the institution, 'This cup is the new covenant in my blood' (1 Cor. 11:25). Thus Paul relates 'the blood' to each of his most important ways of interpreting what Christ did for us and to the great sacrament in which Christians habitually joined. It is an important idea.

Attempts have been made in modern times to show that 'blood' points us essentially to life.[19] Exponents of such views rely heavily on a particular interpretation of Leviticus 17:11, 'the life of the flesh is in the blood: and I have given it to you upon the altar to make atonement for your souls: for it is the blood that maketh atonement by reason of the life'. Now this verse is patient of more than one interpretation. It could mean that the ritual presentation of blood signifies the ritual presentation to God of life, the life of the victim. Or, it could mean that what is ritually presented to God is the evidence that a death has taken place in accordance with His judgment on sin. For blood *in separation from the flesh* is not life but death. Upholders of the view we are considering never seem to consider the possibility that the verse may be understood in this second way. Nor do any of them, as far as my reading goes, make a real attempt to survey the whole of the Old Testament evidence on the subject. Such a survey shows clearly that the Hebrews understood 'blood' habitually in the sense 'violent death' (much as we do when we speak of 'shedding of blood'), and in the sacrifices the most probable meaning is not 'life' but 'life yielded up in death'.[20] And this is surely Paul's meaning. It makes nonsense of the passages we have listed to understand them as pointing to anything other than the death of Christ, and that death not a normal, peaceful death, but a violent death inflicted unnaturally.[21] It is such a death that brings the benefits Paul has been speaking of to those who are Christ's.

[19] See, for example, H. C. Trumbull, *The Blood Covenant*, London, 1887; B. F. Westcott, *Commentary on the Epistles of St. John*, London, 1892, pp. 34ff.; F. C. N. Hicks, *The Fullness of Sacrifice*, London, 1946; S. C. Gayford, *Sacrifice and Priesthood*, London, 1924; Vincent Taylor, *Jesus and His Sacrifice*, London, 1939, etc.

[20] See further A. M. Stibbs, *The Meaning of the Word 'Blood' in Scripture*, London, 1954; and my *The Apostolic Preaching of the Cross*, London and Grand Rapids, 1955, ch. III.

[21] Cf. A. M. Stibbs, 'Blood is a visible token of life violently ended; it is a sign of life either given or taken in death. Such giving or taking of life is in this world the extreme, both of gift or price and of crime or penalty. Man knows no greater' (*op. cit.*, p. 30).

The idea that Christ in His death closely identified Himself with sinful men, the teaching which we have seen in the Gospels and in Acts, meant a good deal to Paul, and he has some very far-reaching statements about it. He tells us that Christ came 'in the likeness of sinful flesh and . . . for sin' (Rom. 8:3),[22] and he applies to Christ's sufferings the words of the Psalmist, 'The reproaches of them that reproached thee fell upon me' (Rom. 15:3). I do not see how this can well be interpreted without the thought that Christ has borne that which men should have borne, that His death is in some sense the sinner's death.

And this is stated in express terms when Paul writes, 'one died for all, therefore all died' (2 Cor. 5:14). On this verse A. B. Macaulay writes, 'the death of Christ had a substitutionary and inclusive character'.[23] I do not see how this estimate can fairly be disputed. One died, not many. But the death of that one means that the many died. If language has meaning, this surely signifies that the death of the One took the place of the death of the many.

Later in the same chapter Paul has one of his most important statements about the death of Christ. After beseeching his readers 'be ye reconciled to God', Paul goes on, 'Him who knew no sin he (i. e., God) made to be sin on our behalf . . .' (2 Cor. 5:20f.). The first point to notice here is that the verb is active and that the subject is God. This passage is often, perhaps even usually, misquoted in such a way as to obscure this.[24] Men say Christ 'was made sin' or 'became sin', making the statement curiously impersonal, and seriously distorting Paul's meaning. Whenever this is done an important truth is obscured. The atonement is not basically an impersonal affair nor a sole concern of the Son. It is rather something in which the persons of both the Father and the Son are exceedingly active. It is not an affair in which Christ takes a firm initiative while the Father adopts a passive role. In every part of the New Testament that we have so far examined the fact that the atone-

---

[22] J. Hoad sees Is. 53 (especially vv. 9b, 10, 11) as underlying this passage and 2 Cor. 5:21. In both these passages he thinks the 'primary pattern' is this: 'Christ (a) who had done no wrong, (b) was made an offering for our sins (c) that we might come into a right relationship with God through Him' (ET, lxviii, p. 254).

[23] *The Death of Jesus*, London, 1938, p. 174. So also R. H. Strachan, 'There can be little doubt that the words "One has died for all" bear a substitutionary meaning . . . . Paul means that Christ bore voluntarily a doom that should have been ours' (*in loc.*).

[24] Denney made his complaint about this long ago: 'It is all-important to observe that it was *God* who made Christ sin; the passage is habitually quoted "He became sin," or, indefinitely, "He was made sin," in a vague sense unconsciously willing to leave God out . . . . Christ, by God's appointment, dies the sinner's death. The doom falls upon Him, and is exhausted there' (ST, p. 112).

ment proceeds from the loving heart of God has been emphasized. And Paul is emphasizing it here. He is not saying that somehow Christ happened to be mixed up with sin. He is saying that *God* made Him sin. God, none less and none else, made Him sin. Christ went to the cross, not because men turned against Him, but because the hand of God was in it. We have seen how this follows on a statement which means that Christ died the death that sinners should have died. Now we read that He did this by the appointment of the Father. It was the Father's condemnation of sin that brought about the atoning death of Christ, that and His burning will to save men.

'Made sin' is not a very usual expression,[25] but I should have thought that it is fairly plain that it means 'treated as a sinner', 'made to bear the penalty of sin' or the like.[26] But in recent times some have denied this. D. E. H. Whiteley, for example, admits that the words could mean 'Made to bear the guilt of sin, treated in a penal substitutionary transaction as if he were a sinner.' But he goes on to reject this in favour of the meaning, 'that in the providence of God Christ took upon himself human nature, which though not essentially sinful, is *de facto* sinful in all other cases'.[27] This seems to me to be evading the sense of the passage, and I do not see how this extraordinary meaning can be extracted from the text at all. All the verbal juggling in the world cannot make 'made sin' mean 'took upon himself human nature'. Moreover, although Paul can write movingly about the incarnation when he wishes to (it is sufficient to refer to Phil. 2:5ff.), he does not see Christ as

---

[25] Cf. T. J. Crawford, 'The abstract word "sin" must necessarily be held to be here put for some concrete. And there is no concrete that we can think of as denoted by it, except either "a sinner," or "one who bears or suffers for sin." Now, that Christ "was made *a sinner* for us" is inconsistent, not only with the testimony which the Scriptures elsewhere bear to His immaculate holiness, but with the express statement in the adjoining clause, that "He knew no sin." Accordingly, we are shut up to the other interpretation, that Christ was "made sin for us" in the sense of being divinely appointed to *bear the burden* or to *suffer the penal consequences* of our transgressions' (*The Doctrine of Holy Scripture respecting the Atonement*, Edinburgh, 1871, pp. 40f.).

[26] As Vincent Taylor puts it, Paul's 'conviction must be that the righteousness of God, and His purpose to justify men and reconcile them to Himself, required that Christ should suffer the condemnation of sin and come under its curse. This, in effect, is what he is saying, in a context, be it noted, in which reconciliation is the main theme' (ANT, p. 88). Cf. also A. B. Macaulay, 'He made Him die that death which is the wages of sin, as our substitute' (*op. cit.*, p. 174). Karl Barth regards the saying as 'almost unbearably severe', and explains it thus: 'He has caused Him to be regarded and treated as a sinner. He has Himself regarded Him and treated Him as a sinner' (CDDR, p. 165).

[27] JTS, n. s. viii, p. 246.

redeeming men from the curse of sin by becoming man, but by hanging on a cross. And when he speaks of God as making Christ sin for us[28] he is using a strong way of affirming that God has caused Christ to bear what we sinners should have borne.[29]

It is not unlike another saying of Paul's, this time in Galatians, where he tells us that 'Christ redeemed us from the curse of the law, having become a curse for[30] us: for it is written, Cursed is every one that hangeth on a tree' (Gal. 3:13). Just as the previous passage we were examining spoke of God as making Christ 'sin', so this speaks of Christ as becoming a 'curse'.[31] As we saw the former to mean that He bore our sin and its consequences, so the latter will mean that He bore our curse.[32] This curse is related to the manner of the death He died, and the quotation from the law of the Old Testament shows that it is the curse of the law that is meant.[33] Indeed Paul has just said, 'as many as are of the works of the law are under a curse' (v. 10). His meaning then is that men have not kept the law of God. Therefore they stand under a curse. But Christ became a curse for them. He bore the curse that they should have borne. He died their death. As Vincent Taylor puts it, 'A spiritual experience of reprobation is meant, and since this cannot be personal, it must be participation in the reproba-

. [28] Whiteley is also guilty, I think, of overlooking the point that we have just made, that the subject of 'made sin' is the Father. He equates 'made sin' with 'took upon himself human nature', thus replacing the Father with the Son as the subject. But this passage is one which tells what the Father did to bring about atonement.

[29] This is supported also by the fact that in the Old Testament words like אשם and חטאת mean both 'guilt', 'sin' and 'the punishment for guilt (sin)'. They can also denote the sacrifice which takes away the sin, which is the justification for the translation of NEB mg. 'God made him a sin-offering for us' (against this is the difficulty of seeing why ἁμαρτία should mean 'sin' at its first occurrence and 'sin-offering' three words later; the transition from 'sin' to 'the consequence of sin' is easier).

[30] The preposition is ὑπέρ. Some deny a substitutionary force in the passage on the grounds that this word does not mean 'in the place of'. This however is not the correct way of stating the case. The word does not necessarily convey the idea of substitution, but it can convey it. See A. T. Robertson, A Grammar of the Greek New Testament in the Light of Historical Research, London, n.d., p. 630; C. Hodge, Commentary on 2 Cor. 5:14; K. Barth, CDDR, p. 230, etc.

[31] The coincidence of language with Dt. 21:23 is closer than appears in the English translation, for the original (קללת אלהים) means 'the curse of God' not 'cursed of God'.

[32] On this point cf. W. D. Davies, Paul and Rabbinic Judaism, London, 1948, p. 284.

[33] Though this form is Jewish it expresses what J. S. Candlish calls 'the divine law in general' (The Christian Salvation, Edinburgh, 1899, p. 28), and J. Scott Lidgett can speak of 'the special and peculiar expression of universal principles' (The Spiritual Principle of the Atonement, London 1897, p. 46).

tion which rests upon sin'.[34] This is a vigorous way of putting it. Paul's vivid language conveys the thought that our sin is completely dealt with, our curse is removed from us forever.[35] And Christ did this by standing in our place. He was one with sinners in His death.

Thus there are various passages which stress the thought that Christ in His death was very much one with sinners, that He took their place. As J. S. Stewart puts it, 'Not only had Christ by dying disclosed the sinner's guilt, not only had He revealed the Father's love: He had actually taken the sinner's place. And this meant, since "God was in Christ," that *God* had taken that place. When destruction and death were rushing up to claim the sinner as their prey, Christ had stepped in and had accepted the full weight of the inevitable doom in His own body and soul.'[36] Nothing less than this seems adequate to the language used. And at the risk of being accused of being unduly repetitious we conclude this section by drawing attention once more to the fact that the divine initiative is stressed throughout these passages. It was God who was in Christ, God who made Him sin, God who sent His Son in the likeness of sinful flesh and for sin.[37] We have been insisting that substitution is

---

[34] *Op. cit.*, p. 88. Dr. Taylor proceeds to examine the idea that the sufferings of Christ are penal. He rejects Ritschl's submission that they are but affliction, not penalty, and says, 'Every one desires a better word than penal, but until we find it we ought not to abandon it because it has been used in ways which revolt the conscience or under the delusion that we can account better for the consequences of sin by invoking the operation of an inevitable law of cause and effect in the moral universe rather than the activity of God' (*op. cit.*, p. 89).

[35] Cf. Karl Barth, 'If God Himself in Jesus Christ bears the *curse* that must fall upon the transgressors of His law, then it really *is* borne; then there can be no thought of our bearing it again further. Then we are acquitted according to the law, yes, declared righteous . . . . If God Himself in Jesus Christ suffers the *punishment* that our existence would have to incur, then that means that He, this Other, has sacrificed His existence for us' (*Credo*, London, 1936, p. 93).

[36] *A Man in Christ*, London, 1947, pp. 240f. Similarly D. Dawson-Walker comments on 2 Cor. 5:21 and Gal. 3:13, 'each expression conveys alike the meaning that Christ saves us by becoming our substitute' (*The Atonement in History and Life*, ed. L. W. Grensted, London, 1936, p. 145); and again, 'Whatever may have happened to the idea of "substitution" in more recent thought, it cannot be eliminated from the thinking of St. Paul' (*op. cit.*, p. 149). Or A. B. Macaulay, 'He made our doom, namely death, His own, death being the curse of the Law. There is no reason why we should seek to explain away the substitutionary force of these passages' (*op. cit.*, p. 174).

[37] James Denney stresses the importance of this idea, together with its correlative of Christ's acceptance of all this, for Paul's message. 'All that sin meant for us — all that in sin and through it had become ours — God made His, and He made His own, in death. He *died* for us. This death, *defined as it must be by relation to our sins*, is that in virtue of which Jesus Christ is a propitiation for sin. Without it and without this interpretation of it St. Paul would have no gospel to preach. The word has been abused, and

the only unforced way of interpreting the passages in this section. But with this we must take the thought that God is active in the process. Substitution is not some external process which takes place with God no more than a spectator. He is involved. He involves Himself in this business of saving mankind.[38]

And if we must not overlook the connection of the Father with what happened on Calvary, neither should we minimize the way men are to link themselves with it. Paul stresses the closeness of the identification of believers with Christ in His death. They are dead with Him (2 Tim. 2:11). They are crucified with Him (Rom. 6:6; Gal. 2:20).[39] They are baptized into His death (Rom. 6:3). They are buried with Him (Rom. 6:4; Col. 2:12). They suffer with Him (Rom. 8:17). Those who are Christ's 'have crucified the flesh' (Gal. 5:24). The world is crucified to them and they to the world (Gal. 6:14). Such strong expressions emphasize the fact that Paul does not take the crucifixion of Christ as something to be understood quite apart from the believer. The believer and the Christ are in the closest possible connection. If it is true that their death is made His death, it is also true that His death is made their death.[40]

DELIVERANCE

In the preceding chapter we noticed that Paul sees man as caught up in a grim and many-sided bondage. Over against that we must now notice that he sees the cross as an act of deliverance on a grand scale. Whatever tyrants lord it over man, their power is broken by Christ's atoning work. Are men slaves to sin? Christ has set His people free from sin. The sixth chapter of Romans rings with

---

false inferences have been drawn from it, but is there a word in the world which covers the essential truth of this gospel better than the word *substitution*? αὐτὸς ἡμῶν τὰς ἁμαρτίας ἀνήνεγκεν. HE bore OUR sins' (*Expositor*, VI, 3 (1901), pp. 446f.).

[38] Cf. J. S. Stewart, 'The essential correlate of the substitutionary idea is that "*God* was in Christ": many critics of the idea have forgotten this' (*op. cit.*, p. 241, n. 5).

[39] 'The effect of His Cross is to draw us into a repentance which is a dying with Him, and therefore a part of the offering in His death; and then it raises us in newness of life to a fellowship of His resurrection' (P. T. Forsyth, WOC, p. 194).

[40] 'The substitutionary work of Christ is not a work that takes place outside of us and which is *subsequently applied* to us. We ourselves die in and with Christ. "His dying implied, and to that extent was, our own dying." His death was the death of all, independent of their attitude to this event . . . . The judgment was not cancelled but was executed in full and deepest earnestness. *Man* — all men — are struck by it and through the death of Christ "are made to disappear." "Man could not be helped other than through his annihilation"' (G. C. Berkouwer, *The Triumph of Grace in the Theology of Karl Barth*, Grand Rapids, 1956, p. 135).

the thought. We 'died to sin' (v. 2);[41] 'our old man was crucified with him, that the body of sin might be done away, that so we should no longer be in bondage to sin; for he that hath died is justified from sin' (vv. 6f.); 'reckon ye also yourselves to be dead unto sin, but alive unto God in Christ Jesus' (v. 11); 'let not sin therefore reign in your mortal body' (v. 12); 'sin shall not have dominion over you' (v. 14); 'ye were servants of sin' (vv. 17, 20; the tenses are past: you were sin's servants but you no longer are); you are 'made free from sin' (vv. 18, 22). And Paul rounds off the section by contrasting 'the wages of sin' with 'the free gift of God' which 'is eternal life in Christ Jesus our Lord' (v. 23). It is plain that Paul looks on sin as something no longer to be feared. Its power is broken. He loves to dwell on the freedom from sin that is his (Rom. 8:2; Eph. 2:1, 5). God's grace shown in Christ abounded far more than sin did (Rom. 5:20f.). God's covenant is concerned with taking sin away (Rom. 11:27). God has resoundingly defeated sin and made this victory real for His people. Sin no longer tyrannizes over them.

One of the most openly disliked and industriously evaded parts of Paul's teaching is that concerning the wrath of God. He is sure that that wrath was extended to all sinners. But he is sure, too, that Christ has delivered us from it. 'For God appointed us not unto wrath, but unto the obtaining of salvation through our Lord Jesus Christ, who died for us' (1 Thes. 5:9f.). 'Much more then, being now justified by his blood, shall we be saved from the wrath of God through him' (Rom. 5:9). Such passages linking the death of Christ with salvation from wrath seem to indicate that Christ's death represents a bearing of the divine wrath.[42] Despite the hesitation of some, this must be accepted as the teaching of Paul. In his massive argument in the early chapters of Romans he develops the thought that all men are under the wrath of God. Then he speaks of 'Christ Jesus: whom God set forth to be a propitiation, through faith, by his blood' (Rom. 3:24f.). The recent tendency to replace 'propitiation' by 'expiation' is, in my judgment, mistaken. It is not linguistically

[41] Cf. C. Gore, 'That old sinful self of ours was put to death, and we passed, as new men, into another life. Henceforth the tyrant sin has no claim on us, for death closes all scores and acquits of all claims. "The man is dead" is a summary and final plea against all claimants, and that is our plea against the claim of sin. We have died to it once and for all' (*The Epistle to the Romans,* i, London, 1902, pp. 208f.).

[42] Cf. P. Althaus, 'Jesus sanctified the wrath of God because, in this double form, He bore it as the punishment of the sins of mankind. He became true man, in the whole depth of their suffering under the hand of God. He can forgive because He took upon Himself the load of humanity in complete solidarity with mankind. He sanctified the wrath in order that He might overcome it. He overcame it in that He sanctified it' (*Mysterium Christi,* ed. G. K. A. Bell and A. Deissmann, London, 1930, p. 209).

sound,[43] and it does not face the demands of the context. Unless this expression means that Christ's death is the way in which God's wrath is averted from man, there is nothing to show how the wrath is turned away. And this after the care with which Paul has laboured to show that God is really wrathful against all sin. Nor should it be overlooked that God's righteousness is linked in this section with His wrath,[44] and that, as in 2 Corinthians 5:21, God is the active one. He 'set forth Christ' in this way. It is because He is the righteous God that He is wrathful against sin, and that He makes the cross the means of meeting both that righteousness and that wrath.[45] This is not a denial of grace. The grace of God is seen in the fact and the way that He chooses to deal with man's sin.[46] Paul is just as sure that God's grace has fully dealt with man's sin and the resultant wrath against him as he is of the reality of that wrath.[47] And he looks out to the future and sees no further cause for anxiety, for Jesus 'delivereth us from the wrath to come' (1 Thes. 1:10). The wrath of God is real. But so is the work of God in Christ. And on account of the latter we no longer fear the former.[48]

Men are hopeless in the face of death, but not so men in Christ. The reign of death has been replaced by the reign of the recipients of the divine grace, and it is specifically said that they will 'reign in life through the one, even Jesus Christ' (Rom. 5:17). Paul can

[43] I have set forth the evidence in *The Apostolic Preaching of the Cross* (London and Grand Rapids, 1955), chs. IV, V, and for ἱλαστήριον in NTS, ii, pp. 33-43. I am not aware that any scholar who maintains that we should abandon the concept of propitiation has really faced the arguments against his position. C. H. Dodd is sometimes said to have demonstrated the point, but his position is not sound, as I have endeavoured to show in the places mentioned. Roger Nicole has made a devastating criticism in WThJ, xvii, pp. 117-157. Indeed, I consider Nicole's case unanswerable. W. E. Wilson takes up a position much like that of Dodd (*The Problem of the Cross*, London, n. d., pp. 86ff.).

[44] Emil Brunner sees the meaning of the cross in this (*The Mediator*, London, 1946, p. 520).

[45] Markus Barth says that in Rom. 1:18-3:20 'God's righteousness is described, not as though it were contrary to God's wrath, but because it triumphs even *in* His wrath. God's juridical action against all unrighteousness and the necessary humiliation of man before God's exclusive righteousness are proclaimed with a ring of triumph' (SJT, viii, pp. 294f.).

[46] Cf. Karl Barth, CDDR, p. 490.

[47] Sometimes a false antithesis is put between the wrath of God and the love of God. Then, since the latter is accepted as basic, the former is rejected. But 'The wrath of God under which the idolatrous, sinfully perverted man stands is simply the divine love, which has become a force opposed to him who has turned against God. The wrath of God is the love of God, in the form in which the man who has turned away from God and turned against God, experiences it, as indeed, thanks to the holiness of God, he must and ought to experience it' (Emil Brunner, *Man in Revolt*, London, 1953, p. 187).

[48] See further pp. 348ff. below.

cry out in anguish, 'O wretched man that I am! who shall deliver me out of the body of this death?' But he immediately cries in triumph, 'I thank God through Jesus Christ our Lord' (Rom. 7:24f.). He is 'free from the law of sin and of death' (Rom. 8:2). Over against the death which is 'the mind of the flesh' he can set the life and peace which are 'the mind of the spirit' (Rom. 8:6). Death is unable to separate us from God's love (Rom. 8:38f.). But the most important passage under this heading is 1 Corinthians 15, where Paul enlarges on the theme of the resurrection and its importance for Christian men, both practically and doctrinally. The whole chapter is concerned with the defeat of death by Christ, and he insists that 'as in Adam all die, so also in Christ shall all be made alive' (v. 22). Death may be the last enemy, but it will be destroyed (v. 26). And Paul brings the chapter to its close with his ringing affirmation of the triumph won over death. 'Death is swallowed up in victory. O death, where is thy victory? O death, where is thy sting? . . . thanks be to God, which giveth us the victory through our Lord Jesus Christ' (vv. 54-57).

It is not otherwise with the law. So long as it is regarded as the way of salvation all that it can result in is condemnation. So Paul insists repeatedly that believers are not 'under law' (or similar term, Rom. 3:21, 28; 6:14; Gal. 5:18). They are 'made dead to the law through the body of Christ' (Rom. 7:4). Christ's death ends the claims of the law, and of those in Christ Paul can say, 'now we have been discharged from the law, having died to that wherein we were holden' (Rom. 7:6).[49] Paul does not think of this as implying any disrespect for the law, and he can speak of Christians as establishing rather than as nullifying the law (Rom. 3:31). He thinks of the Christian's freedom from the domination of law as connected with Christ's atoning work. It is 'a righteousness of God' which is 'apart from the law' that is shown in the cross (Rom. 3:21-26). Christ 'is the end of the law unto righteousness to every one that believeth' (Rom. 10:4). Those who are 'of the works of the law' are under a curse for their failure to keep the law (Gal. 3:10), but Christ has redeemed us from that curse (Gal. 3:13). He came 'to redeem them which were under the law' (Gal. 4:5). And it is in a context

---

[49] S. Mowinckel (referring to the Suffering Servant) speaks of 'the ancient belief that an offence can be atoned for by vicarious payment of compensation ('āsām), or guilt offering, or rite of purification (sin-offering), such as Job used to perform for sins which his children might have committed (Job i, 5). In this way the one who makes atonement becomes the "redeemer" (gō'ēl) of his kinsman. According to the ancient mode of thought the family, the tribe, or the people is a unity; and thus the decisive factor in atonement for an offence is not that the culprit should himself pay the penalty but that the community to which he belongs should do so' (He That Cometh, Oxford, 1956, pp. 209f.). The law's claims must be met, but not always by the offender himself. It is this of which Paul is speaking.

which is explaining the significance of Christ's death that we read that He 'abolished in his flesh the enmity, even the law of commandments contained in ordinances' (Eph. 2:15). Paul never systematizes all this, but once more it would seem that what he means is that Christ has stood in our place. He has taken on Himself the curse that our law-breaking involved, and thus cancelled out our obligations to the law. Therefore we are free from the law.

We saw that Paul looked on all men as standing under divine condemnation. But 'There is . . . now no condemnation to them that are in Christ Jesus' (Rom. 8:1).[50] In the light of God's justifying action Paul asks rhetorically, 'who is he that shall condemn?' (Rom. 8:34). Christ has delivered from condemnation.

And He has delivered from bondage to the flesh. Paul can speak of the days when believers were 'in the flesh' as past (Rom. 7:5). He often uses expressions like 'us, who walk not after the flesh, but after the spirit' (Rom. 8:4; cf. 8:9; 2 Cor. 10:2, 3). All such carry the implication that the bondage of the flesh has been done away for the believer. This underlies also those passages in which there are references to 'mortifying' the flesh or the like (Rom. 8:13; Col. 3:5), or to living without engaging in its lusts (Rom. 13:14; 2 Cor. 7:1; Gal. 5:16). Paul's well-known discussion of the striving of flesh and Spirit, of 'the works of the flesh' (which believers are not to do), and 'the fruit of the Spirit' (which they are to produce), shows plainly enough that Paul considers the power of the flesh to have been broken. That this is connected with the cross is indicated by his statement that 'they that are of Christ Jesus have crucified the flesh with the passions and the lusts thereof' (Gal. 5:24), which surely refers to the union with Christ in His death that we have noted elsewhere. Something of the sort may possibly be in mind also when Paul refers to what Christ did in the flesh to abolish the enmity (Eph. 2:15; Col. 1:22).

Paul is just as sure of Christ's victory over the evil spirits.[51] In

---

[50] 'His death is conceived as putting away sin, because in that death our condemnation came upon Him . . . . It is a death in which the divine condemnation of sin comes upon Christ, and is exhausted there, so that there is thenceforth no more condemnation for those that are in Him' (James Denney, ST, p. 108).

[51] Clinton D. Morrison argues that 'Christ's victory did not have its locus among the powers but in the community of believers' (The Powers That Be, London, 1960, p. 119). For example, he explains Col. 2:15 by Col. 2:20, saying, 'it was not the spirits who were affected, but the believers' (op. cit., p. 116). But he does not really face the accusatives after ἀπεκδυσάμενος and θριαμβεύσας, which indicate that something was done to the spirits as well as to the men over whom they tyrannized. Moreover, such statements as Col. 1:13, 'who delivered us out of the power of darkness', while formally concerned with believers and not the evil power, cannot be explained apart from something done to the evil power.

this connection G. H. C. MacGregor points to the significance of the expression ἀπεκδυσάμενος (Col. 2:15), which he translates 'stripped off from himself'. MacGregor proceeds,

> How "stripped off from himself"? Paul consistently argues that Christ must first subject himself to that from which he is to save others. He made himself, for example, liable to the curse of the Law that he might save from the Law. Now that part of man through which the evil spirit powers can lay hold of man and enslave him is his "flesh". Therefore Christ had taken upon himself the physical constitution of man; God had sent him "in the likeness of sinful flesh" — "flesh" in which the "principalities and powers" still could make a lodgement. And in the act of dying he divested himself of that flesh, and with it "stripped off the principalities and powers", thus breaking their dominion, and carrying with himself in his victory all those who through faith had come to be "in him" and thus shared his experience.[52]

Wherever Paul speaks of the 'principalities and powers' it is with the implication that Christ is supreme over them. He can warn the Ephesians that they are engaged in a struggle with such powers, but the tenor of his message is that the resources that God in Christ has put at the disposal of the Christian are adequate for him to emerge victorious (Eph. 6:12ff.). When he speaks of bondage to the elemental spirits it is in the past (Gal. 4:3). They no longer are victorious. The cross has routed them. This part of Paul's message ought never to be overlooked. We no longer feel ourselves haunted by demons in quite the same way as did the men of earlier days.[53] But we do often feel caught in the grip of forces that are stronger than we, and this is where Paul has a very relevant message for us.[54]

---

[52] NTS, i, p. 23.

[53] We ought not unthinkingly to assume that this is the result of superior enlightenment. J. M. Ross gives eight reasons for 'The Decline of the Devil', and says, when he comes to the eighth, 'Perhaps the real reason for the modern rejection of the devil is that *we do not take evil seriously enough*. We have grown accustomed to a Platonic conception of evil as merely the absence or negation of good; but if evil is more accurately regarded as the counterfeit of good . . . then the counterfeit of God cannot otherwise be thought of than as an active will seeking to thwart His purposes. If this is so, it is no longer necessary to explain away or "demythologize" the references to the devil which appear prominently among our Lord's utterances and elsewhere in the New Testament' (ET, lxvi, p. 61).

[54] Cf. MacGregor. 'We are still conscious that, apart from the victory of Christ, man is a helpless victim in a hostile cosmos. It is little comfort to us that the inexorable fate which was once expressed in terms of the influence of the stars, conceived as personal demons, is now expressed in terms of psychological or physical or economic determinism. We still ask how a man is to triumph over an evil heredity, or how he can be free and victorious

The story with regard to the other troubles in which Paul sees man as standing is the same. Man stands under judgment, but over against that Paul sets the 'free gift' which brings men justification and righteousness of life (Rom. 5:16, 18). The judgment of God is not annulled. It is taken with seriousness. Christ saves men in a way which accords with the divine judgment.[55] But He saves them. They are no longer subject to the judgment He has borne for them. This represents a radical re-thinking of the concept of judgment, and one which enables us to take God's judgment with genuine seriousness at the same time as we hold that men are saved. This is something new in religion. It is easy to see men as saved and God's law treated as of no account. It is not difficult to see men as lost and God's law as upheld. Paul rejects both positions and sees in the cross the upholding of the concept of judgment as well as the means of deliverance from the judgment.[56]

Paul speaks of the whole creation as in bondage to futility, but he looks for a time when 'the creation itself also shall be delivered from the bondage of corruption into the liberty of the glory of the children of God' (Rom. 8:21). There are several references to Christian labour and the like as not being 'in vain'[57] (1 Cor. 15:10, 58; 2 Cor. 6:1; Gal. 2:2; Phil. 2:16; 1 Thes. 2:1). The discussion in 1 Corinthians 15, which connects 'in vain' with the suggestion that there is no resurrection, is meant to show by its emphasis on the actuality of the resurrection that the Christian life, far from being futile, is the most purposeful existence known to man. It is sharply differentiated from the kind of life that non-Christians live (Eph. 4:17). Men are in bondage to the world. But 'Christ . . . gave himself for our sins, that he might deliver us out of this present evil world' (Gal. 1:4). Paul can speak of 'the cross of our Lord Jesus Christ, through which the world hath been crucified unto me, and I unto the world' (Gal. 6:14). The story could go on. Whatever enemy Paul can think of he thinks of as beaten. Christ has conquered it; He has set men free from every spiritual foe.

---

in a world of rigid law and scientific necessity. We still suffer from "astronomical intimidation" — terror at the insignificance of man and the vastness of the material universe encompassing him' (op. cit., p. 27).

[55] P. T. Forsyth sees in this a truth of first importance, 'The one meaning of an atoning Cross is the securing and establishing of God's holy and righteous judgment throughout the moral world to its victory in love — His bringing forth judgment to such victory' (JG, p. 108). Later he rejects the Grotian view on the grounds that 'judgment is an essential' element in Fatherhood, and not a corrective device' (op. cit., p. 177 n.). Cf. also J. Burnaby, Is the Bible Inspired?, London, 1949, p. 78.

[56] Cf. T. R. Glover, Paul of Tarsus, 1925, p. 88.

[57] The expression is κενός, which, of course, denotes basically 'empty' and Paul's view is that Christ fills life full. See the article 'The Abundance of the Gospel', by G. F. Dowden, in Theology, lviii, pp. 173-179.

We should look briefly at one important way of speaking about this deliverance, namely that in which it is viewed as redemption. We have had occasion in earlier chapters to notice that this signifies not simply 'deliverance', but 'deliverance on payment of a price'. Paul sees Christians as redeemed from the law's curse (Gal. 3:13), as redeemed from being under the law (Gal. 4:5). Redemption is persistently associated with Christ. It is 'in' Him (Rom. 3:24; Col. 1:14). It is 'through his blood' (Eph. 1:7; cf. Rom. 3:24f.). He 'was made unto us wisdom from God, and . . . redemption' (1 Cor. 1:30; notice that here again the activity of the Father is stressed in that He 'made' Christ redemption). Sometimes Paul specifically says that we are bought at a price (1 Cor. 6:20; 7:23),[58] the clear implication being that the price was the death of Christ. But all the expressions we have here noted emphasize that a price was paid for our deliverance, that it was paid by Christ, and that He paid it on the cross. And I do not see how this can well be interpreted other than as that He took our place. How else could He pay the price of our sins?[59]

It remains only to notice that Paul thinks of redemption as something that is not fully worked out here and now. He looks for the redemption of our bodies (Rom. 8:23), for the final working out of that redemption of which the Holy Spirit represents 'an earnest' (Eph. 1:14).[60] He speaks of being 'sealed' in the Holy Spirit 'unto the day of redemption' (Eph. 4:30). So rich and wonderful is Christ's redeeming work that the full unfolding of its implications is not to be seen in this life.

From all this it is clear that Paul sees deliverance in many aspects as one important part of the atonement. However many be the tyrants that work to hold men in subjection, and whatever be the means that they employ, Paul sees them as completely frustrated. Christ has delivered His people from them all.

[58] R. Garrigou-Lagrange sees in these passages evidence 'that the death of Jesus on the cross was a redemption by substitution' (*Our Saviour and His Love for Us*, London, 1951, p. 196).

[59] Cf. James Denney, 'And if any one says that this was morally impossible, may we not ask again, What is the alternative? Is it not that the sinful should be left alone with their responsibility, doom, curse, and death? And is not that to say that redemption is impossible?' (DC, p. 157). So also J. G. Simpson, 'Denials of the doctrine of substitution, made though they be in the interest of morality, inevitably tend to minimise, if not to annul, the claim of Redeeming Love to intervene as God in the recovery of man' (*What is the Gospel?* London, 1914, pp. 200f.).

[60] AG define ἀρραβών as '*first instalment, deposit, down payment, pledge,* that pays a part of the purchase price in advance, and so secures a legal claim to the article in question, or makes a contract valid . . . . in any case ἀ. is a payment which obligates the contracting party to make further payments'. The present gift of the Holy Spirit points to a further gift in the life to come.

THE GOSPEL

Paul delights to express the Christian message shortly by referring to 'the gospel'. As we saw in our first chapter, the word basically means 'good news', and the Christian preachers used it because for them there is no good news to compare with the good news of what God has done for man in Christ. Paul is especially fond of the word, using it nearly four times as often as all the other New Testament writers put together.[61]   Clearly the idea conveyed so succinctly by this term mattered immensely to the fiery little man from Tarsus.

Sometimes Paul speaks of 'the gospel of God' (Rom. 1:1; 15:16), putting stress on the divine origin of the message. Or he can speak of 'the gospel of his Son' (Rom. 1:9), reminding us that the good news centres in the action of Christ. Or he might refer to 'my gospel' (Rom. 2:16), with the emphasis on the fact that he has made the truths of the gospel his own personal possession (as we must also do for ourselves). So important is the preaching of the gospel that Paul speaks of it as the primary activity of his mission, even to the exclusion of the sacraments (1 Cor. 1:17). He was 'separated unto' it (Rom. 1:1). We see something of his love for the gospel in the string of references to it in the opening chapter of Philippians. Here Paul stresses his own activity of preaching the message, and welcomes the preaching of others, even of enemies, if so be that the gospel is thereby made more widely known (Phil. 1:5, 7, 12, 16, 27; 'preaching Christ' in vv. 15ff. means the same thing). It is because the gospel is of crucial importance that he can cry, 'Woe is unto me, if I preach not the gospel' (1 Cor. 9:16). We should understand this along with the strong language of Galatians 1:8f., 'though we, or an angel from heaven, should preach unto you any gospel other than that which we preached unto you, let him be anathema.' Solemnly, emphatically, Paul repeats this. 'If any man preacheth unto you any gospel other than that which ye received let him be anathema.'[62]   This is not the raving of narrow-minded fanaticism.

---

[61] There are 60 occurrences of εὐαγγέλιον in the Pauline writings (including 4 in the Pastorals), against 16 in all the rest of the New Testament. Maurice Goguel speaks of the significance of the word for Paul: 'When Paul used it he meant the redemption of the sinful world by the death and resurrection of Jesus Christ, and the preaching of this message of salvation' (*The Life of Jesus*, London, 1958, p. 134).

[62] Cf. the words of another fiery spirit, Martin Luther, 'Here appeareth an exceeding great fervency of spirit in the Apostle, that he dare curse all teachers throughout the whole world and in heaven, which pervert his Gospel and teach any other: for all men must either believe that Gospel that Paul preached, or else they must be accursed and condemned. Would to God this terrible sentence of the Apostle might strike a fear into their hearts that seek to pervert the Gospel of Paul; of which sort at this day (the more it is to be lamented) the world is full' (*St. Paul's Epistle to the Galatians*, London, 1953, p. 69).

It is the expression of a deeply-held conviction that the gospel is divine in origin and in content. To pervert it accordingly or to oppose it is to pervert or to oppose the very purpose of God. Little that Paul says on the atonement, or for that matter on any other theological topic, will be understood unless this point is grasped. Paul was not playing a parlour game. He was proclaiming a God-given message to men on the brink of hell.

He tells us that the gospel is 'veiled in them that are perishing' (2 Cor. 4:3). Unless there is a divine miracle, men do not perceive its relevance. It is not a piece of human wisdom. It does not appeal to the natural man. It is not 'after man' (Gal. 1:11). It includes the message of judgment (Rom. 2:16), and this never attracts man. But, like it or not, there is and can be but one gospel (Gal. 1:6ff.). Since God has given it, any man-made alternative is false. It must be rejected.

The true gospel is effective within those who receive it. It is 'the power of God unto salvation' (Rom. 1:16). Paul delights in this emphasis, and often contrasts mere words with power (1 Cor. 1:18; 4:20; 1 Thes. 1:5). The gospel is effective because the Spirit of God is in it, and not because of any human effort whatever. The gospel brings life, for those who receive it are begotten through it (1 Cor. 4:15). It establishes men (Rom. 16:25). It brings them light (2 Cor. 4:4), peace (Eph. 6:15), and hope (Col. 1:23).

In line with all this is Paul's continual stress on grace (he uses the noun about twice as often as all the rest of the New Testament writers put together).[63] The idea in grace is closely connected with that of joy. Basically grace means 'that which causes joy',[64] and for the Christian there is no joy like the joy the gospel brings. And what God has done for man He has done freely. Grace always implies a freeness in giving. Grace is God's free gift (Eph. 3:7f.). So when we read 'by grace have ye been saved' (Eph. 2:5, 8) the thought is that of salvation by way of divine gift and apart from human merit. So it is with the statement that the grace of God brings salvation (Tit. 2:11), or those which speak of justification as connected with grace (Rom. 3:24; Tit. 3:7), or of the Christian as being 'under grace' (Rom. 6:14f.). Paul brings out God's defeat of sin by speaking of grace as abounding far more than sin abounded,

---

[63] Paul uses χάρις 101 times (including 13 in the Pastorals) as against 56 for the rest of the New Testament (including 2 in speeches of Paul in Acts). Goguel sees Paul's idea of grace as the new thing in his theology. 'The originality of Paulinism in relation to Judaism consists in the fact that it substitutes the idea of grace for that of merit and the observance of the law' (op. cit., pp. 107f.).

[64] GT gives the meaning as, 'prop. that which affords joy, pleasure, delight' (sub voc.), and AG says, 'It seems that χάρις is not always clearly differentiated in mng. fr. χαρά' (sub voc.).

and of grace as 'reigning' (Rom. 5:20f.). The apostle uses some very expressive verbs to refer to the abundance of God's grace such as πλεονάζω (Rom. 6:1f.), ὑπερπλεονάζω (1 Tim. 1:14), ὑπερβάλλω (2 Cor. 9:14), ὑπερπερισσεύω (Rom. 5:20). Karl Barth draws attention to these and comments, 'We find a kind of boundless astonishment on the part of the apostle at the divine intervention acknowledged in the concept grace (or love).'[65] It is grace which makes Paul what he is (1 Cor. 15:10), and he can use grace more or less as a synonym for the gospel (Gal. 1:6; Col. 1:6). Grace has two basic strands in its make-up. There is the thought of the freeness of God's gift, and there is the thought of the power that God gives (cf. 'My grace is sufficient for thee' with reference to Paul's 'thorn in the flesh', 2 Cor. 12:9).[66] This power is not something isolated, a formidable impersonal power. Rather it must be understood in personal terms.[67] As G. W. H. Lampe puts it, grace is 'the active presence of Christ Himself mediated through the Holy Spirit to be the principle of our life in Him'.[68]

We see something of the meaning of grace in the saying, 'ye know the grace of our Lord Jesus Christ, that, though he was rich, yet for your sakes he became poor, that ye through his poverty might become rich' (2 Cor. 8:9). Or again we learn what Paul understands by it from the way he contrasts grace with due. 'Now to him that worketh, the reward is not reckoned as of grace, but as of debt' (Rom. 4:4; in v. 16 faith is closely connected with grace). Similarly grace and works are contrasted (Rom. 11:6). Here Paul says plainly, 'if it is by grace, it is no more of works: otherwise grace is no more grace'. Salvation by grace and salvation by merit are incompatible. Each automatically rules out the other. This is the reasoning also in Paul's argument in Galatians 3, where he contrasts the works of the law with the hearing of faith. If men are to be saved by the deeds they do, that is one thing. If they are to be saved by God in Christ that is quite another. Paul's writings leave us not the slightest doubt as to which he understood to be correct. Notice further that grace is often connected with God the Father (e. g., 2 Cor. 9:14).

---

[65] CDDR, p. 82.

[66] Cf. J. Moffatt, 'At every mention of "grace," he was unbaring the vital heart of Christianity as he understood it; there is a throb and thrill of thankfulness for an undeserved and absolutely effective religion' (*Grace in the New Testament,* London, 1931, p. 140).

[67] Cf. T. F. Torrance, 'As power acting on men it is not impersonal, but intensely personal, as personal as Christ Himself, for it is Christ acting in person, and not in any sub-personal fashion. The great characteristic of the Pauline *charis* is its intimate attachment to the person of Christ Jesus, and as operating only within the personal encounter of Christ with men through the word of the Gospel' (*The Doctrine of Grace in the Apostolic Fathers,* Edinburgh, 1948, p. 32).

[68] *Reconciliation in Christ,* London, 1956, pp. 78f.

That is to say, the ultimate root of grace is in God. Yet, while the number of passages where the exact expression occurs is not so high, it is more characteristic to refer to 'the grace of our Lord Jesus Christ'. While Paul does not minimize the part of the Father, he sees grace above all in what Christ has done for men.[69] Indeed, he often makes some addition to a reference to God's grace to make it clear that it is intimately bound up with Christ and His work for men (e. g., Eph. 2:7).[70] The grace of God and the grace of Christ cannot be separated. We know both from the cross.[71]

THE CONSTRAINING LOVE OF GOD

All this might be expressed in terms of love. So Paul tells us that 'God commendeth his own love toward us, in that, while we were yet sinners, Christ died for us' (Rom. 5:8), and that God 'for his great love wherewith he loved us, even when we were dead through our trespasses, quickened us together with Christ' (Eph. 2:4f.). But whether he explicitly mentions love, or whether he confines himself to terms like 'grace' or 'the gospel', the love of God is always at the basis of what Paul says. Perhaps our deep interest in other aspects of his message causes us to overlook Paul's passionate interest in love, and we do not always realize, for example, that he has much more to say on the subject than has the Fourth Gospel.[72] It is fundamental to him that God is 'the God of love and peace' (2 Cor. 13:11). And nothing is more basic for his thought on salvation than the idea that God's love and not man's merit is the root cause.[73] Salvation rests on what God is and does, and not

---

[69] Cf. J. Moffatt, grace 'is definitely confined to the relationship between God and man through Jesus Christ. When in the climax of the world-order Christ appears, then, and not till then, does Paul mention grace' (op. cit., p. 197).

[70] C. Ryder Smith goes as far as to say, 'Probably in all Paul's hundred uses of charis there is not a single instance where this idea is not present' (The Bible Doctrine of Grace, London, 1956, p. 60).

[71] Cf. T. F. Torrance, 'Two elements are always cardinal to the use of the word in St. Paul: the person of the risen Lord, and the Cross' (op. cit., p. 28).

[72] Thus in the Pauline writings ἀγάπη is used 77 times (including 12 in the Pastorals), as against 7 times in John, while the figures for ἀγαπάω are 34 (2) and 36, and for ἀγαπητός 27 (2) and 0. As the Pauline corpus and this Gospel are of comparable sizes (in the British and Foreign Bible Society's Greek text Paul takes up 87 pages and John 79) the comparison is significant. It should, of course, be added that there is much about love in the Johannine Epistles.

[73] This is sometimes overlooked even by those who write on the love of God. Thus Lonsdale Ragg says, 'The mercy of God, to whom all things are an eternal present, looks upon us in the light of our life's promise. He regards us not as we are, but as we are becoming; so He treats us, so He loves us: "Tales nos amat Deus quales futuri sumus, non quales sumus"' (Aspects of the Atonement, London, 1904, pp. 116f.). But, while it is of

on the activity of any human being. We should not overlook the surprising character of this aspect of Paul's teaching. The cross, on the surface of it, shows us the injustice of man, and the sacrificial love of Jesus. To the casual observer it is the tragedy so often reported in the affairs of men which poses the question 'Does God not care at all?'[74] But Paul was no casual observer. For Him it was clear that God was in Christ and that the cross shows us the love *of God*.[75] God indeed cares. He cares as much as that. With this we must take, of course, Paul's teaching on the love of Christ, for he does not distinguish sharply between the two. He speaks movingly of 'the Son of God, who loved me, and gave himself up for me' (Gal. 2:20). Twice in Ephesians he speaks of Christ as loving believers and giving Himself for them (Eph. 5:2, 25), while his thought that God 'freely bestowed' His grace on us 'in the Beloved' (Eph. 1:6) comes out of the same circle of ideas. The opening section of Colossians likewise refers us to God's saving work in terms of His love of Christ. He 'delivered us out of the power of darkness, and translated us into the kingdom of the Son of his love' (Col. 1:13). Paul links the Father and the Son when he thinks of God as having loved us and given us 'eternal comfort and good hope through grace' (2 Thes. 2:16). And as he ends a letter he can pray, 'Peace be to the brethren, and love with faith, from God the Father and the Lord Jesus Christ' (Eph. 6:23). He leaves no room for a division between Father and Son on this point, as have some who have pictured the loving Son as winning salvation

---

course true that God sees us as we will be, His love is greater than that. The wonderful thing is that His love was made known in Christ's death 'while we were yet sinners'.

[74] H. R. Mackintosh points out that 'there is one question we should expect to be asked very frequently, though in point of fact within Christendom it has seldom been heard. It is this: Why does the crucifixion not so horrify and revolt us as to make sceptics by the thousand? . . . It is an event which appears wholly incompatible with a righteous or loving world-government; why then do our minds not flame with indignation against God Himself on that account?' He answers, 'The reason plainly is that in the cross what is felt to be both present and presented is God's own love; and it is present as enduring a vicarious burden due to human sin' (*The Christian Experience of Forgiveness*, London, 1944, p. 207).

[75] Cf. D. M. Baillie, 'the most remarkable fact in the whole history of religious thought is this: that when the early Christians looked back and pondered on the dreadful thing that had happened, it made them think of the redeeming love of God. Not simply of the love of Jesus, but of the love of God. One might have expected them rather to lose all faith in the love of God, for the crucifixion might well seem to be the final *reductio ad absurdum* of the belief that the world is governed by a gracious providence' (*God Was in Christ*, London, 1955, p. 184).

from a stern and unyielding Father. The Father's love for us is the cause, not the result of our salvation.[76]

Paul often links the love of God with election. He writes to the Thessalonians that he knows 'brethren beloved of God, your election' (1 Thes. 1:4), and again he can say, 'we are bound to give thanks to God alway for you, brethren beloved of the Lord, for that God chose you from the beginning unto salvation' (2 Thes. 2:13). He reminds the Colossians that they are 'God's elect, holy and beloved' (Col. 3:12). The thought comes out a number of times when he is thinking of the position of Israel (Rom. 9:13, 25; 11:28). This is very important, for men often today misunderstand the whole idea of election. It does not fit in with our democratic understanding of life, nor with our deep-rooted conviction that man, and not God, should be the arbiter of salvation. So, rejecting in advance the idea of election, we think of it as an arbitrary device, and caricature it as a means of choosing men without rhyme or reason. And having made it look sufficiently ridiculous we find it totally unacceptable. But the Bible concept of election is not so easily to be dismissed. And in particular it has to be stressed that there is something back of it other than arbitrary caprice. There is the love of God. God chooses men for salvation because He loves them. Whenever we are talking about the biblical idea of election we should not forget that. I do not suggest that this is a key which unlocks all the mysteries of election, so that no further difficulty remains. But I do suggest that we are not doing justice to Paul's thought unless we see salvation as proceeding from election, and election as being the outworking of God's love.

Paul has a good deal to say about the effects of this love in the believer. He constantly regards love as the characteristic attitude of the follower of Christ, so characteristic indeed that in a number of passages 'them that love God' or 'them that love our Lord Jesus Christ' is synonymous with 'Christians' (e.g., Rom. 8:28; 1 Cor. 2:9; 16:22; Eph. 6:24). And we need point no further than 1 Corinthians 13 for the fact that love to one's fellow man is demanded of the believer in preeminent degree. The concluding verse of that chapter assures us that 'now abideth faith, hope, love, these

[76] Cf. Augustine, 'The love, therefore, wherewith God loveth, is incomprehensible and immutable. For it was not from the time that we were reconciled unto Him by the blood of His Son that He began to love us; but He did so before the foundation of the world . . . . Let not the fact, then, of our having been reconciled unto God through the death of His Son be so listened to or so understood, as if the Son reconciled us to Him in this respect, that He now began to love those whom He formerly hated . . . but we were reconciled unto Him who already loved us, but with whom we were at enmity because of our sin' (*Homilies in the Gospel of John*, 110. 6; ed. P. Schaff, Grand Rapids, 1956, p. 411).

three; and the greatest of these is love' (1 Cor. 13:13). Believers
are to be 'rooted and grounded in love' (Eph. 3:17). The church is
built up in love (Eph. 4:16). And all this is not a human achievement. Left to themselves, men would never produce the particular
quality of Christian love.[77] It is part of 'the fruit of the Spirit' (Gal.
5:22). It is clear that for Paul God's love is poured out freely on His
people (Rom. 5:5), not because they are worthy of that love, for
they can never be worthy, but because He is a loving God. He loves
because it is His nature to love and not because He finds in sinful
man something that is attractive to Him. And, when God bestows
His love on men and men respond to that love, His divine love
produces in them an answering love. They come to see men in a
measure as He sees them, and to love them though they are sinners,
recognizing that they are the object of God's love. So the love that
they display as their characteristic attitude is something that they get
from God. It is not their own achievement.[78]

Then we should notice that the love of God has other effects on
believers. 'In all these things', writes Paul, 'we are more than
conquerors through him that loved us' (Rom. 8:37). Love makes us
to triumph. And nothing can separate us from the love of God that is
in Christ Jesus (Rom. 8:35, 38f.). Love is invincible. Small wonder
that he regards the knowledge of the love of Christ as the supreme
good (Eph. 3:19).

We learn a very important truth from the passage in which Paul
assures the Corinthians of the constraint exercised by the love of
Christ. 'The love of Christ constraineth us', he writes, and immediately goes on, 'because we thus judge, that one died for all, therefore all
died' (2 Cor. 5:14). Notice that the love of Christ is connected not
simply with the fact of His death, but with the fact that He died

[77] Cf. C. E. Raven, 'If you could find somewhere, at the moment when
you are conscious of your own guilt, someone who knows you through and
through, not merely the mask which you turn to the world, but all those
dark crannies which you struggle to keep secret, knows you and does
not cease to love you though you loathe yourself, — if you find such a love
you are transformed by its irresistible wonder. That is the love which those
men and women found in Calvary, the love which not only knew, but had
actually suffered, the effects of their ill-dealings, the love which they had
spurned and betrayed, the love which none the less would not let them go,
the love which still yearned and still gave . . . . To all of us He gives that
love in Christ Jesus who knows and does not cast us off' (*Our Salvation,*
London, 1925, pp. 62f.).

[78] This response in man to the love of God is important. The divine love
is concerned that men be lifted out of their self-centredness and their sin,
and brought into a new relationship to men as to God. Ryder Smith reminds
us that the purpose of God's love 'is not primarily the happiness of the beloved, but his perfection; it seeks to help a man to be what God made him
to be. Unlike much so-called "love", it is wholly allergic to sin' (*op. cit.,*
p. 98).

that death which is the death of all. If He had not died our death, His death would have been interesting, perhaps also deeply moving, but it would not exercise the constraint of love as Paul sees it. What gives it this power is that it is precisely our death that He died.

THE SON OF GOD

From what we said earlier about the nature and the extent of the plight of man it is obvious that salvation is no light or easy affair. He who would save mankind from such a fate must Himself be very great. In fact, Paul thinks of Him as the very greatest possible, and his Saviour is not in any degree less than God. To go into Paul's Christology would require a book in itself, but here we notice some passages in which the apostle brings the person and the work of Christ into the closest connection.

Colossians 1 is most significant. Paul gives thanks to the Father who has brought men salvation (Col. 1:12). He has brought men 'out of the power of darkness' and 'into the kingdom of the Son of his love' (Col. 1:13). This leads to the thought of what the Son has done. Men have redemption and forgiveness through Him 'who is the image of the invisible God, the firstborn of all creation' (Col. 1:14f.). Thus from a consideration of salvation Paul finds himself launched into an exposition of the person of Christ. He goes on to speak of His work in creation, His preeminence, His headship over the Church, His triumph over death, His 'fulness'[79] (Col. 1:16-19). Then he comes back to the thought of salvation. Now he views it as a process of reconciliation, of making peace, of presenting God's erstwhile enemies 'holy and without blemish and unreproveable before him' (Col. 1:20-22). Throughout this passage, then, Paul moves easily back and forth between the thought of who Christ is and what He has done. This intermingling of the person and the work of Christ is profoundly significant. For Paul, neither can be understood apart from the other. We cannot estimate the person of Christ aright unless we see that in His love and His mercy He came to earth and died to bring men salvation, unless we see that all the saved are saved through Christ. And we cannot understand

---

[79] F. F. Bruce explains this term thus: 'the peculiar force of its use here lies in the probability that it was employed in a technical sense by the heretical teachers at Colossae (as it was in a number of gnostic systems) to denote the totality of divine emanations or agencies, those supernatural powers under whose control men were supposed to live . . . . Paul undermines the whole of this theosophical apparatus in one simple, direct affirmation: the fulness or totality of divine essence and power has taken up its residence in Christ. In other words, He is the one mediator between God and the world of mankind, and all the attributes and activities of God — His Spirit, word, wisdom and glory — are displayed in Him' (in loc.).

the Christian salvation unless we see that it was wrought by One who is no less than God.

Something of the same thought process underlies the great passage in Philippians 2. Here the apostle starts with the affirmations that Christ was 'in the form of God' and 'on an equality with God' (Phil. 2:6). But He 'emptied himself, taking the form of a servant . . . he humbled himself, becoming obedient even unto death, yea, the death of the cross' (Phil. 2:7f.). Because of this 'God highly exalted him, and gave unto him the name which is above every name' (Phil. 2:9). In this passage there is a majestic movement from heaven to earth and back to heaven again. And this is a movement that cannot be understood apart from the twin truths of the full deity of Christ and of the effective salvation that He accomplished for men.[80]

The truths behind these great passages are found elsewhere, for the mingling of Christ's person and work goes deep into Paul's understanding of things.[81] Thus he can say, 'in him dwelleth all the fulness of the Godhead bodily', and immediately add, 'and in him ye are made full, who is the head of all principality and power' (Col. 2:9f.). He speaks of 'the mystery of God' (which we saw before to be connected with the idea of salvation) and goes on to the greatness of Christ 'in whom are all the treasures of wisdom and knowledge hidden' (Col. 2:2f.). He is 'declared to be the Son of God with power', the deity 'by the resurrection of the dead' (Rom. 1:4), the consummation of the work of redemption. It is in connection with 'the gospel of the glory of Christ' that he speaks of the Lord as 'the image of God' (2 Cor. 4:4). And so we might go on. Paul is in no doubt as to the majesty of his Saviour. For him there is no difference between the Christ and God.[82] And this gives meaning to his whole doctrine of salvation.

JUSTIFICATION

In a number of passages the death of our Lord is described as a legal penalty which the innocent Jesus suffered for the guilty sinner who so richly deserved it . . . . This juristic conception of

[80] See R. P. Martin, *An Early Christian Confession*, London, 1960, for a valuable treatment of this passage, and an account of recent work on it.

[81] M. Black, in an article entitled 'The Pauline Doctrine of the Second Adam' (SJT, vii, pp. 170-179), argues that, though the terms 'the second man' or 'the last Adam' occur in Paul once only (1 Cor. 15:45ff.), yet 'The idea . . . has provided him with the scaffolding for his most characteristic doctrines of redemption and resurrection' (*op. cit.*, p. 179). He cites W. D. Davies and A. E. J. Rawlinson as also bearing witness to the importance of this concept. And this, of course, fits in with what we have been saying. It gives to Christ an exalted title and relates it to the work of salvation.

[82] For a fuller discussion of this point see my *The Lord from Heaven*, London and Grand Rapids, 1958, ch. v.

salvation through the Cross sometimes occurs in close conjunction with the ransom and sacrificial theories as in Ro 3:21-26;
but it is logically quite distinct from them, and is Paul's most
characteristic contribution to the theory of the atonement. We
are "put right with God" or "acquitted" not by our works, but
by the free grace of God received by us through our faith in
Christ, who on the Cross paid on our behalf the debt or penalty
which we owed to God, but could never pay.[83]

In these words A. W. Argyle stresses the importance of the juridical
understanding of the atonement for Paul. The great apostle does
not share the curious modern antipathy to the use of legal terms in
interpreting God's relation to men. He delights in speaking of Christ
as having 'justified' sinners.[84] Justification is essentially a legal term.[85]
It means a verdict of acquittal. To justify means to declare 'not
guilty'. When Paul speaks of men as 'justified', then, he means that
they have God's verdict of acquittal. When they stand before the bar
of God's justice they need have no fear, for the Judge has already
given His verdict in their favour.

Many theologians have maintained that justification means 'to make
righteous'. They assert that the term points to a change in men,
so that, by the grace of God, they become the kind of people they
ought to be.[86] This is to confuse justification and sanctification.[87]

---

[83] ET, lx, p. 255.
[84] G. Schrenk maintains that the forensic use of δικαιόω by Paul is
'universal and indisputable (*einhellig und unbestreitbar*)' (TWNT, ii, p. 219).
He also says that Paul 'manifests quite an interest in clothing God's act of
grace in forensic imagery' (*op. cit.*, p. 219, n. 18).
[85] This point is often neglected. Such a great scholar as G. Aulén can say,
'Justification and Atonement are really one and the same thing; Justification
is simply the Atonement brought into the present, so that here and now
the Blessing of God prevails over the Curse' (*Christus Victor*, London, 1937,
p. 167). This is simply not true. Justification has a meaning of its own
and that meaning must be sought carefully. That Christ's work for men
can be described in terms of atonement, or blessing, or curse, does not give
us license to equate justification with any of these terms.
[86] For example, H. N. Oxenham, 'Justification is the free gift of Christ,
whereby He restores to us our lost inheritance of grace, and in restoring it
cleanses every stain whether of actual or original sin, though concupis-
cence still remains for our trial. But it is more than a simple restoration
of our forfeit birthright, for we are raised by justification to a higher state than
that from which Adam fell, and made through union with the Redeemer partakers of the Divine nature' (*The Catholic Doctrine of the Atonement*,
London, 1895, p. 104). Oxenham, of course, makes no attempt to show that
this is the biblical meaning of the term.
[87] On this frequent confusion N. P. Williams says, 'No doubt St. Paul
never contemplated the possibility of a "justification" which was not in-
variably followed by "sanctification"; justification and sanctification are for
him inseparably connected in fact; but none the less they are absolutely distinct in thought, and the confusion between them (due ultimately to the

The very way we use the term ought to put us on our guard against this error. When we speak of justifying an opinion or an action we do not mean that we change or improve it. Rather we mean that we secure a verdict for it, we vindicate it. And just as the English verb has nothing to do with changing for the better so is it with the Greek verb. It signifies 'to declare righteous', 'to acquit', and not 'to make righteous'. While it is true that the justified man will be deeply concerned with holy living, it is also true that justification is not simply another name for his holy life. It refers to his standing before God, to God's acceptance of him.

In a resounding paradox Paul speaks of Christ as 'him that justifieth the ungodly' (Rom. 4:5), and this gives us the heart of the matter. In many places Paul insists that no law works of any kind will ever avail to justify a man before God (Rom. 3:20; Gal. 2:16; 3:11). Indeed, the whole of the Epistle to the Galatians may be said to be written around this theme. The reason is simple. Man is a sinner. And being a sinner he cannot be acquitted of sinfulness. Thus when he is justified, the only thing that comes from his side is faith, the attitude of complete reliance on God (Rom. 3:28; Gal. 2:16; 3:8, 24).[88] Justification is the outcome of a 'free gift' (Rom. 5:16). Justification means that he is really just, but not on account of any contribution of his own. The paradox is striking.[89]

Just as emphatically as he repudiates the thought that man can secure his own acquittal, Paul sets forth the truth of the matter, that 'It is God that justifieth' (Rom. 8:33). He sees all three Persons of the Trinity as concerned in this. Thus he rests justification securely in the activity of the Father (Rom. 8:30). And he tells the Corinthians that they are 'justified in the name of the Lord Jesus Christ, and in the Spirit of our God' (1 Cor. 6:11). But, as we might expect, he usually concentrates on its connection with Christ (e. g., Gal. 2:16f.). More specifically he links it with Christ's death and

---

rendering in the Old Latin versions of δικαιοῦν by *iustificare*, the factitive form of which fatally misled St. Augustine and his successors) has involved Christian thought in centuries of quite unnecessary controversy' (ET, xlv, p. 8).

[88] David Cox has a section in which he sharply criticizes theologians like C. H. Dodd, Vincent Taylor, C. Anderson Scott, and E. J. Bicknell who make faith the necessary precursor of justification (*Jung and St. Paul*, London, 1959, pp. 85ff.). His point is that they are making faith into a kind of 'work' and this must be avoided at all costs.

[89] Martin Luther expressed it in the well-known words *simul justus et peccator*, which Aulén explains thus, 'the meaning is not that he is at once and in the same sense sinless and sinful. It is that two different principles are present together in him, so that he can be regarded from two aspects: on the one hand, he is a child of God, alive unto God, justified; on the other, he is not worthy of this Divine vocation. And the more deeply he recognises his Divine vocation, the more he becomes conscious of his own sin' (*op. cit.*, p. 172 n.).

resurrection. We are 'justified freely by his grace through the re-demption that is in Christ Jesus' (Rom. 3:24); we are 'justified by his blood' (Rom. 5:9); Jesus was 'delivered up for our trespasses, and was raised for our justification' (Rom. 4:25);[90] we are justified 'by his grace' (Tit. 3:7). In all this he is saying that man, being a sinner, cannot be acquitted before God. But believers will be ac-quitted, indeed they already have the status of acquittal. And they have it as a divine gift; they have it because of Christ's death, a death that is connected with our sins. Penal views are out of favour just now, but it is difficult to see what this means if not that Christ has borne the penalty for our sins.[91] And because He has borne the penalty we no longer face it. It is taken out of the way. The claims of divine law are fully met.

There are other ways of looking at the salvation that Christ secured for us. And some of these others are more satisfying to the men of our day. But this does not give us license to overlook[92] or pervert[93] the meaning of justification. It is a term which had a clear and definite meaning for the men of the first century. Applied to the salvation Christ wrought, as Paul applies it, it means that our salva-tion rests on a sound legal basis. Arising out of this, other blessings follow. But we ought not to confuse them with this initial act of justification.[94] It is not right to empty Paul's forceful and

[90] On this verse F. W. Dillistone says, 'By the death of Jesus, in other words, man's debt of sin had been annulled in a way consonant with God's righteousness' (*The Significance of the Cross,* London, 1946, p. 50).

[91] Even one so far removed from conservatism as John Knox recognizes that the idea of Christ's death as a paying of penalty is found in the New Testament (*The Death of Christ,* London, 1959, p. 150). Objection is often taken to the validity of this concept, as H. Maldwyn Hughes, *What is the Atonement?,* London, n.d., pp. 36f.; W. Fearon Halliday, *Reconciliation and Reality,* London, 1919, p. 142. But the objections usually seem to rest on the view that Christ's death is to be taken as quantitative, whereas we should understand it qualitatively.

[92] D. M. Ross in trying to make the point that reconciliation matters more to Paul than justification goes as far as to say, 'If he does occasionally make use of the idea of justification . . .' (*The Cross of Christ,* London, 1928, p. 162)!

[93] It is difficult to use any other language than this of such a position as that of Dom Gregory Dix who parodies the doctrine by saying that accord-ing to it a man 'needs nothing more, can do nothing more, than be conscious of *feeling* that confidence in the merits of Christ's sacrifice. He must cling to that *feeling* of confidence, for it is all that stands between him and eternal torment' (*The Question of Anglican Orders,* London, 1956, pp. 19f.; Dix's italics).

[94] Denney stresses the centrality for Paul of the doctrines set forth in Rom. 3-5: 'It is Christ our Substitute, Christ who bore our burden, Christ who made our sins His own when He died our death upon the tree, it is that Christ and no other in whom the power dwells, and by whom it is ex-ercised, to draw sinners to Himself and make them one with Him in death

colorful language of its meaning. Rather it is our business humbly
to learn what his terms meant to him and what they can come to
mean to us.[95]

With this idea of justification we must take another Pauline concept, that of 'the righteousness of God'. This is not something that
all men know, but a new thing revealed in the gospel (Rom. 1:17).
Yet far from being some new-fangled contraption, in essentials it is
very old, for it is witnessed to by the law and the prophets (Rom.
3:21). This righteousness is evidently that which is spoken of as
'the gift of righteousness' (Rom. 5:17), i. e., it is not God's righteousness considered as an ethical quality, but the righteousness that men
may have when God gives it them. That is to say it is their standing
as righteous before Him. So this righteousness is 'of faith' (Rom.
9:30; 10:6), it is 'of God' (Rom. 10:3; 2 Cor. 5:21), it is
'of God by faith' (Phil. 3:9). All these passages stress that the
right standing comes to us from God. It may be closely linked
with Christ (Rom. 10:3f.; 1 Cor. 1:30; 2 Cor. 5:21; Phil. 3:9). And
in negating the idea that righteousness comes by the law, Paul
points out that were this so, then Christ's death would have been
in vain (Gal. 2:21). The implication is that Christ's death was not
in vain and that it brought the righteousness of which the apostle
writes. But probably the most important passage in this connection
is in Romans 3 where we read of

> the righteousness of God through faith in Jesus Christ . . . being
> justified freely . . . through the redemption that is Christ Jesus:
> whom God set forth to be a propitiation, through faith, by his
> blood, to shew his righteousness, because of the passing over of the
> sins done aforetime, in the forbearance of God; for the shewing, I
> say, of his righteousness at this present season: that he might himself
> be just, and the justifier of him that hath faith in Jesus (Rom. 3:22-
> 26).

In this passage Paul speaks of God's righteousness as being shown in
the way men are forgiven. Some have misunderstood this as signifying that Paul thinks it is a righteous thing that God should save

---

and life. The sixth, seventh, and eighth chapters of Romans are not a
new gospel for those who do not care for the third, fourth and fifth; they
are not an accidental, or a much needed, supplement to those chapters, having yet no organic connexion with them; they are vitally involved in them,
and in nothing else' (*Expositor*, VI, 4, p. 85).

[95] Theo Preiss makes another point. 'When theology no longer takes
really seriously the biblical statement that Satan is the accuser of men before God and their adversary on the earth we cannot but have a very limited
idea of justification' (*Life in Christ*, London, 1954, p. 54). That which we
ought to notice is that we are seriously accused of sin in a court where this
accusation is not taken lightly. And there is no real doubt of our guilt. If
in this situation we are acquitted, then that is no mere formality. It is to
this miracle that Paul's concept of justification directs us.

sinners.⁹⁶ This may or may not be the case, but it is not what Paul is saying. It is not the *fact* but the *manner* of salvation which shows God's righteousness.⁹⁷ It is not salvation, but *salvation by the way of the cross* which shows God as at one and the same time 'just' and 'the justifier.' It is that salvation wherein a 'propitiation' is effected, i.e., a salvation in which God's concern for the right is safeguarded as well as His concern for sinners.⁹⁸ And His concern for the right is more than a mere abstract desire that justice be done. His justice is creative. It brings about the righteousness He demands.⁹⁹ There is a demonstration of His grace as well as of His justice.

Now and then Paul uses other imagery to express his conviction that Christ has dealt with all the legal consequences of sin. Thus he speaks of Him as 'having blotted out the bond written in ordinances

⁹⁶ C. Ryder Smith gives what he understands as Paul's meaning thus: 'God pleased to make man so that it was possible for him to sin; He also made man so that every sin should spread its evil infection through the mass of mankind; we have just seen the hideous result (Romans i. 18 — iii. 18); God, who must have foreseen this, would not even be righteous if He did not find a way to save men from this; He has found such a way by sending His Son' (BDS, p. 218). But H. E. Guillebaud is nearer the mark when he says, 'That God can punish seems to the modern man to need elaborate explanation: that He can forgive seems to Paul to be what needs to be explained' (*Why the Cross?* London, 1956, p. 67). Ryder Smith is perplexed by the question 'How could God be righteous if He did not forgive?' But Paul is asking rather 'How could God be righteous if He did?' And he finds his answer in the fact that God did not forgive, period. He forgave by the way of the cross.

⁹⁷ James Denney points out the importance of distinguishing between πάρεσις (used in v. 25) and ἄφεσις, 'To take διὰ τὴν πάρεσιν as if it were equivalent to διὰ τῆς ἀφέσεως, in order to make forgiveness itself the manifestation of God's righteousness (i.e., His grace), is not to interpret the apostle, but to rewrite him. It is effectively refuted, to go no further, by the distinction between the past (τῶν προγεγονότων ἁμαρτημάτων), when sins were passed by in God's forbearance, in a way which puzzled, or might have puzzled, the onlooker, and brought God's righteousness into question, and the present (ἐν τῷ νῦν καιρῷ), when on the basis of the ἱλαστήριον His righteousness is evinced' (CDR, p. 158, n.).

⁹⁸ Cf. James Denney, 'He is righteous, for in the death of Christ His Law is honoured by the Son who takes the sin of the world to Himself as all that it is to God; and He can accept as righteous those who believe in Jesus, for in so believing sin becomes to them what it is to Him. I do not know any word which conveys the truth of this if "vicarious" or "substitutionary" does not, nor do I know any interpretation of Christ's death which enables us to regard it as a demonstration of love to sinners, if this vicarious or substitutionary character is denied' (DC, p. 176).

⁹⁹ In his *Love, Power and Justice*, London and New York, 1954, Paul Tillich speaks of 'creative justice' (p. 66; this justice, he says, 'is expressed in the divine grace which forgives in order to reunite'), and of the necessity for justification (p. 86). If we combine the two we get something of Paul's idea.

that was against us, which was contrary to us', and he proceeds, 'he hath taken it out of the way, nailing it to the cross' (Col. 2:14). The uncertainties about the details here[100] do not affect the main point, that Paul sees the sinner as in legal trouble on account of his sin, but as delivered in legal form by what Christ did for him.[101]

Sometimes Paul speaks of righteousness as being 'imputed' or 'reckoned' to men, quite apart from their works (Rom. 4:6, 8, 11).[102] This was the way it was with Abraham (Rom. 4:22f.), and this is the way it will be for us if we believe (Rom. 4:24). Paul returns to the same truth and the same example in Galatians, where he says, 'Abraham believed God, and it was reckoned unto him for righteousness' (Gal. 3:6). Some modern writers find this strand of Pauline teaching objectionable. They speak of the impossibility of a 'fictional righteousness' or the like. But Paul is not arguing for a fiction. He sees righteousness as a right standing before God,[103] and this right standing is obtained, not by any effort of man, but only by God's grace. Imputation is a way of saying that God accords believers that standing that they could never reach of themselves.[104] Paul

---

[100] Notably is this the case with the reference to the nailing to the cross. It is plain enough from the papyri that χειρόγραφον was used of a certificate of debt, a bond (see MM *s.v.*). Such a bond was cancelled by crossing it out with a cross shaped like the letter χ, whence the verb χιάζω. But no custom of driving a nail through a bond appears to be cited. There may have been such a custom which we as yet have not discovered, but it is likely that the meaning is as Bruce suggests that Christ 'nailed it to the cross as an act of triumphant defiance in the face of those black-mailing powers who were holding it over you as a threat' (*in loc.*). See further A. Deissmann, BS, p. 247; LAE, pp. 332ff.

[101] Ambrose connects this passage with 2 Cor. 5:21. 'He condemned sin in order to nail our sins to the Cross. He was made sin for us that we might be in Him the righteousness of God. Thus the taking of our sins is the mark not of sin but of piety. By reason of this sin, the Eternal God Who spared not His own Son, but made Him to be sin for us, acquitted us' (Comm. in Ps. 37:6; cited in H. E. W. Turner, *The Patristic Doctrine of Redemption,* London, 1952, p. 107).

[102] A. Marmorstein reminds us that 'the doctrine of imputed righteousness was never thought of before Judaism proclaimed it' (*The Doctrine of Merits in Old Rabbinical Literature,* London, 1920, p. 29). Paul was not taking up some commonplace of religion, but a truth that was known only in his own nation and applying it to what Christ did for men. For the importance of the doctrine see the article 'Imputed Righteousness' by T. Miller Neatby, *The Churchman,* lviii, pp. 21ff.

[103] See my *The Apostolic Preaching of the Cross,* London and Grand Rapids, 1955, chs. VII and VIII.

[104] G. W. H. Lampe maintains that 'Christ's righteousness is imputed to the sinner who is devoid of any inherent righteousness, because he is *in* Christ. He has put on Christ, and so has confidence before God because by free grace he has received a new status in Christ, for no merit of his own' (*The Doctrine of Justification by Faith,* London, 1954, p. 59). We must not forget that imputation and being 'in Christ' go together.

can put the same truth negatively and speak of God as 'not reckoning unto them their trespasses' (2 Cor. 5:19). Several times he connects righteousness with faith (Rom. 4:13; Gal. 5:5, etc.). And the same truth is in mind when he thinks of righteousness as a gift (Rom. 5:17).

In such ways Paul seeks to bring out Christ's dealing with the legal implications of man's plight. Notice that in salvation the guilt and the power of sin are not the same thing.[105] While Christ effectively deals with both, these are yet distinct aspects, and the passages we have been concerned with in this section speak of the guilt, the legal liability.[106] And Paul is saying that God is concerned with right in the manner of His dealing with our plight. As Anselm put it, 'it beseemeth not God to forgive anything in His realm illegally'.[107] Now that He has dealt with it we know that when we stand before Him on the last great day we will not stand as sinners but as righteous. The righteousness we have is not our own, it comes as God's good gift in Christ. But we will be righteous. Notice that this means more than being pardoned.[108] The pardoned criminal bears no penalty, but he bears a stigma. He is a criminal and he is known as a criminal, albeit an unpunished one. The justified sinner not only bears no penalty; he is righteous. He is not a man with his sin still about him. The effect of Christ's work is to remove his sin completely.

RECONCILIATION

Some modern scholars think of reconciliation as the most important way of viewing the atonement to be found in the Pauline writings, and, indeed, in the whole New Testament.[109] This is difficult to

---

[105] Cf. H. Wheeler Robinson, 'The modern emphasis tends to fall on salvation from the power of moral evil in present experience. The New Testament, without, of course, denying or excluding this element as an accompaniment or even a condition of salvation, finds its centre of gravity in a cosmic event. Christian work and love are reckoned amongst "the things that accompany salvation" ' (op. cit., p. 233).

[106] Cf. A. Hodge, 'Corruption of nature may be removed by divine power, but guilt never' (op. cit., p. 100). Guilt requires that regard be had to what is right.

[107] Cur Deus Homo?, I. 12 (The Ancient and Modern Library of Theological Literature edn., p. 25).

[108] Cf. H. C. G. Moule, 'Justification, in common speech, never means pardon. It means winning, or granting, a position of acceptance. "You are justified in taking this course of action," does not mean, you were wrong, yet you are forgiven. It means, you were right, and in the court of my opinion you have proved it. In religion accordingly our Justification means not merely a grant of pardon, but a verdict in favor of our standing as satisfactory before the Judge' (The Fundamentals, ii, Chicago, n.d., p. 110).

substantiate at least on the grounds of frequency of mention. Paul does not linger on this idea as he does on some of the others that we have dealt with (it is used in only four passages, admittedly all important), and the idea is scarcely found at all outside his letters. It is an important idea, but let us not exaggerate as we treat it.

D. S. Cairns puts what he calls 'The Problem of Reconciliation' thus:

> We all alike believe that the only God worth believing in is the God of absolute moral perfection, and we all believe that man is made for full communion with God. Our moral nature demands the first and our religious nature requires the second. But how is that communion to be attained, kept, and developed? How is the unholy to commune with the holy, the sinner with his Judge? If I am not wholly at ease with my own conscience (and what morally sane man is?), how can I possibly be at ease with the omniscient conscience, who is also the Sovereign Reality and Power?[110]

That is the problem faced by all who take seriously the two facts of the holiness of God and the sin of man. Let us see how Paul faces it.

In Romans 5 he speaks of Christ's death for sinners as proof of the Father's love, and goes on, 'if, while we were enemies, we were reconciled to God through the death of his Son, much more, being reconciled, shall we be saved by his life', and he goes on to speak of 'our Lord Jesus Christ, through whom we have now received the reconciliation' (Rom. 5:10f.). Here he makes the point that men were 'enemies'. Their sin had put them at loggerheads with God. But the death of Christ effected reconciliation. As this is said to have been 'received', it was in some sense accomplished independently of men.

In 2 Corinthians 5 Paul has been speaking of Christ's death as the death of those for whom He died, and he goes on to refer to 'God, who reconciled us to himself through Christ', and he explains 'the ministry of reconciliation' that is given to preachers in these terms: 'God was in Christ reconciling the world unto himself,[111] not reckon-

---

[109] Thus P. Althaus gives as the first of his three points 'of primary importance' in the New Testament understanding of the cross this one: 'God is clearly set forth as the subject of the work of reconciliation — the differentiation from heathenism is sharp and clear — God is not reconciled but He consummates the reconciliation; and yet the way of the Cross is necessary for Him also. God gives His Son, but the Son is active towards God' (op. cit., p. 195).

[110] ET, lvii, p. 66.

[111] G. Aulén cites these words and goes on: 'But Christian faith can at the same time speak of God as being reconciled, that his wrath is "stayed," "is turned away," and so on. Such expressions are legitimate so long as they do not encroach upon, but are rather incorporated into, the fundamental Christian point of view, namely, that reconciliation is throughout a work of God. To Christian faith the matter appears thus, that God is reconciled

ing unto them their trespasses' (2 Cor. 5:18f.). The initiative here is entirely with God, as, indeed, is the whole process. But what is not always recognized in modern discussions is that Paul sees the reconciliation as meaning that God does not reckon to men their trespasses.[112] Most recent exegetes are so much taken up with the great thought that 'God was in Christ' (there has even been a very important book with just this title) that they overlook the fact that the passage is not dealing with the incarnation at all. The words that follow are not supporting evidence designed to show that Christ really was God. They are concerned with salvation, and with salvation in a particular way, namely salvation defined in terms of the non-imputation of sin. This was such a great work that it demanded a divine Person for its execution. There are certainly implications for Christology here. But we should not overlook the main thrust of the passage. Reconciliation in Paul's thought is closely linked with imputation, and, as verses 20f. show, with Christ's being closely identified with sinners in His death.[113] In other words reconciliation is not some respectable idea that modern men may safely employ while holding aloof from concepts like imputation and the death of Christ in the sinner's stead. It is closely linked with both.

In Ephesians 2 Paul deals with the problem of the Gentiles who were, he says, outside the blessings of the covenant, 'having no hope and without God in the world'. But Christ has altered that. Now they 'are made nigh in the blood of Christ'. He has done away with the distinction between Jew and Gentile and 'made both one'. He has 'abolished in his flesh the enmity . . . that he . . . might reconcile them both in one body unto God through the cross, having slain the enmity thereby' (Eph. 2:11-16). The approach is different, but the essential idea is the same. Again we have the thought of 'the enmity'. Sinners were far from God. But Christ's death has altered all that. It was through the death on the cross that the enmity was destroyed. Note that the context here makes it quite plain that the

---

in and through his reconciliation of the world unto himself' (*The Faith of the Christian Church*, Philadelphia, 1948, p. 229). Cf. P. T. Forsyth, Christ 'not only acted from God on man, but from man on God. I do not mean that He changed God's *feeling* to the race. That was grace always, the grace that sent Him. But He did change the *relation* between God and man' (PP, p. 362).

112 'It is the laying-aside of divine wrath rather than the overcoming of human hostility that the apostle has specially in mind when he speaks of the reconciliation of the world to God' (E. D. Burton, *Biblical Ideas of Atonement*, Chicago, 1909, p. 191).

113 Karl Barth interprets this passage by going 'back to the basic meaning of καταλλάσσειν. The conversion of the world to Himself took place in the form of an exchange, a substitution, which God has proposed between the world and Himself present and active in the person of Jesus Christ. That is what is expressly stated in the verse (21) with which the passage closes' (CDDR, p. 75).

enmity to be removed is from the divine side and not the human (the people are clearly without the spiritual privileges which are theirs after the reconciliation; it is what God does of which the apostle is speaking). There is a tendency in some quarters to build too much on the fact that the New Testament never says in so many words that God is reconciled to man, but only that man is reconciled to God. The teaching of Scripture is that the alienation is due to God's demand on man, not to any attitude that man takes up. Reconciliation accordingly takes place in connection with those demands.

In Colossians 1 Paul intermingles thought about the person and the work of Christ. The section of importance to us says: 'For it was the good pleasure of the Father . . . through him to reconcile all things unto himself, having made peace through the blood of his cross; through him, I say, whether things upon the earth, or things in the heavens. And you, being in time past alienated and enemies in your mind in your evil works, yet now hath he reconciled in the body of his flesh through death' (Col. 1:19-22). Again the problem is the sin that makes men 'enemies'. Again the remedy is the cross.

The basic idea in reconciliation is that of making peace after a quarrel, or bridging over an enmity. Now the way to do that is to deal with the root cause of the hostility. In all these passages it is clear that the root cause is the sin of man which inevitably arouses the opposition of a holy God. If there is to be harmony then that sin must not be glossed over, but really dealt with. In one aspect the work of Christ was doing away with the enmity,[114] and He did this by dealing with sin. He judged it.[115] He met the demands of a righteous God concerning it.[116] He defeated it and took it out of the way.[117] Notice that this is a distinctively Christian idea. The

---

[114] This has effects both Godward and manward, for as P. T. Forsyth puts it, 'a real and deep change of the relation between the two means a change on both sides' (WOC, p. 75).

[115] P. T. Forsyth speaks of 'the principle of immanent and ultimate and saving judgment, and of reconciliation by judgment' as 'the principle of the Cross of Christ as *the* moral crisis of God and man, *i. e.* of the universe' (JG, p. 206).

[116] G. C. Berkouwer quotes Karl Barth, 'If God does not meet us jealously, wrathfully, He does not meet us at all' and goes on, 'It is *precisely* God's wrath, according to Barth, that shows that He is *gracious*. . . . The wrath of God does not stand in *antithesis* to forgiveness, but *in* wrath and in judgment *reconciliation takes place*' (*op. cit.*, p. 235).

[117] Emil Brunner stresses that this is more than merely subjective. Dealing with reconciliation, he says, 'It is not primarily the sense of guilt which has to be removed, but the actual stain of guilt itself. Many men have scarcely any sense of guilt at all; it is not aroused in them until they come into contact with Christ. And it is in Christ alone that we all come to know what our guilt really is. The first element, therefore, in the act of reconciliation is not the removal of this subjective sense of guilt, but the knowledge that our guilt has been purged' (*The Mediator*, London, 1946, p. 522).

other religions of the world, in either ancient or modern times, lack a deep sense of the purity and holiness of God and of the ill desert of sin. It is a thought unpalatable to man that God's holiness must be taken seriously in any attempt to solve the problem of reconciliation.[118] Only the Christians thought of forgiveness as something so wonderful as almost to be unbelievable. Only the Christians saw the necessity for the tremendous moral energy of the cross for it to be effected.[119]

With this we should, of course, take the Pauline references to peace. This great word is used often with no express mention of reconciliation, but reconciliation is always implied. This follows from Paul's references to 'enmity', 'enemies', and the like. If sinful men by nature are enemies of God, and if Paul can speak of men as enjoying peace, then obviously the war must be over. But peace means more than an end to hostilities. In the New Testament it is not a negative word.[120] It has a positive content. It points to the presence of positive blessings and not simply to the absence of evil. More particularly, it is concerned with spiritual blessings. First and foremost, peace is peace with God, and arising out of that, peace with man. It is the broadbased prosperity of the whole man. We have peace with God through Christ (Rom. 5:1; Phil. 4:7). So characteristic is peace that God may be spoken of as 'the God of peace' (Rom. 16:20; Phil. 4:9; 1 Thes. 5:23). In the first of these passages God is depicted as bruising Satan, a warlike activity which fits into the biblical concept of peace naturally enough, though to us it is practically a contradiction in terms.[121] It reminds us to interpret

[118] This is a truth on which P. T. Forsyth insists again and again. For example, 'By the atonement, therefore, is meant that action of Christ's death which has a prime regard to God's holiness, has it for its first charge, and finds man's reconciliation impossible except as that holiness is divinely satisfied once for all on the cross . . . . This starting-point of the supreme holiness of God's love, rather than its pity, sympathy, or affection, is the watershed between the Gospel and the theological liberalism which makes religion no more than the crown of humanity and the metropolitan province of the world' (CC, p. viii).

[119] Cf. A. E. J. Rawlinson, 'the death of Christ is a sacrifice freely offered for sinners by One who is sinless, and S. Paul believes that "God was in Christ reconciling the world unto Himself." There are no pagan analogies to such an idea. In Reitzenstein's words, "the tremendous emphasis upon the preaching of sin and atonement is lacking in Hellenism," and the Christian Gospel of the forgiveness of sins is essentially "new"' (*The New Testamant Doctrine of Christ*, London, 1949, p. 152).

[120] See above, p. 137.

[121] There is probably a reference to Gen. 3:15. Godet rejects the idea that ἐν τάχει here is correctly understood of 'the nearness of the event'; rather it denotes 'the celerity with which it is accomplished . . . . Paul means, therefore, not that the victory will be near, but that it will be *speedily* gained, once the conflict is begun' (*in loc.*).

peace carefully. But, however it be expressed, peace is always due to the work of Christ for us. It comes 'through the blood of his cross' (Col. 1:20), and it comes no other way.

LIFE 'IN CHRIST'[122]

'I have been crucified with Christ; yet I live; and yet no longer I, but Christ liveth in me: and that life which I now live in the flesh I live in faith, the faith which is in the Son of God, who loved me, and gave himself up for me' (Gal. 2:20). In these moving words Paul gives succinct expression to his major contribution to our understanding of the Christian life. It comes only from Christ's atoning work. At both the beginning and the end of this verse he refers to Christ's death. There are also the thoughts of mystical union with Christ in His death, of Christ's life within the believer, and of the necessity for faith if the life of which Paul writes is to be lived. All these thoughts are important for Paul.

So he tells us that we are saved by Christ's life (Rom. 5:10), and when we read that we 'reign in life through the one, even Jesus Christ' (Rom. 5:17) there is no doubt that the atonement is in mind. The same is true of the references to 'eternal life through (or in) Jesus Christ our Lord' (Rom. 5:21; 6:23). But the point hardly requires demonstration. That the life of believers springs from Christ's death is fundamental for Paul. And in his notable argument in Romans 6 he makes it clear that this involves a union with Christ in His death.[123] He speaks of being buried with Christ in baptism and of being raised with Him. 'If we died with Christ, we believe that we shall also live with him' (Rom. 6:8).

The thought that the believer's life is bound up with that of his Lord is one to which Paul returns again and again. He can say to the Colossians, 'your life is hid with Christ in God' (Col. 3:3), and again, he speaks of 'Christ, who is our life' (Col. 3:4). For Paul, 'to live is Christ' (Phil. 1:21). He tells the Corinthians, 'we shall live with him through the power of God' (2 Cor. 13:4), and the Thessalonians, that He 'died for us, that, whether we wake or sleep, we should live together with him' (1 Thes. 5:10). He speaks of the early preachers as 'always bearing about in the body the dying of Jesus, that the life also of Jesus may be manifested in our body'.

[122] Ernest Best opens his book, *One Body in Christ* (London, 1955), with the words, 'The phrase or formula, "in Christ", with those allied to it, is the most frequently recurring of all those used by Paul'. Later he says, 'the formula "in Christ" contains two fundamental ideas: believers are in Christ; salvation is in Christ' (*op. cit.*, p. 29).

[123] W. H. Griffith Thomas sees the key to Rom. 6 'in verse 5, which of course refers to the present life, not to the future beyond the grave, and we are taught that the believer has been made vitally one with Christ' (*Romans*, ii, London, 1912, p. 4).

He adds, 'For we which live are alway delivered unto death for Jesus' sake, that the life also of Jesus may be manifested in our mortal flesh' (2 Cor. 4:10f.; cf. his reference to them that will 'live godly in Christ Jesus', 2 Tim. 3:12). Then there is his reference to 'the Spirit of life in Christ Jesus' (Rom. 8:2).

This life is intimately bound up with faith. In one of his best-known sayings Paul quotes the prophet Habakkuk, 'the righteous shall live by faith' (Rom. 1:17; Gal. 3:11). Whether we take this verse in the conventional way, or whether we prefer, with A. Nygren, to translate 'he who through faith is righteous shall live',[124] in either case the words emphasize the place of faith. So does the reference to 'them which should hereafter believe on him unto eternal life' (1 Tim. 1:16).

Sometimes this life is traced back to its source in the Father, as in the reference to 'eternal life, which God, who cannot lie, promised before times eternal' (Tit. 1:2), or that to those whose names are 'in the book of life' (Phil. 4:3). This will be the meaning also when eternal life is spoken of as 'the free gift of God' (Rom. 6:23). Or Paul may relate it to the Spirit (Rom. 8:11; Gal. 5:25). He speaks of its quality as 'newness of life' (Rom. 6:4), and of its direction with his repeated references to living 'unto God' or 'unto the Lord' (Rom. 6:10; 14:8; 2 Cor. 5:15; Gal. 2:19).

There is more. But this is sufficient for us to see that for Paul all real life is owed to God, and in particular to what God did for men in the death of His Son. It is this alone that enables us to live.

OTHER BLESSINGS

Paul sees the cross as bringing men a great variety of blessings. One of them is forgiveness. This may be practically equated with redemption, as one of the results of Christ's death (Eph. 1:7; cf. Col. 1:14). Vincent Taylor maintains that forgiveness is never represented by Paul 'as the object for which Christ died'.[125] This is so only if it means that Paul does not say in set terms that forgiveness was the aim before Christ when He died. Even so, the

---

[124] He maintains that 'The very structure of Romans and the letter as a whole are proof that in its theme ἐκ πίστεως is connected with ὁ δίκαιος and not with ζήσεται. In the first part of the epistle, to the end of chapter 4, Paul gives himself with great precision to the first half of his theme; he discusses the man who through faith is justified. In the second part (chap. 5-8) he affirms the second half of the theme, what is to happen to the one thus justified: he "shall live"' (Commentary on Romans, London, 1952, p. 86; Nygren's italics). F. J. Leenhardt disputes this, maintaining that the other interpretation is preferable (in loc.). He cites authorities on both sides.

[125] ANT, p. 82. He thinks of it as 'a gift of the grace of God especially associated with the salvation which Christ brings, but not the precise end for which He suffered.'

passage to which we have just referred comes close to it when the
apostle says that in Christ we have 'our redemption through his
blood, the forgiveness of our trespasses' (Eph. 1:7). I do not see
how it can seriously be maintained that Paul thought of forgiveness
as brought about by anything other than the death of Christ. He
reminds the Ephesians that 'God also in Christ forgave you' (Eph.
4:32; 'the Lord forgave you', Col. 3:13, probably has a similar meaning). Forgiveness 'in Christ' is impossible to interpret apart from
the cross. The same is true of his words to the Colossians, 'you, I
say, did he quicken together with him, having forgiven us all our trespasses' (Col. 2:13).[126] Both before and after these words Paul
speaks of the cross, and it would be curious exegesis indeed to hold
that when he turns to forgiveness the cross drops out of his mind.

Along the same lines some suggest that nothing other than
penitence is required as the condition of divine forgiveness. Thus
H. Maldwyn Hughes argues that a free pardon granted by a king
'offers no analogy for the forgiveness of man by man or of man
by God'. But 'an individual may forgive when a court of law cannot. A father may forgive his son who has forged his name. He
may be assured of the reality of the son's penitence, and a restoration of personal relations may be possible. But if the case
comes before the court, the judge cannot forgive.'[127] The suggestion
is that the forgiveness of God is to be likened to that of the father
rather than to that of the king. But this is an oversimplification.
While it is true that God is a Father, it is also true that He is a King.
We neglect either aspect to our loss. The divine forgiveness as the
Bible pictures it is much more complex than Dr. Hughes allows.
Certainly Christ's work is involved. We are forgiven for His sake.
Views which see penitence or the like as the one requirement, either
intentionally or otherwise, dismiss the work of Christ as of no account in the matter. They leave Christ out. They speak of a forgiveness brought about without Him. All such views must be
firmly rejected. It is Paul's concern to make the cross of Christ
central. Forgiveness is part of that new life that Paul sees available
to men in Christ and only in Christ.

Sometimes Paul makes use of the metaphor of adoption (Rom.
8:15; Gal. 4:5; Eph. 1:5). The practice was common in the Roman
world. It was the process whereby a person who was not a member

---

[126] F. W. Dillistone brings out the element of freeness of bounty in forgiveness in his comment on the verb used here. 'Thus, in the verb
charizomai, we find both an overwhelming sense of the free self-giving of God
and an indication that it had come to a particular focus in the limitless forgiveness manifested in Christ' (*op. cit.*, p. 87).

[127] *Op. cit.*, p. 14.

of a family was incorporated into that family.[128] He became a family member with both the rights and the privileges that that entails. Paul conceives of men in Christ as having been made members of the family of the heavenly Father. By nature they do not belong to that family. They have no claim. But one result of Christ's work for them is that they are adopted into it.

More than once Paul speaks of believers as being 'sealed' (2 Cor. 1:22; Eph. 1:13; 4:30).[129] Sealing was a common practice in an age when most men could not read. It meant putting on an article a mark which even the illiterate could understand. It made ownership clear for all to see. Paul thinks of the Holy Spirit as being given to believers as 'a seal'. In other words, the presence of the Holy Spirit within them is the sign that they belong to God. They have been bought by the blood of Christ. And as a sign of their new ownership they are marked or 'sealed' with the Spirit of God. Akin to this is the thought we sometimes find that believers 'were made a heritage' or the like expression (Eph. 1:11, 14, 18). They belong to God in a way in which those not bought by Christ do not.

Salvation may be interpreted in terms of glory. Paul speaks of the new dispensation in contrast with the old as characterized by 'the glory that surpasseth' (2 Cor. 3:10). Believers reflect 'as a mirror the glory of the Lord', they 'are transformed into the same image from glory to glory' (2 Cor. 3:18). God has 'shined in our hearts, to give the light of the knowledge of the glory of God in the face of Jesus Christ' (2 Cor. 4:6). The very gospel that they proclaim is 'the gospel of the glory of Christ' (2 Cor. 4:4).[130] Some-

---

[128] R. A. Webb relates adoption to justification and regeneration in this way: 'Justification is that act of grace whereby we sinful subjects of God's government are received into the number of, and given a right and title to, all the privileges of the kingdom of God. Adoption is that act of grace, whereby we fallen sinners are received into the number of, and are given all the rights and privileges of, the sons of God . . . . The one restores to citizenship; the other, to sonship . . . . Regeneration is that act of saving grace which, at least incipiently, reimparts to him his lost filial disposition, while adoption is that act of grace which restores to him his filial standing. By the one, he is given the heart of a child, by the other, he is given the rights of a child' (*The Reformed Doctrine of Adoption*, Grand Rapids, 1947, p. 21).

[129] Σφραγίς is used of a visible attestation of the reality of the spiritual fact . . . . The "seal" openly marked the servants of God as belonging to Him (2 Cor. 1:22), and assured them of His protection. So they were solemnly recognised as His sons (comp. John vi. 27) and on the other hand pledged to His service' (B. F. Westcott, *Saint Paul's Epistle to the Ephesians*, London, 1906, p. 17).

[130] 'AV takes "the glory" as a qualifying genitive signifying *the glorious gospel*. It is more meaningful to take it as an objective genitive in the sense that the gospel reveals the glory of Christ; it enables men to see His essential splendour' (R. V. G. Tasker, *in loc.*).

times Paul uses the concept of glory in other ways, as when he assures the Thessalonians that 'ye are our glory and our joy' (1 Thes. 2:20), or even tells the Corinthians that certain brethren are 'the glory of Christ' (2 Cor. 8:23). He tells the Ephesians in a most unusual use of the term that his tribulations for them 'are your glory' (Eph. 3:13). But characteristically he speaks of 'the riches of the glory' (Eph. 1:18) or the like. 'My God', he tells the Philippians, 'shall fulfil every need of yours according to his riches in glory in Christ Jesus' (Phil. 4:19), and in a memorable phrase he writes to the Colossians of 'Christ in you, the hope of glory' (Col. 1:27). God has called believers into glory (1 Thes. 2:12). God has made known to them its riches (Rom. 9:23). And there are riches yet to be revealed (Rom. 8:18), an 'eternal weight of glory' (2 Cor. 4:17). Believers might be, and in the first century generally were, humble, insignificant and unimportant people. But the Christian life was glorious for all that. Those who were Christ's had within them the very glory of God Himself.

In the Epistle to the Hebrews one of the great ideas is that Christ's death means the inauguration of the new covenant foretold by Jeremiah. The idea is not so prominent in Paul, though he does make use of it (e. g., Rom. 11:27), and can even speak of Christian ministers as 'ministers of a new covenant' (2 Cor. 3:6). In this latter passage, as Erich Sauer points out, there is a sevenfold superiority of the new covenant brought out in a series of contrasts: '(1) stone-flesh (vv. 3, 7); (2) letter-spirit (v. 6); (3) death-life (vv. 6, 7); (4) lesser-greater (vv. 8-10); (5) condemnation-righteousness (v. 9); (6) passing-remaining (v. 11); (7) veiling-unveiling (vv. 12-18).'[131] It cannot be denied that on occasion Paul could use the thought of a covenant that was 'new' with some power. But more fundamental for him is the thought that the covenant that God made with Abraham was fulfilled not in Judaism but in Christianity. In Galatians 3 he makes the point that when a covenant has been confirmed its terms may not be altered (v. 15). The covenant was made with Abraham (v. 16). Therefore the law, hundreds of years after, cannot disannul the covenant (v. 17). The inheritance is by promise rather than by law (v. 18), which means that it comes to those who are in Christ. In another place Paul thinks of the two covenants as symbolized by Hagar and Sarah (Gal. 4:21ff.). He does this to make the point that in Christ there is liberty, whereas under Judaism there is bondage. Again, he links the understanding of the sacrament of the Lord's Supper with the thought of covenant by recording the words of Christ, 'This cup is the new covenant in my blood' (1 Cor. 11:25). In

---

[131] *The Triumph of the Crucified*, London, 1951, p. 91.

their worship believers are reminded that their whole standing depends on Christ's atoning work.[132]

Now and then Paul uses the concept of sacrifice, as when he tells us that 'Christ also loved you, and gave himself up for us, an offering and a sacrifice to God for an odour of a sweet smell' (Eph. 5:2). Or he may refer to a particular sacrifice: 'our passover also hath been sacrificed, even Christ' (1 Cor. 5:7). Such passages show that Paul felt that Jesus had fulfilled all that was foreshadowed in the ancient sacrificial system. What they hinted at He perfectly accomplished. But for Paul this is one way among many of viewing the cross and he does not dwell upon it. He utilizes it for the lessons it teaches, but does not rely exclusively on it. It does point to a real dealing with sin, and this matters immensely.

There are yet other ways of understanding salvation. Paul speaks of it as 'the prize of the high calling of God in Christ Jesus' (Phil. 3:14). It is being translated into Christ's kingdom (Col. 1:13). It is a blotting out of the handwriting that was against us (Col. 2:14). It is 'eternal comfort' and 'good hope' (2 Thes. 2:16). It brings 'the crown of righteousness' (2 Tim. 4:8). And there is more. We cannot deal with the theme exhaustively. But enough has been said to show that Paul sees salvation as a many-sided concept. And all the many sides take their origin from Christ's cross.

VICTORY

In common with the other New Testament writers,[133] though with greater emphasis than most, Paul exults in the resurrection. Sometimes he speaks of Christ as having risen from the dead (e. g., 1 Thes. 4:14), but his habit is to speak rather of the Father as raising Him (Rom. 4:24; 1 Cor. 6:14; Eph. 1:20; Col. 2:12; 1 Thes. 1:10). He thinks of Christ's resurrection as a complete defeat of death. 'Christ being raised from the dead dieth no more; death no more hath dominion over him' (Rom. 6:9). The great resurrection chapter, 1 Corinthians 15, in which Paul sets forth so much of the significance of the resurrection, comes to an almost lyrical conclusion as Paul exults in the complete overthrow of death. He

---

[132] The radical French critic, Charles Guignebert, explains Paul's reference to the sacrament in this way: 'Thus Paul thinks of the death of Jesus as an atoning sacrifice, conferring upon men the forgiveness of sins, reconciling them to God, and assuring them of eternal life' (*Jesus,* London, 1935, pp. 443f.).

[133] J. Mánek, in an article called 'The Apostle Paul and the Empty Tomb' (*Novum Testamentum,* ii, pp. 276-80), argues that, though Paul does not refer in set terms to the empty tomb, his language implies it. 'The only difference between his conception and that of the Evangelists is this, that they proclaim the opened tomb (the stone being rolled away) — not only the empty tomb' (*op. cit.,* p. 280).

sees in death no sting, no victory, 'but thanks be to God, which giveth us the victory through our Lord Jesus Christ' (1 Cor. 15:57).

The resurrection is integral to salvation. If it did not take place, then Christian preaching is empty (1 Cor. 15:14). Its content has gone. Christ 'was raised for our justification' (Rom. 4:25). Belief in the resurrection is regarded as a condition of salvation (Rom. 10:9). Paul can characterize the God in whom he believes as 'God which raiseth the dead' (2 Cor. 1:9), and he includes the resurrection in the short summary of the essentials of the gospel (1 Cor. 15:4).

Paul does not see Christ's triumph over death as something He effects in complete isolation from believers. On the contrary, He 'died, and lived again, that he might be Lord of both the dead and the living' (Rom. 14:9). His resurrection had His relationship to His people in mind. Then, just as He won a victory over death for Himself, so He won it for His followers (Rom. 8:11). He is 'the firstfruits of them that are asleep' (1 Cor. 15:20).[134] Now the very idea of firstfruits means that there are later fruits. The adjective is meaningless apart from this. Christ's resurrection accordingly carries with it the resurrection of those that are in Christ.[135] They are 'raised with him' (Col. 2:12; 3:1). Paul looks for the time when 'the dead in Christ' shall rise (1 Thes. 4:16).

We have already noted in other connections passages which speak of Christians as having a present victory over foes of one kind or another. It is worth repeating that Paul thinks of Christ as having brought a great triumph into the lives of His people. They 'reign in life through the one, even Jesus Christ' (Rom. 5:17). They are 'more than conquerors' (Rom. 8:37). They can cast down imaginations 'and every high thing that is exalted against the knowledge of God,' they can bring 'every thought into captivity to the obedience of Christ' (2 Cor. 10:5). Whatever foe confronts the believer, he has no need to fear. Paul gives no grounds for apprehension. The

---

[134] Cf. C. Hodge, 'The apostle does not mean merely that the resurrection of Christ was to precede that of his people; but as the first sheaf of the harvest presented to God as a thank-offering, was the pledge and assurance of the ingathering of the whole harvest, so the resurrection of Christ is a pledge and proof of the resurrection of his people . . . . *As he rose, so* all his people must; as certainly and as gloriously' (*in loc.*).

[135] 'The resurrection could, of course, be taken as a sign merely of Jesus being vindicated by God apart from the community whose reproach he bore. But the resurrection stands as the inaugural triumph of *the mission* of Jesus, not as a personal triumph. It is as the gathering point for the new community that he appears on earth' (H-H. Schrey, H. H. Walz, and W. A. Whitehouse, *The Biblical Doctrine of Justice and Law,* London, 1955, p. 96).

fighting Christian is victorious, even though the foes confronting him are formidable.[136]

In this context, too, we should notice Paul's frequent emphasis on the second coming. He refers to this doctrine so very often that quotation is quite unnecessary. The second coming stands for the final victory of Christ. It is the V-day corresponding to the D-day of the cross.[137] Calvary represents the critical battle, the decisive victory. There the forces of evil were broken. The victory was won. That does not mean that there are not pockets of resistance, some of considerable size. Mopping up operations continue, and will continue to the end of time. Christians are not likely to forget that they are still in a battle, but the doctrine of the second coming means that the outcome is sure. In the fulness of the time Christ will come again, and then He will abolish 'all rule and all authority and power' as He delivers up 'the kingdom to God, even the Father' (1 Cor. 15:24).

[136] It is only those who seriously reckon with the foe who can know real victory. Cf. the remark of J. S. Whale with regard to Charles Wesley, 'Because he never failed to reckon with tears and sin and death — things which abide — he was able, as few have been, to rejoice in the Gospel which triumphed over them' (SJT, ii, p. 131).

[137] O. Cullmann reminds us that 'the "Victory Day" does in fact present *something new* in contrast to the decisive battle already fought at some point or other of the war,' and points out that there is similarly something new in the end of things. He adds, 'To be sure, this new thing that the "Victory Day" brings is based entirely upon that decisive battle, and would be absolutely impossible without it. Thus we make for the future precisely the same confirmation as we did for the past. It is a unique occurrence; it has its meaning for redemptive history in itself; but on the other hand it is nevertheless founded upon that one unique event at the mid-point' (*Christ and Time*, London, 1951, p. 141).

CHAPTER SEVEN

The Cross in the Pauline Epistles

III. MAN'S RESPONSE

The emphasis in Paul's writings is always on what God has done for man's salvation, not on any human effort whatever. The cross is the means whereby sin is put away. Over and over again Paul stresses the priority of the divine, and with it man's total inability to do anything at all to bring about salvation. Nevertheless, and though its place must be understood carefully, Paul does not think of man's response as lacking importance. It is not in any way meritorious and this truth must not be obscured. It is not the cause of salvation, but it is the means of receiving salvation. Paul thinks of God as having done in Christ all that is necessary for dealing effectively with man's sin. But man must receive the proffered salvation, else he will not have it.

REPENTANCE[1]

If men are to be saved from sin, then they must put away sin. Salvation and sin are incompatible. Like the other New Testament writers, Paul calls for a complete break with every evil thing. Perhaps no passage is more illuminating for his view of repentance than 2 Corinthians 7:9-11. Here Paul says that the Corinthians had been 'made sorry unto repentance'. He points out that 'godly sorrow worketh repentance unto salvation, a repentance which bringeth no regret'. With this he contrasts 'the sorrow of the world'. This, he says, only 'worketh death'. That is to say, a man may be very sorry about his sin, but that brings no salvation. It may result only in death.[2] Paul ascribes no particular merit to grieving over sin. A man may be very regretful in the way we call remorse. This involves depth of grief, but no decisive break with sin, no determined putting away of sin. Paul does not wish to see this 'sorrow of the world'. But being 'made sorry after a godly sort' is very different. 'What earnest care it wrought in you,' he writes, 'yea what clearing of yourselves, yea what indignation, yea what fear, yea what longing, yea what zeal, yea what avenging!' The repentant sinner is not only sorry about his sin, but by the grace of God he does something about it.[3] He makes a clean break with it. Repentance is forward looking as well as backward looking. It points to a life lived in the power of God whereby sin will be forsaken and overcome as well as grieved over. It is integral to the process of salvation. Paul can mourn over 'them

[1] H. J. Cadbury is surprised that Paul does not mention repentance more often. 'That this "Pharisee of the Pharisees" has so little to say . . . about repentance, a doctrine cardinal to Judaism and congenial to Christianity, has never been explained' (*The Making of Luke — Acts*, London, 1958, p. 288). The number of passages may not be large, but they are significant as the discussion, I hope, shows.

[2] There is an attitude which D. R. Davies characterizes as 'Eros in tears'. This, he points out, 'is egoism in a chastened though more determined mood. It is a decision, self-born, to be a good boy — or girl. Repentance is radically different and almost wholly other. Where penitence expresses a determination to tighten up the ego, repentance indicates a decision to abandon the ego . . . . It is the difference between trying to make the old car do by extensive repairs and getting rid of it altogether and going in for an aeroplane — transport in a new element. Repentance is the most fundamental and revolutionary of all human experiences' (*The Art of Dodging Repentance*, London, 1952, p. 13). It may be questioned whether penitence is the best name for this other attitude, but that repentance is unique and thoroughgoing is the important point.

[3] 'Repentance, μετάνοια, was not the rather easy Jewish process of the Day of Atonement, but a genuine sharing of God's outlook at all costs to oneself, a disinterested emotion as opposed to one sprung of self-seeking, an affirmation of God's ways' (T. R. Glover, *Paul of Tarsus*, London, 1925, p. 88).

that have sinned heretofore, and repented not' (2 Cor. 12:21). The absence of repentance means that these men still bear the burden of their sin.

We are apt to think of the atonement as what Christ has done for us, with repentance as our own achievement. But Paul does not see it quite that way. Left to themselves men do not repent. Repentance is a gift of God. In his great passage on judgment in Romans 2, where he has a good deal to say about 'the wrath' and the fate of them that continue in sin, he yet points out that 'the goodness of God leadeth thee to repentance' (Rom. 2:4). The Lord's servant is to be active in setting forth the Christian message to sinners, 'if peradventure God may give them repentance unto the knowledge of the truth' (2 Tim. 2:25). Unless God intervenes sinful men will continue on in their sin. But when he gives men the gift, they turn away from their sin and experience repentance. We may reflect that repentance, true repentance, is such an uncomfortable experience that sinners naturally shun it.[4] They will adopt all kinds of subterfuges to hide from themselves and from others their need of it, and they will engage in all manner of activities in substitution for it.[5] It requires a special gift from God before they realize the necessity for it. This is all the more so in that there are sins of which a man must repent which do not appear to the natural man to be sins at all. Thus in his pride he does not recognize pride as pride, but acts in a spirit of self-righteousness. It takes a complete revolution in the soul, a divine work of re-creation before a man can see that repentance is needed for a whole way of life, his 'good' as well as what was patently evil.[6]

FAITH

Paul never tires of pointing out the important place faith has in the Christian scheme of things. He does not see it as a mere intellectual adherence to certain doctrines,[7] as has sometimes been

[4] Cf. William Law: 'Repentance is but a kind of table-talk, till we see so much of the deformity of our inward nature as to be in some degree frightened and terrified at the sight of it' (*Selected Mystical Writings*, ed. S. Hobhouse, London, 1938, p. 13).

[5] M. Jarrett-Kerr has a chapter entitled 'The Evasion of Penitence' in which he examines the various shifts to which men resort to avoid penitence (*Our Trespasses*, London, 1948, chap. I). He discusses the denial of the need for penitence, the 'psychological' or 'medical' alibi, the 'sociological' alibi, the 'pietistic' alibi, the 'activist' alibi, and the 'intellectualist' alibi.

[6] Cf. David Cox, 'Christian penitence involves a "qualitative" change in natural penitence, because it means the discovery of a whole class of sins which were not before acknowledged, even as errors; sins which, in fact, we cannot know as sins without being confronted by a criterion of perfection from outside ourselves' (*op. cit.*, p. 224).

[7] Cf. M. Goguel, 'Although faith contains an intellectual element, in the Pauline sense of the word it is something quite different from that relative

thought. Faith for Paul is a warm personal trust in a living Saviour. Faith is a transforming attitude.[8] When a man believes his whole personality is affected.[9] The entire Christian life accordingly is a life of faith, or, as Paul puts it, 'we walk by faith, not by sight' (2 Cor. 5:7).

Paul links faith particularly with the reception of salvation. Repeatedly he insists on this. 'It was God's good pleasure', he tells the Corinthians, 'through the foolishness of the preaching to save them that believe' (1 Cor. 1:21). And if it was 'God's good pleasure', then man could do little about it. Paul had not always seen this. In his days as a Jew he had striven for righteousness according to the law (Phil. 3:6). But now he sees that righteousness does not come by way of the law but by faith (Rom. 3:28).[10] All boasting is excluded (Rom. 3:27; Eph. 2:9).[11] Paul's whole emphasis is on faith. 'By grace have ye been saved through faith' (Eph. 2:8). 'Ye are all sons of God, through faith' (Gal. 3:26). The gospel is 'the power of God unto salvation to every one that believeth' (Rom. 1:16). Paul loves to appeal to scripture, and one of the great Old Testament passages for him is Habakkuk 2:4, which he quotes in Romans 1:17 and Galatians 3:11, 'the righteous shall live by faith'. In the gospel he tells us there 'is revealed a righteousness of God by faith unto faith' (Rom. 1:17), which is apparently a way of saying 'faith from first to last'. The 'righteous-

---

certitude which can be experienced in connection with realities which cannot be known directly by the intelligence nor by the senses; faith is supremely mystical union with Christ, a union through which the believer lays hold of all that there is in Christ for him' (*The Life of Jesus*, London, 1958, p. 113).

8 Cf. Emil Brunner, 'To believe means objectively to die — i.e. to die as that false ego which is identical with sin; and likewise to believe means objectively to rise again as the new man — Christ in me' (*Eternal Hope*, London, 1954, p. 110).

9 Cf. C. Anderson Scott, 'But if we ask what it was Paul felt to be present in the consciousness of the believer at the moment of believing it would be best expressed as an utter and entire committal of himself to God in Christ, following an over-mastering impulse of the will to respond with love to the love of God which had been manifested in Christ' (*Christianity According to St. Paul*, Cambridge, 1939, p. 110).

10 Karl Barth points out that Paul can speak of δικαιοσύνη πίστεως (Rom. 4:13), or τῆς πίστεως (Rom. 4:11), δικ. ἐκ πίστεως (Rom. 9:30), δικ. διὰ πίστεως and ἐπὶ τῇ πίστει (Phil. 3:9). 'There is no instance of the combination δικ. διὰ τὴν πίστιν. This means that from the standpoint of biblical theology the root is cut of all the later conceptions which tried to attribute to the faith of man a merit for the attainment of justification or co-operation in its fulfilment, or to identify faith, its rise and continuance and inward and outward work with justification' (CDDR, pp. 614f.).

11 Johannes Munck sees this as one of Paul's 'basic themes — God makes all boasting impossible by creating something out of what is nothing' (*Paul and the Salvation of Mankind*, London, 1959, p. 164).

ness of God' which has just been mentioned he understands as the right standing that a man obtains from God, and this he links with faith repeatedly (e.g., Rom. 3:22; 9:30; 10:6; Gal. 5:5; Phil. 3:9). Faith is counted for righteousness (Rom. 4:5). Paul links various aspects of Christ's atoning work with faith, such as justification (Rom. 5:1; Gal. 3:24), propitiation (Rom. 3:25), or adoption (Gal. 3:26) and access to God (Rom. 5:2; Eph. 3:12). So Christ dwells in the hearts of believers 'through faith' (Eph. 3:17). It is abundantly clear that Paul sees faith as that one right attitude that God seeks in man.[12]

Paul is fond of thinking of Abraham as the Christian's prototype in treading this path of faith. He characterizes that patriarch as 'strong through faith' (Rom. 4:20), and as having 'the righteousness of faith' (Rom. 4:13). It was his faith that made him the 'father' of all believers, circumcised or uncircumcised (Rom. 4:11f.). Thus he sees Christians, believers, as the true sons of Abraham, not the Jews whose connection is only one of lineal descent. 'Know therefore that they which be of faith, the same are sons of Abraham' (Gal. 3:7). In similar vein he tells us that it is 'they which be of faith' who 'are blessed with the faithful Abraham' (Gal. 3:9).

Paul thus thinks of faith as central.[13] Christians stand by faith (Rom. 11:20; 2 Cor. 1:24). They 'walk by faith' (2 Cor. 5:7). But he does not think of faith as static. He tells the Thessalonians of his desire to 'perfect that which is lacking in your faith' (1 Thes. 3:10), and later he renders thanks that the faith of this same group of believers 'groweth exceedingly' (2 Thes. 1:3). Faith is a growing, active thing. There is such a thing as 'your work of faith' (1 Thes. 1:3). Paul has a very descriptive phrase when he writes to the Galatians of 'faith working through love' (Gal. 5:6). It is abundantly clear from the Pauline Epistles that the apostle ascribes a very high place indeed to Christian love. In this verse we see the link between faith and love. For Paul, neither operates in isolation. Love for him is not an attitude that springs from the inner being of the

12 Cf. J. McLeod Campbell, 'our faith is, in truth, the Amen of our individual spirits to that deep, multiform, all-embracing, harmonious Amen of humanity, in the person of the Son of God, to the mind and heart of the Father in relation to man, — the divine wrath and the divine mercy, which is the atonement. This Amen of the individual, in which faith utters itself towards God, gives glory to God according to the glory which He has in Christ; therefore does faith justify' (*The Nature of the Atonement*, Cambridge, 1856, p. 224). J. Scott Lidgett says, 'faith in Christ makes His death *our* sacrifice. That which Christ uttered to God in His death, we by faith utter in Him' (*The Spiritual Principle of the Atonement*, London, 1897, p. 407).

13 'To him faith is the great fundamental human virtue, the indispensable condition of all salvation and life and blessing' (D. S. Cairns, *The Faith that Rebels*, London, 1933, p. 207).

natural man. It is the product of a right Christian faith. And the exercise of a right Christian faith necessarily leads to love. Love is the way faith works.

As in the case of repentance, Paul regards faith as in some sense the gift of God. He can say, 'God hath dealt to each man a measure of faith' (Rom. 12:3).[14] Paul will say nothing that obscures the divine initiative. For him it is basic that salvation proceeds from God. It is divine from first to last. Though there are conditions from the human end if salvation is to be received, yet these conditions do not enable men to claim the credit for any part in their salvation.[15] They could not produce repentance and faith without divine assistance. They come only as God's gift.[16]

This is the basis of Paul's notable argument against human wisdom in 1 Corinthians 1:18-2:16. Here he is arguing that natural wisdom will never lead men to God. The Corinthians, like other Greeks, evidently ascribed a very high place indeed to the exercise of wisdom. That is man's highest excellence. The thrust of Paul's argument in this opening section of his Epistle is that man, left to himself, can never find God. Whatever its value, human wisdom cannot accomplish that. Only those humble enough to accept this truth and walk in the path that God shows them will enter salvation.

The centrality of faith is seen in the way Paul uses it as more or less synonymous with Christianity. Thus he characterizes the gospel as 'the word of faith, which we preach' (Rom. 10:8), and he gives the report of his conversion in the words 'He that once persecuted us now preacheth the faith of which he once made havoc' (Gal. 1:23). He speaks of the church as 'the household of the faith' (Gal. 6:10), including in it even 'him that is weak in faith' (Rom. 14:1). Grace and apostleship, he says, are 'unto obedience of faith' (Rom. 1:5).[17] So he looks to the Colossians to continue in

[14] Perhaps we should add 1 Cor. 12:9, but there the meaning appears to be a special gift of the Spirit confined to certain individuals, rather than that faith which is the distinguishing mark of all Christians.

[15] Even such a perceptive writer as J. Rivière loses sight of this when he writes, 'But for us to secure our Salvation and the application of Christ's merits, some labour is required of us' (*The Doctrine of the Atonement*, London, 1909, i, p. 61).

[16] Cf. R. Bultmann, 'πίστις is the complete surrender of a man to God, and indeed a surrender which a man cannot in any way decide to make of his own accord — for in that case he would remain in the domain of ἔργα — but which can only be a surrender to God's grace, and thus only a response to God's act' (R. Bultmann and A. Weiser, *Faith*, London, 1961, p. 91).

[17] Dietrich Bonhoeffer sees a close connection between obedience and faith: ' "Only those who believe obey" is what we say to that part of a believer's soul which obeys, and "only those who obey believe" is what

the faith, and to be 'stablished' in it (Col. 1:23; 2:7). And his discussion on the resurrection in 1 Corinthians is concerned with the question of whether their faith was 'vain' (i. e., 'empty' or 'futile', see 1 Cor. 15:14, 17). Were faith to be emptied of its force in this way, the implication runs, then Christianity has become an empty shell. It is a well-grounded faith which gives it content.[18]

Paul delights to dwell on faith and its consequences. Often he speaks of believers as being 'in Christ', and sometimes also of Christ as being in them. Faith brings about a union that is so close that it is possible in this way to speak of mutual indwelling. This is a strong way of expressing the truth that the believer surrenders himself completely to Christ and the complementary truth that contact with the living Christ brings man into a new life.

THE LIFE OF THE BELIEVER

Paul's letters abound in exhortations to his converts to lead holy lives. He cannot say often enough or strongly enough how important it is that they should break with every evil thing and cleave to what is good. Their lives must reflect their Christian profession.[19] They are men who 'walk in newness of life' (Rom. 6:4). They must be 'unto the praise of his glory' (Eph. 1:12). The gospel brings forth fruit (Col. 1:6). Paul says, 'I through the law died unto the law, that I might live unto God' (Gal. 2:19). He tells us that 'they that are of Christ Jesus have crucified the flesh with the passions and the lusts thereof' (Gal. 5:24). The world was crucified to Paul, and Paul was crucified to the world (Gal. 6:14).

---

we say to that part of the soul of the obedient which believes. If the first half of the proposition stands alone, the believer is exposed to the danger of cheap grace, which is another word for damnation. If the second half stands alone, the believer is exposed to the danger of salvation through works, which is also another word for damnation' (*The Cost of Discipleship*, London, 1959, p. 58). So also Bultmann can say, 'It was chiefly Paul who emphasised that the nature of faith is that of obedience. For him πίστις is also ὑπακοή, as can be seen by comparing Rom. i.8, 1 Thess. i.8 with Rom. xv.18, xvi.19; or II Cor. x.5f. with x.15. Faith means to him *to give heed* (ὑπακούειν) *to the gospel* (Rom. x.16)' (*op. cit.*, p. 63).

[18] T. C. Edwards points out that if Christ did not rise the gospel 'ceases, therefore, to be a message (κήρυγμα) and becomes a speculative doctrine (φιλοσοφία), which, in the case of a religion designed to save men, is nothing better than a κενὴ ἀπάτη, a hollow deception (Col. ii.8). Christianity becomes an unreal system of notions, like other phantoms of the theatre, if it is not an interpretation of facts. Faith also is no more faith; for faith must act on an external fact and a living person' (on 1 Cor. 15:14).

[19] 'Sanctification is the claiming of all human life and being and activity by the will of God for the active fulfilment of that will' (Karl Barth, CDDR, p. 101).

He prays concerning the Thessalonians that their whole body, soul and spirit be preserved blameless (1 Thes. 5:23).

Much more could be quoted along the same lines. It is basic to Paul that the Christian must be Christlike. This represents something of a novelty in religion. Among most of the religions of antiquity it was accepted that a man might be very religious, though not particularly righteous. Paul would have denied this absolutely. The reality of a man's faith is shown in the way he lives.

Here again Paul insists on the priority of the divine. Christians are 'created in Christ Jesus for good works, which God afore prepared that we should walk in them' (Eph. 2:10). Paul is not prepared to see in good works the evidence of a merely human striving. Men could never do good works other than in the strength that God provides. Paul's doctrine of the Holy Spirit comes in here. Again and again he insists that Christians are distinguished by the fact that the Spirit of God is in them (Rom. 8:9, 14). Paul is sure that in the power of that Holy Spirit of God believers will be strong to overcome evil, strong to do good. They will not be cramped in by the iron grip of their own past.[20]

The note of power runs through much of what Paul writes. He assures the Romans that the gospel 'is the power of God unto salvation to every one that believeth' (Rom. 1:16). The word of God 'worketh in you that believe' (1 Thes. 2:13), which clearly means that the effectiveness of the Thessalonians for Christian service arises from the divine power within them. Paul likes to contrast 'word' and 'power', as when he says, 'the kingdom of God is not in word, but in power' (1 Cor. 4:20), or, 'our gospel came not unto you in word only, but also in power, and in the Holy Ghost' (1 Thes. 1:5). For Paul it is important to be clear that Christ not only tells men what they ought to do, but gives them power and strength to obey His command. This emphasis is not yet out of date.[21]

[20] Cf. P. Althaus, 'Justification or forgiveness in Christ retains the character of the incredibly wonderful. It cannot in any way be ethically rationalised. It is non-ethical, indeed anti-ethical. For it frees man from what he cannot and indeed ought not to free himself, and from what he may not and dare not think himself to be freed, from what accompanies him in his every moment — namely what he has been' (*Mysterium Christi*, ed. G. K. A. Bell and A. Deissmann, London, 1930, p. 220).

[21] F. C. Grant reminds us that 'our modern psychoanalytic interpretation inclines to leave out mysticism, the sense of rebirth, the new power that comes, not from a full "analysis" and a careful probing of sin or of long-forgotten emotional disturbances, but from consecration, the new life in Christ, the power of an endless life brought to bear upon a mortal one, the powers of the age to come already operative in this age . . .' (*An Introduction to New Testament Thought*, New York, 1950, p. 261).

THE CHRISTIAN AND SUFFERING

What we read of Paul in the Acts and in his own Epistles makes it clear that the apostle suffered greatly. Journeying up and down the Roman Empire as he did, he ran into danger constantly. The life of a traveler in those days could certainly be both eventful and difficult, with shipwreck, highway robbers, etc., as nothing other than the normal hazards. Add to this the incessant opposition which was the inevitable lot of a first-century Christian preacher and you see that life for such a one must have been a thing of pain and of anguish and of torment and of constant foreboding. But Paul neither complains about nor is inhibited by his sufferings. He does not like them, but he does not regard them as an unmixed evil. They are part of the service he renders to God. He uses them.[22] He does not simply put up with them, but incredibly, he rejoices in them, and he calls on others to do likewise, saying to the Romans, 'let us also rejoice in our tribulations' (Rom. 5:3), and to the Corinthians, 'I take pleasure in weaknesses, in injuries, in necessities, in persecutions, in distresses, for Christ's sake' (2 Cor. 12:10), and again, 'I overflow with joy in all our affliction' (2 Cor. 7:4). He speaks of dying daily (1 Cor. 15:31). His peril was always with him.

For Paul the great thing about suffering is that it is not aimless, not futile. It is not the result of blind chance. It is not the torture inflicted by an unfeeling Fate. Suffering can come only as an all-powerful and all-wise Father permits. Therefore suffering, for the Christian, is always meaningful. Paul can speak of his sufferings as having 'fallen out . . . unto the progress of the gospel' (Phil. 1:12). Something like this will be the meaning of his reference to himself as 'the prisoner of Christ Jesus in behalf of you Gentiles' (Eph. 3:1; 4:1), and to his tribulations as the 'glory' of his converts (Eph. 3:13). Sufferings can be 'an evident token of . . . salvation, and that from God' (Phil. 1:28). Evidently Paul holds that God's purposes are set forward in the sufferings of His servants.

On occasion we are allowed to see something of these purposes. Thus suffering enables him who has borne it to be a comfort to others (2 Cor. 1:4ff.).[23] In view of the way in which men's lives

---

[22] E. Stanley Jones has a comment on the Christian's suffering which is applicable to Paul: 'When a storm strikes an eagle, he sets his wings in such a way that the air currents send him above the storm by their very fury. The set of the wings does it. The Christian is not spared the pains and sorrows and sicknesses that come upon other people, but he is given an inner set of the spirit by which he rises above these calamities by the very fury of the calamities themselves' (*Christ and Human Suffering*, London, 1934, p. 99).

[23] 'In missionary work sympathy is the great condition of success . . . . the comfort is deliverance, not necessarily from the suffering, but from the anxiety

are intertwined as they live together in community this is no small gain. The Christian may always be sure that his sufferings will help him in his service of others. But for Paul there is a deeper truth than this. Suffering for him is a privilege given by God (Phil. 1:29). Christ suffered even unto death for His people, and Paul speaks of the Christians as 'becoming conformed unto his death' (Phil. 3:10). So, too, he says, 'the sufferings of Christ abound unto us' (2 Cor. 1:5). In a very bold expression he affirms, 'I rejoice in my sufferings for your sake, and fill up on my part that which is lacking of the afflictions of Christ in my flesh for his body's sake, which is the church' (Col. 1:24). It would be a mistake to regard this as indicating that human sufferings are atoning.[24] Paul's writings give abundant evidence of the fact that he held the cross of Christ to be unique, unrepeatable, perfect in its scope and efficacy. Yet the sayings we have quoted indicate that the cross of Christ has transformed suffering for the Christian. For him it is a privilege to suffer for others. T. F. Torrance argues that this is integral to the whole ministry of the church: 'The Church Militant is still under the Cross and it belongs to its life and mission to work out analogically in itself what happened in Christ for the Church, to fill up in its body that which is eschatologically in arrears of the sufferings of Christ and so to fulfil the Word of God (cf. Col. 1:24f.).'[25]

---

which suffering brings. There is the assurance that sufferers are in the hands of a loving Father, and this assurance they can pass on to others in all their afflictions' (A. Plummer, ICC, in loc.).

[24] Cf. E. F. Sutcliffe, 'Christ deigned to leave some share of His work and of His sufferings to His members, not to redeem the world, but to act as His ministers in the application to men of the atoning power of His redemption' (Providence and Suffering in the Old and New Testaments, London, 1953, p. 137).

[25] SJT, vii, p. 257. He also says, 'Jesus Christ was Suffering Servant in a unique sense in that He had a ministry of substitutionary and vicarious atonement in which His act was act of God. The Church is suffering servant like Him but in a different sense. The church participates in His ministry of reconciliation by serving Him' (op. cit., p. 258).

CHAPTER EIGHT

The Cross in the Epistle to the Hebrews

The writer of this Epistle thinks of God as an awe-inspiring Being, and his view of the greatness of God colours all his thinking. That does not mean that he is unmindful of the wonder and the greatness of God's love. Indeed, a good deal of his Epistle is given over to showing what God has done to bring men salvation, i. e., to showing the love of God in action. But for him the love of God is not a truism. In the strict sense of that word, it is wonderful. God is so great, so holy, that men ought to look on Him with awe. They cannot take it for granted that He will think them worth saving. They are very little, and of very little worth. He is very great and supremely to be venerated. And unless we experience the fear of God as the writer of this Epistle experienced it, we cannot begin to understand his thought on the cross. The desperate plight in which man finds himself as the result of his sin can be appreciated

270

only against the background of the awfulness and the holiness of God.[1]

Take, for example, the description of the scene on Mt. Sinai, that 'mount that might be touched, and that burned with fire,' where there was

> blackness, and darkness, and tempest, and the sound of a trumpet, and the voice of words; which voice they that heard intreated that no word more should be spoken unto them: for they could not endure that which was enjoined. If even a beast touch the mountain, it shall be stoned; and so fearful was the appearance, that Moses said, I exceedingly fear and quake (Heb. 12:18-21).

It is true that when he uses this description of events in days of old it is by way of showing that Christians have a different way of approach. But nevertheless these words show us something of the writer's idea of what God is and might do, and of how He affects men's approach to Him. A God like that is not to be trifled with; He is to be regarded with respect and awe and reverence. As our writer puts it elsewhere, 'It is a fearful thing to fall into the hands of the living God' (Heb. 10:31), or again, 'our God is a consuming fire' (Heb. 12:29). It is only when we appreciate this majestic aspect of the divine nature that we see just how acute is the peril into which the sin of man led him.

In modern times men have usually lost the vision of a God like that. May I illustrate from a criticism levelled at Billy Graham at the time of his crusade in Melbourne? There were, of course, people who opposed the evangelist for a variety of reasons, but our concern is with those whose opposition rested on nothing more solid than inadequate views of God. Here is a letter written to the editor of one of the Melbourne daily papers, and which, I fear, is typical of many more.

> After hearing Dr. Billy Graham on the air, viewing him on TV, and reading reports and letters concerning him and his mission, I am heartily sick of the type of religion that insists that my soul (and everyone else's) needs saving — whatever that means.
>
> I have never felt that it was lost. Nor do I feel that I daily wallow in the mire of sin, although repetitive preaching insists that I do.

---

[1] Cf. J. Moffatt, 'This is not the primitive awe of religion before the terrors of the unknown supernatural; the author believes in the gracious, kindly nature of God . . . but he has an instinctive horror of anything like a shallow levity . . . . We might almost infer that in his mind the dominant conception is God regarded as transcendental, not with regard to creation but with regard to frail, faulty human nature. What engrosses the writer is the need not so much of a medium between God and the material universe, as of a medium between his holiness and human sin' (*Hebrews*, ICC, p. xxxvi).

> Give me a practical religion that teaches gentleness and tolerance, that acknowledges no barriers of color or creed, that remembers the aged and teaches children of goodness and not sin.
>
> If in order to save my soul I must accept such a philosophy as I have recently heard preached, I prefer to remain for ever damned.

Now I do not wish to impugn the sincerity of the writer of this letter, but here we find statements made with tremendously far-reaching implications, and made with no basis, no foundation. These statements are no more than the expression of mere personal preference, of private opinion, not to say prejudice. No appeal is made to any authority other than the writer, be it the Bible or the church, or Jesus Christ, or God. Indeed, the name of God is not once mentioned, which is passing strange in a letter professedly about religion. And the trouble is that this is typical of a good deal that affirms itself to be Christian in the modern world. Men ignore God. Then, having removed from the scene anything that might cramp their style, they proceed to set forth their own personal views and dignify them by labeling them 'Christianity'.

If we share such views we will never understand the Epistle to the Hebrews. There God is a living God (Heb. 3:12; 9:14; 10:31), and His word is living and active (Heb. 4:12). There God is a great God and cannot simply be ignored. He is a mighty Ruler, a Being of glory and majesty, the Sovereign Lord of all creation. If He is to be approached by puny man it must be with awe.[2] If men would serve Him, then they must do it with the best they have. They must offer their hearts' devotion. They cannot draw near with a shoddy offering, with that which they do not value and would never miss. Men cannot presume on the God of the Epistle to the Hebrews.

GOD THE JUDGE OF ALL

Among 'the first principles of Christ' our writer lists the teaching 'of eternal judgement' (Heb. 6:1f.). As he looks to the end of this earthly life, he says, 'it is appointed unto men once to die, and after this cometh judgement' (Heb. 9:27). Ideas like these may fairly be held to underlie the argument of the whole Epistle. It is basic that God, who is a great God, and who has made all mankind, will

---

[2] Cf. Vincent Taylor, 'It cannot be denied that the picture is austere; but, on the other hand, there is no suggestion of an offended Deity who needs to be appeased before man can approach Him in penitence and hope . . . . There is nothing in the representation that is unworthy and much that is essential to any true doctrine of God' (ANT, pp. 112f.); 'he has richly served the cause of Christian truth by emphasizing noble aspects of God's Being, and therefore of redemption, which are easily lost sight of by the sentimentalism which accepts His Fatherhood without adequately recognizing its strength as well as its graciousness' (op. cit., p. 114).

in the end call on men to render account of themselves. God may be referred to as 'the Judge of all' (Heb. 12:23).[3] Our author quotes from the ancient Scripture, 'Vengeance belongeth unto me, I will recompense. And again, The Lord shall judge his people' (Heb. 10:30). Small wonder that he concludes, 'It is a fearful thing to fall into the hands of the living God' (Heb. 10:31).

This accountability of all men gives to life a sense of serious purpose. We are not concerned with a passing show of no particular significance which has its little day and speedily disappears to be seen no more. We shall stand before God and face a serious reckoning for what we have done and what we have not done. Something of what this involves is to be seen from God's dealings with men in the past. He has punished evil, as in the case of Esau (Heb. 12:16f.),[4] or in that of the wilderness generation (Heb. 3:7ff., 15ff.). In both cases exclusion from the blessing was permanent. Esau afterwards wished to secure it, our writer says, but could not. There is a sense of urgency, and sinners ought not to be deluded into thinking that they are faced with a choice fraught with small consequences. The writer sees these incidents recorded in the Scripture as an example to us, 'For if they escaped not, when they refused him that warned them on earth, much more shall not we escape, who turn away from him that warneth from heaven' (Heb. 12:25).

When men are called upon to give an account of their deeds before God, it is especially in mind that evil deeds will be punished. There is a special emphasis on this (Heb. 2:2f.; 6:8; 10:29, 31). The writer looks both back and forward. Sinners were punished in days gone by, and sinners cannot look for anything else when they stand before God. Moreover God's judgment is searching. His word

> is living, and active, and sharper than any two-edged sword, and piercing even to the dividing of soul and spirit, of both joints and marrow, and quick to discern the thoughts and intents of the heart.

[3] Antony Snell thinks of 'Judge' as used here in the sense 'deliverer and vindicator, not in the warning or grim sense found at 10:30' (*New and Living Way*, London, 1959, p. 154). This may well be the case but the deliverance is not haphazard. Snell translates 'as vindicator the God of all', thus making it clear that he does not see an indiscriminate salvation of all men here. The words, translate them how we will, point to man's accountability and to God's ultimate judicial activity.

[4] Cf. W. Manson, 'certainly it was unbelief in the divine promise to his house, not mere sensuality, that led Esau to the irrevocable step of bartering away his birthright. No later repentance was able to undo that act (xii.14-17). It is plain that for the writer to the Hebrews religion (cf. vi.4-6) was not a matter only of repenting and obtaining forgiveness, but of irrevocable commitment of life to a supernatural end' (*The Epistle to the Hebrews*, London, 1951, p. 85).

> And there is no creature that is not manifest in his sight: but all things are naked and laid open before the eyes of him with whom we have to do (Heb. 4:12f.).

This means that men cannot comfort themselves with the reflection that their worst sins are covered over, and no one knows of them. Nothing is hid from God, nothing. All our deeds are called into judgment.[5] Our author is sure of the wrath of God (Heb. 3:11; 4:3). Those who draw back from the salvation God proffers do so 'unto perdition' (Heb. 10:39). And for apostates there remains only 'a certain fearful expectation of judgement, and a fierceness of fire. . .' (Heb. 10:27; cf. 6:1-6). Lack of faith is castigated several times (Heb. 3:12, 19; 4:2, 6, 11). It is specially blameworthy when men refuse to believe in God and so to accept the way of salvation He provides.

Because God is so great and His standards so high, and because we shall one day stand before Him, we do well to give heed to the situation in which our sin has placed us. The sinner facing the prospect of judgment before such a Judge is in no good case. This Epistle leaves us in no doubt but that those who are saved are saved from a sore and genuine peril. Christ's saving work is not a piece of emotional pageantry rescuing men from nothing in particular.

THE COMPASSION OF GOD

The fact that this writer puts considerable emphasis on God's activity as Judge does not mean that he sees Him only as sentencing men and destroying sinners. The interest of the Epistle lies in another direction altogether, namely in the salvation of men. And this salvation is always thought of as stemming ultimately from the compassion and the grace of God. It was 'by the grace of God'[6]

---

[5] 'Generally, we are quite proud about our ability to hide our most secret spiritual and psychic tendencies before the gaze of others. We guard the hidden depths of our being against the grasp and judgment of men. But God, who is a Lord over the living and the dead, makes the claim to judge not only our deeds, but also our thoughts and inmost sensations. This claim is valid whether we recognize it or not. God confronts us constantly in His Word as our judge. We have to give an account before the judgment seat of the divine Word. And he who takes God's Word seriously bows under that Word as the norm and measure of his inward and outward life' (Johannes Schneider, *The Letter to the Hebrews*, Grand Rapids, 1957, p. 35).

[6] 'Grace' is a concept of which our author is fond, and he uses it in a variety of ways. See 4:16; 10:29; 12:15, 28; 13:9, 25. A. B. Davidson says, 'With the exception of ii. 9, grace is spoken of in the Epistle not as the principle in God from which the mission of the Son originates, but as the result of His death' (*The Epistle to the Hebrews*, Edinburgh, n.d., p. 215). This statement is rather too sweeping, for, after all, the verse we are discussing, 2:9, does affirm what Davidson denies.

that Christ died for men (Heb. 2:9). God 'appointed' Him to His calling (Heb. 3:2). This same Christ 'became unto all them that obey him the author of eternal salvation' (Heb. 5:9), and He is also 'the author and perfecter of our faith' (Heb. 12:2), which must be held to point to the same thing, since faith is the means whereby we receive salvation (Heb. 10:38f.). There is no limit to what He can do by way of saving men, for He 'is able to save to the uttermost' (Heb. 7:25). Thus our author delights to dwell on the way Christ has wrought salvation and takes the initiative in bringing it to men.

Sometimes he associates salvation with the Father. He thinks of God as a great God, but not as a remote God uninterested in the world's plight. His standards are high. He will call on all men to give account of themselves. But basically He is gracious, loving, eager that men be saved. It is from God that men obtain mercy and grace (Heb. 4:16)[7] and blessing (Heb. 6:14). God has provided us with the way of salvation in Christ, who Himself first spoke to men about it (Heb. 2:3). Those who heard Him passed the message on, and God attested it by enabling the preachers to do the wonderful things that commended the gospel (Heb. 2:3f.; cf. also 4:2 for the preaching of 'good tidings'). Those who are saved are described as 'called' (Heb. 9:15), a term which stresses the divine initiative, while the reference to 'them that shall inherit salvation' (Heb. 1:14), if it does not go as far as that, at least reminds us that salvation comes as a free gift, and is not the result of human striving. It is the same with 'Behold, I and the children which God hath given me' (Heb. 2:13). It is God who brings about their status 'as children. There are other references to salvation as 'inheritance' (Heb. 6:12; 9:15).

Especially is this brought out by referring to God's promises,[8] for if salvation comes from the fulfilling of God's promises, obviously it is His gift and not our earning. It is a fundamental premise of our author that 'he is faithful that promised' (Heb. 10:23; so also 11:11, 13:5f; he speaks also of Christ's faithfulness, Heb. 2:17,

---

Yet the close connection with the death of Christ should not be overlooked. Moffatt can say that in this Epistle, 'although God is never called directly the Father of Christians, his attitude to men is one of grace, and the entire process of man's approach is initiated by him' (*op. cit.,* p. xxxv).

[7] Cf. Andrew Murray, 'The believing supplicant at the throne of grace not only receives mercy, the consciousness of acceptance and favour, but finds grace, in that Spirit whose operation the Father always delights to bestow' (*The Holiest of All,* London, 1934, pp. 172f.).

[8] This writer is especially fond of references to promise. Both the noun ἐπαγγελία and the verb ἐπαγγέλλομαι occur more frequently in this Epistle than in any other New Testament writing (the noun occurs 14 times and the verb 4).

3:2). This bodes no good for men in their sins, for 'now he hath promised, saying, Yet once more will I make to tremble not the earth only, but also the heaven' (Heb. 12:26). Yet even here it should be noted that our author puts his emphasis on one particular result of that shaking, namely that it brings to light the things 'which are not shaken' and which thus remain, so that we receive 'a kingdom that cannot be shaken' (Heb. 12:27f.). Sometimes he shows us the faithfulness of God in that He fulfilled His promises to Abraham (Heb. 6:15; 7:6; 11:9, 17), or to others (Heb. 11:33). But he remembers that those who have received such promises have not received God's greatest gift. For God has provided that they should not have this without us (Heb. 11:39f.; cf. v. 13). The recipients of salvation may be referred to as those who 'inherit the promises' (Heb. 6:12) or as 'the heirs of the promise' (Heb. 6: 17). The new covenant, which is such a feature of the argument of Hebrews, is characterized as one 'enacted upon better promises' (Heb. 8:6). The far-reaching nature of the salvation God gives comes out in the reference to 'the promise of the eternal inheritance' (Heb. 9:15). Entering salvation may be described in terms of promise: 'For ye have need of patience, that, having done the will of God, ye may receive the promise' (Heb. 10:36). So, contrariwise, may failure to enter salvation: 'Let us fear therefore, lest haply, a promise being left of entering into his rest, any one of you should seem to have come short of it' (Heb. 4:1). From all this it is plain that the whole idea of the promise of God is important to this writer.[9] It is a thought to which he returns again and again. Now if salvation is 'promised', then it is something that God had purposed from of old. Otherwise it would not be possible for Him to have promised it. 'Promise' also carries the thought that salvation rests basically on God's faithfulness. Were He not a faithful God, a God who can be implicitly relied upon, His promise would be meaningless. But, God being God, that He has promised means that He will perform. And that He will perform means that salvation is something wrought out by Him in accordance with His promise, and not something achieved by us. Salvation comes to us as a free gift of God, not as a reward for human merit. Here we have a common New Testament thought, but the writer to the Hebrews has his own way of expressing it.

Sometimes the implications of all this are missed. Thus Vincent Taylor can complain of 'the small extent to which the love of

---

[9] Cf. O. S. Rankin, 'The Epistle to the Hebrews more persistently than any other NT writing lays emphasis on God's promises as a means of exhortation to loyalty and belief. Though the writer may speak both of "the promises" (cf. 11:13) and of "the promise" (11:39), he is ultimately only thinking of one promise — namely that of the soul's salvation in the Kingdom of God' (TWBB, p. 178).

God is prominent' in this Epistle. He affirms that the author's God 'is a Being to whom men must draw near with reverence and with awe, but hardly One of whom the prodigal is likely to say: "I will arise and go to my Father." '[10] The trouble with this position is that it can be maintained only if we concentrate our attention on the occurrences of the actual word 'love'. It ignores the facts noted in this present section. The idea of God's love is undoubtedly prominent in the Epistle, though it is expressed in action, and in words like 'grace' and 'promise' and 'inheritance' rather than with the word 'love' itself.[11] We must distinguish between the terminology and the ideas expressed.

We must also keep in mind the purpose of the Epistle. It was written to people who were evidently so sure of the love of God that they did not greatly bestir themselves. They had failed to work out the implications of their salvation, and were in danger of apostasy. They rested on their privileged position as the people of God. People like this need to be shocked into realization of their position and the dangers in which they are placing themselves. A continuing emphasis on the love of God will not do this. As our generation above all should be aware, an emphasis on love to people unmindful of their danger at the judgment of God does nothing but increase their complacency. But we should not therefore conclude that the love of God is an unimportant idea to those prophetic souls who try to arouse them to the realities of their position. And among such we should class our writer. What he says implies the very reverse of any disregard for the tender mercies of God. But the concrete situation with which he was dealing made it hard for him to give it prominence.

THE DEATH OF CHRIST

The means whereby God brings men salvation is the death of Christ. The Lord came to earth specifically in order that He might die for men, for 'we behold him who hath been made a little lower than the angels, even Jesus, because of the suffering of death crowned with

---

[10] ANT, p. 127. He can say, 'For theological purposes the most important question in connexion with the Epistle is why it fails' (op. cit., p. 125). A long succession of humble believers can testify that the Epistle has not failed at all. And in days like our own its message of the utter finality of the work that God's love has wrought in Christ needs stress. It is not that the Epistle has failed. It is that our age has so often failed to get to grips with its fundamental message.

[11] William J. Wolf takes up a position much like that of Taylor. 'Curiously enough there is almost no mention made of the love of God as the motive behind the atoning act' (No Cross, No Crown, New York, 1957, p. 88). This is true only if we fasten our attention on the word 'love' and ignore other ways in which the idea may be expressed.

glory and honour, that by the grace of God he should taste death for every man' (Heb. 2:9). The whole purpose of the incarnation is seen as death. He came to die. He came to die 'for every man'.

The necessity for His death is brought out with an unusual illustration in Hebrews 9, that of a man's last will and testament. When a man makes a will, it is necessary for his death to occur before the terms of the will become operative.[12] As long as he lives, nothing happens. Now the Greek word διαθήκη, which the writer employs for 'will', is used in the Greek Old Testament to translate the Hebrew word ברית, meaning 'covenant'. It is unmistakably the usual Greek word for a 'will'. But there is an air of finality about a will. You cannot dicker with a testator. You accept what he leaves you on the conditions he lays down, or you reject it. You have no other line of action. The one-sidedness of this process seems to have appealed to those who translated the Old Testament into Greek as a better way of characterizing the covenants God makes with men than συνθήκη, the usual word for 'agreement'.[13] This word might be taken as suggesting a relative equality, an ability on man's side to make conditions. This is totally false. Man accepts the covenant on God's terms or he rejects it. He has no other option. Thus the word in Greek at large means a will, and in the Old Testament it means a covenant.[14] In Hebrews 9:16f. it seems that the writer is playing on the double meaning of the word. Jesus establishes the new διαθήκη, or 'covenant', and His death is necessary to establish it, just as necessary as is the death of any testator to establish his διαθήκη, his 'will'. No διαθήκη is of force without a death.[15] The line of

---

[12] There were some wills in antiquity, those involving adoption, where some at any rate of the provisions of the will became operative before the testator's death. But it is not this kind of will that is in mind. in Hebrews.

[13] F. O. Norton, in his study of the word, notes that it is used of wills, and also of 'A disposition of relations between two parties, where one party lays down the conditions which the other accepts' (A Lexicographical and Historical Study of ΔΙΑΘΗΚΗ, Chicago, 1908, p. 31). The one-sidedness is the important thing. Norton goes on to differentiate this from συνθήκη where 'the convention is entirely mutual, both parties being on an equality and having an equal part in arranging the terms' (loc. cit.).

[14] Cf. W. D. Ferguson, 'The usage of the term διαθήκη in the inscriptions is similar to its usage in the Old and the New Testaments in that the initiative is always taken by one person. In the scriptures it is God who takes the initiative, and in the inscriptions it is the testator. . . . The one making the διαθήκη always assumes the right to command, and to withhold his bequest if the conditions attached to it are not fulfilled' (The Legal Terms Common to the Macedonian Inscriptions and the New Testament, Chicago, 1913, p. 46).

[15] This is true, of course, of a covenant just as it is of a will, for a covenant was established by sacrifice and this meant the death of the animal victim.

reasoning is perhaps one that we would not have employed. But we are dealing with a first-century writing, not one from the twentieth century. And the point the writer is making is that the death of Christ is an absolute necessity. A 'will' is completely inoperative until the testator dies. And Christ's new 'covenant' is likewise inoperative until the death of Christ. Without that the whole Christian system would be impossible.

Another argument that our author uses depends on a philosophical distinction derived ultimately from Plato, but apparently widely and loosely used by educated people in general.[16] This distinction was between the perfect 'idea' of any thing, which is in heaven, and the imperfect 'shadow' or 'copy', which is the best we ever see on earth. Our author makes this kind of distinction between the earthly tabernacle and the true tabernacle in heaven (Heb. 8:2, 5), between the 'shadow' (which the law had) and the 'very image' (which the law did not have) (Heb. 10:1). Probably we should understand the 'country' and the 'better country, that is, a heavenly' (Heb. 11:15f.), as another example of the same kind of distinction, and so with the blood of animals and the blood of Christ (Heb. 9:13f.), and with 'the city which is to come' and the cities we have here on earth (Heb. 13:14).[17] This does not mean that our author is to be understood as a profound philosopher, or that he endorsed the essentials of Platonism. Nothing of the kind seems probable. But he found this distinction being widely made, and it is a useful distinction for his purpose. So he adopts it, but he takes it no farther than is required for that purpose.

So, in the world of sacrifices, he thinks that the animals offered on Jewish altars were the imperfect thing, the shadow or copy, whereas Christ's sacrifice was the true, heavenly sacrifice. The Jewish sacrifices point us to the sacrifice of Christ, but it is this sacrifice alone which is efficacious. And our writer can draw this into an argument for the necessity of Christ's death. 'It was necessary therefore', he says, 'that the copies of the things in the heavens should be cleansed with these' (i. e., with the Levitical sacrifices; the ritual purifications of the old ceremonial law may be effected by the animal sacrifices), but 'the heavenly things themselves' of necessity

[16] 'In the history of philosophy it is to be traced back to Plato, but we cannot mistake the fact that we have here Platonism as expounded by Philo and other Jewish-Alexandrian philosophers' (T. H. Robinson, *Hebrews*, MNTC, pp. 107f.).

[17] S. Cave speaks of all this as using 'the apologetic "better"', and proceeds, 'But his apologetic "better" implies the dogmatic "best." Christianity is the final religion of absolute validity, for it perfectly provides the way of access to God' (*The Doctrine of the Work of Christ*, London, 1937, p. 52).

require 'better sacrifices than these' (Heb. 9:23).[18] For a real cleansing from sin, such that it fits a man for entry into heaven, the perfect sacrifice of Christ was needed. Nothing less would do.

In common with the other New Testament writers, the author of this Epistle thinks of God as in continual conflict with the devil. Jesus came to earth expressly in order that He might enter into this conflict and destroy the devil (Heb. 2:14). His whole life might be understood as a struggle against Satan (cf. the witness of the Gospels to the temptations at the beginning of the ministry, and to the casting out of the demons, Satan's henchmen, throughout it). But preeminently is the struggle seen in His death, which is the focal point of it all. Our writer says explicitly that this is the reason for the incarnation: 'Since then the children are sharers in flesh and blood, he also himself in like manner partook of the same; that through death he might bring to nought him that had the power of death, that is, the devil' (Heb. 2:14).[19]

It may be that there is a reference to the condescension involved in all this when we read of Christ as enduring 'such gainsaying of sinners' (Heb. 12:3). The manuscript evidence is divided, and it may be that the gainsaying is 'against themselves' (as RV), but there is good evidence for reading 'against himself'.[20] It is a surprising thing that One so majestic as He should place Himself in a position where He would be subject to the 'gainsaying' of sinful men. But it was part of the way in which salvation would be procured, so He endured even this.

[18] A. S. Peake understands the verse to mean that sin had defiled even heaven, 'the constant sin of Israel had communicated a certain uncleanness to the sanctuary. Similarly the sin of mankind might be supposed to have cast its shadow even into heaven. It hung like a thick curtain between God and man, preventing free fellowship, and that not only because it defiled the conscience, so that man was ill at ease with God, but because it introduced a disturbing element into the life of God Himself' (Century Bible, in loc.). Sin is a very serious matter, but this seems to be going beyond the meaning of the text. E. C. Wickham reminds us that 'Heaven without the sense of atonement would not be heaven — would be no place of untroubled memory' (in loc.). The effect of the atonement reaches into heaven.

[19] F. Delitzsch reminds us that this means substitution: 'However certain it may be that Christ died for our salvation, no less certain is it that He died in our stead. For we were subject to death, and to the fear of death. He, however, has submitted Himself to death, and to the horrors of death, in order to deliver us from both. Consequently He has suffered death in our stead, as being the satanically procured punishment of sin, and as having the guilt of sin for its sting (ch. ii.9, 14f.; v.7)' (Commentary on Hebrews, ii, p. 421).

[20] εαυτον is supported by A P 326 vg^{s,cl} and αυτον (which means the same) by D^c K L pl sy^h ^{vid} sah s. The plural εαυτους is found in ℵ* D* pc vg^w sy^p boh, and αυτους by P13, 46 ℵ^c 33. With such a division of authorities certainty is difficult. But at least there is good reason for seeing in the verse a reference to what people did against Christ.

There are two somewhat curious references to the sufferings of
Christ. One of them speaks of His being 'made perfect' through
suffering: 'For it became him, for whom are all things, and through
whom are all things, in bringing many sons unto glory, to make the
author of their salvation perfect through sufferings' (Heb. 2:10).
The other tells us in addition that it was through His suffering that
He learned obedience, 'though he was a Son, yet learned obedience
by the things which he suffered; and having been made perfect . . .'
(Heb. 5:8f.). In neither of these are we to think of any imperfection
in Jesus prior to the suffering. Such an implication is unnecessary
and unthinkable. Rather the meaning is that sufferings introduce
a new perfection, a perfection of testedness. There is one perfection
of the bud and another perfection of the flower. But the perfection
of the bud is one thing and the perfection of the flower is quite
another. In the same way there is a perfection involved in actually
having suffered,[21] and which is not implied in any previous perfection.
It casts no doubt on the previous perfection, but it adds something
to it. We may reflect in passing that for Christians, as for their
Master, there is a perfection in suffering. Little as we may like them,
the fires of affliction are the place in which qualities of Christian character are forged. No one wants to suffer. No one looks forward to
suffering. But the Christian cannot regard suffering as an unmitigated
evil. He can agree that it is an evil, but he knows also that, borne
in the right spirit, it is the means of an increasing Christlikeness.

THE EXALTATION OF CHRIST

For the Epistle to the Hebrews, as for every other part of the New
Testament, the cross is absolutely central. No one who is true
to the teaching of the New Testament would wish for one moment
to minimize this. But our Epistle teaches us that we must not stop
there. If our author speaks feelingly of the sufferings and death of
Christ he also speaks warmly of the exaltation of the Lord. He does
not speak of the resurrection very often, but he thinks of it as supremely important, for he lists it among 'the first principles of Christ'
(Heb. 6:1f.). His expression is plural, 'resurrection of dead men',
but it would be hyper-critical to maintain that this excludes the
resurrection of Christ, or that he thinks of our resurrection as based
on anything other than our Lord's own rising from the dead. And
at the very end of the Epistle he brings the resurrection into a very

[21] A. B. Macaulay links this with the thought of substitution: 'the
term "Substitute" emphasizes the fact that there is something from which
Jesus in His death saves the sinner — something with which we ourselves
could not deal, with which He alone could deal, with which He could
only deal, in "a perfected personal experience" in death at the hands of
sinners' (*The Death of Jesus,* London, 1938, p. 158).

beautiful benediction, 'Now the God of peace, who brought again from the dead the great shepherd of the sheep with the blood of the eternal covenant, even our Lord Jesus . . .' (Heb. 13:20).[22] The resurrection is not a major emphasis in the Epistle. But it is there and we should not overlook it. Good Friday is meaningless apart from Easter.

Our author has more to say about Christ's subsequent place in heaven. In his majestic opening sentence he speaks of Jesus, who 'when he had made purification of sins, sat down on the right hand of the Majesty on high' (Heb. 1:3), thus taking a position not given to any angel (Heb. 1:13). The regal state of our Lord is brought out with a reference to the throne; He 'sat down on the right hand of the throne of the Majesty in the heavens' (Heb. 8:1), He 'endured the cross, despising shame, and hath sat down at the right hand of the throne of God' (Heb. 12:2). This sitting at God's right hand is related to His atoning work, for 'he, when he had offered one sacrifice for sins for ever, sat down on the right hand of God' (Heb. 10:12). And it may be in mind when it is not specifically mentioned, for the writer frequently applies Psalm 110 to Christ (Heb. 5:6; 6:20, etc.), a Psalm which begins with 'The Lord saith unto my Lord, Sit thou at my right hand' (Ps. 110:1). There are two points to be considered here, the symbolism of being at the right hand, and that of sitting.[23] The former points us to honor, especially when linked with the 'throne'. In the Old Testament being at the right hand signifies honor (Ps. 110:1), bliss (Ps. 16:11), and the like. From God's right hand go law (Dt. 33:2) and strength (Ps. 18:35). The right hand is thus the place of highest honor. To say that Jesus is 'on the right hand of the Majesty on high' is to say that He is in the place of highest honor in all heaven. Our writer is affirming that Jesus is exalted high above all.

The posture of sitting is that of rest. It indicates that one's work is complete. As applied to Christ it indicates that His work of saving men is a completed whole.[24] This is emphasized when our

---

[22] T. Hewitt comments, 'The fact that Christ was raised by God in virtue of the eternal covenant is proof that His redeeming work had been accepted and that salvation for His people is assured. In other words, all that is said about Christ in this Epistle is genuine, for God has set His seal upon it' (in loc.).

[23] These points are dealt with at length by A. J. Tait, The Heavenly Session of our Lord, London. 1912.

[24] Cf. Johannes Schneider, commenting on Heb. 10:11-14, 'the words "stand" and "being seated" play an important role. The earthly priest stands before the altar. He offers, if the lot has fallen to him, the daily burnt offering. The standing posture of the priest is a legal requirement. The author of Hebrews sees in this a deep symbolism. The priest is always in motion. He does not come to rest and his work is never finished. Christ, however, has finished His work; He has entered into rest and occupied the

writer says that 'he, when he had offered one sacrifice for sins for ever, sat down on the right hand of God; from henceforth expecting till his enemies be made the footstool of his feet' (Heb. 10:12f.). The older theologians delighted to speak of 'the finished work of Christ', and there is no doubt that the Epistle to the Hebrews witnesses to this important truth. T. H. Robinson explains the combined ideas in this way:

> To "sit," in oriental phraseology, is to be unoccupied, to be quiescent, and the fact that Jesus should have *seated Himself for all time at the right hand of God*, not merely implies the supreme honour of His exalted position, but suggests that His task is finished and His work is over . . . . Jesus sits because His duties are accomplished once and for all and He has no need to remain at work.[25]

Sometimes this is denied, the stress being placed on the fact of Christ's perpetual priesthood (Heb. 5:6, etc.), and on the words 'he ever liveth to make intercession for them' (Heb. 7:25), this being a priestly act. This side of the teaching of Hebrews receives a good deal of stress in much recent writing. The impression we get from some writers is that this Epistle lays its chief stress on a continuing priestly activity of our Lord in heaven. This is not so. As we have seen, His place seated at God's right hand points to a completed work. This is reinforced by the frequent use of 'once for all' with respect to Christ's priestly work. He offered Himself once for all on the cross. The passages dealing with His heavenly activity are fewer, and they are to be explained in terms of the finality of the cross. Thus it ought to be noticed that 'perpetual priesthood' does not mean 'perpetual offering'. If a priest were a priest only while he was engaged in the act of offering, he would cease to be a priest the moment he stepped down from his altar. This is manifest nonsense. A priest is a priest, not because he is actually offering, but because he is duly qualified to offer, perhaps also because he has in fact made an offering. The aorist tense, denoting completed action, is used of Christ's offering (Heb. 8:3; 10:12; there is an air of utter finality about 'where remission of these is, there is no more offering for sin', Heb. 10:18). The offering made by Jesus is perpetual in its efficacy, but it is not being offered perpetually. Nor

---

place that belongs to Him by God's decree. His sacrificial ministry being finished, He is seated at God's right hand. He now shares in God's sovereign power and dignity. In this way, through a deepened understanding of the words "to stand" and "to be seated," the fundamental difference between the cultic ministry of the priest and Christ's redemptive work is made clear. The work of the priest remains unfinished, though it is constantly repeated. The work of Christ, on the other hand, is marked by the character of completion. His sacrifice is an all-sufficient sacrifice' (*op. cit.*, pp. 94f.).

[25] *Hebrews*, MNTC, p. 140.

should we interpret the perpetual intercession otherwise than along these lines. As Westcott says, 'He pleads, as older writers truly expressed the thought, by His Presence on the Father's Throne'.[26] The picture that Hebrews gives us is one of Christ as having wrought out man's salvation on the cross, and of His now being exalted to the highest place in heaven, where His very presence is a reminder of the work He has accomplished. Neither the exaltation nor its significance is unimportant.

PRIEST AND VICTIM

Throughout the New Testament the death of Christ is seen in sacrificial terms, but nowhere is the sacrificial understanding of the atonement carried through as thoroughly as it is in this Epistle. First, let us notice that the writer delights to refer to Christ as a 'high priest'. Thus he introduces a new and exceedingly valuable picture into the Christian understanding of Christ's work.[27] Now the particular function of a high priest is to offer sacrifice. That is the whole purpose of his existence as high priest. That is what differentiates the high priest from other men, 'For every high priest, being taken from among men, is appointed for men in things pertaining to God, that he may offer both gifts and sacrifices for sins' (Heb. 5:1); 'every high priest is appointed to offer both gifts and sacrifices' (Heb. 8:3). The sacrificial work of a high priest receives emphasis, and we will come back to this point in connection with Christ's high priestly work.

But first let us notice that the epithets 'priest' and 'high priest' are applied to Christ again and again. Particularly does our author speak of Him as a high priest 'after the order of Melchizedek' (Heb. 5:6, 10; 6:20; 7:11, 15, 17). This Melchizedek is a strange and unaccountable figure. He appears for a fleeting moment in Genesis 14:18-20. That narrative says nothing of his parentage or posterity. It tells us that he was a king, that he brought out bread and wine to Abraham when that patriarch was returning from the slaughter of the kings. It tells us that he was a priest 'of God Most High', that he blessed Abraham, that Abraham gave him tithes of the spoil. And

---

[26] Commentary on Hebrews, p. 230. Cf. also A. J. Tait, 'We may not introduce into our conception of that priestly ministration any idea which is out of harmony with the thought of the divine glory and sovereignty into which Christ, as the Incarnate Son, entered at His Ascension, and the permanent enjoyment of which is signified by His Session' (op. cit., p. ix).

[27] Cf. the discussion by O. Cullmann in Chapter 4 of The Christology of the New Testament, London, 1959. He thinks that the High Priest concept in this Epistle 'offers a full Christology in every respect. It includes all the three fundamental aspects of Jesus' work: his once-for-all earthly work (ἐφάπαξ), his present work as the exalted Lord (εἰς τὸ διηνεγκές), and his future work as the one coming again (ἐκ δευτέρου)' (op. cit., pp. 103f.).

it tells us no more. The two points last mentioned matter a good deal to our author. Both point to Melchizedek as taking a superior place, and to Abraham as recognizing that place. 'Without any dispute the less is blessed of the better' (Heb. 7:7). The point of all this is that by New Testament times Abraham was accorded by the Jews a place all his own. He was superior to any other, the founder of the nation, the forefather of the people of God. Scripture has a good deal to say about him, but this was not enough for his enthusiastic admirers, and all manner of legends gathered about his name to supplement the very important information that Scripture conveys about him. To suggest that Melchizedek was superior to Abraham was accordingly to assign him an unbelievably preeminent place. His priesthood was of no mean order. Specifically, it was a greater priesthood than that of the Levitical priests who ministered in the temple. Our author has an ingenious argument in which he points out that 'so to say, through Abraham even Levi, who receiveth tithes, hath paid tithes; for he was yet in the loins of his father, when Melchizedek met him' (Heb. 7:9f.). If Christ was a priest after the order of Melchizedek, then He was far superior in order of priesthood to the priests in the temple.[28]

In all this our author is following a hint given in Ps. 110:4, 'The Lord hath sworn, and will not repent, Thou art a priest for ever after the order of Melchizedek.' The Psalmist likens the messianic priesthood to that of Melchizedek, but he gets no further. He does not develop the thought. He does not even repeat it. Nor does anyone else go even as far as he does, either in the rest of the Old Testament, or in the Jewish non-canonical literature, or even in the New Testament. But our author is more than a little interested in a priest with no ancestors and no descendants,[29] a priest greater than

---

[28] Alexander Nairne says, 'The author has in his mind a priesthood which is universal, has been in the world from the beginning, and possesses an unbroken life of growth running up at last into the perfect achievement of our Lord Jesus Christ' (*The Epistle of Priesthood*, Edinburgh, 1913, p. 148). Later he says, 'If a translation of "priesthood after the order of Melchizedek" into modern language might be risked, it might be rendered "natural priesthood" ' (*op. cit.*, p. 152), and he goes on to speak of the theory of evolution. This is not true to the thought of the writer. He is not talking about something 'natural', but something supernatural. The priesthood he thinks of is due to the call of God (Heb. 5:4-6) and confirmed by the Divine oath (Heb. 7:20f.). It is established to work out the purpose of God.

[29] S. Mowinckel says, 'When the Epistle to the Hebrews speaks of his having neither father nor mother, this is scarcely an invention of the author based on the fact that the Old Testament does not mention his family, but rather an ancient tradition which survived in Judaism and was really intended to express his close relation to the deity' (*He That Cometh*, Oxford, 1956, p. 75).

the famed forefather of the Jewish race and therefore greater than the Jewish priests who were descended from him, a priest who was at the same time a king, a figure of royalty, a priest king whose personal name means 'King of righteousness' and whose title means 'King of peace' (Heb. 7:2). In all this he sees a picture of the priesthood of Christ, and thus he returns to the analogy again and again.

He draws a particularly important conclusion from the absence of all mention of family. He tells us that Melchizedek was 'without father, without mother, without genealogy, having neither beginning of days nor end of life, but made like unto the Son of God' (Heb. 7:3). Notice that he does not say that Christ is like Melchizedek. He says that Melchizedek was 'made like unto the Son of God'. It is the priesthood of Christ that is the standard.[30] Melchizedek is simply an illustration. He helps us to see some things more clearly. This is not because of some superior merit in Melchizedek personally or in his office. It is because God has made him like to the Son of God, and our author would probably have said that this is in order that we may understand a little more plainly something concerning the priesthood exercised by our Lord. And that which Melchizedek helps us to see above all is that Christ's priesthood transcends all limitations of time. Melchizedek 'abideth a priest continually' (Heb. 7:3). So Christ is 'a priest for ever' (Heb. 7:21); 'after the likeness of Melchizedek there ariseth another priest, who hath been made, not after the law of a carnal commandment, but after the power of an endless life' (Heb. 7:15f.). The word here translated 'endless' means rather 'which cannot end' than 'which does not end'.[31] And His priesthood is 'after the power' of a life like that. In other words the quality of Christ's life as indissoluble determines the character of His priesthood. His priesthood must therefore be the final priesthood. It is different from that of Aaron. Aaron's priesthood had its day and passed away. Christ's priesthood will never pass away. It depends on a life which cannot be dissolved. It will never be superseded. Christ being who He is, it cannot be.

Now the essential place of a priest is that of a mediator. He stands in the middle. He stands between God and man. Ideally he should share in the nature of both, though in the case of priests here on earth this requirement can receive no more than a symbolic fulfilment. But what an ordinary priest can do only in symbol Christ does per-

---

30 Cf. G. Milligan, 'Melchizedek is thus not first in possessing certain characteristics which the High-priest of the New Testament afterwards possessed. Christ is first. Melchizedek is compared with Him: not He with Melchizedek. It is Christ who is clothed with the eternal qualifications exhibited in a shadowy manner in the king-priest of the days of Abraham' (*The Theology of the Epistle to the Hebrews*, Edinburgh, 1899, p. 113).

31 The word is ἀκατάλυτος, defined by GT as 'indissoluble; not subject to destruction'; so AG, 'indestructible'.

fectly. On the one hand our author sees Him as divine. The references to the priesthood after the order of Melchizedek point to this, and so especially does the string of passages cited from the Old Testament in chapter 1. These are expressly meant to show that He is higher than the angels, and who is higher than the angels but God? Indeed one of the passages expressly ascribes deity to Him, 'Thy throne, O God, is for ever and ever' (Heb. 1:8). He is described as 'holy, guileless, undefiled, separated from sinners, and made higher than the heavens' (Heb. 7:26). He is 'without blemish' (Heb. 9:14).[32] He can be expressly differentiated from men: 'For the law appointeth men high priests, having infirmity; but the word of the oath, which was after the law, appointeth a Son, perfected for evermore' (Heb. 7:28). But we scarcely need quotation of specific passages. Throughout the Epistle, Christ comes before us as One who shares in the nature of deity, who cannot be understood apart from His connection with the Father.

But on the other hand our author insists just as strongly on our Lord's genuine humanity, His kinship with men:

> For both he that sanctifieth and they that are sanctified are all of one: for which cause he is not ashamed to call them brethren, saying, I will declare thy name unto my brethren, in the midst of the congregation will I sing thy praise (Heb. 2:11f.).

'Since then the children are sharers in flesh and blood, he also himself in like manner partook of the same' (Heb. 2:14). 'For verily not of angels doth he take hold, but he taketh hold of the seed of Abraham' (Heb. 2:16). There were speculations among the thinkers of the first century of a 'man from heaven' or of angelic beings who might come to earth. Our author will have none of this. He says specifically that Jesus was 'made a little lower than the angels' (Heb. 2:9). He sees Jesus as genuinely human. His use of the human name 'Jesus' is noteworthy. He has a way of using it to put emphasis on the fact that its Bearer was true man.[33]

---

[32] Karl Heim emphasizes this point: 'the whole success of the act of atonement is entirely and solely dependent on Christ entering pure into the great battle which we all have to fight.' He cites Heb. 9:14 and proceeds, 'Everything really does depend on this point. He who is perfectly clean and has never fallen away from communion with God, He is the only really strong One in the battle that is fought here . . . the first thing that is all-important to our salvation is, that this strong One is there, who has not, like all the rest of us, found the way home to God through conversion, through repentance, through a break with a solid past — otherwise the accuser would *a priori* be victorious over Him as he is over us' (*Jesus the World's Perfecter*, Edinburgh and London, 1959, p. 76).

[33] B. F. Westcott notes that of the names by which Jesus is known in Hebrews, 'that which is distinctive of the Epistle is the human name, *Jesus*. This occurs nine times, and in every case it furnishes the key to the

Both His essential humanity and the additional point of His complete sympathy with us in our difficulties are brought out in the references to Christ's being tempted (Heb. 2:18; 4:15). Our writer uses very bold language, indeed, when he speaks of Christ as 'in the days of his flesh, having offered up prayers and supplications with strong crying and tears unto him that was able to save him from death, and having been heard for his godly fear' and proceeds to say that He 'learned obedience by the things which he suffered' (Heb. 5:7f.). The passage is not an easy one, and there are divergent explanations of some of its details. But of the main point there is no doubt whatever. The writer is talking of a genuinely human Jesus. The 'strong crying and tears' refer to a man, not some superior angelic being.

His manhood then was part of His qualification as high priest. Taken with His Godhead, it means that He is perfectly qualified for the role of mediator. Note that the manhood has its meaning for His sacrifice. It was not fortuitous. It was integral to the work He came to do.[34] 'Wherefore it behoved him in all things to be made like unto his brethren, that he might be a merciful and faithful high priest in things pertaining to God, to make propitiation for the sins of the people' (Heb. 2:17). His manhood was an essential qualification for the offering of the propitiatory offering.[35] A high priest, any high priest, is 'taken from among men' that he may minister 'for men in things pertaining to God' (Heb. 5:1). This applies to Christ as to others. Christ was not a high priest *although* He was

---

argument of the passage where it is found' (*op. cit.*, p. 33). On Heb. 2:9, he says, 'The suffering of death — the endurance of uttermost penalty of sin — was the ground of the Lord's exaltation in His humanity' (*in loc.*).

[34] We are reminded of Anselm's famous argument that for man's salvation there must be that satisfaction 'which God only can, and man only should, make' so that 'it is needful that it should be made by one who is both God and man' (*Cur Deus Homo?* II, 6; The Ancient and Modern Library of Theological Literature edn., p. 67).

[35] G. Aulén overlooks the significance of Christ's manhood in the work of atonement. He admits that there are two aspects, but all his emphasis is on the one. He says of Hebrews, 'it regards the Sacrifice of Christ both as God's own act of sacrifice and as a sacrifice offered to God. This double-sidedness is always alien to the Latin type, which develops the latter aspect, and eliminates the former' (*Christus Victor*, London, 1937, p. 93). But his own work is open to exactly the criticism he alleges against the Latin type, except that he stresses the act of Christ as God, and the Latins that of Christ as man. One looks in vain for any real treatment of the significance of Christ's manhood. He says the 'classic view' 'represents the work of Atonement or reconciliation as from first to last a work of God Himself, a *continuous* Divine work' (*op. cit.*, p. 21). Such statements abound. And they cannot be fitted into the Epistle to the Hebrews.

man. In part at any rate, He was a high priest *because* He was man.[36] The thought of Christ's manhood is congenial to our day, and many writers stress the community with us that it implies. 'We have not a high priest that cannot be touched with the feeling of our infirmities' (Heb. 4:15). God loved us so much that in the person of His Son He became one with us. But the result of this is that the doctrine of the incarnation becomes, for many, the central doctrine and Christmas the most important festival of the year. But it is impossible to stop here. We must go on and ask Anselm's question, 'Why did God become man?' Why did He not (dare we say, Why could He not?) bring about our salvation as God? The answer appears to be that the work is essentially a substitutionary work. Humanity was essential to Christ's function as high priest. Now if He was high priest because He was *man* this means surely that, as man, He could stand where sinners stand, stand in the place of man, do that which man should do.[37] If He were only God or if He were only man this would not follow. But if God became man, and if the manhood is of the very essence of His priestly work, then it appears to follow that He took man's place.[38] Man stood under the condemnation of God. Christ stepped into our situation and wrought atonement there, where we were, and not in some imaginary situation where we were not.

Now the work of a priest is to offer sacrifice. It is that which

[36] Cf. F. W. Camfield, 'A deed issuing in a direct and unbroken line from the pure God-head would not be atonement. Such a deed would inevitably be "over man's head". In order to be real atonement it must issue forth from man's life. Certainly the atoning deed was not wrought *by* man, it was wrought *for* man, but out of man's life' (SJT, i, p. 292).

[37] Cf. P. T. Forsyth, 'What God sought was nothing so pagan as a mere victim outside our conscience and over our heads. It was a Confessor, a Priest, one taken from among men . . . . His creative, regenerative action on us is a part of that same moral solidarity which also makes His acceptance of judgment stand to our good, and His confession of God's holiness to be the ground of ours' (WOC, pp. 190f.); 'Christ could make no due confession of holiness for us in judgment if He were outside Humanity, if He were a third party satisfying God over our head. The acknowledgement would not be really from the side of the culprit . . .' (*op. cit.*, p. 191).

[38] F. W. Camfield stresses that substitution is the logical implication of incarnation: 'the background of the atoning deed is not the Godhead *per se*, but the God-manhood of Christ. And this is what the Church has ever maintained . . . . But if that be so, then the idea of substitution is inevitable, and is constitutive of the doctrine of the Atonement. All that constituted atonement was wrought in our place and in our stead; wrought verily in *our* place, that is, wrought *for* us and *as our act*. What we could not accomplish Christ accomplished on our behalf. The infliction and judgment which we could not bear, He bore for us. He took our place and on behalf of us all He made satisfaction for our sins . . . . The manhood was integral and essential and not merely instrumental. And that means in the acutest sense, substitution' (*loc. cit.*). So also T. F. Torrance, SJT, vii, p. 251.

separates a priest from other men. Our author does not shrink from saying that Christ *must,* in His capacity as priest, have something to offer: 'it is necessary that this high priest also have somewhat to offer' (Heb. 8:3). He did have something to offer, something unique. He offered Himself (Heb. 9:26). All other priests perforce offered up victims apart from themselves. Only He could be at one and the same time Priest and Victim. His sacrifice is unique, unique in kind and unique in quality.

The uniqueness of His sacrifice is brought out in various ways. Thus it is sometimes emphasized that it was a sacrifice offered once only, whereas the sacrifices under the Levitical system had to be repeated frequently. The repetition is mentioned quite often: 'the priests go in continually into the first tabernacle, accomplishing the services' (Heb. 9:6); 'the high priest entereth into the holy place year by year' (Heb. 9:25); 'the same sacrifices year by year, which they offer continually' (Heb. 10:1); 'every priest indeed standeth day by day ministering and offering oftentimes the same sacrifices' (Heb. 10:11). Our author draws this very fact of the repetition of the sacrifices into an argument for their ineffectiveness. He points out that these sacrifices can never 'make perfect them that draw nigh. Else would they not have ceased to be offered, because the worshippers, having been once cleansed, would have had no more conscience of sins?' (Heb. 10:1f.). The very fact that there is a continuing need for these sacrifices seems to him to show conclusively that they have no real effectiveness. A sacrifice that really takes away sin would not have to be repeated indefinitely.

And Jesus' sacrifice was not repeated.[39] Our writer stresses that it was offered but once. He uses a strong word which means 'once for all' (Heb. 9:26, 28), and an even stronger compound of the same word (Heb. 7:27; 9:12; 10:10).[40] And he points out that this one offering has permanent effects. 'For by one offering he hath

---

[39] Some maintain (curiously, as it seems to me) that this writer teaches that Christ is perpetually offering himself in heaven. The desperate straits to which upholders of such views are reduced may be gauged from the fact that Moffatt, in giving evidence in favour, can cite only Heb. 7:25 (which says nothing at all about offering or sacrifice, being concerned with intercession), and the Vulgate mistranslation of Heb. 10:12 (*op. cit.,* p. xxxviii). Cf. W. Leonard (a Roman Catholic writer), 'There is therefore no heavenly sacrifice of Christ, but the living priest holds all the power of his sacrifice in his living humanity' (*The Authorship of the Epistle to the Hebrews,* London, 1939, pp. 74f.); 'the idea that Christ officiates before the throne of God, by any sort of liturgical action or by any active pleading of his passion, is nowhere to be found in the Epistle to the Hebrews' (*op. cit.,* p. 73).

[40] The words are ἅπαξ, and ἐφάπαξ. The expression εἰς τὸ διηνεκές (10:12, 14) is also emphatic (cf. NEB, 'for all time').

perfected for ever them that are sanctified' (Heb. 10:14).[41]   He
tells us that Christ 'offered one sacrifice for sins for ever' (Heb.
10:12). He says that, in the light of Christ's offering, 'there is no
more offering for sin' (Heb. 10:18). We Christians, he affirms, 'have
an altar' (Heb. 13:10), which undoubtedly points us to the cross.[42]
It is singular. There is but one offering. Taking all this together,
words could hardly express more emphatically the utter finality of
Christ's work of sacrifice.[43]

Another aspect of the effectiveness of Christ's sacrifice is brought
out with a reference to place. Earthly priests offered their sacrifices
in earthly sanctuaries. They could do no other. There were 'ordinances of divine service, and its sanctuary, a sanctuary of this world'
(Heb. 9:1). But Christ's ministry was not accomplished in any
earthly sanctuary. He appears in heaven for us. His ministry has to
do with 'the good things to come' and is exercised in 'the greater and
more perfect tabernacle, not made with hands, that is to say, not
of this creation' (Heb. 9:11).[44] So 'Christ entered not into a holy

[41] This is overlooked by G. Milligan when, in caricaturing the view
of 'the older Protestant Theology', he says it means that 'the Christian life
is led in the strength of a once completed and exhausted offering' (op. cit.,
pp. 141f.). This is nonsense, and cannot be sustained by citing the
Reformation divines (it is perhaps significant that Milligan quotes nobody to substantiate his position). Milligan has not distinguished between an offering which is eternal in its efficacy and one which is ceaselessly
being offered.

[42] Some have curiously applied this to the 'altar' in the Christian church
building, and have drawn an argument for the doctrine of eucharistic sacrifice from it. However, the position seems well met by Westcott, who, after
making an exhaustive examination of the biblical and early patristic evidence, concludes: 'In this first stage of Christian literature there is not
only no example of the application of the word θυσιαστήριον to any concrete,
material, object, as the Holy Table, but there is no room for such an application' (op. cit., p. 458).

[43] O. Cullmann strongly emphasizes this point, and brings out its relevance
for worship. He rejects the Roman Catholic idea that in the mass there is
a 'making present' of Christ's act. 'It is just the sacrifice as such which
cannot be made present in the way it is supposed to happen in the Catholic
mass. The danger of falling back to the level of Old Testament priesthood
arises when the high priest must always present the sacrifice anew. Christian worship in the light of that "one time" which means "once for all
time" is possible only when even the slightest temptation to "reproduce" that
central event itself is avoided. Instead, the event must be allowed to remain
the divine act of the past time where God the Lord of time placed it — at
that exact historical moment in the third decade of our chronology. It is the
saving consequences of that atoning act, not the act itself, which become a
present event in our worship' (op. cit., p. 99).

[44] C. Spicq rejects the view of many of the early Fathers that διὰ τῆς . . .
σκηνῆς refers to Christ's flesh. He thinks rather that 'The first characteristic of
Christ's priestly work is the perfection of the sanctuary where it is accomplished, the heavenly sanctuary through which He passes right up to
God'. He further reminds us that the author of Hebrews 'has always in

place made with hands, like in pattern to the true; but into heaven itself, now to appear before the face of God for us' (Heb. 9:24). He 'ever liveth to make intercession for them' (Heb. 7:25). He is 'a minister of the sanctuary, and of the true tabernacle, which the Lord pitched, not man' (Heb. 8:2). All this lifts Christ's work for men out of the class of the sacrifices that men might see on the altars of this world. They might suggest some ideas which He fulfilled. They might give us some terminology we may usefully employ when we wish to talk about what He has done. But His sacrifice is of an altogether higher order than theirs. There is a note of authority and of finality about His sacrifice. Nothing can be added to a sacrifice offered by One who can appear for men in heaven itself in the very presence of God.

A similar point is brought out by contrasting the blood of Christ with that of animal victims. Bluntly our writer says, 'it is impossible that the blood of bulls and goats should take away sins' (Heb. 10:4). He ascribes to these sacrifices nothing more than a temporary and limited significance. In 'the time now present . . . are offered both gifts and sacrifices that cannot, as touching the conscience, make the worshipper perfect, being only (with meats and drinks and divers washings) carnal ordinances, imposed until a time of reformation' (Heb. 9:9f.). How could sacrifices of animals do other? A man and an animal stand on different planes. Animal victims could never remove sin other than in a conventional and symbolic manner. But the sacrifice accomplished by Christ is different. It was not 'through the blood of goats and calves, but through his own blood' that Christ 'entered in once for all into the holy place' (Heb. 9:12). His sacrifice was not that of some uncomprehending dumb beast, but the sacrifice of Himself. And when He shed His blood His entry 'into the holy place' was not ineffectual or limited in its results. He 'obtained eternal redemption' (Heb. 9:12). The animal sacrifices had never done this. Even the very sins for which they had been offered, the sins 'that were under the first covenant' were dealt with by Christ's sacrifice (Heb. 9:15). No other sacrifice had about it the inherent quality that would enable it to deal with the sins of men.[45]

---

prospect the ceremonial of Expiation and he contrasts Christ's entrance to heaven with that of the high priest into the Holy of Holies "through the veil", verse 3; vi. 19). The very rigorous parallelism in this passage does not allow us to identify the crossing of the Holy Place with the assumption of humanity by the Word' (*in loc.*).

[45] E. L. Kendall maintains that 'in the Person and the Work of Christ the Sin-bearer and the sacrificial Victim are one; that in the high-priestly Sacrifice of Christ are gathered the elements of propitiation, expiation and substitution through which he has made perfect Reparation for human sin' (*A Living Sacrifice*, London, 1960, p. 87).

Or again, our author may contrast the sacrifices with respect to the access to God that they won. Under the old system 'the way into the holy place hath not yet been made manifest' (Heb. 9:8). The high priest went into the holy place (which symbolized the very presence of God) once a year only (Heb. 9:7) on the Day of Atonement. He had no easy access, but was constrained to observe strict precautions. Even so he obtained a very limited access, an access confined to himself alone, and that for a few minutes. By contrast, Christ has opened the way into the holiest of all, and His people are urged, 'Having therefore, brethren, boldness to enter into the holy place by the blood of Jesus . . . let us draw near with a true heart in fulness of faith' (Heb. 10:19-22). Whereas the Jewish high priest, at best, could win access into the holy place for a few minutes while he sprinkled blood before the mercy seat, Jesus opened the way for believers to approach God with no other mediator.[46] They have access to the presence of God, and that not for a fleeting moment, but always. When we consider the elaborate hierarchy provided by the Jewish religion, and indeed, by nearly all the other religions of antiquity, the importance of this becomes clear. Christ's sacrifice has transformed the whole method of approach to God.[47]

Of special importance is the close link between Christ's sacrifice and obedience. His sacrifice represents an active doing of the will of God. In this it forms a contrast with the animal sacrifices which, as we have just seen, were at best passive. The victims understood nothing and could understand nothing of what was being done. They could not enter into the spirit of it and actively forward what was in hand. Not so Christ. Indeed, it is integral to the very nature of His sacrifice that it was something wrought in obedience. Our writer has a very notable passage in which he brings this out:

> Wherefore when he cometh into the world, he saith, Sacrifice and offering thou wouldest not, but a body didst thou prepare for me; in whole burnt offerings and sacrifices for sin thou hadst no pleasure: then said I, Lo I am come (in the roll of the book it is

[46] Cf. Norman L. Robinson, 'Here was a solemn act of worship performed only once a year on behalf of the whole People of God, which expressed in one moving ceremony the truth lying at the very heart of Israel's faith, namely, access through a representative into the presence of the Holy God. Here, says our author, is a shadow and symbol of what Jesus, our true High Priest, has done for us His People, the new and true Israel, through His sacrifice once offered on the Cross' (*How Jesus Christ Saves Men*, London, n.d., p. 61).

[47] Snell stresses the importance of access: 'The availability of this access to God in Christ is a main motive of the whole Epistle . . . . The old Levitical priesthood could not mediate this access to God, since it could not bring forgiveness of sins. As against this inability of the old priesthood, it is the climax of the writer's exposition of our Lord's priesthood that it fully and finally does effect this' (*op. cit.*, p. 97).

written of me) to do thy will, O God. Saying above, Sacrifices
and offerings and whole burnt offerings and sacrifices for sin
thou wouldest not, neither hadst pleasure therein (the which are
offered according to the law), then hath he said, Lo, I am come
to do thy will. He taketh away the first, that he may establish the
second. By which will we have been sanctified through the offering of the body of Jesus Christ once for all (Heb. 10:5-10).

This passage pictures Christ as coming to do the will of God by
replacing the animal sacrifices (in which God had no pleasure) by
the one effective sacrifice of Himself. It is 'through the offering of the
body of Jesus Christ once for all' that we are sanctified. This passage
is often misinterpreted as though it meant that Christ's sacrifice
consisted solely in His obedience,[48] in the complete surrender of His
will to that of the Father. Now while no one in his right senses would
wish to minimize the importance of the obedience that Christ rendered
the Father, yet this is not doing justice to the passage. These very
words make it plain that the obedience in question is not the general
obedience that pervades the whole of His life, but specifically 'the
offering of the body of Jesus Christ'. And if it be said that this
offering of Christ's body is simply the expression of an obedience
that pervaded His whole life,[49] then the answer is that this has to
be read into the passage. It is not what it says.

The fact is that men today prefer to think of the sacrifice of
Christ as consisting in the sacrifice of a yielded will.[50] This yields
more sense to twentieth-century men than the thought of the sacrifice
of the body of Christ. It is congenial to our outlook; it fits into our

[48] Cf. A. C. Headlam, 'The death of Christ was effective because it was
not a formal or mechanical act, but an ethical sacrifice, a voluntary offering
of himself, and therefore it would appeal to our consciences' (The Atonement,
London, 1935, p. 101). This completely ignores the fact that it was 'the
body of Jesus Christ' that was offered so freely.

[49] Cf. H. R. Mackintosh, 'It is misleading, as well as altogether unlike the
concrete thought of scripture, to take the artificially refined position that
Jesus' actual death was somehow a fortuitous concomitant of a sacrifice already complete within; which is as inept as to say that a poem is the thought
it embodies. A poem is thought or feeling taking shape in noble words,
apart from which there is no poem at all; so the sacrifice of Jesus is obedience
vested in that act, at once inward and outward, in which He gave the life needed
by the Father's reconciling will' (The Christian Experience of Forgiveness,
London, 1944, pp. 221f.).

[50] T. H. Hughes expresses this point of view, 'Whatever satisfaction [God]
derived must have sprung from a spiritual reality, rather than a physical fact.
In other words it must have come not from the sufferings and death of
Jesus, but from His willing surrender to the divine will and purpose, from His
obedience to the consciousness of vocation from God, and all this involves'
(The Atonement, London, 1949, p. 35). The point could be documented
from many modern writers.

thought world.[51]   But it is not what the writer to the Hebrews is saying.   His argument is not: 'The sacrifice of Christ did not consist in anything in the way of a material offering, but rather in the spiritual sacrifice of a will completely surrendered to the Father'.   What he is saying is rather: 'Burnt offerings and similar sacrifices are not the way to please God.   But when the Christ came into the world a body was prepared for Him.   Thereby He was enabled to do the will of God more perfectly than was possible with the old sacrifices. He took away the sacrifices of animals and established a new way. He established it through the offering of His body!'   As Vincent Taylor says, 'the writer's purpose is not to assert that obedience is better than sacrifice, but to claim that, in that it fulfilled the will of God, Christ's sacrifice of Himself surpassed and superseded the Levitical sacrifices.'[52]   The passage does indeed stress the importance of Christ's obedience.   But it is not the quality of obedience in contrast to the thought of sacrifice that is in mind (as it was in Samuel's words to Saul, 'to obey is better than sacrifice', 1 Sa. 15:22).   It is the quality of the act in which the obedience finds its expression.[53] The emphasis is on the fact that men are sanctified 'through the offering of the body of Jesus Christ once for all'.   It is impossible to remove from the passage its emphasis on the fact of the cross.[54]

[51] D. W. Simon draws attention to an inconsistency which is often present with those who reject vicarious atonement, but stress Christ's obedience. 'If God can be righteous on our behalf in the form of obedience, why not in the form of suffering? If it be untrue and perverse for Him to endure our penalty and *count* it as ours, nay, *make* it our endurance, why is it not untrue and perverse for Him to render obedience to Himself on our behalf, and make His obedience ours?' (*The Redemption of Man*, London, 1906, p. 289).

[52] ANT, p. 122. So also James Denney, 'Christ's obedience is not merely that which is required of all men, it is that which is required of a Redeemer; and it is its peculiar content, not the mere fact that it is obedience, which constitutes it an atonement' (DC, p. 233).

[53] P. T. Forsyth reminds us of an important point, 'Christ's death was atoning not simply because it was sacrifice even unto death, but because it was sacrifice unto holy and radical judgment. There is something much more than being obedient unto death. Plenty of men can be obedient unto death; but the core of Christianity is Christ's being obedient unto judgment, and unto the final judgment of holiness' (WOC, p. 135).

[54] E. Masure quotes S. Bernard, *non mors, sed voluntas placuit ipsius morientis*, and adds, 'In the context given to it by the uncompromising Cistercian, the doctor and mystic who founded Clairvaux and who made all the Middle Ages weep with a compassionate love, the phrase means simply that the Passion of His Son gave God no pleasure. The Father could rejoice only in the love with which His Son had delivered Himself to death.' He immediately goes on, 'But that does not mean that the blood shed by Christ was useless, nor that only the dispositions of His soul were profitable for salvation' (*The Christian Sacrifice*, London, 1944, p. 61). The comment of Masure might well be heeded by many who delight with Bernard to dwell on the obedience of the Lord.

Nor should we overlook the importance of the 'once for all'. Those who put their emphasis on the perpetual obedience of Christ seem often to disregard the implications of this. Thus Temple can say, 'the perfect sacrifice of Christ is not limited to His Death; it consists not in any momentary offering but in the perfection of His obedience, which was always complete.'[55] That Christ's obedience is not limited to His death is undoubted. His obedience is much wider than any one action. But that it is this general obedience that the writer to the Hebrews has in mind here is quite untenable. His emphasis is on the one action of Christ on the cross done once and for all. The cross was not simply the symbolic action. It was the critical, the decisive action.[56]

THE NEW COVENANT

It would be impossible to deal with the sacrifice of Christ as it is portrayed in this Epistle without noticing that it is the sacrifice which inaugurates the new covenant. When a covenant, a solemn agreement, was initiated in antiquity, it was always done with the offering of a sacrifice. Special rituals underline the solemnity and importance of the action. A good example is given in Exodus 24, where we have a description of the inauguration of the covenant between the Lord and the people of the Lord. By it they became the people of the Lord, they came to stand in a special relationship to God. The covenant is that on which all the rest stands. The whole system of worship, for example, was that for the people in covenant relationship to God. The laws were the laws for the maintenance of the covenant. It is not too much to say that the thought of the covenant dominated the thinking of the men of the Old Testament. For them it was of supreme importance that they stood in such a relation to the Lord as did no other people.

But for the writer to the Hebrews that covenant no longer stood. It has now been replaced by a new covenant because it was completely impotent. It provided sacrifices, but as we saw earlier, these could

[55] *Christus Veritas,* London, 1925, p. 238. He further says, 'It is Christ's union of humanity with God in perfect obedience which is the essential sacrifice, of which the Cross is the uttermost expression and essential symbol' (*loc. cit.*). This is not the teaching of the Bible. Temple is affirming in effect that men are saved by the incarnation. The writer to the Hebrews thinks of them as saved by the cross.

[56] To understand that the death of Christ is a sacrifice is not, of course, to overlook the truth that there are other important things to be said. Cf. K. E. Kirk, 'Sacrifice and conversion, therefore, are two separate acts in the restoration of man; each has its distinct part to play. Only a debased mind will infer, from the necessity of sacrifice, that it can take the place of conversion; only a shallow mind, that conversion is adequate without sacrificial reparation' (*Essays Catholic and Critical,* ed. E. G. Selwyn, London, 1929, p. 266).

never take away sin. The most they could do was to make 'a remembrance' of sins from year to year (Heb. 10:3). But they could
not deal with those sins. The coming of Christ and the work He
did had among other things the effect of highlighting all this. When
God speaks of the 'new' covenant, our writer reasons, He makes the
former covenant 'old'.[57]   And he adds, 'that which is becoming
old and waxeth aged is nigh unto vanishing away' (Heb. 8:13).

But Christ's work was to establish a new way of approach to God
(Heb. 10:20).   He may be spoken of as 'the mediator of a new
covenant' (Heb. 9:15; 12:24), or 'the mediator of a better covenant'
(Heb. 8:6).   These expressions appear to mean that He is the means
of establishing the new covenant. He brought it about. He is also
called 'the surety of a better covenant' (Heb. 7:22), where 'surety'
points to the idea of guarantee. The new covenant is guaranteed by
what Jesus is and does.

The superiority of the new covenant to the old[58] is seen in that it
'hath been enacted upon better promises' (Heb. 8:6). The old
covenant included promises to the people, but it also included a
binding obligation on the people to obey the law of God (Ex. 24:
3, 7). The characteristic thing about the new covenant is rather
its promise of forgiveness. Repeatedly the people under the old
covenant had failed to live up to what was demanded of them, and
the prophets are full of denunciations accordingly. But Jeremiah
looks for a time when things will be better, He envisages a new
covenant in which God will forgive men their sins and in which He
will write His law on their hearts, and when all of them will 'know'
Him (Jer. 31:31ff.). This clearly represents the negation of legalism,
and the giving of an inward strength such as the old covenant had
never been able to accomplish. The writer to the Hebrews sees
Jeremiah's prophecy fulfilled in the work of Jesus. He is particularly
interested in the forgiveness aspect. He has a long quotation from
Jeremiah about the new covenant (Heb. 8:8-12), and finishes it

---

[57] John Owen puts some emphasis on the active, πεπαλαίωκε, which 'denotes an authoritative act of God upon the old covenant'; 'He did it by
a *plain declaration of its infirmity*, weakness, and insufficiency for the great
ends of a perfect covenant between God and the church . . . when God himself comes positively to declare by that prophet that it was weak and insufficient, and therefore he would make another, a better, with them; this
made it old, or declared it to be in a tendency unto a dissolution' (*An
Exposition of the Epistle to the Hebrews*, vi, Edinburgh, 1862, pp. 174, 175).

[58] It is interesting to notice the large number of things about the new way
that this writer speaks of as 'better'. In addition to the covenant itself
he speaks of a better mediator (Heb. 1:4), better sacrifices (Heb. 9:23),
a more excellent ministry (Heb. 8:6), a better priesthood (Heb. 7:7), a
better possession (Heb. 10:34), better promises (Heb. 8:6), a better hope
(Heb. 7:19), a better resurrection (Heb. 11:35), a better thing that God
had provided (Heb. 11:40), a better country (Heb. 11:16).

only when he comes to the words about forgiveness. He gives an abbreviated citation of the same prophecy in a later place, and it is significant that, though he passes over most of the middle section of the prophecy, he makes sure of including the section about forgiveness (Heb. 10:16f.). Above all things, the new system that Jesus had established meant the forgiveness of men's sins. Men are not left to accomplish their own salvation. His blood avails to put them in right relationship to God. The new covenant is thus one that men may enter with assurance. Nor need they fear it will one day be superseded as the former covenant had been. One of the great themes of Hebrews is the finality of the revelation made in Christ. And specifically we read of the covenant that Jesus has established that it is 'the eternal covenant' (Heb. 13:20).[59]

GOD'S REMEDY FOR SIN

An interesting feature of the treatment of the atonement in this Epistle is the large number of ways in which sin is said to have been dealt with. The writer sees sin as reaping a grim reward. He says with respect to the condition of affairs under the old covenant, 'every transgression and disobedience received a just recompense of reward' (Heb. 2:2). But there are even grimmer possibilities for the sinner who neglects the salvation Christ offers than for the man who rejected Moses (Heb. 10:28f.). Our author cannot be accused of lacking a due appreciation of the demerit of sin. But for all that, his Epistle is one which is full of the thought that sin has been completely defeated in the work of Christ.

The Epistle begins with a section in which the writer extols the majesty of the Person of Christ. And immediately, in the very same sentence, he goes on to speak of Him having 'made purification of sins (καθαρισμὸν τῶν ἁμαρτιῶν ποιησάμενος)' (Heb. 1:3).[60] Here, in the manner of Philippians 2 and Colossians 1 we have an intermingling of the thoughts of the Person and the work of Christ. It was because He was such a Being as He was that He was able to accomplish so difficult a task as that of purifying men, of making them clean from their sins. And it was because men must be

---

[59] Johannes Schneider comments, 'Christ as the eternal High Priest is the guarantor of this Covenant. He has sealed the new institution of God through His blood. For the sake of this blood which contains inexhaustible atoning power and which therefore assures the eternal validity of the New Covenant, Christ has been raised from the dead . . . . Christ has been raised from the dead in order that the blood of the eternal Covenant remain an ever valid fact' (*op. cit.,* p. 134).

[60] On this idea James Denney says, 'He achieves, in short, "purgation of sins" (i.3). This is the evangelical truth which is covered by the word "substitute," and which is not covered by the word "representative"' (DC, p. 236).

purified from their sins that such a Being as He appeared on earth.

Sometimes the thought is of the effect sins might have with God. Thus we read that Christ became man 'to make propitiation for the sins of the people' (Heb. 2:17). The just wrath of God was exercised toward men on account of their sin. But Christ dealt with that situation. He made the propitiation that was necessary, and so sin is no longer operative.[61] Twice our author quotes from Jeremiah the prophecy that God will 'remember no more' man's sins (Heb. 8:12; 10:17). So effective is Christ's work in dealing with sin that it is not kept in remembrance. This is the equivalent of Paul's use of the expression 'justification'. The justified man is as though he had not sinned. He is the acquitted man, the man who has no sin that God remembers against him.

Once our writer says that Christ bore 'the sins of many' (Heb. 9:28; the verb is ἀναφέρω).[62] As a reference to Old Testament passages where the idea of bearing sin or bearing transgressions or the like occurs will show, the thought is that of bearing the punishment for sin.[63] The context makes it plain that a once-for-all bearing of sin is meant, so that the reference must be to Calvary, and

---

[61] Much is often made of the fact that there is an accusative of sin here, εἰς τὸ ἱλάσκεσθαι τὰς ἁμαρτίας τοῦ λαοῦ. Since one does not speak of propitiating a sin the suggestion is made that we should translate 'to expiate the sins of the people'. This, however, is too simple. It ignores the use of ἱλάσκομαι elsewhere in the Bible and in Greek generally. It is a word which has to do with the averting of the divine wrath, as I have tried to show in chs. iv and v of *The Apostolic Preaching of the Cross* (see pp. 174-177 for a discussion of the present verse). Moreover, it is not usually noticed that in the few examples of an accusative of sin after ἱλάσκομαι or ἐξιλάσκομαι, the meaning 'make propitiation with respect to' is usually required rather than 'expiate' (see, for example, Sir. 3:30; 5:6; 20:28; 28:5; 34:19; and cf. 16:7 for this author's understanding of ἐξιλάσκομαι). It is in line with the regular use of the verb to take it here in the sense 'to make propitiation with respect to the sins of the people'. To understand it as 'to expiate the sins of the people' is to import a strange, unproven meaning for the verb.

[62] Morna Hooker thinks this verse echoes Is. 53:12 (*Jesus and the Servant*, London, 1959, p. 123). On the thought of the verse, cf. J. K. Mozley, 'It is one thing to admit, indeed gladly to acknowledge, that Christianity is a religion of redemption . . . . It is another to confess that redemption from sin is through atonement for sin, and that He who bears our sins does so not merely by taking them away from us through the arousing in us of a new power, but by taking them upon Himself, so that we have no longer the oppression of guilt-consciousness and of a moral account with God still unsettled' (*The Heart of the Gospel*, London, 1927, p. 19).

[63] Geerhardus Vos sees a reference to Is. 53, 'Christ is offered up for the bearing (*enengkein*) of the sins of many. Here the ritual and the forensic formula meet together. It is here not merely vaguely stated that Christ *removes* the sin: it is plainly stated that *He takes it upon Himself* . . . . The verb *enengkein* is literally taken from the LXX of Isa. 53, which is a purely vicarious passage' (*The Teaching of the Epistle to the Hebrews*, Grand Rapids, 1956, p. 120).

not to a life-long endurance of the sins of men.[64] This is plain, also, from the contrast between the two advents of our Lord, for this depends on the fact that He came at the first to be a sin-bearer, whereas at His second advent He will be 'apart from sin'.[65] Again Christ is said to have offered 'one sacrifice for sins for ever' (Heb. 10:12; 'sacrifice' is θυσία, which occurs again with reference to Christ in 9:26 and by implication in 10:26; in v. 12 'for sins' is ὑπὲρ ἁμαρτιῶν, whereas in v. 26 we have περὶ ἁμαρτίας). A different noun is used of the 'offering for sin' (Heb. 10:18; προσφορὰ περὶ ἁμαρτίας). Again, we read of 'remission' (Heb. 10:18; ἄφεσις), and we are told that Christ has been 'manifested to put away sin' (Heb. 9:26; εἰς ἀθέτησιν τῆς ἁμαρτίας) where the expression means something like 'the disannulling of sin'.[66] It is used of the 'disannulling of a fore-going commandment' in the only other place where it appears in the New Testament (Heb. 7:18). And once he speaks of 'the redemp-tion of the transgressions' (Heb. 9:15), the imagery being that of the purchase of sinners from the slavery into which their sin had brought them. We ought also to heed what is implied in the application to Jesus of the words of Psalm 45:7, 'Thou hast loved righteousness, and hated iniquity' (Heb. 1:9).[67] This sets Christ in uncompromising opposition to all that is evil. But throughout the Epistle believers are pictured as in harmony and love and fellowship with Christ. The implication is inescapable that the Christ, who hates iniquity, has effectively dealt with it so that it no longer appears in His people.

We should notice also another group of expressions which tell us what the former way of dealing with sin could not do. In each case it implied that Christ has now done this. Thus we deduce that He was offered for sins (Heb. 5:3; the verb is προσφέρω). He has taken away sins (Heb. 10:4, 11, the verbs being ἀφαιρέω and περιαιρέω). He has fulfilled what is foreshadowed in 'whole burnt offerings and sacrifices for sin' (Heb. 10:6; ὁλοκαυτώματα καὶ περὶ ἁμαρτίας). He has brought about that cleansing of worshippers which means 'no more conscience of sins' (Heb. 10:2; μηδεμίαν ἔτι συνείδησιν ἁμαρτιῶν).

---

[64] See further pp. 322ff. below.

[65] If He were not bearing our sin in this way He would have been 'apart from sin' at both His advents.

[66] F. W. Farrar sees this as very important: 'Into this one word is con-centrated the infinite superiority of the work of Christ. The High Priest even on the Day of Atonement could offer no sacrifice which could even *put away* (ἀφαιρεῖν) sin (x.4), but Christ's sacrifice was able to *annul* (ἀθετεῖν) sin altogether' (*in loc.*).

[67] Cf. B. F. Westcott, 'The aorist of the LXX gives a distinct application to the present of the Hebr. The Son in His Work on earth fulfilled the ideal of righteousness; and the writer of the Epistle looks back upon that completed work now seen in its glorious issue' (*in loc.*).

We have included in these passages one in which the sin offering is mentioned and where the implication is that Christ has fulfilled all that this sacrifice meant. There is another passage in the Epistle where this sacrifice is not indeed mentioned by name, but where it is very plainly in mind, and where it is directly applied to what Jesus did for men (Heb. 13:11f.).[68] The burning of the bodies of the victims in the case of the sin offering is recalled in connection with the fact that Jesus 'that he might sanctify the people through his own blood, suffered without the gate.' Christ has made the perfect sin offering. C. Ryder Smith further points to the significant fact that our author compares Christ's sacrifice to the *bodies* of the sacrificial victims,

> which were flung outside just because they were so closely identified with the sin of the people that they were too unclean to be offered on the altar or even to be tolerated within the Tabernacle at all. They *were* sin. In other words, the writer thought of Jesus as identifying Himself with sinners in the utmost consequences of their sin.[69]

This is the thought that we see elsewhere in the New Testament in the cry of dereliction or in Christ's being made 'a curse' (Gal. 3:13) or 'sin' (2 Cor. 5:21). But characteristically, in this Epistle it is expressed in terms of Jewish ritual.

The effect of all this is to stress the completeness with which Christ has dealt with sin. Whatever needed to be done He has done, fully, finally. Sin no longer exists as a force. The writer is not concerned to deny that it exists as a fact. His point is that it is no longer the dominant power exercising sway over men. Christ has made it null and void. He has broken its power. And, while the force of the various expressions used varies somewhat, the cumulative effect is to leave us convinced that Christ has dealt with sin by bearing to the full all that it means. He has taken upon Himself

---

[68] F. C. Synge rejects all interpretations of this passage which see a eucharistic reference. He says, 'The point of the passage is this: that Jesus died as a sin-offering, the fulfilment of what was prefigured by the Day of Atonement sin-offering. Because he died as a sin-offering he died outside the camp' (*Hebrews and the Scriptures,* London, 1959, p. 42).

[69] BDS, p. 238. He goes on to show that all the thoughts of 2 Cor. 5 are present here, though with different terminology. It is failure to give attention to the significance of this different terminology which nullifies Vincent Taylor's contention that the writer to the Hebrews 'nowhere speaks of (Christ's) self-identification with sinners and consequent experience of the judgment which falls upon their sin' (ANT, p. 127). Taylor's valuable discussion is seriously marred by this failure to give due weight to the fact that the writer to the Hebrews has his own way of saying most things. When he is giving expression to a thought found elsewhere in the New Testament he does not necessarily repeat the language of the other writers. The ideas he expresses must be sought, and attention not confined to his terminology.

God's judgment.[70] He has stood in our place and we may go free. No matter how sin be understood, Christ is the answer.

SALVATION INTERPRETED

We have already noticed some of the ways in which this writer interprets Christ's work for men, such as the new covenant. The first or old covenant stands for the whole system represented by the Jewish religion. This was done away in Christ. A new way of approach to God was provided. The covenant conception formed a well-known and satisfying illustration of this theme. The atoning work of Christ means a complete revolution, a totally new religion.

Sometimes the atonement is regarded as the perfecting of Christ's people. 'For the law made nothing perfect', we read, and then, 'a bringing in thereupon of a better hope, through which we draw nigh unto God' (Heb. 7:19). Hope has more than one aspect. It is essentially forward-looking, reminding us that the supreme reality yet awaits us. There is a present aspect. The hope has already been 'brought in'. We lay hold of it (Heb. 6:18).[71] But the concept basically points us forward. So also there is the great gallery of heroes in Hebrews 11, with the conclusion, 'God having provided some better thing concerning us, that apart from us they should not be made perfect' (Heb. 11:40). The verb in each case is τελειόω, which we should probably understand not of perfection in our sense of the term, but rather of maturity.[72] The writer envisages that those who have been saved by Christ's work will go on and become mature Christians. A considerable part of his complaint against his readers is that they have not gone on to maturity for which they were meant. But the point of importance for our purpose is not their failure to arrive at it, but the goal at which they might have been expected to arrive. No one who had

---

[70] Cf. T. F. Torrance, 'It belongs to the essence of atonement that Christ bore man's judgment, the judgment of God upon man's sin. In the Cross, God identifies Himself with man just where he is farthest from Him, that is, just where he stands under the divine judgment' (*Intercommunion*, ed. D. Baillie and J. Marsh, London, 1952, p. 329); 'Both in bearing the divine judgment and in offering a perfect obedience, Jesus Christ stood absolutely alone, acting on our behalf. What we could not do, He has done for us. It was a substitutionary atonement' (*op. cit.*, pp. 329f.).

[71] Cf. Karl Barth, 'Christian hope is a present being in and with and by the promise of the future, a being which is seized by the promise of God and called. If a man does not seize this hope, apprehend it, conform himself to it here and now as a man who belongs to the future, he is not one who has Christian hope' (CDDR, p. 121).

[72] It signifies to bring to its τέλος, its end or aim. AS defines it thus: '1. to bring to an end, finish, accomplish, fulfil . . .2. to bring to maturity or completeness . . . .'

not felt Christ's saving power could attain it, but all those who believe in Him should.

The passages in which our author speaks of God's chastening activity belong in part, at any rate, to this discussion. God chastens us 'for our profit, that we may be partakers of his holiness' (Heb. 12:10). He goes on, 'All chastening seemeth for the present to be not joyous, but grievous: yet afterward it yieldeth peaceable fruit unto them that have been exercised thereby, even the fruit of righteousness' (v. 11). God does not simply give His people the status of being saved and leave it at that. Through all the troubles and trials of this mortal life He disciplines them. His loving hand sees to it that these difficulties are the means of forming their character and making them into the kind of people that they ought to be.

Chastening is a mark of sonship, for our author points out that every father chastens his sons. Indeed he goes as far as to say that 'if ye are without chastening, whereof all have been made partakers, then are ye bastards, and not sons' (Heb. 12:8; cf. 12:5f., 7). Sonship is an important category in this Epistle. A very great deal is said about the sonship of Christ (Heb. 1:2, 5, 8; 3: 6, etc.) for everything depends on Him. But it is significant that believers have no less status than that of sons. They belong in the heavenly family. 'God dealeth with you as with sons' (Heb. 12:7). We see this dignity in the way Scripture comes to us. It does not reveal itself as peremptory commands to slaves but 'the exhortation . . . reasoneth with you as with sons' (Heb. 12:5). And this sonship is not regarded as a natural status. It is a result of the work of Christ. 'It became' God, says our author, 'in bringing many sons unto glory, to make the author of their salvation perfect through sufferings' (Heb. 2:10). Because of His sufferings we are sons with all that that means in terms of the glory of the heavenly family.[73]

Then there are references to all manner of good gifts that come to believers in Christ. There is 'eternal redemption' (Heb. 9:12), which emphasizes the never ending consequences of what Christ has done for us, while 'the redemption of the transgressions that were under the first covenant' (Heb. 9:15) reminds us both that redemption is from sin and that even those who lived under the old dispensation had to have their redemption from Christ. Nothing could put away their sin but that alone. So Christ obtained for us 'the eternal inheritance' (Heb. 9:15; cf. 1:14, where the angels are

---

[73] J. S. Lidgett goes so far as to say that 'the master-theme, the unifying conception, of the Epistle to the Hebrews is . . . Sonship and Salvation' (*Sonship and Salvation*, London, 1921, p. 13). This may be going too far, but the concept certainly is important.

regarded as doing service 'for the sake of them that shall inherit
salvation'). Similarly He secured for us 'great recompense of reward' (Heb. 10:35). There are many references to God's 'promise'
or 'promises' (as Heb. 10:36; 11:39). Believers have their place
in 'the general assembly and church of the firstborn who are en-
rolled in heaven' (Heb. 12:23); they receive 'a kingdom that cannot be shaken' (Heb. 12:28). Several times our author refers to
'rest'. Sinners will not enter God's 'rest'; He has sworn it! (Heb.
3:11, 18). But 'we which have believed do enter into that rest'
(Heb. 4:3); 'there remaineth therefore a sabbath rest for the people
of God' (Heb. 4:9).[74] It may be that, when he goes on to say 'he
that is entered into his rest hath himself also rested from his works,
as God did from his' (Heb. 4:10), he is enunciating the doctrine
that Paul makes so much of, that man can do nothing to bring about
his salvation, but must rest on what God has done for him. And we
are near another Pauline concept when we read that Noah 'became
heir of the righteousness which is according to faith' (Heb. 11:7).
Paul prefers to think of Abraham (on whom this writer also dwells),
but the principle is the same. Righteousness is by faith, and it is
to be discerned in the saints of the Old Testament, so is not to be
thought of as a divine afterthought. God has always required
that men come to Him by faith. And Paul's own text is cited, 'But
my righteous one shall live by faith', after which our author adds,
'we are . . . of them that have faith unto the saving of the soul'
(Heb. 10:38f.).

Christ has won the victory over the devil. He became man
specifically 'that through death he might bring to nought him that
had the power of death, that is, the devil' (Heb. 2:14). Christ
accordingly has delivered His people from the fear of death and
their bondage to Satan (Heb. 2:15). The thought of the final
victory is there also in references to the resurrection (Heb. 6:1f.;
13:20), to Christ's continuing life (Heb. 7:25, etc.), and to the
second coming (Heb. 9:28). These thoughts (apart from that of
Christ's continuing life) are not dwelt upon, and it cannot be said
that the victory Christ won represents as major an interest in this
Epistle as in some other parts of the New Testament. But it is
there. It forms part of the way we should understand this writer's
estimate of the atonement.

---

[74] σαββατισμός does not appear to be attested earlier than this passage
and it is possible that the word was coined by our author. Its significance,
in distinction from that of κατάπαυσις, is given by M. F. Sadler thus: 'the
cessation from work peculiar to the Sabbath. This difference is made, no
doubt, to distinguish the spiritual rest into which the people of God, whether
Jews or Gentiles, now enter, from the temporal or earthly rest, into which
they were introduced by Joshua. The rest, so far as it is entered into in this
world, is spiritual and unworldly' (in loc.).

OUR RESPONSE

Curiously there are some writers who think that this Epistle has little to say about our response to what Christ has done for us,[75] either in the way of saving faith, or in the way of godly living. The truth is, of course, that both receive a good deal of emphasis. The saved, by definition, are committed to a life of obedience, for Christ 'became unto all them that obey him the author of eternal salvation' (Heb. 5:9). The saved and the obedient are the same. Conversely, missing God's blessing in salvation may be described in terms of obedience, for 'they to whom the good tidings were before preached failed to enter in because of disobedience' (Heb. 4:6). Good heed should be paid to this bad example: 'Let us therefore give diligence to enter into that rest, that no man fall after the same example of disobedience' (Heb. 4:11). In another connection we are exhorted, 'Let us therefore draw near with boldness unto the throne of grace' (Heb. 4:16), but draw near we must. Salvation does not come to those who idly sit back, and the question can be put, 'how shall we escape, if we neglect so great salvation?' (Heb. 2:3). We must 'lay hold of the hope set before us' (Heb. 6:18). This means much the same as being of 'them that have faith unto the saving of the soul' (Heb. 10:39).

It is worth our taking time to examine the idea of faith in this Epistle, all the more so since it is frequently depreciated. Vincent Taylor, for example, maintains that in this writing, faith 'is not trust in, and self-committal to, Christ in the Pauline sense; it is rather confidence in the reality of the unseen, in the certainty of God's promises, in the truth of Christ's redemptive work'.[76] The facts do not bear this out. Granted that this Epistle does not speak of faith in Christ in exactly the way Paul does, it yet speaks of a faith in God which it is difficult to interpret other than with respect to what God has done in Christ. Faith that rests on God (ἐπὶ θεόν) is one of the first principles of Christianity (Heb. 6:1). We cannot understand the statements in the roll of honour in chapter 11 without seeing that faith here spoken of includes a wholehearted commitment to and a thoroughgoing reliance on God.[77] It is impossible

---

[75] Cf. William J. Wolf: the writer of this Epistle 'is weakest in showing how men are to respond to this work of Christ, whether by faith-union or eucharistic communion as in Paul, or by a fundamental Christ-mysticism as in the writer of the fourth gospel' (op. cit., p. 88). The writer to the Hebrews does not ape Paul or John, but he has his own way of showing that our response is important.

[76] ANT, p. 104.

[77] H. C. G. Moule objects to the idea that Heb. 11:1 gives a definition of faith. He prefers to think of it as a statement about faith. The words of this verse 'are the sort of statement we make when we say, Knowledge is power. That is not a definition of knowledge, by any means. It is a

to exaggerate the extent of the personal commitment in Abraham's faith when that patriarch 'went out, not knowing whither he went' (Heb. 11:8), or when he made himself ready to offer up Isaac (vv. 17ff.). Or when Moses chose 'rather to be evil entreated with the people of God, than to enjoy the pleasures of sin for a season' (v. 25). Or of those who on account of faith were tortured, endured mockings and scourgings, were imprisoned, stoned, sawn in two, and all the rest of it (vv. 35ff.). If this does not mean personal commitment of the most wholehearted kind, words have no meaning. Here, as elsewhere, the writer is emphasizing that a wholehearted commitment to God is the basic religious attitude.[78]

So he tells us that it is through faith that men inherit the promises of God (Heb. 6:12), through faith that they enter into God's rest (Heb. 4:3). Without faith even the word that comes from God does not profit (Heb. 4:2). Without faith it is impossible to please God (Heb. 11:6). Small wonder that our writer can point to Christian leaders and urge his readers to imitate their faith (Heb. 13:7). Christians are distinguished from non-Christians with the description 'them that shrink back unto perdition . . . them that have faith unto the saving of the soul' (Heb. 10:39).

That faith is not understood apart from Christ is clear from such passages as 'having a great priest over the house of God; let us draw near with a true heart in fulness of faith' (Heb. 10:21f.), or 'looking unto Jesus the author and perfecter of our faith' (Heb. 12:2). We 'draw near unto God through him' (Heb. 7:25). It does not seem possible in the face of the evidence to argue that this writer has a conception of faith essentially different from that in the rest of the New Testament. Different emphases, yes. But an essentially different concept, emphatically, no. He has his own way of expressing his thoughts. He does not repeat the Pauline formulas. But essentially he is arguing for the same basic attitude of reliance on God, on God alone, an attitude which is not one

---

description of it in one of its great effects.' He sees Heb. 11 in this light, 'Noah, Abraham, Joseph, Moses — they all treated the hoped-for and the unseen as solid and certain because they all relied upon the faithful Promiser. Their victories were mysteriously great, their lives were related vitally to the Unseen. But the action to this end was on their part sublimely simple. It was reliance on the Promiser. It was taking God at His Word' (*The Fundamentals,* ii, Chicago, n. d., p. 114).

[78] What Karl Heim says of the *sola fides* of the German Reformation applies here: 'It means that with our whole existence we are in a relationship which is at a deeper level than all our psychological functions, in which our certainty as regards the ultimate conditions of thinking and willing is anchored, from which therefore our deepest knowledge and the deepest decisions of our will grow, as a tree with widespread branches grows from a hidden root which lives under the surface' (*Jesus the Lord,* Edinburgh and London, 1959, p. 110).

in word or thought alone but which, taking its starting point from what God has done in Christ,[79] issues in the total committal of the life to God.[80]

Not only must we come near to God through Christ, but when we come we are required to 'offer service well-pleasing to God with reverence and awe' (Heb. 12:28), and our author reminds us that the blood of Christ cleanses our 'conscience from dead works to serve the living God' (Heb. 9:14). We who are Christ's are exhorted that we 'lay aside every weight, and the sin which doth so easily beset us, and let us run with patience the race that is set before us' (Heb. 12:1). We strive against sin (Heb. 12:4). This service which we are to show in our lives is surely referred to when the Holy Spirit is referred to in connection with the writing of God's laws in men's hearts (Heb. 10:15f.). This points us to the importance of living out the will of God, not from some external constraint, but by the power that is within them. So with the prayer that God will make us perfect 'in every good thing to do his will, working in us that which is well-pleasing in his sight, through Jesus Christ' (Heb. 13:21).

Quite a number of passages speak of the enduring of chastening and the like (Heb. 10:32ff.; 11:25f., 36ff.; 12:10ff.; 13:3, 13). It is clear that Christ's sufferings do not mean an easy path for believers. Perhaps we are near to the thought of Acts 5:41, Colossians 1:24, 1 Peter 4:14, etc., that God graciously permits His servants to follow their Lord in the path of suffering. This is the way, too, in which we become 'partakers of his holiness' (Heb. 12:10). The writer notices that it is possible to fall short of the grace of God (Heb. 12:15). But he does not think that his readers will do this, and he expresses confidence in them, 'But beloved, we are persuaded better things of you, and things that accompany salvation' (Heb. 6:9). The implication is that these things accompanying salvation must without fail be performed by the saved. These will include what he calls 'a sacrifice of praise' (Heb. 13:15), the doing good and communicating (Heb. 13:16), and the other practical duties laid down in the concluding chapter. This is to be done

---

[79] Cf. J. Moffatt, 'Jesus has not only preceded us on the line of faith; he has by his sacrifice made our access to God direct and real, as it never could be before . . . . He does not make Jesus the object of faith as Paul does, but he argues that only the sacrifice of Jesus opens the way into the presence of God for sinful men' (op. cit., p. xliv).

[80] Cf. C. Ryder Smith, 'this writer, who can use even the word "faith" in an independent way, bases his thinking upon the same ideas and experience as Paul. The threefold use of the phrase, "We have a High Priest . . . .", is only one illustration of the concept fundamental throughout, that Jesus and Christians are one because there has been choice on both sides. Paul says the same under the words "faith" and "grace" ' (BDS, p. 227).

wholeheartedly, for the writer exhorts, 'let us consider one another to provoke unto love and good works (εἰς παροξυσμὸν ἀγάπης καὶ καλῶν ἔργων)' (Heb. 10:24). Men 'through faith and patience inherit the promises' (Heb. 6:12). They are 'promises'. They are the gift of God. That is not overlooked. But man's part is not overlooked either.[81]

The writer of this Epistle has an individual point of view. No other New Testament writer thought of interpreting the work of Christ for man through the symbolism of Jewish ritual. This approach enables him to bring out certain truths about the atonement which we do not see quite so readily elsewhere. But it is essentially the same doctrine that we have seen elsewhere. For this writer as for all the others, the problem is posed by the holiness of God and the sin of man. For him as for them, our hope is solely in Christ, who alone can deal with our sins. In that situation the individual point of view of this Epistle is that we have been saved by the mediatorial work of a great high priest.

[81] In view of all this I cannot follow Vincent Taylor when he says, 'More remarkable is the slight extent to which the writer has referred to the ethical and spiritual ends of the atoning ministry of Christ' (ANT, p. 111). If these ethical ends are 'slight' may we be preserved from any thoroughgoing demands!

Chapter Nine

The Cross in the Catholic Epistles and Revelation

THE GENERAL EPISTLE OF JAMES

This Epistle has nothing to say in set terms about the atonement, the death of Christ being not once mentioned. From this some have drawn the conclusion that the writer did not believe that Christ died for our sins. This, of course, does not follow. James is writing with a purpose of his own, and this controls what he inserts or omits. His Epistle must be taken for what it is, and not regarded as a general treatise on the essentials of Christianity.[1]

---

[1] 'The idea of "the simple teaching of Jesus", consisting in the principle of self-sacrifice, is a modernist myth, and the claim that this teaching is preserved in the Epistle of St. James springs from a failure to appreciate the true character of the writing . . . . The truth is that the writing is not an epistle at all, but a homily, or rather a series of homilies, on various practical ethical themes. . . . To expect in such a writing information regarding primitive belief about the death of Christ is as unreasonable as it would be to seek it in the document Q' (Vincent Taylor, ANT, pp. 43f.).

But though his purpose is not to set forth his doctrine of atonement, what James says has its implications for such a doctrine, and we should notice four points at least.

1. *The Serious Character of Sin*

James reproduces an idea that we have seen throughout the New Testament that men's evil deeds are not to be shrugged off as matters of no consequence. Throughout his entire Epistle he makes it clear that sin is totally incompatible with the Christian profession. It is the barrier to fellowship with God. Quite early in his writing James refutes the idea that a man can put the blame for his sin on God, an idea which can be found within Judaism and is not unknown elsewhere. His words are: 'Let no man say when he is tempted, I am tempted of God: for God cannot be tempted with evil, and he himself tempteth no man' (Jas. 1:13). We today would not speak directly of God as tempting man, but men do think of temptation as being due to the way they are made, which amounts to much the same thing. James insists on human responsibility. He points out that temptation arises from a man's own lust, 'Then the lust, when it hath conceived, beareth sin: and the sin, when it is fullgrown, bringeth forth death' (Jas. 1:15). The vivid imagery pictures sin as a thing of power and force and life. 'Bringeth forth' is the metaphor of childbirth.[2] Sin takes time to grow, but when it is mature it conceives and the offspring it brings forth is death. The figure stresses the inevitability of death for the sinner. Death will ensue on sin with the inevitability with which the child will at the set time issue forth from the womb. The New Testament contains no more forthright statement of the connection between sin and death.

This is not our writer's only contribution to the subject. James is clear on the universality of sin. 'In many things we all stumble' (Jas. 3:2). And he brings this out by showing that if we break but one commandment we are lawbreakers. We cannot shelter behind a fancied security of having kept some of the commandments, for God's demand is that we keep them all.[3] James says forthrightly,

---

[2] William Barclay says that ἀποκυέω 'is not a human word at all; it is an animal word for birth; and it means that sin *spawns* death. Mastered by desire, man becomes less than a man and sinks to the level of the brute creation' (*in loc.*). If this is the way to understand the word, James means that this whole evil process is an unnatural affair. ἀποκυέω, however, is used of human birth (e. g., Philo, *On the Posterity of Cain*, 114, and cf. the passages cited in LS) so this cannot be pressed.

[3] Cf. P. Loyd, 'The law is one whole: and the reason for that is that it is not just a body of external precepts, but the expression of a principle of life which is intended to mould the hearts of men and to make them what

whosoever shall keep the whole law, and yet stumble in one point, he is become guilty of all. For he that said, Do not commit adultery, said also, Do not kill. Now if thou dost not commit adultery, but killest, thou art become a transgressor of the law (Jas. 2:10f.).

This has its consequences. As R. V. G. Tasker says, 'it is just man's utter failure to obey that law in its entirety that makes it necessary for his salvation to depend, not on his own righteousness, but upon the righteousness of Another — Jesus Christ!'[4] James speaks of those who sin as being 'convicted by the law as transgressors' (Jas. 2:9). He points out that those in more responsible positions, like teachers, will receive all the heavier judgment when they fail (Jas. 3:1).[5] He has a section on sins of the tongue (Jas. 3:2-12) which convicts us all. And he has a very notable statement about the sin of omission, 'To him therefore that knoweth to do good, and doeth it not, to him it is sin' (Jas. 4:17). Such sayings leave not the slightest doubt but that James thought of sin as a universal phenomenon. No one can escape condemnation judged by such a standard as this.

As do other New Testament writers, James shows us the seriousness of this by speaking of God's strong opposition. He addresses evildoers as 'adulteresses' (Jas. 4:4),[6] a figure which reminds us of the Old Testament habit of characterizing idolaters in this way. Those who bow down to idols have acted treacherously against Yahweh, their lawful Husband. James extends the figure. All sin is a breach of trust, an act of despite against love, and God cannot be indifferent to it. James goes on to say that 'the friendship of the world is enmity with God' (Jas. 4:4). God is more than mildly displeased with sinful men. He is their Enemy. Out of this situation James quotes from Proverbs 3:34, 'God resisteth the

---

God wants them to be. Therefore if a man fails to keep one part of the law, by that much he fails to become what God would have him be, and so he *is become guilty of all'* (*Doers of the Word*, London, 1939, pp. 100f.); 'We must not pick and choose which parts we will obey and which parts we will neglect: because it is all His word; and if we disobey Him in anything, we are *become a transgressor of the law'* (*op. cit.*, p. 102).

[4] *Tyndale Commentary, in loc.*

[5] R. J. Knowling connects the 'excessive eagerness to gain the office of teacher or rather Rabbi' with 'the same excessive estimation of mere external orthodoxy above moral practice', and he proceeds to link it with the 'faith without works' controversy (*in loc.*).

[6] Cf. Moffatt, 'he uses the feminine form deliberately, for one turn of special contempt and scorn in the ancient world was to call a community or group by some feminine equivalent. Thus Theopompus the Greek historian denounced the adherents of Philip by saying, "They were called Friends (*hetairoi*) of Philip, but they were his mistresses (*hetairai*)' (*in loc.*).

proud' (Jas. 4:6).[7] He leaves us in no doubt but that sin is universal and that it leaves man with God ranged against him.

2.   *Salvation Comes from God*

In this situation James does not look basically to anything human for the remedy. He says explicitly, 'Of his own will he brought us forth by the word of truth' (Jas. 1:18). The references to birth and to the 'word' as the divine agent remind us of the teaching on regeneration in John's Gospel, while the explicit statement that in this God was doing 'his own will' clinches the priority of the divine. It is not a salvation humanly motivated or engineered of which James writes. As Moffatt puts it, God 'deliberately willed to make us His own choice offspring . . . . To God we owe our new, true life, to God's set purpose and to that alone'.[8] Similarly James exhorts his readers 'receive with meekness the implanted word, which is able to save your souls' (Jas. 1:21). Again the thought is that of what God does within man, and not of anything that man can do of himself. In the same spirit James can look for 'the wisdom that is from above' (Jas. 3:17), and can remember that 'God . . . giveth grace to the humble' (Jas. 4:6). He urges men to be patient 'until the coming of the Lord' (Jas. 5:7), which shows us his deep confidence in the Lord, and his conviction of ultimate triumph at the second coming. He can be confident, for 'the Lord is full of pity, and merciful' (Jas. 5:11).

3.   *Man's Response*

James, then, is clear that all men desperately need salvation, since they are sinners and as sinners the objects of God's hostility. He is clear, too, that God is ready to provide salvation out of His mercy and by His regenerating Word. But if he is convinced of one thing it is that that salvation does not come to men who sit back idly and wait. It is imperative that men respond to God's readiness to save. Indeed, so strongly does James emphasize this that his Epistle has sometimes been misunderstood as though it taught a doctrine of salvation by works. It does nothing of the sort. But James does place stress on the human response and this ought not to be minimized. It was important to him and it is important to us.

Sometimes the response is put in terms of repentance, though he does not use that precise word. But he does urge his readers: 'Draw nigh to God, and he will draw nigh to you' (Jas. 4:8), to which he immediately adds, 'Cleanse your hands, ye sinners; and

---

[7] Cf. Tasker, 'To all such God is permanently opposed. He actively resists them. His wrath abides upon them' (*in loc.*).

[8] *In loc.*

purify your hearts, ye doubleminded . . . . Humble yourselves in the sight of the Lord'. He exhorts the rich: 'weep and howl for your miseries that are coming upon you' (Jas. 5:1). He commands confession, which inculcates that same basic attitude. 'Confess therefore your sins one to another, and pray one for another, that ye may be healed' (Jas. 5:16). Prayer is to be engaged upon in faith, so that sins may be forgiven (Jas. 5:15). And men must be converted if they are to be saved from death (Jas. 5:20).[9] All of this points us to the same basic reversal of attitudes which we have met elsewhere. The New Testament writers universally regard man's plight as hopeless as long as he relies on his own effort for salvation, James along with the others. He must realize that he is basically a sinner and turn from his wicked way, if God's salvation is to become effective in his life. That means conversion, repentance, prayer, forgiveness, and all the rest of which James speaks.

James also speaks of faith, and it is here that the greatest controversy — and also, we should add, misunderstanding — arises. In a very important passage (Jas. 2:14-26) he denies outright that a man can be saved by faith without works, maintaining that 'faith, if it have not works, is dead in itself' (v. 17). He can even go so far as to say that 'by works a man is justified, and not only by faith' (v. 24). He uses the example of Abraham, as Paul did, and quotes of him 'Abraham believed God, and it was reckoned unto him for righteousness' (v. 23), again as Paul did. But he draws from this a conclusion which seems to be totally at variance with what Paul concludes.

When, however, we turn our attention to the idea that James is enunciating and shake ourselves loose from the fascination of words, we see that there is no contradiction. James is not denying the importance of faith. Elsewhere in his Epistle he speaks of faith easily and naturally. He can urge that prayer be offered in faith (Jas. 1:6), and he can speak of holding 'the faith of our Lord Jesus Christ, the Lord of glory' (Jas. 2:1; Moffatt translates, 'as you believe in our Lord Jesus Christ'). He refers to the poor as

---

[9] I regard as untenable Moffatt's contention that it is the sins of the helper that are covered. He translates, 'he who brings a sinner back from the error of his way saves his soul from death and hides a host of sins', and he comments that 'The unselfish Christian love which makes one feel responsible for an erring brother and moves one to *bring him back* to the church, *hides a host of* the good Christian's *sins* . . . . such forgiving, redeeming love to a brother will atone for a great deal.' Neither James, nor any other Christian writer thinks of good deeds that a man may do as availing to atone for his sins. Atonement in the New Testament is a function of Christ alone and we have no reason for thinking that James thought differently from other writers on this point. Certainly this verse does not say so. The meaning is rather as Goodspeed, 'whoever brings a sinner back from his misguided way will save the man's soul from death . . . .'

being 'rich in faith' (Jas. 2:5). He speaks of 'the prayer of faith' as saving the sick, 'and if he have committed sins, it shall be forgiven him' (Jas. 5:15). There cannot be the slightest doubt that James found a large place for faith.

The very fact that he writes as he does shows us the centrality of the cross in the early church. He was clearly combating those who relied on faith and failed to produce good works. How could such a heretical position arise? From the view that Christ, the perfect Teacher, taught men how they should live? From the idea that Christianity means leading a good life? From regarding the Sufferer on the Cross as our perfect example? Such suggestions have only to be enunciated for their falsity to appear.[10] Surely the only view which explains the situation is one in which men saw Christ as doing all that was necessary for men's salvation and in which men are called upon to believe.

James makes no attempt to dispute this basic proposition. But he cannot find words strong enough to condemn those who affirm that they believe, but whose lives belie their words. The kind of 'faith' he is denouncing he describes himself. 'Thou believest that God is one; thou doest well: the devils also believe, and shudder' (Jas. 2:19). The kind of 'faith' he objects to is the 'faith' of devils. A 'faith' that exists without good works is a barren affair (Jas. 2:20). There is no life in it. Not so are we to understand saving faith.

It is important to notice that the kind of 'works' that James has in mind are those that are the outcome of saving faith. While it is true that he and Paul both use Abraham as their example, they are not talking about the same thing. They choose different times in the patriarch's spiritual pilgrimage, and they have different lessons to bring out. Paul speaks of the time when Abraham believed initially and his faith was reckoned as righteousness (Rom. 4:3, 9f.). He is concerned with justification. But James refers to the occasion when Abraham showed himself ready to offer up Isaac (Jas. 2:21), which took place many years later.[11] He is concerned with the

---

[10] Cf. R. W. Dale, 'such a heresy could never have arisen if the Church had been taught to believe that the sole purpose for which Christ came into the world was to redeem us from eternal ruin by making us better men . . . . This conception of the work of Christ has many great defects, but it has one great merit; it is a conception in which the Antinomian heresy can never take root . . . . Had the early Church been taught that the Christian salvation is only a salvation from sin, or that whatever else it may be is the result of salvation from sin, it is inconceivable that any persons bearing the Christian name could have supposed that they might be saved by faith without works' (*The Atonement*, London, 1902, p. 180).

[11] Cf. W. Cunningham, 'the justification of which James speaks, and which he ascribes to works, refers to something in men's history posterior to that great era when their sins are forgiven, and they are admitted to the enjoy-

fruits of justification, the evidence that justification has taken place. He nowhere says anything that would lead us to think that he is opening the way to those works of the law which Moffatt defines succinctly as 'observance of the ritual and ceremonial Law as constituting a claim for merit before God.'[12] It is this that Paul is concerned to oppose, but it is not this that James is concerned to uphold. His view is rather, 'I by my works will shew thee my faith' (Jas. 2:18).[13] Paul is concerned with the means by which a man becomes a Christian, James with the characteristics of his life as a Christian. James does not mean by 'faith' what Paul means by 'faith', and he does not mean by 'works' what Paul means by 'works'. Indeed, James' 'works' look suspiciously like 'the fruit of the Spirit' of which Paul writes.[14] James is not asserting that men may be saved without faith. His whole discussion presupposes that both he and those with whom he is arguing accept the basic importance of faith. But he emphasizes that faith cannot be said to exist apart from good works. The presence of faith is shown by works (Jas. 2:18).[15] Paul would have been the first to agree with him that if there is a real faith there must be changed lives. 'Faith apart from works is dead' (Jas. 2:26).[16]

4. The Place of Suffering

James begins his Epistle by saying (after the greeting), 'Count it all joy, my brethren, when ye fall into manifold trials' (Jas. 1:2,

---

[12] ment of God's favour, — i. e., to the proof or manifestation of the reality and efficacy of their faith to themselves and their fellow-men' (*Historical Theology*, ii, Edinburgh, 1870, p. 67).

[12] On Jas. 2:24.

[13] It is not clear whether James means these words to be part of the speech of his opponent, or whether he is putting them forth as his own retort. See the discussions in the commentaries. But there is general agreement that whatever be the solution he is putting forward as words with which he agrees. Moffatt translates, 'Someone will object, "And you claim to have faith!" Yes, and I claim to have deeds as well; you show me your faith without any deeds, and I will show you by my deeds what faith is.'

[14] 'There is not a great difference of meaning between ἡ πίστις συνήργει τοῖς ἔργοις (James 2:22) and πίστις δι' ἀγάπης ἐνεργουμένη (Gal. 5:6)' (A. Richardson, *An Introduction to the Theology of the New Testament*, London, 1958, p. 241).

[15] 'It is utterly impossible for one man to set up, so to speak, as a specialist in faith and another man to set up as a specialist in works' (Alexander Ross, *in loc.*).

[16] James Buchanan discusses the relation between the teaching of Paul and James (*The Doctrine of Justification*, London, 1961, pp. 253-63). He distinguishes between 'actual' and 'declarative' justification, with Paul dealing with the former and James occupied by the latter. He concludes by reminding us that the two tendencies, to legalism and to antinomianism, are always with us, 'And for this reason, every faithful minister finds it necessary to make use, alternately, of the teaching of Paul and of James.'

mg.). A little later he returns to the thought with, 'Blessed is the man that endureth temptation' (Jas. 1:12). We have here the thought that we have seen elsewhere that suffering is not to be regarded as an evil pure and simple. The Christian should welcome it, for it is part of the discipline of living out his faith. Only the Christian who has been tested and proved in this way is mature. This does not mean that sufferings lead to atonement. It is the thought we have seen elsewhere in the New Testament that the Christians were led to a different view of suffering in the light of the cross. There is no reason for thinking that James came by his view of suffering in any other way.

THE FIRST EPISTLE GENERAL OF PETER

For a short writing, 1 Peter has an astonishing amount to say about the atonement. Most of the Epistle bears on the problem in one way or another, for Peter is concerned throughout with the salvation that God has wrought in Christ. Sometimes his subject is what God did. Sometimes it is man's response. But in one form or another, salvation is always before us as we read this writing.

We may conveniently consider the Epistle's teaching under the headings of the parts played by the three Persons of the Trinity, and then the human response to all this. This is not a hard and fast classification, but it will serve to bring out something of the richness of the Apostle's teaching on our subject.

1. God the Father and Salvation

The Epistle is addressed to 'the elect . . . according to the foreknowledge of God the Father' (1 Pet. 1:1f.).[17] Thus, right at the beginning, the truth that salvation originates with God is brought before the reader. Peter comes back to the thought of election later (1 Pet. 2:9; 5:13; cf. also 2:6), but he prefers to use the terminology of the divine call (1 Pet. 1:15; 2:9, 21; 3:9; 5:10), which expresses essentially the same idea. Divine choosing out amounts to much the same thing as divine calling out. All these passages emphasize one basic truth. Man does not initiate salvation. It is not in him to make the first move. If he is to be saved, then God must first choose him. God must first call him. As Moffatt puts it, 'The hope of ultimate salvation rests on the consciousness of being *predestined*

---

[17] C. E. B. Cranfield comments, 'They are Christians because they are objects of God's gracious choice. Their lives are in His hands. They have a divinely appointed task to fulfil. The foreknowledge of God includes the distinct though closely related ideas of divine purpose, divine choice, divine providence, and carries with it the assurance that their high destiny shall be accomplished' (*in loc.*).

and chosen by *God the Father,* who has taken up their lives into His eternal will and purpose for all time.'[18]

The thought of the divine plan is in mind also when Peter speaks of the prophets as having 'sought and searched diligently' into salvation, as having 'prophesied of the grace that should come', and as 'searching what time or what manner of time the Spirit of Christ which was in them did point unto, when it testified beforehand the sufferings of Christ. . .' (1 Pet. 1:10f.). The bearing of prophecy on the doing of the will of God is plain enough. If God has said through His servants the prophets that such-and-such a thing will come to pass, then it is clear that that thing is in the will of God. It takes place according to the purpose of God. And Peter not only speaks of the prophets as setting forth what God has planned. He tells us in set terms that the will of God is being done in certain concrete situations. This is the case with the whole life of the believer (1 Pet. 2:15; 4:2), and specifically with the sufferings that he is called upon to endure (1 Pet. 3:17; 4:19).[19] Such passages clearly stress the sovereignty of God. God's will is done. Salvation takes place because God has planned it so.

Peter speaks of this salvation as 'the gospel' (1 Pet. 1:12; 4:6, 17; cf. 1:25). It is 'the good news' of what God has done to provide for man's need. Peter's confidence is in the nature of God. 'He careth for you' he says with impressive simplicity (1 Pet. 5:7). Or he remembers the mercy of God (1 Pet. 2:10). Or, and this is his habit, he dwells on the grace of God. He tells us that 'the Lord is gracious' (1 Pet. 2:3).[20] When he speaks of the salvation into which God has called men, he characterizes Him as 'the God of all grace' (1 Pet. 5:10). So fundamental is grace that he can exhort his readers in these terms: 'set your hope perfectly on the grace that is to be brought unto you at the revelation of Jesus Christ' (1 Pet. 1:13). This exhortation reminds us in the first place of the importance of grace as Peter sees it. Men should set their hope on it. Life for the first Christians could not have been easy. They had little to hope for

---

[18] *Commentary* on 1 Pet. 1:2. He translates the greeting, 'to the exiles . . . whom God the Father has predestined and chosen', and comments, '*Chosen* refers to the Land where they are really at home but from which they are at present distant; *exiles* refers to the land where they reside at present but in which they are not at home.' J. W. C. Wand has the curious note on 'called' in 1 Pet. 1:15, 'there is an entire absence of theological implication such as predestination' (*in loc.*). How a divine call can be entirely without theological implication he does not say.

[19] F. W. Beare relates the concept of election to the sufferings of believers: 'The conviction that God had laid His mighty Hand upon them for good was a constant inspiration and strength to men who lived in daily jeopardy, facing trial by fire, and with no earthly refuge or support' (on 1 Pet. 1:1).

[20] The word is χρηστός. In the following passages 'grace' is χάρις.

as this world counts hope. But they were not downcast. They looked
for better things. And Peter thinks of these better things as rooted
in the grace of God. There men should set their hope. And they
should do this not halfheartedly, but perfectly.[21]   In the second place,
the exhortation shows that the implications of grace are not exhausted,
nor will they be until the Lord returns. Grace is God's continuing
habit. Christians should not forget it. We have already noticed that
'the grace that should come unto you' is a topic of prophecy (1 Pet.
1:10), so that it is from of old. Grace is associated with the living
out of the Christian life (1 Pet. 3:7; 5:5), and, indeed, Christians are
to be 'good stewards of the manifold grace of God' (1 Pet. 4:10).
That is to say, God gives them the varied grace that they need for
the multitude of situations in which they find themselves day by day.
And they are held responsible for it. 'Stewards' is a word which
describes the slave set over a large household by the owner so as to
relieve him of the duty of personal supervision. Such a slave had
considerable freedom, but he was responsible and would have to
give account of his administration. Peter uses the figure to show at
one and the same time that Christians have nothing of their own
but owe all to the grace of God, and that they must use given grace
as men who will give account of themselves. Grace does not encourage irresponsibility. Finally in this section let us notice that
the Epistle begins and ends with grace. 'Grace to you and peace'
(1 Pet. 1:2) is perhaps the conventional Christian opening to a letter,
but certainly it sounds right at the beginning the note of dependence
on God.[22]   And Peter can end his letter saying that he has written
'testifying that this is the true grace of God' (1 Pet. 5:12). Grace,
for him, sums it all up.[23] The freeness of God's mercy and bounty

[21] Cf. H. A. W. Meyer, τελείως 'shows emphatically that the hope should be
perfect, undivided, unchangeable ("without doubt or faintheartedness, with
full surrender of soul," de Wette: Wiesinger adds further: "excluding all
ungodly substance and worldly desire, and including the μὴ συσχηματ., ver.
14") . . .' (in loc.). F. J. A. Hort prefers to take τελείως with the preceding
νήφοντες, but this does not seem to be justified. Incidentally he understands
'set your hope on the grace' to mean, 'rest securely on the grace and treat it
as an assurance justifying all possible hope.' He further comments, 'hope
set on the grace implies what is more fundamental still, hope on God Himself,
and of that St Peter speaks v. 21' (in loc.).

[22] 'Before "joy" or "peace" or any other form of well being, which formed
the subject of ordinary good wishes, the Apostles first wished for their converts the smile and the merciful help of the Lord of heaven and earth . . . .
The Incarnation itself was the perfect expression of what was meant by
"grace," and in its light and power all God's good gifts were become new'
(F. J. A. Hort, in loc.).

[23] A. M. Stibbs is of the opinion that this refers 'to the apostle's fundamental
message . . . the message of the gospel of Christ in whom saving grace is
extended to the unworthy and to the humble (x.10; v.5), making them heirs
of life (iii.7), and qualifying them to endure suffering here, and to enjoy
eternal glory hereafter (v. 10)' (Tyndale Commentary, in loc.).

is the very essence of Christianity. In line with this is the thought that salvation is something that is 'received' (1 Pet. 1:9), or that Christians 'by the power of God are guarded' (1 Pet. 1:5), or that 'the eyes of the Lord are upon the righteous, and his ears unto their supplication' (1 Pet. 3:12). In all this is the thought that God gives men salvation, and gives it in such a way that He preserves them to the end. He does not bring them out of their state of condemnation and then leave them to fend for themselves.

Twice Peter refers to God as regenerating believers. He speaks of God 'who according to his great mercy begat us again unto a living hope' (1 Pet. 1:3). Again he tells us that Christians have been 'begotten again, not of corruptible seed, but of incorruptible, through the word of God, which liveth and abideth' (1 Pet. 1:23; cf. also the reference to 'newborn babes', 2:2). Some have tried to trace this idea to the influence of the mystery religions or to other forces in the Hellenistic world. But it is more likely that this is the strand of Christian teaching that we see in John 3.[24] Before men can see the kingdom of God it is necessary that they be born again of spiritual birth. And Peter is maintaining that such birth is due to God, none less. The newness of the life in Christ is such that nothing less than the language of rebirth will describe it.[25] A man cannot will himself into being born, so the imagery necessarily involves the priority of the divine in the process of salvation as well as the effect of the divine power.[26]

We conclude this aspect of the divine work of salvation by noticing that sometimes Peter thinks of God as at work in the mission of Christ. He tells us that we are redeemed by Christ 'who was foreknown indeed before the foundation of the world' (1 Pet. 1:20). He

---

[24] Wand rejects such ideas as that the concept is borrowed 'from the Stoic belief in the rebirth of the world after its periodic destruction by conflagration', or from the Taurobolium. He goes on, 'More probably, however, it is drawn from some such word of the Lord as that in Jn. iii.7' (on 1:3). Selwyn has an important note on 'I Peter and the Mystery Religions' (*The First Epistle of St. Peter*, London, 1949, pp. 305-11). His conclusion is that 'The claim that the author owed any of his leading ideas to the Mystery Religions must be rejected as wholly unproven.'

[25] Cf. F. W. Beare, 'If the doctrine of regeneration found a ready entrance into the Christian teaching, it was because nothing else was adequate to express the sense of newness which men experienced in Christ; the sense that the old life had ended and a new life begun — new, not merely in direction and intention, but in essence; the sense that the supernatural, the heavenly, the divine, had broken in and displaced the earthly, natural, mortal life' (*The First Epistle of Peter*, Oxford, 1947, p. 38).

[26] Some (e. g., Wand) see a reference to baptism. On this Stibbs comments, 'It is dangerous thus to divert attention away from the divinely-wrought spiritual realities to the sign, whose whole *raison d'etre* is to direct attention and faith to the real cause and occasion of regeneration' (on 1 Pet. 1:3).

goes on to speak in the same strain of Him as being manifested, and says that God 'raised him from the dead, and gave him glory' (1 Pet. 1:21). The purpose of all this is 'that your faith and hope might be in God'.

But though Peter is thus sure of the mercy and the grace of God he is equally sure that there is a darker side to the picture. Indeed, it is only because there is the darker side that grace and mercy may be known for what they are. Peter knows there is a place for fear even in the believer. Thus, when he is talking about redemption, where one might expect him to dwell on the joy of the freedom won in Christ, he can say, 'pass the time of your sojourning in fear' (1 Pet. 1:17). He has a good deal to say about fear. A short list of exhortations includes 'Fear God' (1 Pet. 2:17). Wives should display 'chaste behaviour coupled with fear' (1 Pet. 3:2). Believers should be ready always to give a reason for their hope 'with meekness and fear' (1 Pet. 3:15). This does not, of course, mean that Christians are to live their lives in a perpetual state of terror. But it does mean that God is a great God, One who must be regarded with profound respect and reverence and awe.[27] It is the temptation of our age to presume on the love of God, and to overlook the proper creaturely attitude to the Creator. In such a situation Peter's emphasis is timely.

Peter also has something to say about men's accountability. He assures us that 'the face of the Lord is upon them that do evil' (1 Pet. 3:12; Moffatt renders, 'the face of the Lord is set against wrongdoers'). He reminds us that God judges without respect of persons (1 Pet. 1:17), and that He judges righteously (1 Pet. 2:23). He knows of 'the day of visitation' (1 Pet. 2:12), and of Him 'that is ready to judge the quick and the dead' (1 Pet. 4:5; v. 6 speaks of the dead as being 'judged according to men in the flesh'). Nor in this general expectation of judgment may Christians sit back happily enough, hugging to themselves the thought that they, at any rate, are safe. They should realize that 'the time is come for judgement to begin at the house of God' (1 Pet. 4:17).[28] Peter is quite sure

---

[27] Selwyn prefers 'reverently' as the translation of ἐν φόβῳ. He comments, 'The thought of God as Judge would evoke awe, which is compounded of three instincts, fear, wonder, and "negative self-feeling" . . . . reverence is formed, when to these is added the tender emotion aroused by God's mercy' (on 1 Pet. 1:17).

[28] Cf. J. E. Fison, 'as so often ecclesiastically proclaimed, the one thing that the last judgment is never allowed to do is the one thing that in the New Testament it is most designed to do. Its purpose there is to spring a complete surprise not upon the lost pagan souls outside the pale of the church, but upon the complacent ecclesiastical souls whose entire confidence is based upon the fact that they are well within it' (The Christian Hope, London, 1954, p. 249).

that God is 'longsuffering' (1 Pet. 3:20). But there are limits. Men are responsible beings, and one day they will be called upon to give account of themselves.

Thus Peter thinks of God as active in a variety of ways in connection with man's salvation. It is properly His salvation, originating in His will and carried out according to His purpose. Just as plainly as any other New Testament writer, Peter roots salvation in the will of God.

2. God the Son and Salvation

If Peter sees salvation as finding its origin in the will of the Father, he sees it just as clearly as mediated through the work of the Son. He is sure that the death of Christ is the focal point. It is because of what was done on Calvary that men may now be at peace with God. Sometimes this is put in general terms, as when Peter speaks of his readers as offering spiritual sacrifices 'acceptable to God through Jesus Christ' (1 Pet. 2:5). More commonly he refers specifically to the sufferings[29] or to the death of Christ. The sufferings were foretold by the prophets (1 Pet. 1:11; the prophecies of the rejection of the 'stone' mean much the same, 1 Pet. 2:6-8).

Peter has a most interesting series of interpretations of the death of Christ. In his opening he refers to the 'sprinkling of the blood of Jesus Christ' (1 Pet. 1:2). 'Blood' by itself might mean no more than violent death, but 'sprinkling of blood' points us to the sacrifices.[30] There the most solemn moment was when the priest took the blood of the victim and 'sprinkled' it on the altar. This terminology shows that Peter sees Christ's death as a sacrifice.[31] What the sacrifices of the Old Testament foreshadowed, Christ fulfilled.

A little later Peter goes on to speak of the death of Christ as a process of redemption (1 Pet. 1:18f.). As I have noted elsewhere,

[29] F. L. Cross points out that there are twelve occurrences of πάσχω in this Epistle against eleven in the whole of the rest of the New Testament Epistles, 'i.e. the word occurs about twenty-three times as frequently, counting by columns, in 1 Peter as is the average for the rest of the New Testament Epistles'. Similarly he finds πάθημα to occur about eight times as frequently in this Epistle as in the others (I Peter, A Paschal Liturgy, London, 1954, p. 13). I am not persuaded that this necessarily points to the Passover (Cross's intention is to show that this Epistle is linked with the Passover observance). But the emphasis on Christ's sufferings in 1 Peter is not to be gainsaid or overlooked. Cross goes on to 'recognize the centrality of the sufferings of Christ in the writer's thought' (op. cit., p. 22).

[30] The linking of 'obedience' with 'sprinkling of the blood' awakens memories of Ex. 24, where the people pledged their obedience (vv. 3, 7), and were sprinkled with the blood (v. 8). If this chapter is in mind, then Peter will be thinking of Christ's death as a covenant sacrifice.

[31] 'Throughout this Epistle the writer dwells so constantly upon the sacrifice of the Cross that the Blood of Christ can mean nothing else than His Death and Passion' (C. Bigg, ICC, in loc.).

redemption denotes a process of release on payment of a ransom price. The thought of payment is implicit in the conception itself. But Peter does not leave us to infer this. He specifically lays it down that a price was paid for Christians, and this no corruptible thing, like silver or gold. It was 'precious blood, as of a lamb without blemish and without spot, even the blood of Christ.'[32] It may well be that the reference to the blood of an unblemished lamb points us to the sacrifices once more. Indeed, this is probable. But with sacrifice there is conjoined the metaphor of purchase. Christ's blood is at one and the same time the offering of a sacrifice which avails for men, and the payment of a price which avails for men. We are atoned for and we are purchased. Peter is sure that something with far-reaching implications was effected by Christ's death, and something completely objective. Whatever may take place within man, the objective effects are clear and they are important.

But the subjective effects ought not to be overlooked. They also are important, and Peter tells us that, 'Christ also suffered for you, leaving you an example, that ye should follow his steps' (1 Pet. 2:21). He goes on to particularize, showing that Christ was reviled, but did not retort in kind; He was compelled to submit to sufferings, but He did not threaten His tormentors. Sometimes evangelicals, in reaction to theories of the moral influence type, have tended to overlook this aspect of Christ's sufferings or to play it down. But, while it is not by any means the whole of the atonement, it is certainly part of it, and an important part. Among other things, Christ on the cross did set us an example of the patient endurance of injustice. He is our Pattern as well as our Redeemer. And because He is our Pattern we are bound to attempt to reproduce His attitude in our own experience.[33]

Perhaps the most significant passage in the Epistle for an understanding of the atonement is that which follows. Peter proceeds to tell us that Christ 'his own self bare our sins in his body upon the tree, that we, having died unto sins, might live unto righteousness' (1 Pet. 2:24). At first sight this seems to mean that in some way Christ took away our sins, but this has been disputed. Some have understood the bearing of sins to mean that during the days of His

---

[32] 'Man's redemption could not be achieved by any material sacrifices, however costly. It could be achieved only by Christ's personal offering of himself as an expiatory sacrifice, as *the* lamb without blemish or spot, i. e., as the perfect, final, unrepeatable and sufficient oblation on behalf of mankind' (A. Richardson, *op. cit.*, p. 222).

[33] H. E. W. Turner reminds us that 'any theory which separates the obligation of leading a better life from the Redemption brought by Christ has small claim for acceptance by Christians' (*The Patristic Doctrine of Redemption*, London, 1952, p. 46). In ch. II of this book Turner brings out the extent of this teaching in the early church, though making it clear that this is only one strand.

flesh Jesus endured all the evils that sinful men did to Him. They despised Him, rejected Him, opposed Him, betrayed Him, denied Him, scourged Him, and crucified Him. Right up to and including the cross, He bore their evil deeds. God though He was, He yet submitted to every indignity of man, and refrained from any action that would place Him out of reach of such humiliations. He came to show us how to live, and show us how to live He did, even in the face of harsh and unjust treatment.[34]

First let us notice that this interpretation overlooks the expression 'our sins'. The writer is not talking about the sins of the Palestinians who crucified Jesus. He is talking about his own sins and those of his readers. These are the sins Christ bore. And our passage goes on to make it clear that He bore them, not simply by way of example, but by way of expiating them. 'By whose stripes ye are healed.' Then it overlooks the force of the words 'in his body'. If the sins were borne by the patient endurance we have been speaking of, it is difficult to see why the body is singled out for mention. The important thing in such a bearing of sin is the attitude of soul and spirit. The feelings and the resolute will should be mentioned rather than the body. Nor is it easy to see why such sin-bearing should be connected with 'the tree'. Some expression pointing to the whole of life seems required. In fact this interpretation pays very little attention to the language actually used.

But the great difficulty in this way of understanding the passage is that the Bible does not mean this by the expression 'bearing sins'. This manner of speech is not common in the New Testament (it occurs again only in Heb. 9:28),[35] but it is frequent in the Old Testament.[36] We should need very strong reasons indeed for

---

[34] Some take the thought even further and think of the atonement as being concerned not only with all the events of Christ's life, but with an eternal process. Cf. H. Bushnell, 'there is a cross in God before the wood is seen upon Calvary; hid in God's own virtue itself, struggling on heavily in burdened feeling through all .the previous ages, and struggling as heavily now even in the throne of the worlds' (*The Vicarious Sacrifice*, London, 1866, pp. 35f.). This is not what the New Testament teaches. It overlooks what P. T. Forsyth called 'the cruciality of the cross'.

[35] The context in Heb. 9:28 makes it clear that the sin-bearing took place once for all (see vv. 24ff. and note the use of ἅπαξ to qualify προσενεχθείς). Unless we are prepared to defend the thesis that sin-bearing has different meanings for the two writers, this will rule out the thought of a life-long process.

[36] It is found also in other ancient literature with much the same meaning. Thus in the Gilgamish epic the god Ea protests against Enlil's bringing on of the flood in these words: 'O warrior, thou wisest among gods, how thus indiscriminately couldst thou bring about this deluge? (Had thou counselled): On the sinner lay his sin, on the transgressor lay his transgression . . .' (Tablet X1, lines 178ff.; cited from *Documents from Old Testament Times*, ed. D. Winton Thomas, London, 1958, p. 23). I am indebted to Mr. J. A.

thinking that men so fond of their Scriptures and so deeply learned in them as were the first Christians would use a biblical expression in such a non-biblical sense. When we turn to the Old Testament, there does not seem to be insuperable difficulty in finding out what bearing sins means. For example, Israel bore her sins by wandering in the wilderness. When the spies returned to the people after their forty days' search of the land of Canaan and persuaded them not to go up into the land, the Lord decreed that the nation should be punished by wandering in the wilderness for forty years.

> Your children shall be wanderers in the wilderness forty years, and shall bear your whoredoms, until your carcases be consumed in the wilderness. After the number of the days in which ye spied out the land, even forty days, for every day a year, shall ye bear your iniquities, even forty years (Num. 14:33f.).

Similarly the word of the Lord through Ezekiel stresses that every man is responsible for his own sin: 'The soul that sinneth, it shall die: the son shall not bear the iniquity of the father, neither shall the father bear the iniquity of the son' (Ezek. 18:20). Other passages could be cited to the same effect. Sin-bearing is a concept well understood in the Old Testament. It means bearing the penalty of sin.[37] And when Peter tells us that Jesus 'bare our sins in his body upon the tree' there ought not to be the slightest doubt but that he is using this familiar Old Testament manner of speaking.[38] He

---

Thompson for the information that the noun 'sin' is from the root חטא, which we see in the Old Testament, and that the verb rendered 'lay' is the imperative of *emēdu*, a verb with various nuances of meaning connected with 'bear, carry, load, impose, lean etc.' (*The Assyrian Dictionary*, ed. I. J. Gelb *et al.*, iv, Chicago, 1958, pp. 138-147). The idea that 'bearing' sin means bearing the consequences of sin is widespread.

[37] There are passages which speak of the priests as bearing sin during the discharge of their duties, e. g., Ex. 28:38, 'Aaron shall bear the iniquity of the holy things'. On this A. H. McNeile comments, 'Since Aaron is marked out, by the golden diadem, as the "holy one to Yahweh," summing up all the holy things in his own person, he is also ideally responsible for guarding all the holy things from profanation; and therefore upon him must come the guilt, and the punishment for the guilt, if any of them are profaned' (*in loc.*). G. Buchanan Gray explains the similar expression, 'shall bear the iniquity of the sanctuary' (Num. 18:1) in these words, 'shall bear the consequences of any guilt incurred in connection with the sanctuary' (*in loc.*).

[38] A. Deissmann, contends that the construction ἐπί with accusative cannot have this meaning, but must be understood as 'carry up to', i. e., he thinks it is a general expression pointing to the removal of our sins but not saying how this is done. The meaning I have taken he thinks would require ἐπὶ τῷ ξύλῳ (BS, pp. 88ff.). F. W. Beare, however, sees it as an 'erroneous supposition' that ἐπί with accusative means 'up to' but not 'upon'. He says, 'In fact, the accusative at this period is invading the territory of the other cases and is well on the way to the victory which it has won in modern Greek and ἐπί with the accusative frequently does mean "upon".' He sees the meaning here as

means that Jesus in His death endured the penalty for our sins.[39] Lest there be misunderstanding he adds, 'by whose stripes ye were healed'. Because He suffered we do not suffer. Because He bore our sins we bear them no more.[40]

It should not be overlooked that this passage contains several phrases found also in Isaiah 53 ('who did no sin, neither was guile found in his mouth', 'his own self bare our sins', 'by whose stripes ye were healed', 'going astray like sheep'; cf. Is. 53:9, 12, 5, 6). Clearly the writer had long pondered this chapter and came to use its language when he wished to speak of Christ's death and its effects.[41] Like other New Testament writers he saw Jesus as the Suffering Servant.[42]

Peter also speaks of Jesus as 'the Shepherd and Bishop of your souls' (1 Pet. 2:25). This figure reminds us of the good Shepherd who lays down His life for the sheep of whom we read in John 10, and there can be little doubt, in view of the immediately preceding reference to the cross, that it is something like this that Peter has in mind. He remembers that men, left to themselves, are rather like sheep. They are utterly unable to fend for themselves or find the right way. But they are not left to themselves. The Shepherd

---

'bear the consequences', and comments, 'The idea of expiation is not directly brought out, but it certainly underlies the whole passage' (*in loc.*).

[39] Cf. C. E. B. Cranfield, 'The bearing of our sins means suffering the punishment of them in our place (cf. Num. 14:33). On the cross He bore not merely physical pain and sorrow that men could be so blind and wicked, but, what was much more dreadful, that separation from His Father ("My God, my God, why hast thou forsaken me?") that was the due reward of our sins' (*in loc.*).

[40] Cf. J. Rivière, 'Christ underwent on the cross the penalty of our sins in order to cure us of them. We have here the same penal substitution which we noticed in St. Paul, though here it is without the legal form which it had there' (*The Doctrine of the Atonement*, London, 1909, p. 73).

[41] L. L. Carpenter concludes his survey of I Peter by saying: 'a study of these passages which bear on the sufferings and death of Christ should convince any reasonable critic that the author of this epistle saw in Jesus the fulfilment of the idea of the suffering Servant, and that the character of this Isaian figure was constantly before the writer's mind. He does not use the title "Servant" in application to Jesus, but the fundamental idea carried by the title is clearly present and strongly emphasized. In fact, the Epistle testifies to the thorough working out of that analogy between the suffering Servant of Isaiah and the crucified Messiah, the frequent use of which has been noted in the Petrine speeches in Acts. There it was in the formative stage; here it is practically fullgrown' (*The Doctrine of the Servant*, Durham N. C., 1929, p. 98). Morna Hooker, who is so sceptical about references to the Servant in other parts of the New Testament, has no doubts about them here.

[42] A. F. Walls sees a similar tendency in Mark's Gospel and in the speeches of Peter in Acts. He comments, 'Other New Testament writings, of course, are indebted to Isaiah liii, but it is surely not coincidental that these writings connected with Peter's name all bear the impress of the Servant so deeply that, diverse in form as they are, it can be described as their central thought about Christ' (*Tyndale Commentary on 1 Peter*, p. 33).

seeks them out, and at cost, the cost of His own life, makes them secure. 'Bishop' or 'Overseer' carries the thought of supervision. He looks out over us and secures for us that which we could not secure for ourselves. The term is not specific, but in the context points to much the same truth as does 'Shepherd'. He cares for our souls. Therefore He takes what steps are needed to provide for them. And that meant His death.

Again, Peter tells us that 'Christ also suffered for sins once, the righteous for the unrighteous, that he might bring us to God' (1 Pet. 3:18).[43] This connection of His suffering on the one hand with sins, and on the other with bringing us to God, makes it clear that we are moving in the same thought world as when we read of the bearing of sin. The sins that kept us away from God no longer do so, thanks to that death. Christ's sufferings cancelled out our sins. The statement that 'Christ suffered in the flesh' (1 Pet. 4:1) does not explain how the sufferings availed, but it repeats the fact. It is never far from sight throughout this Epistle. It is this which makes the writer characterize himself so naturally as 'a witness of the sufferings of Christ' (1 Pet. 5:1). The sufferings are central. It is they which must be attested. It is the fact that he can perform this attestation that gives the writer his position.

The emphasis on Christ's sufferings means no demeaning of Him. There was no sin in Him (1 Pet. 2:22), so that all He bore was on account of the sin of others. Arising out of this, He is the Lord of His own, and the writer can urge his readers, 'sanctify in your hearts Christ as Lord' (1 Pet. 3:15). He does not think of Christ as defeated but as triumphant. Men rejected Him indeed (1 Pet. 2:4). But God reversed this verdict, and Peter cites several scriptural passages about stones, concentrating on the thought that the verdict of the builders may not be the correct one. God elevates to the highest place that which men in their folly condemn (1 Pet. 2:6-8). So, as Peter thinks of the death of Christ, he thinks also of His resurrection (1 Pet. 1:3; 3:21). He insists that it was God who raised Him from the dead (1 Pet. 1:21), and he adds, 'and gave him glory'. This is not an isolated thought, for the writer speaks of 'the glories that should follow' Christ's sufferings as having been a subject of prophecy (1 Pet. 1:11). Once he goes into particulars, telling us that Christ

---

[43] William Barclay points out with respect to προσάγω in this verse that the verb has two backgrounds, the Jewish reminding us of the access won to the holy place by the High Priest, and the Greek with its 'specialized meaning' which he explains thus: 'At the court of kings there was an official called the *prosagōgeus*, the *introducer*, the *giver of access,* and it was his function to decide who should be admitted to the king's presence, and who should be kept out. He, as it were, held the keys of access. That is to say, it is Jesus Christ, through what He did, who brings men into the presence of God, who gives them access to God, who opens the way to God' (*in loc.*).

'is on the right hand of God, having gone into heaven; angels and authorities and powers being made subject unto him' (1 Pet. 3:22).[44]

This is a rich and many-sided concept of the atonement. Peter is quite sure that God is in it all. There is no pardon wrung from an unwilling deity, but the working out of the grace of God in such wise that the purposes of God in salvation are fully realized. Man is purchased. He has a sacrifice offered for him; his sins are carried, and, unrighteous as he is, he sees the righteous One take his place and die for him, and for his sins. Man has a Shepherd, a Bishop of his soul, a Lord, who provides all that he needs. And the terms used indicate that He provides this by taking man's place. The word 'substitution' does not occur in the Epistle, but it is difficult to see how justice can be done to what Peter says if this concept is rejected.

3. God the Holy Spirit and Salvation

The place of the Spirit in this Epistle is not as prominent as that of the Father or the Son, but it is not overlooked. Right at the beginning Peter associates salvation with all three Persons of the Trinity, and he includes 'sanctification of the Spirit' (1 Pet. 1:2). That is to say, the process whereby the believer realizes his state of being set apart for the service of God is something that is accomplished by the Spirit.[45] The Spirit of God is also associated with believers in their sufferings. When sufferings come, Christians may be assured that 'the Spirit of glory and the Spirit of God resteth upon' them (1 Pet. 4:14). In other words, the Spirit is with men, enabling them to live out the implications of their salvation, even when this is most difficult.

When we read of them 'that preached the gospel unto you by the Holy Ghost sent forth from heaven' (1 Pet. 1:12) we are on the borders of the Spirit's activities in men and with God. The Spirit is

---

[44] Before leaving this part of our subject perhaps we should notice, if only briefly, the descent into Hades (1 Pet. 3:19f.; 4:6). This is a mysterious happening, not fully described here, and not mentioned elsewhere in the New Testament, though it secured a place in the Apostles' Creed. Three things may be said of it. In the first place, it emphasizes the completeness of our Lord's human experience. When He died, He entered the spirit world that men enter at death. Secondly, the emphasis in 1 Peter is on His preaching (the verb in the first passage is κηρύσσω, and in the second εὐαγγελίζομαι) to the spirits there, this being mentioned both times. And thirdly, in the early church the descent was linked with the thought of Christ's complete victory over all demonic forces. 'The vocabulary of violence, from robbery to earthquake, is used to express the shattering effect upon the demons of our Lord's Descent ad inferos' (H. E. W. Turner, op. cit., p. 51).

[45] Cf. A. M. Stibbs, 'This choice and purpose of God take effect through the activity of the Spirit, who deals with men in sanctification to set them apart and make them fit for this heavenly calling. The end in view is obedience' (in loc.).

active in men. The preaching of the gospel may be regarded as a human activity, but it is not a purely human activity. It is effective only when it is done 'by the Holy Ghost sent forth from heaven'.[46] And the Spirit also is involved in the content of the gospel. Part of the good news is that God sends His Spirit into the hearts of believers, giving them a strength not their own and enabling them to triumph over sin. Sometimes Peter associates the Spirit with the Son in the work of salvation. Thus 'the Spirit of Christ' testified long before of the sufferings of Christ (1 Pet. 1:11). Again, Christ was 'put to death in the flesh, but quickened in the spirit' (1 Pet. 3:18). It is not clear whether this refers to the human spirit of Jesus, or to the Holy Spirit. If the latter,[47] we have a further close link of the Spirit with Christ in the work of saving men.

4. The Human Response

Peter does not think of the fruits of Christ's atonement as coming to all men or to any automatically. The way is open wide, but if men would enter into salvation they must make the response. Peter has a good deal to say about this, and we may well consider his contribution to our understanding of it under three main headings.

(a) *Faith*. Men may be said to believe on Jesus Christ (1 Pet. 1:8; 2:6f.). Or Peter may say that God raised Christ 'so that your faith and hope might be in God' (1 Pet. 1:21). But probably we should see no great difference between believing on Christ or on God, for again he speaks of the redeemed as those 'who through him (i. e., Christ) are believers in God' (1 Pet. 1:21).[48] And if faith in this way is associated with the beginning of the Christian experience, it is also linked with its continuance. Christians may be described in regard to their believing, with the converse that others disbelieve (1 Pet. 2:7). Christians are exhorted to withstand the devil 'stedfast in your faith' (1 Pet. 5:9). They, 'by the power of God are guarded through faith' (1 Pet. 1:5), so that their power to continue as Christians throughout this life depends not on their own spiritual power, nor on their knowledge or strength or attainment, but on their faith, i. e., on their reliance on God. 'The end (i. e., "that at which it is aimed", τέλος) of your faith' Peter

---

[46] On the words 'which things angels desire to look into' in this verse William Barclay comments, 'There is no excuse for triviality in preaching. There is no excuse for an earthbound and unlovely message without interest and without thrill. The salvation of God is such a tremendous thing that even the angels long to see it' (*in loc.*).

[47] So apparently, Moffatt. Most students, however, see 'spirit' as the counterpart to 'flesh', and thus as referring to Christ's own spirit.

[48] 'Faith in Christ (v. 8) is also faith in God, who gave Christ glory, whose mercy is the ultimate source of the resurrection, the regeneration, and the gospel generally' (Bigg, *in loc.*).

explains as 'the salvation of your souls' (1 Pet. 1:9). This means that he sees faith as concerned, not with unimportant side-issues, but with man's fundamental destiny. Small wonder, then, that with all these functions in mind, Peter should speak of 'the proof of your faith' as being 'more precious than gold that perisheth' (1 Pet. 1:7). Faith will be tried and tested by the difficulties of life (and for Peter's readers these were many and sore). But Peter thinks it is abundantly worth it all.

Faith, then, occupies a large place in the thought of the writer.[49] This points to the fundamental necessity for the atonement, for faith essentially means a relying on another and not on oneself. Because Christ died, the way of salvation is open wide. And the means whereby a man enters is faith. Peter's continual stress on faith indicates something of the importance he attached to making this response.

(b) *Godly Living.* Our response is not to be one simply of reliance on God (though Peter never hints that anything more is necessary for appropriating the salvation offered by Christ). Genuine faith has important consequences for living and our Epistle does not overlook them. We see this note right at the beginning when 'obedience' is coupled with 'sprinkling of the blood of Jesus Christ' in the opening greeting (1 Pet. 1:2). Men are elect not only to receive salvation through Christ's blood, but also to serve. Obedience is not an optional extra, added to Christianity for those who wish to go into things somewhat more deeply. It is of the very essence of being a Christian. Christians are God's elect for the purpose of obedience. They are 'children of obedience' (1 Pet. 1:14), i. e., obedience to God is their basic characteristic and not merely some passing aspect of their experience.[50] Peter can even say that his readers have purified their souls in their 'obedience to the truth' (1 Pet. 1:22).

Perhaps this is the place where we should notice the connection between baptism and salvation (1 Pet. 3:21). The exact meaning of this passage is not certain. It is usually understood in some such fashion as in Moffatt's translation, 'Baptism, the counterpart of that, saves you today . . . .' Selwyn paraphrases, 'And water now saves you too, who are the antitype of Noah and his company, namely the water of baptism . . . .' Whichever way it be taken, the following 'not the putting away of the filth of the flesh, but the

---

[49] In view of this list of passages, I simply do not understand Vincent Taylor when he says, 'Perhaps the most important element wanting in 1 Peter is teaching about faith in relation to Christ as Redeemer and Saviour. The one reference to faith is in i.21' (ANT, p. 33). Faith is mentioned quite often, considering the shortness of the writing. And it is specifically linked with Jesus in passages referring to salvation (1 Pet. 1:8f., 2:6f.).

[50] The Semitism, to be a 'son of' some quality, means to be characterized by that quality.

interrogation of a good conscience toward God' shows that Peter is not suggesting that men are saved by the due performance of an outward rite. Baptism is eloquent of the divine provision for salvation. Peter is sure of that. And baptism speaks, too, of the necessity for a proper human response.[51]

The transformation of the character of believers is related to their connection with God. They are to be holy men in all their manner of living, not because this is the prescription of some abstract code of rules, but because the God who called them is holy. Peter quotes from scripture to prove his point (1 Pet. 1:15f.). He wants his readers to 'arm [themselves] with the same mind' as Jesus, so that they 'no longer should live the rest of [their] time in the flesh to the lusts of men, but to the will of God' (1 Pet. 4:1f.). Their whole manner of life is dictated by the fact that they have been saved by a holy God through the sufferings in the flesh of their crucified Saviour. Sometimes details are brought out as in the exhortations to compassion, love, tenderness, humility (1 Pet. 3:8). More commonly there is a reference to a 'good manner of life' (v. 16; cf. also 2:2). Negatively, they are 'to abstain from fleshly lusts, which war against the soul' (1 Pet. 2:11). The object of this is the glory of God. The abstaining from lusts is in order that the Gentiles, though they criticize the Christians, yet 'may by your good works, which they behold, glorify God in the day of visitation' (1 Pet. 2:12). A Christian is to perform his various duties 'that in all things God may be glorified'. Even if he suffers he is not to be ashamed, 'but let him glorify God in this name' (1 Pet. 4:11, 16). The same kind of thing is in mind when wives are counselled so to behave that their husbands may be won (1 Pet. 3:1). The people of God should further the purposes of God by showing in their lives what manner of Being God is.

(c) *Suffering.* Throughout the Epistle it is accepted that Christians must suffer. That is one of the consequences of their faith in Christ. They are 'called' to it (1 Pet. 2:21). It is not 'a strange thing' that has happened to them (1 Pet. 4:12). There is an air of inevitability, a readiness to accept suffering as a part of life, in this Epistle, which is not characteristic of our age, and which accordingly we must make a special effort to appreciate.

---

[51] Cf. A. M. Stibbs, 'Just as the flood spoke of a judgment, which those in the ark were both saved from, and saved by, in order to enjoy a new world, so the water of Christian baptism speaks of the death which fell upon Christ, a death due to sinners, which believers into Christ are both saved from, and saved by, and through which they enter into the enjoyment of new life before God' (*in loc.*). He adds that Peter's following statements 'make unmistakably plain that it is not mere participation in the outward form of baptism that saves. It is only Christ who can save through His death and resurrection, not the baptismal water and its administration.'

But Peter does not view suffering with gloom and dismay. He says, 'ye greatly rejoice, though now . . . ye have been put to grief in manifold trials' (1 Pet. 1:6, mg.). He goes on to refer to gold as being 'proved by fire', which indicates that the suffering in which his readers are invited to rejoice is more than some mild discomfort. It is a blessed thing to suffer 'for righteousness' sake' (1 Pet. 3:14). This brings us to another point in Peter's treatment of the subject, namely that believers must give no justification for their ill-treatment. They must not render 'evil for evil, or reviling for reviling' (1 Pet. 3:9), an injunction which incidentally shows that 'evil' and 'reviling' were to be expected. Again and again he speaks of 'suffering wrongfully' (1 Pet. 2:19), suffering 'as a Christian' (1 Pet. 4:16), suffering 'for well-doing' (1 Pet. 3:17), and the like. Once he goes into details, saying, 'let none of you suffer as a murderer, or a thief, or an evil-doer, or as a meddler in other men's matters' (1 Pet. 4:15). All believers, and not merely those to whom he writes, may expect to suffer, for he points out that 'the same sufferings are accomplished in your brethren who are in the world' (1 Pet. 5:9). Suffering for 'a little while' is the prelude to God's perfecting, stablishing and strengthening Peter's readers (1 Pet. 5:10). It seems as though he is saying that suffering is the necessary preliminary to our final perfection.

But for our purpose the most important part of Peter's teaching on suffering is that in which he links man's suffering with the sufferings of Christ. This he does repeatedly (1 Pet. 2:19-24; 3:17f.; 4:13). Christians must suffer 'because' Christ suffered. They are 'partakers' of His sufferings (1 Pet. 4:13).[52] They suffer as God wills (1 Pet. 3:17; 4:19). Here we have the same thought that we see in so many parts of the New Testament, that Christians are given suffering as a privilege. Christ suffered, and because He suffered they too are allowed to suffer. They enter in some way and in some measure into His sufferings. This does not mean that the sufferings of believers atone in any such way (such a thought is never even hinted at). But the atoning sufferings of Christ are such that believers are permitted to be taken up into them. It is this which causes Peter to continue in his exhortations to rejoicing in suffering. Suffering for him has been transformed because Christ suffered.

5. The Christian Salvation

Included in the Christian salvation are all manner of blessings which the bountiful hand of God showers upon His people. While Peter

---

[52] Vincent Taylor thinks that here 'the idea of being "partakers" of Christ's sufferings is not mystical, but concrete and practical: it has no analogy to the Pauline idea of dying with Christ. The readers are to be patient as He was' (ANT, p. 31).

does not dwell on these good gifts he is not unmindful of them. In his second chapter he has a notable passage on the present standing of believers; he thinks of them as 'built up a spiritual house, to be a holy priesthood, to offer up spiritual sacrifices, acceptable to God through Jesus Christ' (v. 5). They are 'an elect race, a royal priesthood, a holy nation, a people for God's own possession' (v. 9). They are 'the people of God' (v. 10). This is a notable transference to the church of concepts applied to Israel in the Old Testament. Though Peter does not speak of the new covenant brought about in Christ, this is what is implied.

The present gift of God does not exhaust the salvation that is ours. Peter speaks of 'an inheritance incorruptible, and undefiled, and that fadeth not away, reserved in heaven' (1 Pet. 1:4). Unlike the earthly Canaan (to which the word 'inheritance' is frequently applied in the Old Testament), the good gift of God to believers is secure from every manner of devastation. The way Peter puts it probably means also that all that was implied in the 'inheritance' of the men of the Old Testament is more than fulfilled in Christ.[53] The final and ultimate realization of all this is connected with the second coming. It is 'a salvation ready to be revealed in the last time' (1 Pet. 1:5). It will be 'at the revelation of Jesus Christ', or of 'his glory' (1 Pet. 1:7, 13; 4:13). This note of glory is struck elsewhere (cf. 1 Pet. 5:1, 10).

From all this it is clear that Peter has his own distinctive view of the atonement. He sees very clearly the over-all sovereignty of God and the way salvation proceeds from Him alone. It comes through the work of Christ, and this work is viewed in a variety of ways. Christ took away our sin. He effectively dealt with the barrier to fellowship with God. He did this by redeeming us, by bearing our sins in His own body, by meeting our need, Shepherd and Bishop as He is. And Peter looks to men to respond to this by their faith, and to enter into the sufferings of Christ as they serve their God. His emphasis on present suffering as a consequence of our association with the Christ who suffered is noteworthy, and, as we have seen, it is a thought found elsewhere in the New Testament. Peter is not an original thinker. We do not find daring speculation in his writing, nor profound new insights. But neither do we find a mere parrot-

---

[53] Cf. F. J. A. Hort, 'St Peter's language here then calls attention to the new life not only as full of ardent hope for the future, but as at the same time the fulfilment of ancient longings of men and ancient promises of God. This double character runs through the whole paragraph: it looks backward to the searchings of the prophets, and forward to the full unveiling of the Son of God' (*in loc.*).

like repetition of what others have said.[54] The writer sets forth in his own way what the cross has come to mean for him, and it is his own way. And as he does this we see that he stands essentially where the other New Testament writers stand.

THE SECOND EPISTLE GENERAL OF PETER

2 Peter has little to say about the atonement in set terms. Its primary interest lies elsewhere. Nevertheless its statements should not be overlooked. And they should be taken in conjunction with what is said on other matters, but which lets us see something at least of what Christ's work for men meant to this writer.

1. The Punishment of the Wicked

This Epistle is primarily concerned with a situation in which false teachers were perverting the faith, and turning men away from the right path. The writer is taken up with the enormity of such conduct, and he is unsparing in his condemnation both of these teachers and of sinners in general. He reminds his readers of the punishments that befell sinning angels, Noah's contemporaries, and the cities of the plain (2 Pet. 2:4, 5, 6). He cannot find words too strong for those who persist in the ways of sin. But those who have received the Christian salvation are delivered from all this. They have 'escaped from the corruption that is in the world by lust' (2 Pet. 1:4). They look for the second coming of Christ, and a considerable part of the Epistle is given over to a consideration of this topic, and of the condemnation reserved for them that reject it. Even this apparently solid and lasting universe is neither solid nor lasting. One day it will be destroyed.[55] It behoves us to look to real values.

2. Salvation as God's Gift

Like all the other New Testament writers, our author thinks of salvation as a gift of God. His opening greeting runs, 'Grace to you and peace be multiplied in the knowledge of God and of Jesus our Lord; seeing that his divine power hath granted unto us all things that pertain unto life and godliness' (2 Pet. 1:2f.). Here we have a conjunction of the first and second Persons of the Trinity in the work of salvation, and this salvation is definitely said to be given. It proceeds from the nature of God, who is elsewhere spoken of as

[54] 'Windisch is entirely justified in saying that the ideas remind us of St. Paul, but are none the less originally formed' (Vincent Taylor, ANT, p. 31).
[55] Cf. Vincent Taylor, 'the fact that the universe is stamped with impermanence, and must one day cease to be, is affirmed just as strongly by men of science today. For all its apparent solidity, man's present home is a dwelling which in the end must be dissolved' (ET, xlv, p. 440).

'longsuffering . . . not wishing that any should perish, but that all should come to repentance' (2 Pet. 3:9). Indeed, 'the longsuffering of our Lord is salvation' (2 Pet. 3:15). Salvation proceeds from the 'calling' or the 'election' of God (2 Pet. 1:3, 10). The initiative is His, not ours. So it is that salvation means the granting of His 'precious and exceeding great promises' (2 Pet. 1:4).[56] References to faith (2 Pet. 1:1, 5) imply the same thing. Faith means reliance on Another, and this means that that Other and not the believer is responsible for salvation.[57] The certainty that God brings men salvation means much to our author, for even when he is dealing with the punishment of evil-doers he remembers that God delivered men like Noah and Lot (2 Pet. 2:5, 7).[58] The punishment of the wicked is sure. God is not indifferent to moral values. But the primary thing is that God does deliver His people.

3. Knowledge

If there is anything distinctive about the treatment of the Christian salvation in this Epistle, it is in its stress on knowledge. Knowledge is, of course, treated in this connection elsewhere in the New Testament, but there is special emphasis placed upon it in 2 Peter. The writer opens his letter, for example, by praying that grace and peace

[56] Moffatt reminds us that 'These words played a large part in bringing John Wesley through his spiritual crisis in 1730. About five o'clock on the morning of May 24th, he opened his Bible at the words, "There are given to us exceeding great and precious promises, even that ye should be partakers of the divine nature"; that day relief came to him' (on 2 Pet. 1:2). In the interests of accuracy it should perhaps be added that John Wesley's conversion took place in 1738, not 1730.

[57] This does not mean that faith is to be equated with sloth. We must bear in mind Moffatt's warning, 'Faith here, as in ver. 1, is the personal belief which is fundamental . . . . Someone has described conventional Christian experience as "an initial spasm followed by a chronic inertia"; what our writer demands is a challenging, vital quality in faith' (on 2 Pet. 1:5).

[58] The deliverance in these verses is primarily from physical disaster, but there is an important truth about salvation in the deeper sense in the words: 'righteous Lot, sore distressed by the lascivious life of the wicked (for that righteous man . . . vexed his righteous soul from day to day with their lawless deeds).' William Barclay reminds us of Newman's saying, 'our great security against sin lies in being shocked at it.' He comments, 'There are many things at which we ought to be shocked and horror-stricken. In our own generation there is the problem of prostitution and of promiscuity, the problem of drunkenness, the extraordinary gambling fever which has the country in its grip, the breakdown of the marriage bond, the problem of violence and crime, death upon the roads, the still-existing slum conditions. And in many cases the tragedy is that these things have ceased to shock in any real sense of the term' (in loc.). We often pride ourselves on our inability to be shocked. We would be better men if our moral sense were more easily aroused.

may be multiplied to his readers 'in the knowledge of God and of Jesus our Lord', and he goes on to speak of 'the knowledge of him that called us' (2 Pet. 1:2, 3), in which place knowledge is, as Wand puts it, 'personal relation to God or Christ'.[59] Other Epistles begin with references to grace and peace, but they do not go on to stress knowledge as does this one. And we are not yet finished. Peter proceeds to tell his readers that they must add to faith virtue, and to virtue knowledge (2 Pet. 1:5).[60] This introduces a list of desirable Christian qualities, at the end of which he speaks of being 'not idle nor unfruitful unto the knowledge of our Lord Jesus Christ' (2 Pet. 1:8). He proceeds to refer to the things that his readers 'know' (2 Pet. 1:12), and to remind them that the content of the Christian message is not 'cunningly devised fables' (2 Pet. 1:16). Men who escape from 'the defilements of the world' do so 'through the knowledge of the Lord and Saviour Jesus Christ' (2 Pet. 2:20). The wicked are not only evil, they are in error (2 Pet. 3:17), while by contrast the saved may be exhorted to 'grow in the grace and knowledge of our Lord' (2 Pet. 3:18).

All this does not mean that our writer thinks of some intellectual process. He is not speaking primarily of the knowledge of propositions, but of the knowledge of a person. His thought is not dissimilar from that expressed in John 17:3, 'this is life eternal, that they should know thee the only true God, and him whom thou didst send, even Jesus Christ.' But at the same time it should be noticed that his emphasis is an abiding protest against the view that faith is an empty credulity. Faith is not a vague trust. It is trust of a known Person.

4. Jesus Christ, Both Lord and Saviour

Throughout this Epistle we are never allowed to lose sight of the greatness of Jesus Christ. Power, majesty, honour and glory are associated with Him when the voice came to Him 'from the excellent glory' (2 Pet. 1:16f.). This leads on to a mention of 'the word of prophecy made more sure', which in this context points once more to the high place of the Saviour to whom the prophecies point (notice the distinction between 'false prophets', 2:1, and 'the holy prophets', 3:2; it is not prophecy in general which is commended, but that which is of God, and this kind of prophecy bears its witness to Jesus). The high point comes right at the beginning when Peter refers to 'the righteousness of our God and Saviour Jesus Christ' (2 Pet. 1:1), where deity is ascribed to Christ.[61] He is spoken of as 'Saviour' also

[59] On 1:5.
[60] 'It is that knowledge which makes the friend as distinct from the servant, John xv.15' (Bigg, *ICC, in loc.*).
[61] J. B. Mayor thinks this possible, but inclines to a distinction between God and Christ on the grounds that they are distinguished in the next verse (*in loc.*).

in 1:11; 2:20; 3:2, 18, and in each case 'Lord' is conjoined. Nor
is the high view of Christ's person confined to the Jesus who walked
the hills of Galilee and the Lord who is now in heaven above. His
future majesty is not out of sight, and there is an important section
of the Epistle taken up with His return in glory (2 Pet. 3:1-13).
Small wonder that the writer concludes with 'To him be the glory
both now and for ever. Amen' (2 Pet. 3:18).

It is not certain whether 'the Lord' who delivers the godly (2 Pet.
2:9) is Jesus or the Father. Grammatically it should refer back to
'God' in verse 4, but 'Lord' commonly refers to Jesus in this Epistle.
Perhaps no sharp distinction is being made. Deliverance is of divine
origin and that is the important thing. There is no doubt, though,
about 'the Master that bought them' (2 Pet. 2:1), nor that the buying
refers to His dying for them on the cross.[62] Here, as elsewhere,
the death of Jesus is regarded as effecting the salvation of men, as
bringing them out of their slavery to sin[63] and making them all His
own.

5. Partakers of the Divine Nature

In a very important passage this writer speaks of our becoming 'partakers of the divine nature' (2 Pet. 1:4). The exact expression is
found nowhere else in the New Testament.[64] But the reality it
describes is surely that of being 'born again' or 'born from above' in
John 3.[65] Peter is thinking of such a divine work in believers that
they are completely transformed by the power of God. This is sometimes spoken of in terms of the Spirit's indwelling. Clearly it is not
a thing that man can encompass. It occurs because of what God
does.

Salvation may also be spoken of in terms of 'cleansing from his old
sins' (2 Pet. 1:9), or of 'entrance into the eternal kingdom of our

---

[62] Moffatt renders, 'the Lord who ransomed them'; Wand is reminded
of Mk. 10:45 and 1 Pet. 1:18.

[63] Cf. E. M. B. Green, 'In 2 Peter, where his recipients needed neither assurance nor comfort, the cross is implicit, but it remains as the basis for
his denunciation of antinomianism; to go on in sin is to forget the cleansing
once received, and to deny the Lord who bought them' (2 Peter Reconsidered,
London, 1961, p. 17).

[64] But if the idea is rare in the New Testament it is far from being
so in the theology of the early church. H. E. W. Turner sees in this
passage 'what is really the proof-text of the whole tradition' specially characteristic of the Eastern church that Christ's work was one of deification of the
believer (op. cit., p. 70). Turner sees two groups of views: 'The former
sees in the Redemption brought through the Logos the endowment of
humanity with the metaphysical fulness of the Being of God, while the latter
describes the goal of Redemption as Deification brought about by the close
association with the Deifying Logos through His Humanity' (op. cit., p. 71).

[65] Bigg thinks it 'means very much the same as St. Paul's κοινωνία Πνεύματος,
2 Cor. xiii.14; Phil. ii.1' (in loc.).

Lord and Saviour Jesus Christ' (2 Pet. 1:11). Christianity is 'the way of the truth' (2 Pet. 2:2), or 'the way of righteousness' (2 Pet. 2:21), and in accordance with this Christians are men who are 'established in the truth' (2 Pet. 1:12). All this points to a transformation. The saving work of God in Christ is such that believers are new men. The divine power is at work within them.

Here again is the conviction that in Christ a new thing has been done. Nobody would accuse this writer of simply repeating the generality of New Testament teaching. But he is saying in his own way, as the others are in theirs, that salvation is important, that it is something wrought by God and not man, that Christ's action is essential. He also points to the response that is required. Men do not drift into salvation. They must enter in, and then, in the power of God, resist the temptations that will come, including and especially the temptation to backslide. But his emphasis on human responsibility should not be allowed to obscure his fundamental dependence on God.

THE GENERAL EPISTLE OF JUDE

This writing is a two-fold message addressed to Christian people. Basically it is a warning against slipping into the errors of certain evil-doers (who are castigated in no uncertain terms). Coupled with this is an exhortation to keep a firm hold on the great verities of the Christian faith. As in the case of 2 Peter, the bulk of the Epistle is concentrated on a forthright condemnation of the sinners the writer is opposing. He condemns them as deficient both in understanding and in moral attainment. With his burning words before them, Christians could never overlook the intense seriousness of sin. Jude speaks of even angels as being 'kept in everlasting bonds under darkness unto the judgement of the great day' (Jude 6). He refers to 'the punishment of eternal fire' (Jude 7). He tells of men 'for whom the blackness of darkness hath been reserved for ever' (Jude 13). He looks for the coming of the Lord 'with ten thousands of his holy ones, to execute judgement upon all' (Jude 14f.).[66]

But if he is sure of the certain and sore punishment of evil, he is equally sure of the deliverance that has been wrought by God in Christ. He addresses his Epistle to 'them that are called, beloved in God the Father, and kept for Jesus Christ' (Jude 1). He writes of

---

[66] Vincent Taylor draws attention to the doxology in verses 24f. and proceeds, 'In the light of the robust religion revealed by these words there is need for consideration whether our modern revolt against the denunciatory note in Jude and 2 Peter may not be due, not merely to the spirit of tolerance, but to a feebler sense of sin and of its baleful effects in the lives of men' (loc. cit.).

qualities like mercy, peace, love, and grace in God (Jude 2, 4).
He writes of 'our common salvation' (Jude 3), and, though some have
understood 'the faith which was once for all delivered unto the saints'
(Jude 3) as a body of doctrines, it is Jude's idea that this faith tells of
the salvation to which he has just referred. The gospel is something
divine in origin, and now committed to God's people. It is this
which is doubtless in mind when he speaks of 'looking for the mercy
of our Lord Jesus Christ unto eternal life' (Jude 21).[67]   There is
no mention here of the cross, but who can doubt that that is what is
primarily in mind when an early Christian writes of Christ's mercy
as leading to eternal life? That he does not speak more explicitly
is probably to be explained in terms of the body of Christian teaching that writer and reader alike assumed. That this is considerable
may be seen from the reflection of Windisch, cited by Wand, 'we
are given there a short description of the Christian life comprising
a tetrad — faith, prayer, love, and hope — and a triad — Spirit, God,
and Christ.'[68]   And, as the magnificent doxology which closes
the Epistle makes so abundantly clear, Jude puts his trust firmly in
God.

THE FIRST EPISTLE GENERAL OF JOHN

By and large the Epistles of John present us with the same view of
the atonement as does the Fourth Gospel. The same language often
occurs in both. The same kind of thinking finds expression in both.
The same essential approach to life in general and Christian life in
particular lies behind both. We are not moving here in a different
world from that of the Gospel, nor do we expect to find radically new
thoughts enunciated. Yet the Epistles make their own contribution.
Some ideas of the Gospel are put more forcibly and more fully here.
We cannot simply assume that the Gospel covers all that the Epistles
say. There may be no radically new doctrines, but there are new
emphases.

LIFE

One of John's major interests is life, and this comes out in the
Epistle as it did in the Gospel. Indeed John says expressly that his
purpose in writing was that his readers might gain the assurance
that they have eternal life (1 Jn. 5:13). But life for him is no abstract conception, nor is it a natural possession. It is a divine gift

---

[67] Cf. Richard Wolff, 'The expression, "the mercy of our Lord Jesus
Christ unto eternal life," may be somewhat unusual, but the thought is clear:
at that day the mercy of Christ will give eternal life unto His own . . . .
Once the Father had accepted the substitutionary sacrifice of Christ, eternal
life follows as a logical consequence' (in loc.).

[68] In loc.

mediated to us through what Christ has done. John loses no time in bringing before us both life and its connection with Jesus, for in his very first verse he refers to 'the Word of life' (1 Jn. 1:1). Whether this be taken as a description of Christ Himself,[69] or, as seems more probable, of the gospel message (as in Phil. 2:16; cf. Jn. 6:68),[70] the life is intimately bound up with Christ and His work for men. John goes on to say, 'and the life was manifested, and we have seen . . .' which associates life with Christ much in the manner of John 14:6. To see Christ is to see life. Then John tells us what he is about, and we find that it concerns life. He is declaring to his readers 'the life, the eternal life' (1 Jn. 1:2). 'Eternal life', as in the Gospel, is life that is proper to the age to come.[71] But this quality of life is God's gift to believers here and now (1 Jn. 2:25; 5:11). It is a life which, though God's gift and thus not earned by human desert, is incompatible with certain human attitudes. Thus 'no murderer hath eternal life abiding in him' (1 Jn. 3:15), while 'the vainglory of life' (1 Jn. 2:16) clearly excludes all real life. The life of which John writes is 'in' God's Son, so that 'He that hath the Son hath the life; he that hath not the Son of God hath not the life' (1 Jn. 5:11f.; cf. 5:20). It is as simple as that. The purpose of God's sending His Son was 'that we might live through him' (1 Jn. 4:9). This was a costly business for the Son, for it meant that He must lay down His life for us (1 Jn. 3:16). Life, in other words, is purchased by sacrificial love. And life so bought will inevitably manifest sacrificial love. Those who have it must be ready to lay down their lives for others (1 Jn. 3:16). Indeed, love for others is the evidence that they do in fact have this life (1 Jn. 3:14).[72] Life and love are inseparable.

Or John may use other ways of showing what life is and how it comes to men. Sometimes he thinks of life as the result of God's 'begetting' of believers. This, too, is connected with love, for 'every one that loveth is begotten of God' (1 Jn. 4:7). And it is connected

[69] So Ross, for example, 'The One who was thus manifested in the reality and fullness of human nature is the Word of Life, the Logos of life' (in loc.).

[70] So Westcott, 'the word of life is the whole message from God to man, which tells of life, or, perhaps, out of which life springs', or Dodd, 'It would be in accord with Johannine ideas to understand "the word of life" in our present passage as the life-giving Word of God which came to men through Christ and is embodied in the Gospel' (in loc.).

[71] See above, p. 165.

[72] Cf. A. Plummer, 'The natural state of man is selfishness, which involves enmity to others, whose claims clash with those of self: to love others is proof that this natural state has been abandoned. Life and love in the moral world correspond to life and growth in the physical: in each case the two are but different aspects of the same fact. The one marks the state, the other the activity' (in loc.).

with faith, 'Whosoever believeth that Jesus is the Christ is begotten of God' (1 Jn. 5:1). Again, John is concerned with the effects of this life in the Christian. The man who is begotten of God lives victoriously. He overcomes the world (1 Jn. 5:4). The Evil One has no power over him (1 Jn. 5:18). He does not give way to sin (1 Jn. 3:9; 5:18). Positively, he does righteousness (1 Jn. 2:29). He and his ilk may be termed 'children of God' (1 Jn. 3:1, 10).

The coming of Christ, then, has released forces which are of the utmost importance for men. Those who have the benefit of Christ's work within them have been absolutely transformed. They are living on a new and higher level. They are not shackled by sin and hate and evil as are other men. Their lives are lived in the divine strength; they share the life of God. In particular they come to know what love is, and to this we now turn.

LOVE

Twice John tells us that 'God is love' (1 Jn. 4:8, 16), while to abide in love is to abide in God (1 Jn. 4:16). This must surely be our starting point. Repeatedly John tells us that we know love only through the cross.[73] 'Hereby know we love, because he laid down his life for us' (1 Jn. 3:16). 'Herein was the love of God manifested in us, that God hath sent his only begotten Son . . .' (1 Jn. 4:9). 'Herein is love, not that we loved God, but that he loved us, and sent his Son to to be the propitiation for our sins' (1 Jn. 4:10). It is well to note this emphasis, for in modern times men often speak as though love were obvious, and as though love were everything. We still need B. B. Warfield's reminder: 'God *is* Love! But it does not in the least follow that He is nothing but love. God *is* Love: but Love is not God and the formula "Love" must therefore ever be inadequate to express God.'[74] It is important to be clear that the love of which John writes is not something that we know naturally. John is not speaking of some universal human quality, or even the object of common human knowledge. He is not talking about a characteristic human attitude. He is talking about something radically new. We know love in the Christian sense only because God sent His Son to die for sinful men.[75] It is the cross,

---

[73] P. T. Forsyth puts emphasis on the significance of this: 'The great Word of the Gospel is not God is love. That is too stationary, too little energetic. It produces a religion unable to cope with crises. But the Word is this — Love is omnipotent for ever because it is holy' (JG, p. 227).

[74] *The Person and Work of Christ*, Philadelphia, 1950, p. 384.

[75] Cf. James Denney, 'God is love, say those of whom we have been speaking, and therefore He dispenses with propitiation; God is love, say the apostles, for He provides a propitiation' (ST, p. 131). He later says forthrightly, 'That God is love is in the New Testament a conclusion from the fact that He has provided in Christ and in His death a propitiation for sins;

nothing less that shows us what love is. This has been argued powerfully by Anders Nygren in his great book, *Agape and Eros*. He reminds us that the Christians, when they wanted to speak about love, passed by the usual Greek words like *eros,* and instead used *agape,* a word for which we search in vain in the classical Greek writings! They used a new term because they had a new idea to convey, the idea that we know love only through the cross whereon Christ died for sinners. Nygren appears to be out of favour in some quarters just now,[76] and it is not unlikely that some modifications of his views ought to be made. He is too sweeping in his antithesis. *Agape* and *eros* are not as mutually exclusive as he would have us think.[77] And there is more to love than these two words convey.[78] But I believe that his basic contention is sound. John (as for that matter the other New Testament writers also) is not putting forth commonplaces. He is speaking of love as an attitude that is not natural to men. Love as men understand it is usually of the nature of *eros.*[79] It has two outstanding characteristics. It is a love of the worthy

---

but for this, the apostles would never have known that God is love; apart from this, they could never have found meaning for the phrase, God is love. The whole proof, the whole meaning, contents, substance, and spirit of that expression, are contained in propitiation, and in nothing else. What, then, are we to say of those who appeal to love against propitiation, and argue that because God is love the very thought of propitiation is an insult to him? We can say this, at least, that they have fundamentally misunderstood the New Testament. We can deny their right to use apostolic language, like "God is love," after carefully emptying it of apostolic meaning' (*op. cit.,* p. 132).

[76] See the important discussions by J. A. T. Robinson, in *Theology,* xlviii, pp. 98-104; R. Niebuhr, *The Nature and Destiny of Man,* ii, London, 1944, ch. 3; cf. also G. V. Jones, ET, lxvi, p. 3; W. Lillie, SJT, xii, pp. 233, 242; M. C. D'Arcy, *The Mind and Heart of Love,* London, 1945, pp. 100, 329, etc.

[77] Cf. T. Boman, 'Nygren maintains that Agapé is the free and unmerited love that comes from God and flows toward man; Eros, he says, is the love that stems from man and strives toward God. That may be quite correct, even though Nygren presents his interpretation too schematically.' He proceeds to cite Hans Ording that Eros and Agapé 'both represent quite heterodox complexes in which Agapé is the divine factor and Eros the human factor in relation to God' (*Hebrew Thought compared with Greek,* London, 1960, pp. 18f.).

[78] Thus J. Burnaby stresses the importance of *Philia,* which 'differs both from Eros and from Agape in being a mutual relation, a bond which links two centres of consciousness in one' (*Amor Dei,* London, 1938, p. 18). C. S. Lewis distinguishes four types of love, which he calls affection, friendship, eros and charity (*The Four Loves,* London, 1960). His discussion leaves no doubt as to the complexity of the reality we sum up with the word 'love'.

[79] Allan Barr reminds us that 'the use of the word "love", however, may trap the unwary reader into making false connexions with romantic ideas of love, with in fact the modern version of the pagan Eros to which the Christian Agape stood in such contrast for the original readers' (SJT, iii, p. 418).

or at least of that which men think worthy, and it is a love which includes the desire to possess. The love that we see in the cross differs in both respects. It is a love of those whom God knows to be unworthy, and it is a love which seeks not so much to possess as to give. It is a love that proceeds from the essential nature of God, not from something of value in men which attracts Him.

God's love gives. 'Behold what manner of love the Father hath bestowed upon us, that we should be called children of God' (1 Jn. 3:1). It is of the nature of this kind of love that it seeks to give, not to get.

Now love as John understands it is a creative thing. 'We love, because he first loved us' (1 Jn. 4:19). 'Love is of God' (1 Jn. 4:7). That is to say, love in God can produce an answering love in man. Indeed, in very bold language John repeatedly speaks of God's love as being 'perfected' in us when we manifest the quality of Christian love (1 Jn. 2:5; 4:12, 16f.; the first passage speaks of keeping God's word, but this certainly includes the command to love). Love is the evidence that God is abiding in us. Nobody has ever seen God, but when brethren love one another we see the evidence that God lives within them (1 Jn. 4:12). Contrariwise, if a man does not manifest the fruits of love, that is evidence that the love of God does not abide in him (1 Jn. 3:17;[80] notice the implication that the love of God may be expected to 'abide'; it is no transient phenomenon). There are continual commands to love one another (1 Jn. 3:11, 23; 4:7, 11). Such love is the evidence of life (1 Jn. 3:14). And if John connects love with life he connects it also with light, for to have such love is to abide in the light (1 Jn. 2:10), while contrariwise to be without it is to be one of 'the children of the devil' (1 Jn. 3:10).

As these passages show, the love of God and the love of the brethren cannot be kept distinct. This point is important and it is repeated. To love 'the children of God' is to love God (1 Jn. 5:2). And love is practical. It is not a matter of what men say, but of what they do (1 Jn. 3:17f.). Those who have been died for must be ready to die for others (1 Jn. 3:16). It is of no use then for a man to claim that he loves God if he does not love his brother. He is a liar. The thing is impossible. Unless he loves his brother he has no real love for God at all (1 Jn. 4:20f.). Sometimes, in our modern dislike of legalism, we put the keeping of commandments

[80] In this verse 'the love of God' certainly includes the thought of love toward God. But I take it to include also the idea of God's love to us as kindling that love to him. Cf. Westcott, 'It appears therefore most probable that the fundamental idea of "the love of God" in St John is "the love which God has made known, and which answers to His nature" . . . . the essential conception that it is a love divine in its origin and character is not lost' (on 1 Jn. 2:5).

as the antithesis of love, but not our writer. He stoutly urges that 'this is the love of God, that we keep his commandments' (1 Jn. 5:3; cf. also v. 2), and he expressly records that God commands that we love our brethren (1 Jn. 4:21). He leaves us in no doubt as to the important place love occupies in the Christian scheme of things. And just as hatred of the brother is incompatible with the love of God, so is the love of the world incompatible with it (1 Jn. 2:15). The 'world' in this Epistle stands for the whole system of earthly life considered as opposed to the things of God. It is that 'worldliness' which finds no place for God. It is concern for the ephemeral at the expense of the eternal.

John thinks of the atonement, then, as something that springs from the divine love. It is the expression of the fact that God loves us.[81] And it reproduces itself in those in whom the atonement has become effectual. They show forth the love of their fellowmen which is the love of God within them.

LIGHT

Just as with love, so with light John begins with the divine. He is not engaging in pious speculation, but proceeding from what God has revealed Himself to be. If it is true that God is love, it is also true that 'God is light, and in him is no darkness at all' (1 Jn. 1:5). And John gives us this, not as his own contribution to theological thought, but as 'the message which we have heard from him'. Since God is light it is obvious that His worshippers must have regard for light. They are not to 'walk in darkness' but 'in the light' (1 Jn. 1:6f.). It is all too possible for men to 'walk in darkness', and John emphasizes that this is what they do when they hate their brothers. When a man does this his plight is serious, indeed, for 'darkness hath blinded his eyes' (1 Jn. 2:9, 11). And it is all so pointless. There is no need for him to walk so, for 'the darkness is passing away, and the true light already shineth' (1 Jn. 2:8). When God replaces darkness with light it is the height of folly to prefer darkness.

KNOWLEDGE

John has a good deal to say about knowledge,[82] and it is clear that he is interested, not in speculation about religious affairs, but in

---

[81] Lesslie Newbigin reminds us of the important truth that, 'the love of God can only be revealed by an act. Words alone cannot reveal love. Even if God were to write the words "God is Love" in letters of fire in the clouds, it would not tell us anything. Love must be expressed in deeds' (*op. cit.,* p. 71).

[82] H. E. W. Turner finds this strand of teaching especially congenial to the Apostolic Fathers: 'The interpretation of the Redemption which Christ brought primarily in terms of knowledge, and of Christ first and foremost a Teacher, is especially characteristic of the Apostolic Fathers' (*op. cit.,* p. 33).

certainty. It appears that he was opposed by teachers who stressed
knowledge, and it is likely that they espoused a system of a kind
that was ultimately to lead to the Gnosticism that we see in the
second century. Such teachers claimed full and secret knowledge,
but John does not yield an inch. He points out not only that we
know God, but that we know that we know Him, and the evidence
is not found in some esoteric formula, but in the fact that we keep His
commandments (1 Jn. 2:3; cf. 2:5f.). There is an ethical basis to
right religious knowledge, and John is the most practical of writers.
If a man does not keep God's commandments it does not matter
what he says. He does not know God (1 Jn. 2:4). Our knowledge of God rests on the incarnation. 'We know that the Son of
God is come, and hath given us an understanding, that we know
him that is true' (1 Jn. 5:20; cf. also 4:2, 6). John also speaks
of certain pieces of knowledge that we have about Him. We know
'that he was manifested to take away sins' (1 Jn. 3:5); that 'he is
righteous' (1 Jn. 2:29); that 'he abideth in us' (1 Jn. 3:24); that
'he heareth us whatsoever we ask' (1 Jn. 5:15). It is clear that
knowledge of and about God matters intensely. And it is clear
that it all stems from what God has done in Christ.[83]

Thus the purpose of the Epistle can be given in terms of knowledge. It is written not that 'ye may have life' (as the Gospel was;
see Jn. 20:31), but 'that ye may know that ye have eternal life'
(1 Jn. 5:13). This carries with it certain corollaries. We who have
this knowledge turn out to have quite a lot of knowledge. We
know the truth (1 Jn. 2:21); we know that 'we abide in him,
and he in us, because he hath given us of his Spirit' (1 Jn. 4:13);
we know 'that we have passed out of death into life' (1 Jn. 3:14);
we know the imperative need for doing righteousness (1 Jn. 2:29);
we know that when the Lord returns 'we shall be like him; for we
shall see him even as he is' (1 Jn. 3:2).

From all this it is plain enough that John was not going to allow
those who claimed superior enlightenment to get away with their
claim. He knew with an unshakable certainty that God had sent
forth His Son, and that knowledge derived from that source was im-
peccable. Thus the note of certainty underlies everything that he
writes. He wants his readers to see that what God has done
for men does not issue merely in wishes and doubts, in uncertain
hopes and fears. It gives them certainty. So he speaks of setting
our hope on God (1 Jn. 3:3). He says we 'shall assure our heart

---

[83] This is important. It is not knowledge as such, but the knowledge of
God and of God's saving act that counts. Cf. Lesslie Newbigin, 'Sin . . .
is not an illusion which can be dispelled simply by knowledge of the truth.
It is a terrible reality which could only be overcome by mighty acts of God'
(op. cit., p. 43).

before him' (1 Jn. 3:19). If it should be that we are timid and our heart condemn us, 'God is greater than our heart, and knoweth all things.' Clearly he looks to men to go on to the place where 'our heart condemn us not' and we have 'boldness toward God' (1 Jn. 3:19-21). This is not a temporary phenomenon, but John looks to the perfecting of the love of God within us 'that we may have boldness in the day of judgement', and he goes on to point out that 'perfect love casteth out fear' (1 Jn. 4:17f.). It is a far-reaching salvation of which he writes.

SIN

John gives us something in the nature of a definition of sin when he says 'Every one that doeth sin doeth also lawlessness: and sin is lawlessness' (1 Jn. 3:4). Similarly, 'All unrighteousness is sin' (1 Jn. 5:17). Curiously, of the first passage Dodd says John's 'maxim *Sin is lawlessness,* if considered as a general definition of sin, must be considered somewhat superficial'.[84] Surely the truth is the very opposite. John is saying that sin is a denial of the fundamental law of man's being. It is the assertion of the self against the law of God. It is the refusal of the creature to submit to the Creator.[85] As Westcott puts it, 'Sin is not an arbitrary conception. It is the assertion of the selfish will against a paramount authority. He who sins breaks not only by accident or in an isolated detail, but essentially the "law" which he was created to fulfil'.[86] There is nothing superficial about such a conception.

John's doctrine of sin must also be seen against the background of his doctrine of God as love. The self asserts itself not against some abstract law but against the law of that God who is love, who has given His Son for men, who yearns over men and in love makes provision for their deepest need. And because it is of the essence of God's nature to give Himself in holy love, sin becomes that heinous thing, the sin against love. As R. S. Franks puts it, sin 'is the rejection of the Divine Love, alike as a standard of conduct and in its transforming power. There is no need to aggravate the weight of sin by bringing in any other extraneous

---

[84] *In loc.* He contrasts this with Paul's treatment of the theme in Romans.

[85] It is 'the assertion of the individual will against and in defiance of the law of God, the refusal to live in accordance with the revealed standards of right and wrong' (*The New Bible Commentary,* ed. F. Davidson, A. M. Stibbs, E. F. Kevan, London, 1953, *in loc.*). Cf. also H. L. Goudge, 'It is personal opposition to God Himself, an injury done to Him . . . . As the prophet says, two cannot walk together unless they are agreed; and since our wills are now opposed to God's we cannot walk with Him' (*Sin and Redemption,* London, 1919, p. 28).

[86] *In loc.*

considerations. Sin is only truly measured by the love which it rejects and refuses. It is failure to trust and obey God.'[87]

John also associates sin with the Evil One. As it is a denial of God it is not surprising that he can write 'he that doeth sin is of the devil' (1 Jn. 3:8). Sin puts him in the camp of the enemy. The love of the world is incompatible with 'the love of the Father' (1 Jn. 2:15), which means much the same thing. This comes out also in John's references to 'the liar' who is equated with anti-christ (1 Jn. 2:22), or to the liar who claims to love his brother and does not love God (1 Jn. 4:20), or to the liar who says he knows God but who does not keep His commandments (1 Jn. 2:4). Lying and wholehearted service of God are mutually exclusive. To be a liar is to range oneself against God. A couple of sayings in this group are not immediately obvious, but they are profoundly important. 'If we say that we have not sinned, we make him a liar' (1 Jn. 1:10); 'he that believeth not God hath made him a liar' (1 Jn. 5:10). The point of these two sayings is that all God's dealings with man presuppose that man is a sinner. That is why God sent His servants the prophets, and why last of all He sent His Son to be man's Saviour. If man is not a sinner, then all this is false. So is God's demand for faith. That demand is justified only if the atonement wrought by Christ is truly the way of salvation. If men are able to earn their own salvation, if they need not to come relying on the way of faith, then what God has said is false. Clearly John thinks of sin as terribly serious, and of all men as involved in it.

We might deduce this latter point also from the positive righteousness John demands. The whole point of his writing is 'that ye may not sin' (1 Jn. 2:1). And he has his well-known sayings about not sinning: 'Whosoever abideth in him sinneth not'; 'Whosoever is begotten of God doeth no sin . . . and he cannot sin, because he is begotten of God'; 'whosoever is begotten of God sinneth not' (1 Jn. 3:6, 9; 5:18). These are strong expressions and they should not be watered down. John is asserting that those who are in Christ have no truck with sin.[88] At the same time it should be borne in mind that the use of the present tense indicates the continuing attitude and not the occasional act.[89] 'Sin is not in the believer the

---

[87] *The Atonement*, London, 1934, p. 152.

[88] E. Haupt protests strongly against minimizing interpretations. He gives the meaning in these words, 'The present does not express precisely the actual now, but a continuing condition: in him in whom the μένειν has become a reality, for μένειν carries with it the idea of abiding continuously. In him there is the abiding condition of the οὐχ ἁμαρτάνειν' (*Commentary* on 1 Jn. 3:6).

[89] It 'describes a character, "a prevailing habit" and not primarily an act' (Westcott, on 3:6).

ruling principle, as it is in the case of the defiant, persistent sinner.'[90] John stresses the importance of keeping God's commandments (1 Jn. 2:3f., 7f.; 3:22-24; 4:21; 5:2f.). He leaves us in no doubt that there are big issues involved in living out our lives, or that the manner of our living shows whose we are and whom we serve.[91]

THE DEATH OF CHRIST

The death of Christ has a revelatory function. 'Hereby know we love, because he laid down his life for us'; 'Herein is love, not that we loved God, but that he loved us, and sent his Son to be the propitiation for our sins' (1 Jn. 3:16; 4:10). We will never understand the love of God if we start from man. Love, *Agape,* is not of human origin. If we start from man we will inevitably end up with some variety of *eros*. But the cross, whereon the Son of God suffered for sinful men, shows us what love really is. The death of Christ has a revelatory aspect. It is our example, for since He laid down His life for us we should lay down our lives for the brethren (1 Jn. 3:16).

But it is more than revelation. John goes out of his way to stress that Jesus came 'by water and blood . . . not with the water only, but with the water and with the blood' (1 Jn. 5:6). He thinks of 'the water, and the blood' as bearing witness along with the Spirit (1 Jn. 5:8). The meaning of this is not completely clear. But these passages seem to indicate the existence of teachers in the ancient church (as in the modern) who so emphasized the revelatory functions of Christ that they overlooked or at least minimized the significance of His death. Not so John. He insists that Jesus came 'with the blood'. 'He is the Saviour of the world' (1 Jn. 4:14), and not merely its Enlightener.[92]

---

[90] A. Ross on 3:6. He stresses the significance of the continuous tenses, '*Every* one who abideth in Him sinneth not, does not sin habitually and deliberately: *evèry* one who *goes on sinning,* sinning habitually and deliberately, has not seen Christ in His sinlessness and purity and has never really known Him.'

[91] Robert Law has a helpful comment: ' "Can a woman forget her sucking child, that she should not have compassion on the son of her womb?" It must be admitted that there are such monstrosities as mothers who can. But if it be *claimed* that a mother can be cruel and neglectful, and that without losing her character as a mother, the right answer, the morally true answer, is an indignant denial. In the same sense it is true that the Christian, because he is "begotten of God," *cannot* sin; and to assert the contrary is to assert a blasphemy, a calumny upon God' (*The Tests of Life,* Edinburgh, 1909, p. 228).

[92] C. H. Dodd, *in loc.* He stresses the uncertainties surrounding the passage but thinks the teaching opposed is of the type which held 'that Jesus was a mere man until at His baptism the divine Christ descended upon Him; that the Christ remained united with Him during His ministry, but left Him

Probably there is no point at which 1 John differs more from the Gospel than in the way it makes explicit the connection between the death of Christ and man's sin. This is plain enough in the Gospel, but it is unmistakable in the Epistle. Thus John tells us that 'the blood of Jesus his Son cleanseth us from all sin' (1 Jn. 1:7). This is not different from the teaching of the Gospel, but it is more explicit.

An expression which has caused a good deal of discussion is that in which John tells us that Jesus was 'the propitiation' for our sins, and he uses it twice (1 Jn. 2:2, 4:10).[93] In the former passage John speaks of the position if a man should sin. Then 'we have an Advocate with the Father, Jesus Christ the righteous: and he is the propitiation for our sins'. 'Advocate' translates the Greek *parakletos* used elsewhere in the New Testament only of the Holy Spirit. In this verse it clearly bears its legal sense of 'counsel for the defence'. Jesus is man's Representative.[94] He appears for man in the presence of God. And this leads right on to the thought of His priestly work in that He 'is the propitiation for our sins'. The word 'propitiation' properly signifies the removal of wrath. In this context it reminds us that the divine anger was exercised towards man's sin, and that it was Christ's propitiatory death that put the situation right, and made it possible for man to come back to God.[95]

Some, however, deny that there is any thought of propitiation. C. H. Dodd, for example, suggests that we should understand the word as 'expiation' (so RSV and other modern translations). He agrees that the predominant meaning of the word in Greek writings generally is propitiation, but he maintains that there is another meaning also, namely expiation. In his commentary he cites no evidence for this. In *The Bible and the Greeks* he cites two passages only.

---

before His crucifixion . . . since it was as mere man that He suffered, His death had no redemptive efficacy.' That this teaching was current is shown by Irenaeus' summary of Cerinthus' doctrines, 'after His baptism there had descended on Him, from that authority which is above all things, Christ in the form of a dove . . . but that at the end Christ had flown back again from Jesus, and that Jesus suffered and rose again, but that Christ remained impassible, since He was a spiritual being' (ERE, *sub* Cerinthus).

[93] See also pp. 225f. above.

[94] L. S. Thornton brings out some of the implications of all this. 'He took our place and was willing to suffer the consequences. For He could deal with Sin only by making an act of expiation in our stead. He paid the cost of being our advocate by taking our place in the dock and making in his own person an "act of redress". This involved his death as the price of our liberty' (*The Common Life in the Body of Christ*, London, 1950, p. 129).

[95] Cf. C. Ryder Smith, 'in John's Epistle the true High Priest is Himself the Paraclete. Himself "righteous", He stands for and atones for, the sinful men who have believed in Him. The text approximates to the Pauline saying, "Him who knew no sin, he made to be sin on our behalf" ' (BDS, p. 254).

I have examined these elsewhere,[96] and have tried to show that the thought of the averting of wrath is probably present in both. At the very least we can say that Dodd's work does not rest on a secure foundation insofar as it depends on these passages. Nor is he in better case with his conclusion that in the Old Testament the word group signifies expiation. Though he has brought some interesting facts to light, his examination has the serious defect that it totally ignores the context. When we pay attention to this we find that, while the word group translates words with meanings like 'forgive', it does so as a rule only when it is plain that the forgiveness in question involves the averting of the divine wrath. In other words the Greek translators of the Old Testament bore in mind the meaning of the word as propitiation.[97] It is impossible to feel that Dodd's case has been made out for all its current popularity.

In the present passage even Dodd has to admit that 'in the immediate context it might seem possible that the sense of "propitiation" is in place: if our guilt requires an advocate before God, we might, logically, need to placate His righteous anger.' Exactly. And nothing that Dodd says further seems to alter the logic of this. If there is 'a righteous anger' of God, and the New Testament is clear that there is, then it cannot be ignored in the process of forgiveness (as Dodd does ignore it in his discussion of forgiveness). Moreover the point made long ago by Denney should be heeded. 'The characteristic words of religion cannot be applied in new ways at will.'[98] Throughout Greek literature, biblical and non-biblical alike, *hilasmos* means 'propitiation'. We cannot now decide that we like another meaning better.

In the other passage, 1 John 4:10, there is only this to add, that the recognition that the term means 'propitiation' brings us one of the great New Testament paradoxes. That which shows us the love

[96] *The Apostolic Preaching of the Cross,* London and Grand Rapids, 1955, pp. 126-9.

[97] Cf. the summary by Roger R. Nicole, 'The LXX translators, insofar as their work may be viewed as a unit, appear to have sensed especially strongly this propitiatory connotation of כִּפֶּר, and, in consequence, they did most commonly choose to translate it by ἐξιλάσκεσθαι. In this connection they developed some essentially new constructions for this verb, sometimes using it with God as the subject, sometimes with the accusative of the sin for which propitiation was sought, paralleling in this very closely the Hebrew constructions of כִּפֶּר, yet without ever demonstrably losing the basic propitiatory significance of the word' (WThJ, xvii, p. 152). See further on this point Nicole's whole article, and my *The Apostolic Preaching of the Cross,* chs. III, IV.

[98] DC, p. 273. He goes on to notice that *hilasmos* is connected with sin and with the divine law. 'This is what is meant when the propitiation is described as Jesus Christ *the Righteous.* All that is divine, all the moral order of the world, all that we mean by the Law of God, has right done by it in the death of Christ' (*op. cit.,* p. 274).

of God is that which is concerned with the removal of the wrath
of God, for the act of propitiation is performed by none less than
God Himself, in the Person of His Son. To quote Denney again,

> So far from finding any kind of contrast between love and propitia-
> tion, the apostle can convey no idea of love to any one except by
> pointing to the propitiation — love is what is manifested there;
> and he can give no account of the propitiation but by saying, "Be-
> hold what manner of love."[99]

Sometimes John prefers to talk in terms of forgiveness, as when
he says, 'your sins are forgiven you for his name's sake' (1 Jn. 2:12).
The 'name' points to all that Christ stands for, and this in such a
context will especially mean His death. This was the express purpose of His coming, for 'he was manifested to take away sins' (1 Jn.
3:5). This brings us the thought of the purpose of God, and this
will be in mind also when we are told that 'he is faithful and righteous to forgive us our sins, and to cleanse us from all unrighteousness' (1 Jn. 1:9).

John is at pains to indicate that, however our sin be viewed, we
are saved from its consequences only by the work of Christ. But we
are saved by that work. His death is the effective means of salvation. And John expressly tells us that 'the Father hath sent
the Son to be the Saviour of the world' (1 Jn. 4:14). He also adds
to the words about His being the propitiation for our sins 'and not
for ours only, but also for the whole world' (1 Jn. 2:2). John
is not writing of some minor happening concerned with the religious
life of a few obscure people. He is concerned with the divine provision for the salvation of all.

VICTORY

A marked feature of this Epistle is the modified dualism that
runs right through it.[100] John has the habit of dealing with opposites

---

[99] *Op. cit.,* p. 276. Vincent Taylor cites Jn. 3:16 and 1 Jn. 4:9f., and
says, 'Less often quoted than the former passage, the latter is the greater
utterance in that it presents the startling thought that the expiation in
the Son is the expression of the love of God' (ANT, p. 141). And the thought
is even more startling when we realize that ἱλασμός is to be understood as
'propitiation' rather than 'expiation'. It is a personal word, concerned with
the putting away of the divine wrath, not an impersonal word referring to
the cancelling of sin regarded as a thing. R. S. Paul reminds us that 'A
criminal may expiate his crime in prison or upon the gallows, but there is
no necessary reconciliation either to the law or to society involved' (*The
Atonement and the Sacraments,* London, 1961, p. 27). Expiation is not a
personal term, and in this it is inferior to propitiation for an understanding of
Christ's work for us.

[100] This duality occurs often in the Dead Sea Scrolls, and is one of the
indications that there is a connection of some sort between the writings
of John and the Qumran literature.

which he sees in conflict. Thus he sometimes sets truth over against falsehood, as when he refers to a certain man who is 'a liar, and the truth is not in him' (1 Jn. 2:4). Similarly 'no lie is of the truth' (1 Jn. 2:21; cf. also 2:22, 27). Again John speaks of 'the spirit of truth, and the spirit of error' (1 Jn. 4:6), and of 'the Spirit of God' and that 'of the antichrist' (1 Jn. 4:2f.). There is a contrast of death and life (1 Jn. 3:14), and another of darkness and light (1 Jn. 1:6f., which also sets truth over against darkness; 2:8-11; and, most significant of all, 1:5, where God is associated with light). Love and hate are put in opposition several times, as with the liar who says 'I love God, and hateth his brother' (1 Jn. 4:20; cf. also 2:10f.; 3:13-16). There are children of God and children of the devil (1 Jn. 3:10), with which we should take doing righteousness and doing sin (1 Jn. 3:7-9).

The contrast between Him 'that is in you' and him 'that is in the world' (1 Jn. 4:4) introduces us to the conflict with the world which is everywhere presupposed. 'The whole world lieth in the evil one' (1 Jn. 5:19). It does not know believers because it did not know God (1 Jn. 3:1). It is not at all surprising that it hates them (1 Jn. 3:13).

Thus John thinks of a conflict which is constant and severe, and which may be described in many ways. But, unlike the men of the Qumran community,[101] he does not think of a conflict now being waged on more or less equal terms. For John the decisive victory has been won. Indeed, the whole point of mentioning the various facets of the conflict is to hammer home more firmly the truth of Christ's triumph. The whole purpose of Christ's being 'manifested' was that He might win His victory over the devil and completely destroy his works (1 Jn. 3:8). John can exult in the victory that thus becomes available to believers. 'This is the victory that hath overcome the world, even our faith' (1 Jn. 5:4).[102] This

[101] According to the *Manual of Discipline* 'God has established the two spirits in equal measure until the last period' (Millar Burrows, *The Dead Sea Scrolls*, London, 1956, p. 375); 'in equal measure God has established the two spirits until the period which has been decreed and the making new' (*op. cit.*, p. 376).

[102] 'The victorious faith of the Christian is trust in God as He is revealed in Jesus Christ His Son. It means committing ourselves to the love of God as it is expressed in all that Jesus Christ was and all that He did' (C. H. Dodd, *in loc.*). Westcott reminds us that this is the only occurrence of 'faith' ($\pi i\sigma\tau\iota s$) in this Epistle (it is not found at all in the Gospel). He sees the content of this faith in the confession that Jesus is 'the Christ, the Son of God', and comments, 'To hold that faith, to enter into the meaning and the power of that conquest through apparent failure, is to share in its triumph. Our faith is not merely victorious: it is the embodiment of *the victory which overcame the world* .... The victory of Christ was gained upon a narrow field, but it was world-wide in its effects' (*in loc.*).

is a victory over the evil one (1 Jn. 2:13ff. — the repetition indicates something of the importance). John knows of 'many
antichrists' (1 Jn. 2:18; cf. 2:22; 4:3). But believers need have no
fear. They have overcome here also (1 Jn. 4:4). The evil one
himself cannot touch them, for Christ Himself keeps them (1 Jn.
5:18). It is in this connection that we should notice John's repeated references to 'boldness' (1 Jn. 2:28; 3:21; 4:17; 5:14). The
Christian does not live his life in coward fear, but in the boldness
that comes from the assurance of victory. Christ has defeated the
devil and all his hosts. That victory bears fruit in the lives of
believers. Let them accordingly live in joyous confidence.

Now and then this is brought out in terms of the eschatological
triumph. Two of the above references to 'boldness' look to the
time of Christ's return. Even when the day of judgment comes, believers will be confident. John knows that 'he that doeth the will
of God abideth for ever' (1 Jn. 2:17), and that in that day 'we shall
be like him; for we shall see him even as he is' (1 Jn. 3:2). For
time and for eternity the believer is delivered from fear. Christ's
victory is complete.

FAITH

We have already noticed that John uses the noun 'faith' in 1 John
5:4, and nowhere else in either the Epistle or the Gospel. The
verb 'believe' is much more common, and it assures us that faith
is central in the Christian's response to what Christ has done for him.
God's commandment is summed up as 'that we should believe in the
name of his Son Jesus Christ' (1 Jn. 3:23). That is to say, the
prime requirement that God lays on men is faith. This is expressed also by saying that the man who believes 'hath the witness
in him' whereas 'he that believeth not God hath made him a liar'
(1 Jn. 5:10). It is the believer who is begotten of God, and who
has eternal life (1 Jn. 5:1, 13). It is the believer that overcomes
the world (1 Jn. 5:5).

Some of these passages give the content of the belief, as 'he
that believeth that Jesus is the Christ' or 'that Jesus is the Son
of God'. This does not mean that faith is regarded as adherence to
a set of propositions. It means that faith has a content, and that
without that content it is not really faith. Unless Jesus really is
the Christ, the One sent by God, unless He is really the Son of
God, sharing in the divine nature and accomplishing the divine
purpose, there is no salvation. To believe in Christ in the full sense
of that term accordingly implies the acceptance of certain truths
about Him. So John can speak indifferently about believing these
great truths or believing 'on the name' of Christ, or even of believing 'the love which God hath in us' (1 Jn. 4:16). Throughout

he is concerned with the truth that we have seen elsewhere, that the work of salvation proceeds from the love of God, and it becomes operative in man only through faith.[103] The very mention of faith implies that salvation is all of God.

THE SECOND AND THIRD EPISTLES OF JOHN

These two short writings have little to say about the atonement. We see the same connection between the commandment and love that we saw in 1 John (2 Jn. 5f.). There are hints at the struggle between good and evil as when we read 'Beloved, imitate not that which is evil, but that which is good. He that doeth good is of God: he that doeth evil hath not seen God' (3 Jn. 11). But the one point of distinction appears to be the emphasis these writings place on truth. The elder speaks of loving in truth (2 Jn. 1; 3 Jn. 1); of all them that 'know the truth' (2 Jn. 1); of walking in truth (2 Jn. 4; 3 Jn. 3, 4). Indeed, he has no greater joy than to hear of his children walking in the truth (3 Jn. 4). There is such a thing as the witness 'of the truth itself' (Demetrius has it, 3 Jn. 12). Truth 'abideth in us, and it shall be with us for ever' (2 Jn. 2). As Dodd says, 'In these epistles "truth" is not merely, as in ordinary speech, that which corresponds with the facts, but also, specifically, the ultimate Reality as revealed in Christ'.[104] There is the thought that we have seen elsewhere that God has acted in Christ, and we stand only on the basis of that action.

THE REVELATION OF ST. JOHN THE DIVINE

Revelation is possibly the most difficult of all the books in the Bible to interpret. Its symbolism is strange to modern readers. Its beasts and bowls and trumpets come from a thought world that is not ours. Though doubtless all this was familiar enough to Christians of the first century, Christians of the twentieth century

---

[103] H. F. Lovell Cocks reminds us that we are saved not *propter fidem* but *propter Christum*: 'Though (faith) is not a "work" of righteousness that God is graciously pleased to accept in lieu of moral perfection, it is none the less the indispensable instrument whereby the benefits of Christ are received and taken home' (*By Faith Alone*, London, 1943, p. 140). He also says 'When the ground of our justification is taken as something in ourselves — whether that be, as the Catholics say, a faith burgeoning into love (*fides caritate formata*), or, as Osiander maintained, a new nature which is God's own righteousness infused into our hearts — the sinner is robbed of his assurance and can no longer rejoice in the Gospel . . . . when the sinner is taught to look in any other direction than to the Cross for evidence of his acceptance by God, he loses the "joy and peace in believing" that are his birthright in Christ' (*op. cit.*, p. 141). The place of faith must be carefully safeguarded.

[104] *Commentary* on 2 Jn. 1.

have lost the key to its interpretation. The result is that the book becomes the happy hunting ground of all sorts of religious cranks. They make it foreshadow strange prophetical schemes, whose strangeness is equalled only by the confidence with which their exponents claim to be able to interpret this ancient writing. Confronted with this mixture of baffling symbolism and confident claims to the only correct interpretation most Christians are confused and inclined to be suspicious. They generally leave the book alone in consequence. Which is a great pity, for, while much of the symbolism of the book is obscure, a very great deal of its teaching is both plain and valuable and relevant to our needs.

THE TRIUMPH OF GOD

Throughout the whole book no theme is more strongly insisted upon than the triumph of God.[105] Take, for example, the magnificent opening chapter. Here Christ, the exalted and glorious Christ, is introduced to us. He is 'the firstborn of the dead, and the ruler of the kings of the earth' (Rev. 1:5). 'The glory and the dominion' are ascribed to Him 'for ever and ever. Amen' (Rev. 1:6). Once He came to earth in lowliness, but a triumphant reversal of what happened during the incarnation is described as the seer looks for the time when 'he cometh with the clouds'. Then there will be no rejection of a lowly Jesus. Instead 'all the tribes of the earth shall mourn over him' (Rev. 1:7). There follows a majestic description of His appearance (Rev. 1:13-16). The effect of the vision on the seer is to cause him to fall down as one dead. He hears the words, 'Fear not; I am the first and the last, and the Living one; and I was dead, and behold, I am alive for evermore, and I have the keys of death and of Hades' (Rev. 1:17f.). The whole chapter is full of the majesty and the glory of the Christ, and it is totally unintelligible apart from the triumph that Christ has won.

The note thus struck in the opening is carried on in various ways throughout the book. We are never allowed to forget for a moment the over-ruling sovereignty of God.[106] He is supreme everywhere.

---

[105] Hanns Lilje stresses this triumph of God in Christ. 'The imposing names which the Old Testament gave to the Messiah — the Lion of the tribe of Judah, the Root of David (Gen. 49; Isa. 11) — are fulfilled in Christ. He has conquered. It is no accident that in the Apocalypse the word victory always stands alone, and absolutely. Jesus is the victor in a far more complete sense than was ever true of the emperors . . . . Jesus Christ is absolute victor; for in this one word the Apocalypse always sums up his whole saving work' (*The Last Book of the Bible*, Philadelphia, 1957, pp. 114f.).

[106] 'It is the idea of God which dominates all (John's) thought. In everything that follows we are meant to remember that God is the sovereign Power in the background. He is the upholder of righteousness,

Nothing is done but what He instigates it or at least permits it. Glory is continually ascribed to God, and there are frequent little songs of praise to Him (Rev. 4:11; 7:12; 11:17; 14:3; 15:3f.; 19:1f.). Sometimes He is linked in this sort of expression with 'the Lamb' (Rev. 5:13; 7:10; 12:10ff.), or the Lamb may be praised for Himself (Rev. 5:12). But in all such expressions we are to see the triumph of God. He has worked out His purpose through the Lamb, and, whether He is expressly mentioned or not, the thought is there. His royalty is open and manifest. In chapter 4 John describes a vision of God. He uses great reserve, and hints at the appearance of God rather than describing it ('he that sat was to look upon like a jasper stone and a sardius', Rev. 4:3). But he leaves us in no doubt as to God's majesty. So with the assurance that 'The kingdom of the world is become the kingdom of our Lord, and of his Christ: and he shall reign for ever and ever' (Rev. 11:15). The mighty multitude of heaven exult, 'Hallelujah: for the Lord our God, the Almighty, reigneth' (Rev. 19:6).

In view of the close connection between God and Christ throughout this book, it is not surprising that the triumph is often linked with the latter. The favourite way of referring to Him is as 'the Lamb'. For us a lamb has associations of meekness and the like, but this is not the way to understand Revelation. In apocalyptic literature in general, and in this book in particular, a horned lamb is the symbol of a conqueror.[107] To refer to Christ as a lamb, then, is for this writer a way of drawing attention to His triumph. Sometimes this is plain for all to see, as when we are told that the Lamb is 'Lord of lords, and King of kings' (Rev. 17:14; 19:16); or when the Lamb 'having seven horns' is worshipped, and songs are sung to Him (Rev. 5:6-10, 12f.). The Lamb stands on Mount Zion in triumph (Rev. 14:1). He is a terrible figure, for 'the wrath of the Lamb' is regarded as something greatly to be feared (Rev. 6:16f.).

But a lamb in antiquity had other associations and John is not unmindful of them. Frequently a lamb was offered up in sacrifice, and our writer makes use of this fact to link with the triumph the wealth of sacrificial associations. 'A Lamb . . . as though it had been slain' (Rev. 5:6) points unmistakably to the sacrifices.[108]

---

and in this interest He overrules all events. He directs them towards an eternal purpose, which He is now to fulfil through His Messiah. Thus the hand of God is felt throughout the book' (E. F. Scott, *The Book of Revelation*, London, 1939, p. 112).

[107] So R. H. Charles, *Revelation, ICC*, p. cxiii, citing passages from 1 Enoch and the *Testaments of the Twelve Patriarchs*.

[108] Cf. E. F. Scott, ' "The Lamb" has come to be nothing else for him than a title of Christ, which can be used almost like a proper name in any context. It always carries with it, however, the idea of a sacrificial death' (*op. cit.*, p. 64).

The Lamb is both the mighty Conqueror and the lowly Victim.[109] Jesus, the Lamb of God, is triumphant indeed. His triumph is never out of mind. But He won His triumph through His death.

John does not confine his account of the triumph of the Christ to those passages where he speaks of Him as the Lamb. He may use quite different imagery, as when he says, 'the Lion that is of the tribe of Judah, the Root of David, hath overcome, to open the book . . .' (Rev. 5:5), or when he depicts the mighty Warrior treading out 'the winepress of the fierceness of the wrath of Almighty God' (Rev. 19:15). But nothing is so striking as the conjunction of triumph and death, the thought of the prevailing power that there is in the death of the Lamb.

And the triumph of God and of the Lamb is in part conveyed to the people of God. They are made 'a kingdom and priests' (Rev. 5:10; so also 1:6); they 'reign upon the earth' (Rev. 5:10). This theme is developed throughout chapters 2 and 3. There we find a series of short letters 'to the churches'. These conform to a set pattern, and all conclude with a promise made 'to him that overcometh'. This overcomer will eat of the tree of life (Rev. 2:7). He will have no part in the second death (Rev. 2:11). He will eat the hidden manna and receive a white stone with a new name on it that only he will know (Rev. 2:17). He will have power over the nations and he will receive 'the morning star' (Rev. 2:26ff.). He will be clothed in white; his name will not be blotted out of the book of life; Christ will confess his name before the Father (Rev. 3:5). He will be a pillar in the temple of God; he will never go out thence; the name of God and of the new Jerusalem and of Christ will be written on him (Rev. 3:12). He will sit down with Christ in His throne (Rev. 3:21). The note of triumph throbs through these passages. Christians here and now may be a depressed, downtrodden minority, to all outward appearance completely insignificant. Yet they belong to the mighty Conqueror who has won a triumph over all His foes, and a triumph which will in due course be made visible to all the earth. And when that day comes they will share in the triumph. Already they are in fellowship with Him, and they may know the victory in themselves. But when they have endured to the end the results of that victory will be obvious to all, and those

---

[109] Thus Charles can say, 'The Lamb is at once the triumphant Messiah, leading His people to victory, and the suffering Messiah who lays down His life for His people' (loc. cit.). Cf. also M. Kiddle, 'Nowadays the gentleness and meekness of Christ are the qualities usually associated with the Lamb, but John's use of the term here is different . . . . the Lamb is a symbol of power — power, moreover, which has been demonstrated in sacrifice' (MNTC, in loc.).

who are now humiliated will receive the various good gifts that we have noted from the hand of the Highest of all.[110]

There are some uncertainties about the date of Revelation, but all agree that it was written in a time of persecution and written out of that situation of persecution. The Seer looks right through this, however, to the end time. A great deal of his book is taken up with the reversal that will then take place in the punishment of evildoers. Now powerful and tyrannical, then they will be justly punished for all their misdeeds. There are spectacular descriptions of the fall of the city disguised under the name 'Babylon' and of the punishment of the evildoers in it (Rev. 14:8; 17; 18). The wrath of God is mentioned several times (Rev. 14:10, 19f.; 15:1-7; 19:15), but especially in chapter 16 where we read of the outpouring on the earth of 'the seven bowls of the wrath of God'. In fact this theme is one of the great themes of Revelation.[111] The author lets us be in no doubt but that God is implacably opposed to every form of evil. Nor are the forces of evil confined to those we normally meet. John speaks of 'war in heaven', a war which has its culmination when 'the old serpent, he that is called the Devil and Satan, the deceiver of the whole world' is cast down to the earth and his angels with him (Rev. 12:7-9). There is a description of a great final battle, 'the war of the great day of God, the Almighty' (Rev. 16:14; see also 19:19). There is specific mention of the battle of Har-Mageddon (Rev. 16:16), but when the forces of evil make war with the Lamb 'the Lamb shall overcome them' (Rev. 17:14). Satan is severely restricted, for when He wills God binds him for a thousand years (Rev. 20:2). Then Satan is released and proceeds to deceive the nations, but to no avail. His final state is to be cast 'into the lake of fire and brimstone' (Rev. 20:8-10). The theme of these chapters might be held to be 'strong is the Lord God' (Rev. 18:8). The forces of evil are mighty, but the Lord God omnipotent is mightier still. The Seer sees with crystal clarity that those who persecute are far from having the last word. Their fate is to be utterly destroyed. Even in the midst of trial he can exult in final triumph.

THE BLOOD OF THE LAMB

Chapter 7 introduces us to a multitude 'which come out of the great tribulation, and they washed their robes, and made them white in

---

[110] W. Hendriksen entitles his study of Revelation *More Than Conquerors,* thus drawing attention to this major theme.

[111] Cf. A. T. Hanson, 'The concept of the wrath of God is more prominent in the Book of Revelation than in any other part of the New Testament' (*The Wrath of the Lamb,* London, 1957, p. 159). Indeed he finds the teaching about wrath in this book 'a completion and crown of all that is said about the wrath in the rest of the Bible' (*loc. cit.*).

the blood of the Lamb' (v. 14). The expressive imagery emphasizes that the blood of Christ is the effective cause of salvation. The same idea seems to be in mind when the saints are said to be clothed in white linen (Rev. 19:14). Naturally we might be held to be unrighteous and hence filthy. But we are washed clean from every defilement through the blood of Christ. Our robes are spotlessly white.[112]

But blood does not necessarily signify cleansing. Christ is thought of as 'him that loveth us, and loosed us from our sins by his blood' (Rev. 1:5).[113] Here the thought is that of redemption, of loosening a bond at cost. Our sins hold us fast. We cannot break free. But the blood of Christ is the price which sets us free. Similar is the metaphor of purchase. John speaks of 'a new song' sung in heaven which says, 'thou wast slain, and didst purchase unto God with thy blood men of every tribe, and tongue, and people, and nation' (Rev. 5:9). The same process is in mind in the reference to the one hundred and forty-four thousand as having been 'purchased from among men' (Rev. 14:4). The triumph of the church, and more especially of the martyrs, is ascribed to the death of Christ. 'They overcame [the devil] because of the blood of the Lamb, and because of the word of their testimony' (Rev. 12:11).

Or the death of Christ may be referred to without the use of the term 'blood'. John speaks once of the crucifixion (Rev. 11:8). He speaks of the Lamb 'as though it had been slain' (Rev. 5:6), or of 'the Lamb that hath been slain from the foundation of the world' (Rev. 13:8).[114] This last passage connects the thought of the slain Lamb with that of 'the book of life'. Those whose names are not found written there are regarded as in serious plight, indeed. Towards the end of the book this is made clearer when it is pointed out that no evil person will enter the heavenly city, 'but only they which are written in the Lamb's book of life' (Rev. 21:27). In another place John speaks of 'an eternal gospel' (Rev. 14:6), which, in view of the usage we have seen to prevail throughout the New Testament, we must take to point us to the news of what God

---

112 In Rev. 19:8 we read in RV, 'the fine linen is the righteous acts of the saints.' This seems to me out of harmony with New Testament teaching. I have given reasons for thinking that δικαίωμα never means 'righteous act' in Scripture in *The Apostolic Preaching of the Cross*, pp. 263f. It is rather 'the judicial sentences of God' (*ICC*, on Rev. 15:4).

113 Some MSS read 'washed' for 'loosed', but 'loosed' seems the true text.

114 'Slain' in both these last references is a perfect participle; the Lamb continues permanently in the character of One who was slain for men. The crucifixion is not regarded simply as a happening that took place and is all over. While there is a once-for-all aspect to it, there is also the aspect which sees it as of permanent validity and continuing effect.

has done in Christ. It is another reminder that there is no other way to God but through the atoning death, and that this is, indeed, good news to those who put their trust in Him.

From all this it is clear that John thought of the triumph of which his book is so full as resting on the atoning death of Christ. It is 'the Lamb that hath been slain' who is 'worthy . . . to receive the power, and riches, and wisdom, and might, and honour, and glory, and blessing' (Rev. 5:12). He is not simply repeating the commonplaces of apocalyptic thought, but putting before his readers the essential Christian message with the help of apocalyptic imagery.[115] And it is a daring innovation to use the Lamb symbol,[116] the sign of triumph, in the closest connection with the thought of being slain. The crucifixion is not for him a sign of defeat, a difficulty to be explained away. The cross is the place of victory. The crucifixion is the triumph.

THE SUFFERINGS OF THE SAINTS

The writer of the book introduces himself in this way, 'I John, your brother and partaker with you in the tribulation . . .' (Rev. 1:9). In this somewhat oblique fashion he indicates that he himself is suffering for his faith and that his readers are in similar plight. It it not surprising accordingly that the note of suffering is often sounded throughout the rest of the book. There are references to 'toil and patience' (Rev. 2:2; cf. 2:19); to tribulation (Rev. 2:9f.); and to the great tribulation (Rev. 7:14). There are several places where martyrdom is mentioned. Thus Antipas is described as a martyr in Revelation 2:13, while there is a reference to 'the souls of them that had been slain for the word of God' (Rev. 6:9). These souls look for their blood to be avenged, but they are answered that this will not be 'until their fellow-servants also and their brethren, which should be killed even as they were, should be fulfilled' (Rev. 6:10f.). Clearly it was anticipated that many more would suffer for their

---

[115] E. F. Scott speaks of 'John's grand innovation on all apocalyptic thought. He transforms the Messiah into the Lamb, the sacrificial Victim who accomplished His work through His death. This, for John as for Paul, was the distinctive act of Christ' (*op. cit.,* p. 118).

[116] E. F. Scott comments, 'Perhaps the name of "the Lamb," taken as it is from the great prophecy in Isaiah, is meant to carry with it the prophetic idea that "the Lord hath laid on him the iniquity of us all." Christ has redeemed us because He was the sacrifice which made atonement for sin' (*loc. cit.*). C. Ryder Smith also sees a reference to Is. 53. He points out that in Rev. 13:8; 5:6, 9, 12, 'the ruling ideas are suffering, salvation, and glory. There is no example of these three ideas, *taken together,* in the ritual system, but they are just the three found in the last of the Songs of the Servant . . . . It seems clear, therefore, that the Seer's symbol of "the Lamb" is derived from a verse in the fifty-third of Isaiah: "as a lamb that is led to the slaughter" ' (BDS, p. 193).

faith. Martyrdom is thought of as a continuing feature of the history of the church. So there are references to the shed blood of saints and prophets (Rev. 16:6; 17:6; 18:24), and to those 'that had been beheaded for the testimony of Jesus' (Rev. 20:4). 'Blessed are the dead which die in the Lord' (Rev. 14:13) may refer to the same thing.[117] In any case it looks to believers departing this life 'in the Lord' which will imply faithfulness unto death.

Yet for all the many references to suffering it is noteworthy that there is no tendency to dwell on the physical agony of the saints. In later times this was common, but our writer's emphasis is elsewhere. As Lohmeyer says: 'This book, which is so full of passion and bloodshed, has no descriptions of the sufferings of Christians, as there are in later records of martyrdom; it regards suffering and death for the sake of the faith not as an eschatological "woe," but as glorification.'[118] This is a God-centered book. While the sufferings of believers are faced they are not put into the spotlight. They have no interest in themselves but only in the way in which they bear on the furtherance of the divine plan. And in any case, while suffering is real, and is insisted upon, the major emphasis of the book is placed on triumph. Suffering is only to be seen in this perspective.

The sufferings and even martyrdom of God's servants does not mean that the universe has passed out of the control of God. These things do not happen because He is powerless to prevent them. The message to the church in Laodicea runs, 'As many as I love, I reprove, and chasten' (Rev. 3:19). The tribulations through which any believer or group of believers are passing are God's way of working out His good and perfect will. If His people sin it may be necessary to discipline them, and their trials are to be interpreted at least in part in this light.[119] Certainly they are not to be thought of as the result simply of evil men or evil spirits wreaking their own foul will. Throughout the book any power that the forces of evil may wield is expressly said to be 'given' to them. They can do nothing at all unless God permits. And all suffering is to be understood in the light of the cross.

> The horrors and sufferings of the last days are not to weigh upon men like a dull unending pain. For the "sealed," that is, for those who have implicitly become God's own people, the tribulations of these days are illuminated by the Passion of Christ, and therefor they have become transparent and intelligible.[120]

---

[117] So Kiddle, 'John is clearly speaking of the martyrs, of those who are to follow the example of "faithful Antipas" (ii. 13), in braving the Imperial sword' (in loc.).

[118] Cited by H. Lilje, op. cit., p. 129.

[119] 'Love is never cruel, but it can be severe' (R. H. Charles, in. loc.).

[120] H. Lilje, op. cit., p. 137.

Christ's sufferings have transformed the whole concept of suffering for John as for others of the New Testament writers. It is not thereby rendered attractive. But it is rendered meaningful.

THE SINNER'S PERIL

Our writer never takes sin lightly. The messages he records to the seven churches include several calls for repentance (Rev. 2:5, 16, 21f.; 3:3). Believers are warned that if they do not repent their candlestick may be taken out of its place, or they may find that the Lord is warring against them, or they may be punished in other ways. Permitting the false prophetess Jezebel to continue to do her evil deeds is severely castigated (Rev. 2:20ff.). The Lord's hatred of Nicolaitans is given emphasis (Rev. 2:6, 15). Specific sins are often denounced, as idolatry, murder, sorcery, fornication and theft (Rev. 9:20f.), and there is an emphasis on failure to repent. These are stubborn sinners, rejecting God's way and going on still in their paths of self-will and disobedience.[121] There are frequent references to the divine wrath, as we saw earlier. This is such a grievous thing that it can make men call for the mountains and rocks to fall on them to hide them from it (Rev. 6:16f.). All such devices are necessarily in vain, but they show us how seriously the divine hostility to sin is to be taken, and how certainly it will ultimately be manifested.[122] Sometimes we read of the death penalty, usually in the plagues this book depicts so vividly (Rev. 2:23; 6:4, 8; 8:9; 9:18). And even in the end, when he is depicting the joys of heaven, the writer turns aside to remind us that 'for the fearful, and unbelieving, and abominable, and murderers, and fornicators, and sorcerers, and idolaters, and all liars, their part shall be in the lake that burneth with fire and brimstone; which is the second death' (Rev. 21:8).

The devil is depicted as incessantly active. Sometimes he is acting specifically against believers (Rev. 2:10, 13). Sometimes he is concerned with war in heaven and its consequences (Rev. 11:7; 12:7ff.). But wherever the Evil One is mentioned the thought is always of his hostility to the purposes of God. To walk in his ways is accordingly a serious matter. Those who are caught up in his mis-

---

121 'Their heinousness consists not only in the nature of the crimes themselves, but also in the accompanying attitudes: "they repented not" (9:21), and "they repented not to give him glory" (16:9). Impenitence and unwillingness to recognize the sovereignty of God are the fatal aspects of sin' (Merrill C. Tenney, *Interpreting Revelation*, London, 1958, p. 199).

122 'Whenever, in the entire history of the world, any individual remains impenitent and hardens himself in answer to the *initial* manifestation of God's displeasure in judgments, the *final* outpouring of divine wrath will follow sooner or later' (W. Hendriksen, *More Than Conquerors*, Grand Rapids, 1956, p. 40).

deeds will inevitably suffer the consequences. 'Fear God' said the angel (Rev. 14:7). And the whole of this book shows that this is good advice.

THE SEARCHING GLANCE OF GOD

John looks forward with certainty to the judgment of God when all will be suitably recompensed for their ill deeds. He saw 'a great white throne' with the dead, 'the great and the small', standing before it, and 'the dead were judged out of the things which were written in the books, according to their works' (Rev. 20:11f.). Twice God's judgments are said to be 'true and righteous' (Rev. 16:7; 19:2). Men need not fear that justice will not be done. It will. But precisely because of that must sinners tremble.[123] So an angel 'saith with a great voice, Fear God, and give him glory; for the hour of his judgement is come' (Rev. 14:7). A couple of chapters are given over to 'the judgement of the great harlot' Babylon (Rev. 17, 18), and John expressly points out that 'strong is the Lord God which judged her' (Rev. 18:8). No man can expect to escape judgment, when even so mighty a city received full and just recompense. And when the Lord returns it will be 'to render to each man according as his work is' (Rev. 22:12).

The Seer makes it quite clear that there is no escaping from the consequences of one's sin. The Son of God tells the church in Thyatira that 'I am he which searcheth the reins and hearts: and I will give unto each one of you according to your works' (Rev. 2:23). He knows when a church has a name that it lives, but is really dead (Rev. 3:1). He knows who did and who did not 'defile their garments' (Rev. 3:4). He is 'he that openeth, and none shall shut, and that shutteth, and none openeth' (Rev. 3:7). He sees through the subterfuge of the Laodiceans who think themselves to be rich when they are 'wretched . . . and miserable and poor and blind and naked' (Rev. 3:17). From such a God nothing can be hid. Men must not think that they can sin and get away with it. They will not and they cannot. All things are open before Him.

---

[123] Yet this must not be understood in such a way as to obscure the love of God. L. H. De Wolf reminds us that love and justice are not to be separated: 'Justice and love are often described as in polar tension, or paradoxical opposition. Actually this is true only of unjust love and loveless justice. Thus, if it be assumed that justice in criminal law means the evenhanded application of a *lex talionis,* while love means only being kind to the prisoner at the bar, then the two are opposed. But retaliation, however evenhanded, is highly inadequate justice, while love requires concern for all and not only for the prisoner at the bar. To know what love requires is not an easy task for the presiding judge, nor is it easier to know justice. But justice and love are one' (*The Case for Theology in Liberal Perspective,* Philadelphia, 1959, p. 150).

FULL SALVATION

If it is true that this book announces violent punishment upon the wicked, if it stresses that evil will certainly be detected and that sin is serious, it is also true that the writer dwells lovingly on the glories of salvation. He gives us that unforgettable picture of Christ knocking at the door and then coming in to sup with him that opens (Rev. 3:20). He thinks of salvation as belonging 'to our God' (Rev. 19:1; cf. 7:10). In chapter 7 there is an exquisitely beautiful picture of the bliss of the saved:

> They shall hunger no more, neither thirst any more; neither shall the sun strike upon them, nor any heat: for the Lamb which is in the midst of the throne shall be their shepherd, and shall guide them unto fountains of waters of life: and God shall wipe away every tear from their eyes (Rev. 7:16f.).

And at the end of his book John gives two chapters over to the description of the new heaven and the new earth. All things are made new (Rev. 21:5). He has vivid descriptions of the beauty of the heavenly city, but the important things are not the gold and the precious stones, but the fact that the city has no temple and no sun or moon to shine upon it,[124] 'For the Lord God the Almighty, and the Lamb, are the temple thereof . . . . for the glory of God did lighten it, and the lamp thereof is the Lamb' (Rev. 21:22f.). Though this description is brought out in its fullest at the end of the book, the truths it tells forth are implied elsewhere, as in the reference to 'the temple of God that is in heaven' (Rev. 11:19). Or take the memorable saying, 'Blessed are the dead which die in the Lord from henceforth: yea, saith the Spirit, that they may rest from their labours; for their works follow with them' (Rev. 14:13). The joy of heaven is brought out with the reference to 'the marriage supper of the Lamb' (Rev. 19:9). Salvation is made available to men 'of every tribe, and tongue, and people, and nation' (Rev. 5:9; 7:9).

---

[124] 'The reiteration of this idea stresses the brilliance and the glory of the new life which is planned for the saints of God' (Merrill C. Tenney, *op. cit.*, p. 93).

CHAPTER TEN

Conclusion

From the foregoing survey it is plain enough that there is a variety
of thought in the New Testament on the atonement. There is not
the slightest suggestion of docile witnesses obediently putting out the
ancient equivalent of 'the party line'. These writers are men of
integrity and conviction. They write out of deep personal experience, and they set forth the truth about Christ's saving work
as they see it and in the way that comes most natural to them. Each
gives an individual viewpoint. There is no danger of our con-
fusing for example the picture we get in Hebrews of our great
High Priest with anything else in the New Testament. And so
with each of the other writers. Some have a more distinctive
style than others. Some are deeper thinkers than others. But that
each puts down the truth as it has been revealed to him there can be
no doubt.

In view of this it is important to notice that there is a basic
agreement on the essentials, and this applies to the atonement

364

as to all else, indeed to the atonement above all else.[1] For the cross
dominates the New Testament. Notice how naturally it is referred
to as summing up the content of Christianity. 'We preach Christ
crucified' (1 Cor. 1:23); 'I determined not to know anything among
you, save Jesus Christ, and him crucified' (1 Cor. 2:2); 'I delivered
unto you first of all . . . how that Christ died for our sins' (1 Cor.
15:3); 'far be it from me to glory, save in the cross of our Lord
Jesus Christ' (Gal. 6:14). The Gospel is 'the word of the cross'
(1 Cor. 1:18). The enemies of Christianity are 'the enemies of the
cross of Christ' (Phil. 3:18). Baptism is baptism into Christ's
death (Rom. 6:3), and it is not without its interest that, while
Christ did not enjoin His followers to commemorate His birth, or
any event in His life, He did call on them to remember His death.
While it may not be expressly the theme in every place, yet it is because of the cross that every writer writes as he does. The cross
stands as the divine answer to the fundamental problem, the problem
of man's sin. Each New Testament writer writes as one who has
come to know salvation by the way of the cross. He writes, moreover, as one who longs to bring others into that same knowledge of
salvation. And because the writers are men who have themselves
experienced this salvation, and because they are convinced that
there is no other way of salvation than this alone, and because they
have such a deep and genuine concern for others, the cross dominates
everything that they write. Thus it is that we can take, say, the
letters of St. Paul, letters for the most part written to meet the
day-to-day needs of the churches of that apostle's foundation (and
some others), and not at all to set forth in order an exposition of
systematic theology in general or of the atonement in particular,
and use them to bring out the meaning of the death of Christ. So
central is the cross that it affects all that Paul writes. Even when he
is not consciously setting forth its significance the cross shapes his
writing because it has shaped his thinking and his living.

There is in the New Testament both diversity and agreement as to
the significance of the cross. Let us notice some of the principal
points of agreement.

(1) All men are sinners

Sometimes the universality of sin is expressed in set terms, as when
Jesus said, 'If ye then, being evil . . .' (Mt. 7:11; Lk. 11:13), or,

---

[1] G. W. H. Lampe outlines the Pauline view of the atonement and proceeds, 'even if such an interpretation is pre-eminently Pauline, the rest of
the New Testament confirms it, or at the very least, does not anywhere contradict it' (*Reconciliation in Christ*, London, 1956, p. 38). He proceeds to
look at other New Testament writers and then says, 'Varying degrees of
emphasis are laid upon the different facets of the Atonement, but in the
broad lines of their understanding of Christ's death and resurrection the New
Testament writers agree fairly closely with each other' (*op. cit.*, p. 52).

'none is good save one, even God' (Mk. 10:18; similar are Mt. 19:17; Lk. 18:19), or when Paul cites the Psalm that says, 'There is none righteous, no, not one' (Rom. 3:10), or gives his own conclusion in the words, 'all have sinned, and fall short of the glory of God' (Rom. 3:23). But whether we come across express statements such as these or not, the presupposition of the entire New Testament is that all men are united in sin. Nothing makes sense on any other presupposition. This must be recognized as a distinctive Christian note. The Greeks and other thinkers of the ancient world thought of man as basically in a healthy moral condition. It is possible for him to be corrupted, and individual cases of evil are not difficult to find. But these, it was thought, are exceptional. Man's nature is sound. Given reasonable opportunity, his innate goodness would blossom and flourish. And this kind of sunny optimism has reappeared down through the ages. Despite the phenomena of two world wars, with a depression in between, despite the cold war, despite a world wherein the great nations spend fabulous sums on armaments and allow the masses of the underprivileged in backward countries to lack even necessary food, some seem able to hold on to this with all the fervour of those whose dogmatic convictions will not allow them to face reality.[2] There is no shallow sentimentality about the New Testament writers (though there is deep love). They face the sinfulness of man realistically. They are not shocked. They are not given to theatrical exaggeration. But they are not complaisant either. They see sin for the evil thing it is, and they see it in all men. All that they say proceeds from this realistic appraisal.

(2) *All sinners are in desperate peril because of their guilt*

There is a sense in which the New Testament writers accept sin, as we have just seen. It is one of the facts of life. There is another sense in which they do not accept it. Sin is, in the literal sense of the term, a damning fact. Unless something is done about it sinners will perish eternally. There are different ways of putting this. The

---

[2] W. H. Moberly warns against taking our own experience as the norm: 'It would be rash to conclude that, because the intellectual explanations of Atonement are obscure or even repellent, there can have been no experienced reality to be explained . . . . We must not take the kind of experience that is common in a particular people or a particular generation as necessarily exhaustive. John Bull is not the measure of the spiritual possibilities of the human race' (*Foundations,* London, 1913, p. 271). It may be that our generation is not capable of the depth of experience required to see sin for the hideous thing that it is, and to see the need for atonement. But this lack of ours does not mean that these great spiritual truths have now become false. They remain, be our shortcomings what they are.

Synoptists tells us that Jesus spoke of hell[3] (Mt. 23:33; Mk. 9:43, 45, 47; Lk. 12:5). John refers to a present judgment (Jn. 3:19). Paul assures us that 'as many as have sinned without law shall also perish without law: and as many as have sinned under law shall be judged by law' (Rom. 2:12). There are differences. But there is one grim reality which underlies all such statements. Sinners will reap the due reward of their misdeeds. That reward is uniformly regarded throughout the New Testament as the most unpleasant one imaginable.

Many modern writers, in reaction against a theology which emphasized the lurid details of the infernal geography and took a grim delight in picturing the tortures of the damned, have gone to the other extreme and deny the eternal consequences of sin. They suggest that the love of God is incompatible with the idea of eternal death with all that that means.[4] The result is that the consequences of sin as they are thus set forth are not nearly so severe as they are for the Bible writers. At best all men will be saved,[5] and at worst the bad will cease to exist. While some such modern writers do try to bring out the seriousness of sin, seen now as sin against love, yet it is difficult to deny that they have made of sin something less serious than the Bible writers did. In other words, if we are trying to understand the New Testament teaching, we must not be led astray by certain modern notions. Whether these are right or wrong, they are not the ideas in the Bible.

Nor as a matter of fact do they correspond to our best human insights. Serious reflection on life's experiences has convinced most thinkers that sin is not to be trifled with. It erects barriers between man and man. It corrupts character. It reaps a dreadful harvest, both in the life of the sinner and in the lives of others round about him. Great writers have made this their theme in the tragedies of every language throughout the centuries. And it is not uncommon, either in great literature or in common life, to find the sinner's own

[3] The idea of hell is widely rejected today while that of heaven is not. It is worth noting the point made by N. Micklem: 'Heaven is popularly supposed to be a place or a state that will be very, very nice, and we are content to leave it at that. Heaven a nice place? The problem is how it could be endurable for one moment to any one of us . . . . We are to be at home with God, and how can such as we are be at home with God? "They shall see him whom they have pierced." If our Lord were to look upon us with those eyes with which he looked upon St. Peter in the hall, should we be in heaven or in hell?' (*The Doctrine of our Redemption*, Oxford, 1960, p. 10).

[4] T. F. Torrance points out that doctrines which minimize the seriousness of the situation are not really the expression of love (SJT, ii, p. 318).

[5] Like the vessel overheard by Omar Khayam, they dismiss the thought of final judgment, and lightheartedly assume that God will see things their way: 'They talk of some strict testing of us — Pish! He's a Good Fellow, and 'twill all be well' (*Rubaiyat*, 64).

conscience coming to see the necessity for an atonement. Sin must be dealt with. It cannot be simply ignored.[6]

Not only do many modern writers think little of the penalty of sin, but they often deny man's responsibility. Sin, they say, is simply the result of the way we are made. Karl Heim has registered a notable protest against this way of thinking, and quite a long section of his book, *Jesus the World's Perfecter,* is given over to a discussion of guilt. He points to the fact that many in his nation (and what is true of Germany is true also of the rest of the world) regard fate rather than guilt as the significant thing. We are fated to sin, and that is all there is to it. Indeed, some even hold it to be a good thing to sin. Heim cites Wilhelm Hauer as saying, 'There is no growth without guilt. That is why guilt is man's destiny. That is why, if we see its deepest connexions, guilt is God's decision'; 'The epic songs of the Edda . . . are saturated with the tremendous sensation that the hero who goes the way he ought to go becomes guilty.'[7] This is not guilt at all, for guilt means personal responsibility or it means nothing! This is fate, welcoming evil as a means of growth. Heim rejects all such approaches. He points out that this means the overthrow of the foundations of society. He proceeds to draw a series of contrasts between fate and guilt, the third of which brings out the seriousness of guilt. 'Guilt alone is the absolute evil, the absolutely terrible and unbearable, the simple irrevocable loss. Compared to guilt all else that may be terrible in the world is very slight indeed.'[8] The reason for this is that sin is against God. Sin is satanic rebellion against God. To take part in sin is thus to cut ourselves off from communion with God and therefore from our best good. A thoughtful consideration of guilt lends to a recognition of the seriousness of sin.

This emphasis on the significance of guilt is timely. There is no possibility of an ultimately satisfying life or an ultimately satisfying theology if more shallow views of sin and guilt prevail. The New Testament writers see men as in a terrible plight, indeed. Their view of salvation is meaningless apart from that.

(3) *Salvation takes place only because God in His love wills it and brings it about*

Basic to the New Testament doctrine of atonement is the thought that it all proceeds from God. The simplest thing is to connect it with

---

[6] Cf. W. F. Lofthouse, 'It is the same with the lie told by a man to his friend. The friendship cannot be the same after the lie as before it. The wrong, unatoned for, would live on to interfere with all the confidence and openness without which friendship is but a name. Until this need of satisfaction has been recognized by injured and injurer alike, the restoration of real friendship is impossible' (*Ethics and Atonement,* London, 1906, p. 101).

[7] *Jesus the World's Perfecter*, Edinburgh and London, 1959, pp. 6f.

[8] *Op. cit.,* p. 15.

the love of God (Jn. 3:16; Rom. 5:8, etc.). That is to say, the salvation that was wrought in Christ is something that proceeds from the loving heart of the Father. The doctrine of the Reformers has often been caricatured as though it meant setting the Father in opposition to the Son. A loving Son is pictured as winning salvation for men from a just, but unrelenting, Father. This is unjust to the Reformers and it is unjust to the New Testament writers from whom they drew their doctrine. It must be said as firmly as it can be said that there is no understanding of the atonement at all unless it is seen as a fully divine work. Atonement is wrought basically because God loves men.

This is sometimes misunderstood to mean that therefore sin will go unpunished. Since God is loving, runs the thought, He will not be hard on sinners. He will forgive them. He will bring them back to Himself.[9] If this is all that there is to it, it is hard to see why the Christ should have suffered at all. If God simply forgives, then nothing more is needed. The cross is not needed. The cross is no more than a piece of useless embroidery. The cross is emptied of its meaning.

But that is not the way the apostles saw the cross. For them the love of God does not mean that sin can be lightly passed over or dismissed with a wave of the hand.[10] For them the love of God means that sin is dealt with. In point of fact the New Testament does not speak of the love of God as a truism, as though it were quite obvious. It does not even speak of it as something revealed in the sufferings and death of Christ. It is the sufferings and death of Christ *as dealing with our sins* which the New Testament writers see as showing the divine love. If the classic passages connecting the love of God and the cross be examined it will be seen that there

[9] Cf. P. Wernle, 'How miserably all those finely constructed theories of sacrifice and vicarious atonement crumble to pieces before this faith in the love of God our Father, who so gladly pardons. The one parable of the prodigal son wipes them all óff the slate. Sin and its burden lie far away from the disciples of Jesus, and still further is the theology of sin and propitiation' (*The Beginnings of Christianity*, i, London, 1903, p. 109).

[10] H. Cunliffe-Jones has a relevant comment: 'We must take the wrath of God against the sin of man seriously. In a well-known hymn, the writer, having begun a verse rightly

> There is no place where earth's sorrows
> Are more felt than up in heaven;

continues his thought on an emptier plane:

> There is no place where earth's failings
> Have such kindly judgment given.

The judgment of God is compassionate, but it is also costly. It is not kindly, as though he minimized the sin or his own wrath, but redemptive and he himself bears the cost of the hatefulness of sin' (*Deuteronomy*, London, 1951, p. 73).

is always some reference to our deliverance from the plight into which our sins had placed us (e. g., Jn. 3:16; Rom. 5:8; 1 Jn. 4:10). The love and holiness of God must be understood together.[11]   As D. M. Baillie has put it, the sacrifice of Christ 'is an *expiatory* sacrifice, because sin is a dreadfully real thing which love cannot tolerate or lightly pass over, and it is only out of the suffering of such inexorable love that true forgiveness, as distinct from an indulgent amnesty, could ever come.   That is the objective process of atonement that goes on in the very life of God.'[12]   The distinction between 'true forgiveness' and 'an indulgent amnesty' is one which is not always made.   But 'an indulgent amnesty' settles nothing.   Expiation is a necessity *because of* God's love, not something that is mistakenly imagined to have taken place despite that love.

Sometimes Scripture speaks of salvation as taking place according to the will of God (Acts 2:23; Eph. 1:11, etc.).   Or Christ may be spoken of as 'sent' by the Father (Mk. 9:37; Lk. 4:43; and often in John). These passages mean basically the same thing as those we have just been looking at. They root salvation in the divine nature. To say that God willed that men be saved through the death of His Son is the same as to say that He loved men so greatly that He saved them through the death of His Son. The divine will is not to be separated from the divine love.[13]

---

[11] P. L. Snowden points out that 'while it is nowhere said "God is love, love, love," yet both in the Old and New Testaments, by the Prophet Isaiah and by St. John himself, the angelic hosts are represented as proclaiming "Holy, holy, holy, is the Lord of hosts, the Lord God Almighty"' (*The Atonement and Ourselves,* New York, 1918, pp. 41f.). The references are to Is. 6:3 and Rev. 4:8. Snowden, of course, is not minimizing the importance of the truth that God is love, but reminding us that the love is not to be understood in such a way as to belittle the holiness.

[12] *God was in Christ,* London, 1955, p. 198. W. G. T. Shedd distinguished between indulgence and mercy. Indulgence, he says, 'is foolish good nature. It releases from punishment without making any provision for the claims of law . . . . It costs an effort to be just, and it does not like to put forth an effort. Indulgence, in the last analysis, is intensely selfish. Mere happiness in the sense of freedom from discomfort or pain is the final end which it has in view. Consequently, the action of indulgence as distinguished from mercy is high-handed. It is the exercise of bare power in snatching the criminal away from merited suffering. It is might, not right' (*Dogmatic Theology,* Edinburgh, 1889, ii, p. 448). To assert that nothing is necessary for the divine forgiveness other than benevolent good nature is to suggest that in forgiving men God works on the principle that might is right, a horrible and completely unbiblical thought.

[13] J. Burnier speaks of the necessity for Jesus to give proof 'of His own utter loyalty to the will of the holy God to whom the sinner is odious and who perforce pronounces on him the sentence of death. Hence Jesus could only deliver men from the enslavement of sin by undergoing in their presence the punishment which was their due' (*The Vocabulary of the Bible,* ed. J. J. von Allmen, London, 1958, p. 350).

This may be carried back into the past as in the many statements that scripture was fulfilled in the events surrounding the passion. This is such a favourite practice of the New Testament writers in general that quotation is superfluous. And it witnesses to a deeply held conviction that salvation is no afterthought. It takes place because God, foreseeing man's sin, made provision that man be saved. The events in the life and death and resurrection and ascension of Christ then represent the working out of the plan purposed long before and foretold through the prophets. This is the implication also of such concepts as predestination and election. In earlier sections I have pointed out that these should not be understood as contradicting the thought of the divine love. Rather they are its outworking. Because God loves men He has chosen out His saints, He has predestined salvation. This is a major strand of New Testament teaching, and it must receive due emphasis.

(4) *Salvation depends on what God has done in Christ*

This seems so obvious as scarcely to need stating. It becomes necessary because there are many who claim that God in His love is always ready to forgive the penitent, and who leave the statement there.[14] It is, of course, true that God is always ready to forgive the penitent, but on New Testament principles this is not due to any particular merit in penitence, nor to some careless attitude to sin on the part of God.[15] It is due to the fact that God has sent His Son to deal with the problem of man's sin. It is due to the atonement that was wrought out on Calvary's cross. It is because the way is open wide that the penitent sinner may come.

The objectionable feature of the position which we are discussing is that it leaves Christ out of the process of forgiveness. It assumes that all that is necessary is a good disposition on the part of the sinner corresponding to the already good disposition from the side of God. This is to make Calvary meaningless. If His death did nothing to bring about our forgiveness, then exactly why did Christ die?

The New Testament makes the cross central.[16] The Gospels are

---

14 'Our age is apt to think of the moral law as "something which God can set aside with a sort of large-hearted generosity." The belief that throughout the Universe "bills must be paid" is alien to the modern conception of God as an indulgent parent' (Marcus Donovan, *The Faith of a Catholic,* London, 1937, pp. 33f.).

15 Cf. William Temple, 'Free forgiveness is immoral if it is lightly given . . . . The promise of free forgiveness on condition of repentance to men so blind and callous as we are would be demoralising' (*Christus Veritas,* London, 1925, p. 260).

16 This is overlooked by some who stress the eternal nature of suffering love. This point of view was well expressed long ago by H. Bushnell when he said, 'It is as if there were a cross unseen, standing on its undiscovered

basically books about the cross. They make the cross the climax
to which all else leads up. If their interest were primarily bio-
graphical or the like, they would not give such a disproportionate
amount of space to the events associated with the cross. And if it
were the fact of the death and not its significance, they would have
devoted more space to details, to the physical agony and the like.
In point of fact they treat the physical sufferings of Christ with
great reserve. They are not concerned to portray agony for agony's
sake (in the manner of the modern horror story). They are concerned
with God's provision for our salvation, and they see the death of
Christ as the very central thing. The Acts takes up the story
by telling how the good news of what God had done in Christ was
proclaimed far and wide. The Epistles, written as they are to meet
the needs of the churches, unfold the implications of this salvation.
Everywhere Christ is central, and everywhere it is the cross of Christ
on which attention is focussed in particular. That is the one indispensable thing. Without the death of Christ there could have
been no salvation. With that death the salvation of God becomes a
glorious reality.

(5) *Both the Godhead and the manhood of Christ are involved
in the process*

It is plain enough that the New Testament pictures Jesus Christ as
God incarnate. That is to say, it shows Him as fully God and fully
man at one and the same time. The history of doctrine is plentifully
besprinkled with examples of the dangers that attend such an exclusive emphasis on one of these truths that the other is lost sight
of or not allowed its full force. It is not always so clearly realized
that this is true also of the doctrine of the atonement. Man's salvation proceeds from the work of One who was both God and man,
and this salvation is inexplicable apart from both. We have already
stressed the importance of the Godhead. Unless Jesus was fully
God, our salvation did not originate from God. Rather it would have
been wrung from Him. At best we would be left to think that God
did not greatly mind our being saved. But this is not the witness
of the New Testament. There we see a God who cares intensely for
His people, cares enough, in fact, to take painful steps to bring
them to Himself. It is the love and the moral energy and the deep
concern for the right of God Himself that we see so vividly dis-

---

hill, far back in the ages, out of which were sounding always, just the same
deep voice of suffering love and patience, that was heard by mortal ears
from the sacred hill of Calvary' (*The Vicarious Sacrifice,* London, 1866, p. 31).
This is said finely and with deep religious feeling. But it takes the centrality
out of Calvary and distorts the teaching of the New Testament. There the
cross has a once-for-all quality.

played on the cross. Thus it is that the Fourth Gospel, that book about salvation written expressly to tell men how they can obtain eternal life (Jn. 20:31), begins with a section setting forth the infinite dignity of Jesus as the Logos, who can be described as being with God and as being God. Thus it is also that Paul can intertwine the thoughts of the Person and the work of Christ as he does in Colossians 1 and Philippians 2. The news that thrilled the New Testament writers was the news that none less than God Himself had acted for their salvation.

But the New Testament writers insist just as strongly on the manhood of Jesus. Every reference to the death of Jesus means just this, for God does not die. Sometimes the implication is drawn out, as when the writer to the Hebrews insists that Jesus' manhood was an integral part of His priesthood. And we have noticed that most of the New Testament writers in one way or another bring out the point that Jesus made Himself one with sinners. For our salvation He came right where we are.[17] It was as man that He suffered, as man offered His sacrifice, as man rendered obedience to the Father, as man endured the insults and ill-treatment of His enemies.

The omission of either side of this paradox is bound to lead us into error. Aulén emphasizes strongly the way the Latin theory of the atonement puts its stress on the manhood. Jesus the man offers the propitiation, while the Father does little more than accept it. This opens the way for a cleavage in the Godhead. The Son is seen as providing the satisfaction and the Father only as demanding it. The Latin theory has not always been stated quite like this, but, whenever this is its thrust, it is in error. Whenever the atonement is understood in any such way, the biblical doctrine is woefully distorted.

But there is also harm done when it is insisted, as it is by Aulén himself, that the atonement is all of God. Though he sometimes speaks of the human element in Christ's offering this theologian puts all his emphasis on the divine. Over and over he insists that the atonement is from first to last God's work.[18] He concentrates on the theme that God in Christ has won the victory over all the forces of evil. The manhood of our Lord has no real part to play in the

---

[17] Karl Barth points out that the Christian message 'says that God has made Himself the One who fulfils His redemptive will, that He has become man for us, that in the power of His Godhead He might take up our cause in our place' (CDDR, p. 19).

[18] This is emphasized in *Christus Victor*. The same point of view is put forward by A. Nygren in *Essence of Christianity* (London, 1960). He outlines his view thus: "in Christianity there can be no thought of atonement and reconciliation as something accomplished by man. *The atonement is from first to last a work of God.* This statement must be given full weight, and must also be applied without qualification to the atoning work of Christ" (*op. cit.*, p. 97).

work of atonement. The incarnation seems to be meaningless, at least as far as the atonement is concerned.[19] Moreover, this particular concentration on the Godhead to the exclusion of the manhood of Christ leads to an emphasis on the note of victory to the exclusion of that of justice. On this view there is grave danger of coming to the conclusion that might is right with God. God appears as concerned not at all with justice, but only with defeating His enemy, Satan. The thought that persists after reading Aulén is that of the overpowering divine might, of the inability of any creature to stand before Him and of the resounding victory He secured when Satan put Him to the test.

If it were as simple as Aulén implies the long arguments about theories of the atonement would surely never have taken place. The reason that men have differed so very greatly is that the New Testament teaching on the subject is far from simple. And in particular it does not think of it as no more than a display of divine power. There is divine power as the preceding survey has shown. But there is more than that. There is a deep concern for the right, a passionate concern that justice be done. And if the doing of justice in a situation where the strict application of the principle means disaster for the sinner is combined with a determination to save men, then we need not be surprised if the result admits of no simple explanation. The point we are concerned to make just now is that the New Testament insists that both the Godhead and the manhood of Christ are concerned in this process of atonement. It is this which presents us with not the least of our difficulties.

(6) *Christ was personally innocent*

This is another theme which is proclaimed far and wide through the New Testament. The death of Christ cannot possibly be interpreted as the due penalty for personal sin. The Gospel writers depict for us the perfect life of Him 'who went about doing good' (Acts 10:38). They tell us that Pilate bore his testimony to Christ's innocence (Lk. 23:14f.; Jn. 19:6). The writer to the Hebrews assures us that He was 'in all points tempted like as we are, yet without sin' (Heb. 4:15). The life that He lived was spotless, a life of perfect obedience to the Father. The death that He died accordingly was the death of a pure Victim. And a pure Victim everywhere in the Bible is regarded as the only Victim which can take away sins.

---

[19] He can say 'Incarnation and Atonement stand in no sort of antithesis' (*Christus Victor*, London, 1937, p. 50). But there is no part to be played by the incarnation save that of providing an instrument for the Godhead. 'The redemptive work is accomplished *by* the Logos *through* the Manhood as His instrument' (*loc. cit.*). And Aulén does not show us why this particular instrument is necessary, or even desirable.

Christ's sinlessness is an indispensable qualification for His role as Saviour.[20] Had He had the least spot of sin about Him He would have needed to have His own sin removed. He would not have been able to take away the sins of others. But as it is the Scriptures reveal Him as the perfect Saviour.

(7) *While the importance of the life of Christ is not to be minimized, central importance is attached to His death*

The tremendous importance the New Testament attaches to the death of Jesus should not be overlooked. The cross is at the heart of all New Testament teaching. This is a distinctive of the Christian religion. No special importance is attached to the death of anyone in the Old Testament.[21] In all cultures martyrs are highly venerated, but nowhere do we find men regarding the death of their heroes in anything like the way that the New Testament writers regard that of Christ. The Christian emphasis on the cross is distinctively different from the common attitude to the heroic dead.[22]

No Christian in his right mind would want to suggest that the life of Christ is anything but superlatively important. Under heading (6) we were looking at something of this importance. But there is a school of thought today which to all intents and purposes roots salvation in the incarnation. Bethlehem, not Calvary, becomes the focus of attention. A noteworthy recent example is G. S. Hendry's treatment of the theme, *The Gospel of the Incarnation*.[23] The writer several times says that he is not minimizing the place of the death of Christ, and that, in fact, the death can be understood rightly only by seeing it as he does, from the perspective of the life. But the emphasis is all on the life. Statements abound like,

> if the incarnation be interpreted in the "existentialist" terms of the Biblical testimony rather than in the "essentialist" categories of Greek philosophy, if, that is to say, it be understood, not merely as the assumption of our nature, but as the living of the incarnate

[20] Heim puts a great deal of emphasis on this (*op. cit.*, pp. 75f.).

[21] Cf. Dyson Hague, 'There were plenty of martyrs and national heroes in Hebrew history, and many of them were stoned and sawn asunder, were tortured and slain with the sword, but no Jewish writer attributes any ethical or regenerative importance to their death, or to the shedding of their blood' (*The Fundamentals*, xi, Chicago, n. d., p. 25).

[22] Cullmann reminds us of the importance of the worship of the first Christians as indicating their thought on this matter. 'The primitive Church was far more interested in Christ's death and resurrection than in his incarnation. Every Lord's Day (later called Sunday) was a "day of resurrection" and, in addition, there was a single Christian festival, that of Easter, which, along with the holy days associated with it, celebrated Christ's death and resurrection' (*The Early Church*, London, 1956, p. 23).

[23] Philadelphia, 1958.

> life in personal relations with men at the human level, then we
> may say with truth that salvation is by incarnation.[24]

And when he comes to deal with the question 'Why did Christ die?'
he takes up this position:

> death was inherent in his mission as the bearer of the forgiveness
> of God to men.   Forgiveness has its reality in a personal relation-
> ship in which alienation is countered by an acceptance that tran-
> scends it.   Opposition is opposed by a love that overcomes it.
> The encounter of divine grace and human sin has the nature of a
> collision, and as such it necessarily involves suffering.   The cross
> marks the climax of this suffering.[25]

All this appears to mean that there is no particular significance in
the death of Christ.   Its significance is that which it shares with
His life, and that which it shares with the death of other good men
('Indeed, its nonuniqueness is an implicate of the incarnation'[26]).
That and no more.   It is impossible to agree that this is the teaching
of the New Testament.   There the life of Jesus is important, but its
importance is brought out in ways which do not obscure the centrality of the death.   For, as James Denney puts it, 'even Christ's
life, taking it as it stands in the Gospels, only enters into the Atonement, and has reconciling power, because it is pervaded from beginning to end by the consciousness of His death.'[27]   Indeed it is
only as we recognize what His death wrought that we can rightly
appreciate His life,[28] for the two must be understood together.   We
appreciate the life and the Person only when we bear in mind that
they are the life and the Person of Him who by His death wrought
salvation for mankind.   Professor Hendry does not really face this.

And if Professor Hendry's treatment is not scriptural, it is also

[24] *Op. cit.,* pp. 139f.   So also he says, 'Christ saves us, not merely by
the constitution of his person, but by the life he lived among us' (*op. cit.,*
p. 167).

[25] *Op. cit.,* p. 142.

[26] *Op. cit.,* p. 143.   He later says, 'he is unique who died on the cross'.
The uniqueness is not in the death nor in what it accomplished, but solely
in the Person who died.

[27] *The Atonement and the Modern Mind,* London, 1910, p. 108.   He
further speaks of Christ's life as 'part of His death: in deliberate and conscious
descent, ever deeper and deeper, into the dark valley where at the last hour
the last reality of sin was to be met and borne . . . . Our Lord's Passion *is*
His sublimest action — an action so potent that all His other actions are
sublimated in it, and we know everything when we know that He *died*
for our sins' (*op. cit.,* p. 109).

[28] Cf. O. C. Quick, 'It was, we may reasonably conjecture, as forgiver of
sin, and saviour from the wrath which was its penalty, that Jesus first stood
forth in Jewish eyes as a divine person.   Thus it was through the realization
of atonement that Jewish Christians felt their way towards a full doctrine of
the incarnation' (*Doctrines of the Creed,* London, 1949, p. 78).

true that it is not satisfying. It leads to some most unsatisfactory conclusions. Thus he tells us that the New Testament 'nowhere suggests that forgiveness is a problem for God'.[29] We see what this means when we read that Christ

> came as the bearer of forgiveness, which is the gift of the grace of God from all eternity. He dispensed forgiveness to men from the beginning of his public ministry, with never a suggestion that it was contingent upon any work that he did, but only that it was present in him in a unique way. Nor did he ever suggest that only with his mission had God begun to be gracious, or that there had been no forgiveness for men before he came. Any such suggestion would be utterly at variance with the message of the Old Testament.[30]

In the light of this we are surely justified in asking, 'Then just what *did* Jesus do?' If Professor Hendry is right, His death is not the cause of forgiveness, nor for that matter is His life. Even before He came, men were forgiven on no other basis than the grace of God. And if He had not come, surely on these premises they could have gone on being forgiven in the same way. Despite the fact that Professor Hendry argues his case with learning and skill and with transparent devotion, I trust we may be forgiven for refusing to accept a theory which is so calamitous in its implications. With whatever blunderings and false conceptions, some of the theories which Professor Hendry rejects at least set forth with emphasis the truth that Christ actually *did* something for men. His life and His death accomplished something which could not have been accomplished apart from Him. They mean something when they call Him 'Saviour', and when they ascribe our salvation solely to Him. But for Professor Hendry, Christ appears to have done no more than point men to a forgiveness which was there independently of Him and always had been. Traditionally Christians have seen His death as effecting something. In the final analysis Professor Hendry does not.[31]

---

[29] *Op. cit.*, p. 121.

[30] *Op. cit.*, p. 134. W. G. T. Shedd has a different idea of the significance of forgiveness. 'Penal suffering in Scripture is released, or not inflicted upon the guilty, because it has been endured by a substitute. If penalty were remitted by sovereignty merely, without any judicial ground or reason whatever; if it were inflicted neither upon the sinner nor his substitute; this would be the *abolition* of penalty, not the remission of it' (*op. cit.*, p. 392). The last expression will bear thinking over. What do we mean by remission?

[31] He does say 'We have forgiveness only in personal relation with God incarnate' (*op. cit.*, p. 148). But I do not see why he adds the final word. There seems nothing in his argument that demands it, and much which contradicts it, e. g., the suggestion that men had forgiveness before God became incarnate. He keeps insisting that forgiveness depends solely on the grace of God. In the same paragraph from which these words are taken he

G. F. Moore puts the Jewish view of forgiveness this way: 'The Mishnah . . . makes repentance the indispensable condition of remission of every kind of sin, and this, with the other side of it, namely, that God freely and fully remits the sins of the penitent, is a cardinal doctrine of Judaism; it may properly be called the Jewish doctrine of salvation.'[32]   In the last resort it is hard to see a difference between this view and that of Professor Hendry.[33]   But if salvation comes solely on the condition of repentance there is no need, no real need of Christ's work.   It may be valuable to have Him tell us these things. But it cannot be said to be *necessary* on these premises.   Professor Hendry's view no more than that of Judaism finds Christ's work as a necessary work.

Such views are not rare.   On the contrary it is quite common to find modern theologians taking the emphasis off the death and insisting that it is no more than the fitting conclusion to the life.[34]   The atonement, we are told, is something eternal, not an event in time.[35] Some prefer to speak of Christ's sacrifice as glimpsed for a moment on Calvary, but as taking place in eternity.[36]   We are creatures of time, immersed in the time-process.   But we must endeavour to shake ourselves free if we are to appreciate the true nature of Christ's eternal offering.   There is something which makes this kind of thing congenial to thinkers of our day.   But it does not square with the

---

says of forgiveness: 'Its only ground is the grace of God.' He insists that men before Christ could and did receive forgiveness. It seems to me to be avoiding the logic of his position accordingly when he speaks of 'the free gift of God *in Jesus Christ*' and the like. The plain truth is that if forgiveness can come about independently of Jesus Christ, then neither His person nor His work, neither His life nor His death nor anything else about Him can be *necessary* to forgiveness. Professor Hendry cannot have it both ways. If men could be forgiven quite apart from Christ then forgiveness is not 'in Jesus Christ'.

[32] *Judaism,* i, Harvard, 1927, p. 500.

[33] Contrast K. E. Kirk, 'great penitents throughout the ages have recorded for their fellow-Christians the conviction, "Penitence is not enough." Here is a truth to which Christianity is fully and absolutely committed. Penitence is not enough' (*Report of the Anglo-Catholic Congress,* London, 1927, p. 86).

[34] E.g., Nels Ferré, *The Christian Understanding of God,* London, 1952, p. 206.

[35] E.g., Dom Gregory Dix, *The Shape of the Liturgy,* London, 1954, p. 242.

[36] I do not think this has been better expressed than it was by C. A. Dinsmore, 'As the flash of the volcano discloses for a few hours the elemental fires at the earth's centre, so the light on Calvary was the bursting forth through historical conditions of the very nature of the Everlasting. There was a cross in the heart of God before there was one planted on the green hill outside of Jerusalem. And now that the cross of wood has been taken down, the one in the heart of God abides, and it will remain so long as there is one sinful soul for whom to suffer' (*Atonement in Literature and Life,* London, 1906, pp. 232f.).

New Testament, and that is its condemnation.[37] It must accordingly be emphatically rejected. In the New Testament there cannot be the slightest doubt but that the cross is the great central divine act which brings men salvation.[38] 'Crucial' is a significant word.

(8) *In His death Christ made Himself one with sinners. He took their place*

The modern world is ready to pay its homage to the Carpenter of Nazareth, who lived simply, taught beautifully, was betrayed shamefully, and died courageously.[39] He is given an honoured place among 'the noble army of martyrs' who have suffered for their convictions throughout the ages and throughout the world. But that was not the way the men of the New Testament saw His life and death. It is important to be clear on this. His death was not simply a martyrdom.[40] As the New Testament writers saw it, He came to save sinful men and His death was the central feature in His accomplishment of salvation. It was not simply a martyrdom. It was a taking of the place of sinful men so that His death should avail for them.

As early as Matthew 3:15 we read that Jesus submitted to a baptism that numbered Him with transgressors and pointed forward to the death that He would die for them. Throughout His ministry

[37] R. H. Fuller has a section entitled 'The Cruciality of the Cross' in which he emphasizes this for the Gospels (*The Mission and Achievement of Jesus*, London, 1954, pp. 77f.).

[38] Cf. A. M. Ramsey, *The Gospel and the Catholic Church*, London, 1956, p. 23.

[39] See, for example, Upton Sinclair's imaginative reconstruction, *A Personal Jesus*, London, 1954, where the death of Christ has much less than the place the New Testament assigns it.

[40] E. Stauffer has a valuable summary of 'The Principal Elements of the Old Biblical Theology of Martyrdom' (*New Testament Theology*, London, 1955, pp. 331-4), in which he cites both biblical and non-biblical texts on the subject. His list of 47 items shows that the ancient world was deeply interested in the whole subject, but that it rarely attached atoning value to the sufferings of the martyrs. The New Testament attitude toward the sufferings of Jesus is in marked contrast. H. Wheeler Robinson also brings out the difference between the general attitude to the martyrs and the Christian attitude toward the death of Jesus. He speaks of the Maccabean martyrs and points to the importance of their link with others of their race. He goes on, 'In one sense, this, of course, takes something away from the sacrificial aspect of their deaths, as Koeberle points out: "If they suffer for the people, it is because they too are Jews. There is wanting the most important element, viz. that the pious man voluntarily takes the sin of others into his consciousness, and experiences it as his own through love — that he becomes one with the guilty on moral lines, and not on the ground of physical association." That difference should be remembered when we come to consider the vicarious suffering of the Cross of Christ' (*The Cross in the Old Testament*, London, 1955, p. 96).

He stood aloof from the orthodox religious party and continually sought out sinful men. This strand of teaching is found outside the Gospels as when Paul tells us that God sent Him 'in the likeness of sinful flesh' (Rom. 8:3), and when the writer to the Hebrews says 'it behoved him in all things to be made like unto his brethren' (Heb. 2:17).

But particularly is the point made with respect to His death. We have seen reason for thinking that Jesus was held to be the Suffering Servant of Isaiah 53 who 'was wounded for our transgressions', who 'was bruised for our iniquities'. On Him was 'the chastisement of our peace', on Him was laid 'the iniquity of us all'. All of which means substitution. He suffered where we should have suffered. The same thought is behind the ransom saying of Mark 10:45, with Christ giving His life 'a ransom for ($\dot{a}\nu\tau\acute{\iota}$) many'. The agony in Gethsemane and the cry of dereliction point us to the same thing. It is difficult to give either of them an adequate interpretation if we exclude the thought that Christ's death was in our stead. In the Fourth Gospel there is the prophecy of Caiaphas 'that one man should die for the people, and that the whole nation perish not', explained as it is as a genuine prophecy signifying 'that Jesus should die for the nation; and not for the nation only, but that he might also gather together into one the children of God that are scattered abroad' (Jn. 11:50ff.). With these we should take the Johannine statements that Christ in His death was 'the propitiation for our sins' (1 Jn. 2:2; 4:10).

The thought of substitution is clear in the Pauline writings. Notable is the statement that 'Christ redeemed us from the curse of the law, having become a curse for us' (Gal. 3:13). Paul also tells us that God made Him sin for us (2 Cor. 5:21). These passages must surely mean that Christ bore the full consequences of our sin. This reasoning also underlies Romans 3:21-26, where the Apostle argues that God's justice has been manifested in the means whereby sin is forgiven. The same thought of substitution seems implied in passages which stress the close identification of the Saviour with sinners in His death (e. g., Rom. 6:3ff.; 2 Cor. 5:14). The thought is that when Christ died, the sinner died. And Christ is referred to as 'a substitute-ransom ($\dot{a}\nu\tau\acute{\iota}\lambda\upsilon\tau\rho\sigma\nu$)' for men (1 Tim. 2:6).

Elsewhere we should notice as especially important the idea that Christ bore our sins (1 Pet. 2:24; Heb. 9:28). As we saw when we discussed these passages, the thought is that Christ bore our penalty. In other words, He took our place. This is involved also in the statement that He 'suffered for sins once ($\ddot{a}\pi a\xi$), the righteous for the unrighteous' (1 Pet. 3:18).

This is a persistent strand of New Testament teaching and it must not be overlooked. When Christ came to do His great work for sinners, it involved being where the sinners were. To use a phrase from Ezekiel, He 'sat where they sat', and this, not only in the sense that He entered into a perfect sympathy with them as He shared their earthly lot, but also in that He took their place as He died.[41] This view is out of favour just now, but nothing less seems adequate to the New Testament evidence. We shall return to the point.

(9) *By His life, death, resurrection and ascension Christ triumphed over Satan and sin and every conceivable force of evil*

It is the special merit of Aulén's treatment of the subject to have drawn attention to the importance of this element of New Testament teaching. It was prized in the early church, as we see from the exuberance with which it was used and the picturesque, even grotesque, imagery that was employed to express it.[42] Thus Satan was pictured as caught on a fish-hook, and as snared in a mouse-trap. The imagery is forceful. The Fathers exulted in the victory Christ had won, and they voiced their exultation in exuberant language with a lordly disregard for possible implications that might be drawn by men of greater precision and less imagination.[43] But in the course of time the emphasis came to be put on their forceful metaphors, and not on the truth to which they pointed. Pedestrian minds grasped nothing beyond the literal meaning and in time this led to the eclipse altogether of this facet of scriptural teaching. It was never without its exponents (Aulén claims Luther, though this is not conceded by all; that is to say, Aulén's exclusive claim is denied, while it is recognized that this Reformer did stress the victory as well as other

[41] Cf. J. E. Fison, 'Here is no Amos diagnosing evil from the outside with all the pitiless clarity of the spectator's view. Here is another and a greater Hosea implicated himself in the sin and sorrow and suffering of others, who was compelled to pass judgment upon his people and yet only did so by entering mysteriously into that judgment himself in the vicarious alchemy of the cross' (*The Christian Hope*, London, 1954, p. 130).

[42] But we must be on our guard against accepting it as a consciously held theory, held in the same manner as later theories. Cf. A. D. Galloway, 'Where Aulén seems to me to go more seriously astray is in his tendency to treat this "classical" view as though it were a definite and fairly clearly defined conception, comparable to any of the modern views of the Atonement. This gives rather a distorted picture of what seems to have been the actual historical situation' (*The Cosmic Christ*, London, 1951, p. 61). The Fathers at times use expressions compatible with several later theories. They did not so much evolve a precisely defined theory, as give vigorous expression to the thought of Christ's triumph which Aulén is able to work into a theory.

[43] N. Micklem shows that a slight change of language helps us to see their essential meaning: 'Like a magnet he drew upon himself all the forces and reserves of evil; he compelled them to a supreme and final test; they must break him, or he will infallibly break them . . . . If we substitute "magnet" for "bait", the image no longer seems grotesque, and we have some insight into what is meant' (*op. cit.*, p. 51).

aspects of Christ's work). Our hymns, particularly our Easter hymns, have a way of returning to the thought of the triumph of the Christ. But it cannot be denied that this was not in the forefront of theological teaching. Aulén's emphasis has recalled theology to the truth that for the first Christians the victory that Christ had won for them mattered intensely. They were mostly from the depressed classes with little to hope for in this world. And they pictured a host of demons as dominating life anyway. It came as a welcome relief to have assurance that the last word was not with their oppressors, human or supernatural. So the note of victory was sounded with joyous confidence. And we in our day need it no less than they.[44] It is as well that we have been recalled to it. And if we feel that we cannot go along with those enthusiastic exponents of the victory view in their exclusiveness and refusal to see other elements as equally important, that does not dim our gratitude for the fact that they are reminding us of something that ought never to be forgotten.[45]

(10) *Not only did Christ win a victory, but He secured a verdict. He wrought salvation powerfully, but also legally*

The typical Reformation emphasis was on the legal aspects of the atonement. The Reformers thought of man as having broken the law of God. They saw Christ as paying the penalty man had incurred. Thus our forgiveness rests upon the fact that our penalty has been borne for us. And since the penalty has been borne, it cannot be imposed on us again.

[44] H. E. W. Turner speaks of 'the concept of release from the cosmic forces which oppose mankind and its spiritual progress', and proceeds, 'Perhaps in a period in which economic insecurity, international disorder, and ideological conflict form the backcloth against which is set the life of ordinary people, we are better able than our fathers to enter with sympathy and understanding into the motives which led the early Christians to frame in these terms at least part of their teaching about the redemption wrought by our Lord. Some at least of the elements which the psychologist would describe by the concepts of complex, frustration, divided self-hood, and the like would be included under this rubric in the early centuries' (*The Patristic Doctrine of Redemption*, London, 1952, p. 47).

[45] Some modern writers put such emphasis on the resurrection that the cross appears as little more than a necessary preliminary. The two should not be separated. They belong together. But we should not forget that if they are separated the New Testament puts the emphasis on the cross. Cf. Erich Sauer, 'The cross is the greatest event in the history of salvation, greater even than the resurrection. The cross is the victory, the resurrection the triumph; but the victory is more important than the triumph, although the latter necessarily follows from it. The resurrection is the public display of the victory, the triumph of the Crucified One. But the victory itself was complete. "It is finished" (John 19:30)' (*The Triumph of the Crucified*, London, 1951, p. 32).

But in time came reaction. Scholars could not reconcile this with the New Testament emphasis on love.[46] They thought of God as a Father rather than as a Judge. They felt that legal imagery is sub-personal and rejected it.[47] They disliked the tendency of this theory to put division within the Godhead, so that the Son effects salvation and the Father simply demands punishment. They did not like the conflict between the divine justice and the divine mercy which they thought this theory implies.[48] They did not care for a theory which professed a concern for *justice,* but rested on the proposition that the innocent suffered instead of the guilty, a procedure which is not *just,* whatever else may be said about it.[49] The objections multiplied, and were not stilled when a certain hardness sometimes crept into the attitude of the defenders. And the result is that in

[46] Yet this is surely to misunderstand the meaning of Christian love. Of the statement, 'Love transcends justice', Paul Tillich says, 'This seems rather evident, but it is not!' He reasons thus: 'The relation of love to justice cannot be understood in terms of an addition to justice which does not change its character . . . . A man may say to another: "I know your criminal deed and, according to the demand of justice, I should bring you to trial, but because of my Christian love I let you go." Through this leniency, which is wrongly identified with love, a person may be driven towards a thoroughly criminal career. This means that he has received neither justice nor love, but injustice, covered by sentimentality. He might have been saved by having been brought to trial after his first fall. In this case the act of being just would have been the act of love' (*Love, Power and Justice,* London, 1954, pp. 13f.).

[47] E. g., A. Sabatier, in *The Atonement in Modern Religious Thought, A Theological Symposium,* London, 1900, p. 212.

[48] Though he criticized penal theories very strongly, A. Ritschl pointed the way to a truth which supports them when he spoke of God as 'the moral power which satisfies the highest human interests with an orderly system of ends, and with an order of public law that is in harmony with His very being' (*A Critical History of the Christian Doctrine of Justification and Reconciliation,* Edinburgh, 1872, p. 209). It is an error to think of law as something set over God and to which He is in subjection. But, since law 'is in harmony with His very being' He will act in harmony with the highest law.

[49] Thus L. W. Grensted criticizes the view of Turretin, 'When all is said the "just judge" remains alternately over-cruel and over-lenient, demanding penalty when it is not due, and remitting penalty where it should be enforced' (*A Short History of the Atonement,* Manchester, 1920, p. 246). This ignores the unity between the Father and the Son on the one hand, which means that the 'over-cruel' Judge Himself bears the suffering of His people, and that between the Son and the believers on the other, so that the 'over-lenient' Judge takes no action against those whose penalty has been borne. Paul Tillich points out concerning 'Paul's and Luther's doctrine to accept as just him who is unjust' that 'nothing seems to contradict more the idea of justice than this doctrine, and everybody who has pronounced it has been accused of promoting injustice and amorality. It seems to be utterly unjust to declare him who is unjust, just. But nothing less than this is what has been called the good news in Christian preaching. And nothing less than this is the fulfilment of justice' (*op. cit.,* p. 86).

modern times there are few who care to espouse a theory which includes the thought that Christ bore the penalty for our sins.

But one may legitimately inquire whether the reaction has not gone too far. The plain fact is that the Bible writers, Old Testament as well as New, did not share in the slightest degree the modern distaste for legalism. They seem, on the contrary, to have loved a good legal metaphor. Over and over again they appeal to legal processes to explain God's dealings with men. And if this is so in general, it is not at all surprising that it should be so also in the case of the atonement in particular. Here the possibilities leap to the mind. God is a just Judge. He has given His people His laws. But neither His special people, the Jews, nor any other people have kept them. Thus all the world is guilty before God. To a people who loved legal imagery what could be more natural than to express all this in legal terms?

And when salvation is won, why should it not also be set forth with legal imagery? And that in point of fact is what is done. Paul in particular uses the language of justification (though it is not exclusively his; cf. Lk. 18:14, where the Lord spoke of the publican as 'justified', or Acts 13:39). Paul speaks of God as being shown to be just in the very act by which He justified ungodly men (Rom. 3:26). He speaks of the law's curse as being removed (Gal. 3:13). Theo Preiss has reminded us of the large extent of juridical argument and imagery in the Fourth Gospel.[50] To deny that the New Testament sometimes makes use of legal imagery to describe Christ's work for us is to refuse to face reality. It is the theological equivalent of the man who, confronted for the first time with a giraffe, exclaimed 'There ain't no such animal!' There are other ways of talking about the atonement, but that does not justify us in shutting our eyes to this particular fact. And the fact is that there is legal language in the New Testament.

Moreover, it is there in some quantity. This is sometimes overlooked by theologians who, anxious to refute what they consider the errors of penal views, charge exponents of such views with reading their own views into the evidence. Thus Norman L. Robinson writes of Denney, Forsyth, and Brunner,

> In reading their expositions of the doctrine of the Atonement it is impossible to resist the impression that they bring to the interpretation of the work of Christ upon the Cross a view of the moral order already formed, which they take for granted as axiomatic. They accept what Brunner has called an "iron framework" of moral law, into which, like some bed of Procrustes, they try to fit Christ's revelation of God and His redeeming work upon the Cross.[51]

[50] *Life in Christ*, London, 1954, ch. 1.
[51] *How Jesus Christ Saves Men*, London, n. d., p. 107.

The truth is, of course, the very opposite. The use of legal categories is abundant in the New Testament and it is those theologians who profess to expound the New Testament but who find no place for law who are employing the bed of Procrustes. The New Testament writers, unlike some modern writers, find no difficulty in the category of law. They use it freely.

Nor should we dismiss this as unimportant. There is a moral law and the witness of the conscience of all mankind is that this moral law is important. Superior might is no substitute for it.[52] Are we to think that God treated the moral law as of no account, as a bylaw which may be set aside at will in the process of bringing about our salvation?[53] The mind and the conscience revolt at the thought.

This is sometimes overlooked in modern discussions on the nature of punishment. It is accepted as axiomatic in many quarters that punishment is essentially reformatory in an enlightened society. It will also have deterrent aspects, but it is thought hopelessly out of date to hold it to be retributive. But the matter is not so easy. In the first place, we have strictly no *right* to punish merely for reformatory and deterrent purposes. Unless a man deserves to be punished we ought not to make him suffer. We are at fault when we inflict pain unless there is ill desert. L. Hodgson cites a forthright statement on the subject from F. R. Bradley:

> Punishment is punishment, only where it is deserved. We pay the penalty, because we owe it, and for no other reason; and if punishment is inflicted for any other reason whatever than because it is merited by wrong, it is a gross immorality, a crying injustice, an abominable crime, and not what it pretends to be. We may have regard for whatever considerations we please — our own convenience, the good of society, the benefit of the offender; we are fools, and worse, if we fail to do so. Having once the right to punish, we may modify the punishment according to the useful and the pleasant; but these are external to the matter, they cannot

---

[52] Cf. C. J. Cadoux, 'The figure of a victory won suggests the forcible suppression of unwilling opponents, and can therefore in this connexion be at best but a very subsidiary illustration, and by no means the central truth' (*The Historic Mission of Jesus*, London, 1941, p. 261).

[53] Cf. E. F. Scott, 'Could (Paul) not have said in plain words that God forgives sin, and that Christ brought us the message of this free forgiveness? Paul, however, is an honest thinker who never shuts his eyes to unwelcome facts. In his own way he anticipates the modern scientific position that the world is governed by inexorable laws which allow no place for any loophole. All that is done, whether it be good or evil, must find its due recompense, for God is just, and cannot by a mere word arrest the consequence of sin, any more than He can forbid a falling stone to reach the ground. If sin is not to produce its effect there must be some positive act which cancels it, and Paul believes that Christ by His death performed that act' (*Paul's Epistle to the Romans*, London, 1947, p. 38).

give us a right to punish, and nothing can do that but criminal desert.[54]

These words are not too strong. This is an important point and it ought not to be overlooked as unfortunately it so often is. When we have the right to punish it is legitimate to exercise that right for reformatory ends. But these reformatory ends do not give us the right to punish. They may lay upon us other duties and give us other rights, but it is only desert which gives us the right to punish. And, of course, if mere reformation does not give us the right to punish still less does deterrence.

Then in the second place punishment must in fact be retributive if it is to be reformatory. If a man holds that he is being punished unjustly, then he will not be reformed. He will be infuriated and hardened.[55] Before punishment can have its reformatory effect, it must be the just reward of the evildoer's crimes, and it must be seen by him to be such. When it is recognized as just, punishment may even be welcomed.[56] But it cannot be stressed too strongly that it is first necessary that its justice be established. In other words, there is deep down within us a conviction that good ought to be rewarded, and sin ought to be punished. Apart from the operation of this conviction, punishment is sterile. A. E. Taylor recognizes this when he speaks of 'the *retributive* character of punishment' as 'a doctrine really indispensable to sound ethics.'[57] This is very important. So long as a man is concerned with the punishment alone, whether he regards it as reformatory or deterrent or what you will, he has not really come of age morally. He must see not simply that wrongdoing is punished but that it ought to be punished. He must learn to fear not so much the penalty as the fact of deserving penalty, the guilt rather than the punishment.[58]

54 *The Doctrine of the Atonement*, London, 1951, p. 54.

55 H. R. Mackintosh stresses this: 'penalties simply demoralise and infuriate the victim when they are seen to be unjust; and thinkers who deny the retributive character of punishment never seem to ask themselves why this should be so. They overlook the fact, which is surely obvious once it has been pointed out, that if the sinner's punishment is to do him any good, it must be felt to be his sin coming home to its author — the moral reaction of things which he has no option but to recognize as his due' (*The Christian Experience of Forgiveness*, London, 1944, p. 166).

56 Thus R. Mackintosh, in dissociating himself from the 'way of escape' that denies that there is any such thing as retributive punishment, quotes 'the immortal, the boundlessly significant confession, "We indeed suffer justly, for we receive the due reward of our deeds." ' He adds, 'To be unable to join in that confession, when one's sin has found one out, is a measureless spiritual loss' (*Historic Theories of Atonement*, London, 1920, p. 158).

57 *The Faith of a Moralist*, Series I, London, 1951, p. 183.

58 Thus E. Caird says, 'the highest educational result of punishment is to awake a consciousness, not simply that the crime gets or will get punishment, but that it is *worthy* of punishment. It is to make men fear the

We cannot think that God's forgiveness will be such as does despite to such deep-seated moral convictions. We cannot get rid of the idea of the justice of God.[59] Sin does deserve punishment and sin will accordingly not be lightly dismissed as though it carried no ill desert. The cross is the result.

Now it may be that we find it difficult to explain on the principles of human jurisprudence how Christ's death can avail for man's sin, how He can bear our penalty. That kind of substitution is not permitted in the legal systems with which we are familiar.[60] But then we are not being saved with reference to our legal systems. We are being saved with reference to the eternal law of God,[61] and we are not justified in assuming that this law runs in all points exactly like all our human laws. It may be that it allows more room for mercy than do our law codes. But whether we are right in our tracing out of such differences or not, and whether we can follow out all the implications of our condemnation under the divine law or not is beside the point. What matters is that the New Testament writers

---

guilt, and not the penalty' (*The Critical Philosophy of Immanuel Kant*, Glasgow, 1889, ii, p. 377). See further my *The Biblical Doctrine of Judgment*, London, 1960, p. 47, n. 2.

[59] James E. Sellers refers to 'the profound liberal theology of the last century which unfortunately tended to dismiss the notion of the wrath of God as an antiquated myth, and to place the stress on the love of God as the only effective force.' He goes on, 'When the Biblical notion of the justice of God is excluded in one place, it reappears in another' (*Theology Today*, xviii, p. 431). The justice of God is too fundamental a concept to be dismissed.

[60] People who wish to establish the truth of Christ's substitution sometimes employ illustrations taken from our law courts in which the judge sentences the prisoner according to the law and then pays the fine himself. Such illustrations help us to see that there are occasions, even in human experience, wherein concern for justice and deep love for the offender go hand in hand. But they must be used with great caution. They cannot be taken as examples of what Christ did, for He gave His life, not a sum of money. We must bear in mind the distinction made, for example, by David Smith, 'in a pecuniary debt the consideration is not *who pays* but *what is paid*, and in accepting a vicarious payment of his due the creditor shows no indulgence or remission to the debtor. But sin is more than a debt. It is a crime; and here the consideration is not only *what is paid* but also *who pays*. The punishment must be borne by the sinner; for, as the law demands proper and personal obedience, it exacts also proper and personal punishment' (*The Atonement in the Light of History and the Modern Spirit*, London, n. d., pp. 54f.).

[61] Cf. John Pye Smith, 'The question, whether sinners shall be pardoned, is not one that can be referred to arbitrary will or absolute power. It is a question of law and government, and it is to be solved by the dictates of wisdom, goodness, justice, and consistency' (*Four Discourses on the Sacrifice and Priesthood of Jesus Christ*, London, 1828, p. 139). This divine of a bygone age was quite clear that salvation is by way of law, not by arbitrary fiat. Yet he saw that law goes hand in hand with wisdom and goodness.

interpret our salvation partly in terms of law.[62] They see nothing but condemnation awaiting men. Then they see Christ as suffering in such a way as to remove from God the stigma of being unjust in remitting our penalty. And as a result of that suffering they see us as 'justified', i. e., 'declared "not guilty".' Salvation then is a salvation that accords with law. And it is a salvation that gives us the security of the law. There is no accusation that can be preferred against those whom God has acquitted (Rom. 8:33). Our salvation is a legally valid salvation.[63]

The argument that Aulén has used with such force in the case of the ransom theory may be applied here. Aulén pointed out that a theory which appealed to so many Christians over so many years cannot be totally without significance, and he set himself to discover that significance. And when a theory of the atonement has made such a deep appeal to so many souls both acute and profound, over so long a period as this, it is idle to dismiss it cursorily as of no account.[64] Moreover, as C. A. Dinsmore has shown, it is reinforced by the views of literary giants of many different periods and cultures. While not arguing for the penal theory, he yet shows that there is impressive agreement among those who, by common consent, have plumbed man's nature the deepest, that forgiveness is possible only when due regard is paid to the realities of satisfaction and the claims of the moral law. Dinsmore examines the writings of such diverse geniuses as Homer, Aeschylus, Sophocles, Dante, Shakespeare, Milton, George Eliot, Hawthorne, etc., and concludes, 'It is an axiom in life and in religious thought that there is no reconciliation without satisfaction.'[65] There is a reality here and we neglect it to our loss.[66]

---

[62] This appears to be overlooked in such a statement as that of Aulén, that 'the divine act of forgiveness cannot be contained within the order of justice, and that in reality it transcends all merely ethical points of view. The forgiveness of divine Agape cannot be motivated by ethical considerations. Faith *cannot* find any other basis of forgiveness than inscrutable, divine love' (*The Faith of the Christian Church*, London, 1954, p. 295). It is one thing to say that the atonement means more than righteousness and justice. It is quite another to exclude them in this fashion.

[63] Cf. J. McIntyre, 'any adequate doctrine of Atonement must come to terms with the justice of God and not simply treat it as if it were removed by God's love or mercy' (*St. Anselm and His Critics*, Edinburgh, 1954, p. 103; he is summarizing Anselm's position).

[64] H. A. Hodges writes against the view but still can say, 'Yet it is so widespread and so persistent, and (may we add?) it awakens such echoes in the soul that it can hardly be without a core of vital truth, however hard it may be to formulate it satisfactorily' (*The Pattern of Atonement*, London, 1955, p. 46).

[65] *Op. cit.*, p. 226.

[66] Cf. L. W. Grensted, *op. cit.*, p. 221; G. S. Hendry, *op. cit.*, pp. 120f.

(11) *In His death Christ revealed the nature of God as love*

That God is love is not, as many today seem to think, a truism. In point of fact it is a truth that most religions of the world have not attained. And the New Testament does not lay it down as something so obvious that it needs only to be stated to be accepted. It regards it as something that had to be revealed to us. As indeed it had. 'Nature red in tooth and claw' draws attention to one aspect of this world in which we live, and reminds us that to an impartial observer it is not at all obvious that God is love, or even that God loves men. But the men of the New Testament were not impartial observers. They were men whose lives had been transformed by what God had done in Christ. Because of the cross, they knew with an unshakable conviction that God is love, nothing less than love. 'Herein is love . . . that he loved us, and sent his Son to be the propitiation for our sins' (1 Jn. 4:10). 'Christ died for us while we were yet sinners, and that is God's own proof of his love towards us' (Rom. 5:8, NEB). Men often confuse love with sentimentality, and we should see clearly that it is love that is revealed. The cross shows something of the demands of love, we might say the sternness of love. It shows us that love does not gloss over sin, but grapples with it.[67] There is a revelatory aspect to the atonement, and this should not be overlooked in the vigorous discussions as to the place and importance of such aspects as victory over evil, the payment of penalty, and the like. We would not know the reckless, sacrificial love of God were it not for what is revealed in the cross.

(12) *In His death Christ is man's supreme example*

The death of the Lord, as we have tried to make clear in earlier sections, had results quite objective to man. But it also had results within man. The death of Christ is indeed an example, inspiring and ennobling those who contemplate it rightly. If exemplarist theories are to be rejected when they claim to give us the whole truth about the atonement, or even the essential truth about it,[68] they are nevertheless to be accepted inasmuch as they remind us of some-

---

[67] Cf. P. L. Snowden, 'Love no less than justice demands that reparation for sin should be made, and of the two the demands of love are the more imperious. Justice may perhaps be able to forgo its claims and penalties, but from its very nature love must desire the highest and best at whatever cost of suffering. In the eyes of true love no suffering is an evil compared to that of guilt not atoned for' (*op. cit.*, p. 106).

[68] Loraine Boettner remarks that 'Christ's expiatory death is no more an object for our imitation than is the creation of the world' (*The Atonement*, Grand Rapids, 1941, p. 32). The essential part of Christ's atoning work is not a matter for imitation.

thing of great importance.[69]   Nothing shows us so plainly as the cross the kind of men we ought to be.   Nothing humiliates and inspires us as does the cross.   Probably the best known and best loved of all hymns on the passion is 'When I Survey the Wondrous Cross'.   Go through it verse by verse and line by line and there is nothing in it but the subjective theory, the poetic expression of the effect on me of a contemplation of what Christ did in dying on the cross.   And this hymn rings true.   None of us but can sing it with deep feeling, knowing that this corresponds to something deep in our innermost being. These words are true.   Christ is our Inspiration and our Example.

(13) *Men are invited to make a threefold response in repentance, faith, and holy living*

The way of salvation does not depend on anything that we do, but only on what Christ has done for us.   Yet, paradoxically, unless we make our response we do not receive His good gift.   It is like a man receiving title deeds to property.   The property is his, but until he enters on his possession he does not really possess it.   The ingredients of the Christian response to Christ's atoning work are expressed in slightly different ways, but basically the New Testament is agreed on the three points we have just mentioned.

First, there must be repentance.   There is a negative aspect to Christianity, and this consists in a thoroughgoing renunciation of the self-seeking life.   To be aiming at personal success and to be a Christian is a contradiction in terms.   It is noteworthy that the first preachers did not water down their demands on account of the weakness of the flesh or of local ideas.   To take one example, throughout the ancient world it was universally held that chastity is an unreasonable demand to make upon a man.   Men simply are not made that way, reasoned antiquity.   All that can be done is to limit or regulate extra-marital relations.[70]   The Christian preachers made no attempt to meet this position halfway.   They insisted that if men were to become Christians they must break completely with this evil thing.   And break with it they did, thus introducing a new thing

---

[69] G. B. Stevens can say, 'The teaching of Jesus gives us no warrant to speak so slightingly as is commonly done of his *mere example*. Theology is generally so eager to hurry on into its own special sphere that it can barely take time to mention in passing the saving power of the personal influence of Jesus' (*The Christian Doctrine of Salvation*, Edinburgh, 1930, p. 41).

[70] W. E. H. Lecky sums up the Greek attitude thus, 'a combination of circumstances had raised (the whole class of courtesans), in actual worth and in popular estimation, to an unexampled elevation, and an aversion to marriage became very general, and extra-matrimonial connections were formed with the most perfect frankness and publicity' (*History of European Morals*, London, 1877, ii, p. 297).

into the history of morals.[71]   And what went for this particular sin
went for others.   The whole New Testament witnesses to a concern
for righteousness that is expressed in a decisive break with all past
evil.   Repentance is required of all.

This does not mean that repentance is viewed as a virtue, which is
accepted in lieu of the legal and moral demands which proved so
hard to fulfil.   Especially is this the case in view of the fitful and
half-hearted nature of our repentance.[72]   Repentance is painful.
We do not like it and we perform it badly.   Indeed, but for the grace
of God we would not perform it at all.   But, even in the imperfect
form in which we manifest it, it means a renunciation of sin, and
this attitude is important.

The characteristic Christian attitude is one of faith.   Faith is the
means whereby the believer identifies himself with Christ's atoning
work and makes it his.   Faith is the means whereby he reckons
himself to be dead as regards all that is sinful and alive to that which
is good.   Faith means that a man ceases to rely on his own efforts
and instead relies on what God has done for him in Christ.   Faith
means trusting Christ, Christ alone for full salvation.   It ought not
to be necessary to say that faith is not a matter of intellectual
adherence to certain dogmas (though the truth ought not to be overlooked that it is impossible to have a worthwhile faith without some
intellectual content).   Faith is a warm personal trust in a vital and
living Saviour.

The positive answering to the negative of repentance is godly living.   This is insisted upon throughout the New Testament.   The inspired writers never tire of telling us that nothing that we can do,
nothing at all, can merit our salvation.   We must rely wholly on
Christ.   But they never cease to tell us, too, that the gospel 'bringeth
forth fruit' (Col. 1:6, AV).   If our faith in Christ is real, then we
will show that in the manner of our living.   Good works do not
cause our salvation, but they necessarily follow it.[73]   They are not

[71] Cf. William Barclay, 'It has been said that chastity was the one completely new virtue which Christianity introduced into the pagan world'
(*Flesh and Spirit*, London, 1962, p. 27).   Barclay amply documents the degradation of the Graeco-Roman world of the period and emphasizes the
strong contrast in the Christian attitude (*op. cit.*, pp. 24-28).

[72] K. E. Kirk makes very strongly the point that our repentance is at
best imperfect.   Experience teaches us 'that no acknowledgement of sin before God of which we are capable is wholly free from selfish sentiments and
motives' (*Essays Catholic and Critical*, ed. E. G. Selwyn, London, 1929, p.
267).

[73] Cf. R. S. Paul, 'as we are reminded by P. T. Forsyth, although the
eighteenth century was dominated by humanitarian philosophers and scientists,
those who showed real compassion in Christian missions, and we might add,
concern for the slaves, for the illiterate and for the prisoner, were not the
broad-minded thinkers but men whose deepest convictions were governed by

the root, but they are certainly the fruit. Or to change the metaphor, they are not the foundation, but they are assuredly to be found in the superstructure.

In many recent discussions of the atonement, man's response in his use of the sacraments receives a good deal of attention. The point of all this is that the sacraments are not magical rites. They have no efficacy apart from what Christ has done. They are 'sacraments of the gospel' and it is the gospel that gives them meaning. The gift we receive in the due performance of either is ours only because Christ died for us. The sacraments continually point us to the cross.[74]

(14) There is a cross for the Christian as well as for the Christ

The cross of Christ transforms values for the follower of Christ. He sees suffering in the light of that cross not as a wholly unmixed evil, but as the pathway to good. The suffering of Christ, though an evil from the point of view of those who inflicted it, and also in part from the point of view of Him who endured it, is wrongly viewed as essentially an evil. It is the source of untold blessing to all the saved throughout the world and throughout the centuries. And His cross transforms all suffering for His followers. No longer can suffering appear as simply an evil. An evil it is in part, but, rightly borne, it is also fruitful of good. Christ Himself told those who would follow Him that the path of service means a daily taking up of one's cross (Lk. 9:23). The choice of word can scarcely be accidental and the Christian's cross is surely to be interpreted in the light of the Master's cross. That is not to say that it is atoning like His.[75] The New Testament is insistent that there is but one atoning sacrifice. Christ's sacrifice is perfect and complete, and nothing can be added to it.

The meaning rather would seem to be firstly that the Christian is to be ready for the ultimate in self-sacrifice (there is nothing easy or self-centred or luxurious about taking up a cross). Then, secondly,

---

what we should regard as a very narrow religious creed: "a gospel deep enough has all the breadth of the world in its heart." This depth they had in the doctrine of the Atonement that stood at the center of their faith and experience' (The Atonement and the Sacraments, London, 1961, p. 138).

[74] Cf. Neville Clark, both sacraments 'are concerned with incorporation into Christ, with death and resurrection; both are made powerful by the operation of the Holy Spirit; both stand under the sign of the cross' (An Approach to the Theology of the Sacraments, London, 1956, p. 83).

[75] Cf. John Murray, 'Christ has indeed given us an example that we should follow his steps. But it is never proposed that this emulation on our part is to extend to the work of expiation, propitiation, reconciliation, and redemption which he accomplished. We need but define atonement in Scriptural terms to recognize that Christ alone made it' (Redemption — Accomplished and Applied, Grand Rapids, 1955, p. 64).

he is to bear his sufferings calmly remembering that Christ trod this way before. He should not rebel in the manner of the worldling. If the Master bore a cross, what else should the servant expect?[76] Thirdly, he is to understand that the sufferings that come his way are not futile pain but meaningful agony. They are not the sufferings of a worldling, but those of a follower of Christ.[77] And fourthly, in the words of St. Paul, 'I . . . fill up on my part that which is lacking of the afflictions of Christ in my flesh for his body's sake, which is the church' (Col. 1:24). His sufferings are the means of setting forward the purpose Christ achieved in His atoning death. In other words Christian service is costly. The taking of the gospel to those for whom it is intended is to tread the path of the cross. There is also the thought that in some sense Christ and His people are one. F. F. Bruce thinks of the concept of corporate personality: 'the identity of the Servant, which narrowed in scope until it was concentrated in our Lord alone, has since His exaltation broadened out again and become corporate in His people.' He cites Paul's words in Acts 13:47 and proceeds, 'That is to say, the Servant's mission of enlightenment among the nations is to be carried on by the disciples of Christ. But here Paul goes farther: the Servant's sufferings are also to be carried on by the disciples of Christ'.[78] And, while this particular form of expression is found only here, the thought — that the suffering of the Christian is meaningful and important and is to be interpreted in the light of Christ's cross — is to be found throughout the New Testament.

These fourteen propositions seem to me to be extremely important as being attested throughout the New Testament. They give us what we might call the basic, commonly shared point of view. But the

[76] 'The cross which the Christian must carry is not the Cross of Calvary, but his own, yet it can be borne only by one who knows that his Lord endured the agony of Golgotha for him and is with him still continually' (J. G. Riddell, *Why Did Jesus Die?* London, 1938, p. 209).

[77] Cf. Dietrich Bonhoeffer, 'To endure the cross is not a tragedy: it is the suffering which is the fruit of an exclusive allegiance to Jesus Christ. When it comes, it is not an accident, but a necessity. It is not the sort of suffering which is inseparable from this mortal life, but the suffering which is an essential part of the specifically Christian life. It is not suffering *per se* but suffering-and-rejection, and not rejection for any cause or conviction of our own, but rejection for the sake of Christ' (*The Cost of Discipleship,* London, 1959, p. 78).

[78] NICNT, *in loc.* He also points out that it is absurd to take up the position that Paul thought of his own sufferings as atoning. 'When Paul is so concerned as he is here to assert the sole sufficiency of Christ as Saviour and Mediator, it would be absurd to suppose that he means that he himself, by the hardships he endures, is in some way supplementing the saving work of Christ' (*loc. cit.*).

individual writers have their individual contributions and these are far from being unimportant. We need them all if we are to see what this great central truth of Christianity means. Thus the Synoptic Gospels unfold for us the perfect life of the incarnate Lord. They let us see Him as He went about doing good. They bring out the fact of His mission, the truth that He did not drift aimlessly through life, in opportunist fashion, making the most of every occasion on which He could teach men more about God. They show Him purposefully going about the task on which He was engaged, pressing on with the preaching of the good news of the Kingdom.[79] They give a good deal of teaching which brings out the cost of discipleship and show us that to associate with Christ is to take our part in God's great redeeming purpose for the world. And they put their emphasis on the climax to which they lead up, the story of the passion of the Lord. That is their topic. Notice that they are not concerned with suffering as suffering. They do not describe the details nor emphasize the agony. They are concerned with the fact, and with the meaning of the fact.

John tells a similar story, but he tells it in his own way. He puts a good deal of emphasis on present judgment, on the fact of sin and on the way men judge themselves by their participation in evil, their love for darkness. Over against that he sets life, the eternal life which God makes available for men through what Christ has done. And he often speaks of the will of God. His Gospel has a strongly predestinarian strain, and he insists that the will of God is done in men's salvation. Men do not choose to come to God. They come only as He draws them, and without His drawing they could never be saved. And above all John insists that the will of God was wrought out on Calvary. More than anyone else, he shows us Jesus moving inexorably to Calvary. Nothing can interfere with that divinely ordained progress.

When we pass to Acts we move into a different atmosphere. Here we sense the excitement of the early church as these first believers exulted in the salvation Christ had wrought for them. Here we see the eager calling into use of any and every category which will help us understand a little more of the infinite significance of the Person and work of Jesus Christ. There is not much in the way of orderly theological system, but there is a good deal of vigorous expression of the truth that Christ in His death has won

---

[79] R. W. Dale made a noteworthy protest against the view that the primary aim of Christ's coming was that He should preach the gospel: 'The real truth is that while He came to preach the gospel, His chief object in coming was that there might be a gospel to preach' (*The Atonement*, London, 1902, p. 46). There is a very important truth here, but it must not be overpressed, as it is by some, as though Christ did not preach the gospel. Scripture is explicit that He did (Mk. 1:14f.; Lk. 4:18; 20:1).

for men a salvation surpassingly wonderful. There is an emphasis on responsibility. Those who were behind the crucifixion are reminded of their crime, and sinners generally are called upon to repent. And throughout we have the setting forth of the work of the Holy Spirit emphasizing that the end result of the atonement is to be seen in the Spirit-filled life.

Paul has more to teach about the atonement than has any other New Testament writer. None else has grasped so fully the extent of the sinner's plight, and none other accordingly writes so much or so feelingly of the fate of the sinner. Paul sees him in the grip of sin, the law, wrath, the flesh, demonic forces, and the rest. And he sees the grip of every one of them burst wide open by what Christ has done for men. Paul has a bewildering variety of ways of looking at the cross. Now he sees it as reconciliation, now as redemption, now as the formation of a new covenant, now as an act of justification, now as a removal of curse, now as God making Christ 'sin' for us, now as the removal of the bond that was against us, and so on. The richness of his thought is one of the reasons why it is so hard to pin him down and have him support a particular theory. There is no difficulty in finding Pauline passages to support almost any of the theories that have been put forward from time to time. The trouble arises when we try to make him the supporter of one theory exclusively. His thought is kaleidoscopic. Because he sees man's plight from a variety of angles, and because he thinks of Christ as winning a salvation adequate to the needs of all men, he necessarily thinks of the atonement as a complex process. And as he never tries to relate all the facets of his thought on the subject to any one master-theory we are in difficulties when we essay the task.

Probably Paul's greatest contribution to the study of the atonement is his insistence on the legal aspects.[80] 'Justification by faith' is sure to arouse thoughts of Paul. I have indicated earlier that this is not confined to Paul. Others of the New Testament writers do make use of legal imagery for an understanding of the atonement. But none of them has done it as wholeheartedly as the great apostle. He revels in this particular approach and he returns to it again and again. The removal of our condemnation was a large factor in the way he saw salvation.

And Paul is just as emphatic about the importance of our response. He keeps on talking about the necessity for faith, and he keeps on talking about the importance of godly living. It is in-

---

[80] Cf. William J. Wolf, 'The picture of military victory and of a king establishing his sovereignty are two of Paul's principal metaphors to describe salvation. His chief metaphor for atonement, however, is the law court' (*No Cross, No Crown*, New York, 1957, p. 84).

teresting to study the way in which his Epistles have the habit of inserting a 'therefore' just at the point where the opening doctrinal section gives way to Paul's treatment of the Christian life.[81] He begins with an exposition of what Christianity is about, with special emphasis on what God has done for us in Christ. Then he says 'therefore . . .'. Because of what Christ has done certain consequences follow. Our lives must be lives of a Christ-like kind. But this is not the result of a care for abstract ethics. It is not the urging of men to following some nebulously held view of 'the good life'. It is the outcome of the atoning death of Christ. Because Christ has died for us, and because we believe in Him, we must be a certain kind of people. Paul makes the point again and again.

The Epistle to the Hebrews sees the atonement against a background of the greatness of God. He is an awe-inspiring Being, and sin against Him is therefore a heinous evil. The writer sees it as necessary in such a situation that there should be a Mediator who should be one with God and also one with man. Nobody in the New Testament stresses more fully than does this writer the full deity and the full manhood of Christ. Both are necessary as he sees the atonement. So he draws his picture of our great High Priest, that Priest 'after the order of Melchizedek' whose death once and for all dealt with sin. The utter finality of the death of the Lord is emphasized and underlined. From another point of view he emphasizes the new covenant that Christ has brought into being, a covenant that cost Him His blood and is based on forgiveness. And finally he brings out the complete finality with which sin has been dealt with an amazing variety of expressions to indicate that it is completely put out of the way.

And so it goes on. The Epistle of James is concerned that we make the right response to what Christ has done for us. First Peter brings out the concern of all Three Persons of the Trinity with the atonement, and in a very notable saying affirms that Christ bore our sins in His body on the tree (1 Pet. 2:24). 2 Peter and Jude stress the punishment of the wicked and the reality of God's gift to His people. The Johannine Epistles ring with words like love and light and life, like knowledge and cleansing and victory. And in Revelation we are never allowed to forget the triumph of the Lamb, nor the fact that He was slain for men.

It is plain enough from all this that there is a wide variety of teaching on the atonement to be found in the New Testament.[82]

---

[81] See Rom. 12:1; Eph. 4:1; Phil. 4:1; Col. 3:5; etc.

[82] The magnitude and variety of this evidence does not receive adequate attention in such treatments of the subject as that by A. Ritschl. He can say, 'for Christ His sufferings served as a means of testing His faithfulness to His vocation — this and nothing else' (*Justification and Reconciliation*, Edinburgh, 1902, p. 480). It is the last four words that are objectionable.

That is not to say that the various writers are in perpetual conflict. They are not. What is very impressive is the way in which with their varied backgrounds, and their very different way of putting things they should agree so closely on the great central thing, that we are saved, if we are saved at all, only through the death of Jesus Christ for us. Their differences pale into insignificance alongside their impressive agreement on the great central truth. It is not so much that they are in disagreement on the atonement as that the atonement is many-sided. One feature of it makes a greater appeal to one writer, another to another. It is not unlike our situation today, when there are those who find a great deal of help in the thought that Christ has reconciled us to God, while others rest more securely in the conviction that He has won for us the victory. This does not mean that either denies the truth held by the other. And we need not read back such a disagreement into the New Testament. There we have the writings of a group of men who found their lives transformed by a great divine act. Each tries to give the meaning of it as it has come home to him. And it is very important that we give heed to the variety of expression that results. For the atonement cannot be understood within the petty confines of any one theory. It is a great divine act with many facets. We may have a more or less good grasp on one facet (or more). But that does not give us license to deny either the existence or the importance of the other facets.[83]

By common consent the manifold theories of the atonement that have made their appearance during the history of the church may be divided broadly into three groups, those which stress the victory that has been won, those which see satisfaction of some sort as having been offered to the Father, and those which stress the effect on the believer.

The first group includes the ransom theory, which in one form or other was prominent in the church during the first thousand years.[84]

---

[83] R. S. Franks, for example, seems to me to make this mistake when he says, 'an expiation or satisfaction in the strict sense of the words would make forgiveness not only unnecessary but also actually impossible. If a debt is paid, even by another, the same debt cannot be forgiven. Payment and forgiveness are contrary in character: each excludes the other. Forgiveness is in its nature entirely free' (*The Atonement*, London, 1934, p. 158). This reasoning is admittedly specious. Yet it ignores the fact that the New Testament *does* speak of payment ('ye were bought with a price', 1 Cor. 6:20) as well as of free forgiveness. We must not try to reduce the New Testament's colorful variety to a flat uniformity.

[84] It is often said to have 'dominated' the church during the first millennium, but this may give a false impression. Other views are to be found. Thus J. K. Mozley cites Eusebius as speaking of Christ as 'chastised for us, and undergoing a penalty which He did not owe but we for sins, and so gaining for us forgiveness of sins' (*Dem. Ev.* x. 1); Hilary of Poitiers, 'The Passion

This was capable of being stated in strange ways, and some of its formulations are passing strange. It appears here and there in later writers and in recent times G. Aulén has given it new life. It is favored by quite a number of contemporary writers. And as we have seen in our survey it is to be found in the New Testament. There are many passages which emphasize the triumph of the Christ.

The second group is exemplified in the Latin theories from Anselm onwards. Here there is always the thought of a satisfaction[85] to be paid to God's wounded honour,[86] or His broken law or the like. It sees man as being in danger, not from hostile forces of evil, but from a holy God whom he had offended by his sin. And it sees Christ as taking upon Himself the responsibility, as bearing the divine judgment, as winning a new standing for those who are in Him.[87]

The third group is associated particularly with the name of Abelard, though the full flowering of this type of atonement theory had to await the nineteenth century. Exponents of such views have stated them in various ways,[88] but by and large we can say that they reject the mythology of the first group of theories and the legalism of the second. They concentrate on the effect on sin-

---

was voluntarily accepted to satisfy a penal necessity' (in Ps. 53:12); while Ambrose 'represents a very similar point of view . . . . His death both satisfied and destroyed the penalty of death to which sinners were subject' (*De Fug. Saec.* vii. 44) (*The Doctrine of the Atonement,* London, 1915, pp. 108, 119f.).

[85] E. L. Kendall prefers the idea of reparation to that of satisfaction. She says, 'The main connotations of the notion of Reparation are restoration, restitution and compensation' (*A Living Sacrifice,* London, 1960, p. 13); and again, 'in the Person of Jesus the sacrificial Victim and the Sin-bearer are one, and thus . . . by taking upon himself the weight of the world's sin and by offering himself in perfect self-sacrifice even to the point of death, Jesus "took away" the sin of the world by making perfect reparation to God the Father for it' (*op. cit.,* p. 72). W. J. Sparrow Simpson also interprets the cross in terms of reparation (*The Redeemer,* London, 1957, see especially chs. XII, XIII).

[86] J. McIntyre points out that Anselm's view is basically substitutionary.

[87] J. J. Lias stresses the importance of this subjectively as well as objectively: 'It is this doctrine of Satisfaction that is the strength of Christianity. Remove it; supply its place by a proclamation of pardon, made by one who is a perfect example, and you throw men back into all the perplexities from which Christ has set them free' (*The Atonement,* London, 1888, p. 89).

[88] Of this view cf. H. M. Relton, 'It is, (Bushnell) says, one of the most remarkable facts in the history of Chistian doctrine that what the critical historians call the "moral view" of the Atonement, in distinction from the expiatory, has been so persistently attempted and so uniformly unsuccessful' (*Cross and Altar,* London, n. d., p. 95).

ners of the love of God as shown in the cross.[89] This demonstration moves men to repentance, to faith in Christ, to love for God, to amendment of life. So Christ wins men out of their sin and brings them into salvation. He does it by being a Revealer, and an Example[90] and a source of inspiration. He shows them a better way and inspires them to reach it.[91]

It is a commonplace of discussions on the atonement that theories of the atonement are right in what they affirm and wrong in what they deny. This is perhaps an over-simplification, for there are some denials that are worth making. But there is also a basic and an important truth in the statement, and the reason for it is the sheer complexity of New Testament teaching on the subject. Our survey of the doctrine throughout the New Testament has uncovered a bewildering variety of ways of looking at Christ's work. Redemption, for example, is a figure derived from the slave market or the freeing of prisoners of war. It has to do with setting the captive free on payment of the price.[92] Justification is a legal metaphor. It interprets salvation through the law court and sees it as a verdict of acquittal.[93] Reconciliation refers to the making up after a quarrel,

[89] In criticism of this view J. K. Mozley says, 'Repentance and love have indeed discovered in the Cross that which draws out their utmost resources, but if either the direct aim or most far-reaching result of the Cross was to make men penitent or to awaken them to love, the New Testament is a misleading book, with its emphases continually misplaced' (*The Heart of the Gospel*, London, 1927, p. 29).

[90] M. Jarrett-Kerr says of this theory 'it will not do because it would really be nothing but a subtle form of intimidation. When I was small I can remember reading, I think, in *Little Men*, of the schoolmaster (Bhaer, was it?) who overcame the resistance of the naughtiest boy in the school by having him into the study and ordering the boy to give him (the headmaster) the strokes with the cane that the boy himself deserved. Whenever I read it, I got a lump in my throat. But I know also that ever since then on cool reflection I have always thought that it was taking a monstrous unfair advantage of the boy's tender feelings. We all know how cruelly tyrannical ostentatious martyrdom can be' (*The Hope of Glory*, London, 1952, p. 77).

[91] William J. Wolf's criticism is devastating, 'On its own premises the impressiveness of Christ's dying for others is reduced to minimal proportions if no essential meaning can be assigned to his suffering and to his death. The real relationship of this theory to the others is that of a parasite to its host organism. That is to say, when it attempts to stand by itself it fails and whatever real power it has is derived from presupposing elements of other theories' (*op. cit.*, p. 116).

[92] Redemption is a word which is used very loosely in much modern writing. See Deissmann, LAE, pp. 319-330 for an account of redemption in the first century.

[93] It is a legal term and must be understood in a legal fashion. Sometimes this is overlooked. Even Karl Barth can say, 'Jesus Christ is the One who was accused, condemned and judged in the place of us sinners. But we can say the same thing in this way: He gave Himself to be offered up as a sacrifice to take away our sins' (CDDR, p. 277). This does not seem to be

the doing away of a state of hostilities. Propitiation has to do with anger. It reminds us of the wrath of God exercised towards every evil thing and also of the fact that Christ has removed that wrath. How are these figures to be gathered together under one theory? It cannot be done. And we have only just begun. The richness of New Testament teaching comprises a good deal more than this. The point I want to make is that the mind of man is not able to comprehend all the various facets of New Testament teaching on the atonement simultaneously. No theory of the atonement so far put forward has ever been able to win universal assent, and it is fairly safe to say that none ever will. And this is not because the teaching of the New Testament is not clear. Granted that some of it is obscure, yet most is plain enough. But the fact is that it is too great in extent and too complex in character for us to comprehend it all in one theory. If we do succeed in formulating a neat theory, we do so at the expense of a good deal of the evidence.[94]

This ought not to be surprising. After all, atonement is a complex process. In the first place men find it difficult to see sin as a serious matter, so difficult indeed that most men do not see it that way at all. And in the second place, when they do come to see it as serious, they do not know how it can be removed. Sin itself is complex. Long ago Turretin pointed out that sin must be regarded as at least threefold, it is a debt, it is hostility to God, it is a crime.[95] All three aspects must be dealt with in atonement. But it is difficult for the mind of man to grasp how one atoning act can handle all three aspects. We find it hard enough to cope with one aspect at a time. The plain fact is that we do not know enough about sin and atonement to know what is the process by which sin is removed, and what are the conditions for its removal. If I may borrow an illustration from the space age, we are like laymen watching the scientists put a satellite into orbit. It can be done. We see it. But, unless we are scientific experts, we do not know how it can be done. Left to myself I would never devise a means of getting a satellite into orbit. And when it comes to the atonement, we are dealing with something that is not merely beyond the understanding of ordinary men and fit only for

sufficiently precise. Granted that both legal and sacrificial terms may legitimately be used of the atonement this does not make them the same thing. Each set of terms must be understood in its own light. We impoverish our understanding of the atonement if we neglect this, and attempt to force into an unnatural conformity concepts so diverse as justification and sacrifice.

[94] Cf. J. S. Stewart, 'We may take it for certain that any formula or system which claims to gather up into itself the whole meaning of God's righteousness, or of Christ's redeeming work, is *ipso facto* wrong' (*A Man in Christ*, London, 1947, p. 3).

[95] Cited by L. W. Grensted, *op. cit.,* p. 242.

the most eminent theologians. It is beyond the wisest of men. That does not mean that there is nothing that we can affirm about atonement. Nor does it mean that such knowledge as we have about atonement is worthless. There is a very great deal that is very worth-while saying, and in my judgment every endeavour that is made to extend our knowledge in this matter is worth making. If we can learn only a little more of the ways of God, we shall be able to live the more adequately and serve Him the better.

But what I am concerned to contend for is a decent humility in this matter. We ought not to act as though any of our petty theories had comprehended the whole. The atonement is too big and too complex for our theories. We need not one, but all of them, and even then we have not plumbed the subject to its depths. There has always been a tendency for men to think that one theory is sufficient. Thus it has not been uncommon for upholders of the Abelardian view to suggest that other theories are on the whole crude and unsatisfying: they belong to a day when men evaluated the problems of atonement differently; with our modern insights, we do well to reject them and to see in the cross the readiness of the perfect Man to suffer the worst that sinners could do to Him. All the emphasis is put here. Other theories are discarded. Similarly upholders of the penal theory have sometimes so stressed the thought that Christ bore our penalty that they have found room for nothing else. Rarely have they in theory denied the value of other theories, but sometimes they have in practice ignored them. In recent years Aulén has done much the same in his insistence on his 'classic' view. The paying of penalty, the offering of sacrifice, and the rest are discarded. Victory is all that matters.

A number of theologians have done the same thing with the sacrificial theory. This time there is the added complication that upholders of such views assert that they are preserving what is of value in other theories, so that theirs is the truly comprehensive view. O. C. Quick, for example, finds in the Epistle to the Hebrews 'a *narrowly* sacrificial theory' (Quick's italics), which lacks 'the language of love'.[96] Quick accordingly makes good (as he sees it) this deficiency. He maintains that when this is done 'we can fuse the sacrificial and juridical and Abelardian interpretations of it into a single theory, and we can include and reconcile together the language of all three.'[97] This is a large claim, but even so it is

---

[96] *The Gospel of the New World*, London, 1945, p. 104.

[97] *Op. cit.*, pp. 104f. Quick also says, 'by thus dying Christ changed penalty into sacrifice and shame into glory, and by his risen life enables his faithful followers to do the same. Thus it is that the fundamentally sacrificial theory of the atonement can include the others and supply what by themselves they lack' (*op. cit.*, p. 103). This sunny optimism will not meet the facts. Sacrifice is an important concept, but, as noted in the text, it does not include a good deal of New Testament teaching.

not large enough, for Quick does not profess to include Aulén's view. But in any case most will dispute his claim to have fused together those he names. The bearing of penalty, for example, does not appear to mean the same for Quick as for the classical exponents of the penal theory. Nor does his theory include the biblical teaching on a number of points — redemption, to take but one example. Nor does it face the fact that sacrifice is not the dominant New Testament view of the atonement. For all its popularity in some circles, the sacrificial view does not really include what other views stress. It is inadequate, like all the other theories.

And it has a further very serious defect. It is not intelligible. How can a sacrifice take away sin? Quick says, 'What is needed to take away sin is the blood of a life which itself has conquered sin by undergoing and overcoming temptation',[98] and he thinks of Christ's blood as fulfilling these specifications. What he does not tell us is what this means. Why should such blood take away sin? How does it work? At first sight, at least, there is no connection at all between 'the blood of a life which itself has conquered sin' and the sins of all mankind. If this is to be made the lynch pin of a theory of atonement it must be explained and its truth demonstrated. The sacrificial theory compares unfavourably with other theories in this respect. The penal theory, for example, tells us that sinners deserve punishment, that Christ stepped in and took their penalty, and that they now go free. Agree with it or not, the theory is intelligible. So with the Abelardian view. One can see what its exponents are driving at and either accept their view or oppose it. But exactly what does the sacrificial theory mean? Why should a sacrifice take away sin? What is there about the sacrifice of One who has conquered sin Himself which annuls the sin of others? The answers do not appear. And in their absence we cannot agree that this is the theory to replace all the others.[99]

The position then is that all our theories seem to have a measure of truth in them, and none, taken by itself, is adequate. It is not

[98] *Op. cit.,* p. 104.

[99] Turner has the idea that the concept of deification, so dear to the Eastern Fathers, is perhaps the clue to the whole: 'The *Logos Paidagogos* leading his people into an ever-increasing experience of Illumination; the Christ Victim conjoined with the Passion Mysticism of the Medieval period; the *Christus Victor* offering vicarious victory to mankind, all appear as partial significances of that truth upon which the deification theory fundamentally insists: that Redemption, essentially, centrally, consists in Transfiguration, the lifting of human life out of a setting which primarily defeats and baffles because it is set too low by participation, through all that the Historical Christ was, and achieved, in the very life and character of the Triune God Himself' (*op. cit.,* p. 122). But here again one theory is made to do too much. The New Testament teaching on propitiation, for example, to cite but one instance, is more than difficult to bring under this heading.

unlike the situation in the world of physics where scientists are not agreed on the nature of light. The corpuscular theory and the wave theory both have their supporters. It is difficult to see how these two are to be reconciled with one another. Yet neither can be abandoned, for some of the facts support one view and some the other. The reality must transcend both, but so far we do not know what this reality is. So with the atonement. We cannot fit all the evidence into one neat pattern. But that does not give us license to abandon that part of the evidence we do not like. We must simply recognize that the atonement is too vast for men to take it all in, and welcome the insights that the various theories afford us.

Our theories are of value so long as we use them and do not let them tyrannize over our understandings. They help us to organize a certain amount of the evidence, and that is their value. But when they persuade us to shut our eyes to that part of the evidence that they cannot include they hinder instead of help. We ought to be quite clear that no full and final theory of the atonement has yet been given and that this is not simply because we have not yet been fortunate enough to hit on the right solution. It is because we are not good enough as men and not profound enough as thinkers ever to get to the bottom of the subject. The problem is too big for us. Our minds cannot take in at one and the same time all the complexities involved. But the problem is not only a mental one. It is salutary to reflect that those who understand the atonement best seem not necessarily to be great scholars (though some are). They are rather those who have suffered deeply and who are sufficiently pure in heart to see God. We will need H. R. Mackintosh's reminder that the basic reason why we do not understand the atonement is that we are not good enough.[100]

Of the attempts made to sum up the teaching of the Bible particular mention ought to be made of Calvin's use of the three offices of prophet, priest, and king. By showing that Christ fulfilled all that each of these implies, he was able to bring out the teaching office (with all that this implies of example, and of man's response), the priestly office (with 'Christ both priest and victim' as the

[100] He says, 'We are constantly under a temptation to suppose that the reason why we fail to understand completely the atonement made by God in Christ is that our minds are not sufficiently profound. And doubtless there is truth in the reflection that for final insight into the meaning of the cross we are not able or perspicacious enough. But there is a deeper reason still. It is that we are not good enough; we have never forgiven a deadly injury at a price like this, at such cost to ourselves as came upon God in Jesus' death. We fail to comprehend such sacrificial love because it far outstrips our shrunken conceptions of what love is and can endure' (*The Christian Experience of Forgiveness*, London, 1944, pp. 190f.).

theme) and triumph implicit in the kingly office.[101] It is easy to criticize all this, and many have done so. Yet we ought not to overlook the fact that this was a striking and original way of using Christ's work, nor that Calvin was able to comprehend under this triple scheme far more than most theologians before or since.[102] He did not fall into the trap of making the atonement simple, the accomplishment of all that is implied in one particular figure. Calvin's scheme was tremendously popular for a long period; then, under the criticisms of Ritschl and others, it fell into a decline. But recently its merits have been appreciated once more.[103] It is significant that W. A. Visser 't Hooft in a book which aims at interpreting the European churches to those of America[104] should begin with an emphasis on the threefold office.

SUBSTITUTION

One thing I am concerned to contend for is that, while the many-sidedness of the atonement must be borne in mind, substitution

---

[101] Cf. Erich Sauer, 'As *Prophet* He brings knowledge, i.e., light, delivers the understanding from sin's darkness, and establishes the kingdom of truth.

'As *Priest*, He brings the sacrifice, cancels the guilt and thereby the consciousness of guilt, thus delivering the feelings from the crippling pressure of misery and an accusing conscience, and establishes the kingdom of peace and joy.

'As *King*, He rules the will, guides it in paths of holiness, and establishes the kingdom of love and righteousness' (*op. cit.*, pp. 18f.).

[102] Cf. the verdict of R. S. Franks, 'What, however, concerns us most of all in Calvin's theology, is the emergence of a new doctrine of the work of Christ, distinct from either the patristic or the medieval, *viz.* the doctrine of the threefold office. This doctrine, the really characteristic Protestant doctrine of the work of Christ, is highly synthetic in character. It has not merely the value of presenting the whole work of Christ in a single view, but also of presenting it in such a manner that it shows how it terminates in the production of faith (*fiducia*) through the Gospel. It is thus of an eminently practical character: the objective aspect of the work of Christ is here duly completed by the subjective aspect' (*A History of the Doctrine of the Work of Christ*, i, London, n.d., p. 441).

[103] Thus Emil Brunner takes this as the basis of his examination of Christ's work in vol. ii of his Dogmatics, *The Christian Doctrine of Creation and Redemption*, London, 1952, pp. 171ff. J. F. Jansen has a useful discussion of the threefold office in his *Calvin's Doctrine of the Work of Christ*, London, 1956, though he himself prefers a twofold office (omitting prophet) and claims that this in fact is dominant in Calvin's thought. The threefold office appears in J. G. Riddell, *The Calling of God*, Edinburgh, 1961. T. F. Torrance accepts it in his essay 'The Priesthood of Christ' (*Essays in Christology for Karl Barth*, ed. T. H. L. Parker, London, 1956, pp. 153-173).

[104] *The Kingship of Christ, An Interpretation of Recent European Theology*, London, 1948. In this task he says 'it is necessary to dwell on the deeper currents of thought and life which manifest themselves in European churches' (*op. cit.*, p. 8).

is at the heart of it.[105] I do not mean that when we have said 'substitution' we have solved all our problems. We have not. In a way we have only begun, for substitution itself must be understood with some care. But I do not think that we can escape substitution if we proceed on biblical premises.[106] Thus, if we revert to the metaphors we were referring to a short while back, redemption is substitutionary, for it means that Christ paid that price that we could not pay, paid it in our stead,[107] and we go free. Justification interprets our salvation judicially, and as the New Testament sees it Christ took our legal liability, took it in our stead. Reconciliation means the making of people to be at one by the taking away of the cause of hostility. In this case the cause is sin, and Christ removed that cause for us. We could not deal with sin. He could and did, and did it in such a way that it is reckoned to us. Propitiation points us to the removal of the divine wrath, and Christ has done this by bearing the wrath for us. It was our sin which drew it down; it was He who bore it.

And so we might go on.[108] The richness of New Testament teaching on this subject centres on Christ, and again and again the key to the understanding of a particular way of viewing the cross is to see that Christ has stood in our place.[109] The value of this way of viewing the atonement is its flexibility combined with its adaptability to the different ways of stating our need.   Was there a price to be paid? He paid it. Was there a victory to be won? He won it. Was there a penalty to be borne? He bore it. Was there a judgment to be faced? He faced it. View man's plight how you

---

[105] Cf. J. Rivière, 'if He suffered, it was for us alone, literally for us — i.e., in our stead; thus we come to say that Christ took on Him the penalty due to our sins. This idea of a substitution is the very soul of Christian piety and of Christian preaching' (op. cit., p. 9).

[106] Karl Barth puts strong emphasis on Christ's substitutionary activity. Cf. his summary at the end of the section in which he has dealt with Anselm's question: Cur Deus Homo? 'To this question we have given four related answers. He took our place as Judge. He took our place as the judged. He was judged in our place. And He acted justly in our place' (CDDR, p. 273). Each of Barth's four answers means substitution.

[107] Cf. J. C. MacDonnell, 'The prominent idea in ransom is that of payment — of vicarious substitution — of one thing standing in place of another' (The Doctrine of the Atonement, London, 1858, p. 124).

[108] H. F. Lovell Cocks says that Christ 'stands before God as our substitute and representative' and proceeds 'Various titles and conceptions are used in the New Testament to express this substitutionary and representative character of Christ's work. Messiah, Mediator, High Priest, Passover, Sacrifice, Second Adam, the Firstborn among many brethren . . .' (By Faith Alone, London, 1943, p. 157).

[109] Cf. N. Snaith, 'One fact stands out stark and plain. That death on the Cross was a substitution. He was hanging on that Cross, and by rights that is where we ought to be. Most of what is said about the Cross is by way of an attempt to make this clear' (I Believe in . . ., London, 1949, p. 75).

will, the witness of the New Testament is that Christ has come where
man ought to be and has met in full all the demands that might be
made on man.

A. M. Hunter makes it clear that substitution is found in the
teaching of Christ Himself. He reminds us of the three types of theory of the atonement and of one of them says,

> Under this head we may include all theories which deal in
> "satisfaction" or substitution, or make use of "the sacrificial prin-
> ciple." It is with this type of theory that the sayings of Jesus
> seem best to agree. There can be little doubt that Jesus viewed His
> death as a representative sacrifice for "the many." Not only is
> His thought saturated in Isa. liii (which is a doctrine of representa-
> tive suffering), but His words over the cup — indeed, the whole
> narrative of the Last Supper — almost demand to be interpreted
> in terms of a sacrifice in whose virtue His followers can share. The
> idea of substitution which is prominent in Isa. liii, appears in
> the ransom saying. And it requires only a little reading between
> the lines to find in the "cup" sayings, the story of the Agony,
> and the cry of dereliction, evidence that Christ's sufferings were
> what, for lack of a better word, we can only call "penal."[110]

I do not see how this summary of the thought of our Lord can fairly
be evaded. The Gospels do witness to substitution.

Nor is it otherwise with Paul.[111] Like the Gospel writers, he
pictures Jesus as becoming one with sinners. Indeed, he goes further
than anyone else when he tells us that God made Him 'sin for us'
(2 Cor. 5:21). And, as we saw earlier, it is difficult to empty
the thought of substitution out of his words when he speaks of Christ
as having been made 'a curse' for us (Gal. 3:13). It is in my judgment impossible to face squarely the words, 'one died for all, therefore all died' (2 Cor. 5:14), and not recognize that they involve
substitution. If His death, a death for us, means that 'all died',
then He surely died the death that the 'all' should have died.[112]
And Paul makes frequent use of conceptions like justification, redemption, the blood of Christ, propitiation, reconciliation, and the

---

[110] *The Work and Words of Jesus*, London, 1956, p. 100.

[111] Cf. G. B. Stevens, 'Paul did regard Christ's sufferings as serving the
ends of punishment and as a substitute for the punishment of the world's
sin' (*op. cit.*, p. 65).

[112] G. W. Wade sees Paul's use of figures of speech like redemption as suggesting 'that the Apostle considered that Christ's death was in some sense vicarious, and that on the Cross He, the guiltless (2 *Cor.* v.21), underwent the fate
deserved by the guilty (cf. *Gal.* i.4, ii.20, *Rom.* iv.25, v.6, 8). He adds, 'The
same conclusion is deducible from the metaphors drawn from the Jewish
sacrificial system' (*New Testament History*, London, 1922, p. 648). These
statements are all the more noteworthy in that Wade does not find substitution
in the teaching of our Lord, nor does he hold it himself. Clearly Paul's teaching is compelling.

new covenant, which, if not necessarily substitutionary in themselves, are yet substitutionary in the way Paul employs them. They are most naturally understood of a salvation in which Christ stood in our place, suffering the death that sinners ought to have suffered.[113] Sometimes this is strangely denied, as it is, for example, by D. E. H. Whiteley who says that Paul 'believes that Christ made salvation possible for us at the great cost of his own life, not that God accepted his death instead of ours.'[114] Yet even such a critic as this, who firmly rejects the thought of substitution, is constrained to admit at the end of his examination that 'there are several places where the thought of substitution cannot be excluded.'[115] Substitution so runs through Paul's thought that it cannot be removed without distortion of his meaning.[116]

The whole idea of substitution is out of favour in recent discussions. Yet the evidence to which we have directed attention undoubtedly exists. How then do scholars deal with it? The favourite device is to suggest that the New Testament teaches representation but not substitution. It is often alleged that to speak of Christ's death as representative guards all that is of value in the substitutionary idea, while not being open to the objections. Since such ideas are widely held, it may be worth our while to examine them.

In the first place, the concept of representation as commonly used suffers from lack of accurate definition. Very few who accept this and reject substitution take the trouble to give a definition of either term. But it may be doubted whether a very great difference can

---

[113] I have examined each of these concepts at some length in *The Apostolic Preaching of the Cross,* London and Grand Rapids, 1955, and it may suffice to refer to that discussion.

[114] JTS, n. s., viii, p. 240.

[115] *Op. cit.,* p. 225. Whiteley's view is that, 'if St. Paul can be said to hold a theory of the *modus operandi,* it is best described as one of salvation through participation: Christ shared all our experience, sin alone excepted, including death, in order that we, by virtue of our solidarity with him, might share his life' (*op. cit.,* p. 240). That this does not seem to me a fair verdict on Pauline teaching is evident from my examination of the evidence in the earlier chapters. Moreover, like Quick's view, which we noted above, this is an 'explanation' which does not explain. Theories of atonement like the winning of a victory, or the bearing of penalty, or the inspiring of men to repent, may be right or they may be wrong, but they are intelligible. But how does 'participation' bring about salvation? I am not the less a guilty sinner because Christ came to share my lot.

[116] Hastings Rashdall makes the interesting point that Is. 53 'is only once actually quoted in St. Paul. Yet it is not too much to say that it is always being paraphrased by him, and even when the passage was not actually present to his mind, he had before him the tradition of the Church which was mainly based upon that section of Isaiah, and in the light of which he found the same doctrine in other prophecies' (*The Idea of the Atonement in Christian Theology,* London, 1919, p. 102).

be put between them, at least as regards the atonement.[117] The
Oxford English Dictionary gives a meaning of representation
that is relevant to our subject, 'The fact of standing for, or in
place of, some other thing or person, esp. with a right or authority to
act on their account; substitution of one thing or person for another.'
The same *Dictionary* gives the meaning of substitution as 'The putting of one person or thing in place of another.'[118] Apply such
definitions to the death of Christ and it is difficult to see what is
gained by referring to it as representative. The term in this context
seems to mean much the same as substitutionary, but without quite
the same clarity.[119] If we say that suffering is representative it
is very difficult indeed to deny that it is substitutionary.[120]

In the second place, where we can separate the idea of representation from that of substitution it does not seem as though the
former is really to be preferred to the latter. My representative is
surely one whom I have appointed or chosen, either alone or in
conjunction with others. The element of personal delegation of
responsibility seems to be the point at which we may legitimately
distinguish representation from substitution and give it a distinctive
content of its own. And this is the very point at which it becomes
unsuitable for Christian theology, for it rests the initiative squarely
in the hands of men. As H. W. Clark says,

> to speak of Christ as "the representative man" causes us . . . to
> picture immediately a relationship originating from man as its
> source. A representative sums up, so to say, what exists in those

[117] Cf. the remark of A. Ian Dunlop, 'The conception of "substitution" is
deeply embedded in St. Paul's doctrine and we need not be afraid of the
word, although some theologians have preferred the word "representative"
and often have meant the same thing' (SJT, xiii, p. 389).

[118] The word 'vicarious' is another word sometimes used with a meaning
other than substitution. The *Oxford English Dictionary* defines it as
'That takes or supplies the place of another thing or person; substituted
instead of the proper thing or person'. When used of punishment etc., it
signifies 'Endured or suffered by one person in place of another; accomplished
or attained by the substitution of some other person, etc., for the actual
offender'. It is clear that 'vicarious' means 'substitutionary'.

[119] E. L. Mascall makes much the same point in dealing with the work
of the ministry: 'to represent somebody is to take his function upon your
self and perform it in his place' (*The Recovery of Unity*, London, 1958, p. 8)

[120] Cf. G. Aulén, 'It is clear, however, that the affirmations of Christian
faith to the effect that the work of Christ was "for us," "for our sake,"
ultimately include the conception "in our stead." The first expressions tend
to be superseded by the latter. This approach to the work of Christ is
intimately connected with the idea of his struggle and victory over the
demonic forces. This struggle and victory have occurred for our sake, for
our salvation and redemption. But since we have been unable to accomplish
this work ourselves, it has manifestly been done in our stead' (*op. cit.*,
p. 235).

whom he represents: he acts for those who stand behind him in accordance with the inspirations and instructions they transmit to him, translating these into whatever speech or action successive occasions may require; and such a relationship is constructed and construed, be it noted, along a line which starts from the *constituency*, not from the *representative himself*. That is in fact the essence of the matter.[121]

And because that is the essence of the matter, I should think that representation is ruled out, at least as the basic way of looking at the matter.[122]

For reasons such as these I do not think that representation can be held as the explanation of the atonement. But those many who object to the concept of substitution do so on the grounds that it is unthinkable. And so it is, if it be understood in the external mechanical way in which it is often pictured. Thus God is thought of as one individual, Christ as another, and the sinner forms a third entity. The sinner has deserved punishment. God, the Judge, arbitrarily substitutes the innocent Christ for the guilty sinner, and lets the latter go free. It is this kind of thing that W. Fearon Halliday castigates as 'self-evidently immoral'.[123]

Now it is not this crude thing that the New Testament teaches as substitution. But before going into this, I want to point out that there are far-reaching implications in rejecting substitution as immoral.[124]

[121] *The Cross and the Eternal Order,* London, 1943, p. 158. Similarly James Denney says, 'a representative not produced by us, but given to us — not chosen by us, but the elect of God — is not a representative at all in the first instance, but a substitute' (*op. cit.,* p. 99).

[122] If representation be taken along with substitution and if the thought of personal delegation be excluded, that is another matter. So long as the divine initiative is safeguarded, an aspect in which Christ is our representative may be discerned. Thus Leonard Hodgson says, 'We do not have to choose between so-called substitutionary and representative doctrines as though they were mutually exclusive alternatives. Our examination of the two concepts of punishment and forgiveness has shown that there is truth in saying that Christ suffered in our stead ($\dot{a}\nu\tau\grave{\iota}\ \dot{\eta}\mu\hat{\omega}\nu$) and truth also in saying that He suffered on our behalf ($\dot{\upsilon}\pi\grave{\epsilon}\rho\ \dot{\eta}\mu\hat{\omega}\nu$)' (*The Doctrine of the Atonement,* London, 1951, p. 142).

[123] He says, 'we are entitled to ask whether it is moral and right that one man should undergo death as a penalty for another? That the suffering of the innocent should be taken in itself in lieu of the suffering of the guilty is self-evidently immoral. There is in this, moreover, no logical implication that the evil man is changed; he goes scot-free, and plainly does not get what he deserves. The human judge who so acted would rouse the indignation of any modern civilised community' (*Reconciliation and Reality,* London, 1919, p. 19).

[124] As H. Maldwyn Hughes does, for example, 'the actual transference of sin and guilt is morally and psychologically inconceivable' (*What is the Atonement?* London, n. d., p. 45). Similarly T. H. Hughes, 'In reality the transference of guilt or penalty is morally and spiritually impossible' (*The*

To put it bluntly and plainly, if Christ is not my Substitute, I still occupy the place of a condemned sinner. If my sins and my guilt are not transferred to Him, if He did not take them upon Himself, then surely they remain with me. If He did not deal with my sins, I must face their consequences. If my penalty was not borne by Him, it still hangs over me. There is no other possibility. To say that substitution is immoral is to say that redemption is impossible. We must beware of taking up such a disastrous position.

When we try to understand the New Testament doctrine of substitution we must bear in mind first the close unity between God the Judge and Christ the Saviour. In the process of salvation God is not transferring penalty from one man (guilty) to another man (innocent). He is bearing it Himself.[125] The absolute oneness between the Father and the Son in the work of atonement must not for a moment be lost sight of.[126] When Christ substitutes for sinful man in His death that is God Himself bearing the consequences of our sin, God saving man at cost to Himself, not at cost to someone else.[127] As Leonard Hodgson puts it, 'He wills that sin shall be punished, but He does not will that sin shall be punished without also willing that the punishment shall fall on Himself.'[128] In part the atonement is to be understood as a process whereby God absorbs in Himself the consequences of man's sin.[129]

Atonement, London, 1949, p. 45). I try not to avoid the issue these theologians are raising. Yet if they are right Christ cannot redeem a man. Ultimately his salvation comes back to his own efforts, or perhaps to God's forgiveness apart from Christ.

[125] R. W. Dale points out that there would be substance in objections like that of Martineau only 'Had God insisted that before He would forgive sinful men, some illustrious saint or some holy angel should endure the agonies of Gethsemane and the awful sorrow of the cross'. He asks, 'But is there any "immorality," any "crime," anything to provoke "a cry of indignant shame," in the resolve of God Himself, in the person of Christ, to endure suffering instead of inflicting it?' (*op. cit.*, pp. 395f.).

[126] H. E. W. Turner says with respect to protests that substitution is immoral: 'These objections might well be sustained if the transference were regarded as an accidental or wholly external transaction . . . . The morality or otherwise of the transference of punishment depends entirely upon the wider context, both divine and human, within which it is placed' (*The Meaning of the Cross*, London, 1959, pp. 36f.).

[127] W. H. Moberly points out that 'it is easy for a juryman to vote for the "acquittal" of a guilty prisoner, if he is never to see any more of him. But if it means . . . a renewal of intimate personal relations . . . then it will be much harder' (*op. cit.*, p. 319). It is precisely because God is concerned with 'intimate personal relations' that His acquittal of sinners is no casual affair but the extraordinarily costly process we see in the cross.

[128] *Op. cit.*, p. 77.

[129] Cf. C. F. D. Moule, 'Then at least it became clear — however mysterious and unsearchable God's ways must always remain to us — that here was no overlooking of guilt or trifling with forgiveness; no external treatment of

Nor should we overlook the unity between Christ the Saviour and man whom He saves.[130] Throughout our discussion of the New Testament evidence we have been concerned to show at point after point that the various writers bear witness to the truth that Christ became one with sinners. He did not simply become incarnate. Being incarnate, He underwent that baptism at the hands of John that sinners undergo, and from then on He is constantly pictured as being 'reckoned with transgressors' (Lk. 22:37). When He suffered for men He did not accordingly suffer as one who is in all points distinct from sinners and who is arbitrarily drafted to take their place.[131] Situations do arise in this life wherein the suffering of one (or a few) is accepted instead of that of all. Thus the ringleader(s) of a revolt may suffer and the followers be allowed to return to their normal allegiance unscathed. Selected members of a tribe may undergo punishment for an offence which has involved all the members. In all such cases the important point is the connection of the substitute(s) with the other offenders. It is only because there is a unity that such a procedure can be adopted. I am not contending that these examples afford us good illustrations of exactly what happened on the cross. Obviously they are defective, and chiefly because in such cases those who suffer are usually principal offenders (though it is not impossible to envisage situations in which the innocent might be selected or offer themselves as victims). But the difficulty in understanding the atonement arises partly because of its magnitude (we cannot take it all in at once),

---

sin, but a radical, a drastic, a passionate and absolutely final acceptance of the terrible situation, and an absorption by the very God himself of the fatal disease so as to neutralise it effectively' (*The Sacrifice of Christ*, London, 1956, p. 28).

130 P. Van Buren's summary of Calvin's position is an excellent statement of the connection between substitution and union with Christ: 'By standing in our place, Christ has not simply endured our punishment for us, so that we might be set free to go our own way, but He has set us in an indissolvable relation to Himself, so that we are bound to Him. By the very closeness of this union, comparable to the unity between a body and its head, the death of a part is the death of the whole. Only the head need die for the whole body to die. And if the head then be given life on behalf of the body, that body is already on the way to life, although the full realization of this life may be delayed. But all this is true only so long as the body is in union with the head' (*Christ in Our Place*, London, 1957, p. 87).

131 Cf. L. Pullan, 'no theory which regards Christ as our substitute can be true unless it implies the solidarity of the human race which He represents, and that no punishment is inflicted by God which is not in accordance with the working of moral laws' (*The Atonement*, London, 1907, p. 94). Cf. also E. L. Mascall, 'the essence of redemption lies in the fact that the son of God has hypostatically united to himself the nature of the species he has come to redeem and, by offering himself to God the Father in their nature, has offered them to God the Father in him' (*Christian Theology and Natural Science*, London, 1956, p. 38).

and partly because of its uniqueness. It is *sui generis,* and because there is nothing else quite like it there is nothing else which will serve as a complete illustration of what it does. All our illustrations are no more than means of enabling us to see a little better some small fraction of this great event. So in the present case we are able to see that intimate connection with the offender is a qualification for suffering on his behalf.[132] Perhaps it is better to put it the other way round and say that unless there is close connection between the two there is no ground for substitutionary suffering.[133] Objection made to the atonement understood as substitution usually rests on a failure to recognize that He who suffers is one with those for whom He suffers as well as one with God.[134]

One great merit of the substitutionary way of viewing the atonement is that it makes a genuine attempt to face the problem of the past. Granted that any religion that claims to be adequate for men's needs must bring present peace of mind and the assurance of a transformed future, yet it is little short of astonishing to see how many writers on the Christian salvation content themselves with giving thought to the present and the future. They write as though good intentions were all-important, and treat the past as of no

---

[132] Cf. R. L. Ottley, 'Christ was our substitute, not through some arbitrary arrangement by which the innocent was compelled to suffer for the guilty, but in virtue of His representative character as the head and flower of our race, in whom humanity is "summed up" ' (*The Doctrine of the Incarnation,* London, 1904, p. 635).

[133] A. Hodge thinks 'it must be conceded by all that justice cannot demand and execute the *punishment* of a sin upon any party that is not truly and really responsible for it; and that the sin of one person cannot be really expiated by means of the sufferings of another, unless they be in such a sense legally one that in the judgment of the law the suffering of the one is the suffering of the other' (*The Nature of the Atonement,* London, 1868, p. 286).

[134] Cf. R. C. Moberly, 'A stranger, hired for money to undergo a loss of limb or liberty, would always be an insult to true equity. But one who was very closely identified with the wrong-doer in condition, or blood, or affection; a tribesman dedicating himself for a tribal wrong; the willing representative of a conquered nation, or army; the father, on behalf of his own child; the husband, for the sake of his wife; is it impossible to conceive circumstances under which a willing acceptance of penalty on the part of some one of these, would as truly be the deepest hope of the transformation of the guilty, as it would be the crown of his own nobleness?' (*Atonement and Personality,* London, 1924, p. 78). W. G. T. Shedd maintains that 'a creature cannot be substituted for a creature for purposes of atonement', but that this lies in the nature of his position as a creature, owing duties to both God and man (*op. cit.,* p. 389). Christ is not limited in this way, and therefore can do what man can not. But it still is important that there be community. Without His close connection with sinners He could not be their substitute.

account.[135] They see salvation as, perhaps, a process of reconciliation and put all their emphasis on the restoration of communion between man and God. Or they see it as a victory, whereby the believer is delivered from his bondage to evil and set free to live righteously. Their stress is on the transformation of life, and the evil past, the time of defeat, is quietly ignored. Or they may prefer to think of it as akin to a process of inspiration, wherein the believer, seeing God's great love so movingly depicted on the cross, gets the vision of sacrificial living and goes on his way a better man. The power of positive thinking means much to modern men. We like the forward look, and phrases like 'morbid preoccupation with past sins' come easily to our lips. We take to heart the injunctions of our psychiatrists and feel ourselves immensely superior to the men of earlier generations who brooded and fretted over their misdeeds.

There is certainly something in this, for it is not good to be so taken up with the past that we inhibit the future. It is surely better to be positive than negative. And yet the suspicion persists that our casual attitude to the past is both unhealthy and unwise. Certainly we cannot treat the past as of no consequence in other spheres of human activity. The business man, for example, is not permitted to wipe out all his debts, bewailing his former evil practice, and simply start anew. The criminal may not sorrow over his crimes and without further ado settle down as a law-abiding citizen. The student who fails in his first year examination cannot shrug off the unpleasant fact and proceed happily to the second year. The past is important. It cannot be shaken off. It cannot be ignored. It reaches into the present and affects our status and our actions. Why should we think it otherwise when God's judgment is in question? The heart and the conscience of men know that it is not otherwise. Neither here nor anywhere else in our experience can the past be ignored. It rises up to haunt us and to demand that justice be done to it. The problem of guilt is not solved by pretending it is not there.[136] Sin

---

[135] The attitude is widespread and may even be found in each one of us. C. S. Lewis can say, 'We have a strange illusion that mere time cancels sin. I have heard others, and I have heard myself, recounting cruelties and falsehoods committed in boyhood as if they were no concern of the present speaker's, and even with laughter. But mere time does nothing either to the fact or to the guilt of a sin. The guilt is washed out not by time but by repentance and the blood of Christ' (*The Problem of Pain,* London, 1943, p. 49).

[136] Cf. E. Brunner, 'guilt is that element in sin by which it belongs unalterably to the past, and as this unalterable element determines the present destiny of each soul. Guilt means that our past — that which can never be made good — always constitutes one element in our present situation. Therefore we only conceive our life as a whole when we see it in this dark shadow of guilt' (*The Mediator,* London, 1946, p. 443).

must be faced and dealt with. Otherwise we must live with a perpetual sense of guilt and helplessness.[137] We cannot know peace at the deepest level until we have come to see that, though our guilt is real, so is God's forgiveness. Christ has dealt with our past.[138] Repentance is admitted by all to be a primary demand. Why? Surely because the past is important. The very notion of repentance involves a backward as well as a forward look. And the impressive agreement, among Christians through the centuries, that repentance is a fundamental demand witnesses to the importance of the past.

It is an outstanding merit of the substitutionary view, then, that it does not gloss over the past. It recognizes it for the serious and significant thing that it is. But it affirms that Christ has taken care of our past as He has taken care of every aspect of our need.[139] He has paid the penalty. He has wiped out the sin. He has freed us from the entail of the past.

This has consequences for our view of the nature of God. He is not a God who sits loose to sin. In an expressive statement of James Denney, 'God condones nothing: His mercy itself is of an absolute integrity.'[140] No Christian, of course, would suggest that

---

[137] Cf. the experience of Hanns Lilje, 'To look back at one's own past gives one a sense of utter helplessness. It is impossible to alter it by a hand's breadth. It is over and done with; yet there it is. But it was this very sense of utter helplessness which enabled me to throw myself on the mercy of God' (*The Valley of the Shadow*, London, 1950, p. 90).

[138] F. W. Camfield speaks forthrightly on this point. 'Now it is strange how little alive thought is to the problem of the past. Philosophy scarcely seems to have faced it. Even the modern Existential philosophy can hardly be said to have addressed itself to it in any thorough-going fashion, otherwise it would have seen in the Christian doctrine of the Atonement its solution . . . . And what is perhaps more remarkable still, modern theories of the Atonement almost without exception ignore this recalcitrant problem of the past . . . . A significant experience of Kierkegaard may be alluded to this connexion. He has left it on record, that though he had learned and had come to believe that God had forgiven his sin, he could not reach real liberation and peace until he had become convinced that God had also forgotten it. This is Christian experience of the very centre. This is psychology of the deepest depths. Kierkegaard could not be satisfied without such atonement as literally buried his sin in Christ's grave; without such atonement as made his sinful past as if it had never been' (SJT, i, pp. 290f.).

[139] H. Vogel says, 'Here in Christ is a substitution or an exchange, full of wonder and of comfort. Christ experienced our death and entered our Hell; we experience his life and enter his blessed state. Just as he takes for his own everything that is ours, including our guilt and our death, so all that is his, his holiness and his eternal life, become ours' (*op. cit.*, p. 156). William J. Wolf insists that 'Christ redeems the past, the present, and the future' (*op. cit.*, p. 136), and carefully expounds all three (*op. cit.*, pp. 136-173). Such a balance is a necessity for a valid view of atonement.

[140] *The Expositor*, VI, 3, p. 449.

God does condone evil. But when the past is ignored, when all the emphasis is put on God's hostility to the sinful life we are pursuing and this is coupled with a demand for newness of life, then in practice no expression is given to God's hostility to *all* evil. The impression is left that the sinner can compound his past misdeeds by a due regard to the ways of God for the future. In however imperfect a way, the substitutionary view does attempt to give expression to God's implacable hostility to all sin, past as well as present and future. It witnesses to His absolute integrity as it tells of a God who in forgiving men takes account of their past, and deals with it fully and adequately.

An objection to this view arises from the intensely personal nature of guilt. My misdeeds are my own, and all the verbal juggling in the world cannot make them belong to someone else. P. Althaus can say:

> Reconciliation and forgiveness belong together, but not equivalence and forgiveness. The conception of substitution must be separated absolutely from that of equivalence. The emphasis placed on equivalence overlooks the fact that an atoning adjustment is impossible in the face of the seriousness of the demands of God's holiness, which drives home the fact that all my yesterdays are mine and those of other men are theirs.[141]

It is the case that my yesterdays belong to me. It is also the case that if atonement consists simply in ignoring this, and putting the punishment arising from my yesterdays upon someone else, then a grave wrong has been done. Sin is not to be regarded as a detachable entity which may be removed from the sinner, parcelled up, and given to someone else. Sin is a personal affair. My guilt is my own.

What are we to say then? In the first place that no one thinks of substitution as the whole story. Salvation is an exceedingly complex process with many facets, and, while substitution is a very helpful concept for bringing out some of the truth, it must be supplemented where other aspects are in question.[142] Thus if it is true that salvation may helpfully be described in terms of Christ's bearing of my penalty, it is also true that it is to be described further in terms of new birth (Jn. 3:3, 5, 7), in terms of my dying with Christ and rising with Him (Rom. 6:8; Col. 3:1-3), in terms of my becoming partaker of the divine nature (2 Pet. 1:4), and in other ways. Substitution is not to be regarded as a magic key

---

[141] *Mysterium Christi,* ed. G. K. A. Bell and A. Deissmann, London, 1930, p. 204.

[142] Cf. Lewis B. Smedes, 'Our point is that while the substitutionary death of Christ is not everything in redemption, nothing else is enough without it' (*The Incarnation,* Kampen, n. d., p. 160, n. 6).

which unlocks all the doors. And substitution that leaves those substituted for exactly as they were, penalty apart, is not the biblical substitution.

Earlier we were thinking of the importance for substitution of seeing that Christ is one with those for whom He died. Then our point was that no substitutionary bearing of penalty is conceivable unless there is a very close bond uniting the Substitute with those for whom He substitutes. Now we return to this thought of oneness, but look at it the other way. Not only did Christ become one with us and take our doom upon Him, but we become one with Him and now see things from His point of view, not that of the natural man. T. F. Torrance speaks of

> a substitution where the guilty does not shelter behind the innocent, but such a substitution that the guilty is faced with the Light, that man is dragged out of his self-isolation and brought face to face with God in His compassion and holiness.

He goes on, and the point is important,

> Because it is God Himself who here steps into man's place and takes his status upon Himself, man is not sheltered from God but exposed to His judgment, for in our place He claims to displace us and demands that we renounce ourselves for Him, in order to be one with Him.[143]

This is the kind of substitution that the New Testament teaches, a substitution which means that Christ died in our stead, that He did in our place what we could never do, but which does not leave us unchanged. It is a substitution of persons and our whole personality is affected.[144] The consequence of this is at least twofold. In the first place substitution awakens those for whom it has taken place to the greatness of the peril to which they have been exposed, and to their ill desert which brought them into such peril, and which

---

[143] SJT, vii, p. 252. Cf. N. Snaith, 'In our surrender to God, we give ourselves not only for ourselves, but for our "neighbour", since we are bound indissolubly with him. And our "neighbour" is every man. It is in this sense that the sacrifice of Christ, Christ's gift of Himself, is for us. It is instead of us, that is, instead of the whole race of man. But it is not instead of us in the sense that His sacrifice avails for me quite apart from any self-giving of mine' (*Mercy and Sacrifice*, London, 1953, p. 118). I would not care to put it quite like this, but I do want to draw attention to Snaith's emphasis on our self-giving as integrally bound up with Christ's death viewed as substitution.

[144] We must bear in mind, as J. C. MacDonnell, for example, points out, that there is always a distinction between a substitution of things and a substitution of persons. The former is mechanical and is a mere matter of barter and exchange. But the latter is not. MacDonnell says, 'In neither the substitute, nor those for whom He suffers, are God's righteous dealings with men as responsible beings suspended or reversed' (*op. cit.*, p. 169).

involved their Saviour in such a fate. There is nothing like the recognition that what Christ suffered He suffered in our place and stead for causing us to see sin for the evil thing it is and ourselves for the guilty people we are.[145]

Then in the second place, they come to see sin, at any rate in some measure, as He sees it. The fact that they are 'in' Christ, one with Him, saved in and by Him, means that from henceforth His attitude toward sin is theirs. They turn from it. They seek the help of the Holy Spirit to strengthen them as they amend their lives. They find themselves fully committed to the service of God.[146] Nothing less than this is adequate to the biblical view of oneness with Christ as the necessary correlate of substitution. It means not only that Christ died for the believer, but that he died with Christ. And not only does he experience a death to sin, but also a rebirth to righteousness, not only a cleansing from the guilt of sin but also a freeing from the dominion of sin so that the fruit of the Spirit becomes apparent in his life. The biblical substitution is not a purely external, more or less academic kind of substitution. It is a substitution in which the believer is existentially involved. He is caught up in the struggle. He is transformed. Substitution is inclusive.[147]

Substitution is thus a many-sided concept. Understood as it is in the Bible, it is a rich and satisfying way of viewing Christ's work for men. Add to this that it is well attested in the New Testament and it is not surprising that it has always made its appeal to men. And, though it is rejected by some scholars and perhaps even dis-

[145] Paul Tillich sees in the fact that Anselm's view does justice to the psychological situation the reason 'why his doctrine was the most effective one, at least in Western Christianity'. He later says, 'For the believing Christian, this means that his consciousness of guilt is affirmed in its unconditional character. At the same time he feels the inescapability of that punishment which is nevertheless taken over by the infinite depth and value of the suffering of the Christ. Whenever he prays that God may forgive his sins because of the innocent suffering and death of the Christ, he accepts both the demand that he himself suffer infinite punishment and the message that he is released from guilt and punishment by the substitutional suffering of the Christ' (*Systematic Theology*, ii, London, 1957, p. 199).

[146] H. F. Lovell Cocks speaks of Christ as bearing the judgment of our sin and as making 'on our behalf that confession of God's holy love and renunciation of our loveless egoism which we could not make for ourselves.' He goes on, 'He did this as our substitute, but also as committing us to the same surrender and obedience' (*op. cit.,* p. 166).

[147] William J. Wolf rejects substitution in the sense that 'we are relieved from all responsibility', and accepts it 'in that (Christ) does what we could never do by our own power, but it is a representative and inclusive "substitution"' (*op. cit.,* p. 64).

missed out of hand as unworthy of serious consideration, it still seems the most satisfactory way of looking at the cross.[148]

In the last resort it seems that we are shut up to three possibilities: the moral view (that the effect of Christ's death is its effect on us), the view that Christ as our Substitute bore what we should have borne, and the view that Christ did not bear our suffering but something different which effects more or less the same thing. The first of these views is obviously inadequate. While it contains a truth, it is yet unable to meet the statements of scripture which persistently speak of something as being effected outside man, and that something as the most important part of the process. The third view has been rejected wherever it has been put forward and studied seriously. It is essentially Duns Scotus' view of *acceptilatio*, defined as 'the optional taking of something for nothing, or of a part for the whole.'[149] It is Grotius' view that Christ did not bear our penalty, but such sufferings as would show the ill desert of sin. Always such views have been found inadequate, and, for all the earnestness with which they are argued, the modern equivalents seem no more satisfying.[150] Like Anselm's view, they find no *necessary* connection between Christ's sufferings and us. If we reject the moral view as inadequate, there seem only two possibilities — either Christ took my sins and bore their consequences, or He

---

[148] William Barclay defines substitution in this way: 'The substitutionary view of the work of Jesus holds definitely and distinctly that Jesus Christ on his Cross bore the penalty and the punishment for sin which we should have borne, and that he did so as an act of voluntary and spontaneous and sacrificial love' (*Crucified and Crowned*, London, 1961, p. 116). He notes that many recoil from this, 'But two things have to be said. First, there is the quite general truth that the heart of man witnesses that there is something here which is fundamentally true . . . . The second general truth is this: this is an interpretation and understanding of the Cross which has existed without break since the beginning of Christian thought' (*op. cit.*, pp. 117f.). To substantiate this last point he cites passages from Paul, Tertullian, Cyprian, Hilary, Ambrose, and Augustine, and concludes, 'There is no age in Christian thought to which the idea of Jesus Christ as the Saviour, whose death was voluntary, vicarious, sacrificial, substitutionary, has not been dear' (*op. cit.*, p. 118).

[149] A. Hodge, *op. cit.*, p. 224. He says that Duns Scotus, 'referring the necessity for the Atonement ultimately to the will and not to the nature of God, consequently maintained that God could have forgiven sin without any satisfaction; that if he had so willed, he might have proposed conditions of forgiveness other than those fulfilled by Christ; and that the temporary and finite sufferings of Christ are accepted by God, in the gracious exercise of sovereign prerogative, as a substitute, but not as a full, legal equivalent for the eternal sufferings of men' (*loc. cit.*).

[150] Cf. H. M. Relton, 'No theory of the Atonement rings true either to the Biblical teaching or to the deepest experience of the penitent heart which fails to do justice to this element of substitution in the Cross of Calvary' (*op. cit.*, pp. 108f.).

did not take my sins, in which case they are still on me, and I bear the consequences. Such views do not explain the atonement. They reject it. We are left with the thought of substitution.

The chief impression that a study of the atonement leaves with us is that of the many-sidedness of Christ's work for men. When He died for us on the cross, He did something so infinitely wonderful that it is impossible to comprehend it in its fulness. However man's need be understood, that need is fully and abundantly met in Christ. The New Testament writers are like men who ransack their vocabulary to find words which will bring out some small fraction of the mighty thing that God has done for us. And yet, though it is so complex and so difficult, it may be put very simply: 'the life which I now live in the flesh I live by the faith of the Son of God, who loved me, and gave himself for me' (Gal. 2:20, AV).

Appendix

PASSAGES REFERRING TO CHRIST'S DEATH

It will be useful to many readers to have a short classified statement of all the New Testament references to the death of Christ. R. W. Dale, of course, adapted T. J. Crawford's full account and included it at the end of his book on the Atonement, but this is not always readily accessible. I was interested to learn that Dr. Wilbur M. Smith has made a new classification on different principles, which appears in Dr. Smith's book, *Great Sermons on the Death of Christ*, published by W. A. Wilde Company. It appears here by kind permission of Dr. Smith and Mr. Thomas H. Wilde.

A CLASSIFIED ARRANGEMENT OF ALL REFERENCES TO THE DEATH OF CHRIST OCCURRING IN THE NEW TESTAMENT

I have included some passages in which, while the specific nomenclature of *death* does not occur, yet death is clearly implied, e.g., "three days and three nights in the heart of the earth," Matthew 12:40; "depart out of this world," John 12:1; 13:36; 16:5, 7; etc. On the other hand I have not included, though they might easily be, such passages as Luke 2:35; 12:50; John 7:33; Galatians 3:13.

I have felt justified in including all passages in which Christ's resurrection *from the dead* is declared, because such statements are direct testimonies to the fact of His having died. On the other hand, I have *not* included passages affirming only the fact of Christ's resurrection, if the concept of *from the dead* is not also included. I have not felt it necessary to include the thirty-three passages in which the *tomb* (or *sepulchre*) of Joseph of Arimathea is referred to.

Most will be surprised at three truths that such a classification as this so clearly reveals: (1) The number of *different predictions* that Christ would die at the hands of His enemies — there are nineteen of them (thirty-one, including parallel accounts). (2) The great number of different Greek words used to describe the putting of Christ to death — there are eleven of them. (3) The vast, profound, and eternal consequences that result from the death of Christ, and how tragic are the present state and eternal doom of all who are not reconciled to God by the death of His Son.

A. *PREDICTIONS OF CHRIST'S DEATH IN THE GOSPELS*

    I. Declared by John the Baptist, John 1:29, 36

    II. Discussed by Moses and Elijah at the time of the Transfiguration, Luke 9:31

    III. Predictions by Christ Himself

        A. In the Synoptics

            1. reference to Jonah, Matthew 12:40
            2. suffer many things and be killed, Matthew 16:21; Mark 8:31; Luke 9:22
            3. "till the Son of Man is risen from the dead," Matthew 17:9; Mark 9:9
            4. delivered up and be killed, Matthew 17:22, 23; Mark 9:31; Luke 9:44
            5. first He must suffer many things, Luke 17:25
            6. that He would be crucified, Matthew 20:18, 19; Mark 10:33, 34; Luke 18:33; cf. John 18:32
            7. He would give His life a ransom, Matthew 20:28; Mark 10:45
             8. the Son of man shall suffer, Matthew 17:12; Mark 9:12
            9. delivered up to be crucified, Matthew 26:2
          10. anointed for burial, Matthew 26:12; Mark 14:8; John 12:8
          11. must eat the Passover before He suffered, Luke 22:15
          12. His words at the Last Supper (listed under F)
          13. in a parable, Matthew 21:39; Mark 12:7, 8

        B. In the Fourth Gospel

            1. destroy this temple, 2:19, 21
            2. concerning eating His flesh, etc., 6:51-56
            3. the good Shepherd to lay down His life, 10:11, 15, 17, 18
            4. "I, if I be lifted up," 12:32, 33
            5. "I go away," etc., 13:1, 36; 14:28; 16:5, 7, etc.

    IV. By Caiaphas, John 11:31

B. *DETERMINATION OF THE JEWS TO PUT JESUS TO DEATH*

1. They took counsel together against Him how they might destroy Him, Matthew 12:14; Mark 3:6
2. They sought how they might destroy Him, Mark 11:18; Luke 19:47
3. The Jews sought to kill Him, John 7:1; cf. vv. 20, 25
4. They took counsel to put Him to death, John 11:53
5. The chief priests sought how they might kill Him, Luke 22:2; Mark 14:1
6. That they should destroy Jesus, Matthew 27:20
7. "He ought to die," John 19:7
8. "Let Him be crucified," Matthew 27:22, 23; Mark 15:13; Luke 23:21, 23; John 19:15
9. "His blood be on us," Matthew 27:25

Note: It is very significant that while the verb translated *destroy, apollumi* (often translated *perish*: John 3:15, 16; 6:27; 10:10, 28, etc.), is the verb used to indicate the *purpose* of the enemies of Christ, it is never once used of any aspect of their actually putting Christ to death, i.e., no one ever *destroyed* Jesus.

C. *TESTIMONIES TO THE FACT OF HIS DEATH*

1. The soldiers, Mark 15:44, 45; John 19:30
2. The angels, Matthew 28:5, 7; Mark 16:6; Luke 24:7
3. The evangelists — all references to the fact that Christ was *crucified* (see below) and John 2:22; 20:9; 21:14
4. St. Luke, Acts 1:3
5. The Jews, Acts 5:28
6. Festus, Acts 25:19
7. Apostle Peter, Acts 2:23, 24, 32; 3:15; 4:10; 5:30; 7:52; 10:39, 41; 1 Peter 1:2, 3, 11, 19, 21; 2:21, 23, 24; 3:18; 4:1, 13
8. Apostle Paul, Acts 13:28, 29, 30, 34, 37; 17:3, 31; 26:23; Romans 1:4; 4:24, 25; 5:6, 8, 9, 10; 6:3, 4, 5, 8, 9, 10; 7:4; 8:11, 32, 34; 10:9; 14:9, 15; 1 Corinthians 1:18, 23; 2:2, 8; 5:7; 8:11; 10:16; 11:25, 26, 27; 15:3, 12, 20; 2 Corinthians 4:10; 5:14, 15; 13:4; Galatians 1:1, 4; 2:20, 21; 3:1; 5:11; 6:12, 14; Ephesians 1:7, 20; 2:13, 16; 5:2, 25; Philippians 2:8; 3:10, 18; Colossians 1:18, 20, 22, 24; 2:12, 14, 20; 1 Thessalonians 1:10; 2:15; 4:14; 5:10; I Timothy 2:6; 2 Timothy 2:8, 11; Titus 2:14
9. Epistle to the Hebrews, 1:3; 2:9, 10, 14, 17; 5:8; 7:27; 9:12, 14, 15, 26, 28; 10:10, 12, 14, 19, 29; 12:2, 24; 13:12, 20
10. St. James, 5:6
11. St. John, 1 John 1:7; 5:6, 8; Revelation 1:5; 5:6
12. Groups in heaven, Revelation 5:9, 12; 7:14; 12:11
13. Christ Himself, Luke 24:46; Revelation 1:18; 2:8

D. *VARIOUS TERMS USED TO INDICATE HOW CHRIST DIED*

1. *Crucified — stauroo*
   Matthew 20:19; 26:2; 27:22, 23, 26, 31, 35, 38; 28:5; Mark 15:13, 14, 15, 20, 24, 25, 27; 16:6; Luke 23:21, 23, 33; 24:7, 20;

John 19:6, 10, 15, 16, 18, 20, 23; Acts 2:36; 4:10; 1 Corinthians 1:23; 2:2, 8; 2 Corinthians 13:4; Galatians 3:1; Revelation 11:8, also *prospegnumi* — Acts 2:24

2. *On a cross — stauros*

Matthew 27:32, 40, 42; Mark 15:21, 30, 32; Luke 23:26; John 19:17, 19, 25, 31; 1 Corinthians 1:17, 18; Galatians 5:11; 6:12, 14; Ephesians 2:16; Philippians 2:8; 3:18; Colossians 1:20; 2:14; Hebrews 12:2

3. *He was hung on a tree*

Acts 5:30; 10:39; 13:29; 1 Peter 2:24; cf. Galatians 3:13

4. *He suffered*

Verb — pascho

Matthew 16:21; 17:12; Mark 8:31; 9:12; Luke 9:22; 17:25; 22:15; 24:26, 46; Acts 1:3; 3:18; 17:3; Hebrews 2:18; 5:8; 9:26; 13:12; 1 Peter 2:21, 23; 3:18; 4:1

Noun — pathema

2 Corinthians 1:5, 6, 7; Philippians 3:10; Hebrews 2:9, 10; 10:32; 1 Peter 1:11; 4:13; 5:19

5. *He gave up the ghost*

Matthew 27:50; Mark 15:37; Luke 23:46; John 19:30

6. *His decease — exodus*

Luke 9:31

7. *He shed His blood — ekkuno*

Matthew 26:28; 27:4, 6, 8, 24, 25; Mark 14:24; Luke 2:22, 44; John 6:53, 54, 55, 56; Acts 1:19; 5:28; 18:6; 20:28; Romans 3:25; 5:9; 1 Corinthians 10:16; 11:25, 27; Ephesians 1:7; 2:13; Colossians 1:14, 20; Hebrews 9:12, 14; 10:19, 29; 12:24; 13:12, 20; 1 Peter 1:2, 19; 1 John 1:7; 5:6, 8; Revelation 1:5; 5:9; 7:14; 12:11

8. *He was killed (slain)*

(in the order of frequency — many passages are referred to in other sections, and I have not attempted to repeat all of them)

(1) *apokteino* — to kill, Matthew 16:21; 17:23; 21:38, 39; 26:4; Mark 8:31; 9:31; 10:34; 12:7, 8; 14:1; Luke 9:22; 18:33; 20:14, 15; John 5:16, 18; 7:1, 19, 25; 8:37, 40; 11:53; Acts 3:15; 1 Thessalonians 2:15

(2) *thanatoo* — to put to death, Matthew 26:59; 27:1; Mark 14:55; 1 Peter 3:18. Also with use of the noun *thanatos*, Matthew 20:18; Mark 10:35; Luke 24:20; Hebrews 2:9, 14, etc.

(3) *tithemi* — to lay down, hence to lay down His life, John 10:11, 15, 17, 18; 1 John 3:16

(4) *anaireo* — to lift up, to slay, Luke 22:2; 23:2; Acts 2:23; 10:39; 13:28

(5) *sphazo* — to put to death by violence, Revelation 5:6, 9, 12; 13:8

(6) *phoneuo* — to murder, James 5:6. The noun form "murderer" occurs in Acts 7:52

(7) *diacheirizomai* — to lay hands on, Acts 5:30

9. Pierced — Revelation 1:7; John 19:34

E. *CHRIST'S DEATH AS A DIVINE TRANSACTION BETWEEN THE FATHER AND THE SON*

1. He was delivered by the determinate counsel and foreknowledge of God, Acts 2:23
2. The Father loved Him because He laid down His life, John 10:11, 15, 17, 18
3. He gave Himself up, Galatians 2:20
4. He gave Himself up an offering to God, Ephesians 5:2; Hebrews 10:10, 14; *prosphora*
5. He gave Himself up a sacrifice to God, Ephesians 5:2; Hebrews 9:26; 10:12; 11:4; *thusia*. The verbal form, 1 Corinthians 5:7
6. A propitiation — *hilasmos*, 1 John 2:2; 4:10; *hilasterion*, Romans 3:25; *hilaskomai*, Hebrews 2:17
7. A ransom — *lutron*, Matthew 20:28; Mark 10:45; *antilutron*, 1 Timothy 2:6
8. Through the eternal Spirit He offered Himself without blemish unto God, Hebrews 9:14

F. *THE VAST CONSEQUENCES OF CHRIST'S DEATH*

I. Its Universal Efficacy
1. For all, 2 Corinthians 5:14, 15, "for us all," Romans 8:32; 1 Corinthians 8:11
2. "for every man," Hebrews 2:9
3. "for many," Hebrews 9:28
4. "for us," Romans 5:8; Titus 2:14
5. for those for whom He died, Romans 14:15
6. "for me," i.e. for Paul, Galatians 2:20

II. In its Relation to Sin
1. Basically — He died for sin, Romans 4:25; 1 Corinthians 15:3; Galatians 1:4; Hebrews 10:12; 1 Peter 3:18
2. He shed His blood for the remission of sins, Matthew 26:28; Mark 14:24; Luke 22:20
3. to bear the sins of many, Hebrews 9:28; He bare our sins in His own body on the tree, 1 Peter 2:24
4. for the purification of sins, Hebrews 9:14
·5. to put away sin, Hebrews 9:26

III. Two Consequences for Christ Himself
1. He learned obedience, Hebrews 5:8
2. He was made perfect through suffering, Hebrews 2:10

IV. For the Redeemed — By His Death
1. We are redeemed, Ephesians 1:7; 1 Peter 1:19
2. We are made nigh to God, Ephesians 2:13
3. We are reconciled to God, Colossians 1:20, 21; Romans 5:10
4. Jew and Gentile are now made one, Ephesians 2:16
5. We are cleansed, Hebrews 9:14; 1 John 1:7
6. We are justified, Romans 5:9
7. We are sanctified, Hebrews 10:10; 13:12

8. We are perfected forever, Hebrews 10:14
9. We have been purchased unto God, Revelation 5:9
10. The bond that was against us has been nailed to the cross, Colossians 2:14
11. We have boldness to enter into the holy place, Hebrews 10:19
12. We are loosed from our sins, Revelation 1:5
13. We may overcome by the blood of the Lamb, Revelation 12:11
14. By His cross peace with God has been secured, Colossians 1:20
15. His blood establishes a new covenant, 1 Corinthians 11:25; Hebrews 12:20
16. His death was to redeem us from all iniquity, Titus 2:14

V. In Relation to the Church "which He purchased with His own blood," Acts 20:28

VI. In Relation to Heaven — Purification, Hebrews 9:12

VII. In Relation to Evil Powers
1. On the cross He made an open show of principalities and powers, Colossians 2:15
2. Through His death He brought to nought the Devil, who had the power of death, Hebrews 2:14

VIII. The finality of Christ's Sacrifice, Romans 6:9, 10; Hebrews 10:12; 7:27; 9:26, 28

IX. The Death of Christ fulfilled the relevant prophecies of His Death in the Old Testament, Mark 9:12; Luke 18:31; 24:26, 46; Acts 3: 18; 26:23; 1 Corinthians 15:3; 1 Peter 1:11

G. *OUR RESPONSE TO CHRIST'S DEATH*

1. We have faith in the efficacy of His blood, Romans 3:25
2. We are to glory alone in the Cross of Christ, Galatians 6:14
3. We should determine to know nothing save Jesus Christ and Him crucified, 1 Corinthians 2:2
4. We are to look upon Christ's offering of Himself as an example, and to follow in His steps, 1 Peter 2:21
5. We are to overcome by the blood of the Lamb, Revelation 12:11
6. We are to reckon ourselves crucified with Christ, and continually seek to be made conformable unto His death — Romans 6:3, 4, 5, 8; Galatians 2:20; Philippians 3:10; Colossians 2:12; 2 Timothy 2:11; 1 Peter 4:13
7. We are to preach Christ crucified, 1 Corinthians 1:23
8. We are to "proclaim the Lord's death till He come," in our observing the Lord's Supper, 1 Corinthians 11:26; cf. "a communion of the blood of Christ," 1 Corinthians 10:16

GENERAL INDEX

427

INDEX OF AUTHORS

434

INDEX OF BIBLICAL REFERENCES